EXAM PREP

MCSA/MCSE 70-291

Implementing, Managing, and Maintaining a Microsoft Windows Server 2003 Network Infrastructure

Will Schmied

MCSA/MCSE 70-291 Exam Prep: Implementing, Managing, and Maintaining a Microsoft Windows Server 2003 Network Infrastructure

International Standard Book Number: 0-7897-3649-7

Library of Congress Cataloging-in-Publication Data
Schmied, Will.
MCSA/MCSE 70-291 exam prep : implementing, managing, and maintaining a Microsoft Windows server 2003 network infrastructure / Will Schmied.
p. cm.
ISBN 0-7897-3649-7 (pbk.)
1. Electronic data processing personnel--Certification. 2. Microsoft software--Examinations--Study guides. 3. Microsoft Windows server. I. Title.
QA76.3.S35555 2007
005.4'476--dc22
2006027803

Printed in the United States of America

First Printing: October 2006

09 08 07 06 4 3 2 1

Trademarks

Warning and Disclaimer

Bulk Sales

Que Publishing offers excellent discounts on this book when ordered in quantity for bulk purchases or special sales. For more information, please contact

U.S. Corporate and Government Sales
1-800-382-3419
corpsales@pearsontechgroup.com

For sales outside the U.S., please contact

International Sales
international@pearsoned.com

PUBLISHER
Paul Boger

ACQUISITIONS EDITOR
Betsy Brown

DEVELOPMENT EDITOR
Deadline Driven Publishing

MANAGING EDITOR
Patrick Kanouse

PROJECT EDITOR
Mandie Frank

COPY EDITOR
Jill Batistick

INDEXER
Larry Sweazy

PROOFREADER
Jessica McCarty

TECHNICAL EDITOR
Marc Savage

PUBLISHING COORDINATOR
Cindy Teeters

MULTIMEDIA DEVELOPER
Dan Scherf

DESIGNER
Gary Adair

PAGE LAYOUT
Bronkella Publishing LLC

Safari BOOKS ONLINE ENABLED

This Book Is Safari Enabled

The Safari® Enabled icon on the cover of your favorite technology book means the book is available through Safari Bookshelf. When you buy this book, you get free access to the online edition for 45 days.

Safari Bookshelf is an electronic reference library that lets you easily search thousands of technical books, find code samples, download chapters, and access technical information whenever and wherever you need it.

To gain 45-day Safari Enabled access to this book:

- Go to http://www.quepublishing.com/safarienabled
- Complete the brief registration form
- Enter the coupon code HFQG-CF2P-9YCS-JYQF-C38N

If you have difficulty registering on Safari Bookshelf or accessing the online edition, please e-mail customer-service@safaribooksonline.com.

Contents at a Glance

Table of Contents

About the Author

Will Schmied, BSET, MCSE, CWNA, TICSA, MCSA, Security+, Network+, A+, is a Senior Systems Administrator for a world renowned children's research hospital. As a freelance writer, Will has worked with many publishers, including Microsoft Press and Pearson Education. Will has also worked directly with Microsoft in the MCSE exam-development process and is the founder of the popular Internet certification portal, www.mcseworld.com.

Will holds a bachelor's degree in mechanical engineering technology from Old Dominion University along with his various IT industry certifications. Before becoming a civilian, he served in the U.S. Navy for over 12 years in the nuclear power field.

Will currently resides in northern Mississippi with his wife, Chris; their children, Christopher, Austin, Andrea, and Hannah; their dog, Charlie; and their cats, Smokey, Evin, and Socks. When he's not busy working, you can find Will enjoying time with his family, taking in a hockey game, or vegetating in front of the Xbox 360.

About the Technical Editor

Marc Savage is a National Technical Advisor and Senior Technical Trainer for Nexient Learning Inc.. Combined with more than 11 years of experience in microcomputer training and systems development in the private, public, and non-profit organization sectors, his professional expertise is focused particularly on providing companies with a clear vision and direction in regards to Microsoft products.

Marc currently holds the following certifications: MCT, MCSE NT4, MCSE 2000, MCSA 2000, MCSA 2003, MCSE 2003, CNE, A+, NETWORK+ and HDA.

Marc as worked as a technical editor and author on many tittles with New Riders and Que Publishing.

Marc lives in Ottawa, Canada with is lovely wife Lynne and two daughters, Isabelle and Carolyne.

Dedication

To my wonderful and very understanding family: Thank you for your support on all those late nights. You make projects like this book worth doing!

Acknowledgments

I would like to thank all of the outstanding staff at Que Publishing, especially Betsy Brown who brought this project to life. Thanks to Marc Savage for providing key insight into the ways that we could make this book better than its predecessor and who helped get all the bits and bytes in the right order in such a timely fashion.

We Want to Hear from You!

As the reader of this book, *you* are our most important critic and commentator. We value your opinion and want to know what we're doing right, what we could do better, what areas you'd like to see us publish in, and any other words of wisdom you're willing to pass our way.

As publisher for Que Publishing, I welcome your comments. You can email or write me directly to let me know what you did or didn't like about this book—as well as what we can do to make our books better.

Please note that I cannot help you with technical problems related to the topic of this book. We do have a User Services group, however, where I will forward specific technical questions related to the book.

When you write, please be sure to include this book's title and author as well as your name, email address, and phone number. I will carefully review your comments and share them with the author and editors who worked on the book.

Email: scorehigher@pearsoned.com

Mail: Paul Boger
Publisher
Que Publishing
800 East 96th Street
Indianapolis, IN 46240 USA

Reader Services

Visit our website and register this book at www.examcram.com/register for convenient access to any updates, downloads, or errata that might be available for this book.

Microsoft 70-291 Exam Objectives

Implementing, Managing, and Maintaining a Microsoft Windows Server 2003 Network Infrastructure

Exam Number: 70-291

Associated Certifications: MCP, MCSA on Windows Server 2003, MCSE on Windows Server 2003

Length: 40–45 questions, including simulations

Exam Description

The Implementing, Managing, and Maintaining a Microsoft Windows Server 2003 Network Infrastructure exam is one of three core exams required of candidates pursuing the Microsoft Certified Systems Administrator (MCSA) on Windows Server 2003, and it is one of six core exams required of candidates pursuing the Microsoft Certified Systems Engineer (MCSE) on Windows Server 2003. This exam tests basic networking and security-related topics to which the candidate will be exposed on the job. Each top-level exam objective is related to a job skill that the candidate is expected to have and to demonstrate in the workplace.

Exam Objectives

Exam 70-291 consists of the following five objectives, each with several sub-objectives.

Continues on Following Page

Objective Matrix Continued

Unit/Objective/Sub-objective	Page
Implementing, Managing, and Maintaining Network Security	
Implement secure network administration procedures.	**282**
▶ Implement security baseline settings and audit security settings by using security templates.	283
▶ Implement the principle of least privilege.	282
Install and configure software update infrastructure.	**326**
▶ Install and configure software update services.	326
▶ Install and configure automatic client update settings.	339
▶ Configure software updates on earlier operating systems.	395
Monitor network protocol security. Tools might include the IP Security Monitor Microsoft Management Console (MMC) snap-in and Kerberos support tools.	**557**
Troubleshoot network protocol security. Tools might include the IP Security Monitor MMC snap-in, Event Viewer, and Network Monitor.	**557**
Implementing, Managing, and Maintaining Routing and Remote Access	
Configure Routing and Remote Access user authentication.	**364**
▶ Configure remote access authentication protocols.	364
▶ Configure Internet Authentication Service (IAS) to provide authentication for Routing and Remote Access clients.	371
▶ Configure Routing and Remote Access policies to permit or deny access.	379
Manage remote access.	**398**
▶ Manage packet filters.	398
▶ Manage Routing and Remote Access routing interfaces.	401
▶ Manage devices and ports.	405
▶ Manage routing protocols.	408
▶ Manage Routing and Remote Access clients.	411

Unit/Objective/Sub-objective	Page
Manage TCP/IP routing.	**471**
▶ Manage routing protocols.	474
▶ Manage routing tables.	471
▶ Manage routing ports.	500
Implement secure access between private networks.	**416**
Troubleshoot user access to remote access services.	**435**
▶ Diagnose and resolve issues related to remote access VPNs.	435
▶ Diagnose and resolve issues related to establishing a remote access connection.	437
▶ Diagnose and resolve user access to resources beyond the remote access server.	439
Troubleshoot Routing and Remote Access routing.	**440**
▶ Troubleshoot demand-dial routing.	440
▶ Troubleshoot router-to-router VPNs.	441
Maintaining a Network Infrastructure	
Monitor network traffic. Tools might include Network Monitor and System Monitor.	**582**
Troubleshoot connectivity to the Internet.	**604**
Troubleshoot server services.	**608**
▶ Diagnose and resolve issues related to service dependency.	608
▶ Use service recovery options to diagnose and resolve service-related issues.	608

Introduction

MCSA/MCSE 70-291 Exam Prep: Implementing, Managing, and Maintaining a Microsoft Windows Server 2003 Network Infrastructure is designed for advanced end users, technicians, system administrators, and systems engineers who are seeking to pass Exam 70-291, "Implementing, Managing, and Maintaining a Microsoft Windows Server 2003 Network Infrastructure," in pursuit of a Microsoft Windows certification. Passing Exam 70-291 qualifies you as a Microsoft Certified Professional (MCP) and counts as core credit toward the Microsoft Certified Systems Administrator (MCSA) and Microsoft Certified Systems Engineer (MCSE) certifications.

Exam 70-291 measures your ability to install, manage, monitor, configure, and troubleshoot Domain Name System (DNS), Dynamic Host Configuration Protocol (DHCP), remote access, network protocols, IP routing, and Windows Internet Name Service (WINS) in a Windows Server 2003 network infrastructure. In addition, the exam measures the skills required to manage, monitor, and troubleshoot basic server and network security, including digital certificates, security policies, and the auditing and updating of computers.

Who Should Read This Book

This book is designed to help you meet your certification goals by preparing you for Exam 70-291. In a Windows Server 2003 network, the ability to install, support, and troubleshoot the various networking components and services included with Windows Server 2003 is critical to the success of an administrator. Windows Server 2003 tightly integrates services such as DHCP and DNS into the core operating system as well as Active Directory, and it requires that these services be configured correctly in order to function. This exam touches on all the major networking components that are critical to a successful Windows Server 2003 implementation. Although volumes of information are available on the history, theory, and underlying applications, this book does not cover these portions of the services in detail. The purpose of this book is to provide an introduction to these services in general, provide an in-depth look at the Windows Server 2003 implementations of these network services, and prepare you to take the exam. One additional area that is new to this exam is the emphasis on security. In keeping with the Microsoft Trustworthy Computing initiatives, Microsoft is putting much greater emphasis than in the past on the security facets of all of its Windows Server 2003 exams.

Because a great deal of related information exists that this book is not able to cover, each chapter in this book contains a section called "Suggested Readings and Resources" that points you to sources that can fill in the blanks. So, for example, although you might not be a virtual private network (VPN) expert by the time you complete this book, you'll know how to configure Windows Server 2003's Routing and Remote Access Service (RRAS) to allow VPN connections and ensure that IP Security (IPSec) is working. You'll also have a recommendation for some additional reading if you need to understand exactly what the makeup of an Authentication Header (AH) packet looks like.

One of the most common questions with any of the Microsoft certification tests is, "Do I need to take a class to pass this test?" Although the author has endeavored to ensure that all of the information you need to pass the exam is in this book, one thing that is difficult for any book to provide is hands-on experience with the product. If you can set up an environment that enables you to perform the exercises outlined in this book (you'll find hardware and software recommendations for this environment at the end of this introduction), you're going to be in good shape. You'll be in especially good shape if you have the opportunity to work with Windows Server 2003 in a production environment. To pass the exam, you do not need to take a class in addition to buying this book. However, depending on your personal study habits or learning style, you might benefit from taking a class in conjunction with studying from this book.

Microsoft assumes that the typical candidate for this exam will have a minimum of one year's experience implementing and administering network operating systems in a medium to very large network environment.

How This Book Helps You

This book takes you on a self-guided tour of all the areas covered by Exam 70-291 and teaches you specific skills you will need as you work to achieve MCSE certification. You'll also find helpful hints, tips, real-world examples, and exercises, as well as references to additional study materials. Specifically, this book is set up to help you in the following ways:

- **Organization**—This book is organized by individual exam objectives. Every objective you need to know for Exam 70-291 is covered in this book. We have attempted to present the objectives in an order that is as close as possible to how Microsoft would teach the information. However, we have not hesitated to reorganize where needed to make the material as easy as possible for you to learn. We have also attempted to make the information accessible in the following ways:
    - The full list of exam topics and objectives is included in this introduction.
    - Each chapter begins with a list of the objectives covered in that chapter.
    - Each chapter also begins with an outline that provides an overview of the material and the page numbers where particular topics can be found.

- The objectives are repeated where the material most directly relevant to it is covered (unless the whole chapter addresses a single objective).

- **Instructional features**—This book is designed to provide you with multiple ways to learn and reinforce the exam material. Following are some of the helpful methods:

  - **Exam alerts**—These provide specific exam-related advice. Such alerts might address what material is likely to be covered (or not covered) on the exam, how it is covered, or particular quirks of that exam.

  - **Key terms**—A list of key terms from the chapter appears at the end of each chapter.

  - **Notes**—Notes contain various kinds of useful information, such as tips on technology or administrative practices, historical background on terms and technologies, and side commentary on industry issues.

  - **Warnings**—When using sophisticated information technology, the potential for mistakes always exists; catastrophes can even occur because of improper application of the technology. Warnings alert you to such potential problems.

  - **In the Field sidebars**—These relatively extensive discussions cover material that may not be directly relevant to the exam but that is useful as reference material or in everyday practice. In the Field sidebars may also provide useful background or contextual information that is necessary for understanding the larger topic under consideration.

  - **Exercises**—Found at the end of the chapters in the "Apply Your Knowledge" section and in the "Challenge Exercises" found throughout the chapters, exercises are performance-based opportunities for you to learn and assess your knowledge.

  - **Step by Steps**—These are hands-on tutorial instructions that walk you through tasks and functions that are relevant to the exam objectives.

- **Extensive practice test options**—The book provides numerous opportunities for you to assess your knowledge and practice for the exam. The practice options include the following:

  - **Review questions**—These open-ended questions appear in Appendix C, "Review Questions," at the end of the book. They enable you to quickly assess your comprehension of what you just read in the chapter. Answers to the review questions are provided later in the section.

  - **Practice exam**—A practice exam is included in the "Final Review" section of the book. The "Final Review" section and the practice exam are discussed later in this Introduction.

- **Final Review**—This part of the book provides the following valuable tools for preparing for the exam:
  - **Fast Facts**—This condensed version of the information contained in the book is extremely useful for last-minute review.
  - **Practice Exam**—A practice exam is included in this book. As much as possible, questions on this practice exam are written in styles similar to those used on the actual exam. Use the practice exam to assess your readiness for the real thing. Use the extensive answer explanations to improve your retention and understanding of the material.

The book includes several other features, such as the "Suggested Readings and Resources" section at the end of each chapter that directs you to additional information that can aid you in your exam preparation and your real-life work. Valuable appendixes are provided as well, including a glossary and a description of what is on the CD-ROM.

For more information about the exam or the certification process, contact Microsoft at 800-636-7544 or MCPHelp@microsoft.com or visit www.microsoft.com/learning/.

Hardware and Software You Will Need

As a self-paced study guide, this book is meant to help you understand concepts that you must refine through hands-on experience. To make the most of your studying, you need to have as much background on and experience with Windows Server 2003 as possible. The best way to do this is to combine studying with working on real networks, using the products on which you will be tested. This section describes the minimum computer requirements you need in order to enjoy a solid practice environment.

The minimum computer requirements to ensure that you can study everything on which you'll be tested are one or more workstations running Windows 2000 Professional or Windows XP Professional, and two or more servers running Windows Server 2003—all connected by a network. Many of the examples, exercises, and references in this book refer to Internet Web sites, so an Internet-connected network would be a benefit. Because this book looks at the core networking capabilities of the Windows Server 2003 family, the minimum requirements listed are specific to Windows Server 2003 Standard Edition, which has all the features that are covered by this exam and the lowest minimum hardware requirements.

To get the full benefit of the exercises in this book, you need the following lab equipment:

- **Workstations**—The workstation configuration should meet the following requirements:
    - Computer listed on the Microsoft Hardware Compatibility List (HCL)
    - Pentium 150MHz or better (Pentium processor 233MHz or better for Windows XP)
    - 64MB RAM (128MB for Windows XP)
    - 2GB hard disk with a minimum of 650MB free space (1.5GB free space for Windows XP)
    - 3.5-inch 1.44MB floppy drive
    - VGA video adapter (Super VGA adapter for Windows XP)
    - VGA monitor (Super VGA adapter for Windows XP)
    - Mouse or equivalent pointing device
    - CD-ROM drive
    - Network interface card (NIC)
    - Presence on an existing network or use of a hub to create a test network (Internet connection beneficial for some exercises)
    - Microsoft Windows 2000 Professional or Windows XP Professional
- **Servers**—The server(s) should meet the following requirements:
    - Two computers listed on the Microsoft HCL
    - Pentium 133MHz or better—Microsoft recommends a 550MHz processor
    - 256MB RAM (128MB is the minimum supported, but performance will suffer with just 128MB)
    - 1GB free hard disk space
    - 3.5-inch 1.44MB floppy drive
    - VGA video adapter
    - VGA monitor
    - Mouse or equivalent pointing device
    - CD-ROM drive

- NIC
- Presence on an existing network or use of a hub to create a test network
- Microsoft Windows Server 2003 Standard Edition (Enterprise Edition will also work but is not needed)

It is generally easiest to obtain access to the necessary computer hardware and software in a corporate business environment. It can be difficult, however, to allocate enough time within the busy workday to complete a self-study program. Most of your study time will likely occur after normal working hours, away from the everyday interruptions and pressures of your regular job.

Advice on Taking the Exam

Although this list is not all inclusive, here are a few bits of advice to keep in mind as you study and prepare for your 70-291 exam:

- Read all the material. Microsoft has been known to include on its exams material not expressly specified in the objectives. This book includes additional information not reflected in the objectives in an effort to give you the best possible preparation for the examination—and for the real-world network experiences to come.
- Do the Step by Steps and complete the exercises in each chapter. They will help you gain experience in using the specified methodology or approach. All Microsoft exams are task and experienced based and require you to have experience actually performing the tasks on which you will be tested.
- Use the review and exam questions to assess your knowledge. Don't just read the chapter content; use the questions to find out what you know and what you don't. If you are struggling at all, study some more, review, and then assess your knowledge again.
- Review the exam objectives. Develop your own questions and examples for each topic listed. If you can develop and answer several questions for each topic, you should not find it difficult to pass the exam.
- Find a study buddy. This might sound corny, but it works. You should find a co-worker or friend who is also preparing for the exam and use him or her to improve your knowledge. Quiz each other and assist each other with sections where you feel your knowledge is weak.

NOTE

Exam-Taking Advice Although this book is designed to prepare you to take and pass Exam 70-291, there are no guarantees. Read this book, work through the questions and exercises, and when you feel confident, take the Practice Exam and additional exams, using the *Measure Up* software. That should tell you whether you are ready for the real thing.

When taking the actual certification exam, make sure you answer all the questions before your time limit expires. Do not spend too much time on any one question. If you are unsure about an answer, answer the question the best you can; then mark it for review when you have finished the rest of the questions.

Be sure to read each question carefully and read all the answers before you make a selection. A question might have an answer that is close, but one of the other answers might, in fact, be a better answer. If you select an answer before reading all the choices, you might miss the best answer.

Get a good night's sleep before the exam. If you don't know the exam information by the night before the exam, an all-night cram session will just make you tired when you are taking the exam. You need to be at your sharpest when you take this exam; don't handicap yourself with sleep deprivation.

Remember, the primary objective of this book is not the exam; it is to ensure that you understand the material. After you understand the material, passing the exam should be simple. Knowledge is a pyramid; to build upward, you need a solid foundation. This book and the MCP programs are designed to ensure that you have that solid foundation.

Good Luck!

Study and Exam Prep Tips

This element of the book provides you with some general guidelines for preparing for any certification exam, including Exam 70-291, "Implementing, Managing, and Maintaining a Microsoft Windows Server 2003 Network Infrastructure." It is organized into four sections. The first section addresses learning styles and how they affect preparation for the exam. The second section covers exam preparation activities and general study tips. This is followed by an extended look at the Microsoft certification exams, including a number of specific tips that apply to the various Microsoft exam formats and question types. Finally, changes in Microsoft's testing policies and how they might affect you are discussed.

Learning Styles

To best understand the nature of preparation for the test, it is important to understand learning as a process. You are probably aware of how you best learn new material. You might find that outlining works best for you, or, as a visual learner, you might need to see things. Or you might need practices or examples, or maybe you just like exploring the product. Whatever your learning style, test preparation takes place over time. Obviously, you shouldn't start studying for a certification exam the night before you take it; it is very important to understand that learning is a developmental process. Understanding learning as a process helps you focus on what you know and what you have yet to learn.

Thinking about how you learn should help you recognize that learning takes place when you are able to match new information to old. You have some previous experience with computers and networking. Now you are preparing for this certification exam. Using this book, software, and supplementary materials will not just add incrementally to what you know; as you study, the organization of your knowledge actually restructures as you integrate new information into your existing knowledge base. This leads you to a more comprehensive understanding of the tasks and concepts outlined in the objectives for this exam and of computing in general. Again, this happens as a result of a repetitive process rather than a singular event. If you keep this model of learning in mind as you prepare for the exam, you will make better decisions concerning what to study and how much more studying you need to do.

Study Tips

There are many ways to approach studying. However, the tips that follow should work well for the type of material covered on Microsoft certification exams.

Study Strategies

Although individuals vary in the ways they learn information, some basic principles of learning apply to everyone. You should adopt some study strategies that take advantage of these principles. One of these principles is that learning can be broken into various depths. Recognition (of terms, for example) exemplifies a rather surface level of learning in which you rely on a prompt of some sort to elicit recall. Comprehension or understanding (of the concepts behind the terms, for example) represents a deeper level of learning than recognition. The ability to analyze a concept and apply your understanding of it in a new way represents further depth of learning.

Your learning strategy should enable you to know the material at a level or two deeper than mere recognition. This will help you perform well on the exams. You will know the material so thoroughly that you can go beyond the recognition-level types of questions commonly used in fact-based, multiple-choice testing. You will be able to apply your knowledge to solve new problems.

Macro and Micro Study Strategies

One strategy that can lead to deep learning includes preparing an outline that covers all the objectives and subobjectives for the particular exam on which you are working. You should delve a bit further into the material and include a level or two of detail beyond the stated objectives and subobjectives for the exam. Then you should expand the outline by coming up with a statement of definition or a summary for each point in the outline.

An outline provides two approaches to studying. First, you can study the outline by focusing on the organization of the material. You can work your way through the points and subpoints of your outline, with the goal of learning how they relate to one another. For example, you should be sure that you understand how each of the main objective areas for Exam 70-291 is similar to and different from the others. Then, you should do the same thing with the subobjectives; you should be sure you know which sub-objectives pertain to each objective area and how they relate to one another.

Next, you can work through the outline, focusing on learning the details. You should memorize and understand terms and their definitions, facts, rules and tactics, advantages and disadvantages, and so on. In this pass through the outline, you should attempt to learn detail rather than the big picture (the organizational information that you worked on in the first pass through the outline).

Research has shown that attempting to assimilate both types of information at the same time interferes with the overall learning process. If you separate your studying into these two approaches, you will perform better on the exam.

Active Study Strategies

The process of writing down and defining objectives, sub-objectives, terms, facts, and definitions promotes a more active learning strategy than merely reading the material does. In human information-processing terms, writing forces you to engage in more active encoding of the information. Simply reading over the information leads to more passive processing.

You need to determine whether you can apply the information you have learned. You can do this by attempting to create examples and scenarios on your own. You should think about how or where you could apply the concepts you are learning. Again, you should write down this information to process the facts and concepts in an active fashion.

The hands-on nature of the exercises at the end of each chapter provides further active learning opportunities that will reinforce concepts as well.

Common-Sense Strategies

You should follow common-sense practices when studying: You study during the time of day you are most alert and thus, most productive. In addition, you should reduce or eliminate distractions by turning off email and not answering the phone. Lastly, it's always a good practice to refresh and recharge by taking a 5–10 minute break every hour or so.

Pretesting Yourself

Pretesting allows you to assess how well you are learning. One of the most important aspects of learning is what has been called *meta-learning*. Meta-learning has to do with realizing when you know something well or when you need to study some more. In other words, you recognize how well or how poorly you have learned the material you are studying.

For most people, this can be difficult to assess. Review questions, practice questions, and practice tests are useful in that they reveal objectively what you have learned and what you have not learned. You should use this information to guide further studying. Developmental learning takes place as you cycle through studying. After studying, you assess how well you learned, then you review, and start the cycle over by assessing again until you feel you are ready to take the exam.

You might have noticed the practice exam included in this book. You should use it as part of the learning process. The *MeasureUp* test simulation software also provides you with an excellent opportunity to assess your knowledge. You should set a goal for your pretesting. A reasonable goal would be to score consistently in the 90 percent range.

See Appendix A, "Accessing Your Free MeasureUp Practice Test—Including Networking Simulations!" for further explanation of the test simulation software.

Microsoft Exam Prep Tips

After you have mastered the subject matter, the final preparatory step is to understand how the exam will be presented. Make no mistake: A Microsoft Certified Professional (MCP) exam will challenge both your knowledge and your test-taking skills. The following sections describe the basics of exam design, the exam formats, and hints targeted to each of the exam formats.

The Exam

Every Microsoft MCP exam is released in one of two exam basic formats: fixed-form and simulation. Each exam format uses the same types of questions. These types or styles of questions include multiple-rating (or scenario-based) questions, traditional multiple-choice questions, and simulation-based questions. It's important to understand the types of questions you will be asked and the actions required to properly answer them.

Understanding the exam formats is key to good preparation because the format determines the number of questions presented, the difficulty of those questions, and the amount of time allowed to complete the exam.

Exam Format

The basic format for the MCSE exam is the traditional fixed-form exam. As its name implies, the fixed-form exam presents a fixed set of questions during the exam session.

Fixed-Form

A fixed-form computerized exam is based on a fixed set of exam questions and is the most likely form you will encounter for Exam 70-291. The individual questions are presented in random order during a test session. If you take the same exam more than once, you won't necessarily see the exact same questions. The reason is that two or three final forms are typically assembled for every fixed-form exam Microsoft releases. They are usually labeled Forms A, B, and C.

The final forms of a fixed-form exam are identical in terms of content coverage, number of questions, and allotted time, but the questions are different. You may notice, however, that some of the same questions appear on, or rather are shared among, different final forms. When questions are shared among multiple final forms of an exam, the percentage of sharing is generally small. Many final forms share no questions, but some older exams may have a 10–15 percent duplication of exam questions on the final exam forms.

Fixed-form exams also have a fixed time limit in which you must complete the exam. Finally, the score you achieve on a fixed-form exam, which is typically reported for MCSE exams on a scale of 0–1000, is based on the number of questions you answer correctly. The exam's passing score, currently 700, is the same for all final forms of a given fixed-form exam.

The typical format for the fixed-form exam is as follows:

- 50–60 questions.
- 75–90 minute testing time.
- Question review is allowed, including the opportunity to change your answers.

Simulation Questions

A variety of question types can appear on MCSE exams. Examples of multiple-choice questions and scenario-based questions appear throughout this book and the MeasureUp software. Simulation-based questions are new to the MCSE exam series.

Simulation-based questions reproduce the look and feel of key Microsoft product features for the purpose of testing. The simulation software used in MCSE exams has been designed to look and act, as much as possible, just like the actual product. Consequently, answering simulation questions in an MCSE exam entails completing one or more tasks just as if you were using the product itself.

The format of a typical Microsoft simulation question consists of a brief scenario or problem statement along with one or more tasks that must be completed to solve the problem.

This advice sounds obvious, but your first step when you encounter a simulation is to carefully read the question. Do not go straight to the simulation application! You must assess the problem being presented and identify the conditions that make up the problem scenario. Note the tasks that must be performed or outcomes that must be achieved to answer the question and review any instructions on how to proceed.

The next step is to launch the simulator by using the button provided. After clicking the Show Simulation button, you will see a feature of the product presented in a dialog box. The window of the simulation application will partially cover the question text on many test center machines. Feel free to reposition the simulation or move between the question text screen and the simulation by using hotkeys, by using point-and-click navigation, or even by clicking the simulation launch button again.

It is important to understand that your answer to the simulation question will not be recorded until you move on to the next exam question. This gives you the added ability to close and reopen the simulation application (using the launch button) on the same question without losing any partial answer you may have made.

The third step is to use the simulator as you would the actual product to solve the problem or perform the defined tasks. Again, the simulation software is designed to function, within reason, just as the product does. But don't expect the simulation to reproduce product behavior perfectly. Most importantly, do not allow yourself to become flustered if the simulation does not look or act exactly like the product.

There are two final points that will help you tackle simulation questions. First, respond only to what is being asked in the question; do not solve problems that you are not asked to solve. Second, accept what is being asked of you. You may not entirely agree with conditions in the problem statement, the quality of the desired solution, or the sufficiency of defined tasks to adequately solve the problem. Always remember that you are being tested on your ability to solve the problem as it is presented. If you make any changes beyond those required by the question, the item will be scored as wrong on an MCSE exam.

Putting It All Together

As you can see, Microsoft is making an effort to utilize question types that go beyond asking you to simply memorize facts. These question types force you to know how to accomplish tasks and understand concepts and relationships. You should study so that you can answer these types of questions rather than those that simply ask you to recall facts.

Given all the different pieces of information presented so far, the following sections present a set of tips that will help you successfully tackle the exam.

More Pre-Exam Preparation Tips

Generic exam-preparation advice is always useful. Tips include the following:

- Become familiar with the product. Hands-on experience is one of the keys to success on any MCP exam. Review the exercises and the Step by Steps in the book.
- Review the current exam-preparation guide on the Microsoft Training & Certification Web site. The documentation Microsoft makes available on the Web identifies the skills every exam is intended to test.
- Memorize foundational technical detail, but remember that MCP exams are generally heavier on problem solving and application of knowledge than on questions that require only rote memorization.
- Take any of the available practice tests. We recommend the one included in this book and the ones you can access via the MeasureUp's website. See Appendix A for more information.
- Look on the Microsoft Learning Web site for samples and demonstration items. These items tend to be particularly valuable for one significant reason: They help you become

familiar with any new testing technologies before you encounter them on an MCP exam.

During the Exam Session

The following exam-taking advice that you've heard for years applies when you're taking an MCP exam:

- Take a deep breath and try to relax when you first sit down for your exam session. It is very important that you control the pressure you might (naturally) feel when taking exams.
- You will be provided scratch paper. Take a moment to write down any factual information and technical detail that you have committed to short-term memory.
- Carefully read all information and instruction screens. These displays have been put together to give you information relevant to the exam you are taking.
- Accept the nondisclosure agreement and preliminary survey as part of the examination process. Complete them accurately and quickly move on.
- Read the exam questions carefully. Reread each question to identify all relevant detail.
- In fixed-form exams, tackle the questions in the order in which they are presented. Skipping around won't build your confidence; the clock is always counting down.
- Don't rush, but also don't linger on difficult questions. The questions vary in degree of difficulty. Don't let yourself be flustered by a particularly difficult or wordy question.

Besides considering the basic preparation and test-taking advice presented so far, you also need to consider the challenges presented by the different exam designs, as described in the following sections.

Tips for Fixed-Form Exams

Because a fixed-form exam is composed of a fixed, finite set of questions, you should add these tips to your strategy for taking a fixed-form exam:

- Note the time allotted and the number of questions on the exam you are taking. Make a rough calculation of how many minutes you can spend on each question, and use this figure to pace yourself through the exam.
- Take advantage of the fact that you can return to and review skipped or previously answered questions. Record the questions you can't answer confidently on the scratch paper provided, noting the relative difficulty of each question. When you reach the end of the exam, return to the more difficult questions.

- If you have session time remaining after you complete all the questions (and if you aren't too fatigued!), review your answers. Pay particular attention to questions that seem to have a lot of detail or that require graphics.
- As for changing your answers, the general rule of thumb here is *don't*! If you read the question carefully and completely and felt like you knew the right answer, you probably did. Don't second-guess yourself. If you later find that one of your answers clearly stands out as being incorrect, you should of course change it. But if you are at all unsure, go with your first impression.

Tips for Answering Simulation Questions

Following are tips for answering the simulation questions:

- Avoid changing any simulation settings that don't pertain directly to the problem solution. Solve the problem you are being asked to solve and nothing more.
- Assume default settings when related information has not been provided. If something has not been mentioned or defined, it is a noncritical detail that does not factor into the correct solution.
- Be sure your entries are syntactically correct, paying particular attention to your spelling. Enter relevant information just as the product would require it.
- Close all simulation application windows after completing the simulation tasks. The testing system software is designed to trap errors that could result when using the simulation application, but trust yourself over the testing software.
- If simulations are part of a fixed-form exam, you can return to skipped or previously answered questions and change your answer. However, if you choose to change your answer to a simulation question or even attempt to review the settings you've made in the simulation application, your previous response to that simulation question will be deleted.

Final Considerations

Finally, a number of changes in the MCP program affect how frequently you can repeat an exam and what you will see when you do:

- Microsoft has an exam retake policy. The rule is "two and two, then one and two." That is, you can attempt any exam twice with no restrictions on the time between attempts. But after the second attempt, you must wait two weeks before you can attempt that exam again. After that, you are required to wait two weeks between subsequent attempts. Plan to pass the exam in two attempts or plan to increase your time horizon for receiving the MCP credential.

- New questions are always being seeded into the MCP exams. After performance data is gathered on new questions, the examiners replace older questions on all exam forms. This means that the questions appearing on exams regularly change.

These changes mean that the brute-force strategies for passing MCP exams have lost their viability. So if you don't pass an exam on the first or second attempt, it is likely that the exam's form could change significantly by the next time you take it. It could be updated from fixed-form to adaptive or, even more likely, it could have a different set of questions or question types.

Microsoft's intention is not to make the exams more difficult by introducing unwanted change, but to create and maintain valid measures of the technical skills and knowledge associated with the different MCP credentials. Preparing for an MCP exam has always involved not only studying the subject matter, but also planning for the testing experience itself. With the continuing changes, this is now truer than ever.

PART I

Exam Preparation

CHAPTER ONE

Configuring and Troubleshooting TCP/IP Addressing

Objectives

The capability to allow computers to communicate with each other is the fundamental principle of the modern computer network. Just as people from various parts of the world may have different native languages, different operating systems have typically had different native networking protocols they could use. This has changed recently, however, as TCP/IP has become the networking protocol of choice for nearly all operating systems and networks. The capability of all computers on a network to communicate effectively is dependent on having a properly implemented common network protocol.

Microsoft lists the following objectives for the "Implementing, Managing, and Maintaining IP Addressing" section of Exam 70-291, "Implementing, Managing, and Maintaining a Microsoft Windows Server 2003 Network Infrastructure":

Configure TCP/IP addressing on a server computer.

- A Windows Server 2003 computer needs connectivity with other computers and network devices to effectively accomplish its mission. You, as the administrator, need to be knowledgeable about the fundamentals of Transmission Control Protocol/Internet Protocol (TCP/IP)—the primary network communications protocol used in Windows Server 2003 networks.

Troubleshoot TCP/IP addressing.

- **Diagnose and resolve issues related to Automatic Private IP Addressing (APIPA).**
- **Diagnose and resolve issues related to incorrect TCP/IP configuration.**
- Having an incorrect IP address assigned to a computer prevents the computer from establishing and maintaining norma!, effective network communications with other hosts. Although APIPA IP addresses can be helpful in some small networks, they really serve no purpose in an enterprise network that runs Windows Server 2003 and uses Dynamic Host Configuration Protocol (DHCP) for IP address assignment. In addition, having an incorrectly entered TCP/IP configuration prevents normal network communications from succeeding. You need to be able to determine the source of problems and correct problems such as these to keep communications flowing on a network.

Outline

Study Strategies

- Make sure that you understand the basics of TCP/IP. Windows Server 2003 is extremely reliant on TCP/IP; in fact, you cannot even uninstall TCP/IP from Windows Server 2003. This exam focuses heavily on the more complex issues of TCP/IP and how it works with several aspects of Windows Server 2003. You should take some time to review the basics of IP and then build from there.
- Become familiar with the available TCP/IP troubleshooting tools you have at your disposal. Each of them can be used to perform one or more specific tasks, but no single one of them provides a solution by itself. You can use these tools not only on your own network, but also on hosts located on the Internet and other networks (within reason, of course) to see how they behave differently when the computer on the other end of the connection is located remotely. You should commit to memory the functions of the various switches and modifying commands that each tool has; these are often the basis for very simple exam items that you should not miss.
- Get your hands dirty. The Step by Step exercises throughout this book provide plenty of directions and exercises, but you should go beyond these examples and create some of your own. If you can, experiment with each of the topics we discuss in this chapter to see how they work and why you would use each one.

Introduction

Not that many years ago, TCP/IP *was not* the king when it came to network communication protocols. Windows NT 4.0 relied on the venerable NetBIOS Extended User Interface (NetBEUI) protocol by default and NetWare servers could be counted on to understand only IPX/SPX. With the introduction of the Internet to the masses, TCP/IP slowly started to creep into private networks of all sizes and purposes. Administrators and network designers began to see the power and flexibility that TCP/IP offered them, and Microsoft and Novell took note of the shift.

Soon all operating systems provided support for TCP/IP, but it still was not the networking protocol of choice. With the introduction of Windows 2000, Microsoft made TCP/IP and the Domain Name System (DNS) integral parts of Windows 2000 Active Directory networks. With the introduction of Windows XP on the client side and Windows Server 2003 on the server side, TCP/IP has become a mandatory networking protocol—installed by default and not able to be removed. This chapter examines the basics of TCP/IP as it applies to you, the network administrator.

Understanding TCP/IP and Related Concepts

TCP/IP is the network communications protocol of choice in Windows Server 2003. It permeates Windows from end to end as the preferred network protocol. But what is TCP/IP, and how does it work? Before you can get to the business of configuring this flexible protocol, you need to have a basic understanding of its key points.

TCP/IP is a suite of protocols that allows hosts, networks, and operating systems to communicate with each other. As you might know, TCP/IP was originally built for the U.S. Department of Defense (DoD) to allow its mainframes and servers to chat with each other locally and remotely.

TCP/IP actually evolved from a network created by a vast research agency—the Advanced Research Projects Agency (ARPA)—which performed advanced technical research for the DoD. This collection of networks, called ARPAnet, connected research centers, such as universities, to each other and with DoD sites, such as the Pentagon. ARPAnet was designed to provide a redundantly reliable network that could survive the loss of one or more hosts. The thought was—and it was a very realistic thought at the time—that in the event of a nuclear war, it was very likely that several cities would be destroyed, taking with them their network hosts. ARPAnet was designed to allow continued communications between remaining locations.

ARPAnet ran on top of the original routing protocol, Network Core Protocol (NCP). NCP was composed of the TCP and IP protocols—two separate protocols that are examined later in this chapter. The basic design of TCP/IP is simple, fault tolerant, routable, and vendor neutral.

Originally, TCP/IP was used to connect mainframes. However, the 1980s saw the evolution of Unix and personal computers (PCs). Although it faced some resistance, Unix eventually led the way, at the University of California, Berkeley, in integrating TCP/IP to connect these PCs. The Macintosh world used the AppleTalk protocol, and much of the Windows world stuck with either the NetBEUI protocol or the NWLink IPX/SPX-compatible protocol for connectivity with NetWare servers. One day, almost out of nowhere, this thing called the World Wide Web happened; because of the WWW, everyone needed TCP/IP, and they needed it right away.

The Mechanics of IP

Internet Protocol (IP) allows data to travel from one computer to another, either on a local network or through a router to a remote network. How does this work?

If you have eight computers in Chicago connected on the same Ethernet network, you've got a local area network (LAN). There's no routing—and no need for it. In an Ethernet network, each computer receives every packet, regardless of whether the packet is intended for that computer. The physical address (that is, the Media Access Control [MAC] address) of the network card determines whether a packet is to be accepted or discarded.

When Computer A needs to send a packet to Computer B on the same Ethernet network via TCP/IP, the packets don't have to pass through a router. What has to happen, however, is that Computer A needs to know the IP address of Computer B. Then IP resolves that IP address to the MAC address of the network adapter card in Computer B. That MAC address is in the header of the packets sent out on to the network, and only Computer B will accept those headers because only Computer B has that exact MAC address on its network card.

But what about when Computer A in Chicago needs to talk to Computer E in Atlanta (see Figure 1.1)? Now you have a wide area network (WAN), so you need a router. A *router* is a device that routes packets from network to network to network and eventually to the host. When Computer A needs to communicate with Computer E, the packets are forwarded on to the router because the destination is not on the local network.

The router then forwards the packet, based on its routing table, to the next router and onward, until eventually the packet ends up at the final network and on the target computer.

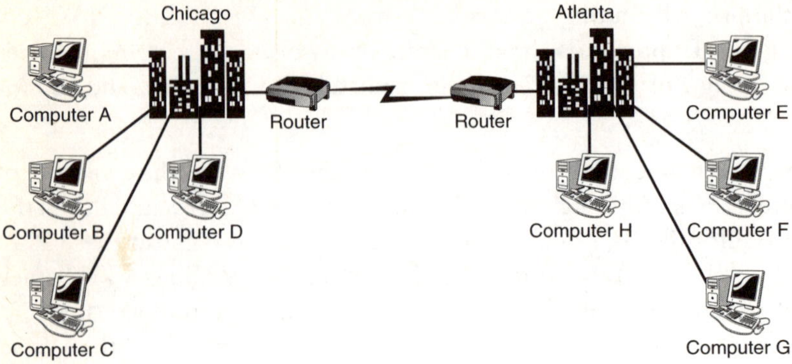

FIGURE 1.1 TCP/IP makes communicating over WANs an easy task.

IP Addresses

For routing to happen, a network design must be based on specific rules. The first rule of TCP/IP is that you must use a valid IP address. An *IP address* is a series of numbers that represents your computer—for example, 131.108.116.55. Each of the numbers in the IP address is an *octet*, made up of 8 bits; the whole IP address is 32 bits. If you were to look at 131.108.116.55 in binary, as the computer sees it, you would see 10000011 01101100 01110100 00110111.

IP addresses are typically displayed in decimal format, called *dotted-decimal notation*. Each host that requires connectivity on a TCP/IP network requires its own unique IP address. A network address in dotted-decimal notation is easier for humans to read than an address in binary form. However, having the address in dotted-decimal notation is not convenient for the computer, which uses binary form. It is sometimes helpful to understand what the computer is doing when it works with network addresses, such as when it is identifying which route may be used for a particular address, determining the binary representation of a subnet mask, or in general, troubleshooting TCP/IP.

The easiest way to convert dotted-decimal notation to binary is to understand the mechanics of the binary system. By knowing that the smallest value an IP address octet can take is 0 and the largest value an IP address octet can take is 255, you can then make a chart such as the one shown in Table 1.1.

TABLE 1.1 Decimal-to-Binary Conversion Basics

	128 (2^7)	64 (2^6)	32 (2^5)	16 (2^4)	8 (2^3)	4 (2^2)	2 (2^1)	1 (2^0)
255	1	1	1	1	1	1	1	1
0	0	0	0	0	0	0	0	0

Table 1.1 represents the 8 binary digits that make up a single IP address octet. So, if you have a value of decimal 255, its binary equivalent is 11111111. Conversely, if you have a value of decimal 0, its binary equivalent is 00000000. But what about those numbers in the middle? Let's examine the decimal values 127 and 93 in binary notation. Table 1.2 presents these values.

TABLE 1.2 Converting Decimal Numbers to Binary

	128 (2^7)	64 (2^6)	32 (2^5)	16 (2^4)	8 (2^3)	4 (2^2)	2 (2^1)	1 (2^0)
127	0	1	1	1	1	1	1	1
93	0	1	0	1	1	1	0	1

How is the conversion made? It's simple: 127=64+32+16+8+4+2+1 in decimal notation equals 01111111 in binary notation. In addition, 93=64+16+8+4+1 in decimal notation equals 01011101 in binary notation. The same process can be performed for any other values between 0 and 255.

EXAM ALERT

Binary Math Although you're not likely to be tested extensively on binary math on Exam 70-291, it's a good idea to create a chart something like that shown in Table 1.1 when you get into the testing center. This will make it easier for you to quickly perform decimal-to-binary math conversions and also assist you in working with variable length subnet masks (VLSM).

When you know how to convert one octet, you simply apply the process to each remaining octet, and you are in business. With some time and practice, you will be able to quickly convert many common binary values in your head.

Because of the extremely large possible number of IP address—2^{32} (4,294,967,296)—IP addresses are organized by class. There are three basic classes: Class A, Class B, and Class C. Table 1.3 defines the range and number of hosts included with each class of network.

TABLE 1.3 IP Address Classes

Class	Address Range	Number of Network IDs	Number of Host IDs
A	1–126	126	16,777,214
B	128–191	16,384	65,534
C	192–223	2,097,152	254

Subnets and Subnet Masks

If you assume that an IP address identifies a computer, it's fair to say that a subnet identifies where the computer is. The component of an IP address that determines whether packets are to be sent locally or through a router is the *subnet mask*. The subnet mask tells the protocol whether the local host and the destination host are on the same subnet.

A subnet mask effectively breaks a complete IP address into two parts: the network identifier and the host identifier. Think of this in relationship to your home street address, which also has two parts: the street name (the network identifier) and the house number (the host identifier).

Basically, when the subnet bits match, the host and destination host are on the same subnet, and no routing is needed. When the subnet bits don't match, the destination host is on a remote network, and the packets are sent to the router.

The Internet community has standardized default subnet masks for each of the three IP address classes. The subnet masks for these address classes are defined in Table 1.4.

TABLE 1.4 Default IP Class Subnet Masks

Address Class	Bits for Subnet Mask	Subnet Mask
A	11111111 00000000 00000000 00000000	255.0.0.0
B	11111111 11111111 00000000 00000000	255.255.0.0
C	11111111 11111111 11111111 00000000	255.255.255.0

If a computer has an IP address of 142.146.102.45 with a subnet mask of 255.255.0.0, the first two octets (142.146) identify the network, and the last two octets (102.45) identify a specific host on that network.

Variable Length Subnet Masks (VLSM)

When you're working with TCP/IP, one of the most difficult topics to understand is the concept of Variable Length Subnet Masks (VLSM). As the use of TCP/IP has grown more widespread, it has become obvious that sometimes assigning even a full Class C address with 254 available hosts is a waste of address space; this would be the case, for example, in a branch office with five employees, a file server, and a printer. An IP address range must be broken into smaller pieces to allow for more efficient use of the address space. Using VLSM (also known as *subnet addressing*) is a method for "borrowing" bits from the host ID portion of an IP address and applying them to the network ID.

Suppose that you have been assigned the Class C address 193.18.5.0 and you need to create five separate networks, one for five different offices, from your one IP address range. To do so, you will need to borrow three bits from the host ID field, thus creating the subnet mask of 255.255.224.0. By using this subnet mask, you actually end up being able to create six separate subnets, which is the closest match to your needs since you can't create five subnets and the next smallest amount is four subnets using the 255.255.192.0 subnet mask as you'll see a bit later on.

To see how subnet addressing works, let's first convert the IP address 193.18.5.0 to binary form:

```
11000001 00010010 00000101 00000000
```

Remember, in a default Class C address, the first 24 bits are the network ID, and the last 8 bits are the host ID.

To indicate that bits are being borrowed from the host ID, you use a subnet mask, which is also a 32-bit binary number. To make clear the purpose of the subnet mask, you need to examine it in conjunction with the binary IP address, like this:

`11000001 00010010 00000101 00000000` represents the IP address assigned to you. `11111111 11111111 11100000 00000000` represents the subnet mask required.

In dotted-decimal notation, the subnet mask address is 255.255.224.0. The rules of subnet masking are simple:

- 1 in the network mask indicates that a bit in the IP address is part of the network ID.
- 0 in the network mask indicates that a bit in the IP address is part of the host ID.

This example has 27 bits in the network mask, so within the network ID are 27 bits for addressing. This subnet mask allows the following subnetworks (that is, subnet IDs) to be used within the Class C address range:

```
10101100 00010010 11111111 11100000
10101100 00010010 11111111 00100000
10101100 00010010 11111111 01000000
10101100 00010010 11111111 01100000
10101100 00010010 11111111 10000000
10101100 00010010 11111111 10100000
10101100 00010010 11111111 11000000
10101100 00010010 11111111 00000000
```

If you do the math to convert the binary addresses to decimal, you will find that the subnet mask 255.255.255.224 lets you construct eight subnets with the following IP address ranges:

- 193.18.5.0–193.18.5.31
- 193.18.5.32–193.18.5.63
- 193.18.5.64.–193.18.5.95

- 193.18.5.96–193.18.5.127
- 193.18.5.128–193.18.5.159
- 193.18.5.160–193.18.5.191
- 193.18.5.192–193.18.5.223
- 193.18.5.224–193.18.5.255

Recall that the 224 in the subnet mask 255.255.224.0 comes from the fact that we are borrowing bits from the host ID and using them for the network ID. Referring back to Table 1.1, we can see how the value was obtained. 224=128+64+32 in decimal notation equals 11100000 in binary notation. The subnet mask actually becomes part of the configuration of each host on the network, enabling the hosts to discriminate between network ID, subnet ID, and host ID.

To determine the available IP addresses in each subnet, you simply perform the binary math again on the host ID portion of the third octet. The second range, 193.18.5.32–193.18.5.63, yields host IDs in the fourth octet from 32 to 63. The IP address 193.18.5.32 itself is not valid for host use because it is the broadcast address for that subnet, so the first IP address that a host could use would be 192.18.5.33. In this case, 33=0+0+32+0+0+0+0+1 equals 00100001 in binary notation.

NOTE

Controlling the Numbers By now, you might be wondering how the rules and regulations for IP addresses and IP addressing are laid down and who regulates them. The Internet Assigned Numbers Authority (IANA) is responsible for assigning IP address blocks to organizations (ISPs and large companies) as well as maintaining three private IP address ranges (10.0.0.0/8, 172.16.0.0/12, and 192.168.0.0/16) that are intended for use on private networks. You can learn more about IANA's activities by visiting www.iana.org.

NOTE

Let's take a short break before moving on to the next topic and examine what some sample subnetting charts might look like. Obviously this is much more detail than you'd need to create for your exam to answer a single exam question, but seeing it here should help you to understand the relationship between the subnet mask, the subnet network address, the host IP address ranges, and the subnet broadcast address.

Sample Class C Subnetting Chart Using the IP Address of 192.168.15.0

Subnet Mask	Number of Subnets	Number of Hosts per Subnet	Network Address	Usable IP Range	Broadcast Address
255.255.255.0 /24	1	254	192.168.15.0	192.168.15.1–192.168.15.254	192.168.15.255
255.255.255.128 /25	2	126	192.168.15.0	192.168.15.1–192.168.15.126	192.168.15.127
			192.168.15.128	192.168.151.29–192.168.15.254	192.168.15.255
255.255.255.192 /26	4	62	192.168.15.0	192.168.15.1–192.168.15.62	192.168.15.63
			192.168.15.64	192.168.15.65–192.168.15.126	192.168.15.127
			192.168.15.128	192.168.15.129–192.168.15.190	192.168.15.191
			192.168.15.192	192.168.15.193–192.168.15.254	192.168.15.255
255.255.255.224 /27	8	30	192.168.15.0	192.168.15.1–192.168.15.30	192.168.15.31
			192.168.15.32	192.168.15.33–192.168.15.62	192.168.15.63
			192.168.15.64	192.168.15.65–192.168.15.94	192.168.15.95
			192.168.15.96	192.168.15.97–192.168.15.126	192.168.15.127
			192.168.15.128	192.168.15.129–192.168.15.158	192.168.15.159
			192.168.15.160	192.168.15.161–192.168.15.190	192.168.15.191
			192.168.15.192	192.168.15.193–192.168.15.222	192.168.15.223
			192.168.15.224	192.168.15.225–192.168.15.254	192.168.15.255
255.255.255.240 /28	16	14	192.168.15.0	192.168.15.1–.14	192.168.15.15
			192.168.15.16	192.168.15.17–.30	192.168.15.31
			192.168.15.32	192.168.15.33–.46	192.168.15.47
			192.168.15.48	192.168.15.49–.62	192.168.15.63
			192.168.15.64	192.168.15.65–.78	192.168.15.79
			192.168.15.80	192.168.15.81–.94	192.168.15.95
			192.168.15.96	192.168.15.97–192.168.15.110	192.168.15.111
			192.168.15.112	192.168.15.113–192.168.15.126	192.168.15.127
			192.168.15.128	192.168.15.129–192.168.15.142	192.168.15.143
			192.168.15.144	192.168.15.145–192.168.15.158	192.168.15.159
			192.168.15.160	192.168.15.161–192.168.15.174	192.168.15.175
			192.168.15.176	192.168.15.177–192.168.15.190	192.168.15.191
			192.168.15.192	192.168.15.193–192.168.15.206	192.168.15.207
			192.168.15.208	192.168.15.209–192.168.15.222	192.168.15.223
			192.168.15.224	192.168.15.225–192.168.15.238	192.168.15.239
			192.168.15.240	192.168.15.241–192.168.15.254	192.168.15.255

We'll leave the last two subnets (.248/29 and .252/30) for you to complete on your own later!

Recall that the /24 subnet mask is the default Class C subnet mask, and one that you'll typically see in production, but not so much during your exam. Another common subnet mask is /16, or 255.255.0.0. When working with that subnet mask, you can use the same basic subnetting logic as we've seen thus far. The next table illustrates how subnetting works for a Class B IP address.

Sample Class B Subnetting Chart Using the IP Address of 172.16.0.0

Subnet Mask	Number of Subnets	Number of Hosts per Subnet	Network Address	Usable IP Range	Broadcast Address
255.255.0.0 /16	256	254	172.16.0.0	172.16.0.1–172.16.0.254	172.16.0.255
			172.16.1.0	172.16.1.1–172.16.1.254	172.16.1.255
			...	...	...
			172.16.255.0	172.16.255. 1–172.16.255.254	172.16.255.255
255.255.128.0 /17	128	508	172.16.0.0	172.16.0.1–172.16.0.254 and 172.16.1.1–172.16.1.254	172.16.1.255
			172.16.2.0	172.16.2.1–172.16.2.254 and 172.16.3.1–172.16.3.254	172.16.3.255
			...	...	...
			172.16.254.0	172.16.254.1–172.16.254.254 and 172.16.255.1–172.16.255.254	172.16.255.255
255.255.192.0 /18	64	1016	172.16.0.0	172.16.0.1–172.16.0.254 and 172.16.1.1–172.16.1.254 and 172.16.2.1–172.16.2.254 and 172.16.3.1–172.16.3.254	172.16.3.255
			...	...	...
			172.16.252.0	172.16.252.1–172.16.252.254 and 172.16.253.1–172.16.253.254 and 172.16.254.1–172.16.254.254 and 172.16.255.1–172.16.255.254	172.16.255.255

EXAM ALERT

Private IP Address Ranges You should know that within each IP address class range there exists a private IP address range. Addresses in these private ranges are to be used only on private networks and are thus not routable on the Internet. These ranges are 10.0.0.0/8, 172.16.0.0/12, and 192.168.0.0/16. Chances are that your organization is using one or more subnets from one or more of these private address ranges.

Default Gateway

A *default gateway* is the IP address of the router that the packets from a host should use to leave the subnet. The typical process of how a packet leaves a host and gets to a destination is as follows:

1. Computer A looks up the IP address of Computer E by using a query to a DNS server.
2. Computer A determines whether the IP address of Computer E is local or remote by comparing its own IP address to that of Computer E.
3. If the address is remote, Computer E sends the packets to the default gateway's MAC address. The MAC address of the default gateway is determined via an Address Resolution Protocol (ARP) broadcast.
4. The default gateway forwards the packets on to the next router, according to its routing table.
5. If Computer E's IP address is on the same subnet as Computer A, the IP address of Computer E is resolved to the MAC address through an ARP broadcast.
6. Computer A and Computer E communicate with one another, and there is no need for routing.

This section briefly explained the basics of TCP/IP, including its evolution, mechanics, and components. With this basic knowledge, you can move forward and configure TCP/IP on a Windows Server 2003 computer.

Challenge

You are a consultant who has been hired by Gidget's Widgets LLC, a small widget manufacturing company that has four departments. You have been hired by Gidget's Widgets to evaluate and recommend a design for a new Windows Server 2003–based network they plan to install in their new building. All computers on the network will be either Windows XP Professional or Windows Server 2003.

The president of Gidget's Widgets has told you that he wants each department to be on its own separate IP subnet with room for future growth. Each department must be on a separate IP subnet due to regulatory

(continues)

(continued)

requirements imposed on the widget manufacturing industry. The company has three IP addresses assigned to it for external use by their ISP, but the company wishes to use IP addresses from the 192.168.100.0/24 private range for its internal needs. Should the company grow substantially and need additional IP addresses in the future, it will take them from the 192.168.101.0/24 subnet.

Each computer on the internal network is to be assigned its own statically configured IP address per the CIO's instructions. In cases in which there are more computers in a department than there are usable IP addresses in a subnet, two subnets may be assigned to the same department. For security reasons, a firewall will be used to prevent unauthorized inbound access to internal network clients from the Internet.

The departments and total number of computers are as follows:

- Administration: 25 computers
- IS: 45 computers
- Engineering: 55 computers
- Sales: 35 computers

Your task is to plan the required subnets for Gidget's Widgets using the IP range and instructions given to you by the president of the company.

Try to complete this exercise on your own, listing your conclusions on a sheet of paper. After you have completed the exercise, compare your results to those given in the following paragraphs.

Answers

You need to create four subnets from the given IP address block of 192.168.100.0/24. By applying the subnet mask 255.255.192.0 or 192.168.100.0/26, you can create these four IP subnets:

- 192.168.100.1–192.168.100.62
- 192.168.100.65–192.168.100.126
- 192.168.100.129–192.168.100.190
- 192.168.100.193–192.168.100.254

By using the VLSM /26, you create four valid subnets, each with a total of 62 usable addresses, allowing room for some growth on each IP subnet.

You can now assign each division its own subnets, as outlined here:

- Administration: 192.168.100.1–192.168.100.62
- IS: 192.168.100.65–192.168.100.126
- Engineering: 192.168.100.129–192.168.100.190
- Sales: 192.168.100.193–192.168.100.254

Configuring TCP/IP

Objective:

Configure TCP/IP addressing on a server computer.

Several important changes and improvements have been made to TCP/IP in Windows Server 2003:

- **`netsh` can be used to reset TCP/IP**—A new `netsh` command has been added that allows you to reset TCP/IP back to its defaults. This takes the place of being able to remove and reinstall TCP/IP for troubleshooting in versions of Windows prior to Windows Server 2003.
- **`netstat` can display PIDs**—A new option has been added to the `netstat` command that displays the process identifier (PID) of the process that is holding the active connection. You can use the Task Manager to associate a PID with a specific application. This ability can be extremely useful in determining what applications are putting data on the network on your servers, especially in a troubleshooting situation.
- **Internet Group Management Protocol version 3 (IGMPv3) is supported**—Because Windows Server 2003 has built-in IGMPv3 support, hosts can request to receive multicast traffic from a specific source or from all sources except a specific source. In addition, source-specific routing allows multicast-capable routers to prevent delivery of multicast traffic to subnets with no multicast clients.
- **TCP/IP can determine the interface speed route metric**—TCP/IP can now automatically determine the metric of a route, based on the speed of its interface. Interfaces with a speed of 10Mbps get a metric of 30, and interfaces with a speed of 100Mbps get a metric of 20. This allows the server to automatically treat an interface with a greater speed as preferred over one with a lower speed.
- **IPv6 is supported**—Support for the forthcoming IPv6 is provided in Windows Server 2003 for future compatibility and growth options.

EXAM ALERT

`netsh` and TCP/IP Perhaps the most likely item to appear on your exam is the fact that you will use the `netsh` command to reset TCP/IP back to its defaults instead of removing and reinstalling TCP/IP for troubleshooting in versions of Windows prior to Windows Server 2003.

Introducing IPv6

It's no secret that we're running out of IP addresses under the current IPv4 addressing system. Under IPv4, an IP address is a 32-bit number that consists of four binary octets separated from each other by periods, such as `11000000.10101000.00000000.10011010`, which is 192.168.0.154 in dotted-decimal notation. This way of providing IP addresses provides for 2^{32} (that is, 4,294,967,296) possible addresses, of which a small number is reserved for private networks and cannot be routed in the Internet.

The IPv6 addressing system aims to solve this problem by making use of a 128-bit number to represent a unique IP address. Using 128 bits gives you 2^{128} (that is, 340,282,366,920,938,463,463,374,607,431,768,211,456, or 3.4×10^{38}) possible addresses. That is enough IP addresses to provide 655,570,793,348,866,943,898,599 (that is, 6.5×10^{23}) addresses for every square meter of the earth's surface. That *should* help solve the shortage of available public IP addresses. Of course, the true power of the IPv6 addressing system is that it allows multiple hierarchical levels of organization and flexibility in design. Both are currently lacking from the IPv4 Internet of today.

A 128-bit IPv6 address, as you might suspect, looks different from what you are used to seeing in IPv4. An IPv6 address in binary form looks like this: `0010000111011010 0000000011010011 0000000000000000 0010111100111011 0000001010101010 0000000011111111 1111111000101000 1001110001011010`. This translates into `21DA:00D3:0000:2F3B:02AA:00FF:FE28:9C5A` in hexadecimal format.

Looks confusing, doesn't it? Well, it certainly can be if you're not accustomed to looking at IPv6 addresses. The IPv6 protocol and addressing system should all but put an end to memorizing IP addresses!

Using the IPv6 protocol, IP classes and classless interdomain routing (CIDR) will be things of the past. The three commonly used private IP ranges (10.0.0.0/8, 172.16.0.0/12, and 192.168.0.0/16) will be replaced by one site-local address range (FEC0::/48). The familiar loopback address of 127.0.0.1 will be replaced by ::1.

So what's up with the :: in IPv6? In the interest of making things easier, you can use a double colon (::) to represent contiguous strings of zero values. Therefore, the loopback address 0:0:0:0:0:0:0:1 can become simply ::1. Of course, you can use a double colon only once in an IPv6 address—for obvious reasons.

In addition, you can use leading zero suppression to remove the leading zeros within an individual 16-bit string. Thus, `21DA:00D3:0000:2F3B:02AA:00FF:FE28:9C5A` becomes `21DA:D3:0:2F3B:2AA:FF:FE28:9C5A`. Of course, the drivers within the operating system and the infrastructure hardware devices (routers, switches, and so on) will handle all these conversions automatically, and they will be invisible to you.

For more information on IPv6, you can visit the official IPv6 site, located at www.ietf.org/html.charters/ipv6-charter.html, or visit the Microsoft Web site about IPv6, located at www.microsoft.com/windowsserver2003/technologies/ipv6/default.mspx.

EXAM ALERT

No IPv6 Don't expect to be tested on IPv6 on your exam as it is still quite some time from broad mainstream adoption.

With knowledge in hand of how IP addressing works, you can now proceed to configuring a computer's network adapter with the required TCP/IP information. You can configure a Windows Server 2003 computer with an IP address in two ways. The first is through DHCP, as discussed in Chapter 2, "Implementing, Managing, and Troubleshooting DHCP." Using DHCP has many advantages, including the following:

- Allows for centralized management
- Enables you to make changes at the server rather than on each computer
- Resolves conflicts of IP addresses
- Resolves problems when hosts move from subnet to subnet
- Saves time because you no longer need to visit each computer to set the IP properties

CAUTION

What IP Address Should I Use? If you're working in a large network, there's probably a group of people responsible for adding and removing the IP addresses assigned to the network. You should check with these gurus before you arbitrarily add an IP address to the network. A wrong IP address on your end could mean big headaches on theirs.

If you're isolated from a production environment, however, you can use whatever IP address you want.

The second way to configure a Windows Server 2003 computer with an IP address is to manually assign the IP address and other TCP/IP properties on the computer. For workstations, this method is not often chosen due to the complexity and difficulty of maintaining a large number of statically assigned IP address. For servers, however, the situation is much different. Any server that offers a service to the network should have a static IP address. The following list contains some of the more common server types that offer services to clients and thus require statically assigned IP addresses:

- Domain Controllers
- DNS, DHCP or WINS servers
- File or print servers
- Database or Web servers
- Exchange servers

NOTE

Know Your Connections The term *connection* refers to a network component that represents how one host connects to another host. Examples of connections include Local Area Network (LAN), Wide Area Network (WAN), or Dial-Up Networking (DUN).

Step by Step 1.1 describes the process of configuring the TCP/IP properties for a Windows Server 2003 computer's network adapter.

STEP BY STEP

1.1 Configuring TCP/IP

1. Open the Network Connections window by selecting Start, Settings, Network Connections. The Network Connections window, shown in Figure 1.2, displays all configured connections on the computer.

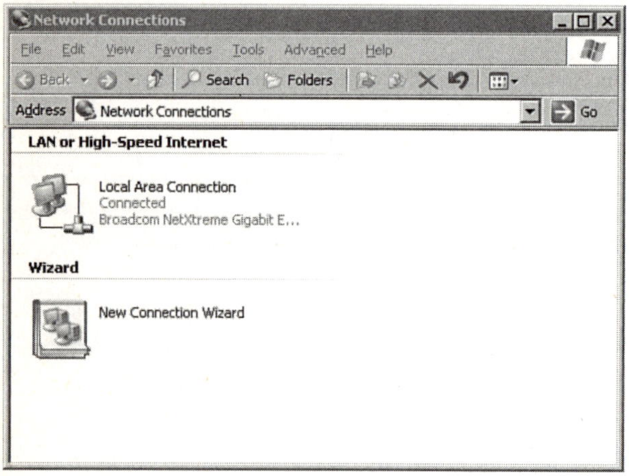

FIGURE 1.2 The Network Connections window displays all configured network connections for a computer.

2. Double-click the Local Area Connection icon to bring up the Local Area Connection Status dialog box, as shown in Figure 1.3.

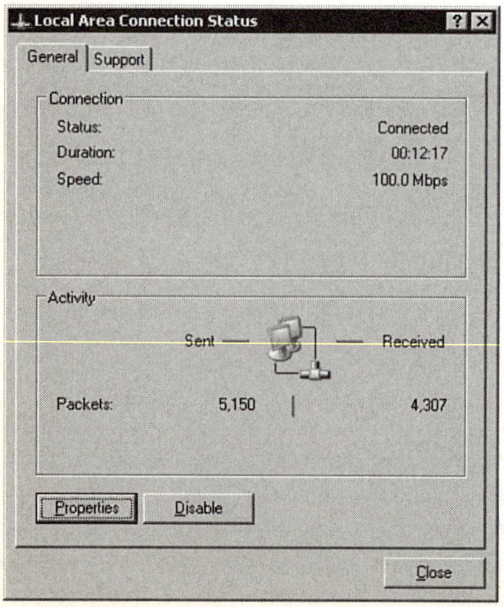

FIGURE 1.3 The Local Area Connection Status dialog box displays general statistics about the network connection.

3. Click the Properties button to open the Local Area Connection Properties dialog box, as shown in Figure 1.4.

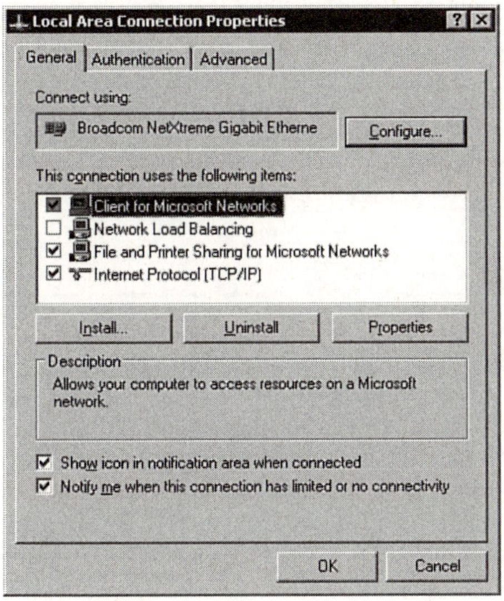

FIGURE 1.4 The Local Area Connection Properties dialog box allows you to configure network connection properties.

4. On the General tab, select Internet Protocol (TCP/IP) and then click Properties. The Internet Protocol (TCP/IP) Properties dialog box opens, as shown in Figure 1.5.

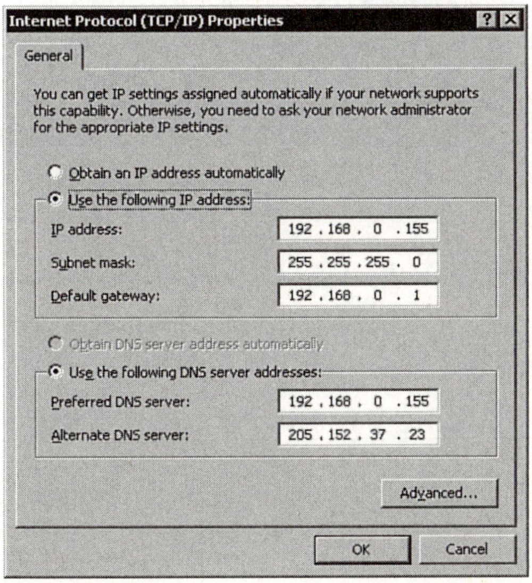

FIGURE 1.5 The Internet Protocol (TCP/IP) Properties dialog box is used to configure TCP/IP settings for a network connection.

5. As you can see in Figure 1.5, the IP address, subnet mask, default gateway, and DNS servers are statically assigned. The server in this example is providing network services, including DNS and DHCP, to network clients and thus requires a static IP address. If you want to have the network adapter acquire its IP address information from a DHCP server, select the options Obtain an IP Address Automatically and Obtain DNS Server Address Automatically. You can also have the IP address information provided by DHCP and manually specify the DNS server addresses if you choose. After you make your selections, click OK to accept them.
6. Click Close to close the Local Area Connection Properties dialog box.

NOTE

DNS Servers DNS servers provide a crucial network service for networks of all sizes. DNS servers provide forward (domain name-to-IP address) and reverse (IP address-to-domain name) lookups to network clients. Using DNS allows you to remember an easy domain name, such as www.microsoft.com, instead of an IP address, such as 207.46.134.190. When you enter www.microsoft.com into a browser, one or more Internet DNS servers provide name resolution services for you, allowing you make a connection to the Microsoft Web site. The same concept applies to private networks. DNS is discussed in more detail in Chapter 3, "Implementing and Managing DNS."

EXAM ALERT

Configuring a Gateway The discussion about whether the default gateway is a required portion of a valid IP address is an ongoing one in many circles. If you recall the fact that a default gateway is required only when a computer must route packets off its own subnet, you can say that it is not always a required portion of the TCP/IP configuration information. In some cases, you might have a very good reason not to configure a default gateway, as in the example of a server that you do not want to be able to communicate with clients outside its own subnet; not having a default gateway adds a small bit of extra security in this case. However, when you take your exam, you should *always assume* that a default gateway is required and should be configured on a server unless specifically told otherwise.

The following section describes how to make additional configuration settings, if required.

Advanced TCP/IP Configuration

After you've performed the initial configuration of TCP/IP, you might still need to configure some additional settings on the protocol. On the TCP/IP Properties dialog box, you can access these settings by clicking the Advanced button, which causes the Advanced TCP/IP Settings dialog box, shown in Figure 1.6, to appear.

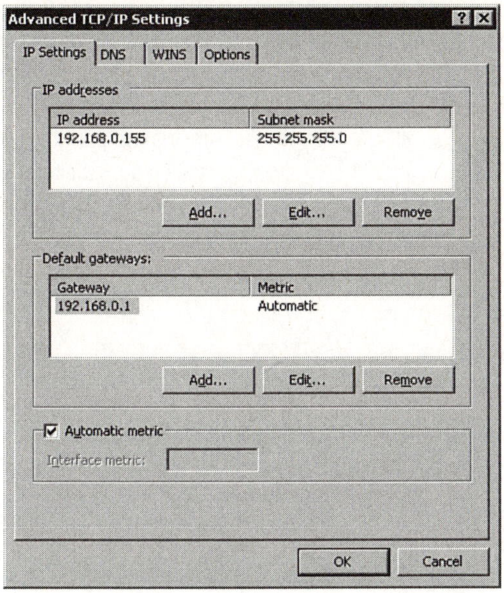

FIGURE 1.6 The Advanced TCP/IP Settings dialog box is used to configure additional, advanced TCP/IP settings for a network connection.

As you can see in Figure 1.6, the IP Settings tab displays the currently configured IP address and default gateway. From this tab, you can add additional IP addresses to the network adapter. This option is rarely used for most servers; however, it might be used if the computer hosts one or more Web sites. You can assign two IP addresses to one adapter. Each IP address represents a different domain name hosted on the server.

You can also specify additional default gateways, including the option to manually configure the route metric associated with each gateway. The *route metric* can be thought of as the "cost" of using a specific route: Each hop along the route has a specific cost that is dependent on several factors, including the actual monetary cost of the link and the speed of the link. Lower metrics typically equal faster routes and thus are preferred. Recall that Windows Server 2003 automatically assigns metrics based on the speed of the network interface. As mentioned earlier in this chapter, interfaces with a speed of 10Mbps get a metric of 30, and interfaces with a speed of 100Mbps get a metric of 20. The lower the number, the more preferred the route is.

The DNS tab of the Advanced TCP/IP Settings dialog box, shown in Figure 1.7, allows you to configure additional multiple DNS servers that the network connection should use and the order in which they should be contacted. In addition, you can modify the behavior of Windows in relationship to domain name suffixes.

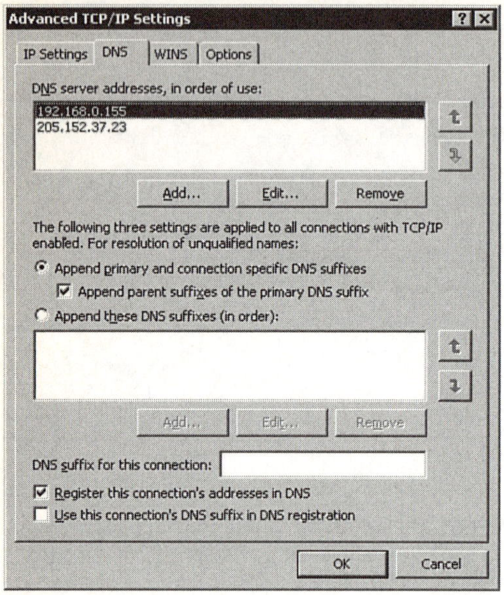

FIGURE 1.7 You can specify granular configuration information on the DNS tab of the Advanced TCP/IP Settings dialog box.

Selecting the Append Primary and Connection Specific DNS Suffixes option specifies that name resolution for unqualified names that are queried on the computer is to be limited to the domain suffixes of the primary and connection-specific suffixes. For example, suppose that your primary DNS suffix is corp.quepublishing.com and you attempt to `ping` a computer by issuing the following command:

```
ping filesvr042
```

In this case, your server will query the DNS servers for filesvr042.corp.quepublishing.com. If you have a connection-specific suffix domain name configured on an adapter, such as indianapolis. corp.quepublishing.com, your computer will also query for filesvr042. indianapolis.corp. quepublishing.com.

Alternatively, you can manually specify DNS suffixes that the computer should query by selecting Append These DNS Suffixes (in Order) and adding them as appropriate. For example, suppose you have selected this option and configured the DNS suffixes sales. quepublishing.com and production.quepublishing.com. Now if you attempt to ping filesvr042, the computer will attempt to query for filesvr042.sales.quepublishing.com and filesvr042. production.quepublishing.com only.

You can specify the connection-specific DNS suffix in the DNS Suffix for This Connection box. Selecting the Register This Connection's Address in DNS option specifies that the computer is to register the fully qualified domain name (FQDN) of the computer in DNS via dynamic DNS (DDNS). If you select the Use This Connection's DNS Suffix in DNS

Registration option, an additional update will be made to DNS with the connection-specific information.

Before DNS was king in Microsoft Windows-based networks, WINS was used to resolve NetBIOS hostnames to IP addresses on a network. Although it is no longer required in networks running all Windows 2000 or better computers, WINS still exists to support legacy systems on networks.

To specify WINS servers that are to be used, you need only click the Add button seen in Figure 1.8, which opens the TCP/IP WINS Server input box shown in Figure 1.9. You can use the arrows to move them up and down as required to set them in the preferred order of usage. Windows Server 2003 follows in the footsteps of Windows 2000 Server by allowing you to add as many as 12 different WINS servers.

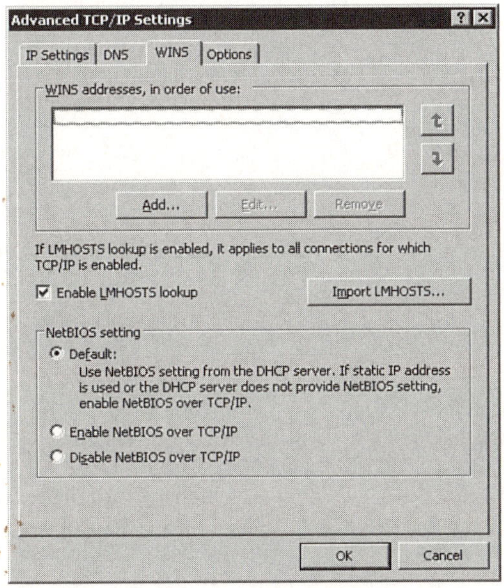

FIGURE 1.8 The WINS tab of the Advanced TCP/IP Settings dialog box allows you to specify how the network adapter behaves in relationship to WINS and NetBIOS.

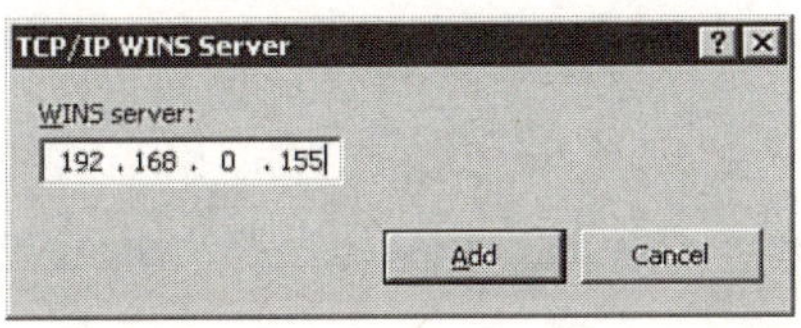

FIGURE 1.9 You can add any WINS servers, if required, by using the TCP/IP WINS Server input box.

The `lmhosts` file is the WINS equivalent of the DNS `hosts` file: It contains static mappings of NetBIOS hostnames-to-IP addresses. If you still have an `lmhosts` file in use, you can specify to have it used. In addition, you can opt to import the `lmhosts` file to the local computer.

The last item you can configure on the WINS tab is whether you will allow NetBIOS over TCP/IP (NetBT). You can opt to use the DHCP server setting, to enable NetBT support, or to disable NetBT support. If you are operating in an environment where no legacy WINS clients exist, you can safely disable NetBT support.

The Options tab of the Advanced TCP/IP Settings dialog box, shown in Figure 1.10, contains only one item in Windows Server 2003: TCP/IP Filtering. Windows Server 2003 allows you to control the type of TCP/IP information that is sent to a computer. You can configure a universal rule for the type of data that reaches all network connections in the server, or you can configure each connection individually.

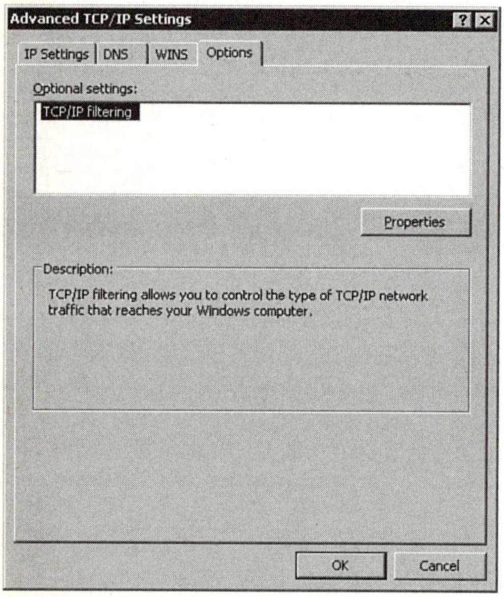

FIGURE 1.10 The Options tab of the Advanced TCP/IP Settings dialog box contains few options in Windows Server 2003; it allows you to configure only TCP/IP filtering.

Common TCP/IP Ports

TCP provides guaranteed packet delivery. Table 1.5 lists the common TCP ports to which you can allow or deny access.

TABLE 1.5 Common TCP Port Numbers

TCP Port Number	Description
20	FTP data channel
21	FTP control channel
22	SSH Remote Login Protocol
23	Telnet

TABLE 1.5 Continued

TCP Port Number	Description
25	Simple Mail Transfer Protocol (SMTP)
53	Domain Name System (DNS)
69	Trivial File Transfer Protocol (TFTP)
80	Hypertext Transfer Protocol (HTTP)
110	Post Office Protocol version 3 (POP3)
137	NetBIOS Name Service (NBNS)
138	NetBIOS Datagram Service
139	NetBIOS Session Service
161	Simple Network Management Protocol (SNMP)
389	Lightweight Directory Access Protocol (LDAP)
443	Secure HTTP using SSL/TLS (HTTPS)

EXAM ALERT

Know Your Ports The list of TCP ports in Table 1.5 is a good start to those ports that you should memorize before exam day. This information will also come into play during your daily administrative tasks after you've passed your exam.

User Datagram Protocol (UDP) does not provide guaranteed packet delivery; rather, it makes a best-effort attempt for delivery. Table 1.6 lists common UDP ports to which you can allow or deny access.

TABLE 1.6 Common UDP Port Numbers

TCP Port Number	Description
20	FTP data channel
21	FTP control channel
22	SSH Remote Login Protocol
23	Telnet
25	SMTP
53	DNS
69	TFTP
80	HTTP
110	POP3

(continues)

TABLE 1.6 Continued

TCP Port Number	Description
137	NBNS
138	NetBIOS Datagram Service
139	NetBIOS Session Service
161	SNMP
389	LDAP
443	HTTPS
520	Routing Information Protocol (RIP)

NOTE

IP Port Numbers You can get a full list of all the IP port numbers at www.iana.org/assignments/port-numbers.

Common TCP/IP Protocols

IP is composed of several different protocols. Table 1.7 lists common Internet protocol numbers to which you can allow or deny access.

TABLE 1.7 Common Internet Protocol Numbers

Protocol Number	Protocol
1	Internet Control Message Protocol (ICMP)
2	Internet Group Management Protocol (IGMP)
3	Gateway-to-Gateway Protocol (GGP)
4	IP in IP (encapsulation)
5	Stream (ST)
6	TCP
7	Computer-base training (CBT)
8	Exterior Gateway Protocol (EGP)

NOTE

Internet Protocol Numbers You can get a full list of all the Internet protocol numbers at http://support.microsoft.com/default.aspx?scid=KB;en-us;289892.

TCP/IP Packet Filtering

TCP/IP packet filtering allows you to determine the type of TCP ports that can be accessed, the UDP ports that are accessed, and more directly, which Internet protocols can access a computer. For example, you can filter port 80, which is used by HTTP. By filtering this port, you can deny access to all Web servers.

Step by Step 1.2 guides you through the process of creating an IP packet filter.

STEP BY STEP

1.2 Configuring IP Filtering

1. Open the Network Connections window by selecting Start, Settings, Network Connections.
2. Double-click the Local Area Connection icon to bring up the Local Area Connection Status dialog box.
3. Click the Properties button to open the Local Area Connection Properties dialog box.
4. On the General tab, select Internet Protocol (TCP/IP) and then click Properties. The Internet Protocol (TCP/IP) Properties dialog box opens.
5. From this General tab of the Internet Protocol (TCP/IP) Properties dialog box, click the Advanced button. The Advanced TCP/IP Settings dialog box opens.
6. Click the Options tab (refer to Figure 1.9) and click the Properties button to open the TCP/IP Filtering dialog box, as shown in Figure 1.11.

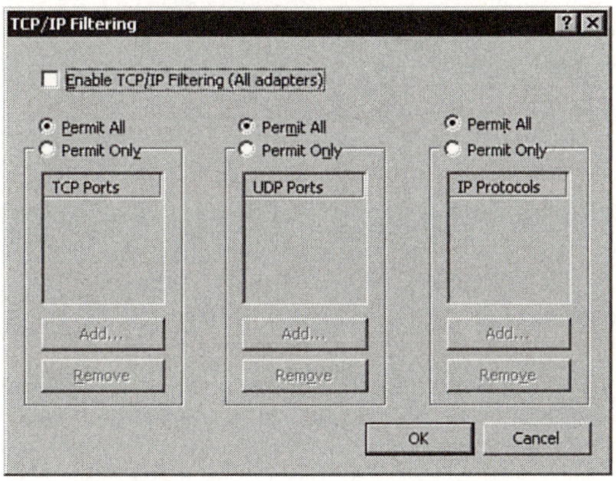

FIGURE 1.11 You configure TCP/IP filters for a network connection from the TCP/IP Filtering dialog box.

7. Select the Enable TCP/IP Filtering (All Adapters) option to enable TCP/IP filters.
8. Above TCP Ports, select the Permit Only option and then click the Add button. The Add Filter dialog box opens.
9. Specify port number 23 for Telnet sessions, and then click OK.

10. Click Add and enter port number 80 for Web access, and then click OK.
11. Select the Permit Only option for UDP ports and then click the Add button.
12. Enter port number 69 for TFTP sessions, and then click OK.
13. Click Add and enter port number 161 for SNMP, and then click OK.
14. Click OK to approve these settings, which allow only TCP ports 23 and 80 and UDP ports 69 and 161 to be accessed on the server.

CAUTION

Don't Rely Solely on TCP/IP Filters The TCP/IP filters provided in Windows can't ever replace a full-featured network protective device such as a firewall. Microsoft never intended TCP/IP filters to fulfill this role, and you should not either. In addition, you need to be aware that the TCP/IP filtering in Windows Server 2003 does not make any differentiation between outgoing and incoming requests, so you might get unexpected results.

Troubleshooting TCP/IP Addressing Problems

Even in the best planned and implemented networks, problems arise from time to time. Some problems can be traced back to users making unauthorized changes to client computer settings, and others may be due to network connectivity problems such as downed or saturated links. Whatever the case may be, you need to quickly identify and correct problems related to TCP/IP addressing if network communications are to occur smoothly on your network.

In your troubleshooting efforts, you can make use of several tools that are built into Windows Server 2003. These tools include the venerable `ping` command, which has been around as long as TCP/IP (well, almost as long) and some newer tools, such as the `pathping` command and the Network Diagnostics tool that can be run within the Windows graphical user interface (GUI). Of course, there are many useful third-party tools and applications available, but you do not need to worry about them for the exam.

Troubleshooting APIPA

Objective:

Troubleshoot TCP/IP addressing.

- Diagnose and resolve issues related to Automatic Private IP Addressing (APIPA).

APIPA is a double-edged sword when it comes to TCP/IP configuration. Introduced in Windows 98, APIPA allows a DHCP-configured computer to automatically assume (or take on) an IP address from the range 169.254.0.1–169.254.255.254 with a subnet mask of 255.255.0.0 when a DHCP server cannot be contacted. IP addresses in this range are sometimes referred to as 169.254.x.y.

So far, it sounds like APIPA is the best thing to come along in the networking world since TCP/IP itself—so why did we call it a double-edged sword? Although APIPA does provide a client with an IP address if a DHCP server cannot be contacted, the only guarantee that is made is that the IP address the client assumes will not belong to any other computer on its IP subnet. Past that, all bets are off. APIPA does not provide any other information to the computer beyond the IP address and subnet mask. This means that computers possessing APIPA IP addresses will not be able to communicate with other computers working with correctly assigned IP addresses and subnet masks. In addition, APIPA computers receive no default gateway and thus are unable to communicate outside their IP subnet.

If one computer cannot communicate with the rest of the network, you can start your troubleshooting search with APIPA. By issuing the `ipconfig/all` command, you will quickly determine the status of the computer's network adapter. Figure 1.12 shows the output you can expect to see when a DHCP-enabled computer cannot locate a DHCP server.

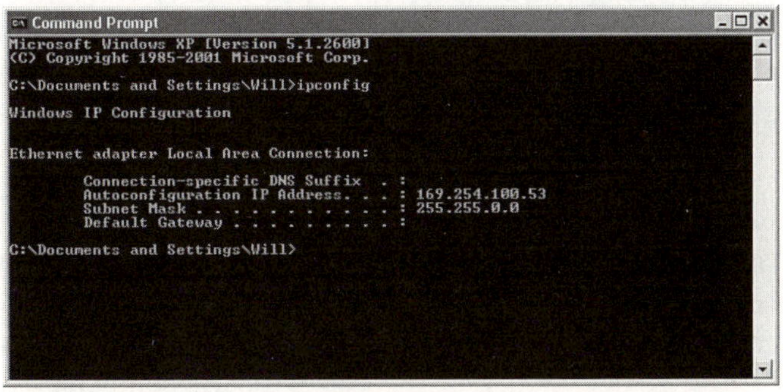

FIGURE 1.12 Network adapters with APIPA IP addresses display the IP address 169.254.x.y

As usual, identifying a problem is only half the battle. The other half is correcting it. Should you have a computer with an APIPA IP address that is having trouble communicating, you need to determine exactly why that computer is not able to communicate with the DHCP server. The possibilities are virtually endless and range from a disconnected network cable to network traffic problems to incorrect TCP/IP configurations.

Client computers who have an APIPA IP address will not be able to connect to any network resources, will not be able to properly process a user logon (although the client computer may be able to perform a logon using cached credentials if Group Policy allows it), and generally will cause a call to the Help Desk. The next section describes how to troubleshoot and diagnose some of these problems.

Troubleshooting Incorrect TCP/IP Configurations

Objective:

Troubleshoot TCP/IP addressing.

- Diagnose and resolve issues related to incorrect TCP/IP configuration.

Having incorrectly configured TCP/IP settings is a problem that you should strive to avoid if at all possible. The best way to avoid having TCP/IP configuration problems is to implement and use DHCP on a network to handle the assignment of IP addresses and other network information. DHCP is discussed in Chapter 2.

If you cannot use DHCP or still have TCP/IP configuration problems, even with DHCP on the network, you can use the tools that Windows Server 2003 provides to determine where the problem lies. Three of these tools—`ping`, `ipconfig`, and the Network Diagnostics tool—are discussed in the following sections.

EXAM ALERT

Know Your Tools You'll want to have a good understanding of the tools used in basic TCP/IP troubleshooting on test day. This knowledge will also carry over into your daily routine as a system administrator.

`ping`

The `ping` command is practically as old as TCP/IP networking itself. You can use the `ping` command to test basic network connectivity between two computers over local and remote networks. The basic syntax of the `ping` command is `ping` *`computerIP`*. This command causes Windows to send to the remote computer four special ICMP packets, which will then be returned to the local computer. Figure 1.13 shows the output of a simple `ping` command against an internal network server.

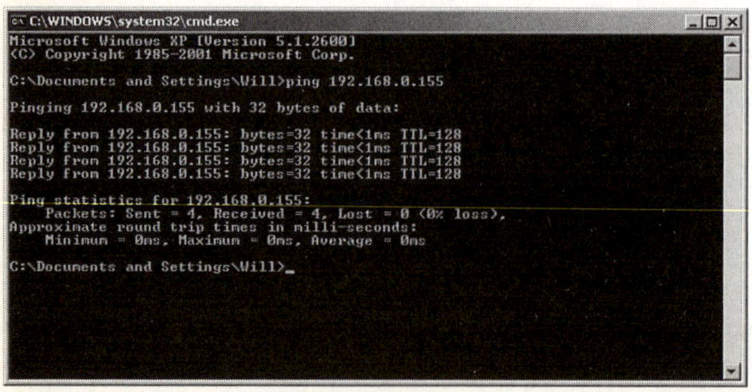

FIGURE 1.13 You can use the `ping` command to verify that basic connectivity exists between two computers.

The following is the full syntax of the `ping` command:

```
ping [-t] [-a] [-n count] [-l size] [-f] [-i TTL] [-v TOS]
[-r count] [-s count] [{-j HostList ¦ -k HostList}] [-w timeout]
```

The switches used with the `ping` command are described in Table 1.8.

TABLE 1.8 The `ping` Command Switches

Switch	Description
`-t`	Specifies that the `ping` command should continue sending echo request (ICMP) messages until manually interrupted. This is useful for establishing and monitoring a constant connection between two hosts.
`-a`	Specifies that reverse name resolution is to be performed on the destination IP address. (Name resolution is discussed in Chapter 3.)
`-n` *`count`*	Specifies how many echo request messages are to be sent to the destination computer. The default is 4.
`-l` *`size`*	Specifies the length of the data field on the echo request, up to a maximum of 65,527 bytes. The default is 32 bytes.
`-f`	Specifies that the echo request messages shall not be fragmented by routers along their path. This setting can be used to troubleshoot maximum transmission unit (MTU)–related problems.
`-i` *`TTL`*	Specifies the value of the Time to Live (TTL) field in the IP header for echo request messages sent. The default is the default TTL value for the host. The maximum TTL is 255.
`-v` *`TOS`*	Specifies the value for the Type of Service (TOS) field in the echo request. The default value is 0, and valid values range from 0 to 255.
`-r` *`count`*	Specifies that the Record Route option in the IP header is used to record the path taken by the echo request message and corresponding echo reply message. The count must between 1 and 9.
`-s` *`count`*	Specifies that the Internet Timestamp option in the IP header is used to record the time of arrival for the echo request message and corresponding echo reply message for each hop. The count must be between 1 and 4.
`-j` *`HostList`*	Specifies that the echo request messages use the Loose Source Route option in the IP header with the set of intermediate destinations specified in *`HostList`*. When you're using loose source routing, successive intermediate destinations can be separated by one or multiple routers. You can enter a maximum of nine addresses or hostnames in *`HostList`*.
`-k` *`HostList`*	Specifies that the echo request messages use the Strict Source Route option in the IP header with the set of intermediate destinations specified in *`HostList`*. When you're using strict source routing, the next intermediate destination must be directly reachable. You can enter a maximum of nine addresses or hostnames in *`HostList`*.
`-w` *`timeout`*	Specifies the amount of time, in milliseconds, to wait for the echo reply message to be received. The default timeout is 4000 milliseconds (4 seconds).

> **NOTE**
>
> **The Story of `ping`** If you want to read about the history of the `ping` command and learn some other interesting `ping`-related trivia, be sure to visit the page of the late Mike Muuss, creator of the `ping` application. You can find it at http://ftp.arl.mil/~mike/ping.html.

Although the `ping` command has many options available, you will most often find yourself using it as demonstrated previously, perhaps by appending the `-t` and/or `-a` switches to it. This provides a constant, verifiable connection and name resolution for your troubleshooting efforts.

`ipconfig`

You can use the `ipconfig` command to quickly determine what settings have been configured for the network adapters in computers. In addition, you can use this command to release and renew DHCP-assigned IP addresses and flush the local DNS cache. Figure 1.14 shows the output of the `ipconfig/all` command on a healthy adapter—that is, one that has no network connectivity problems.

FIGURE 1.14 You can use the `ipconfig` command to verify the configuration status of a network adapter.

The following is the full syntax of the `ipconfig` command:

```
ipconfig [/all] [/renew adapter] [/release adapter] [/flushdns]
[/displaydns] [/registerdns] [/showclassid adapter]
[/setclassid adapter ClassID]
```

The switches for the `ipconfig` command are described in Table 1.9.

TABLE 1.9 The `ipconfig` Command Switches

Switch	Description
`/all`	Specifies that the full TCP/IP configuration is to be displayed for all installed network adapters.
`/renew` *`adapter`*	Specifies that the DHCP configuration for the specified adapter (or all adapters, if none is specified) is to be renewed.
`/release` *`adapter`*	Specifies that the DHCP configuration for the specified adapter (or all adapters, if none is specified) is to be released by sending a `DHCPRELEASE` message to the DHCP server.
`/flushdns`	Specifies that the contents of the local DNS resolver cache are to be flushed. This is useful in times of DNS-related troubleshooting.
`/displaydns`	Specifies that the contents of the local DNS resolver cache are to be displayed onscreen.
`/registerdns`	Specifies that a manual dynamic registration for the DNS name and IP address assigned to the computer is to be performed. This is most useful when you're troubleshooting DNS-related issues.
`/showclassid` *`adapter`*	Specifies that the DHCP class ID for the specified adapter is to be displayed. This is useful when you're troubleshooting DHCP options that are assigned by class ID.
`/setclassid` *`adapter ClassID`*	Specifies that the DHCP class ID for the specified adapter is as provided in the *`ClassID`* space. This removes the currently assigned class ID if no value is specified.

You will most often find yourself using the `/all`, `/renew`, `/release`, and `/flushdns` switches in troubleshooting TCP/IP.

The Network Diagnostics Tool

In an effort to continuously improve the tools available to you and make your job a bit easier, the Network Diagnostics tool is available in Windows XP and Windows Server 2003. You can use this tool to perform many of the same tests shown in the preceding section, plus many more, all from within the Windows GUI. As an example, the Network Diagnostics utility can `ping` SMTP and POP3 gateways, if it is configured to do so. All output is clearly and concisely provided and can be saved to an HTML file if desired.

The easiest way to find the Network Diagnostics tool is to select Start, Help and Support. Then you click Use Tools to view your computer information and diagnose problems. From the list on the left side that then appears, you click the Network Diagnostics link. To configure how the scan will be performed, you can click the Set Scanning Options link. Figure 1.15 shows the options that you can configure to control how the scan is performed.

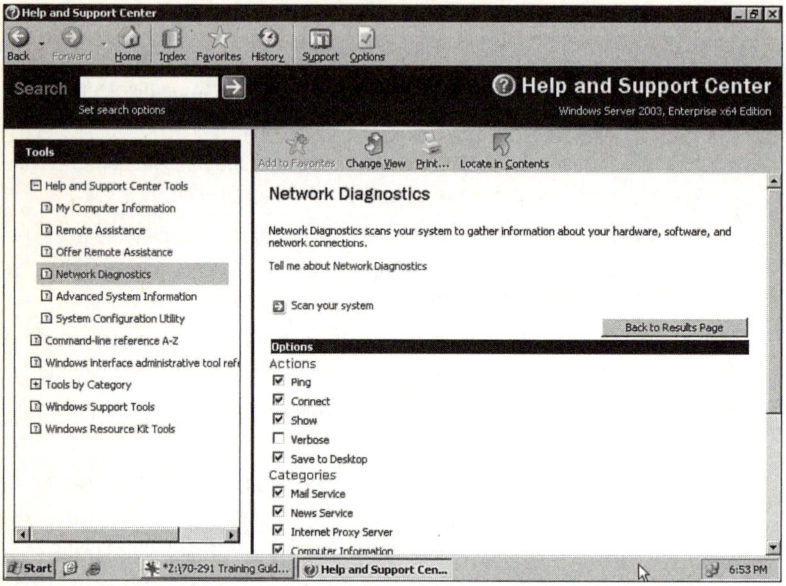

FIGURE 1.15 You can configure a wide array of options to be examined by the Network Diagnostics tool.

When you are ready to perform the scan, click the Scan Your System link. The results of a typical scan are shown in Figure 1.16.

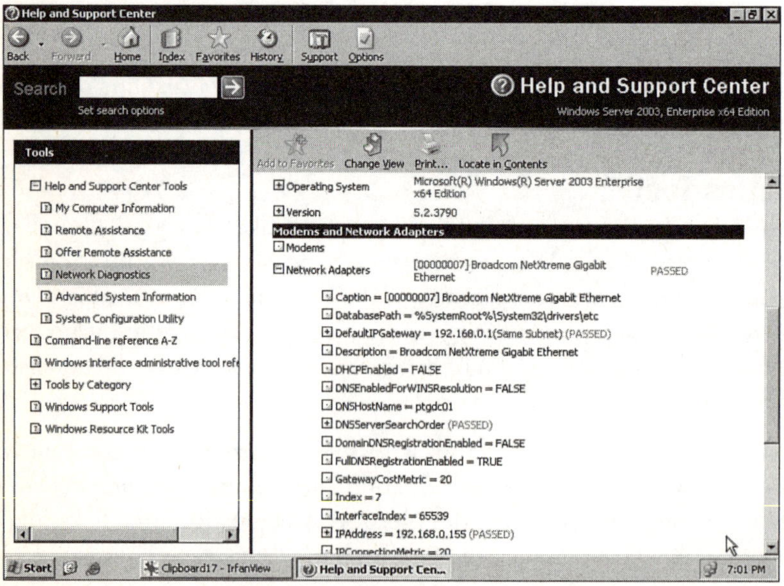

FIGURE 1.16 You can use the Network Diagnostics tool to easily generate a graphical display of TCP/IP network configuration problems.

You can configure the Network Diagnostics tool to examine as much or as little of a TCP/IP configuration as you like. It runs fairly quickly and, as mentioned previously, provides the ability to save the output to HTML files for later viewing.

netsh

The `netsh` command is an advanced configuration and troubleshooting command that provides that ability to manage almost any networking-related component on your Windows Server 2003 computer, but it does require you to have knowledge of the task you're trying to achieve. The `netsh` command can be used interactively or via scripting to manage networking-related configurations such as those for the Windows Firewall, DHCP, WINS, TCP/IP configuration and IP Security (IPSec) settings, as well as many other tasks.

Unlike the relatively easy to understand and use `ping` or `ipconfig` commands we examined earlier, `netsh` can seem significantly more complex to use due to its context-based operation. In other words, you don't simply append switches to the `netsh` command as you've seen previously with `ping` or `ipconfig`; instead, you first must set the context in which `netsh` operates. For instance, you would use interface context to manage network adapters or firewall context to manage the Windows Firewall.

Figure 1.17 demonstrates the context-based approach; that is, we've set the context to mange the TCP/IP properties of the network adapters in a Windows Server 2003 computer. In this case, as shown in the figure, we've simply opted to display the basic configuration of the network adapter.

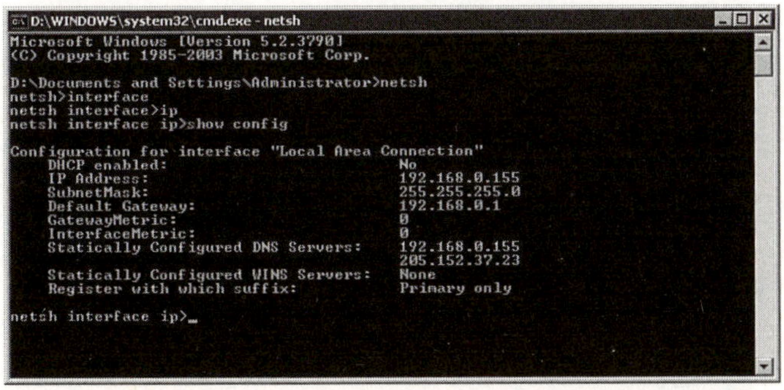

FIGURE 1.17 The `netsh` command can be used to manage almost any networking related setting.

As we mentioned at the start of this section, the `netsh` command has been enhanced in Windows Server 2003 to provide you a means to reset the TCP/IP stack back to its default values should the need arise. This replaces the ability in previous versions of Windows to remove and reinstall TCP/IP for troubleshooting. This advanced troubleshooting and repair action of `netsh` is also accessed from the `netsh interface ip` context you saw previously in Figure 1.17 and is shown as an available command in Figure 1.18.

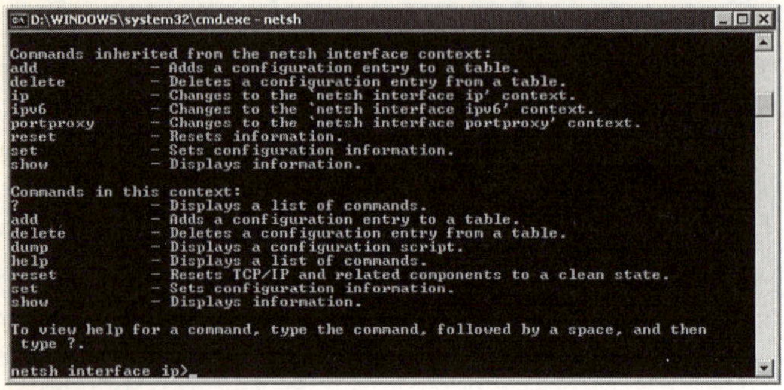

FIGURE 1.18 `netsh` allows you to reset the TCP/IP stack to its defaults for advanced network troubleshooting in Windows Server 2003.

Chapter Summary

To have a reliable, routable network, you need to do effective planning.

In Windows Server 2003, TCP/IP is installed by default. Many features of Windows Server 2003 rely on TCP/IP; thus, in this version of Windows, TCP/IP cannot be uninstalled from a computer's network adapters. TCP/IP requires a valid IP address, subnet mask, default gateway, and DNS servers to operate properly in a large network environment. This information may be entered manually at each client computer and server, or it can be done automatically through DHCP (this is the preferred option). DHCP assigns the client computer an IP address when it is needed. If you're using Windows Server 2003 along with older NetBIOS-reliant operating systems, chances are that you'll be using WINS as well. WINS resolves NetBIOS names, such as `Computer5`, to IP addresses, such as 192.168.0.125. You can access the WINS properties through the WINS tab of the Advanced TCP/IP Settings dialog box.

When something goes awry with a TCP/IP configuration, you need to be able to determine the cause and the required corrective action. Windows Server 2003 (and Windows XP) provides you with a suite of tools that you can use to troubleshoot TCP/IP configuration. You will most commonly find yourself relying on the `ping` and `ipconfig` command-line tools. You can also use the Network Diagnostics tool to collect and display information in the Windows GUI. The more advanced, and more powerful, `netsh` command is also available to manage almost any networking setting.

Key Terms

- Class A IP address
- Class B IP address
- Class C IP address
- default gateway
- IP address
- `ipconfig`
- `ping`
- `netsh`
- subnet mask
- TCP/IP
- TCP/IP filter
- VLSM

Apply Your Knowledge

In this chapter, you have examined the basic history, configuration, implementation, and troubleshooting of TCP/IP in Windows Server 2003. In the following exercises, you will practice some of the concepts and methods discussed in this chapter.

Exercises

1.1 Testing TCP/IP

This exercise guides you through the process of retrieving IP address information. Then you use a few command-line entries to test the configuration and connectivity of the IP address.

Estimated time: 5 minutes

1. Select Start, Run. Then type **CMD** in the Run dialog box and press Enter.
2. At the command prompt, type the command **`ipconfig`** and press Enter. What is your IP address? What is your subnet mask? Can you determine the IP address of the DNS server?
3. Enter **`ipconfig/all`**. What additional information can you now see?
4. Enter **`ping 127.0.0.1`**. This is a special loopback test that tells you whether your network interface card is dead, just playing sick, or, hopefully, just fine.
5. Enter **`ping`** ***XX***, where ***XX*** is your favorite Web site.
6. If you have another computer on this network, `ping` the IP address of that computer.
7. `ping` the name of the computer.

Did all your communications occur successfully? If not, you might need to perform some additional investigation and troubleshooting to determine where your problem lies.

1.2 Creating a TCP/IP Packet Filter

This exercise walks you through the process of creating a TCP/IP filter on a computer.

Estimated time: 20 minutes

1. Open the Network Connections window by selecting Start, Settings, Network Connections.
2. Double-click the Local Area Connection icon to bring up the Local Area Connection Status dialog box.
3. Click the Properties button to open the Local Area Connection Properties dialog box.
4. On the General tab, select Internet Protocol (TCP/IP) and then click Properties.
5. On the General tab of the Internet Protocol (TCP/IP) Properties dialog box, click the Advanced button.
6. Select the Options tab and then click the Properties button to open the TCP/IP Filtering dialog box.

7. Select the Enable TCP/IP Filtering (All Adapters) option to enable TCP/IP filters.
8. Above TCP Ports, select the Permit Only option and then click the Add button.
9. Specify port number 23 for Telnet sessions, and then click OK.
10. Click Add and enter port number 80 for Web access, and then click OK.
11. Select the Permit Only option for UDP ports and then click the Add button.
12. Enter port number 69 for TFTP sessions, and then click OK.
13. Click Add and enter port number 161 for SNMP, and then click OK.
14. Select the Permit Only option for IP protocols and then click the Add button.
15. Enter **2** for IGMP and then click OK.
16. Click OK to approve these settings. Then restart the computer to test the changes.
17. After the computer restarts, go to another computer on the network. Open a command prompt on that computer and `ping` the IP address of the server that has IP filtering configured. Are you able to `ping` the computer?
18. Open the TCP/IP Filtering dialog box on the original computer again. In the Permit Only IP Protocol section, add **1** for ICMP. Approve these settings and restart the computer.
19. Go to another computer on the network and try to `ping` the computer. Does it work now?
20. Return once more to the original computer and remove all the IP packet filters. Approve your changes, reboot, and test the `ping` command again.

1.3 Manually Configuring TCP/IP

In this exercise, you will manually configure TCP/IP on a network adapter.

Estimated time: 10 minutes

1. Open the Network Connections window.
2. Open the Local Area Connection Status dialog box.
3. Click the Properties button to open the Local Area Connection Properties dialog box.
4. On the General tab, select Internet Protocol (TCP/IP) and then click Properties.
5. On the Internet Protocol (TCP/IP) Properties dialog box, manually enter the IP address, subnet mask, default gateway, and DNS servers for this network adapter. If you need to make advanced settings, click the Advanced button. After you make your selections, click OK to accept them.
6. Click Close to close the Local Area Connection Properties dialog box.
7. Check your settings by opening a command prompt and using the `ipconfig/all` command.

1.4 Getting Familiar with `netsh`

In this exercise, you will use the `netsh` command to return configuration information about your server.

Estimated time: 10 minutes

1. Select Start, Run. Then type **CMD** in the Run dialog box and press Enter.
2. At the command prompt, type the command **`netsh`** and press Enter.
3. The `netsh>` prompt appears; type **?** to see a list of available contexts.
4. Enter the interface context by typing **`interface`** and pressing Enter.
5. The `netsh interface>` prompt appears; type **?** to see a list of available sub contexts.
6. Enter the ip context by typing **`ip`** and pressing Enter.
7. The `netsh interface ip>` prompt appears; type **?** to see a list of available subcontexts.
8. Display the show menu by typing **show** and pressing Enter.
9. Enter **`show config`** to display the TCP/IP properties for your network adapter.
10. After you're done examining this information, type **`exit`** and press Enter to close `netsh` and return to the command prompt.

Exam Questions

1. Chris is a departmental systems administrator for Widgets, Inc. Her network consists of 15 Windows Server 2003 computers, 5 of which are domain controllers. The remaining 10 servers are file and print servers for her 750 Windows XP Professional workstation clients. The previous administrator had carefully assigned every computer a static IP address, equally split up among five Class C subnets. Now some users have started moving their computers from one location in the building to another; this trend will be the norm for Widgets, Inc. in the future. After moving, the users complain to Chris that they can no longer access network resources. What is the most likely cause of this problem, and what should Chris do about it? The senior systems administrator has DHCP servers available for Chris to use, should she decide to use them.

   ❍ **A.** There are not enough client access licenses (CALs) for the Windows Server 2003 computers. Chris should purchase the required number of CALs.

   ❍ **B.** The statically configured IP addresses are no longer valid on the subnet to which the computers have been moved. Chris should reconfigure the computers with the correct static IP addresses.

   ❍ **C.** The statically configured IP addresses are no longer valid on the subnet to which the computers have been moved. Chris should reconfigure the computers so that they are DHCP clients.

   ❍ **D.** The port to which the computers are connecting on the switch may be failing. Chris should replace the switches where computers cannot connect to network resources.

2. As the systems administrator of a small legal firm, you are in the process of converting some IP addresses from decimal to binary. What would be the binary value of 209.168.241.158?

   ❍ **A.** 11010001.10101000.11110001.10011110

   ❍ **B.** 11001001.10101000.11110001.10011110

   ❍ **C.** 11010001.10101000.11101001.10011110

   ❍ **D.** 11010001.10101010.11110001.10011110

3. You are the systems administrator for your company. Your task is to configure the IP addresses of your network. You decide to implement DHCP to automate the process and reduce downtime. You have decided, however, to manually enter static IP addresses for certain hosts on the network. Of the following, which would be good candidates to have statically configured IP addresses? (Choose all that apply.)

   ❍ **A.** A laptop that moves around within the company's building throughout the week

   ❍ **B.** A DNS server

   ❍ **C.** An Exchange server

   ❍ **D.** A print server

4. Hannah, a user from the Accounting Department, calls you, the systems administrator, to report that she's having a tough time connecting to resources on your Windows Server 2003 domain. You ask for more information, and Hannah reveals that she is trying to connect to a server in Washington. Other users can connect to that server, but she cannot. Hannah can `ping` the IP address of other hosts on her segment, her default gateway, and even the IP address of the server in Washington, but when she uses the server's hostname to enter the name of the server, she cannot connect. What do you suspect is the problem?

   ❍ **A.** Hannah has a blank or invalid DNS server IP address.

   ❍ **B.** Hannah has a blank or invalid subnet mask.

   ❍ **C.** Hannah has a faulty network adapter card.

   ❍ **D.** Hannah needs to renew her IP address by running the command `ipconfig/release` and then `ipconfig/renew`.

5. You are the systems administrator for Tock's Clocks LTD. All your Windows XP Professional client computers are configured to get DHCP leases from your Windows Server 2003 DHCP server. This morning, one of your client computers no longer had connectivity with the rest of the network. The user claims that she did not change any network settings and has verified that the network cable is properly connected to both the network adapter and the wall jack. What is the most likely reason for the problem that the computer is experiencing?

❍ **A.** The network cable has been damaged and is no longer passing a signal.

❍ **B.** The computer was not able to contact a DHCP server and has assigned itself an APIPA IP address.

❍ **C.** The computer is not a member of the domain and is being refused an IP address.

❍ **D.** The TCP/IP stack on the computer is corrupt and needs to be reset.

6. You are trying to break down an IP subnet into smaller groups of IP addresses. Given the IP address 192.168.50.1/27, what is the corresponding dotted-decimal value subnet mask?

❍ **A.** 255.255.192.0

❍ **B.** 255.255.255.224

❍ **C.** 255.255.255.240

❍ **D.** 255.255.255.192

7. You are the systems administrator for Not Quite Right Sales, Inc. You are configuring a new Windows Server 2003 server to be a file server for your home office intranet that will be used only by local users. Which of the following will you need to have to suitably configure the IP address with a statically assigned address? (Choose all that apply.)

❍ **A.** A valid IP address for the server

❍ **B.** A valid WINS server IP address

❍ **C.** A valid subnet mask

❍ **D.** A valid default gateway

8. You are the systems administrator for Gilligan's Island Tours, Inc. You have recently hired a new assistant systems administrator. You are trying to explain to your assistant how two computers on the same subnet communicate with each other. Which of the following statements should you use to explain to your assistant the process that two computers use to communicate with each other on the same IP subnet?

❍ **A.** The packets will be sent to the MAC address of the default gateway for routing to the destination computer's IP address.

❍ **B.** The packets will be sent to the MAC address of the destination computer.

❍ **C.** The packets will be sent to the IP address of the destination computer.

❍ **D.** The packets will be sent to the IP address of the default gateway for routing to the destination computer's MAC address.

9. You are the systems administrator for Not Quite Enough, Inc. You manually assign IP address information to your network computers. You have three DNS servers on your network that you want to configure in the TCP/IP properties for a new computer that you are configuring. How will you configure three DNS servers for this computer?

❍ **A.** You need to create a dns.ini file and place it in the Startup folder of the computer.

❍ **B.** You cannot configure three DNS servers because there is room for only two entries on the Internet Protocol (TCP/IP) Properties dialog box.

❍ **C.** You need to configure the third DNS server from the DNS tab of the Advanced TCP/IP Settings dialog box.

❍ **D.** You need to add the third DNS server by using the `netsh` command.

10. While troubleshooting a Windows XP Professional computer, you discover that it has an IP address of 169.254.176.132, a subnet mask of 255.255.0.0, and no configured default gateway. What is the most likely reason this computer has gotten these IP settings?

❍ **A.** The user of the computer has configured new settings without fully understanding how routed IP networks function.

❍ **B.** The TCP/IP stack on the computer is corrupt.

❍ **C.** The DHCP server scope has become corrupt.

❍ **D.** The computer has been unable to contact a DHCP server.

11. You are troubleshooting network connectivity between two computers on a routed IP network. What command can you use to send a continuous flow of ICMP echo request packets to the destination IP address?

- ❍ **A.** `ping -a`
- ❍ **B.** `ping -t`
- ❍ **C.** `ping -l`
- ❍ **D.** `ping -f`

12. You are troubleshooting a network adapter that does not appear to have an IP address assigned to it. What command could you issue to cause this network adapter to acquire a DHCP lease?

- ❍ **A.** `ipconfig/acquire`
- ❍ **B.** `ipconfig/refresh`
- ❍ **C.** `ipconfig/renew`
- ❍ **D.** `ipconfig/lease`

13. You are part of the team of systems administrators for SunShine Networks. Your task is to segment your Class C IP address, 210.115.64.0, into three subnets. You must allow for the number of networks to increase. The maximum number of hosts per subnet will never surpass 14 hosts. What subnet mask would allow you to segment the network and allow for the required growth?

- ❍ **A.** 255.255.255.224
- ❍ **B.** 255.255.255.240
- ❍ **C.** 255.255.255.248
- ❍ **D.** 255.255.255.255

14. As a junior systems administrator, you are trying to troubleshoot one of your DNS servers. It seems that your computers running Windows XP Professional have not registered dynamically with your DNS server. You would like to force these computers to register with DNS. What should you do?

- ❍ **A.** Get the user to reboot the system.
- ❍ **B.** At the command prompt, type **`ipconfig/renew`**.
- ❍ **C.** At the command prompt, type **`ipconfig/registerdns`**.
- ❍ **D.** At the command prompt, type **`ipconfig/release`**.

Answers to Exam Questions

1. **C**. In this case Chris should definitely make the move to using DHCP to assign and manage IP address assignments. Even though it will be a fair amount of work initially, it will provide for ease of management later on, especially if more workstations will be moved around in the building. Purchasing CALs is not indicated in the problem and would present Chris with other indicators. Manually configuring the correct IP address settings provides only a temporary quick fix for the problem, but it will not help Chris in the long run. Chris should not replace network infrastructure devices, such as switches, without further investigation. In this situation, the problem is more likely due to the movement of workstations than anything else. For more information, see the section "Configuring TCP/IP."

2. **A**. When converting from decimal to binary, 209.168.241.158 is equal to 11010001.10101000.11110001.10011110. For more information, see the section "IP Addresses."

3. **B**, **C**, **D**. Typically, any server that provides a network service to clients should have a statically configured IP address. This includes DNS servers, Exchange (mail) servers, print servers, file servers, SQL (database) servers, routers, firewalls, and many other types of network devices. For more information, see the section "Configuring TCP/IP."

4. **A**. If Hannah can successfully `ping` local and remote hosts, including the server to which she is trying to connect, most likely she has either a missing DNS IP address or a DNS IP address that has been configured incorrectly. For more information, see the section "Configuring TCP/IP."

5. **B**. In the majority of cases in which a computer configured for DHCP suddenly cannot communicate with the rest of the network, the cause is due to the computer having assigned itself an APIPA IP address. Having a damaged network cable (or any other damaged network device) is certainly a possible cause of this problem, but it is not the most common one. For more information, see the section "Troubleshooting APIPA."

6. **B**. The VLSM 192.168.50.1/27 would be the dotted-decimal equivalent of 255.255.255.224. For more information, see the section "Variable Length Subnet Masks (VLSM)."

7. **A**, **C**, **D**. You need to have a valid IP address, subnet mask, and default gateway configured. Configuring other items, such as a WINS server or DNS server, is not required but will assist in network communications. For more information, see the section "Configuring TCP/IP."

8. **B**. The packets are originally sent to the IP address of the destination computer, but IP uses ARP to determine the MAC address of the destination computer. The MAC address is in the header of the IP packets, and only the network adapter that has that MAC address accepts the packets. For more information, see the section "The Mechanics of IP."

9. **C**. You need to add the third DNS server from the DNS tab of the Advanced TCP/IP Settings dialog box. You can add all three servers from here if you want, and you can change the order in which they are queried by the computer by using the up and down arrows. For more information, see the section "Advanced TCP/IP Configuration."

10. **D**. The most likely reason to see an IP address in the 169.254.0.1–169.254.255.254 range is due to a client computer not being able to contact a DHCP server. IP addresses in this range have a subnet mask of 255.255.0.0 and no configured default gateway—thus preventing any communications outside the local IP subnet and also preventing communications with other client computers that are receiving the proper IP addresses from a DHCP server. For more information, see the section "Troubleshooting APIPA."

11. **B**. By issuing the `ping -t` command, you can send a continuous stream of ICMP echo request packets to the destination IP address. You can stop the stream of packets by using the Ctrl+C key combination. For more information, see the section "`ping`."

12. **C**. You can issue the `ipconfig/renew` command to force the network adapter to acquire a DHCP lease from a DHCP server. For more information, see the section "`ipconfig`."

13. **B**. Because you will never exceed 14 hosts per subnet, your subnet mask should be 255.255.255.240. For more information, see the section "Variable Length Subnet Masks (VLSM)."

14. **C**. To get a client computer to register dynamically with a DNS server at the command prompt, type **`ipconfig/registerdns`**. For more information, see the section "`ipconfig`."

Suggested Readings and Resources

1. Stevens, W. Richard. *TCP/IP Illustrated, Volume 1: The Protocols*. Addison-Wesley, 1994.

2. "Deploying Network Services," http://technet2.microsoft.com/WindowsServer/en/Library/119050c9-7c4d-4cbf-8f38-97c45e4d01ef1033.mspx.

3. "Technical Overview of Windows Server 2003 Networking and Communications," www.microsoft.com/windowsserver2003/techinfo/overview/netcomm.mspx.

4. "Windows Server 2003 Reviewer's Guide," www.microsoft.com/windowsserver2003/techinfo/overview/reviewersguide.mspx.

5. "Windows Server 2003: Product Help," www.microsoft.com/technet/prodtechnol/windowsserver2003/proddocs/entserver/sag_NPStopnode.asp.

CHAPTER TWO 2

Implementing, Managing, and Troubleshooting DHCP

Objectives

Microsoft lists the following objectives for the DHCP portion of the "Implementing, Managing, and Maintaining IP Addressing" section of Exam 70-291, "Implementing, Managing, and Maintaining a Microsoft Windows Server 2003 Network Infrastructure":

Manage DHCP.

- **Manage DHCP clients and leases.**
- **Manage DHCP Relay Agent.**
- **Manage DHCP databases.**
- **Manage DHCP scope options.**
- **Manage reservations and reserved clients.**
- One of the first few network services you will likely deploy and configure when rolling out a production Windows Server 2003 network is the DHCP service. DHCP is highly integrated with both Active Directory and the dynamic DNS (DDNS) service. To meet this objective, you must have a thorough understanding of the workings of DHCP and also how to configure it for use in a network.

Troubleshoot DHCP.

- **Diagnose and resolve issues related to DHCP authorization.**
- **Verify DHCP reservation configuration.**
- **Examine the system event log and DHCP server audit log files to find related events.**
- **Diagnose and resolve issues related to configuration of DHCP server and scope options.**
- **Verify that the DHCP Relay Agent is working correctly.**
- **Verify database integrity.**
- Installing and configuring the DHCP service does not relieve you of monitoring and managing it over time. The ability to monitor, manage, and troubleshoot the DHCP service on a network is critical to the ongoing health of the network as a whole. You should be able to use all the tools available to you to ensure that the DHCP service is operating properly, providing service to network clients.

Outline

Study Strategies

- Be sure you understand what DHCP is, how it works, why it was created, and what enhancements Microsoft Windows Server 2003 DHCP server service adds to the protocol. DHCP has been used in Transmission Control Protocol/Internet Protocol (TCP/IP)–based networks for quite a while. Microsoft has extended the functionality of DHCP as part of its Windows Server 2003 operating system. DHCP is used to dynamically allocate IP addresses, and it also plays a critical role in registering hosts with the Domain Name Service (DNS).
- Be sure you understand the types of scopes that Windows Server 2003 DHCP server service supports, how each works, and when you should use each in a production environment.
- Get your hands dirty. The Step by Step exercises throughout this book provide plenty of directions and exercises, but you should go beyond those examples and create some of your own. If you can, experiment with each of the topics we discuss in this chapter to see how they work and why you would use each one.

Introduction

TCP/IP is the de facto standard for computer networking and appears to have no challengers in the networking protocol arena. If you are going to work with Windows Server 2003, you should expect to work with TCP/IP. One of the keys to successfully working with TCP/IP is having an understanding of the concept of TCP/IP addresses. The designers of TCP/IP wanted an identification scheme that was independent of any one computer or network equipment design, so they established a scheme of IP addresses.

If you've ever surfed the Web, you have probably seen IP addresses at one time or another (numbers such as 192.168.144.77). As you administer TCP/IP on a network, a considerable part of your time will be devoted to IP address assignment because IP addresses don't just magically get assigned to network hosts—they have to be provided through manual configuration or some other means. When a computer is added to a network, it needs an IP address to communicate on that network. When the computer moves to a new location, it is likely to need a new IP address. If you are just starting out with managing a large TCP/IP network, you might find the notion of managing all those addresses a bit daunting. If you move a DNS server to a new subnet, you may have to reconfigure every client computer. If you move a client computer to a new subnet, you may have to update its IP address. This does not endear you to road warriors who travel among several offices, especially those who are regional managers. If you manually manage IP addresses, almost any change to the network will require a visit to one or more computers to update TCP/IP configurations—not a happy prospect. Fortunately, the people who brought us DNS to replace the `hosts` file also came up with a solution to this dilemma.

DHCP was the Internet community's answer to dynamically distributing IP addresses. DHCP is open and standards-based, as defined by the Internet Engineering Task Force (IETF) in their Requests for Comments (RFCs) 2131 and 2132. (The IETF is the main standards organization for the Internet.) This chapter examines the basics of DHCP as it applies to you, the systems administrator, and how you can use it to make your life and your network better.

Understanding DHCP

Public IP addresses are registered with the Internet Assigned Numbers Authority (IANA) so that IANA can keep track of IP addresses that are being used on the Internet. In some cases, a network will not be connected to the Internet and will not need to use registered public IP addresses. In other cases, the network is connected to the Internet with special hardware and software that can be configured to allow the network to use private addresses in conjunction with address translation, commonly referred to as Network Address Translation (NAT). By using NAT, you can (in simple terms) place an entire private network behind a single public IP address. As an example, the organization I work for has over 5,000 hosts on its internal network. When I or anyone else visits a Web site on the Internet, we all appear to be coming from a single IP address. That's NAT in action!

> **NOTE**
>
> **What Are RFCs?** RFCs are used to propose changes to existing standards and to help create new standards that specify the way the Internet and IP behave. If an RFC can garner enough interest, it might eventually become a standard. Topics of RFCs range from File Transfer Protocol (FTP; originally RFC 0114 but updated by RFC 0141, RFC 0172, and RFC 0171) to the Hitchhiker's Guide to the Internet (RFC 1118). The first RFC was posted in 1969 by Steve Crocker, and the topic of that document was host software. You can find listings of all the RFCs at a number of sites throughout the Internet. One place is www.rfc-editor.org.

Quite often, systems administrators use private (unregistered) addresses on their internal networks to ensure that there are enough readily available addresses for all users. This model works great on a network that is not tied directly to the Internet. However, with the shortage of Class A and Class B (and even Class C) IP addresses, some environments use small pools of registered addresses to service larger numbers of DHCP clients; the idea is that not every client computer would need access simultaneously. These environments require aggressive leasing policies to ensure that everyone can get an address.

In addition to IP addresses, DHCP can also provide gateway addresses, DNS server addresses, and Windows Internet Name Service (WINS) server addresses—in essence, everything the client computer needs to participate in the network. This means that all available IP addresses can be stored in a central database, along with associated configuration information, such as the subnet masks, gateways, and addresses of DNS servers.

DHCP

DHCP provides the mechanism for dynamically distributing IP addresses on a network—but it doesn't happen magically. Here's how a client computer gets an address:

1. After boot up, the client computer broadcasts a `DHCPDISCOVER` message that is intended for the DHCP server(s) on the network. If a router sits between the DHCP server and the client, it needs to be configured with the IP address of the DHCP server as well as be configured to forward BOOTP. BOOTP is discussed in the next section, "BOOTP."

2. Each DHCP server that receives the `DHCPDISCOVER` message responds with a DHCP offer message. That message includes an IP address that is appropriate for the subnet where the client computer is attached. The DHCP server determines the appropriate address by looking at the source subnet for the broadcast `DHCPDISCOVER` message.

3. The client computer considers the offer messages and selects one (usually the first offer it receives). It sends a request (DHCPREQUEST) to use the address to the DHCP server that originated the offer. If there are multiple DHCP servers, they need to be carefully configured. It is easy to inadvertently configure servers and end up with them conflicting, so it is important if you have multiple DHCP servers on a network that they do not have the capability to offer duplicate IP addresses. Because DHCP servers do not communicate with one another, they have no way of telling whether an address has already been issued by another DHCP server.
4. The DHCP server acknowledges the request and grants the client computer a lease to use the address.
5. The client computer uses the IP address to bind to the network. If the IP address is associated with any configuration parameters, the parameters are incorporated into the client computer's TCP/IP configuration.
6. For the first renewal of the IP address, when 50 percent of the configured lease time has elapsed, the client sends another DHCPREQUEST message to the DHCP server that granted its lease, asking to renew and extend its current lease. All subsequent lease renewal will be at 75 percent.
7. If the DHCP server is reachable, it responds with a DHCPACK message to the client, renewing and extending the DHCP lease as requested.
8. If the DHCP server is not reachable, the client continues trying to reach it until 87.5 percent of the lease time has elapsed. At this point, the client attempts to renew its lease with any DHCP server that responds. If this is unsuccessful, the client starts the process of acquiring a new DHCP lease.

EXAM ALERT

DHCP Solitude Be sure to remember that DHCP servers do not communicate with one another, therefore they have no way of telling whether an address has already been issued by another DHCP server. It is for this reason that you will never create identical DHCP scopes on multiple DHCP servers.

The first step of this process indicates that DHCP clients request their addresses by using broadcast messages. If you are familiar with routing, particularly TCP/IP routing, you are probably familiar with the fact that one of the benefits of routing is that the router segregates broadcast domains. In other words, broadcasts do not generally cross routers. Does that mean that DHCP works only on the local segment and you need 50 DHCP servers for 50 subnets? No, that is not the case, not if you configure your routers or other Windows Server 2003 computers to act as DHCP relay agents.

Configuring a router or server as a DHCP relay agent causes it to begin using BOOTP. BOOTP was the precursor to DHCP, and it was the first protocol used to assign IP addresses dynamically. BOOTP was specially designed to pass across a router, and it continues to be used to allow DHCP broadcasts to propagate across routers. You'll learn about the installation and configuration of DHCP relay agents later in this chapter, in the section "Configuring and Implementing a DHCP Relay Agent."

BOOTP

Before we discuss installing and configuring the DHCP service in Windows Server 2003, a brief discussion about BOOTP is necessary. A number of DHCP's features had their beginnings in BOOTP. BOOTP was originally designed in 1985 by Bill Croft and John Gilmore to automate the configuration of network devices. To use BOOTP, the systems administrator must create a table with a list of client computers, their IP addresses, and network configurations. When a client computer comes on to the network, it broadcasts a request that the BOOTP server receives. The BOOTP server looks up the client computer in the table and responds with the configuration information stored in the table, allowing the client computer to communicate on the network.

Because BOOTP worked well, it was used extensively in the early 1990s in conjunction with diskless workstations. (A BOOTP chip was a common option on a network interface card [NIC], and many networks thrived on BOOTP.) The downside of BOOTP was that it provided only the configuration information entered in the table. The administrator still needed to configure the table. The limitations of BOOTP effectively prevented any automation of these tasks, so it was eventually replaced with DHCP. BOOTP and DHCP packets look virtually identical, and DHCP even takes advantage of the BOOTP forwarder functionality of many routers and switches. DHCP offers the automation features BOOTP was lacking.

Now that we've completed the history lesson, you should have a pretty good understanding of the theory of DHCP. Before moving on to the workings of DHCP in Windows Server 2003, let's examine the new DHCP features that Windows Server 2003 provides.

What's New with Windows Server 2003 DHCP

DHCP is not a new service in Windows Server 2003, but it has undergone some changes from both Windows 2000 and Windows NT 4.0. The following list summarizes some of the major changes in DHCP in Windows Server 2003, as compared to Windows 2000 Server and Windows NT 4.0:

- **DHCP integration in DNS**—Windows Server 2003 DHCP servers can trigger dynamic updates in the DNS database for all clients to which it leases IP addresses. Windows 2000 and newer clients can automatically update their DNS records if they are authorized to do so. Legacy clients can have their records updated by the DHCP server if it is authorized to do so.
- **Rogue DHCP server detection**—Unauthorized, or *rogue*, DHCP servers can cause a wide variety of problems, including denial of service (DoS) to clients. To prevent such problems, Windows Server 2003 provides for authorizing DHCP servers and detecting and shutting down unauthorized servers. Active Directory is required for the detection of rogue DHCP servers to occur.
- **Superscope and multicast scope support**—Superscopes allow you to group several standard DHCP scopes into a single administrative group without causing any service disruption to network clients. Multicast scopes allow you to lease Class D IP addresses to clients for participation in multicast transmissions, such as streaming video and audio transmissions. Multicast scopes are discussed in more detail in the section "Understanding Multicasting and Multicast Scopes" later in this chapter.
- **Local security groups for DHCP management**—Two new local administrative security groups are created when the DHCP service is installed: DHCP Users and DHCP Administrators. The DHCP Users group can be used to provide read-only console access to the server to allow group members to view, but not modify, DHCP data. The DHCP Administrators group provides full administrative control of the DHCP service without granting its members full administrative control over the entire server.
- **Improved monitoring and reporting**—DHCP is a critical network service that must be kept running. The key to discovering problems early is monitoring, so Windows Server 2003 provides a full set of performance monitoring counters that can be used to monitor DHCP server performance.
- **Custom DHCP option classes**—User- and vendor-specified option classes can be used to distribute specific options to the clients that need them. For example, you can use option classes to distribute a specific default gateway or parent domain name to one group of computers on a network.
- **In-console backup and restore**—For the first time ever, Windows Server 2003 provides the administrator with the ability to perform DHCP scope backups and restorations from within the DHCP console itself.

Now that we've briefly examined the improvements made in the DHCP service in Windows Server 2003, we can talk about configuring and implementing it on the network.

Configuring and Managing DHCP

The first question many managers ask when presented with a request to install Windows Server 2003 DHCP is this: "Can't we just use our existing DHCP?" The answer to this question is both yes and no. If you are maintaining a legacy domain and WINS network, Windows Server 2003 can receive DHCP information from any DHCP server with which Windows NT 4.0 or Windows 2000 works. However, if you want to take advantage of the features of Active Directory and migrate away from the legacy WINS architecture, you need the Windows Server 2003 DHCP service.

The following sections discuss how to install and configure DHCP for a network.

Installing the DHCP Server Service

When you install Windows Server 2003, you have the ability to install DHCP as one of the optional services. To prepare for Exam 70-291, you need to know how to install DHCP on an existing server that does not already have DHCP installed.

NOTE

A DHCP Server Cannot Also Be a DHCP Client If you currently have a server configured as a DHCP client, the DHCP installation will prompt you to enter a static IP address for the server.

Before you install DHCP, you must configure the server with a static IP address, as discussed in Chapter 1, "Configuring and Troubleshooting TCP/IP Addressing." After the DHCP server's network adapter is configured with a static IP address, you can go about the process of installing the DHCP service onto the server. To install the DHCP service on your server, perform the steps described in Step by Step 2.1.

STEP BY STEP

2.1 Installing the DHCP Service

1. Select Start, Settings, Control Panel, Add or Remove Programs.
2. On the Add or Remove Programs page, click Add/Remove Windows Components to open the Windows Components Wizard.
3. Select Networking Services, as shown in Figure 2.1.

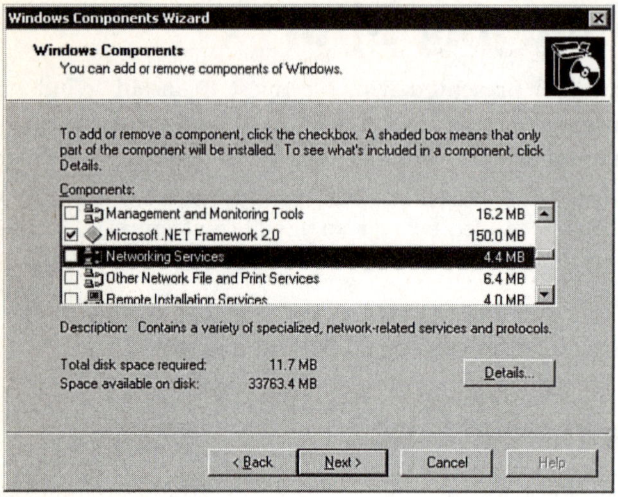

FIGURE 2.1 DHCP is located in the Networking Services group in the Windows Component Wizard.

4. Click the Details button to open the Networking Services window, shown in Figure 2.2.
5. Select Dynamic Host Configuration Protocol (DHCP) and click OK.

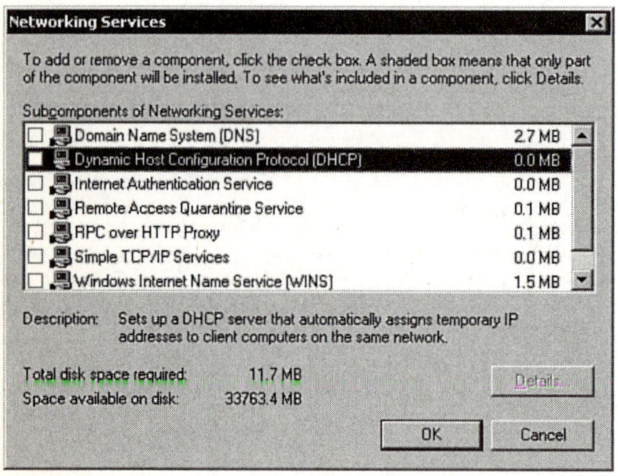

FIGURE 2.2 You select the Dynamic Host Configuration Protocol (DHCP) option to install the DHCP server.

6. Back in the Windows Components Wizard page, click Next to begin the installation.
7. If you are prompted to supply the location of your Windows Server 2003 CD-ROM or installation files, provide the correct location. Windows installs the DHCP service files on your computer.
8. When prompted that installation is complete, click Finish to close the Windows Components Wizard.

After you've installed the DHCP service, you next need to begin configuring the DHCP server so that it can service network clients. Before you can begin the configuration process, you first need to get an understanding of the types of DHCP scopes in Windows Server 2003.

Understanding DHCP Scopes

A *scope* is a range of IP addresses that are available for dynamic assignment to hosts on a given subnet. The scope for a particular subnet is determined by the network address of the broadcast DHCP request. In addition to address information, a scope can include a set of configuration parameters to be assigned to client computers when the address is assigned. This list of configuration parameters can include DNS servers, WINS servers, default gateways, the subnet mask, a NetBIOS scope ID, IP routing information, and WINS proxy information.

You should make the scope as large as you can. Later in the scope-creation process, you have the ability to exclude addresses, and you can also define reservations for particular addresses that exist within the scope.

NOTE

At Least One Scope After you install the DHCP service, you must define at least one scope on the server. Otherwise, the service will not respond to DHCP requests.

EXAM ALERT

Planning for Redundancy Although most of the examples in this chapter assume that you have only one DHCP server on the network, that is most often not the case. The discussion here is oriented this way to help you get the important knowledge down without adding any confusion.

In reality, you will want to have two or three or perhaps even more DHCP servers to service clients. Let's examine, for example, a situation in which you have two DHCP servers servicing network clients. The network has these two DHCP scopes configured with IP addresses: 192.168.50.10–192.168.50.169 and 192.168.51.10–192.168.51.169. Your first thought might be to just place one complete IP address range on each server. This would not be the best solution, however.

For redundancy and protection in the event that disaster strikes, you should place a portion of each IP address range on each DHCP server. You should consider using either the 80/20 or the 70/30 rule (the most common DHCP distribution methods in use today). If you used the 80/20 rule, you would create a scope on the first DHCP server with 80 percent of the first IP address range (192.168.50.10–192.168.50.127) and another scope with 20 percent of the second IP address range (192.168.51.128–192.168.51.169). You would then create a scope on the second DHCP server with 80 percent of its IP address range (192.168.51.10–192.168.51.127) and a second scope with 20 percent of the other IP address range (192.168.50.128–192.168.50.169).

This design prevents the failure of one DHCP server from completely preventing network clients from obtaining DHCP leases and accessing network resources. In addition, you can cluster DHCP servers to provide another form of redundancy in even larger networks.

Understanding DHCP Superscopes

The *superscope* type of scope was introduced to the Windows NT product family with Service Pack 2 for Windows NT 4.0. A superscope allows you to support a supernetted or multinetted network with a Windows Server 2003 DHCP server.

A supernetted network is a network that has multiple network addresses or subnets running on the same segment. This configuration is common in a network environment with more than 254 hosts on a subnet and in an environment in which certain hosts need to be isolated from the rest of the logical network for security or routing reasons. Superscopes support a local multinet or a multinet that is located across a router and configured to use the BOOTP forwarder service.

When to Use Supernetting

Visualize a large company that has been assigned the IP address block 198.142.1.0–198.142.6.254 by its ISP. The company occupies five floors in a building. On each of these floors are approximately 300 users, all on the same physical network. Traditional network design would have a routed backbone running between the floors, and each floor would be its own IP network. But there's one problem: There are too many users on these floors to be handled by a single Class C subnet. What are the alternatives?

You could place a router somewhere on each of the floors to further segment the network. This is an expensive and support-intensive solution and is generally considered to be impractical.

You could purchase a block of Class B addresses, but this could get costly and is generally very wasteful.

The last thing you could do is place multiple IP networks on the single-routed segment. In other words, you could create a supernet. This capability is supported by any of the routers on the market today, including the operating system–based routing services in Windows Server 2003, Novell NetWare, and any of the Unix flavors. So when you think about a supernet, think about a floor in a building with too many users for 254 IP addresses.

Understanding Multicasting and Multicast Scopes

Multicasting is the act of transmitting a message to a select group of recipients. This is in contrast to the concept of a *broadcast*, in which traffic is sent to every host on the network, or a *unicast*, in which the connection is a one-to-one relationship and there is only one recipient of the data.

Let's look at an example using an email message. If you send an email message to your manager, that email is a unicast message. If you send an email message to every user on the system, you have sent a broadcast. If you send an email message to a mailing list, you have sent a multicast message, which falls between a unicast message and a broadcast message. Teleconferencing and videoconferencing use the concept of multicasting, as does broadcast audio, in which the connection is from one source computer to a selected group of destination computers. At this time, only a few applications take advantage of multicasting, but with the growing popularity of multicast applications, we might see more multicast applications in the future.

The following are a few terms you need to understand before we discuss the Windows Server 2003 multicast capabilities:

- **Multicast DHCP (MDHCP)**—An extension to the DHCP standard that supports dynamic assignment and configuration of IP multicast addresses on TCP/IP-based networks.
- **Multicast forwarding table**—The table used by an IP router to forward IP multicast traffic. An entry in the IP multicast forwarding table consists of the multicast group address, the source IP address, a list of interfaces to which the traffic is forwarded (that is, the *next-hop interfaces*), and the single interface on which the traffic must be received to be forwarded (that is, the *previous-hop interface*).
- **Multicast group**—A group of member TCP/IP hosts configured to listen for and receive datagrams sent to a specified destination IP address. The destination address for the group is a shared IP address in the Class D address range (224.0.0.0–2239.255.255.255).
- **Multicast scope**—A scope of IP multicast addresses in the range 239.0.0.0–239.254.255.255. Multicast addresses in this range can be prevented from propagating in either direction (send or receive) through the use of scope-based multicast boundaries.

Windows Server 2003 makes use of the concept of a multicast scope. The DHCP service has been extended to allow the assignment of multicast addresses in addition to unicast (single-computer) addresses. A proposed IETF standard (RFC 2730), Multicast Address Dynamic Client Allocation Protocol (MADCAP), defines multicast address allocation. MADCAP (also known as MDHCP in Microsoft lingo) would allow administrators to dynamically allocate multicast addresses to be assigned in the same fashion as unicast addresses. The Windows Server 2003 DHCP multicasting capability also supports *dynamic membership*, which allows individual computers to join or leave a multicast group at any time. This is similar to registering to receive an Internet broadcast or joining and leaving an email mailing list. Group membership is not limited by size, and computers are not restricted to membership in any single group.

How do client computers join and leave a multicast group? The answer is via MDHCP and the MDHCP application programming interface (API). Client computers using MDHCP must be configured to use the MDHCP API. MDHCP assists in simplifying and automating configuration of multicast groups on a network, but it is not required for the operation of multicast groups or for the DHCP service. Multicast scopes provide only address configuration and do not support or use other DHCP-assignable options. MDHCP address configuration for client computers should be done independently of how the client computers are configured to receive their primary IP addresses. Computers using either static or dynamic configuration through a DHCP server can also be MDHCP clients.

EXAM ALERT

Class D IP Addresses for the Multicast Scope Remember that along with a primary IP address, a computer receives a multicast address, and that address is for multicasts only and uses the Class D IP addresses specified in the multicast scope. Multicast addresses are not used for regular network traffic such as Web traffic or other IP-based applications.

Now that you have knowledge of the different types of scopes supported in Windows Server 2003, you can move forward to creating scopes on a DHCP server.

Creating a DHCP Scope

Objective:

Manage DHCP.

- Manage DHCP clients and leases.
- Manage DHCP scope options.

Now that you are familiar with the different types of scopes, you can create one. To create a standard DHCP scope, you perform the steps described in Step by Step 2.2.

EXAM ALERT

Preparing Before Performing Before you actually start to create a DHCP scope, you should ensure that you have gathered all required information. You typically need the starting and ending IP addresses, the subnet mask, the DNS server IP address, and the gateway IP addresses.

STEP BY STEP

2.2 Creating a DHCP Scope

1. Open the DHCP console by selecting Start, Programs, Administrative Tools, DHCP.
2. Right-click the DHCP server and select New Scope from the context menu.
3. Click Next to dismiss the opening page of the New Scope Wizard.

4. On the first page of the wizard, the Scope Name page, enter a name and description for the new scope, as shown in Figure 2.3. You should make this name something that will allow you to easily identify this scope in the event that you have multiple scopes on the DHCP server. When you're done entering the information, click Next to continue.

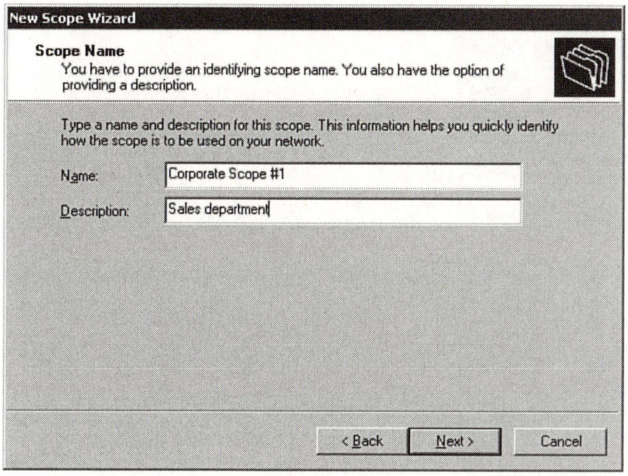

FIGURE 2.3 You should enter an intuitive name and description for the new scope.

5. On the next page of the wizard, the IP Address Range page, enter the IP address range and subnet mask that you need for the network, as shown in Figure 2.4. You can define the subnet mask by using the standard octet method (for example, 255.255.255.0) or by using the more router-centric mask length field (for example, 24 bits). When you're done entering the information, click Next to continue. If you need a refresher on subnet masks, refer to Chapter 1.

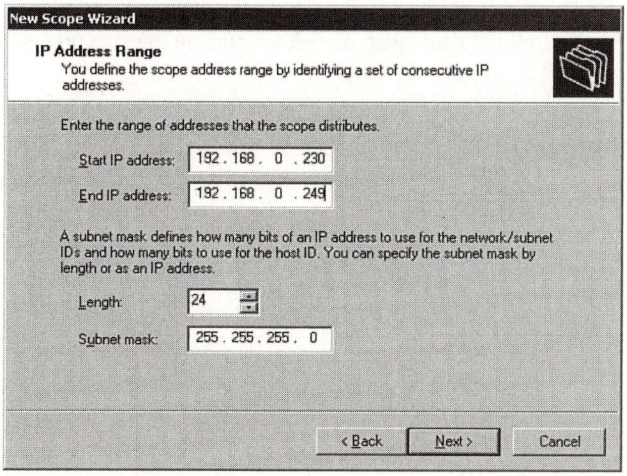

FIGURE 2.4 Configuring the IP address range and subnet mask information defines the scope boundaries.

6. On the next page of the wizard, the Add Exclusions page (see Figure 2.5), you can configure a range of IP addresses that will not be leased to client computers. These are typically addresses assigned to application servers, routers, printers, or other infrastructure equipment that requires static addresses. You can have multiple excluded IP addresses or ranges for each scope. When you're done entering the information, click Next to continue.

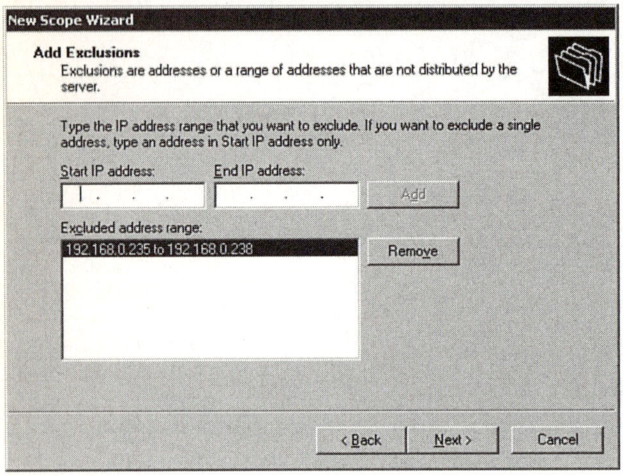

FIGURE 2.5 Configuring IP address exclusions allows you to prevent addresses within the scope from being leased out.

7. On the next page of the wizard, the Lease Duration page, you can configure the amount of time for which a DHCP lease is valid, as shown in Figure 2.6. The default setting is 8 days and can be changed to any value between 1 minute and almost 1,000 days (999 days, 23 hours, 59 seconds, to be exact). For the average network, the default setting of 8 days is sufficient. In a network that has a large number of computers connecting at various locations, such as portable computers on wireless connections, you might want to reduce the lease duration. Conversely, in a network with clients that do not change location, you might consider increasing the lease duration to cut down on DHCP traffic on the network. When you're done entering the information, click Next to continue.

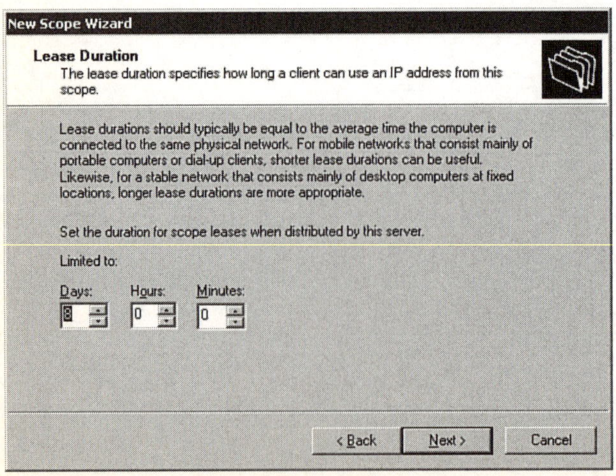

FIGURE 2.6 You should configure the lease duration that seems appropriate for the network.

8. On the next page of the wizard, the Configure DHCP Options page, you are given the choice to configure additional options for your scope now or later. It is usually best to configure these options at the time of scope configuration, and thus you should do that now. Table 2.1, later in this chapter, presents the entire list of DHCP scope options that can be configured, although you will only be able to configure three of them at this time. Select Yes, I want to Configure These Options Now and click Next to continue.

NOTE

Options Levels You can configure DHCP options at four different levels for each DHCP server:

- **Server options**—These are DHCP options that are applied, by default, to all scopes on the DHCP server.
- **Scope options**—These are DHCP options that are applied only to the specific scope on the DHCP server. When a scope option conflicts with a server option, the scope option wins and that value is made a part of the scope. If the conflicting scope option is later removed, the server option once again becomes effective in the scope.
- **Class options**—These are DHCP options that are applied only to clients identified as members of specified user or vendor classes.
- **Reservation options**—These are DHCP options that are applied only to a single specific computer.

9. On the next page of the wizard, the Router (Default Gateway) page, enter the default gateway for the network or the subnet that the scope serves, as shown in Figure 2.7. When you're done entering the information, click Next to continue.

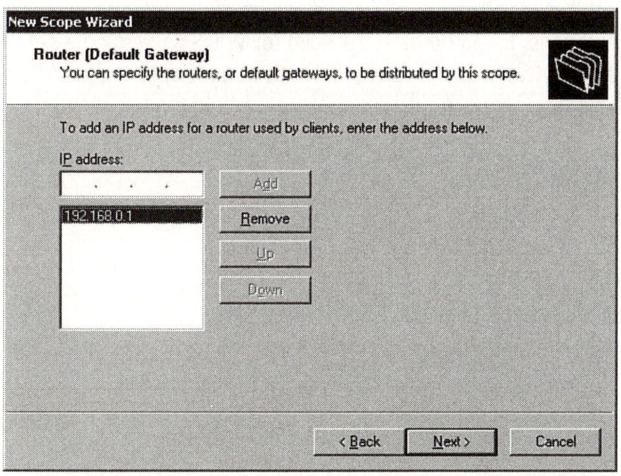

FIGURE 2.7 If you configure multiple gateways, you need to ensure that you place them in preferred order from top to bottom.

10. On the next page of the wizard, the Domain Name and DNS Servers page, configure the parent domain of which all DHCP clients should be made part as well as any number of DNS servers you require, as

shown in Figure 2.8. It is recommended that you enter at least two DNS servers for your clients to use. If you need to resolve a server name to an IP address, you can enter the server's name and then click the Resolve button. Configuring the DNS service is discussed in Chapter 3, "Implementing and Managing DNS." When you're done entering the information, click Next to continue.

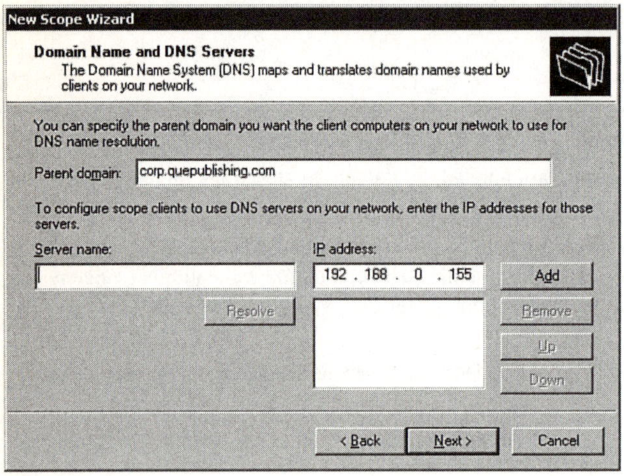

FIGURE 2.8 If you configure multiple DNS servers, you should ensure that you place them in preferred order from top to bottom.

11. On the next page of the wizard, the WINS Servers page, enter the IP addresses of the network's WINS servers, as shown in Figure 2.9. WINS servers are used to convert NetBIOS names to IP addresses for legacy clients on the network. As in the Domain Name and DNS Servers page, you can use the Resolve button to resolve a hostname to an address. If a network is purely Windows 2000 or better, you do not need to have a WINS server on the network because Windows 2000, Windows XP, and Windows Server 2003 use DNS by default for all name resolutions. If you do have the need for WINS servers on a network, it is recommended that you enter at least two of them here. When you're done entering the information, click Next to complete the scope creation process.

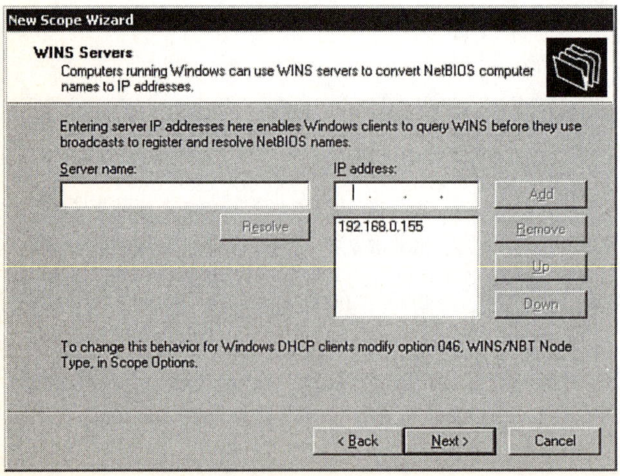

FIGURE 2.9 WINS servers are not required for networks that use only Windows 2000, Windows XP, or Windows Server 2003 computers.

12. On the next page of the wizard, the Activate Scope page (see Figure 2.10), you are given the option to active the configured scope now or later. In most cases you want to activate the scope right away. Select Yes, I Want to Activate This Scope Now and click Next to activate the configured scope.

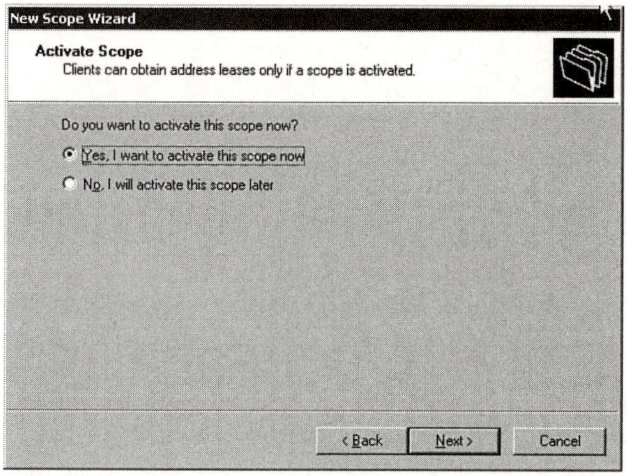

FIGURE 2.10 You typically want to activate the scope immediately after configuring it.

13. Click Finish to close the New Scope Wizard. Note that the DHCP won't issue any IP address from your new scope unless it has already been authorized in Active Directory, which we discuss a little bit later in this chapter.

NOTE

Configuring Scope Ranges The common practice when configuring a new DHCP scope is to configure it and leave out enough addresses to cover all servers and other infrastructure devices that require statically assigned IP information without needing all the other options provided in a DHCP scope, such as DNS servers, WINS servers, and default gateways. For example, you might configure a scope of 192.168.0.10–192.168.0.200, with the remaining IP addresses available for servers, routers, switches, and other infrastructure equipment on that subnet. This practice prevents the possibility of forgetting a configured reservation and ending up with duplicate IP addresses.

EXAM ALERT

When to Use the New Multicast Scope Option Creating a new scope and creating a new multicast scope are two different tasks. If you get a question on the exam regarding the procedure for creating a multicast scope, remember that you need to start the process by selecting New Multicast Scope, not New Scope.

Configuring Scope Properties

Objective:

Manage DHCP.

- Manage DHCP clients and leases.
- Manage DHCP scope options.
- Manage reservations and reserved clients.

After you've created a scope, you might want to modify its properties. To modify a scope's properties, you perform the steps described in Step by Step 2.3.

NOTE

Changing Scope Properties It's worth it to point out that you cannot change every option a scope has. For example, if you need to change the subnet mask that DHCP clients are receiving as part of their DHCP lease, you'll need to create a new DHCP scope reflecting this change and then remove the existing DHCP scope. Clients will then get the new information when they renew their lease the next time.

STEP BY STEP

2.3 Configuring a DHCP Scope's Properties

1. Right-click the scope and select Properties from the context menu.
2. The Properties dialog box opens, as shown in Figure 2.11.

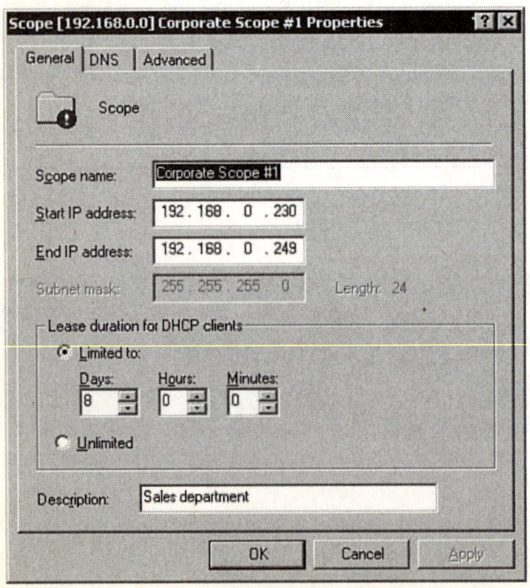

FIGURE 2.11 You can use the Scope Properties dialog box to change scope properties after you create a scope.

3. On the General tab, change the scope name, IP address range, lease duration, and scope description if you want to.
4. If you want to change the options on the DNS tab, do so now. The options on the DNS tab are discussed later in this chapter, in the section “Configuring DHCP for DNS Integration.”
5. On the Advanced tab, select options related to BOOTP clients, as shown in Figure 2.12. If you have BOOTP clients on your network, select either the BOOTP Only option or the Both option, depending on your network configuration. The default setting is DHCP Only. Click OK to close the Scope Properties dialog box after you make your changes.

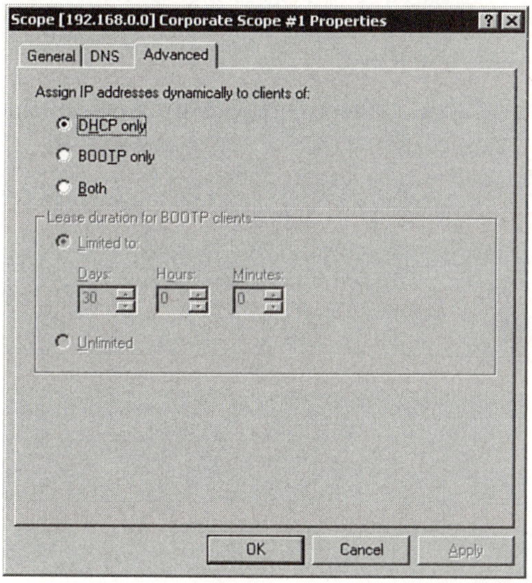

FIGURE 2.12 You can configure the scope to service BOOTP clients on the Advanced tab of the Scope Properties dialog box.

6. To view the address pool and configured exclusion ranges, click the Address Pool node of the DHCP console, as shown in Figure 2.13.

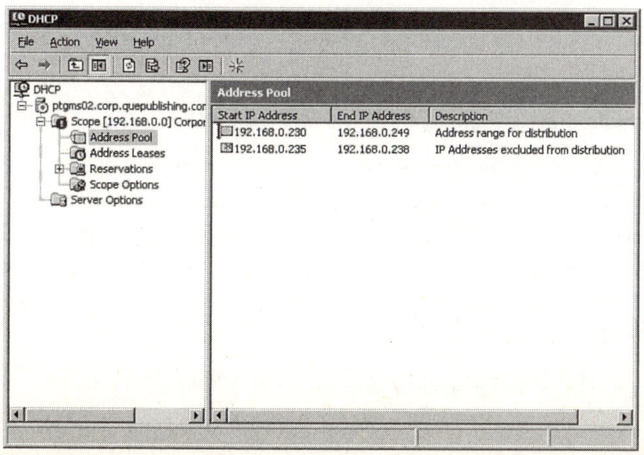

FIGURE 2.13 You can quickly view all configured scope ranges and exclusion ranges from the Address Pool node.

7. To add a new exclusion range, right-click Address Pool and select New Exclusion Range from the context menu. The Add Exclusion window appears (see Figure 2.14). Click Add after you enter your new exclusion range.

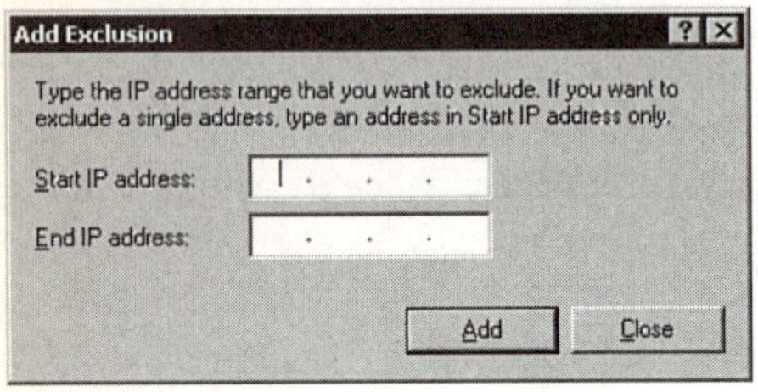

FIGURE 2.14 You can add a new exclusion range to a configured DHCP scope by using the Add Exclusion dialog box.

8. To view the addresses that have been leased, click the Address Leases node, as shown in Figure 2.15. (Of course there won't be any leases shown here until you authorize the DHCP server, as discussed later in this chapter, in the section "Authorizing a DHCP Server in Active Directory.")

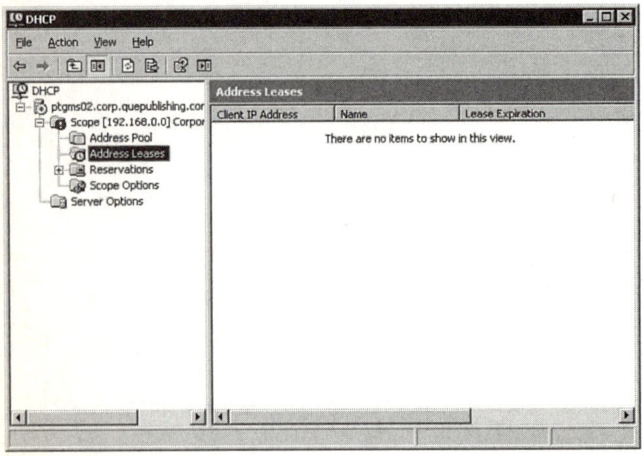

FIGURE 2.15 You can view all active scope leases from the Address Leases node.

9. If you want to manually revoke an active client lease, right-click it in the right pane of the Address Leases node and select Delete from the context menu.
10. To view the configured reservations, click the Reservations node of the DHCP console.
11. You can configure a new address reservation by right-clicking Reservations and selecting New Reservation from the context menu. You can configure a reservation for any device that you want to have a DHCP-assigned IP address that never expires. Configure the reservation as shown in Figure 2.16 and click Add to add it. Click Close to close the New Reservation input box after you're done configuring reservations for this scope. After you've configured a reservation, you can see it in the Reservations node of the DHCP console, as shown in Figure 2.17.
12. You can view existing scope options by clicking the Scope Options node, as shown in Figure 2.18.

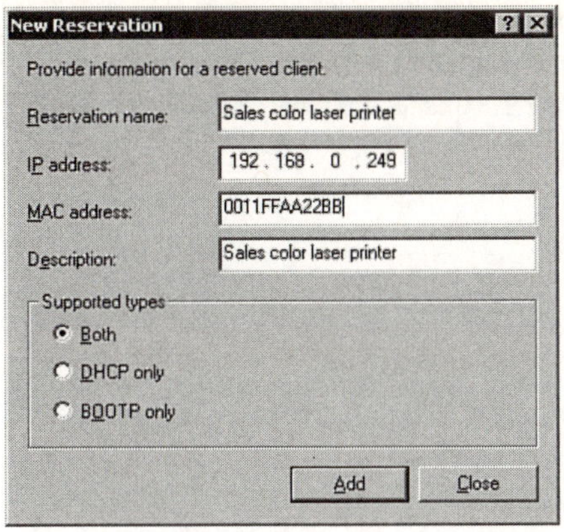

FIGURE 2.16 You can configure a new DHCP reservation, which is typically done for printers and other static infrastructure devices.

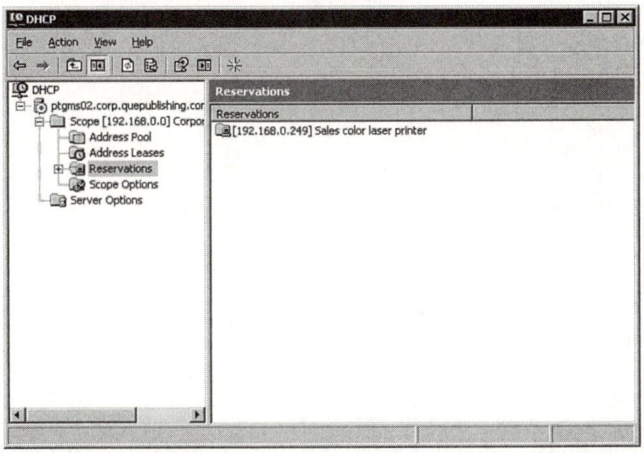

FIGURE 2.17 You can view all scope reservations from the Reservations node.

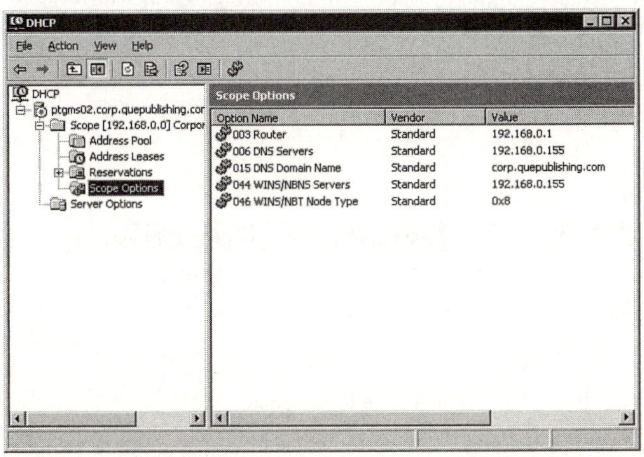

FIGURE 2.18 The Scope Options node lists all currently configured scope options.

13. To configure a new scope option, right-click the Scope Options node and select Configure Options from the context menu. Configure the options in the Scope Options window (see Figure 2.19). Table 2.1 lists the common DHCP options available for configuration. Table 2.2 explains the Microsoft-specific DHCP options that are available for configuration.

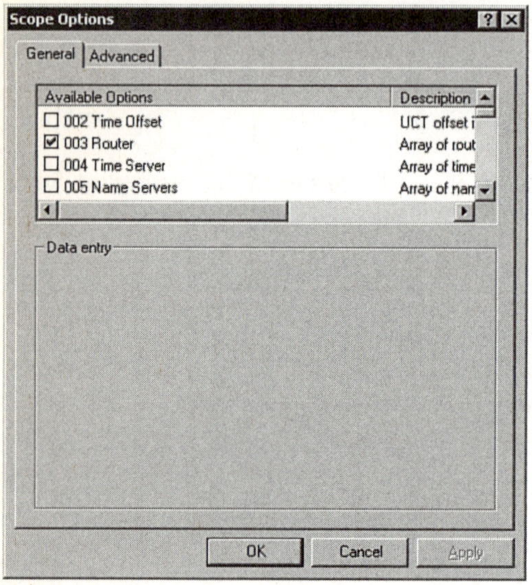

FIGURE 2.19 You can configure extra scope options from the Scope Options dialog box.

EXAM ALERT

Configuring Server Options You can configure server-wide DHCP options as mentioned in Step by Step 2.3. To configure server DHCP options that apply to all scopes on the DHCP server, right-click the Server Options node in the DHCP console and select Configure Options from the context menu.

Some of the more common DHCP scope options are presented in Table 2.1.

TABLE 2.1 Common DHCP Scope Options

Code	Option Name	Option Description
2	Time Offset	Specifies the offset of the client's subnet in seconds from UTC.
3	Router	Specifies a list of IP addresses for routers on the client's subnet.
4	Time Server	Specifies a list of RFC 868 time servers available to the client.
5	Name Servers	Specifies a list of name servers available to the client.
6	DNS Servers	Specifies a list of DNS servers available to the client.

TABLE 2.1 Continued

Code	Option Name	Option Description
9	LPR Servers	Specifies a list of RFC 1179 line printer servers available to the client.
15	DNS Domain Name	Specifies the domain name that the client should use when resolving hostnames via DNS.
27	All Subnets Are Local	Specifies whether the client can assume that all subnets of the IP network to which the client is connected use the same MTU as the subnet of the network to which the client is directly connected.
28	Broadcast Address	Specifies the broadcast address in use on the client's subnet.
44	WINS/NBNS Servers	Specifies a list of RFC 1001/1002 NBNS servers, listed in order of preference.
46	WINS/NBT Node Type	Allows NetBT clients, which can be configured as described in RFC 1001/1002.
47	NetBIOS Scope ID	Specifies the NetBT scope parameter for the client, as specified in RFC 1001/1002.

There is a provision in DHCP for manufacturer-specific DHCP options to be configured. You can select these options by opening the DHCP management console and selecting the scope for which to configure options, as described in Step by Step 2.3. Selecting the Advanced tab allows you to select Microsoft Options from the drop-down list in the Vendor Class window. Table 2.2 shows the manufacturer options that are defined by Microsoft.

TABLE 2.2 Microsoft-Specific DHCP Options

Code	Option Name	Option Description
1	Microsoft Disable NetBIOS	This option can be used to selectively enable or disable NetBT for DHCP-enabled computers running Windows.
2	Microsoft Release DHCP Lease on Shutdown	This option can be used to control whether DHCP-enabled computers running Windows send a release for their current DHCP lease to the DHCP server when shutdown occurs.
3	Microsoft Default Router Metric Base	This value is a specified router metric base to be used for all default gateway routes.

Authorizing a DHCP Server in Active Directory

For security reasons, a new DHCP server must be authorized in Active Directory before it can assign IP addresses by an administrator with Enterprise Admin credentials. This prevents unauthorized DHCP servers from running on the network. One of the nastiest things a troublemaker can do is to put up a rogue DHCP server and have it issue addresses that conflict with infrastructure devices' addresses. The nice thing about this feature is that if you are running Windows 2000 or better client computers and they are using Active Directory, the computers will not accept DHCP addresses from an unauthorized server. To authorize a DHCP server in Active Directory, you perform the steps described in Step by Step 2.4.

STEP BY STEP

2.4 Authorizing a DHCP Server in Active Directory

1. Open the DHCP console by selecting Start, Programs, Administrative Tools, DHCP.
2. Right-click the DHCP server and select Authorize from the context menu.
3. The authorization process might take some time, depending on network conditions. Refresh the DHCP console by pressing F5, and you should see the window shown in Figure 2.20. When authorization is complete, the status is shown as Active and the server is ready to issue addresses when it receives DHCP requests. Note also that the status arrow on the server itself is now pointing up instead of down as before.

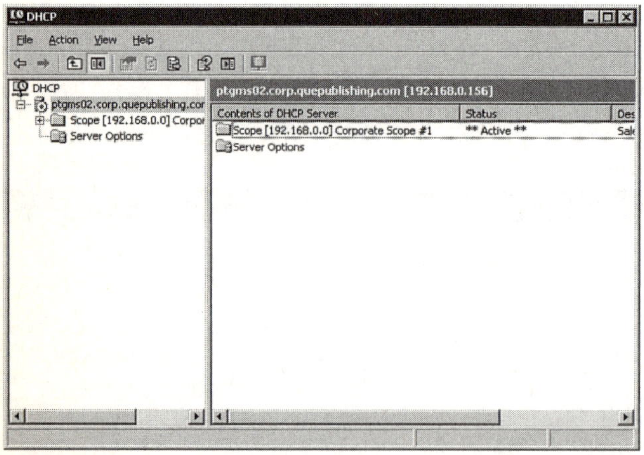

FIGURE 2.20 When a DHCP server is authorized, DHCP server scope information shows up in the right pane of the DHCP console window.

Windows Server 2003 and Windows 2000 Server DHCP servers that are not authorized do not provide DHCP services to network clients. These unauthorized servers also check every five minutes to see if their authorization status has changed, thus allowing them to begin servicing clients.

You have now installed, configured, and authorized a Windows Server 2003 DHCP server. We next examine configuring DHCP for DNS integration.

Configuring DHCP for DNS Integration

One of the keys to effectively implementing an Active Directory environment is the capability for Windows 2000 and Windows XP workstations using DHCP to be automatically registered in DNS. You can set the following settings for DNS integration (see Step by Step 2.5):

- **Dynamically Update DNS A and PTR Records Only If Requested by the DHCP Clients**—This is the default behavior of the Windows Server 2003 DHCP server, and it causes the DHCP server to register and update client information with the authoritative DNS server of the zone in which the DHCP server is located, according to the DHCP client's request. The DHCP client can request the way in which the DHCP server performs updates of its host (A) and pointer (PTR) resource records. If possible, the DHCP server will accommodate the client's request for handling updates to its name and IP address information in DNS. This selection requires the Enable Dynamic DNS Updates According to the Settings Below option to be selected.
- **Always Dynamically Update DNS A and PTR Records**—When this option is selected, the DHCP server will always update the client's fully qualified domain name (FQDN), IP address, and both the A and PTR resource records, regardless of whether the client has requested to perform its own updates. This selection requires the Enable Dynamic DNS Updates According to the Settings Below option to be selected.
- **Discard A and PTR Records When Lease Is Deleted**—This option, which is selected by default, instructs the DHCP server to cause the DNS server to delete the client's A and PTR records when the lease has expired or otherwise has been deleted. This selection requires the Enable Dynamic DNS Updates According to the Settings Below option to be selected.
- **Dynamically Update DNS A and PTR Records for DHCP Clients That Do Not Request Automatic Updates**—This option allows legacy clients, such as Windows NT 4.0 and Windows 9*x* clients, to participate in DNS dynamic updates. This selection requires the Enable Dynamic DNS Updates According to the Settings Below option to be selected.

NOTE

New Group Policy Object Options Although it is beyond the scope of Exam 70-291, you can also configure the DNS options discussed here from Group Policy. The options are located in the Computer Configuration, Administrative Templates, Network, DNS Client node.

Because DNS dynamic updating is controlled by the DHCP server, you will need to perform all of the applicable DNS configuration from the DHCP console. The DHCP server automatically updates any DNS server configured as part of the server's TCP/IP network properties. It is important to be sure that the primary DNS server is configured as one of the DNS servers because any updates sent to it will be propagated to the rest of the DNS servers for that domain. However, the DNS server in question must support DDNS. DNS is discussed in more detail in Chapter 3. The Windows Server 2003 DNS server supports these updates, as do a number of other DNS servers.

To configure a DHCP server for DNS integration, you perform the steps described in Step by Step 2.5.

STEP BY STEP

2.5 Configuring DHCP for DNS Integration

1. Open the DHCP console by selecting Start, Programs, Administrative Tools, DHCP.
2. Right-click the DHCP server and select Properties from the context menu. Select the DNS tab of the DHCP Server Properties dialog box, as shown in Figure 2.21.

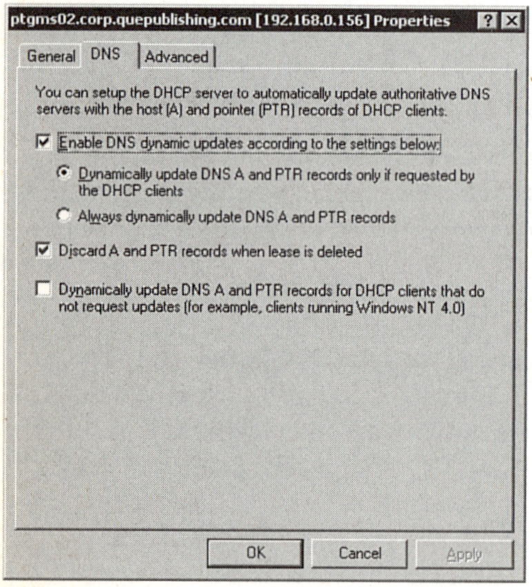

FIGURE 2.21 You can configure DDNS options on the DNS tab.

3. To enable DHCP integration with DNS, ensure that the Enable Dynamic DNS Updates According to the Settings Below check box is selected.
4. Select to have the DHCP server update A and PTR records when requested or to always update A and PTR records.
5. To help keep the DNS database clean and consistent, allow the DHCP server to cause expired leases to lead to A and PTR record deletion.

6. If there are legacy clients on the network, ensure that dynamic updating is configured for them.
7. If you are using secure dynamic updates, you should consider configuring a dedicated network user account for dynamic updating. You can enter the account credentials by switching to the Advanced tab of the DHCP Server Properties dialog box, as shown in Figure 2.22.

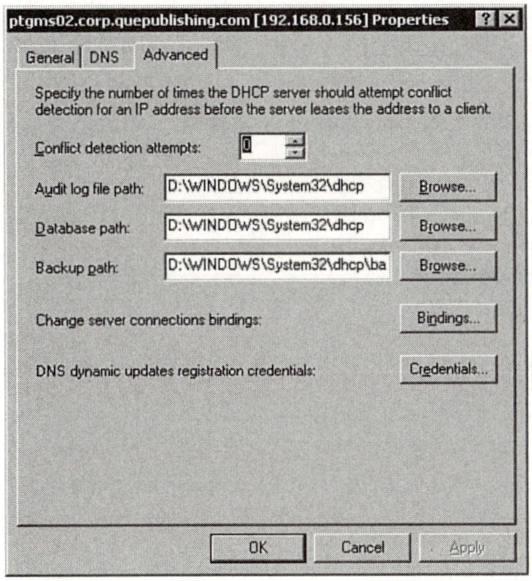

FIGURE 2.22 You need to click the Credentials button to enter the account username and password for DDNS.

8. Click the Credentials button to open the DNS dynamic update credentials window, which is shown in Figure 2.23.

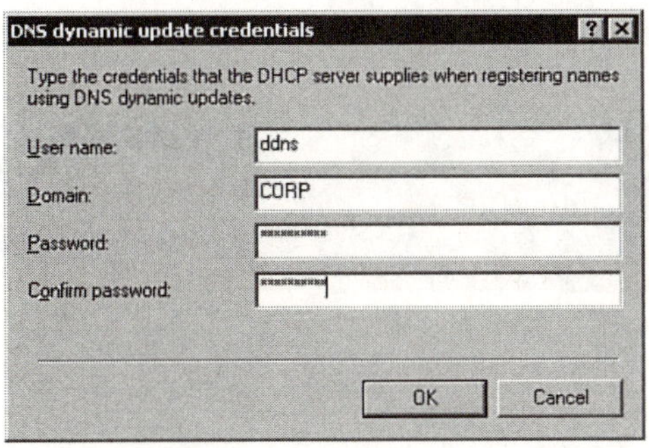

FIGURE 2.23 You need to enter the dynamic updates account credentials on the DNS dynamic update credentials dialog box.

9. Enter the domain user account name, domain, and password in the DNS dynamic update credentials dialog box. Click OK to accept the credentials or Cancel to avoid entering credentials at this time.
10. Click OK to close the DHCP Server Properties dialog box.

DHCP option code 81 is required in order to make dynamic update work. Let's look at two examples that explain the basic dynamic update process.

The first example looks at a Windows 2000 Professional client computer that has requested a DHCP lease from a Windows Server 2003 DHCP server configured with the default options:

1. During the DHCP lease negotiation process, the Windows 2000 Professional client sends a `DHCPREQUEST` message. By default, the client includes DHCP option 81 in this message, informing the DHCP server that it is requesting that its PTR record be registered in DNS by the DHCP server. The client will be responsible for registering its A record on its own.
2. The DHCP server replies with a `DHCPACK` message, granting the requested DHCP lease. This message includes DHCP option 81. With the default DHCP server settings, the DHCP server informs the client that it will register the PTR record and that the client will be responsible for registering the A record in DNS.
3. The client registers its A record, and the DHCP server registers the client's PTR record in DNS.

The second example looks at a Windows NT 4.0 Workstation client computer that has requested a DHCP lease from a Windows Server 2003 DHCP server configured with the default options:

1. During the DHCP lease negotiation process, the Windows NT 4.0 Workstation client sends a `DHCPREQUEST` message. DHCP option 81 is not included in this message.
2. The server returns a `DHCPACK` message to the client, granting its DHCP lease request.
3. The DHCP server updates the DNS server with the client's A and PTR records.

EXAM ALERT

DHCP and DNS It is important to remember that Windows 2000 and Windows XP client computers update the A records in DNS without any assistance from the DHCP server. The only client computers for which DHCP updates DNS are older legacy clients.

CAUTION

DDNS Updates and Domain Controllers To perform DDNS updates, you should not configure the DHCP service on a computer that is also a Domain Controller. If a DHCP server exists on a domain controller, the DHCP server has full control over all DNS objects stored in Active Directory because the account under which it is running (the domain controller computer account) has this privilege. This creates a security risk that should be avoided. You should not install the DHCP server service that is configured to perform DDNS updates on a domain controller; instead, you should install it on a member server if you're performing DDNS updates.

As an alternative, you can use a new feature in Windows Server 2003 DHCP. This feature allows you to create a dedicated domain user account that all DHCP servers will use when performing DDNS updates.

Configuring and Implementing a DHCP Relay Agent

Objective:

Manage DHCP.

- Manage DHCP Relay Agent.

Today, most networks that use DHCP are routed. As discussed previously, DHCP messages are broadcast messages. By default, nearly all routers do not pass broadcast traffic in the interest of reducing overall network traffic levels. Fortunately, you can get around this design limitation by configuring a DHCP relay agent to pass BOOTP messages across routers.

There are three basic configurations in which you can set up a DHCP relay agent. The first involves entering the IP address or addresses of the DHCP server(s) into the router itself, instructing it to pass DHCP messages to a specified IP address for action. The second method involves using the Windows Server 2003 Routing and Remote Access Service (RRAS) component as a router (in the place of a hardware-based router) and configuring the DHCP relay agent within it. The third solution, and the one that we examine in this section, is to use a Windows Server 2003 computer located on a subnet without a DHCP server to act as a DHCP relay agent. This option requires the use of the RRAS components, but it does not involve the creation or configuration of a router as the second solution would. What's important to understand is that the server providing the DHCP relay agent service does not have to be dedicated to that purpose; it could be a file server, print server, or any other type of Windows Server 2003 (or Windows 2000 Server) server on that subnet. Figure 2.24 shows how this arrangement would look on a network.

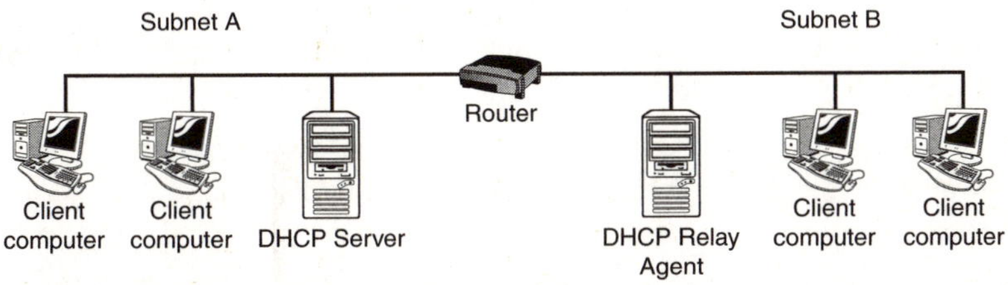

FIGURE 2.24 The DHCP relay agent allows clients on the other side of a router to communicate with the DHCP server.

EXAM ALERT

DHCP Relay Agent Recall that the DHCP relay agent is needed only to help pass DHCP traffic across a router that otherwise cannot pass that traffic. As such, the server acting as the relay agent is not going to be the same server providing DHCP and will be located on the subnet on the *other side* of the router in question. Referring back to Figure 2.24, the DHCP server is located on subnet A whereas the DHCP relay agent is located on subnet B.

In Step by Step 2.6, you enable the DHCP relay agent on a Windows Server 2003 computer. This exercise assumes that you have not previously configured and enabled RRAS on the computer.

STEP BY STEP

2.6 Configuring a DHCP Relay Agent

1. Select Start, Programs, Administrative Tools, Routing and Remote Access to open the Routing and Remote Access console, which is shown in Figure 2.25. (If you've previously configured and enabled RRAS, you can skip to Step 7.)

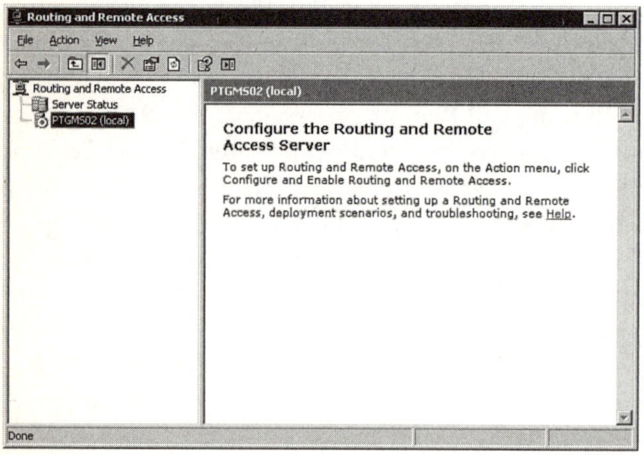

FIGURE 2.25 The Routing and Remote Access console is initially empty.

2. Right-click the server name and select Configure and Enable Routing and Remote Access from the context menu. The Routing and Remote Access Server Setup Wizard appears. Click Next to dismiss the opening page.
3. On the Configuration page of the wizard, shown in Figure 2.26, select the Custom Configuration option and click Next to continue.
4. On the Custom Configuration page of the wizard, shown in Figure 2.27, select the LAN routing option and click Next to continue.
5. When the summary page is displayed, review your selections and then click Finish to continue.
6. You are prompted to start RRAS. Click Yes to start the service.
7. Back at the Routing and Remote Access console, expand the following nodes: Routing and Remote Access, *ServerName*, IP Routing, and General, as shown in Figure 2.28.

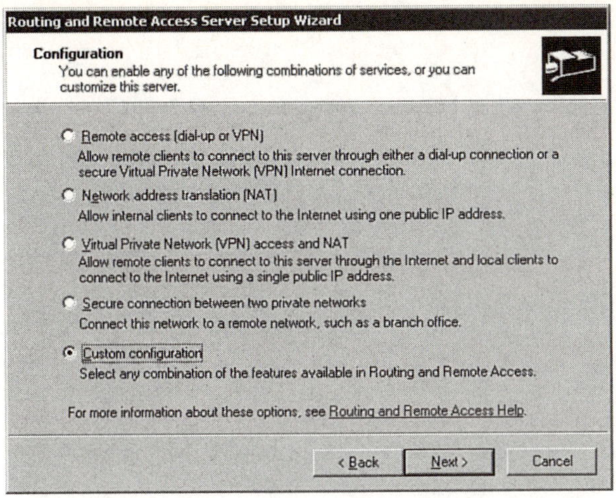

FIGURE 2.26 You need to specify a custom configuration in order to perform a basic DHCP relay agent setup.

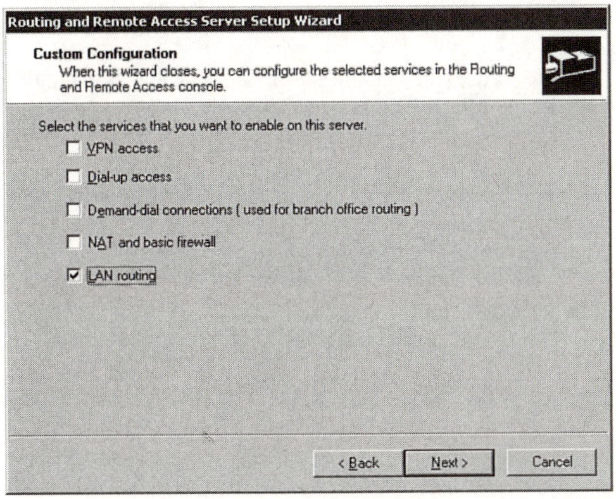

FIGURE 2.27 The LAN routing option is the bare minimum you need to support later installation of the DHCP relay agent.

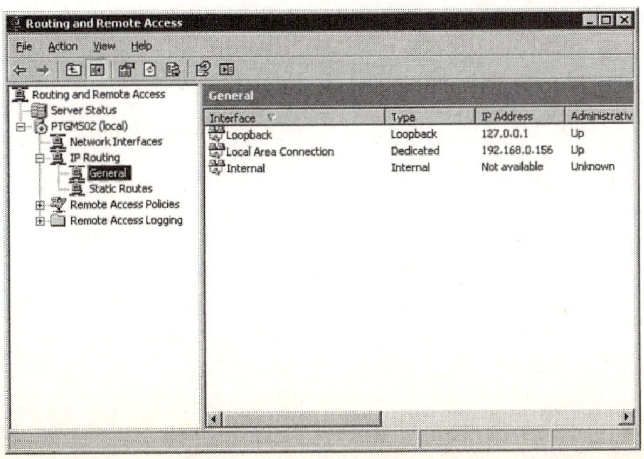

FIGURE 2.28 You need to add the DHCP relay agent from the General node.

8. Right-click the General node and select New Routing Protocol from the context menu. This opens the New Routing Protocol dialog box.
9. From the New Routing Protocol dialog box, shown in Figure 2.29, select DHCP Relay Agent. Click OK to confirm your configuration.

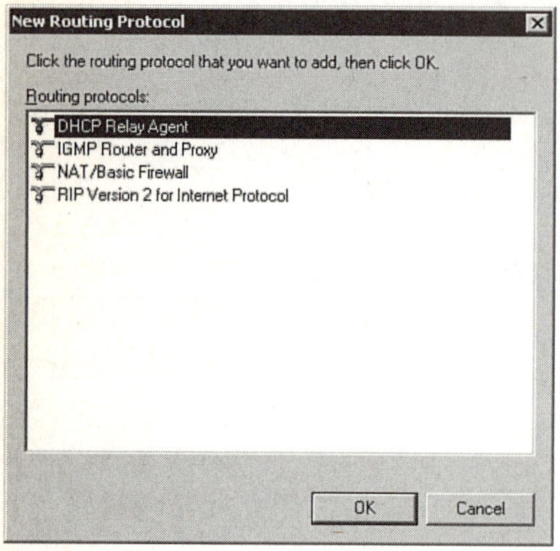

FIGURE 2.29 You can add the DHCP relay agent in addition to standard IP routing protocols.

10. To select a network interface for the DHCP relay agent to run on, right-click the DHCP Relay Agent node in the RRAS console and select New Interface from the context menu.
11. On the New Interface for DHCP Relay Agent page, shown in Figure 2.30, select the network interface that you want to be available for the DHCP relay agent. Click OK to continue. The DHCP Relay Properties dialog box, shown in Figure 2.31, opens.

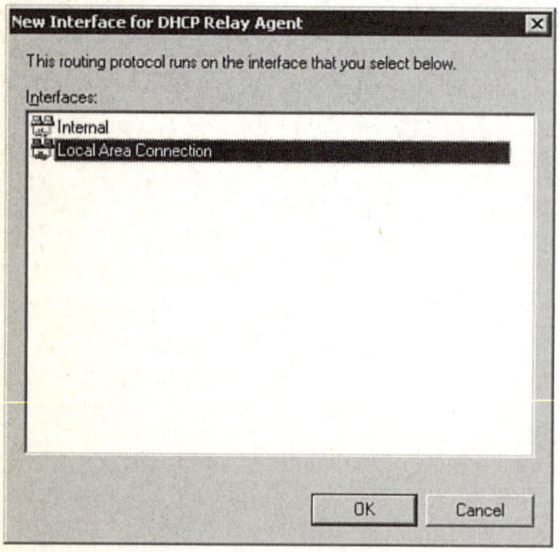

FIGURE 2.30 You need to select one or more installed network adapters for use by the DHCP relay agent.

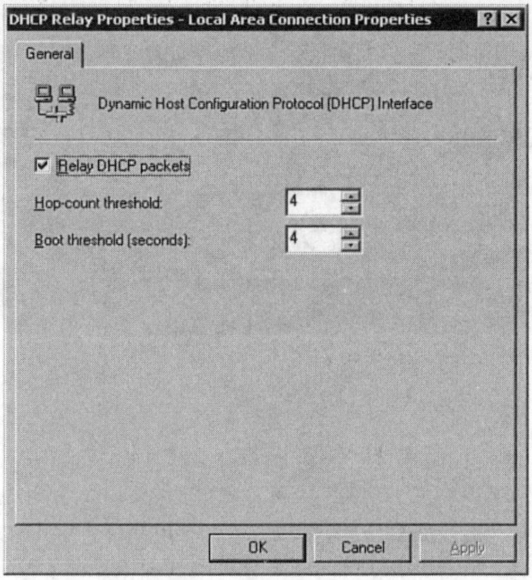

FIGURE 2.31 You need to configure the maximum hop count and length of delay time for the DHCP relay agent.

12. In the DHCP Relay Properties dialog box, configure the required values for hop-count threshold and boot threshold. The default value for each of them is 4. Click OK to confirm your settings.

13. The last configuration you need to perform is to assign the DHCP server IP addresses to which the DHCP relay agent forwards DHCP messages. Right-click the DHCP Relay Agent node in the RRAS console and select Properties to open the DHCP Relay Agent Properties dialog box, which is shown in Figure 2.32. Enter one or more remote DHCP servers into the list and click OK to confirm your settings.

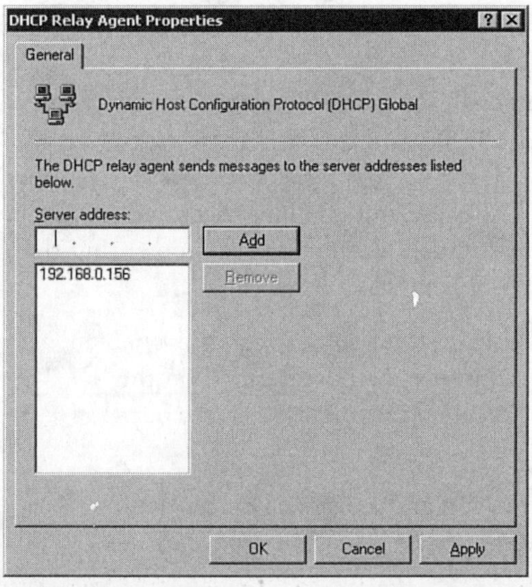

FIGURE 2.32 You need to provide one or more remote DHCP servers to which the DHCP relay agent can forward DHCP messages.

EXAM ALERT

DHCP Relay Agent Options The Hop-Count Threshold option allows you to configure a value for the maximum number of DHCP relay agents that are allowed to handle DHCP-relayed traffic. The maximum value is 16 hops—meaning that you can have only 16 DHCP relay agents (typically on different connected subnets) between a client and a DHCP server.

The Boot Threshold option allows you to specify how long the DHCP relay agent waits before forwarding DHCP messages. By configuring DHCP relay agents with different values, you can establish one that is to respond first and then one or more DHCP relay agents that are to forward DHCP messages if required.

Configuring Security for DHCP

Although there are no administrative tasks that outwardly appear that they will help secure your DHCP infrastructure, there are some best practices and other actions that you can follow that will provide a more secure (and thus, more reliable) DHCP implementation in your environment. We briefly examine them here:

- **Use the 80/20 address allocation rule**—Use DHCP servers in pairs to provide leases to each of your network subnets. One server should be configured with 80 percent of the available addresses (in a scope) on it, and the other server should have a corresponding scope configured with the remaining 20 percent of the available addresses. The scopes should be balanced between the two servers such that each server has approximately the same number of 80-percent scopes (its own scopes) and 20-percent scopes (scopes that belong to the other server). By using this configuration, you can ensure that leases will still be made available to clients requesting them in the event a single server is under a DoS attack.
- **Create and use DHCP server clusters**—By enabling a DHCP server cluster, you remove a single server as a single point of failure (SPOF). By having two (or more) servers in a cluster acting a single DHCP entity, a failure of a single server (or multiple servers depending on your configuration) will not result in a failure to provide leases to clients. Clustering can be expanded on by creating two clusters and implementing the 80/20 address allocation rule for maximum redundancy.
- **Examine the DHCP audit logs regularly**—Ensure that audit logging is enabled, as shown in Figure 2.33. The audit logs are stored in the location defined on the Advanced tab, which was shown in Figure 2.22. The location is `%systemroot%\system32\dhcp\` by default.
- **Harden servers**—You can get detailed information and assistance on hardening Windows Server 2003 servers from the *Windows Server 2003 Security Guide*.

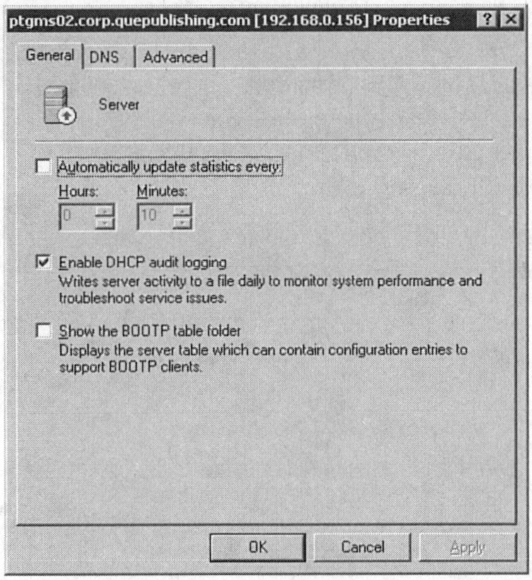

FIGURE 2.33 DHCP audit logging is enabled from the General tab of the DHCP server Properties dialog box.

EXAM ALERT

Clusters? **The topic of configuring and managing server clusters using Windows Server 2003 is one that is beyond the scope of the 70-291 exam, so don't worry about it if you're not all that knowledgeable about them right now. We do examine clustering in detail in the *MCSE 70-293 Exam Prep: Planning and Maintaining a Microsoft Windows Server 2003 Network Infrastructure* by Will Schmied in preparation for that exam, so rest at ease.**

Challenge

You are the systems administrator for NR Widgets, Inc., a computer manufacturing company. NR Widgets, Inc., is just about to migrate to a purely Windows Server 2003 environment. You have two user networks—Sales and Engineering—and a corporate backbone network where all servers and other key infrastructure equipment are located.

The Sales network has more than 400 users and is multinetted to provide an adequate number of addresses for everyone. The Engineering network has only 75 users, but that network also contains a number of printers, plotters, and test equipment, so there are only 40 addresses for the users' computers. The users work three shifts in Engineering, with 25 engineers working each shift.

A major brand router separates the two user networks from each other and also from your corporate backbone. The multinetted Sales network has been implemented using a major brand switch configured to create Virtual Local Area Networks (VLANs).

(continues)

(continued)

Today, all of the hosts use static addresses, which works okay for the Sales network, but it means that to avoid IP address resolution problems, the engineers have to be careful about which computers are left connected to the network. Yesterday your manager suggested, "While you're migrating to Windows Server 2003, why don't you fix the IP address problems on the network?"

Your task is to implement a DHCP solution for NR Widgets, Inc., to eliminate the need to manually assign static IP addresses to the Sales and Engineering networks.

Try to complete this exercise on your own, listing your conclusions on a sheet of paper. After you have completed the exercise, compare your results to those given.

Answers

Some key questions to which you will need to provide answers to successfully complete this task are as follows:

1. How can you configure enough DHCP addresses for the 400 clients located on the Sales network?
2. Assuming you have the hardware resources available to configure and implement only a single DHCP server at this time, on what network should you place the new DHCP server?

Given what you know, your best option will be to configure and implement the new DHCP server on the corporate backbone network where your other servers are located (this is a general best practice). This location, however, assumes that you will be able to create a DHCP scope that contains more than the 40 IP addresses that are currently assigned to the Engineering department and that you will be able to configure the router to pass DHCP traffic. Following along with this design, you would then create the following scopes on the DHCP server:

- A single scope for the Engineering network that contains a full Class C subnet worth of IP addresses (254) to eliminate the need to have only a certain number of hosts online at any one time.
- A superscope for the Sales network. The superscope allows you to combine multiple scopes for easier management. The Sales network requires multiple scopes (three of them, in fact) due to the large number of hosts on the network. Alternatively, you could opt to create a single larger scope using a Class B subnet.

Before you can call your solution complete, however, you will need to complete at least two more tasks if you haven't already done so:

- After the DHCP service has been installed, you need to authorize the server in Active Directory before it will be able to give leases to domain clients.
- You need to be sure that the router has been configured to pass the DHCP traffic back and forth from the corporate network to the Sales and Engineering networks. If this is not possible, you will need to place a DHCP relay agent on each of the client networks to facilitate DHCP traffic transfer through the router.

In the unlikely event that you are not able to procure more IP addresses for use by the Sales network, your design may end a bit differently, especially if network traffic from DHCP is a concern. In this scenario, your design will be different in the following ways:

- The DHCP server will likely be placed on the Engineering network as there will be more DHCP traffic occurring on that network due to the limited number of IP addresses available.
- The lease time for the Sales DHCP scopes should be configured at a longer value, such as 30 days, due to the availability of more than addresses. This will minimize DHCP traffic across the router from the Sales network to the Engineering network.
- The lease time for the Engineering DHCP scope should be configured much shorter than the default value, perhaps 4 hours, so that addresses are available for the incoming shift as the previous shift leaves for home. The lease time will likely require some trial and error to tune it to the needs of the specific implementation.

Regardless of the restrictions and criteria that are imposed on you in this scenario, using Windows Server 2003 DHCP can produce a solid solution.

DHCP Server Management and Monitoring

Objective:

Manage DHCP.

- Manage DHCP databases.

We have spent some time now examining the installation and configuration of the Windows Server 2003 DHCP service. The final piece of the DHCP puzzle is managing and monitoring the server after it is installed and configured. The Windows Server 2003 DHCP server bundles enhanced monitoring and statistical reporting for precisely that purpose.

The DHCP console has several features that can be accessed by selecting the server and clicking the Action menu or by right-clicking the server. We examine these management and monitoring features in more detail in the following sections.

Examining the DHCP Server Statistics

The Display Statistics command opens the Server Statistics window, which is shown in Figure 2.34.

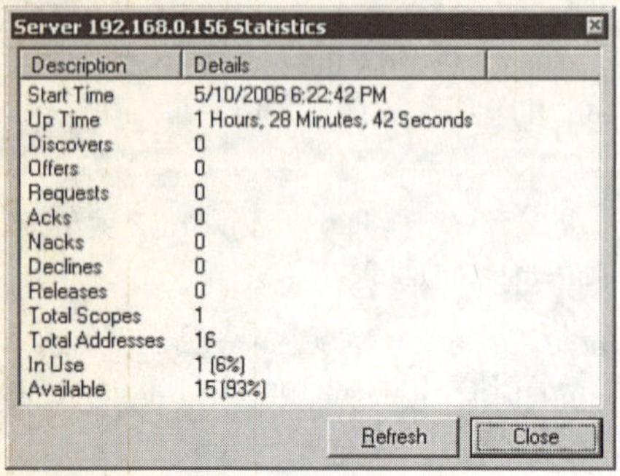

FIGURE 2.34 The Server Statistics window quickly displays pertinent DHCP statistics.

The Server Statistics window displays the following statistics:

- **Start Time**—The date and time the service was started.
- **Up Time**—The total uptime for the DHCP service. If you restart the service, this number resets to zero, even if the DHCP server has not been restarted.
- **Discovers**—The number of `DHCPDISCOVER` packets the server has received.
- **Offers**—The number of `DHCPOFFER` packets the server has sent.
- **Requests**—The number of `DHCPREQUEST` packets the server has received.
- **Acks**—The number of `DHCPACK` packets the server has sent.
- **Nacks**—The number of `DHCPNACK` packets the server has sent.
- **Declines**—The number of `DHCPDECLINE` packets the server has received.
- **Releases**—The number of `DHCPRELEASE` messages the server has received.
- **Total Scopes**—The total number of scopes that are active on the server.
- **Total Addresses**—The total number of addresses available. This number includes the number of addresses for all the active scopes on the server.
- **In Use**—The number of addresses presently leased to DHCP client computers.
- **Available**—The number of addresses available for lease for the total address pool.

DHCP Server Backup and Restore

As mentioned earlier in this chapter, DHCP server backup and restore is one of the new features found in the DHCP service in Windows Server 2003. Two types of backups from the DHCP console are supported:

- **Synchronous**—A synchronous backup occurs automatically on the configured interval. The default interval is 60 minutes and can be changed from the registry location `HKEY_LOCAL_MACHINE\SYSTEM\CurrentControlSet\Services\DHCPServer\Parameters\BackupInterval`.
- **Asynchronous**—An asynchronous backup is a manual backup that is performed by using the Backup command from within the DHCP console.

Both types of DHCP backups place their data in the same location, which is `%systemroot%\System32\Dhcp\Backup` by default. You can then use Windows Backup (`NTBACKUP.exe`) or any other backup application to safely back up this data to another location. You can change the database backup folder by selecting a different local folder during a manual backup or by changing the backup folder location in the DHCP server properties.

Backups of the DHCP data from the DHCP console include the following items:

- All scopes
- All reservations
- All leases
- All options, including server options, scope options, reservation options, and class options
- All registry data in the following registry location: `HKEY_LOCAL_MACHINE\SYSTEM\CurrentControlSet\Services\DHCPServer\Parameters`

NOTE

Dynamic Update Credentials Regardless of how you back up DHCP data, the DNS dynamic update credentials that the DHCP server uses for registering DHCP client computers in DNS will not be backed up.

EXAM ALERT

Performing a Backup You do not need to stop the DHCP service on the server to perform either an asynchronous backup or a synchronous backup unless you will be migrating the database to a different DHCP server.

You can manually perform a backup by selecting Action, Backup. In addition, you can perform the restoration of the DHCP data by selecting Action, Restore. If you want to change the backup path, you can do so from the Advanced tab of the DHCP Server Properties dialog box.

NOTE

DHCP Database Restoration Caveats You can restore DHCP databases only to the same language version of Windows from which they were backed up. For example, you cannot restore an English language version DHCP database to a DHCP server running the Japanese version of Windows Server 2003.

During the restoration process, the DHCP service is stopped for a short period of time on the server. During this time, clients are not able to contact the DHCP server.

Reconciling the DHCP Database

Objective:

Troubleshoot DHCP.

- Verify database integrity.

When you reconcile scopes on your DHCP server, you are comparing the information contained in the DHCP database against the information stored in the registry. Typically, reconciliation of scopes is performed when you are observing problems with the DHCP server and want to verify the configured addresses. The Reconcile All Scopes command allows you to perform this comparison should you need to. You can click the Verify button in the Reconcile All Scopes dialog box (shown in Figure 2.35) to check the consistency of the database and get a report of any errors.

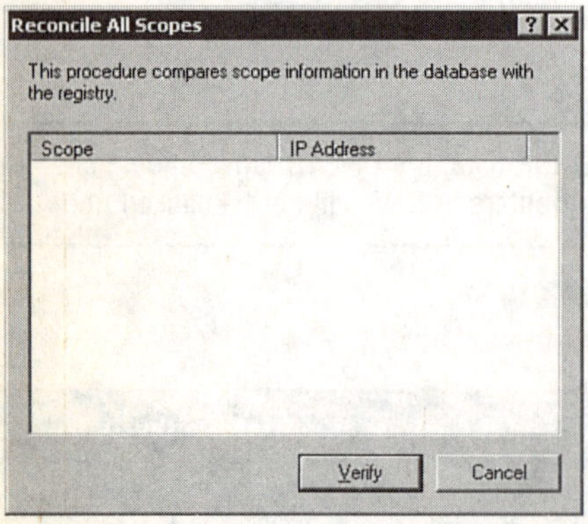

FIGURE 2.35 You can reconcile all scopes from the Reconcile All Scopes dialog box.

Stopping the DHCP Server

Sometimes you'll want to prevent a DHCP server from giving out leases so that you can perform maintenance on the server or make configuration changes to scopes on the server. You can cause this happen by either unauthorizing the server or by stopping the DHCP server service. The Unauthorize command removes the DHCP server from the list of authorized DHCP servers in Active Directory. You are warned before removal occurs, as shown in Figure 2.36.

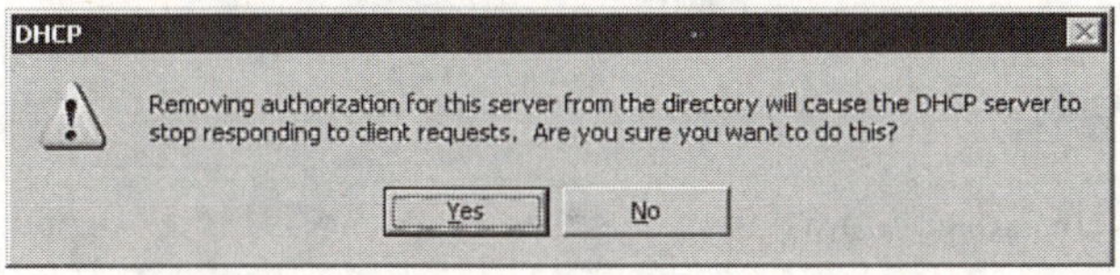

FIGURE 2.36 Unauthorizing a DHCP server prevents it from servicing client requests.

The advantage of unauthorizing a server versus stopping the DHCP server service, as shown in Figure 2.37, is that you can still perform scope and server configuration and modification while the server is unauthorized. That is not possible when the DHCP server service has been stopped on the server.

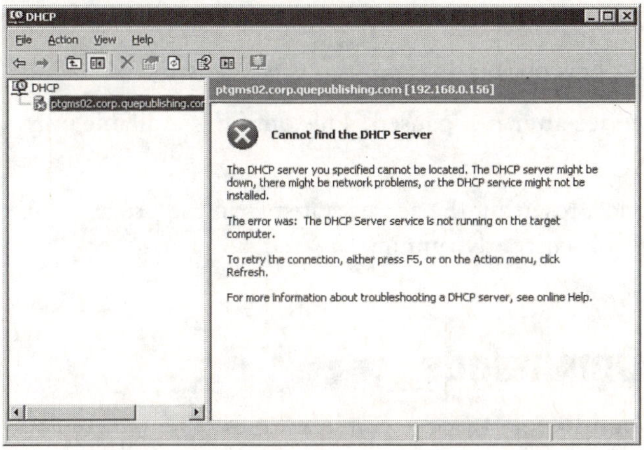

FIGURE 2.37 Stopping the DHCP server service removes the ability to perform configuration on it.

Configuring Options and Classes

The options Define User Classes, Define Vendor Classes, and Set Predefined Options are beyond the scope of Exam 70-291. You will probably not use them in the context of a standard DHCP installation, but you should be aware of what user classes and vendor classes are in general so that your knowledge of DHCP will be complete.

- **User classes**—User classes are generally created for administrative purposes, similar to user groups. They can be used to identify all the DHCP clients in a specific department or location. User classes are used to assign DHCP options to groups of DHCP clients.

- **Vendor classes**—Vendor classes are generally used to provide vendor-specific DHCP enhancements. For example, the Windows Server 2003 DHCP service has the capability to disable NetBT on its DHCP clients.

Changing the Server State

Should you want to change the state of the server, perhaps pause or stop the DHCP server altogether, you can do this from the Action menu. Selecting Action, All Tasks opens a submenu that allows you to control the operational state of the DHCP server. The following options are available:

- **Start**—Starts the DHCP service. This option is available only if the service is stopped or paused.
- **Stop**—Stops the DHCP service. This option is available when the service is running or paused. This option causes the server statistics to be reset.
- **Pause**—Pauses the DHCP service. This option does not reset the statistics.
- **Resume**—Resumes the DHCP service after it is paused. This option is available only when the service is paused.
- **Restart**—Restarts the DHCP service, resetting the server statistics in the process. This option is available only if the service is currently running.

DHCP Server Common Commands

The three commands Delete, Refresh, and Export List are common ones. The Delete command deletes the DHCP server. The Refresh command causes all the displayed information to be refreshed with a current status. The Export List command allows you to export the information displayed in the right pane of the console window to a tab- or comma-delimited text or Unicode text file. You can export a list of various nodes by clicking them before selecting the Export List command.

The Properties command opens the Properties dialog box for the selected DHCP server. The Properties dialog box (shown previously in Figure 2.33) opens to the General tab, which allows you to configure the following options.

- **Automatically Update Statistics Every**—This option allows you to set the automatic refresh of the statistics, as well as the interval at which the statistics are refreshed.
- **Enable DHCP Audit Logging**—This option allows you to log all the DHCP activity to a text file located in the `%systemroot%\System32\dhcp` folder, which can be opened

in Notepad or any other text editor. This is an excellent option to select if you are troubleshooting a DHCP problem and want to see what activity is taking place on the server.

- **Show the BOOTP Table Folder**—This option deals with BOOTP backward compatibility and allows you to view the table that contains the BOOTP configuration entries. After you select this option, the BOOTP Table node appears in the DHCP console, as shown in Figure 2.38. From this node you can configure boot images for BOOTP clients. Remember, however, that you still need to provide your own third-party TFTP server.

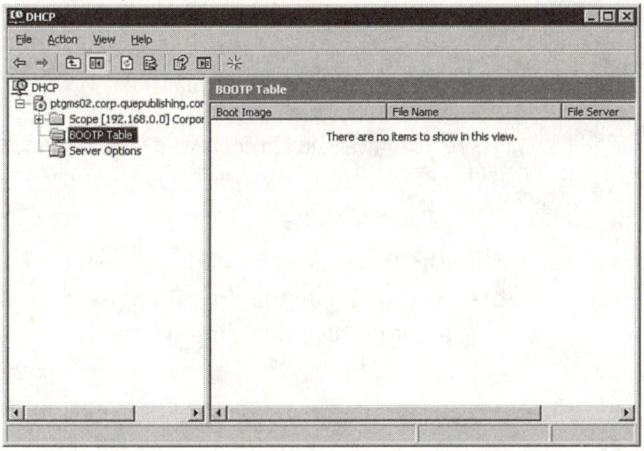

FIGURE 2.38 When the BOOTP Table folder is enabled, you can perform configuration of BOOTP boot images.

The DNS tab of the Properties dialog box is discussed in detail earlier in this chapter, in the section “Configuring DHCP for DNS Integration.” You can use the Advanced tab, shown in Figure 2.39, to perform more advanced and less common configuration tasks.

The Advanced tab has the following configuration options:

- **Conflict Detection Attempts**—This option causes the DHCP server to check for conflicting IP addresses on the network before issuing an address. Although this sounds like a great way to make sure there are no address conflicts, it can add significant overhead to the server, and you should use it only while you’re troubleshooting address conflict issues. By default, this option is set to 0.

- **Audit Log File Path**—If audit logging is enabled, the log file is located in the `%systemroot%\System32\dhcp` directory. You can modify the location to be any location on the local computer (including mapped drives).

- **Database Path**—This option allows you to specify the location of the DHCP database. By default, it is in the `%systemroot%\System32\dhcp` directory. You can modify the location to be any location on the local computer (including mapped drives).

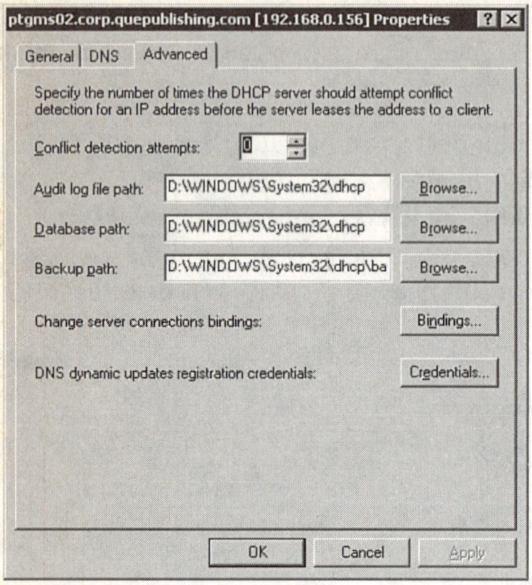

FIGURE 2.39 The Advanced tab contains all the options that don't fit anywhere else.

- **Backup Path**—This option allows you to specify the location of the DHCP backup file. By default, it is in the `%systemroot%\System32\dhcp\backup` directory. You can modify the location to be any location on the local computer (including mapped drives).
- **Change Server Connection Bindings**—This option allows you to view the connections through which the DHCP server is providing addresses. If you have multiple network adapters in a DHCP server, you might want to configure DHCP for only selected interfaces. You can click the Bindings button to view and configure the binding on your computer, as shown in Figure 2.40.

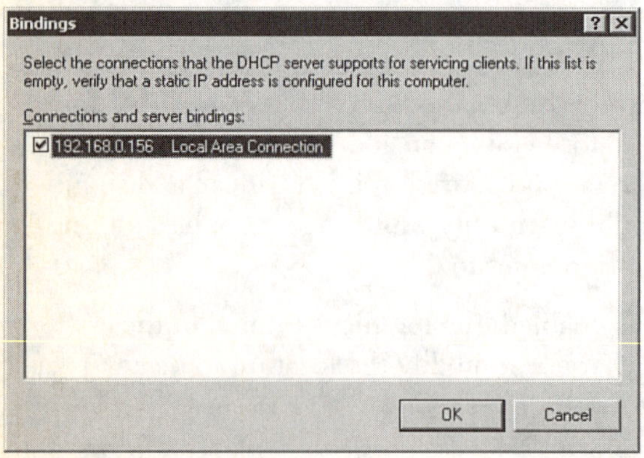

FIGURE 2.40 You can view and change the DHCP bindings from the Bindings window.

- **DNS Dynamic Updates Registration Credentials**—As discussed previously, this option allows you to specify a domain user account to be used during DNS dynamic updates.

EXAM ALERT

Resolving Conflict Problems When you start seeing a large number of declines per second (as discussed in the next section, "Troubleshooting DHCP"), you might want to enable conflict detection on the DHCP server. Conflict detection causes the server to look for conflicts before issuing an address, and it should take care of conflict problems until you can find the problem. You should do this only until the problem is addressed. Forcing the DHCP server to detect conflicts every time it issues an address adds a lot of overhead to the server and the DHCP service, and it should be avoided on a long-term basis. After you have resolved a problem, be sure to turn off this feature.

Troubleshooting DHCP

Although DHCP is typically one of the easiest of the common network services to configure and maintain, from time to time, you might encounter problems. More often than not, the DHCP-related problems that you will have will be due to misconfiguration in a scope, unauthorized DHCP servers on the network, or network connectivity problems. You might also have instances in which information has changed in some way, but the change has not been reflected in your DHCP configuration, as in the case of DHCP reservations (which are tied to MAC addresses) or the changing of a DHCP server's IP address. Network connectivity issues are addressed in Chapter 1, and the following sections examine some troubleshooting tasks you can do in an effort to quickly determine the cause of DHCP woes and get this vital network service back into proper operation.

Troubleshooting DHCP Server Authorization Problems

Objective:

Troubleshoot DHCP.

- Diagnose and resolve issues related to DHCP authorization.
- Diagnose and resolve issues related to configuration of DHCP server and scope options.

As discussed previously, one of the first indicators you might see of an unauthorized or rogue DHCP server is an unexpected increase in the number of DHCPNACK messages. You can monitor this statistic over time by using the Performance console. The Performance console includes several counter objects that you can use to monitor and troubleshoot your DHCP server:

- **Acks/Sec**—This counter monitors the number of DHCPACK messages sent per second by the DHCP server to client computers. The DHCP server uses the DHCPACK messages to acknowledge requests for an address. An increase in this number indicates that a large number of client computers are probably trying to renew their leases with the DHCP server. This could be because of a short lease time configuration or because a number of new computers are entering the network.
- **Active Queue Length**—This counter monitors the current length of the internal message queue of the DHCP server. This number represents the number of unprocessed messages received by the server. A large number here could indicate an unusually large amount of network traffic or a heavy load on the server.
- **Conflict Check Queue Length**—This counter monitors the current length of the conflict check queue for the DHCP server. Before a Windows Server 2003 DHCP server issues an address, it checks whether any IP address conflicts exist. The conflict check queue holds the messages not responded to while the DHCP server performs address conflict detection. A large value here could indicate heavy lease traffic at the server. You might also want to check the Conflict Detection Attempts parameter, which could be set too high.
- **Declines/Sec**—This counter monitors the number of DHCPDECLINE messages that the DHCP server receives per second from client computers. This counter indicates that the DHCP client computer has declined the IP address issued by the server. You see this number rise when client computers start having address conflict problems, and it could indicate a network problem, computers with static addresses also being part of a scope, or having a rogue DHCP server on the network.
- **Discovers/Sec**—This counter monitors the number of DHCPDISCOVER messages received per second by the server. The DHCPDISCOVER message is the initial request a client computer sends when it first enters the network and is looking for a DHCP server to issue an address. A sudden increase in this counter could indicate that a large number of client computers are attempting to initialize and obtain an IP address lease from the server at the same time. You might see this first thing in the morning, when users power on their PCs, or after a power failure, when all the PCs might be powered on at about the same time.
- **Duplicates Dropped/Sec**—This counter monitors the number of duplicate packets per second dropped by the DHCP server. Duplicate packets on a network are never a good sign, and they can indicate that DHCP clients are timing out before the server can respond. This can be caused by client computers timing out too fast or the server not responding quickly enough.

- **Informs/Sec**—This counter monitors the number of `DHCPINFORM` messages received per second by the DHCP server. `DHCPINFORM` messages are used when the DHCP server queries the directory service for the enterprise root and when dynamic updates are being done on behalf of client computers by the DNS server. This is part of the DDNS integration, and an unusual increase in this number could indicate a large number of addresses being issued.
- **Milliseconds Per Packet (Avg)**—This counter monitors the average time, in milliseconds, the DHCP server takes to process each packet it receives. This is a very subjective number that depends on the server configuration; therefore, having a baseline for this number is a good idea. A sudden increase in this counter could indicate a disk problem or an increased load on the server.
- **Nacks/Sec**—This counter monitors the number of DHCP negative acknowledgment (`DHCPNACK`) messages sent per second by the DHCP server to client computers. A `DHCPNACK` message indicates that the server is unable to fulfill the DHCP request. A very high value for this counter could indicate a network problem or misconfiguration of client computers or the server. You should keep an eye out for a deactivated scope as a possible culprit.
- **Offers/Sec**—This counter monitors the number of `DHCPOFFER` messages that the DHCP server sends per second to client computers. A `DHCPOFFER` message is the message the server returns to the client computer after the client computer sends a `DHCPDISCOVER` message, and it indicates that the server is offering to issue an address to that client computer. A sudden increase in this value could indicate heavy traffic or a heavy load on the server.
- **Packets Expired/Sec**—This counter monitors the number of packets per second that expire and are dropped by the DHCP server. This situation is caused by a packet remaining in the server's internal message queue too long. A large number for this counter indicates that the server is either taking too long to process some packets or causing other packets to wait in queue, or that the traffic on the network is too heavy for the DHCP server to handle. It is important to note that high numbers for this counter can indicate pure network traffic problems and not necessarily DHCP-related problems.
- **Packets Received/Sec**—This counter monitors the number of message packets received per second by the DHCP server. A large number indicates heavy DHCP message traffic to the server. These message packets might be requests for addresses, renewals, or releases.
- **Releases/Sec**—This counter monitors the number of `DHCPRELEASE` messages that the DHCP server receives per second from client computers. A `DHCPRELEASE` message is sent only when the client computer manually releases an address, such as when the

`ipconfig /release` command is used or the Release All button in the `winipcfg` utility is used at the client computer. Because most users do not manually release their addresses, this number should be low in all but the most unusual network environment.

- **Requests/Sec**—This counter monitors the number of DHCPREQUEST messages that the DHCP server receives per second from client computers. These messages are the requests that the client computer sends to request an IP address after it has found a server that can issue addresses. An increase in this number indicates that a large number of client computers are probably trying to renew their leases with the DHCP server. This could be caused by a short lease time configuration or because a number of new computers are entering the network.

Configuring the Performance console to monitor and collect data about a DCHP server is a simple process, as outlined in Step by Step 2.7.

STEP BY STEP

2.7 Monitoring DHCP Performance

1. Select Start, Program, Administrative Tools, Performance to open the Performance console.
2. Click System Monitor, as shown in Figure 2.41.

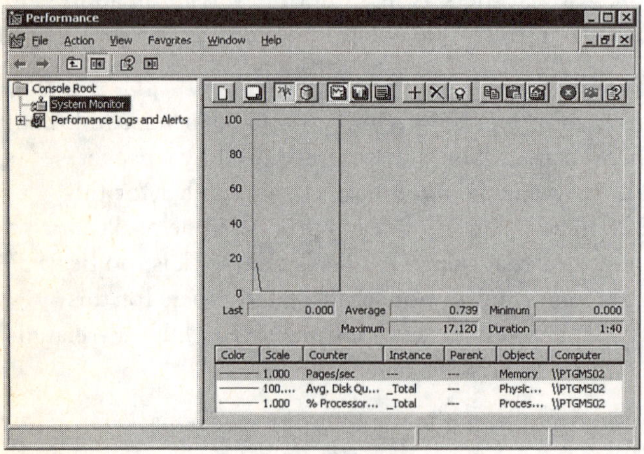

FIGURE 2.41 You can view server performance statistics by using the Performance console.

3. To create an entry in System Monitor, click the + icon. The Add Counters dialog box shown in Figure 2.42 opens, allowing you to begin adding counters.

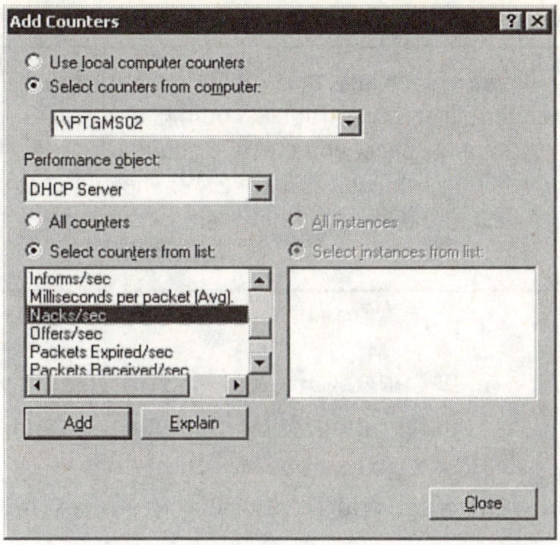

FIGURE 2.42 You can add counters to begin monitoring DHCP server statistics.

4. Select the DHCP Server performance object in the Performance object drop-down list box. You then see the list of counters available for selection that relate to the DHCP service. If you need to know what a counter means, select the counter and click the Explain button.
5. When you have decided what counter you want to monitor, click Add. You can add multiple counters either by selecting each counter and clicking Add or by holding down the Ctrl key while you select all the counters you want to monitor and then clicking Add. Click Close when you are finished. Your counters are graphed like those shown in Figure 2.43.

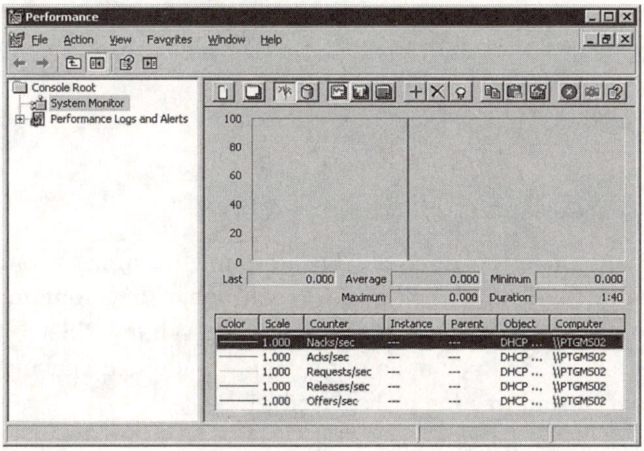

FIGURE 2.43 You can monitor DHCP server statistics in real time.

NOTE

Creating Server Baselines If you create baselines on servers, you will be able to compare the performance at any given time to a known value. This can be very useful in performing troubleshooting, and it also helps in periods when configurations are being modified. To create a baseline, you create a counter log from the Counter Logs option of the Performance Logs and Alerts node shown in Figure 2.42. The configuration and usage of a counter log is nearly identical to the creation and usage of the System Monitor, as described in Step by Step 2.7.

If you notice a trend of higher-than-normal numbers of `DHCPNACK` messages, you need to determine what the source is. The most common cause is that a rogue DHCP server has been set up on the network. You can also examine the DHCP lease properties of clients to determine whether any of them have different information than what you have configured in your DHCP scopes.

It's important to remember that Windows 2000 and Windows XP clients in an Active Directory environment that are configured to use DHCP do not accept leases from unauthorized DHCP servers. Older clients accept these leases and can contribute to the number of `DHCPNACK` messages when they attempt to renew their DHCP leases.

You can also examine the DHCP server daily audit logs, located in the `%systemroot%\sysytem32\dhcp` folder, to look for rogue detection events. The DHCP audit logs are discussed in the next section.

Using the DHCP Logs

Objective:

Troubleshoot DHCP.

- Examine the system event log and DHCP server audit log files to find related events.

The DHCP server daily audit logs are often overlooked as a valuable source of information. You have learned how to enable the audit logs; now let's have a look at what they contain. Unlike the logs produced by the Windows 2000 Server DHCP service, the Windows Server 2003 daily audit logs are natively in text format, and you open them simply by double-clicking them. A sample of what you might expect to find in a log is displayed here:

```
ID,Date,Time,Description,IP Address,Host Name,MAC Address
00,04/27/06,20:08:38,Started,,,,
55,04/27/06,20:08:39,Authorized(servicing),,lab1.area51partners.com,,
24,04/27/06,20:44:10,Database Cleanup Begin,,,,
25,04/27/06,20:44:10,0 leases expired and 0 leases deleted,,,,
25,04/27/06,20:44:10,0 leases expired and 0 leases deleted,,,,
24,04/27/06,21:44:12,Database Cleanup Begin,,,,
```

```
25,04/27/06,21:44:12,0 leases expired and 0 leases deleted,,,,
25,04/27/06,21:44:12,0 leases expired and 0 leases deleted,,,,
11,04/27/06,19:39:46,Renew,192.168.0.231,
    xpclient01.corp.quepublishing.com,00E07DC13E70,
31,04/27/06,19:39:46,DNS Update Failed,
    192.168.0.231,xpclient01.corp.quepublishing.com,-1,
10,04/27/06,19:43:07,Assign,192.168.0.230,
    iMac01.corp.quepublishing.com,00306509D772,
30,04/27/06,19:44:14,DNS Update Request,192.168.0.231,
    xpclient01.corp.quepublishing.com,,
31,04/27/06,19:44:14,DNS Update Failed,192.168.0.231,
    xpclient01.corp.quepublishing.com,-1,
30,04/27/06,19:47:03,DNS Update Request,192.168.0.231,
    xpclient01.corp.quepublishing.com,,
11,04/27/06,19:47:03,Renew,192.168.0.231,
    xpclient01.corp.quepublishing.com,00E07DC13E70,
30,04/27/06,19:47:03,DNS Update Request,
    192.168.0.231,xpclient01.corp.quepublishing.com,,
11,04/27/06,19:47:03,Renew,192.168.0.231,
    xpclient01.corp.quepublishing.com,00E07DC13E70,
32,04/27/06,19:47:03,DNS Update Successful,192.168.0.231,
    xpclient01.corp.quepublishing.com,,
32,04/27/06,19:47:03,DNS Update Successful,192.168.0.231,
    xpclient01.corp.quepublishing.com,,
```

As you can see from this example, the DHCP server cleans up the database hourly. You can also see that two clients requested leases. One of them, an Apple iMac, requested and was assigned the IP address 192.168.0.230, with no further actions. Another client, a Windows XP Professional computer, requested and received the IP address 192.168.0.231, with several failed DNS updates (evidenced by ID 31). After the DNS dynamic update account was properly configured, the DHCP server was able to make the DNS dynamic updates and generate an ID of 32. Table 2.3 explains the ID codes used in the DHCP daily audit logs.

TABLE 2.3 The DHCP Daily Audit Log ID Codes

ID	Description
00	The log was started.
01	The log was stopped.
02	The log was temporarily paused due to low disk space.
10	A new IP address was leased to a client.
11	A lease was renewed by a client.
12	A lease was released by a client.
13	An IP address was found to be in use on the network.
14	A lease request could not be satisfied because the scope's address pool was exhausted.

(continues)

TABLE 2.3 Continued

ID	Description
15	A lease was denied.
16	A lease was deleted.
17	A lease was expired.
20	A BOOTP address was leased to a client.
21	A dynamic BOOTP address was leased to a client.
22	A BOOTP request could not be satisfied because the scope's address pool for BOOTP was exhausted.
23	A BOOTP IP address was deleted after a check was made to see that it was not in use.
24	The IP address cleanup operation has began.
25	IP address cleanup statistics are provided.
30	A DNS update request to the named DNS server was made.
31	The DNS update failed.
32	The DNS update was successful.
50+	These IDs are used for Rogue Server Detection information.

In addition to the DHCP daily audit logs, events related to the DHCP service are also generated and placed in the system log, as shown in Figure 2.44.

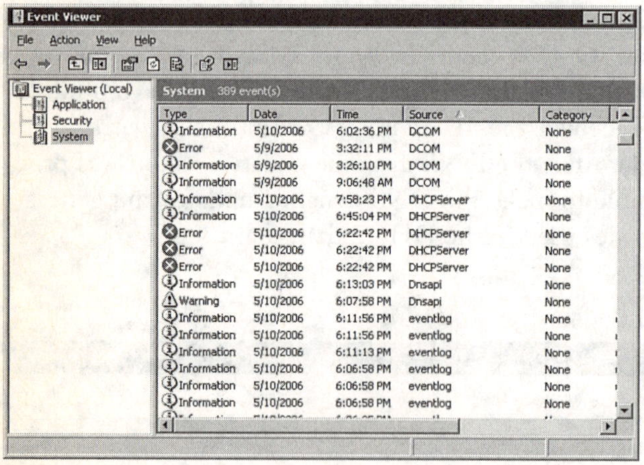

FIGURE 2.44 The system log contains events related to the DHCP service.

As you can see in Figure 2.45, there is a DHCP server on the network that has not been authorized in Active Directory. The system log contains many useful log events about all aspects of a server and is an area you should review often.

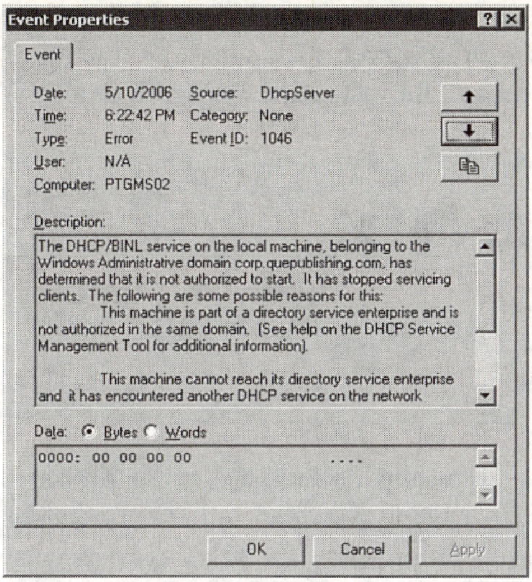

FIGURE 2.45 An unauthorized DHCP server cannot start the DHCP service.

Troubleshooting DHCP Reservations

Objective:

Troubleshoot DHCP.

- Verify DHCP reservation configuration.

For the most part, the only problem that prevents a DHCP reservation from functioning properly is a misconfigured MAC address. If you have a misconfigured DHCP reservation, you should see it show up in the Address Leases node of your DHCP server, with the status Reservation (Inactive). Reservations that are configured properly show the status Reservation (Active). If you look back at Figure 2.16, you'll see the reservation we created had a bad MAC address and thus was the cause of the problem seen in Figure 2.46.

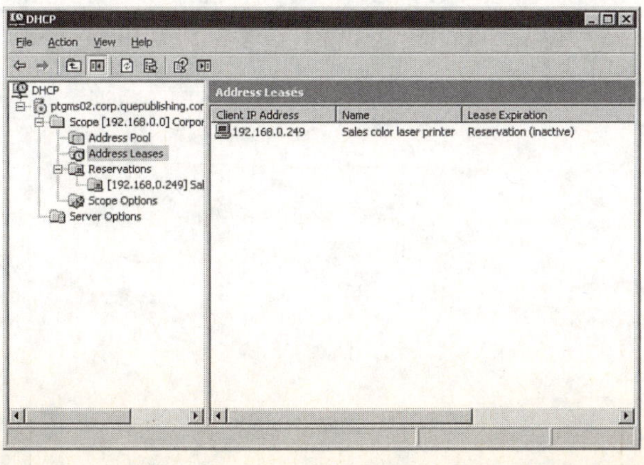

FIGURE 2.46 A DHCP reservation that is not active usually indicates a misconfiguration.

To verify that a reservation is configured properly, you can compare the MAC address of the component that is to have a reserved DCHP address (a print server, for example) to the MAC address entered in the reservation Properties dialog box. The vast majority of the time, this will reveal the source of the problem.

Troubleshooting the DHCP Relay Agent

Objective:

Troubleshoot DHCP.

- Verify that the DHCP Relay Agent is working correctly.

The DHCP relay agent, like a DHCP reservation, typically doesn't present a problem. However, there may be cases when relay services are not being provided to network clients. Some of the most common problems that you might encounter with the DHCP relay agent include the following:

- The network interface on the DHCP relay agent server that is connected to the subnet where the DHCP clients are located has not been selected for use with the DHCP relay agent. You can verify whether the interface has been added or add it from the DHCP Relay Agent node of the DHCP console. You should also verify that the Relay DHCP Packets check box is selected on all adapters that have been selected for use.
- An incorrectly entered DHCP server IP address on the DHCP Relay Agent Properties dialog box (refer back to Figure 2.32) prevents the successful relaying of packets. You can verify and correct this problem from the properties dialog box of the DHCP Relay Agent node of the DHCP console.
- Remote DHCP servers may not be reachable due to network or server problems. In this case, you need to troubleshoot basic network connectivity, as discussed in Chapter 1. You should troubleshoot the server status as discussed in this chapter.
- DHCP traffic may be being filtered. In this case, you need to ensure that no IP filters exist for UDP ports 67 and 68 at any point between the DHCP servers and the remote DHCP clients.

Chapter Summary

In this chapter, we've examined how to implement, manage, and troubleshoot DHCP in Windows Server 2003. Some points of interest to take away from this chapter include the following:

- Windows Server 2003 DHCP supports three types of scopes: standard scopes, superscopes, and multicast scopes. A superscope is a grouping of one or more standard DHCP scopes, whereas a multicast scope is used for special Class D IP addresses for multicasting to clients.
- DHCP servers must be authorized in Active Directory to service clients. Windows Server 2003 DHCP servers that have not been authorized cannot offer leases to DHCP clients.
- DHCP can be integrated with DNS to provide dynamic updating of DNS A and PTR records for DHCP clients. This serves to keep the DNS database accurate and up-to-date as DHCP assigns leases to client computers.
- You can perform monitoring and troubleshooting on a DHCP server by using the DHCP counters in the Performance console.

Key Terms

- BOOTP
- DNS
- DHCP
- DHCP server
- DHCP client
- exclusion
- lease
- multicast scope
- registered IP address
- RFCs
- DHCP reservation
- scope

- supernetted network
- superscope
- TCP/IP
- unicast address

Apply Your Knowledge

In this chapter, you have learned what DHCP is and how it works to make IP address assignment easier, quicker, and more accurate. In the following exercises, you will practice some of the concepts and methods discussed in this chapter.

Exercises

2.1 Creating a DHCP Scope

This exercise guides you through the process of creating a standard DHCP scope. This exercise requires you to have a Windows Server 2003 computer with the DHCP service installed.

Estimated time: 20 minutes

1. Open the DHCP console by selecting Start, Programs, Administrative Tools, DHCP.
2. Right-click the DHCP server and select New Scope from the context menu.
3. Click Next to dismiss the opening page of the New Scope Wizard.
4. On the Scope Name page, enter the name **`SCOPE1`** and an appropriate description for the new scope. Click Next to continue.
5. On the IP Address Range page, enter the IP address range **`10.0.0.2`**–**`10.0.0.100`**, and the subnet mask **`255.255.255.0`**. Click Next to continue.
6. On the Add Exclusions page, enter the IP address ranges **`10.0.0.5`**–**`10.0.0.10`** and **`10.0.0.15`**–**`10.0.0.20`** as exclusions. Click Next to continue.
7. On the Lease Duration page, you can leave the default setting of eight days. Click Next to continue.
8. Select to configure advanced options and click Next to continue.
9. On the Router (Default Gateway) page, enter the default gateway IP address **`10.0.0.1`**. Click Next to continue.
10. On the Domain Name and DNS Servers page, enter the IP addresses **`10.0.0.250`** and **`10.0.0.251`** for the DNS servers. Specify the parent domain as **`testlab.local`**. Click Next to continue.

11. On the WINS Servers page, enter the IP addresses of the WINS servers if you have legacy clients that still need WINS services. Enter the IP addresses **10.0.0.250** and **10.0.0.251** for the WINS servers. Click Next to continue.
12. Opt to activate the scope now and click Finish to complete the wizard.

2.2 Creating a Superscope

This exercise shows you how to manage multiple scopes by creating a superscope. You need to have completed Exercise 2.1 in order for this exercise to work.

Estimated time: 20 minutes

1. Open the DHCP console by selecting Start, Programs, Administrative Tools, DHCP.
2. Right-click the DHCP server and select New Scope from the context menu.
3. Create a second scope, using the IP address range 10.0.0.102–10.0.0.200, using the same default gateway, DNS servers, and WINS servers as detailed in Exercise 2.1, with no exclusions. Name the scope **SCOPE2**.
4. Right-click the DHCP server and select New Superscope from the context menu.
5. Click Next to dismiss the opening page of the New Superscope Wizard.
6. On the Superscope Name page, enter **SUPERSCOPE1** and click Next to continue.
7. On the Select Scopes page, select SCOPE1 and SCOPE2 by holding down the Ctrl key and clicking both scopes. Click Next to continue.
8. Verify your configuration on the Completing the New Superscope Wizard page. Click Next to complete the superscope creation process.
9. The Completing the New Superscope Wizard dialog box gives you a summary of the selections you made throughout the wizard. Click Finish to create the superscope.

2.3 Configuring a DHCP Relay Agent

This exercise walks you through the process of creating and configuring a DHCP relay agent for a network.

Estimated time: 15 minutes

1. Open the Routing and Remote Access console.
2. Expand the console nodes so that you can access the IP Routing, General node.
3. Right-click the General node and select New Routing Protocol.
4. Select the DHCP relay agent.

5. Right-click the DHCP Relay Agent node and select New Interface from the context menu to select the interface to be used for the DHCP relay agent.
6. Configure your required values for hop-count threshold and boot threshold.
7. Right-click the DHCP Relay Agent node and select Properties. Enter one or more remote DHCP servers into the list and click OK to confirm your settings.

2.4 Authorizing a DHCP Server in Active Directory

This exercise walks you through authorizing a DHCP server in Active Directory. This exercise requires that you have an Active Directory environment with an installed DHCP server.

Estimated time: 5 minutes

1. Open the DHCP console by selecting Start, Programs, Administrative Tools, DHCP.
2. Right-click the DHCP server and select Authorize from the context menu.
3. The authorization process may take some time, depending on network conditions. Refresh the DHCP console by pressing F5. The DHCP server status is shown as Active when the authorization is complete. The server is then ready to issue addresses when it receives DHCP requests.

2.5 Configuring DHCP for DNS Integration

This exercise walks you through configuring a DHCP server for DNS integration. This exercise requires that you have an Active Directory environment with an installed DHCP server and DNS server. To complete this exercise, you need to have completed Exercise 2.4.

Estimated time: 15 minutes

1. Open the DHCP console by selecting Start, Programs, Administrative Tools, DHCP.
2. Right-click the DHCP server and select Properties from the context menu. Switch to the DNS tab of the DHCP Server Properties dialog box.
3. To enable DHCP integration with DNS, ensure that the Enable Dynamic DNS Updates According to the Settings Below check box is selected.
4. Select to either have the DHCP server update A and PTR records when requested or to always update A and PTR records.
5. To help keep your DNS database clean and consistent, you should allow the DHCP server to cause expired leases to lead to A and PTR record deletion.
6. If you have legacy clients on the network, ensure that dynamic updating is configured for them as well.
7. If you are using secure dynamic updates, you should consider configuring a dedicated network user account for the dynamic updating. You can enter the account credentials by switching to the Advanced tab.

8. Click the Credentials button on the Advanced tab to open the DNS Dynamic Update Credentials dialog box.
9. Enter the domain user account name, domain, and password.

Exam Questions

1. You are the systems administrator for Wild Widgets, Inc. You are training a new employee on the use of the DHCP service in Windows Server 2003. She asks you how the client computer requests and receives an address from the server. Which of the following answers is correct?

   ❍ **A.** The client computer broadcasts a `DHCPDISCOVER` message. The DHCP server offers an IP address. The client computer accepts the address and uses it to communicate on the network.

   ❍ **B.** The client computer broadcasts a `DHCPDISCOVER` message. The DHCP server offers an IP address. The client computer accepts the address and sends a request to use that address back to the DHCP server. The client computer uses the address to communicate on the network.

   ❍ **C.** The client computer broadcasts a `DHCPDISCOVER` message. The DHCP server offers an IP address. The client computer accepts the address and sends a request to use that address back to the DHCP server. The DHCP server acknowledges the request and grants the client computer a lease to use the address. The client computer uses the address to connect to the network.

   ❍ **D.** The client computer broadcasts a `DHCPDISCOVER` message. The DHCP server offers an IP address. The client computer accepts the address and sends a request to use that address back to the DHCP server. The DHCP server acknowledges the request and grants the client computer a lease to use the address. The client computer responds with an acknowledgement of the lease and uses the address to connect to the network.

2. You are the system administrator for Phil's Phill-up Stations, a chain of gas stations. As part of the network, you maintain a Windows Server 2003 DHCP server to dynamically assign addresses. You have three superscopes set up, and within each superscope are four scopes. One day, you start experiencing problems with one of the scopes issuing bad addresses. You check the server and suspect that there is a database problem. How can you verify that the database is intact?

   ❍ **A.** Open the DHCP console. Select the scope in question and select Action, Reconcile Scope.

   ❍ **B.** Open the DHCP console. Select the superscope that contains the scope in question and then select Action, Reconcile All Scopes.

   ❍ **C.** Open the DHCP console. Select the DHCP server that contains the scope in question and then select Action, Reconcile All Scopes.

   ❍ **D.** Open the DHCP console. Select the DHCP server that contains the scope in question and then select Action, Reconcile DHCP Database.

3. You are the LAN administrator for Get Stuffed Taxidermy, and you are responsible for maintaining the company's Windows Server 2003 DHCP server. While doing your daily system checks, you notice that the number of DHCPDISCOVER packets spiked at 9:00 this morning. What could cause the Discovers/Sec counter to spike at 9:00 a.m.?

❍ **A.** A network problem

❍ **B.** The DHCP service being restarted

❍ **C.** A large number of computers entering the network at approximately the same time

❍ **D.** A rogue DHCP server issuing duplicate addresses

4. You are the systems administrator for Hank's Harmonicas, Ltd. Your Active Directory–based network consists of all Windows Server 2003 server computers and Windows 98, Windows 2000 Professional, and Windows XP Professional client computers. This morning one of the users of a Windows 98 computer called you and said that she could no longer connect to network resources. Upon further investigation, you discover that several other Windows 98 clients are experiencing the same problem. You determine that the cause of the problem is due to an incorrectly configured DHCP lease. What is the most likely reason that only your Windows 98 clients are exhibiting this problem?

❍ **A.** The DHCP service in Windows 98 is not as stable as that in Windows 2000 or Windows XP, and this sometimes results in corrupted lease information.

❍ **B.** An unauthorized DHCP server has been set up on the network.

❍ **C.** A misconfigured DHCP server has been set up on the network.

❍ **D.** The Windows 98 clients were unable to renew their DHCP lease and have thus assumed APIPA IP addresses instead.

5. You are the lead systems administrator for Little Faith Enterprises, and a customer has asked you to install the DHCP service on her Windows Server 2003 computer, get one scope configured, and issue addresses. What minimum steps do you need to take in order to accomplish this?

❍ **A.** Install the DHCP service from the Windows Components Wizard. After the service is installed,.authorize it in Active Directory. Next, create the scope. Finally, configure the DNS integration.

❍ **B.** Install the DHCP service from the Windows Components Wizard. After the service is installed, create the scope and then configure the DNS integration.

❍ **C.** Install the DHCP service from the Windows Components Wizard. After the service is installed, create the scope. Create a superscope and add the scope to it. Authorize the server in Active Directory.

❍ **D.** Install the DHCP service from the Windows Components Wizard. After the service is installed, create the scope. Authorize the server in Active Directory.

6. You are the systems administrator for the Hittem Boxing Glove Corporation. The corporation is running a routed network with a centrally located Windows Server 2003 DHCP server. The server is able to issue addresses to users on the local segment but cannot issue addresses to any of the sites that are across a router. What is the most probable cause of this problem?

   ❍ **A.** The DHCP forwarder service is not enabled on the DHCP server.

   ❍ **B.** The BOOTP forwarder service is not enabled on the DHCP server.

   ❍ **C.** The DHCP forwarder service is not enabled on the routers.

   ❍ **D.** The BOOTP forwarder service is not enabled on the routers.

7. You manage the Windows Server 2003 DHCP servers for the Really Big Screwdriver Corporation. You are running in a purely Windows Server 2003 environment with all Windows XP Professional clients, and you need to make sure that workstations are registered properly in DNS for Active Directory integration. How should you configure DNS integration?

   ❍ **A.** Set DNS integration to automatically update DHCP client information in DNS.

   ❍ **B.** Set DNS integration to discard A and PTR records when a lease is deleted.

   ❍ **C.** Set DNS integration to enable updates for DNS clients that do not support dynamic updates.

   ❍ **D.** Set DNS integration to enable DNS keepalives.

8. You are the systems administrator for UR Write publishing, a bookseller. Your Windows Server 2003 DHCP server issues a block of 40 addresses to 120 salespeople on the Sales network. These users are frequently in and out of the office, so no more than 40 users are ever on the network at one time. What do you need to do to ensure that users get addresses when needed?

   ❍ **A.** Set the DHCP lease duration to 60 minutes.

   ❍ **B.** Set the DHCP lease duration to 5 days.

   ❍ **C.** Configure a reservation for each user.

   ❍ **D.** Configure an exclusion for each user.

9. You are the distributed computing administrator for Talk to Me Telephone. The company has Windows Server 2003 installed, with the DHCP service running. Mixed in with the DHCP client computers, the company still has some old workstations on the network with BOOTP chips on their Ethernet cards. You need to add support for BOOTP for these computers. How do you ensure that support?

❍ **A.** Add the BOOTP service to the server.

❍ **B.** In the Advanced tab of the scope Properties dialog box, configure the server to issue addresses to BOOTP clients.

❍ **C.** In the Advanced tab of the server Properties dialog box, configure the server to issue addresses to both DHCP and BOOTP clients.

❍ **D.** In the Advanced tab of the scope Properties dialog box, configure the server to issue addresses to both DHCP and BOOTP clients.

10. You manage the Windows Server 2003 DHCP servers for the Really Big Hammer Corporation. It is a mixed environment, with Windows 2000, Windows XP, and Windows 98 workstations. You need to make sure workstations are registered properly in DNS for Active Directory integration. What do you need to do?

❍ **A.** Set DNS integration to automatically update DHCP client information in DNS.

❍ **B.** Set DNS integration to discard A and PTR records when a lease is deleted.

❍ **C.** Set DNS integration to enable updates for DNS clients that do not request dynamic updates.

❍ **D.** Set DNS integration to enable DNS keepalives.

11. You are the systems administrator for BT Editing Unlimited. You have a 50-host network and are running a Windows Server 2003 DHCP server to assign IP addresses. You also have five IP-based printers with static IP addresses. Your assistant administrator has been working on the DHCP server and has made some changes. Now, your users cannot print to one of the printers. What is most likely the problem?

❍ **A.** The scope from which the printers were receiving their IP addresses has been deleted.

❍ **B.** The existing scope has been modified so that it overlaps the addresses reserved for the printers.

❍ **C.** The existing scope has been modified so that it overlaps the addresses reserved for the printers, and a workstation has been assigned the same address as one of the printers.

❍ **D.** The DHCP service was inadvertently stopped.

12. You are the systems administrator for the Little Faith Department Store. You are responsible for maintaining the company's Windows Server 2003 DHCP server. The company recently added a new router and routed a segment to the network. Now that segment must be added to the DHCP server. The address of the router port is 10.10.25.1, and the router is subnetted with a Class C subnet mask. You need to provide 40 addresses, starting at 10.10.25.20. What needs to occur for you to get DHCP working on that segment?

❍ **A.** You need to install and configure an additional DHCP server on that segment to provide DHCP services.

❍ **B.** You need to add to the DHCP server a scope that contains the addresses from 10.10.25.20 through 10.10.25.59. The scope needs a subnet mask of 255.255.255.0. You need to configure the BOOTP forwarder for the new segment's router, using the address of the DHCP server. You need to activate the scope.

❍ **C.** You need to add to the DHCP server a scope that contains the addresses from 10.10.25.20 through 10.10.25.60. The scope needs a subnet mask of 255.255.255.0. You need to configure the BOOTP forwarder for the new segment's router, using the address of the DHCP server. You need to activate the scope.

❍ **D.** You need to add to the DHCP server a scope that contains the addresses from 10.10.25.20 through 10.10.25.60. The scope needs a subnet mask of 255.255.255.0. You need to configure the BOOTP forwarder for the new segment's router, using the address of the DHCP server. You do not need to activate the scope because that happens automatically when the scope is created.

13. You are the network manager for IntCo Manufacturing. You are running in a mixed environment, and you are using a Windows Server 2003 DHCP service to support three network segments. Your client computers consist of Windows 2000 Professional, Windows NT Workstation, and Windows 98 SE workstations. What do you need to do to ensure that all the client computers can receive DHCP addresses?

❍ **A.** Configure a scope for each network segment. Configure each client computer to receive IP addresses dynamically. Configure the DHCP service for backward compatibility.

❍ **B.** Configure a scope for each network segment. Configure each client computer to receive IP addresses dynamically. For the Windows NT Workstation client computers, ensure that the DHCP update from Service Pack 6 has been installed.

❍ **C.** Configure a scope for each network segment. Configure each client computer to receive IP addresses dynamically. Configure the DHCP service for mixed mode.

❍ **D.** Configure a scope for each network segment. Configure each client computer to receive IP addresses dynamically.

14. You are the systems administrator for BT Editing, and you are running a purely Windows Server 2003 network using Active Directory and the Windows Server 2003 DHCP service. A user in another department has installed a DHCP server on a Unix server. How do you prevent your client computers from receiving DHCP addresses from that server?

❍ **A.** Disable the unauthorized server in Active Directory.

❍ **B.** Make sure all your domain client computers are running Windows 2000 or higher.

❍ **C.** Reconfigure BOOTP on the router.

❍ **D.** Go to each client computer and enter the address of the production DHCP server in the Internet Protocol (TCP/IP) Properties dialog box.

15. You are the systems administrator for Area 51 Partners, a consulting firm that is not involved in any way, shape, or form with alien activity in Nevada. You have a customer who would like to ensure that only authorized DHCP servers can make dynamic updates to the DNS database. What will you configure for the customer in order to make this happen? (Choose all that apply.)

❍ **A.** Create a new domain user account called DNSDYNUPD.

❍ **B.** Enter the credentials for the DNSDYNUPD account in the scope options for your DHCP server.

❍ **C.** Enter the credentials for the DNSDYNUPD account in the DNS Dynamic Update Credentials dialog box for your DHCP server.

❍ **D.** Add the DNSDYNUPD account to the Enterprise Administrators group.

Answers to Exam Questions

1. C. The client computer cannot use the address until the DHCP server grants the lease. After the DHCP server acknowledges the DHCP request and grants the lease, the client computer is able to use the address. Before a client computer can actually use an offered address, it must request to do so and receive an acknowledgement from the offering DHCP server; thus Answers A, B, and D are incorrect. No additional step is required in the process. For more information, see the section "DHCP."

2. C. You need to reconcile all the scopes on the server. Answer A is almost correct because you can reconcile a single scope, but the correct command is Reconcile, not Reconcile Scope. You cannot reconcile scopes at the Superscope level, as stated in Answer B. The command in Answer D does not exist. For more information, see the section "Reconciling the DHCP Database."

3. C. The DHCPDISCOVER packet is sent when a computer first requests an address. The most likely reason for the Discovers/Sec counter to spike would be a large number of concurrent requests occurring, which could happen when a large number of client workstations request addresses at the same time. A network problem would have the opposite effect because no DHCPDISCOVER packets would reach the server; thus Answer A is incorrect. A DHCP service restart or a rogue

DHCP server couldn't affect the number of DHCPDISCOVER packets because the packets are generated by client PCs; thus Answers B and D are incorrect. For more information, see the section "Troubleshooting DHCP Server Authorization Problems."

4. **B**. In this scenario, the most likely cause for the problem is that an unauthorized DHCP server has been set up on the network. Windows 2000 and Windows XP clients in an Active Directory domain do not take DHCP leases from DHCP servers that have not been authorized in Active Directory. The DHCP service in Windows 98 would not likely cause this sort of problem; thus Answer A is incorrect. A misconfigured DHCP server that was authorized would give bad DHCP lease information to all clients—not just to Windows 98 clients; thus Answer C is incorrect. In addition, if clients were unable to reach a DHCP server, the Windows 2000 and Windows XP clients would also assign themselves APIPA IP addresses; thus Answer D is incorrect. For more information, see the section "Troubleshooting DHCP Server Authorization Problems."

5. **D**. If the task is to install the DHCP service and get it issuing addresses, you do not need to configure DNS, but you do need to authorize the server in Active Directory; thus Answers A and B are incorrect. Even though you learned how to create a superscope in this chapter, you do not need a superscope for the server to function; thus Answer C is incorrect. For more information, see the section "Configuring and Managing DHCP."

6. **D**. To issue addresses using DHCP across a router, the router needs to have the BOOTP forwarder service enabled and configured; thus Answer C is incorrect. DHCP relay is configured on a router or a Windows Server 2003 computer running Routing and Remote Access; thus Answer A is incorrect. There is no such thing as the BOOTP forwarder server; thus Answer B is incorrect. For more information, see the section "Configuring and Implementing a DHCP Relay Agent."

7. **A**. In a purely Windows 2000, Windows XP, and Windows Server 2003 environment, you need to configure DHCP to automatically update DNS to ensure that the client computers appear on the network correctly. Setting the DNS integration to discard lookups after a lease is deleted also works with a purely Windows 2000 network, but it has nothing to do with the computers registering properly; thus Answer B is incorrect. Windows 2000, Windows XP and Windows Server 2003 all support dynamic updates; thus Answer C is incorrect. Keepalives are associated with HTTP sessions, not DNS; thus Answer D is incorrect. For more information, see the section "Configuring DHCP for DNS Integration."

8. **A**. To ensure that addresses are available, the DHCP lease needs to be set to a short interval; thus Answer B is incorrect. Reservations won't help since you have too few leases already; thus Answer C incorrect. There was no mention of a need for exclusions and thus no need to configure them; therefore Answer D is incorrect. For more information, see the section "Creating a DHCP Scope."

9. **D**. You need to configure the scope to issue addresses to both DHCP and BOOTP clients; thus Answers A, B, and C are incorrect. For more information, see the section "Creating a DHCP Scope."

10. **C**. Because the non-Windows 2000 (or non-Windows XP) machines lack the capability to directly update the DNS server themselves, you need the DHCP server to make the updates to DNS. Using DNS integration to enable updates for DNS client computers that do not support dynamic updates enables the DHCP server to perform this service. The options mentioned in Answers A and B do not exist; thus they are incorrect. Keepalives are associated with HTTP sessions, not DNS; thus Answer D is incorrect. For more information, see the section "Configuring DHCP for DNS Integration."

11. **C**. The address from the printer has probably been issued to another computer. Because the printers use static addresses, the only change to the DHCP server that could have affected printing would be another host having the same address. Deleting the scope would cause problems, but not likely right away; thus Answer A is incorrect. Answer B is close, but just creating an overlapping scope is not a problem until the overlapping addresses are assigned. As with deleting the scope, stopping the DHCP service would cause problems, but not unless a client needed a new address; thus Answer D is incorrect. For more information, see the section "Configuring and Managing DHCP."

12. **B**. A single DHCP server can serve multiple segments, so you do not need an additional server. To get 40 addresses, the range must be from 10.10.25.20 to 10.10.25.59, which is an inclusive range. Also, the last step of the New Scope Wizard is to authorize the new scope. The actions listed in Answer A are not enough to perform the required task; thus Answer A is incorrect. Answers C and D each provide 41 addresses; in addition Answer D has you not activating the scope, which you must do this in order to use the scope. Therefore Answers C are D are incorrect. For more information, see the section "Configuring and Managing DHCP."

13. **D**. You do not need to make any special configurations to the DHCP service; it can communicate with non-Windows 2000 or non-Windows XP client computers without problems. Thus Answers A and C are incorrect. You also do not need to update any of the client computers. Windows NT and Windows 98 are capable of utilizing DHCP without needing updates applied; thus Answer B is incorrect. You just need to configure the appropriate scope and configure the client computers to utilize that scope. For more information, see the section "Configuring and Managing DHCP."

14. **B**. Because a Unix server cannot be enabled in Active Directory, Windows 2000 (and Windows XP) client computers do not accept DHCP addresses from the server. Answer A is not correct because you cannot disable a server that isn't joined to the Active Directory domain. Changing the BOOTP configuration on the router might prevent remote users from receiving addresses, but local users would still be vulnerable; thus Answer C is incorrect. In Answer D, there is nowhere to enter the address of the DHCP server. For more information, see the section "Authorizing a DHCP Server in Active Directory."

15. **A, C**. Windows Server 2003 allows you to use a preconfigured domain user account to perform DNS dynamic updates. This ensures that only authorized DHCP servers are performing dynamic updates and that all DHCP servers can update and modify DNS entries. In addition, this prevents problems previously associated with allowing a DHCP server running on a domain controller to perform DNS dynamic updates. The best course of action is to create a dedicated domain user account for this purpose. The account information to be used for dynamic updates is configured at the server level; thus Answer B is incorrect. The account used for dynamic updates does not need to be a member of the Enterprise Administrators group; thus Answer D is incorrect. For more information, see the section "Configuring DHCP for DNS Integration."

Suggested Readings and Resources

1. Davies, Joseph, and Lee, Thomas. *Microsoft Windows Server 2003 TCP/IP Protocols and Services Technical Reference.* Microsoft Press, 2003.
2. Stevens, W. Richard. *TCP/IP Illustrated, Volume 1: The Protocols.* Addison-Wesley, 1994.
3. "Deploying Network Services," http://technet2.microsoft.com/WindowsServer/en/Library/119050c9-7c4d-4cbf-8f38-97c45e4d01ef1033.mspx.
4. "Technical Overview of Windows Server 2003 Networking and Communications," www.microsoft.com/windowsserver2003/techinfo/overview/netcomm.mspx.
5. "Windows Server 2003 Reviewer's Guide," www.microsoft.com/windowsserver2003/techinfo/overview/reviewersguide.mspx.
6. Windows Server 2003 Online documentation: "Network Services," www.microsoft.com/technet/prodtechnol/windowsserver2003/proddocs/entserver/sag_NPStopnode.asp.
7. "Dynamic Host Configuration Protocol (DHCP) Operations Topics," http://technet2.microsoft.com/windowsserver/en/operations/dhcp.mspx.
8. "Windows Server 2003 Security Guide," http://www.microsoft.com/technet/security/prodtech/windowsserver2003/W2003HG/SGCH00.mspx.

CHAPTER THREE

3

Implementing and Managing DNS

This chapter discusses network infrastructure with Domain Name System (DNS), one of the earliest of the many name resolution services available today. Whenever you surf the Web, you take advantage of DNS. This chapter covers the "Installing, Configuring, Managing, Monitoring, and Troubleshooting DNS in a Windows Server 2003 Network Infrastructure" objectives for Exam 70-291, "Implementing, Managing, and Maintaining a Microsoft Windows Server 2003 Network Infrastructure." One of the most important services in a Transmission Control Protocol/Internet Protocol (TCP/IP) infrastructure—particularly one running Active Directory—is DNS. This chapter examines all the facets of running the DNS server service in a Windows Server 2003 network.

Microsoft lists the following objectives for the "Installing, Configuring, Managing, Monitoring, and Troubleshooting DNS in a Windows Server 2003 Network Infrastructure" section of Exam 70-291:

Objectives

Install and configure the DNS server service.

- **Configure DNS server options.**
- **Configure DNS zone options.**
- **Configure DNS forwarding.**
- One of your first tasks when getting ready to deploy a production Windows Server 2003 network environment is to ensure that DNS is installed and configured correctly. DNS is the foundation on which Active Directory relies, and you need to have a thorough understanding not only of the Windows Server 2003 DNS server service, but also of how DNS itself functions. This objective expects you to be able to install DNS, configure it for use in an Active Directory network, and test it to make sure it is functioning.

Manage DNS.

- **Manage DNS zone settings.**
- **Manage DNS record settings.**
- **Manage DNS server options.**
- This objective requires you to be able to maintain a DNS server after it is installed and configured. Your DNS server will be of little use if you cannot properly administer it, and with Active Directory's reliance on DNS, a poorly administered DNS server can lead to a host of other problems.

Monitor DNS. Tools might include System Monitor, Event Viewer, Replication Monitor, and DNS debug logs.

- This objective requires you to be able to monitor a DNS server after it is installed and configured. The ability to monitor the DNS server's activities and ensure that the server is functioning properly is critical to the ongoing administration of a Windows Server 2003 network, particularly a network that relies on Active Directory.

Outline

Study Strategies

- Understand what DNS is, how it works, why it was created, and what enhancements Microsoft made to DNS for Active Directory. DNS provides the name resolution backbone for the Internet today. With the introduction of Active Directory, it is now also the backbone of Microsoft's name resolution solution.
- Understand the relationship between DNS and Dynamic Host Configuration Protocol (DHCP) and how dynamic DNS (DDNS) works.
- Understand the variety of zone types and DNS server types that Microsoft Windows Server 2003 DNS server service supports. You need to know how the zone and DNS server types work and when you might use them in a production environment.
- Closely review the Step by Steps and the exercises at the end of this chapter so that you can completely prepare for the questions on Exam 70-291.
- Take the next step, and experiment with the system. The Step by Steps in this chapter provide good guidelines, but you should see what happens when you select other settings, delete entries or entire servers, and do anything else you can think of. It is best to make mistakes in a lab environment; these mistakes will help you prepare for the exam.

Introduction

One of the most important network services in use on any network today is name resolution. How can you translate the cryptic hardware address of a network host to something intuitive that will allow an end user to access his or her resources? Asking someone to map a drive to 00-10-B5-06-25-21 or 10.10.111.24 is probably not going to go over too well.

As the industry recognized this problematic issue, several solutions were designed to allow users to utilize easy-to-remember names instead of the hard-to-remember addresses. Microsoft's contribution to this effort was the Windows Internet Name Service (WINS), which allowed Windows systems using NetBIOS to discover system names by using broadcasts. WINS was later scaled to support larger TCP/IP-based networks. The other major designer of name resolution solutions was the Unix/Internet community, which needed a dynamic way to resolve addresses on what would eventually become the Internet. This community's answer was DNS, which was actually designed and implemented before WINS.

As the popularity of the Internet grew, it became evident that the Internet's solution for name resolution was becoming the predominant solution, and in the latest version of the Windows operating system, Microsoft has further improved its support for DNS.

NOTE

More on WINS We spend Chapter 4, "Implementing and Managing WINS," looking at WINS and learning how it is installed, configured, and maintained.

Introducing DNS

If you have ever connected to a Web site by name, you have used DNS. DNS is a service that is used on the Internet for resolving *fully qualified domain names (FQDNs)* to their actual Internet Protocol (IP) addresses. For example, suppose you were preparing to take the latest Windows Server 2003 certification exam. You've asked your co-workers about the best study guide available, and they recommend that you check out Que Publishing's Web site to see what is available. Your obvious question is, "Where can I find Que Publishing's Web site?" Before DNS, the answer would have been 63.240.93.132, and if you are like most people, you might have remembered that IP address for about 30 seconds. Given the likelihood of you forgetting that IP address, you never would have been able to use it to find Que Publishing's site (or get that study guide you were looking for).

DNS puts a user-friendly face on that obscure numeric address. With DNS, your friend can tell you to go to www.quepublishing.com, and the DNS infrastructure of the Internet translates the name to the correct address, 63.240.93.132. It's like a big phone book. You put in a name, and DNS gives you the correct number. Fortunately for those of us with a limited ability to memorize strings of numbers, the Internet community recognized the benefits of a name resolution system as a critical part of the infrastructure that would make up the original Internet architecture. And DNS was born.

NOTE

Domain Name System or Domain Name Service You may have heard that DNS stands for "Domain Name Service," yet it is referred to as "Domain Name System" in the previous sections of this chapter. These names are interchangeable, although Microsoft tends to use "Service," whereas most Internet users use "System." From here on in the chapter, we use the term "System" for consistency.

DNS is a hierarchical database that contains names and addresses for IP networks and hosts, and it is used almost universally to provide name resolution. This is true now more than before because Microsoft has embraced DNS as its name resolution method for Windows Server 2003 (and Windows 2000 Server before it), in place of the more proprietary, less accepted Windows Internet Name System (WINS). Before we tackle DNS in a Windows Server 2003 network, we should cover a little of the history and makeup of DNS in general, how DNS zones work, and what the DNS server roles are.

The History of DNS

Back in the early days of the Internet, when it was known as the Advanced Research Products Agency Network (ARPAnet) and the number of hosts on the network was less than 100, there used to be a master list of names and IP addresses called the `HOSTS` file. It was maintained by the Stanford Research Institute's Network Information Center (known as the SRI-NIC at the time), and it worked very well, as long as the number of hosts was low and changes were infrequent. Everyone using the network would periodically download a copy of the `HOSTS` file, and they would have a local table of names and addresses with which to connect to computers by name. Windows Server 2003 (and most TCP/IP stacks in general) still has this functionality, although it is seldom used in conjunction with the Internet any longer. This method of name resolution was great for a while, but as the number of computers grew, this solution ran into a few problems, including the following:

- **Traffic**—As more and more people tried to access the `HOSTS` file, the load on the SRI-NIC network and servers became excessive.
- **Consistency**—As the number of hosts and the number of changes grew larger and larger, propagation of the `HOSTS` file became nearly impossible. As the file was being propagated to the most distant servers, new servers were being added to the network, rendering obsolete the file that had just been distributed.

- **Flat-file limitations**—Windows NT 4.0 domain administrators are familiar with flat-file limitations. Because the HOSTS file was a flat file (similar to the way domain objects are stored under Windows NT 4.0 domains), a requirement existed that every name be unique. No hierarchical capabilities were built into the naming structure. As a result, coming up with unique names that were also intuitive became more and more difficult.

EXAM ALERT

Comparing DNS with HOSTS Files For Exam 70-291, you need to be familiar with the advantages of DNS over the flat-file method of name resolution provided by a HOSTS file.

The network needed a better answer than a text file for name resolution. In 1983, in RFCs 882 and 883, Paul Mockapetris introduced DNS. These RFCs have since been superseded by RFCs 1034 and 1035, the current DNS specifications. You should also be aware of RFC 2136, which defines the standards for DDNS on which Windows Server 2003 relies.

NOTE

A Note on RFCs Request for Comments (RFC) documents are used to create proposals regarding the Internet and Internet technologies. If an RFC can garner enough interest, it may eventually become a standard. You can review all the existing RFCs by going to www.rfc-editor.org. We reference RFCs for standards-based protocols wherever possible throughout the book.

The DNS Database

DNS is a distributed database that allows local control of DNS for segments of the namespace while still maintaining a logical architecture to provide the local information throughout the network. Each piece of the DNS database resides on a server known as a *name server*. The architecture of DNS is designed so that there can be multiple name servers for redundancy, and caching of names to the local server is also supported, further enhancing DNS's robustness. In addition, with parts of the overall namespace placed on separate computers, the data storage and query loads are distributed to thousands of DNS servers throughout the Internet. The hierarchy of DNS is designed in such a way that every computer on or off the Internet can be named as part of the DNS namespace.

To effectively install, configure, and support the Windows Server 2003 DNS server service, you must understand the underlying architecture of today's DNS. Rather than having you read the RFCs (although you are encouraged to do so to improve your understanding of DNS), the following sections discuss the DNS namespace architecture and how individual DNS servers support their portions of the overall namespace as well as the specifics of the Windows Server 2003 DNS server service.

DNS Domains Defined

As mentioned earlier in this chapter, you probably have already used DNS, regardless of whether you were familiar with the underlying mechanism. Domain names such as www.microsoft.com or www.quepublishing.com are easy to comprehend. All you need is the ability to read. However, this simplicity comes at a price: The DNS namespace is complex. DNS names are created as part of a hierarchical database that functions much like the directories in a file system. Hierarchies are powerful database structures because they can store tremendous amounts of data while making it easy to search for specific bits of information. Before we examine the specifics of the DNS namespace hierarchy, let's discuss hierarchies in general.

> **NOTE**
>
> **A Simple Example of a Hierarchy** Microsoft's Active Directory is an excellent example of a hierarchical database. Of course, given that the Active Directory hierarchy is created on top of the existing rules for a DNS namespace, the information on the DNS hierarchy directly relates to the construction of Active Directory.

Hierarchies

You need to understand the following terms related to hierarchies:

- **Tree**—A tree is a type of data structure in which each element is attached to one or more elements directly beneath it. In the case of DNS, this structure is often called an inverted tree because it is generally drawn with the roots at the top of the tree.
- **Top-level domain (TLD)**—A TLD is related to the suffix attached to an Internet domain name. There are a limited number of predefined suffixes, and each one represents a TLD. The most common TLDs (at least in the United States) are `com`, `edu`, `gov`, `mil`, `net`, and `org`.
- **Node**—A node is a point where two or more lines in a tree intersect. In the case of DNS, a node can represent a TLD, a subdomain, or an actual network node (that is, a host).
- **FQDN**—An FQDN is a domain name that includes all domains between the host and the root of DNS. For example, www.microsoft.com is an FQDN.
- **Leaf**—A leaf is an item at the very bottom of a hierarchical tree structure that does not contain any other objects. In DNS, leaves are called *nodes*. In the earlier example, www would be the leaf of FQDN www.microsoft.com.
- **Second-level domain (SLD)**—This is the domain that includes the TLD and the next organizational unit of the FQDN. quepublishing.com is an example of an SLD.

- **Zone**—A DNS zone is a logical grouping of hostnames within DNS. For example, quepublishing.com is considered the forward lookup zone for Que Publishing. It is where the information about the Que Publishing host is contained within DNS.

If you told typical end users that they have been working with a hierarchy since the first time they turned on a computer, many would have no idea what you were talking about. In fact, a fair number of administrators would have to think about it as well. However, it's true: MS-DOS version 2 introduced a hierarchy to PCs in the form of the file system, and systems such as mainframes and Unix used hierarchical file structures much earlier than did MS-DOS. Why do computers need a hierarchical file system? Because storing files as an endless alphabetic listing is inefficient; the files can be stored much more efficiently in related groups. Today all computers use hierarchical structures for organizing file storage.

In DNS, the containers are called *domains*. The hierarchy starts with a root container, called the *root domain*. The root domain doesn't have a name, so it is typically represented by a single period. Directly below the root domain are the top-level domains (TLD), which are also sometimes called *first-level domains*. Lower-level domains are second-level, third-level, and so on (see Figure 3.1). Every domain name has a suffix that indicates the TLD to which it belongs. There are only a limited number of such domains.

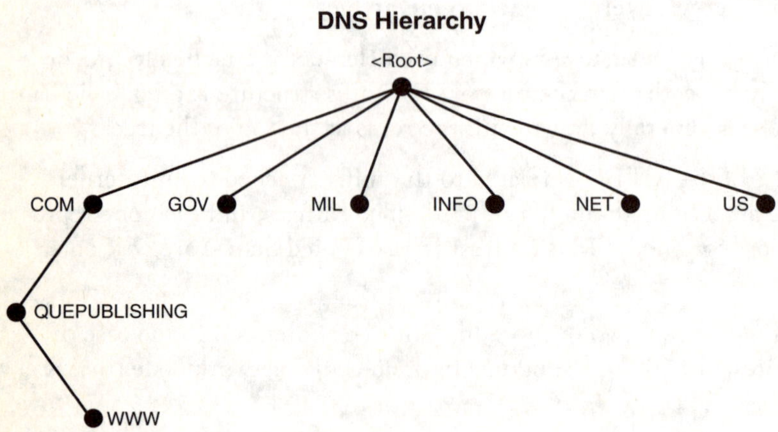

FIGURE 3.1 This portion of the DNS hierarchy shows the location of www.quepublishing.com in the DNS database in relationship to other parts of the DNS database.

The following are some examples of TLDs:

- `com`—Originally, the `com` domain was supposed to contain only commercial entities, but `com` has become the overwhelming favorite TLD, and everyone wants his or her personal subdomains to be in `com`. Because `com` has been overused and abused, it's nearly impossible to come up with a sensible new name for a `com` subdomain. The crowding within `com` is the main impetus behind the definition of new TLDs. An example of a `com` domain is quepublishing.com.

- **`org`**—The `org` domain is supposed to accommodate organizations that are noncommercial in nature. `org` is a good place for nonprofit organizations, professional groups, churches, and other such organizations. An example of an `org` domain is stjude.org.
- **`edu`**—The `edu` domain was originally supposed to embrace all types of educational institutions, but it began to fill up quickly as schools gained access to the Internet. Now it is primarily reserved for higher education institutions. Primary and secondary schools are supposed to register in their state domains, which are subdomains of their country domains. An example of the `edu` domain is berkeley.edu.
- **`gov`**—The `gov` domain contains agencies of the U.S. federal government. It does not include the military, however, which uses the `mil` domain. An example of the `gov` domain is whitehouse.gov.
- **`net`**—The `net` domain supports Internet service providers (ISPs) and Internet administrative computers. An example of the `net` domain is qwest.net.
- **Country domains**—Each country is assigned a unique TLD. Some examples include the following:
    - **`au`**—Australia
    - **`ca`**—Canada
    - **`uk`**—United Kingdom
    - **`us`**—United States
- **New domains**—A number of additional domains have been created, including `biz`, `coop`, `info`, `museum`, `name`, and `pro`. These have been added for a variety of purposes, and the list continues to grow as the need for new domains expands. By the time this book makes its way into your hands, there will probably be even more TLDs available.

Originally managed by the Internet International Ad Hoc Committee (IAHC), creation and management of TLDs is now done based on the guidelines detailed in the Generic Top Level Domain Memorandum of Understanding (www.gtld-mou.org). This memorandum divides management of the TLDs between the U.S. Department of Commerce's National Telecommunication and Information Administration (NTIA; www.ntia.doc.gov) and Internet Corporation for Assigned Names and Numbers (ICANN; www.icann.org). The ICANN site related to TLDs is www.icann.org/tlds. Management of TLDs varies from name to name; the ICANN site details the organizations responsible for managing each TLD.

Unfortunately, due to slow adoption by the general public, the creation of these additional domains has not completely alleviated the crowding of the original `com` and `net` domains.

People still consider the com namespace to be the only acceptable namespace, and until the new TLDs become more widely accepted, you can expect to work with one of the original TLDs in most situations.

As discussed previously, DNS is used to translate a hostname to an IP address. The DNS name typically looks something like this:

```
isaac.publishing.quepublishing.com
```

This DNS name is known as the host's FQDN because it lists the host's precise location in the DNS hierarchy. The DNS name in the example represents the host `isaac` in the subdomain `publishing` (this is frequently a department or division in a company), which is in the domain `quepublishing` (this is frequently the name of the company or organization that has registered the domain), which is in the TLD `com`. For the name to be complete, you also need a trailing dot, which indicates the root of the namespace.

When an organization wants to establish a domain name on the Internet, it must register the domain name with one of the authorized registration authorities. One such organization with which many people are familiar is VeriSign, Inc., which purchased Network Solutions, which was formerly the InterNIC. (You will still find references to the InterNIC in DNS-related documentation, so you need to realize that it is now a defunct TLD registrar.)

You can research new domain names and access registration forms at www.networksolutions.com. You can also contact your ISP for assistance; most ISPs offer domain name registration as part of their service. To register a domain, you need at least two name servers to provide resolution information for your domain. Some of the registrars will host your domain on their DNS servers for an additional fee, and most ISPs will also host your zone for you on their DNS servers. That's great, but what exactly is a DNS zone? Read on to find out.

EXAM ALERT

Understanding FQDNs For the exam, make sure you have a good understanding of what an FQDN is and how it is represented.

DNS Zones

It is very easy to get lost in the maze of acronyms and buzz words surrounding DNS, especially if you are having a conversation with someone who has been working with IP networking and DNS for a while. You have primary masters for each zone, which is also a domain, unless it's a reverse lookup zone, and then you have zone transfers happening when you least expect it. To the uninitiated, this can sound alarmingly like some arcane networking ritual in which you pay homage to the DNS deities. However, it's not nearly as bad as it sounds.

Before we get any deeper into the Windows Server 2003 DNS infrastructure, we need to discuss what exactly is meant by *DNS zone*. First, although typically abbreviated in the world of DNS, a *zone* is actually a *zone of authority*, which means it contains the complete information on some part of a domain namespace. In other words, it is a subset of a domain. The name server is considered to have authority for that zone, and it can respond to any requests for name resolution from that zone. So when you look at the DNS name www.quepublishing.com, you know that `quepublishing.com` is a DNS zone within the `com` hierarchy. `www` denotes the DNS record of a host contained within the `quepublishing.com` zone. This conceptual representation of a zone also has a physical counterpart: All the information related to a particular zone is stored in a physical file known as the *zone database file* or, more commonly, the *zone file*. If the DNS zone is not stored in Active Directory, under Windows Server 2003, this file will be found in the directory `%systemroot%\system32\dns`.

NOTE

The Difference Between a Zone and a Domain Although the terms "zone" and "domain" can seem as if they are used interchangeably, there is a difference. A DNS domain is a segment of the DNS namespace. A zone, on the other hand, can contain multiple, contiguous domains. For example, `quepublishing.com` is a DNS domain. It contains all the information for that specific portion of the DNS namespace. `sales.quepublishing.com` is another example of a domain, and it is contiguous with the `quepublishing.com` domain—in other words, the two domains "touch." So if you were to create a DNS forward lookup zone on a DNS server, it could contain records for both domains. Zones allow for the logical grouping and management of domains and resource records on DNS servers.

NOTE

Active Directory and DNS We examine the integration and operation of DNS and Active Directory later in this chapter in the section "Integrating Active Directory and DNS."

The Windows Server 2003 DNS service supports three basic types of zones:

- Forward lookup zones
- Reverse lookup zones
- Stub zones

The following sections take a closer look at these zone types, which make up the underlying structure of DNS.

Forward Lookup Zones

Forward lookup zones provide the hostname-to-IP address resolution for which DNS is most frequently used. A forward lookup zone contains resource records that contain the information about the resources that are available within that zone. Windows Server 2003 relies on the SRV (service) resource record to provide IP address information about servers and services within a zone, so that workstations can locate needed services such as Lightweight Directory Access Protocol (LDAP). The SRV record is also used to provide a single service over multiple hosts, assign priorities to hosts for a particular service, and move services from host to host easily. More information on the SRV record can be found in RFC 2782, "A DNS RR for specifying the location of services (DNS SRV)."

Reverse Lookup Zones

A reverse lookup zone (as you may have guessed from the name) provides the opposite resolution from a forward lookup zone: It resolves IP addresses to hostnames. This is discussed in greater detail later in this chapter, in the section "Reverse Lookups."

Stub Zones

Microsoft introduced support for stub zones for the first time in Windows Server 2003. A stub zone contains only those resource records that are necessary to identify the authoritative DNS servers for that zone. Such resource records include Name Server (NS), Start of Authority (SOA), and possibly glue host (A) records. (Glue host records provide A record pointers to ensure that the master zone has the correct name server information for the stub zone.) Stub zones are frequently used for the following:

- **To keep delegated zone information up-to-date**—Because a stub zone is used to provide pointers to a delegated zone, updating the stub zone causes the DNS server hosting both the parent zone and the stub zone to maintain a current list of authoritative DNS servers for the delegated zone.
- **To improve name resolution performance**—Because a stub zone enables a DNS server to perform recursive resolution by using the stub zone's list of name servers, the DNS server making the request does not need to query any Internet name servers or internal name servers to get the resolution.

As an example of when you might want to use stub zones, consider the scenario where two organizations are closely linked and often need to access resources on each other's networks. If you are the systems administrator in organization A, and you created a stub zone that uses one or more name servers within organization B, your users would simply issue a DNS query to an organization A DNS server, which then forwards the query to one of organization B's name servers to resolve. This solution provides a simpler and more efficient means of helping your users resolve those host names without the burden of maintaining another secondary zone on your DNS servers.

Zone Delegation

With *zone delegation*, one DNS server can assign the administration of a domain to another DNS server. For example, let's look at the `quepublishing.com` domain. Let's say that the IT Department is responsible for the `quepublishing.com` zone, which contains the domains `quepublishing.com`, `sales.quepublishing.com`, and `developers.quepublishing.com`. The IT Department maintains the DNS records for all three zones, but the developers who are working on software projects are always adding and removing hosts to and from their domain and want to be able to update their resource records without having to place a request with the IT Department each time. To take care of this, the IT Department can delegate the administration of the `developers.quepublishing.com` zone to a DNS server that is maintained by the developers. The main zone, `quepublishing.com` (zones are typically named for the "uppermost" domain in the DNS hierarchy), would maintain a delegation entry that points queries about the `developers.quepublishing.com` domain to the developers' DNS server.

EXAM ALERT

Zone Delegation Be sure you understand what zone delegation entails. In a distributed environment with local administration, delegation can be critical to a successful DNS implementation.

Zone Transfers

A *zone transfer* involves the copying of the zone database from one DNS server to another. This is typically done to ensure name resolution availability and DNS server fault tolerance. Given the critical nature of DNS name resolution in a Windows Server 2003 environment, using a single server to support name resolution is a bad idea. If that server is not responding or is off the network, queries for names in the zone can fail. However, if you are using multiple DNS servers for high availability, you need a mechanism to allow the primary master DNS server (the only server with a read/write copy of the zone database) to replicate and synchronize the zone database on all the DNS servers that host the zone.

Windows Server 2003 supports incremental zone transfers by DNS servers. When a new DNS server is added as a host of a zone, a full transfer of the zone database is done. After that, an incremental zone transfer transfers changes to the zone database only, as opposed to the full transfer that is required with many of the older implementations of DNS. This reduces network traffic and speeds the transfer of the zone changes.

EXAM ALERT

Zone Transfer Types Two types of zone transfer are supported by Windows Server 2003: full zone transfer and incremental zone transfer. You might see these types abbreviated as AXFR (full zone transfer) and IXFR (incremental zone transfer).

DNS Server Roles

There are a number of roles that a DNS server can perform based both on configuration and on the requirements of the site or network to which the server is connected. These server roles include the following:

- **Primary master**—The primary master DNS server has the only read/write copy of the zone database. As a result, any updates to the zone database must be completed on this server. This is similar to the Windows NT 4.0 primary DC. The primary master server is also known as the *authoritative server* for the zone.
- **Secondary master**—A secondary master DNS server has a read-only version of the zone database. This allows it to resolve any name resolution requests, but it prevents any changes from being made to the zone database. When a secondary server starts, it contacts the name server it updates from (the authoritative server) and gets the latest copy of the zone data.
- **Caching-only server**—A caching-only DNS server is a DNS server that does not contain any zone information or copies of any zone database files. Instead, it builds its resolution table from the successful resolutions it has performed for its client computers.

NOTE

Why Use a Caching-Only Server? Caching-only servers are useful for several reasons. They do not generate any zone transfer traffic, which can be useful for keeping unneeded traffic off slow WAN links, and they can be placed on the far side of a slow WAN link and used to provide local DNS resolution for remote users. When a sufficient address cache has been built, calls across the WAN are virtually eliminated.

- **DNS forwarder**—A DNS forwarder is a DNS server that passes recursive DNS requests to another DNS server. (In other words, it forwards recursive DNS requests to another DNS server.) This can be useful if you do not have local copies of your internal DNS zone and want to have your local DNS server forward DNS queries to a central DNS server that is authoritative for the internal DNS zone. Caching-only servers make good DNS forwarders. If the DNS forwarder does not receive a valid resolution from the server to which it forwards the request, it attempts to resolve the client request itself.
- **DNS slave server**—A DNS slave server is a DNS forwarder server that does not try to resolve a resolution request if it doesn't receive a valid response to its forwarded DNS request. You typically see this type of DNS server implemented in conjunction with a secure Internet connection.

After you have identified the two (or more) name servers (or have arranged to have your domain hosted on someone else's DNS servers), you are ready to register your domain. To register a domain name at www.networksolutions.com, you use the process outlined in Step by Step 3.1. (This process is similar at any of the major registrars.)

STEP BY STEP

3.1 Registering a DNS Domain

1. Search www.networksolutions. com to find a domain name that isn't already in use. If the domain you selected is not available, the search engine suggests possible alternatives.
2. Get the IP addresses of two domain name servers—a primary (or master) and a secondary (or backup) that will be authoritative for your domain. If your ISP will be providing your name servers, obtain the IP addresses of them from your ISP. You can also use DNS names, if your DNS servers either have or will have entries in DNS.
3. Register the domain name at www.networksolutions.com, which includes online forms for registering and changing domain names.
4. If you actually want to register a domain (you don't need to do so as part of this exercise), you need to pay the registration fee, which varies depending on the options you select.

NOTE

Active Directory and DNS Domains Because of Active Directory's critical reliance on the underlying DNS infrastructure, it is a good idea to use a registered DNS name whenever you create a Windows Server 2003 network infrastructure. This ensures that your rights to use that name will never be in question. Conversely, you can also opt to create a private namespace on your internal network using a TLD such as `local`, `corp`, or `int`. In reality, most organizations do not actually use the same exact namespace, such as `quepublishing.com`, both internally and externally. Externally, `quepublishing.com` might be a good namespace, but internally, it might be implemented as `corp.quepublishing.com` or `quepublishing.corp`, depending on the requirements and desires of the architects planning and implementing the solution.

The Name Resolution Process

When you've registered a domain and you understand the DNS hierarchy, the next step is to understand how DNS works. In other words, after you enter a hostname, how does it get translated to an IP address?

The DNS name server resolves a name to an IP address by using the following process:

1. The client computer makes a request to the local DNS server. This generally occurs when an application tries to make a connection by using a hostname, such as when you enter www.quepublishing.com into a Web browser and the resolution is not found in the client's DNS cache.
2. The DNS server looks in a local memory cache for names it has recently resolved. If the requested name is found in the local cache, the name server returns the IP address the client computer requires. Most DNS servers cache both local and remote domain names in memory, so even a DNS request for a host on your local network may be in cache.
3. The name server looks in the DNS server's host tables to see if there is a static entry (or, in the case of DDNS, a dynamic entry) for the hostname-to-IP address lookup. If an entry exists, the DNS server forwards the IP address to the client computer.
4. If the request has not been resolved, the name server refers the request to a root name server. (Root name servers support the root of the namespace hierarchy.) At present, 13 computers support the root domain.
5. The root name server refers the request to a name server for the TLD in the hostname. (For example, if you have requested a host address for the `quepublishing.com` domain, the root name server forwards the request to the `quepublishing.com` DNS server.) The TLD name server refers the request to a name server for the second-level domain in the hostname, and so on, until a name server is encountered that can resolve the complete hostname.
6. The first name server that can resolve the hostname to an IP address reports the IP address to the client computer.

NOTE

How Root Servers Find a Domain When you register a domain, you are required to provide the names and addresses of two (or more) DNS servers that will be providing DNS services for the domain. The root name servers have access to these names and addresses and thus know where to send the requests.

For the process to work in your environment, you need to ensure the following are true:

1. Make sure that your network has at least one name server, and preferably more than one. These name servers can be ones that you configure and implement, or they can be those provided by your ISP.

2. Make sure your client computers are all configured to use these servers for DNS lookups.

The rest of the process generally just works. You do not need to maintain the root name servers list or the lookup process, although the list of root name servers is typically updated in service packs if any changes have occurred.

Reverse Lookups

We have discussed how to get the most common form of DNS lookups, known as forward lookups, in which you enter a name and the DNS server returns the IP address. As mentioned earlier in this chapter, there is another kind of lookup, known as a reverse lookup. A reverse lookup works much as the name implies: You query the DNS server with an IP address, and it returns (if there is an entry) the DNS name for that host. The ability to perform a reverse lookup can be useful if you are trying to keep track of network usage, trying to track down a host that is causing problems on the network, or trying to verify the identity of a host. At one time, it was popular to use reverse lookups for the downloading of 128-bit software to ensure that the user attempting to download the software was within the United States or Canada. The different record types are discussed later in this chapter, in the "DNS Record Types" section, but for now, it is important for you to know that reverse lookup tables use PTR records to resolve IP addresses to names. (A PTR record is a pointer to a location—an FQDN—in the DNS domain.)

NOTE

Reverse Lookups and the `nslookup` Command If you want to be able to correctly and completely use the `nslookup` command, you'll need to have correctly configured and populated reverse lookup zones on your DNS servers.

EXAM ALERT

The Function of the Reverse Lookup Table Because they are used less and thus are less understood than forward lookup tables, reverse lookup tables are an excellent topic for exam questions.

SPAM Emails and Reverse Lookups

In today's world, you are likely to find that you are using reverse lookups in the fight against spam, also known as UCE (unsolicited commercial email). Email servers use many tools to reduce the volume of spam; one tool is the reverse lookup, which email servers use to verify the validity of an email domain. When the mail server receives an email message, it checks whether the reverse lookup of the originating IP address matches the domain portion of the email address. If the two do not agree, the filter rejects the email message because this typically indicates that the return address of the email is a fake, commonly referred to as a *spoofed* address. A lot of spammers have used fictitious or false domains in an attempt to hide their real identities.

Spam has become virtually ubiquitous to anyone with an Internet email address, and the flood seems to increase with each passing year. In addition to being annoying for the user, it also eats up significant amounts of network bandwidth and frequently contains false, misleading, or obscene content.

What does this mean to you? If you are setting up DNS on the Internet and want to be able to send and receive email from that domain, you need to be sure to include a reverse zone for your mail servers. Otherwise, you can expect your mail to be filtered out as spam in many instances.

The naming convention for a reverse lookup zone is this:

```
<first octets of the IP address (reversed)>.in-addr.arpa
```

Thus, the address of the reverse table for the IP network 205.133.113.87 is `113.133.205.in-addr.arpa`.

It is important to know that the Active Directory Installation Wizard does not automatically add a reverse lookup zone and PTR resource records to the server. You need to add them manually because it is possible that another server may control the reverse lookup zone. You will want to add a reverse lookup zone if this is not the case. Although a reverse lookup zone is not necessary for Active Directory to work, it is useful for the reasons listed previously.

DNS Record Types

Before we continue our discussions of DNS, you should take a quick look at Table 3.1, which lists the different types of records you can create in a DNS domain in Windows Server 2003. In the table, you will also find the pertinent RFC for each type, which can help you do additional research.

EXAM ALERT

Don't Memorize the Table of DNS Record Types Although you must understand the commonly used DNS record types, uncommon entries such as the Andrew File System database server record will not likely be on the exam. The most commonly used record types are A, CNAME, MX, PTR, SRV, and SOA.

TABLE 3.1 DNS Record Types

Record Type	RFC	Description
AFSDB	RFC 1183	Andrew File System Database Server record. An AFSDB entry indicates the location of either an AFS volume location server or a Distributed Computing Environment (DCE) server.
CNAME	RFC 1035	Canonical Name record. A CNAME entry indicates an alias domain name for a name already specified as another resource type in this zone. CNAME is the acronym for canonical name.

TABLE 3.1 Continued

Record Type	RFC	Description
ATMA	RFC 2601	ATM Address record. An ATMA record maps a DNS name to an ATM address.
A	RFC 1035	Address record. An A record maps a DNS name to an IP version 4 address.
AAAA	RFC 1886	AAAA record. An AAAA record is similar to the A record. It is used to map a DNS name to an IP (version 6) address.
ISDN	RFC 1183	Integrated Services Digital Network record. An ISDN record maps a DNS name to an ISDN telephone number.
MX	RFC 1035	Mail Exchanger record. An MX record is used to provide message routing to a specific mail exchanger host for a specific DNS name.
MG	RFC 1035	Mail Group record. An MG record is used to add mailbox records as members of a domain mailing group.
MB	RFC 1035	Mailbox record. An MB record maps a specified domain mailbox name to the host that hosts the mailbox.
MINFO	RFC 1035	Mailbox or Mailing List Information record. An MINFO record specifies a domain mailbox name to contact. It can also specify a mailbox for error messages.
PTR	RFC 1035	Pointer record. A PTR record points in the domain. This is typically used for reverse lookups or IP-address-to-DNS-name lookups.
MR	RFC 1035	Renamed Mailbox record. An MR record is used to specify a domain mailbox that is the proper rename of an existing mailbox record.
RP	RFC 1183	Responsible Person record. An RP record specifies the domain mailbox for a responsible person for which text (TXT) records exist.
TXT	RFC 1035	Text record. A TXT record is used to hold a string of characters that serve as descriptive text to be associated with a specific DNS name.
RT	RFC 1183	Route-through record. An RT record provides an intermediate route through binding for internal hosts that do not have their own direct WAN address.
SRV	RFC 2052	Service record. An SRV record allows administrators to use several servers for a single DNS domain, to easily move a TCP/IP service from host to host, and to designate primary and backup service hosts.
WKS	RFC 1035	Well-known service record. A WKS record is used to describe well-known TCP/IP services supported by a particular protocol (that is, TCP or UDP) on a specific IP address.
X25	RFC 1183	X25 record. An X25 record is used to map a DNS name to a Public Switched Telephone Network (PSTN) address.
SOA	RFC 1035	Start of Authority record. An SOA is the first resource record in each correctly configured zone. It contains information about the zone and tells the DNS server that it is authoritative for a zone.

DNS Naming Conventions

Table 3.2 shows the restrictions for creating a DNS name and an FQDN.

TABLE 3.2 DNS Name Restrictions

Restriction	Standard DNS	DNS in Windows Server 2003 (As Well As Windows 2000)
Characters	Supports RFC 1123, which permits A to Z, a to z, 0 to 9, and the hyphen (-).	Supports several different standards, including the RFC 1123 standard, RFC 2181, and the character set specified in RFC 2044 (UTF-8).
FQDN length	63 bytes per label and 255 bytes for a whole FQDN.	63 bytes per label and 255 bytes for a whole FQDN. DCs are limited to 155 bytes for an FQDN.

The Windows Server 2003 DNS Server Service Supports Additional Standards

Microsoft has one problem with its direction of a DNS-based directory service, and it has been a problem for years. NetBIOS, the legacy Microsoft naming mechanism, does not conform to the naming standards in RFC 1123. This means that in some environments, companies could be forced to rename all their Microsoft devices if they want to move to a naming standard supported by Active Directory. To avoid this, Microsoft has included support for RFCs 2181 and 2044, which allows legacy NetBIOS names to be supported under DNS. An example of a character supported by Windows Server 2003 DNS but not by other DNS implementations is the _ (underscore) character, used commonly in NetBIOS naming as a separator; it is not valid under many DNS implementations.

There's a catch to Microsoft's proposed support for RFCs 2181 and 2044, however. If you move to a naming convention that takes advantage of the new standards, you might run into problems with non-Windows Server 2003 DNS servers, including Windows NT 4.0 DNS servers. Most servers do not support the standards Microsoft is proposing. The reason for this is that RFC 2044 calls for the support of the character-encoding Unicode Translation Format 8 (UTF-8). UTF-8 supports characters from a variety of foreign languages that are not supported by some non-Windows 2000/Server 2003 versions of DNS.

What's New with Windows Server 2003 DNS

DNS is certainly not a new service in Windows Server 2003, but it has undergone some changes from both Windows 2000 and Windows NT 4.0. The following list summarizes some of the major changes in DHCP in Windows Server 2003 from Windows 2000 Server and Windows NT 4.0:

- **Integrated zones**—With the Windows Server 2003 DNS server service, you can integrate DNS into Active Directory, and resource records are stored in Active Directory and can be updated by any DC running DNS. This integration is a proprietary feature of the Windows Server DNS, but it can yield a much more secure, robust, and fault-tolerant implementation than standard DNS. Integrated zone files appear in Windows 2000 Server.

- **Incremental zone transfers**—The standard model for DNS zone transfers is to transfer the entire zone whenever an update is made. Transferring entire zones is very inefficient. Windows Server 2003 DNS allows secondary servers to request incremental updates, which contain changes that have occurred only since the last transfer. Incremental zone transfers first appear in Windows 2000 Server.
- **Secure DNS updates**—Changes to records in a zone can be restricted to those coming only from trusted sources.
- **DNS/DHCP integration**—The power of DDNS lies in its integration of DHCP with DNS. Any Windows Server 2003 DHCP client computer is automatically added to the DNS table at the time that its IP address is issued. DNS/DHCP integration first appears in Windows 2000 Server.
- **Support for stub zones**—A stub zone contains only those resource records that are necessary to identify the authoritative DNS servers for that zone.
- **Conditional forwarding**—Conditional forwarding allows administrators to direct DNS requests to other DNS servers based on domain. Previous versions of Microsoft DNS would support only one forwarder, so if forwarding were enabled, all requests would be sent to a single server. Conditional forwarding is used frequently when you want requests made to the internal network to be forwarded to a master DNS server that stores internal DNS zones, but you want to have resolution requests that are made to Internet domains sent to the Internet by using the standard resolution process.
- **Enhanced debug logging**—The Windows Server 2003 DNS service offers extremely detailed debug logging for advanced DNS troubleshooting.
- **DNS security (DNSSEC) extensions**—In keeping with Microsoft's secure computing initiatives, Windows Server 2003 DNS provides basic support for the DNSSEC extensions defined in RFC 2535.
- **Additional round-robin DNS capabilities**—Round-robining of all resource record types is supported under Windows Server 2003 DNS. This additional functionality first appears in Windows 2000 Server.
- **Support for application directory partitions**—An application directory partition stores dynamic, application-specific data. An application directory partition can store any type of object except security principals and is not replicated to the global catalog. Replication of application directory partitions can be tightly controlled, and application directory partitions can be replicated only to a Windows Server 2003 DC.

EXAM ALERT

Active Directory Relies on DNS Because Active Directory relies completely on DNS for name resolution and the Active Directory structure is also modeled on DNS, you can expect DNS to make a very good topic for exam questions.

Installing and Configuring the DNS Server Service

Objective:

Install and configure the DNS Server service.

- Configure DNS server options.
- Configure DNS zone options.
- Configure DNS forwarding.

Manage DNS.

- Manage DNS zone settings.
- Manage DNS server options.

Now that you have a solid background on DNS, you can install, configure, and test the Windows Server 2003 DNS server service. The following sections show how.

Installing the DNS Server Service

To install the Windows Server 2003 DNS server service, follow the procedure outlined in Step by Step 3.2.

NOTE

Using a Dynamic IP Address If you are using a dynamically assigned IP address on the system on which you are installing DNS, you will get a warning message stating that you should use static IP addresses only for a DNS server. You are then given the option to set a static IP address from there. If this occurs in a lab environment or you have a reservation for the server on your DHCP server so that it will always have the same dynamic IP address, you can ignore this warning. If you are using dynamic addressing for production servers, you might want to rethink that IP address strategy. For the purpose of this exercise, you can ignore the warning.

STEP BY STEP

3.2 Installing the DNS Server Service

1. Log on to Windows Server 2003 using the Administrator account or another account that has administrator privileges.

2. Open the Control Panel and then open the Add/Remove Programs applet. The Add or Remove Programs dialog box appears (see Figure 3.2).

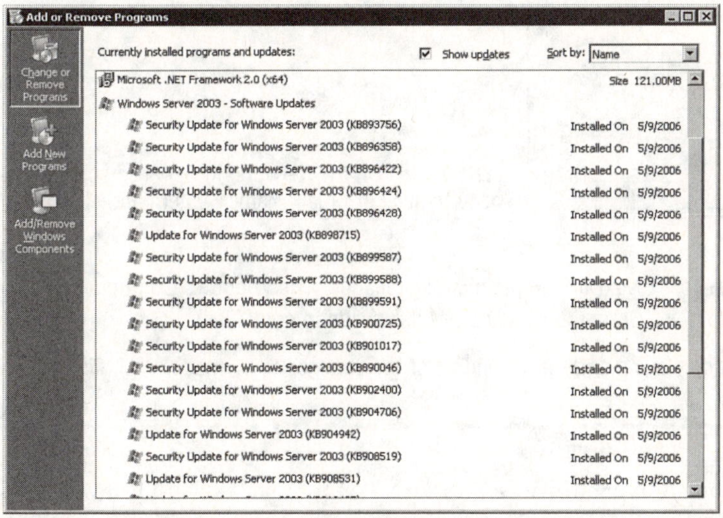

FIGURE 3.2 The Add or Remove Programs dialog box provides useful information about installed applications, including application size and in some cases the frequency of use of an installed application.

3. Click Add/Remove Windows Components on the left side of the Add or Remove Programs dialog box. The Windows Components Wizard dialog box appears (see Figure 3.3).

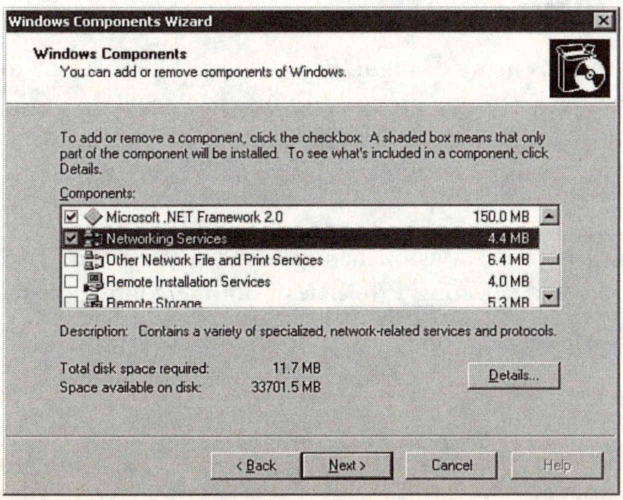

FIGURE 3.3 The Windows Components Wizard allows you to install, remove, or configure the various components of Windows Server 2003.

4. Select Networking Services and click Details. The Networking Services dialog box, shown in Figure 3.4, appears. Select Domain Name System (DNS) and then click OK.

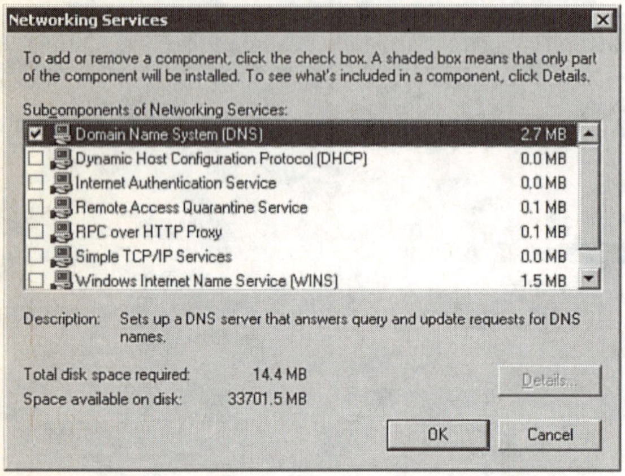

FIGURE 3.4 On the Networking Services screen, you need to select Domain Name System and click OK.

5. On the next screen that appears, click Next to complete the installation. The Windows Component Wizard prompts you for the Windows Server 2003 CD-ROM if it needs to copy files.
6. When the wizard is finished, it displays a summary window of the changes to be made. Click Finish to complete the installation.

You can also use the Manage Your Server utility (see Figure 3.5) to install DNS. We won't go through all the steps in doing so, but you should know that it is another option. This application opens following the installation of Windows Server 2003, and you can reopen it by selecting Start, Manage Your Server.

Examining DNS Server Options

Windows Server 2003 DNS is complex and has many configuration options. The best way to understand these many options is to examine them one group at a time, as we will do in the following sections. To get to these options, you will need to first open the DNS management console by clicking Start, Control Panel, Administrative Tools, DNS. The DNS console seen in Figure 3.6 will open.

The server Properties dialog box, seen in Figure 3.7, is opened by right-clicking the DNS server in the left pane of the DNS console and selecting Properties from the context menu. The DNS server Properties dialog box appears.

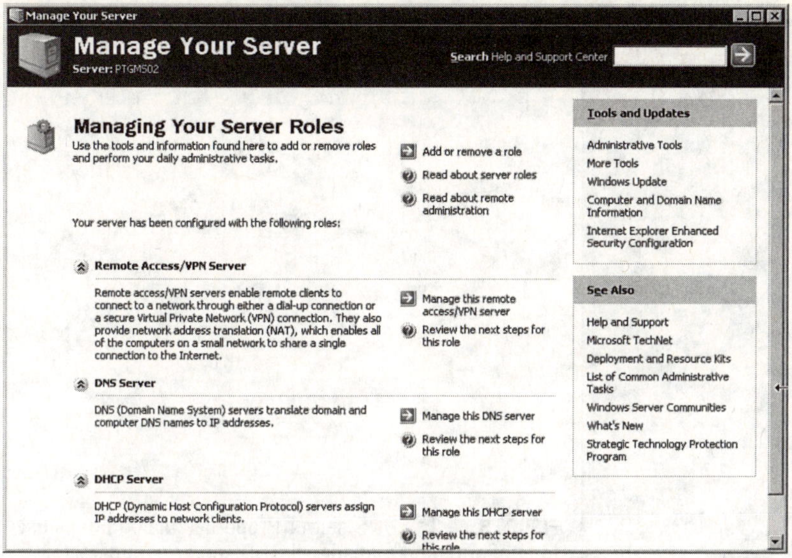

FIGURE 3.5 The Manage Your Server utility provides a very simple, easy-to-use interface for configuring a server for a variety of roles, including DNS server.

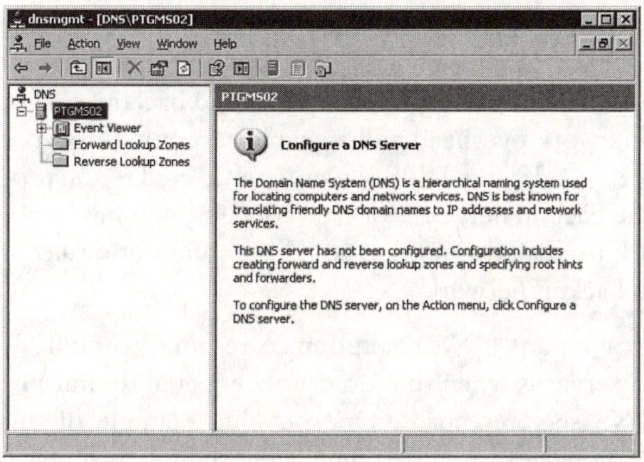

FIGURE 3.6 The DNS console is used to manage the DNS service, including setting options and creating and managing zones.

The Interfaces Tab

Figure 3.7 shows the Interfaces tab of the DNS server Properties dialog box. From this screen, you can set the server options that determine which of the network interfaces of the server will respond to DNS queries. You can either specify all interfaces or choose specific interfaces to respond to queries. When would you need to choose specific interfaces to respond to queries? There are two circumstances in which you might not want your server to respond to DNS queries on all interfaces.

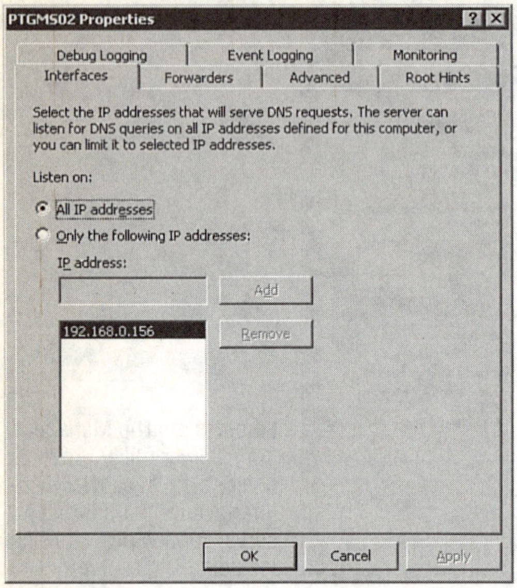

FIGURE 3.7 The DNS server Properties dialog box is used to configure and manage all DNS server parameters.

The first circumstance involves the use of a dedicated, non-routable network used for system-to-system data transfers and data backup. This type of network is commonly found in large data centers, where traffic such as database synchronization and network-based backups is kept off the production network to reduce the network overhead and to avoid saturating network interfaces used by end users to access applications. If your DNS server is connected to the production network for DNS queries and to the backup network for data backups, you might not want the connection to the backup network to respond to queries. This configuration keeps additional overhead off the interface to the backup network.

Another circumstance in which you might not want DNS resolution to respond to multiple interfaces on a Windows Server 2003 DNS server is when the server is connected to multiple discrete networks that utilize different DNS server records. One possible example of this might be a Windows Server 2003 that is connected to an extranet network and an internal network. You might not want that server to respond to DNS queries on the extranet network because you might want to avoid exposing internal name resolutions to customers or business partners who connect to the extranet.

The Forwarders Tab

Figure 3.8 shows the Forwarders tab of the DNS server Properties dialog box. As discussed earlier in this chapter, a DNS forwarder is a DNS server that passes recursive DNS requests to another DNS server; in other words, it forwards them to another DNS server. On the Forwarders tab, you can set the server(s) to which DNS queries should be forwarded.

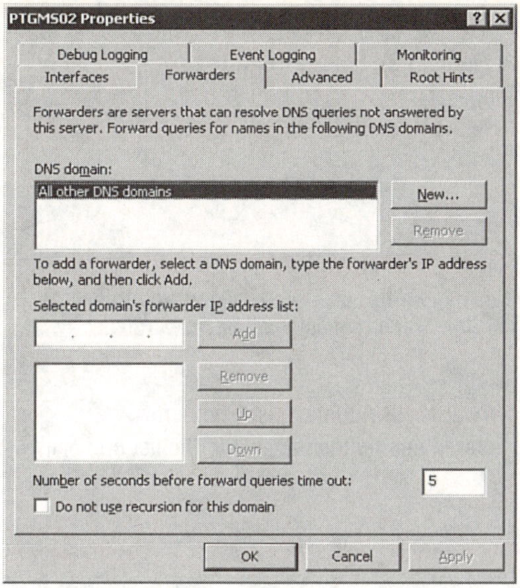

FIGURE 3.8 The Forwarders tab is used to configure where the server will send DNS requests if another DNS server will be supplying some or all of the DNS resolution for that server.

Let's say you have a single internal domain called `intranet.quepublishing.com`. You need to forward any queries to that domain directly to the primary DNS server for the `intranet.quepublishing.com` domain. The Windows Server 2003 DNS service allows you to configure forwarding for a single domain, a group of domains, or all domains. Earlier versions of the Windows DNS service supported forwarding only for all domains—it was an all-or-nothing proposition. Being able to split forwarding between multiple servers while still resolving some domains locally is known as *intelligent forwarding*.

EXAM ALERT

Conditional Forwarding Because the ability to do intelligent forwarding is a new capability with Windows Server 2003 DNS, you need to be familiar with how it works and when you might need to use it.

To configure a single-domain DNS forwarder, you follow the procedure outlined in Step by Step 3.3.

STEP BY STEP

3.3 Setting Up a DNS Forwarder

1. Select Start, Control Panel, Administrative Tools, DNS. The DNS console appears.
2. Right-click the DNS server in the left pane of the DNS console and select Properties from the context menu. The DNS server Properties dialog box appears.

3. Select the Forwarders tab (refer to Figure 3.8).

4. Click New. The New Forwarder dialog box appears (see Figure 3.9). Enter **`intranet.quepublishing.com`** and click OK to add the domain.

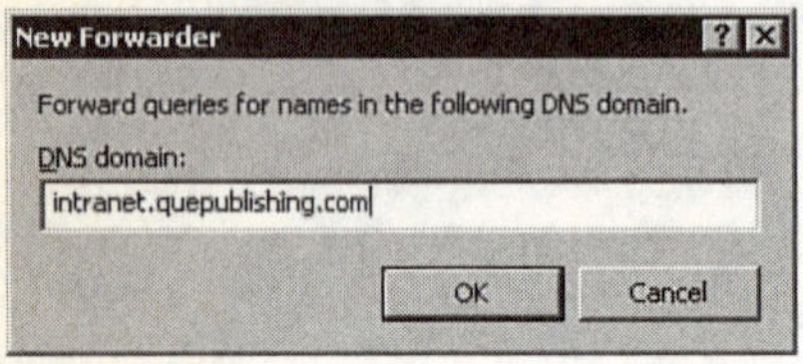

FIGURE 3.9 The New Forwarder dialog box allows you to set the name of the domain for which requests will be forwarded.

5. Back at the Forwarders tab, in the Selected Domain's Forwarder IP Address List field, enter **`192.168.1.165`** and click Add. The IP address you entered should then appear in the list box below, as shown in Figure 3.10.

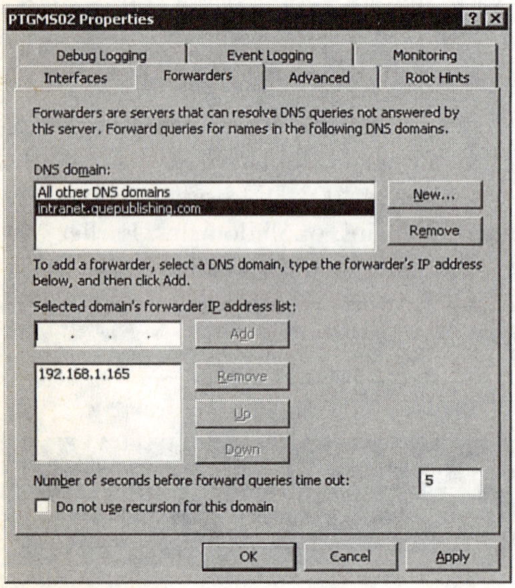

FIGURE 3.10 You can enter multiple servers to forward requests to each forwarded DNS domain.

6. Click OK to close the DNS server Properties dialog box.

NOTE

Deleting Your Forwarder To avoid conflicts with later Step by Steps, you should go back and delete the forwarder you just configured.

CAUTION

Recursion and Forwarding If you disable recursion by selecting Do Not Use Recursion for This Domain in the DNS server Properties dialog box, you will not be able to use a forwarder. Forwarding DNS requests requires that the DNS server be able to make recursive queries.

The Advanced Tab

Figure 3.11 shows the Advanced tab of the DNS server Properties dialog box.

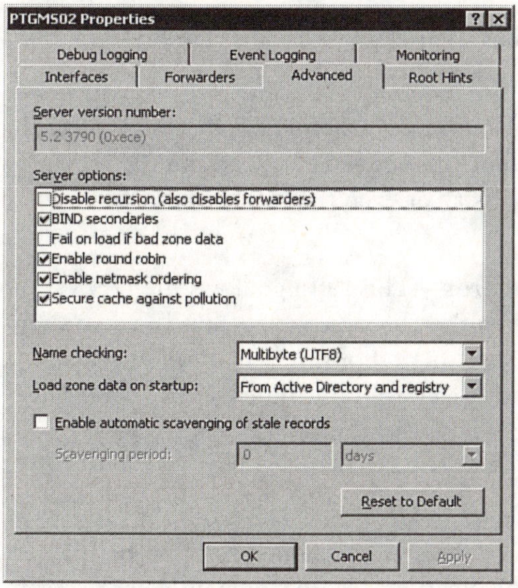

FIGURE 3.11 You typically access the obscure settings on the Advanced tab of the DNS server Properties dialog box only if you are running a nonstandard DNS implementation.

The Advanced tab's settings include the following:

- **Disable Recursion**—This setting (which you might remember from the Forwarders tab) disables recursive DNS queries on the server as well as any forwarders that may be configured.
- **BIND Secondaries**—This setting is used when communicating with Berkeley Internet Name Domain (BIND) servers. In the event that you have old BIND servers that cannot handle fast-transfer DNS updates, you might need to disable this setting.
- **Fail on Load If Bad Zone Data**—This setting, if enabled, prevents the DNS service from loading data from a zone if it is incorrect or corrupt. By default, the Windows Server 2003 DNS service logs the error(s) and continues to load the good zone data.
- **Enable Round Robin**—Round robin (also known as "poor man's load balancing") allows the DNS service to rotate the resource records associated with a query result.

Round robin allows you to use DNS to help spread the load on a group of servers by allowing you to tie multiple IP hosts to a single resource record. Each time a resolution is requested, DNS returns the "next" record in the list of addresses.

- **Enable Netmask Ordering**—Netmask ordering allows the DNS server to determine which resource record to respond with based on the IP address of the requesting host.
- **Secure Cache Against Pollution**—As the name implies, this setting allows the DNS service to monitor the cached entries for possible bad or insecure responses, and it deletes them. This setting is enabled by default, and it probably should be left enabled in almost all cases.
- **Name Checking**—Name checking determines what character set is supported by the DNS server for requested DNS names.
- **Load Zone Data on Startup**—This setting determines from where the server loads its DNS data on startup. By default, the server looks to Active Directory and the registry, but you can configure it to look just to the registry or even to a file for its domain information.
- **Enable Automatic Scavenging of Stale Records**—This setting allows the DNS service to prune records from the DNS cache when they become stale—that is, when they have not re-registered with DDNS within the set period of time. In an office with a very transient user population, you might want to shorten this interval. For very static environments, lengthening this period reduces the overhead on the server slightly because the process doesn't run as often.

A good general rule for the Advanced tab is to leave the settings alone until you have a very good understanding of the intricacies of DNS. These settings can have unanticipated results on DNS resolution if you are not absolutely sure of what each setting does. The most common reason you will configure a setting on the Advanced tab is to enable and configure scavenging of stale records.

The Root Hints Tab

Figure 3.12 shows the Root Hints tab of the DNS server Properties dialog box. The root hints identify the DNS servers that hold the root of the DNS tree. Because the Windows Server 2003 DNS server cannot use the DNS name of a root server to find a root server, it must have a static list of root servers so that it can find the root of the tree to find a DNS server to resolve its request. For example, if you were trying to connect to www.quepublishing.com, you would need to start at the root of the name, `com`, to find the DNS server that is authoritative for the `quepublishing.com` domain. The root hints contain the addresses of the DNS servers that are authoritative for the TLDs, including `com`. The authoritative root server for `com` would direct the request to the DNS server that was authoritative for the `quepublishing.com` domain, and that DNS server would resolve the query.

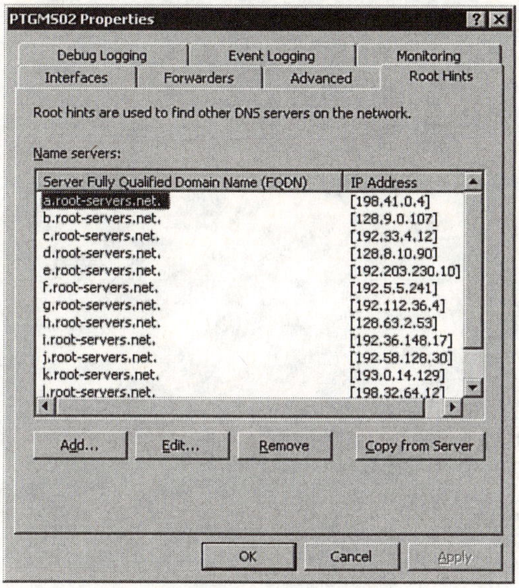

FIGURE 3.12 The Root Hints tab of the DNS server Properties dialog box contains the list of DNS servers that are authoritative for the TLDs.

The Debug Logging Tab

Figure 3.13 shows the Debug Logging tab of the DNS server Properties dialog box. Debug logging is discussed in more detail later in this chapter in the "Monitoring the DNS Service" section, but at this point, you should know that it is used to do detailed logging of DNS traffic and is typically used only when troubleshooting DNS issues with the server. Its limited use is due to the amount of data logged.

The Event Logging Tab

The Event Logging tab of the DNS server Properties dialog box (see Figure 3.14) offers more traditional logging than the Debug Logging tab. The log file for these events can be found at `%SystemRoot%\system32\dns\dns.log`. `%SystemRoot%` is usually the Windows system file directory. Event logging is discussed in more detail later in this chapter in the "Monitoring the DNS Service" section.

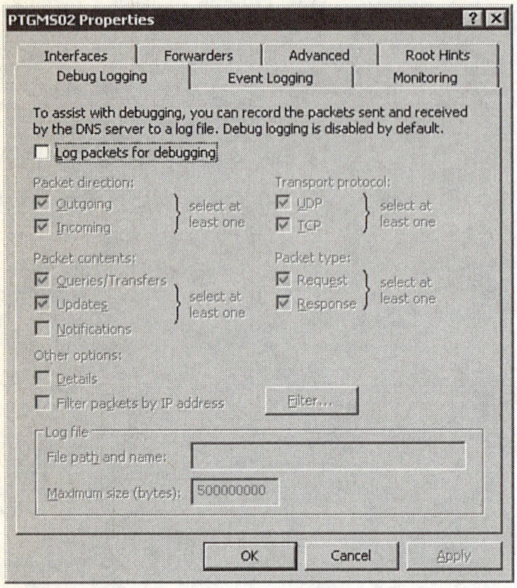

FIGURE 3.13 The Debug Logging tab of the DNS server Properties dialog box provides detailed logging information about DNS traffic.

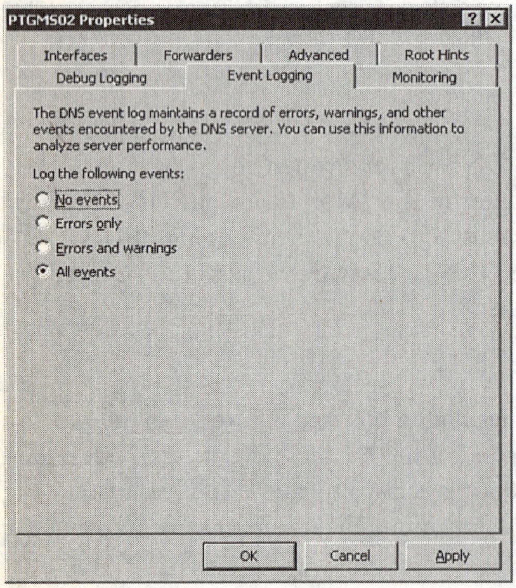

FIGURE 3.14 Event logging records information on errors, warnings, and other DNS-related events.

The Monitoring Tab

Figure 3.15 shows the Monitoring tab of the DNS server Properties dialog box. The Monitoring tab allows you to automate the testing of the DNS service, which is discussed in detail later in this chapter, in the "Testing the DNS Service" section.

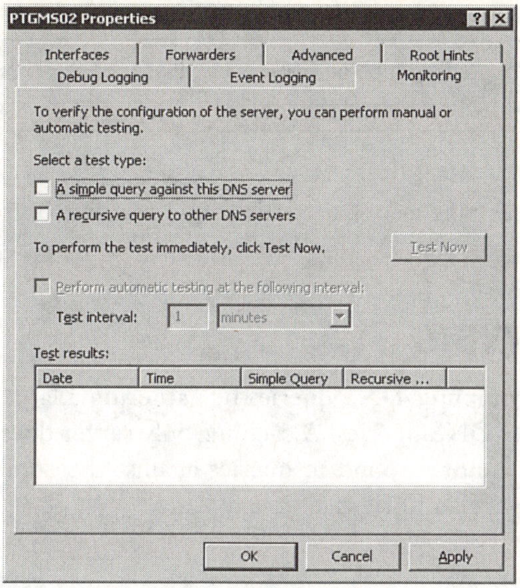

FIGURE 3.15 The Monitoring tab of the DNS server Properties dialog box allows you to automate the testing of the Windows Server 2003 DNS service.

The Security Tab

The Security tab of the DNS server Properties dialog box allows you to configure the rights to the DNS service (see Figure 3.16). This tab should look familiar to you because it is the standard rights assignment screen for any rights, from those for the file system to those for DNS privileges. If you want certain users or groups to have permissions on the DNS service, you can assign their rights from the Security tab.

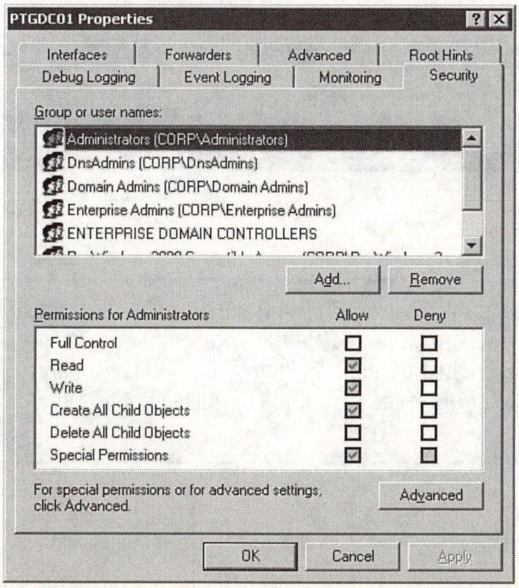

FIGURE 3.16 If you want to configure granular privileges for DNS, you can do so on the Security tab of the DNS server Properties dialog box.

NOTE

The Security Tab The Security tab will not be available for configuration on DNS servers that are not installed on a Domain Controller.

With the DNS service installed at a basic level, let's take a look at setting up a caching-only server.

Configuring Caching-Only Servers

Caching-only servers are used to speed up client computer DNS queries by gathering a large number of cached records based on client computer DNS queries. A caching-only server does not have a copy of the zone table and therefore cannot respond to queries against the zone unless they are already cached. A caching server is not authoritative on any zone.

NOTE

Room for Cached Information All the cache entries on a caching-only server are stored in RAM. You need to be sure that your caching server has plenty of RAM; otherwise, it will not be effective.

Let's assume that you have an existing Windows Server 2003 DNS server and you want to convert it to a caching-only server that can resolve internal DNS entries. The procedure outlined in Step by Step 3.4 guides you through this process.

EXAM ALERT

Doing It the Easy Way By default, when you install the Windows Server 2003 DNS service, it automatically acts as a caching-only server—albeit one that is able to resolve only Internet-accessible DNS entries—until you start creating zones and setting parameters.

CAUTION

This Step by Step Is Optional You do not need to complete this Step by Step if you have only one DNS server available. If you opt to complete this Step by Step, you should not delete the Root Hints as instructed in Step 6. Additionally, you should delete the record you created during this Step by Step after you are done. This will ensure that your DNS server will be ready to perform the rest of the exercises in this and following chapters.

STEP BY STEP

3.4 Creating a Caching-Only DNS Server

1. Log on to Windows Server 2003 using the Administrator account or another account that has administrator privileges.

2. Open the DNS console by selecting Start, Control Panel, Administrative Tools, DNS. Expand the tree view of the DNS server and delete any zones listed under either Forward Lookup Zones or Reverse Lookup Zones. A caching-only server cannot be authoritative on any zones.

3. Double-click the Root Hints entry in the right pane, and the DNS Server Properties dialog box appears with the Root Hints tab selected, as seen in Figure 3.17.

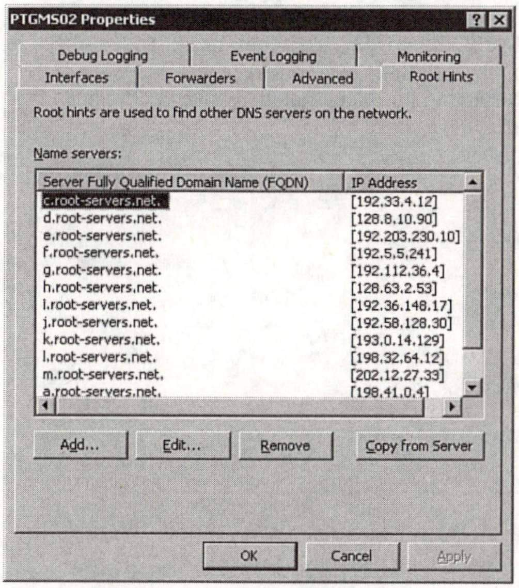

FIGURE 3.17 The root hints entries contain the IP addresses of the root Internet DNS servers and tell the DNS server where to forward requests that cannot be resolved locally.

4. Click the Add button; the New Resource Record dialog box appears, as seen in Figure 3.18. Add a resource record for every DNS server for which you want this server to cache lookups. These name servers must already exist in your DNS hierarchy. In this case, you can enter the FQDN and IP address of the server you just installed.

5. Click OK when you are done entering the FQDN and IP address. The name server you added appears on the Root Hints tab of the DNS server Properties dialog box, as seen in Figure 3.19.

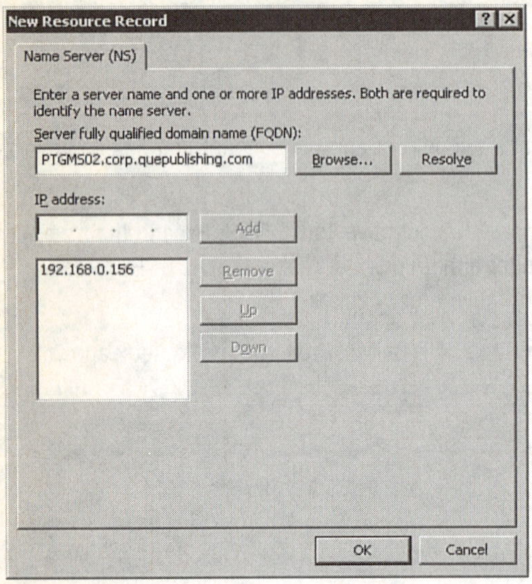

FIGURE 3.18 To create a caching-only server, you need to add to the Root Hints list the server that you want to perform resolution for the entries that have not yet been cached.

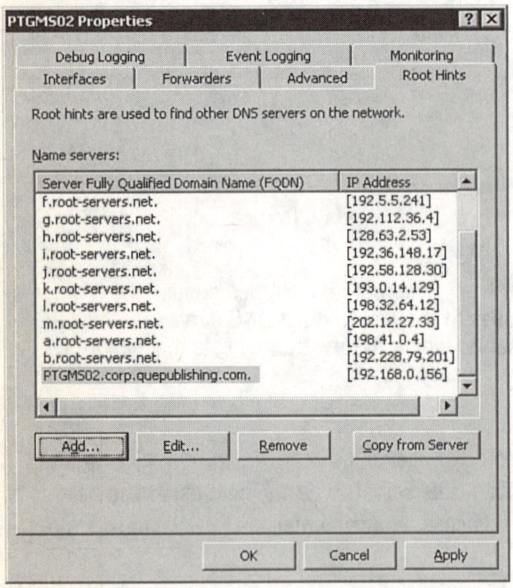

FIGURE 3.19 You need to make sure that the server that will be performing resolution of systems not in the cache is on this list before you delete all the other entries.

6. Now that you have the forwarding DNS server in the list, delete all the other entries on the Root Hints tab, unless this is your only DNS server. This restricts all local name resolution to the DNS cache and causes requests for noncached entries to be forwarded to the specific server you have configured. When a response is received from that server, it is added to the cache of this server.
7. Click OK to return to the DNS console. The creation of the caching-only server is complete.

To verify that the caching function is working, you can `ping` several hosts by DNS name from a workstation configured to use your caching-only DNS server for DNS resolution. This builds the cache. Then you should go to another workstation that is also using the caching-only server for DNS and `ping` the same hosts. This time, the response should be much quicker because the DNS server will be able to get the DNS name of the host from the cache instead of forwarding the request to another DNS server.

We have discussed how to set the server options. Now let's talk about configuring DNS zones so that the new server can perform name resolution.

Configuring Zones

Although it is possible to manually configure the text files that DNS creates, the DNS console makes it much easier to manage the DNS namespace configuration. When you first install your DNS server, you will need to configure your DNS server with its first zones before it works properly. We will look at how to do this by using the wizard and then take a look at how to do this if you need to add additional zones later.

EXAM ALERT

The DNS Console Equals the MMC The DNS console is really nothing more than the MMC with the DNS Management snap-in installed. Microsoft provides this version of the MMC to make managing systems easier for new users of Windows Server 2003, so don't be confused if you see references to the MMC in the exam. That's all the DNS console is.

Using the MMC and Manually Adding Snap-ins

If you are an advanced user and would like to skip using differently configured versions of the MMC for each of the services installed on Windows Server 2003, there is an easy way to manage everything from a single configuration. You simply open the MMC by selecting Start, Run, MMC. This opens the MMC shell, which is empty the first time you load it. Next you select Console, Add/Remove Snap-in. When the Add/Remove Snap-in dialog box appears, you click the Add button. In the Add Standalone Snap-in dialog box that appears next, you can select any or all of the snap-ins for Windows Server 2003 services.

As discussed earlier in this chapter, the most common types of DNS zones are forward lookup zones, which are used to translate hostnames to IP addresses, and reverse lookup zones, which provide IP-address-to-hostname translations. Now let's look at how you would set up a new forward lookup zone and a new reverse lookup zone on a DNS server.

To configure the zones on your DNS server for the first time, you follow the procedure outlined in Step by Step 3.5.

STEP BY STEP

3.5 Configuring a Forward Lookup Zone and a Reverse Lookup Zone

1. Log on to Windows Server 2003 using the Administrator account or another account that has administrator privileges.
2. Open the DNS console by selecting Start, Control Panel, Administrative Tools, DNS. Right-click the new server and select the Configure a DNS Server option from the context menu. The Configure a DNS Server Wizard, seen in Figure 3.20, opens.

FIGURE 3.20 The Configure a DNS Server Wizard guides you in configuring your new DNS server.

3. Click Next, and the Select Configuration Action screen appears, as seen in Figure 3.21.

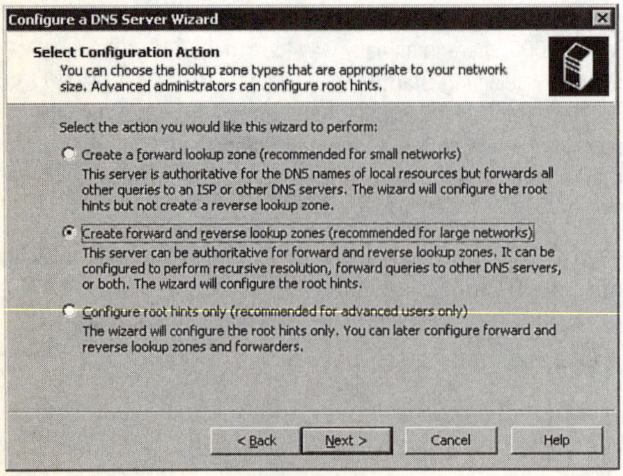

FIGURE 3.21 The Select Configuration Action screen allows you to select which activities you need to perform based on the size of the network or other requirements.

4. Select the Create Forward and Reverse Lookup Zones option and click Next. The Forward Lookup Zone screen appears, as seen in Figure 3.22.

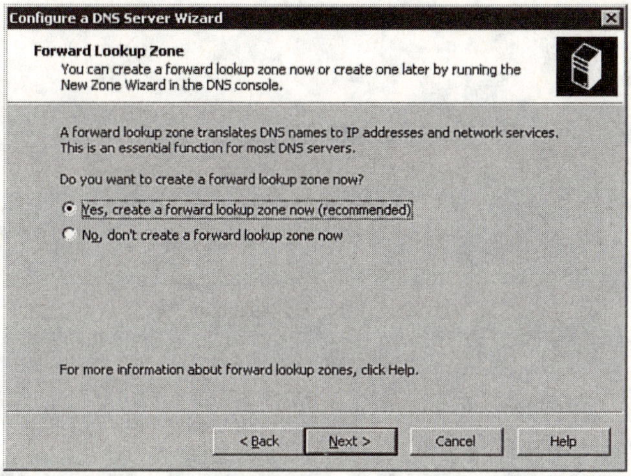

FIGURE 3.22 The Forward Lookup Zone screen verifies that you really want to create a forward lookup zone.

5. On the Forward Lookup Zone screen, you are asked to confirm that you do in fact wish to create the zone. Select Yes and click Next. The Zone Type screen appears, as seen in Figure 3.23.

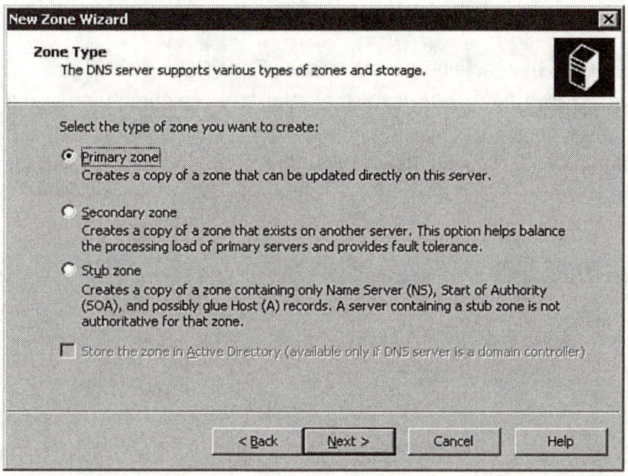

FIGURE 3.23 The Zone Type screen allows you to create a primary, secondary, or stub zone.

6. Select Primary zone to make this DNS server authoritative for the zone you are creating and click Next. The Zone Name screen appears, as seen in Figure 3.24.

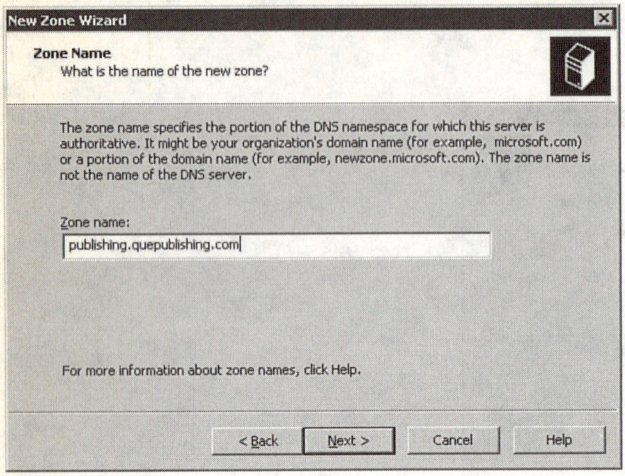

FIGURE 3.24 As we discussed, it is generally a good idea to use a registered domain name whenever you are creating a zone.

> **NOTE**
>
> **Active Directory–Integrated** If your DNS server were also a DC, you would have the option Store the Zone in Active Directory available to you (see Figure 3.23). For the purposes of this exercise, we're going to create a standard DNS zone as we'll examine Active Directory integration with DNS in more detail later in this chapter.

7. Enter the name of the domain for which you will be resolving names into the Zone Name field. The example in Figure 3.24 uses `publishing.quepublishing.com`, but you can use something else if you like. If you are on a network that is not connected to the Internet and will not be resolving names for users outside your internal network, this name can be anything. Click Next, and the Zone File screen appears, as seen in Figure 3.25.

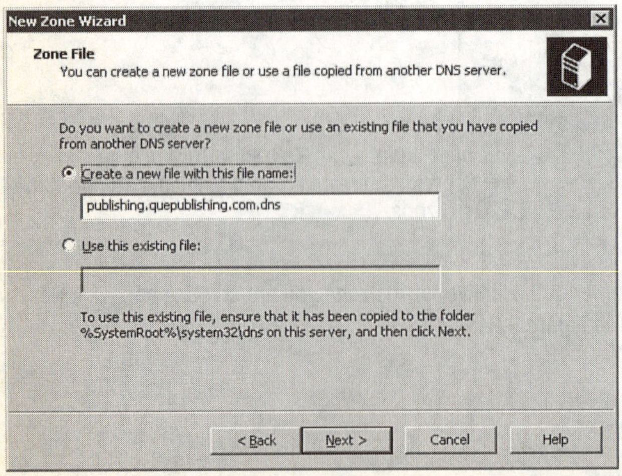

FIGURE 3.25 You should usually select the suggested default zone file name.

8. On the Zone File screen, you will most likely leave the default selection intact. After making your selection, click Next. The Dynamic Updates screen appears, as seen in Figure 3.26.

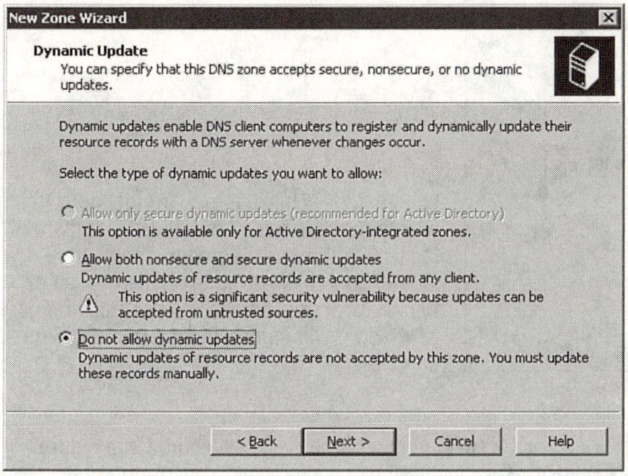

FIGURE 3.26 Dynamic updates can be configured to make record management easier for an administrator.

9. On the Dynamic Updates screen, you can opt to allow nonsecure and secure dynamic updates if you want, but for the purposes of this exercise, select the Do Not Allow Dynamic Updates option as we'll configure them later. Click Next, and the Reverse Lookup Zone screen appears, as seen in Figure 3.27.

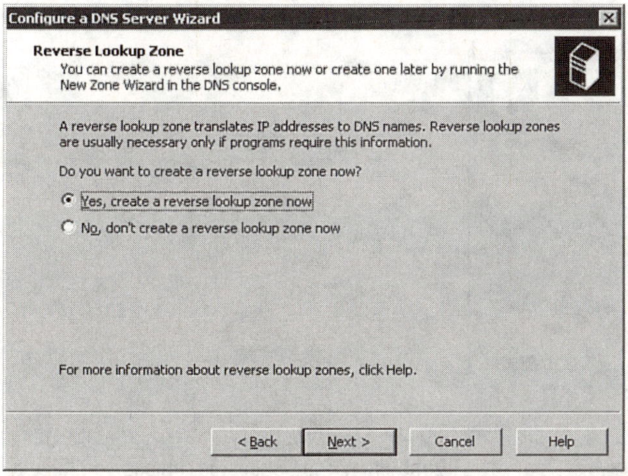

FIGURE 3.27 The Reverse Lookup Zone screen verifies that you really want to create a reverse lookup zone.

10. Select Yes, Create a Reverse Lookup Zone Now, and click Next to continue. The Zone Type screen appears. This should look familiar because it is the same screen that you used to create a forward lookup zone (refer back to Figure 3.23).

11. Select Primary Zone, but do not opt to store the data in Active Directory. Click Next, and the Reverse Lookup Zone Name screen appears, as seen in Figure 3.28.

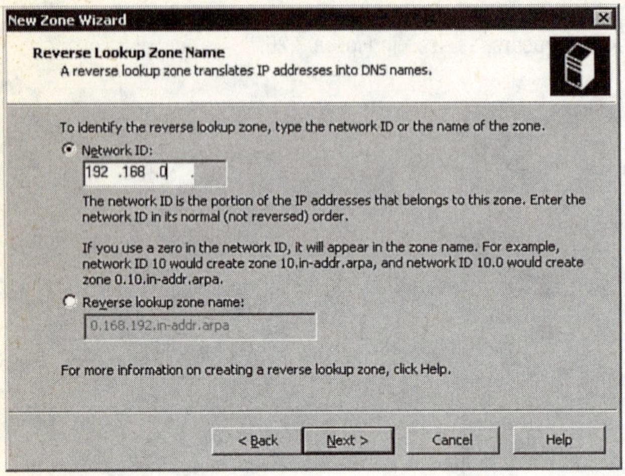

FIGURE 3.28 Unlike a forward lookup zone, whose name is based on the DNS domain of the Active Directory domain, a reverse lookup zone has its name created based on the network portion of the IP address range to which it will be providing reverse lookup services.

12. Identify the reverse lookup ID by the network ID or by specifying a name. The name shown in Figure 3.28 uses the standard naming convention, which is the network ID (in this case, 192.168.0.x) in reverse order, with `in-addr.arpa` appended. This results in the name `192.168.0.in-addr.arpa`. Notice the `arpa` in the name. If you were guessing that this naming convention has been around since the Internet was called the ARPAnet, you would be correct. As discussed earlier in this chapter, in the section "Reverse Lookups," this is the Internet-standard naming convention, and you should try to stick with it. Click Next. The Zone File screen appears as seen in Figure 3.29.

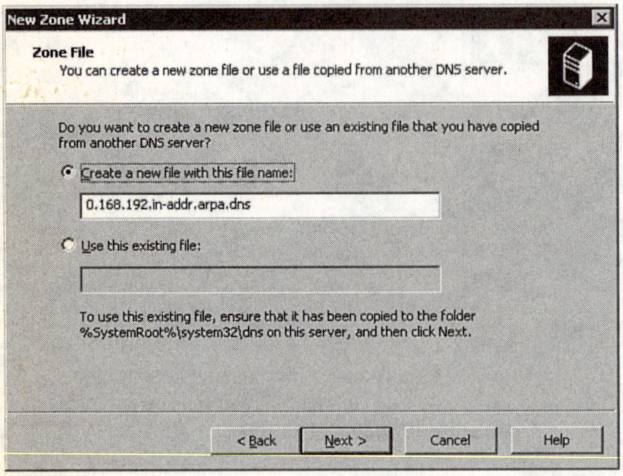

FIGURE 3.29 You should select the default zone file name suggested, unless you have a specific reason otherwise.

13. On the Zone File screen, you will most likely leave the default selection intact unless you have a specific reason to change it. After making your selection, click Next. The Dynamic Updates screen appears, as seen previously in Figure 3.26.

14. On the Dynamic Updates screen, select the Do Not Allow Dynamic Updates option. Click Next and the Forwarders screen appears, as seen in Figure 3.30.

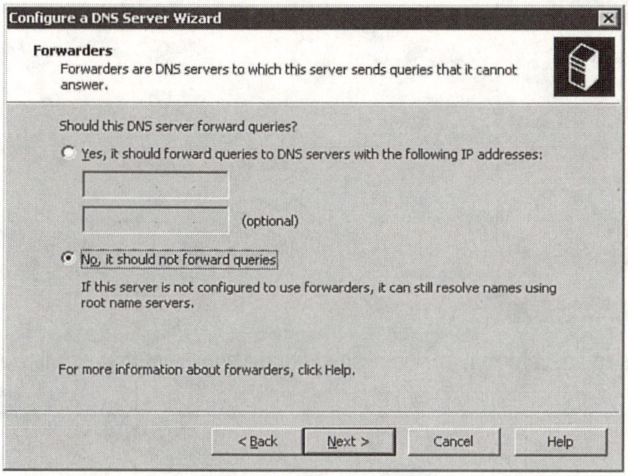

FIGURE 3.30 Microsoft has added the capability to set a DNS server as a forwarder by using the Configure a DNS Server Wizard.

15. For the purposes of this exercise, select No, It Should Not Forward Queries and click Next. The Completing the Configure a DNS Server Wizard dialog box appears, as seen in Figure 3.31. This screen allows you to review the configurations you selected and either go back to correct mistakes or cancel the wizard before the changes are committed.

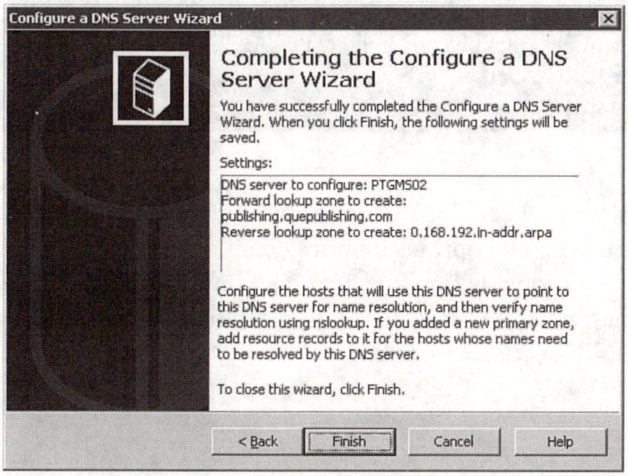

FIGURE 3.31 You need to double-check your information before committing the changes you just made.

16. Click Finish to complete the configuration. Notice in Figure 3.32 that the zones that were configured by the wizard now appear in the DNS console.

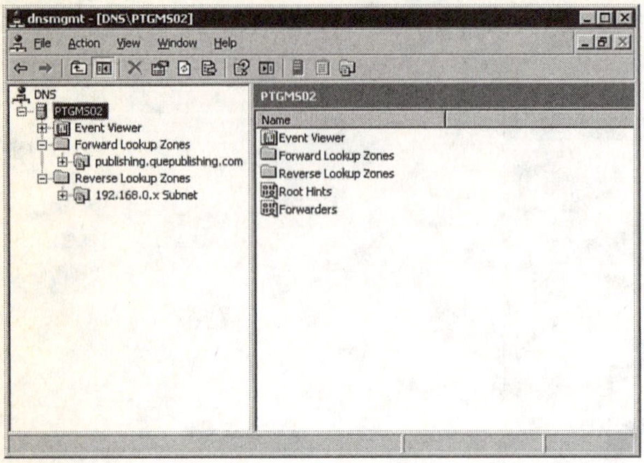

FIGURE 3.32 The DNS console gives you access to any information you need about the zones configured on that DNS server.

EXAM ALERT

Changing DNS Names Used with Active Directory When choosing a domain name to use when installing DNS, it is always a good idea to register a domain name with the appropriate domain name registration agency and use that name even if your internal network is isolated (that is, not connected to the Internet). Doing so ensures that your domain name is not in use somewhere else. A famous example of this is the `xyz.com` domain, used in some old Windows documentation as a sample domain. Someone actually has that domain registered and is using it. If you set up Active Directory by using this domain name and are connected to the Internet, you can cause conflicts. The good news is that with Windows Server 2003, you can rename the domain without breaking Active Directory—this is a new feature with this release of Windows. The fact that the DNS name used with Active Directory can now be changed would make an excellent exam question.

Now that you have created new forward and reverse lookup zones by using the Configure a DNS Server Wizard, we'll look at configuring zone options in more detail. We will also come back to these zones later in the chapter and look at how they can be converted into Active Directory–integrated zones (provided that your DNS server is also a Domain Controller) in the "Integrating Active Directory and DNS" section of this chapter.

Examining Zone Options

For the most part, once they have been created and configured, DNS zones pretty much work without any problems. In this section, we examine the basic zone options available to you and how they are configured.

To access a zone's options, you simply need to select the zone, right-click it, and select Properties from the context menu. The Properties dialog box opens to the General tab, as seen in Figure 3.33.

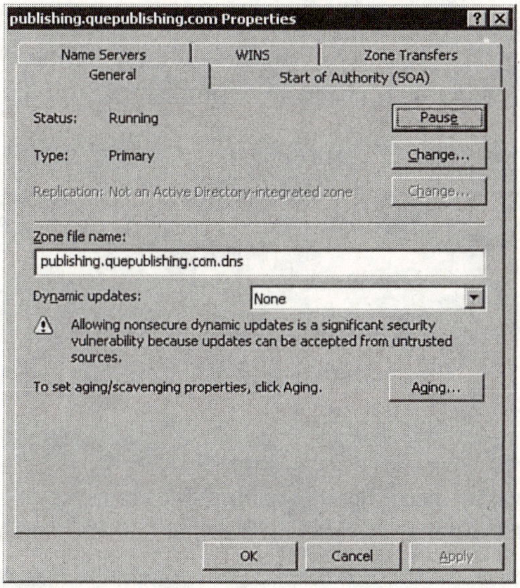

FIGURE 3.33 The zone Properties dialog box allows you to fully manage the configuration and status for a domain.

The General Tab

From the General tab, as seen in Figure 3.33, you can configure basic options about how the zone itself operates and behaves. If for some reason you needed to stop name resolution from occurring against that zone, you could click the Pause button to pause the zone. This could be useful when configuring changes or troubleshooting the zone.

The Change button in the Type section of the tab allows you to change the zone type, such as from a primary zone to a secondary zone or from a primary zone to a stub zone. Beware that changing a standard primary zone to a secondary zone has the implications of leaving no primary zone afterwards, so you will need to change a secondary zone to a primary zone for DNS to work correctly.

On DNS servers that reside on a Domain Controller, the Change button in the Replication section of the tab will be available to you. You can change how the zone is replicated, such as from a standard primary zone to an Active Directory–integrated zone, and also configure the scope of replication within Active Directory. We will examine these options later in the "Integrating Active Directory and DNS" section of the chapter.

You can also configure and change the zone file name, the type of dynamic updates that the zone will process, and the aging and scavenging properties for the zone. Under normal circumstances, there should never be a reason to change the zone file name; however, the ability to do so exists. We examine the configuration of dynamic updates in the next section and the configuration of aging and scavenging later in the "Configuring Aging/Scavenging" section of this chapter.

Configuring Zones for Dynamic Updates

One of the major advantages of running a Windows Server 2003 network is the capability to use DDNS. To configure a DNS zone for dynamic updates, you follow the procedure outlined in Step by Step 3.6.

STEP BY STEP

3.6 Configuring a Zone for Dynamic Updates

1. Log on to Windows Server 2003 using the Administrator account or another account that has administrator privileges.
2. Open the DNS console by selecting Start, Control Panel, Administrative Tools, DNS.
3. Right-click the zone you want to configure to receive dynamic updates (for example, `publishing.quepublishing.com`). From the context menu, select Properties. The Properties dialog box shown previously in Figure 3.33 appears. (Note that the title bar of the dialog box reflects the name of the zone.)
4. For a DNS server that is not running on a Domain Controller, the only option to select is Nonsecure and Secure. If the zone were running on a Domain Controller and were Active Directory integrated, you would also have the option to enable secure updates, as we'll see later in the "Integrating Active Directory and DNS" section of the chapter. For now, select the Nonsecure and Secure option, click OK to confirm the selection, and close the Properties dialog box.
5. You will need to repeat this process for each of your forward and reverse lookup zones that are to utilize dynamic updates.

DDNS is specified in RFC 2136, "Dynamic Updates in the Domain Name System (DNS UPDATE)." It is the foundation of a successful Active Directory implementation. As discussed in this chapter, DNS is used to resolve a name to an IP address, or vice versa, using a defined hierarchical naming structure to ensure uniformity. DDNS takes that architecture to the next level. This section describes the Windows Server 2003 implementation of the dynamic update process.

In Windows Server 2003, client computers can send dynamic updates for three types of network adapters: DHCP adapters, statically configured adapters, and remote access adapters. We will examine these configurations in more detail in the next section, "Configuring DNS Client Computers."

DDNS integrates DHCP and DNS, as described in RFC 2136. Every time a computer requests a new address or renews its address, the computer sends an option 81 and its fully qualified domain name to the DHCP server and requests that the DHCP server register an entry in the reverse lookup DNS zone on its behalf. The DHCP client computer also requests an entry in the forward lookup zone on its own behalf. The end result is that every DHCP client computer has an entry in the DNS zones, both forward and reverse. This information can be used by other Windows Server 2003 computers in place of WINS for identifying the names and IP addresses of other hosts.

NOTE

Option 81 Option 81 (also known as the FQDN option) allows the client computer to send its FQDN to the DHCP server when it requests an IP address.

By default, the dynamic update client computer dynamically registers its resource records whenever any of the following events occur:

- The TCP/IP configuration is changed.
- The DHCP address is renewed or a new lease is obtained.
- A Plug and Play event occurs.
- An IP address is added to or removed from the computer when the user changes or adds an IP address for a static adapter.

By default, the dynamic update client computer automatically deregisters name–to–IP address mappings whenever the DHCP lease expires.

You can force a re-registration by using the command-line tool `ipconfig`. For Windows Server 2003–based client computers, you type the following at the command prompt:

```
ipconfig /registerdns
```

This command also works for Windows XP and Windows 2000 computers.

Now let's take a quick look at the dynamic update process and see how a Windows Server 2003 host gets dynamically registered with DNS. A dynamic update occurs in the following manner:

1. The DNS client computer queries its local name server to find the primary name server and the zone that is authoritative for the name it is updating. The local name server performs the standard name resolution process to discover the primary name server, and it returns the name of the authoritative server and zone.

2. The client computer sends a dynamic update request to the primary server. The authoritative server performs the update and replies to the client computer regarding the result of the dynamic update.

The Start of Authority (SOA) Tab

From the Start of Authority (SOA) tab, as seen in Figure 3.34, you can configure the fields that appear on the SOA record. Each DNS zone has one and only one server that is considered to be the primary name server for that zone (even in Active Directory–integrated zones where all DNS servers are otherwise considered equal). The *root name server* of a domain is the name server that is acting as the SOA for that DNS zone and is the one referenced by the Windows Server 2003 DNS services as the primary server. The SOA record is the first record in the database, and it has the following format:

```
IN SOA <primary server> <contact email> <serial number> <refresh time>
<retry time> <expiration time><time to live>
```

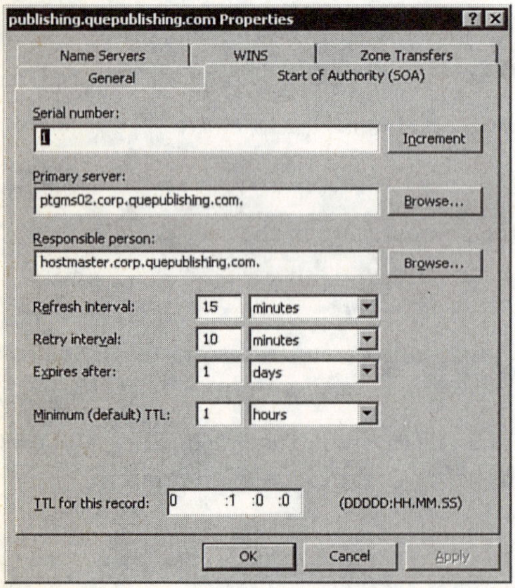

FIGURE 3.34 The Start of Authority (SOA) tab allows you to configure the SOA record.

These are the sections of the SOA field (in the order in which they appear on the tab in Figure 3.34):

- **`serial number`**—This is important. It acts as the version number for the database file, and it should increase each time the database file is changed. The file with the highest serial number takes precedence during zone transfers.
- **`primary server`**—This is the DNS server that maintains this file.

- ***responsible person***—This is the Internet email address for the person responsible for this domain's database file. See the note "Don't Use a Standard Email Address for the SOA" for important formatting information.
- ***refresh interval***—This is the elapsed time (in seconds) that a secondary server will wait between checks to its master server to see whether the database file has changed and a zone transfer should be requested. This is set to 15 minutes by default, but it can be increased in an environment where DNS doesn't change often.
- ***retry interval***—This is the elapsed time (in seconds) that a secondary server will wait before retrying a failed zone transfer. The default for Windows Server 2003 is 10 minutes, and this setting can be increased or decreased as needed for the environment.
- ***expires after***—This is the elapsed time (in seconds) that a secondary server will keep trying to download a zone. After this time limit expires, the old zone information is discarded. This is set to one day by default, and it can be modified as needed. You might want to increase this number for areas with intermittent connectivity where outages are common, such as with DNS across a VPN.
- ***time to live***—The time to live (TTL) is the elapsed time (in seconds) that a DNS server is allowed to cache any resource records from the database file.

NOTE

Don't Use a Standard Email Address for the SOA One very important fact about the contact email in the SOA is that it does not use the standard Internet email format. Instead, you replace the @ symbol in the email address with a period. For example, `billg@microsoft.com` would be `billg.microsoft.com` in the zone file.

The Start of Authority (SOA) tab also has a configuration field that allows you to configure a different TTL for the SOA record itself, if desired.

The Name Servers Tab

From the Name Servers tab, as seen in Figure 3.35, you can configure which name servers are to be considered authoritative for the zone. For standard zones, this will include the server that holds the primary zone and all servers that hold secondary copies of the zone. For Active Directory–integrated zones, this will include all DNS servers that hold the zone.

You can manage the list of authoritative name servers using the Add, Edit, and Remove buttons on this tab.

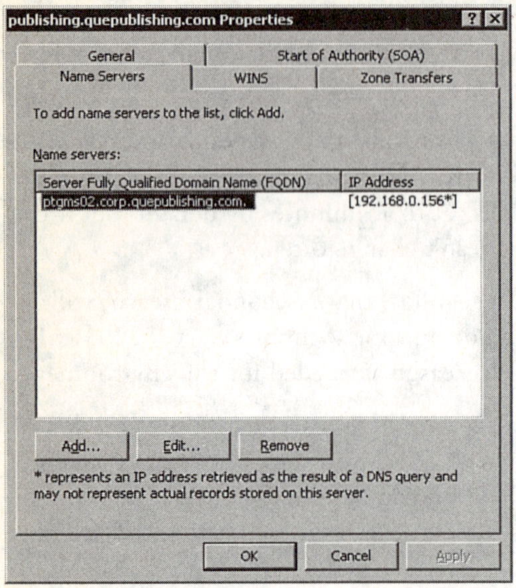

FIGURE 3.35 The Name Servers tab allows you to add and remove authoritative name servers for the zone.

The WINS Tab

From the WINS tab, as seen in Figure 3.36, you can configure the zone for WINS lookup integration. If your network still relies on WINS, then you will likely need to configure the options on this tab to provide the best name resolution services available to your clients. We discuss this integration in Chapter 4, "Implementing and Managing WINS."

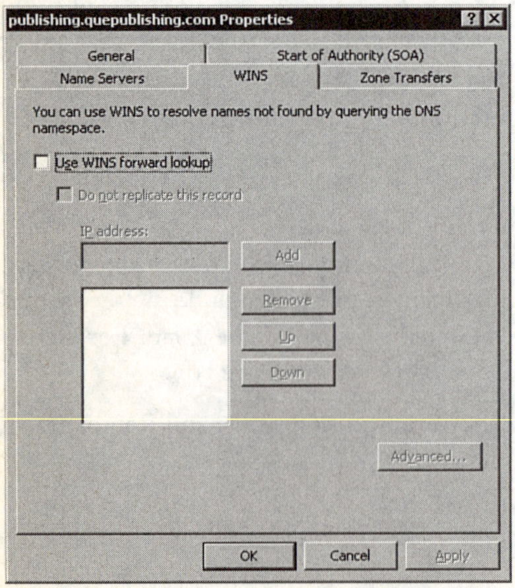

FIGURE 3.36 The WINS tab allows you to configure the zone for WINS integration if you need to support legacy WINS clients.

The Zone Transfers Tab

From the Zone Transfers tab, as seen in Figure 3.37, you can configure how the zone will perform zone transfers.

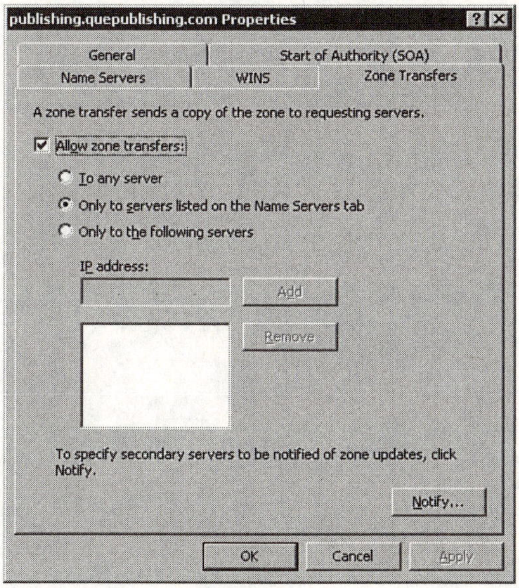

FIGURE 3.37 The Zone Transfers tab allows you to configure the zone transfer properties.

In most cases, the default selection of Only to Servers Listed on the Name Servers Tab will be the best selection. However, there are times when you may need to change the selection. The available options are as follows:

- **Allow zone transfers**—If this option is unchecked, the options below it become unavailable and no zone transfers will be allowed for the server. Turning off zone transfers (for standard zones) is useful only in cases in which no other DNS servers that would need a zone transfer exist; this is typically an unlikely scenario. By default, Active Directory–integrated zones do not allow zone transfer as the zone data is replicated by Active Directory itself and is not stored in a flat text file.
- **To any server**—This least-secure option allows any server that requests a zone transfer of your zone file to have it.
- **Only to servers listed on the Name Servers tab**—The default option allows zone transfers with those authoritative name servers that you configured on the Name Servers tab.
- **Only to the following servers**—This option allows you to explicitly specify which servers (by IP address) will be allowed to perform zone transfers with this zone.

The Security Tab

From the Security tab, as seen in Figure 3.38, you can configure additional zone security. Recall that the Security tab in the server Properties dialog box does not appear unless the DNS server is running on a Domain Controller. Likewise, the Security tab in the zone Properties dialog box will not appear unless the zone is an Active Directory–integrated one, which is discussed in the "Integrating Active Directory and DNS" section later in this chapter.

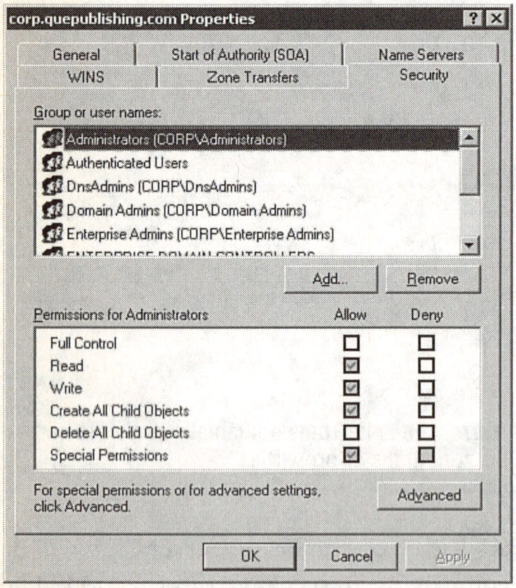

FIGURE 3.38 The Security tab will be available only for Active Directory–integrated zones.

Now that you have finished the basic configuration of a Windows Server 2003 DNS server and its zones, let's move on and examine additional DNS-related management and configuration tasks you'll need to understand.

Configuring DNS Client Computers

Now that you have installed and configured the DNS server portion of Windows Server 2003 DNS, you should take a look at how to properly configure DNS on a Windows XP Professional client computer. The key to configuring DNS on a Windows XP client computer (and on a Windows 2000 client computer as well) is to keep in mind that DNS is installed in two places. First, DNS is configured as part of the TCP/IP interface. If you have ever installed DNS on a Windows NT 4.0 or Windows 2000 computer, this process should be familiar.

EXAM ALERT

You Need Windows XP or Windows 2000 for DDNS Remember that the Windows 9x and Me operating systems were designed for use by home users, who do not typically need to register with a DNS server to interact with Active Directory appropriately. These operating systems do not participate in DDNS. For that reason, this chapter looks only at the business operating systems, such as Windows XP Professional and Windows 2000.

The second place you may need to configure DNS on a client computer is in the System Properties dialog box. The DNS information configured here is used as the DNS suffix for building FQDNs and is similar to the suffix information configured under the Internet Protocol (TCP/IP) Properties dialog box on other Windows operating systems. It is also used as part of the process for registering a computer in DDNS. Step by Step 3.7 describes how to configure the Internet Protocol (TCP/IP) Properties.

STEP BY STEP

3.7 Configuring a Windows XP Professional DNS Client Computer

1. Log on to a Windows XP Professional DNS client computer using the Administrator account or another account that has administrator privileges.
2. Open the Control Panel and double-click the Network Connections applet. The Network Connections window appears, as seen in Figure 3.39.

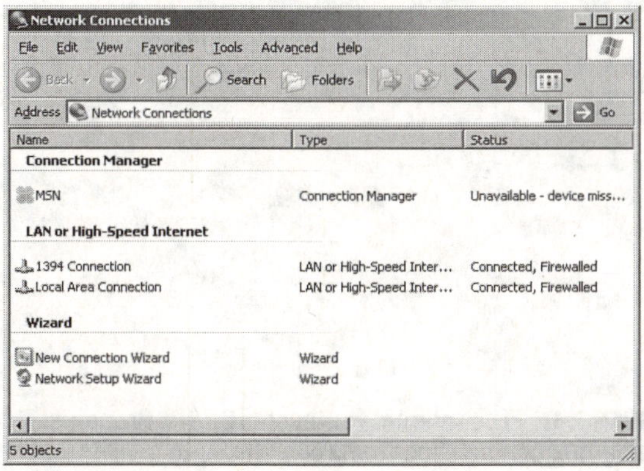

FIGURE 3.39 The Network Connections window allows you to see all the configured connections on the client workstation, including both LAN and dial-up connections.

3. Right-click the Local Area Connection icon and select Properties from the context menu. The Local Area Connection Properties dialog box appears, as seen in Figure 3.40.

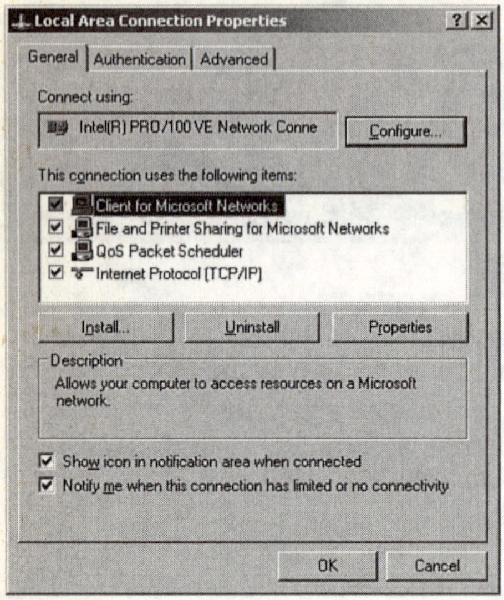

FIGURE 3.40 The local area connection properties include all the protocols and services configured to run on this connection.

4. Select Internet Protocol (TCP/IP) and click the Properties button. You can accomplish the same effect by double-clicking the Internet Protocol (TCP/IP) entry. The Internet Protocol (TCP/IP) Properties dialog box appears, as seen in Figure 3.41.

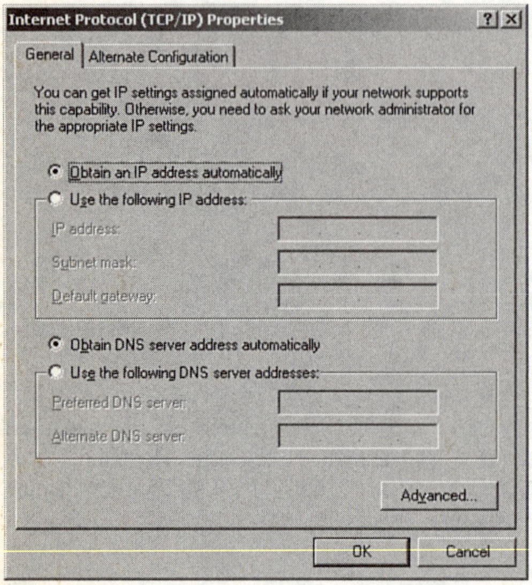

FIGURE 3.41 The Internet Protocol (TCP/IP) Properties dialog box can be used to make changes to a TCP/IP configuration, including not only DNS, but also DHCP, WINS, and even TCP/IP filters.

5. In the bottom section of the Internet Protocol (TCP/IP) Properties dialog box, you can choose to have DNS configured automatically via DHCP or specify the preferred and alternate DNS servers. Click Advanced for additional DNS options. The Advanced TCP/IP Settings dialog box appears. Select the DNS tab to see the DNS options shown in Figure 3.42.

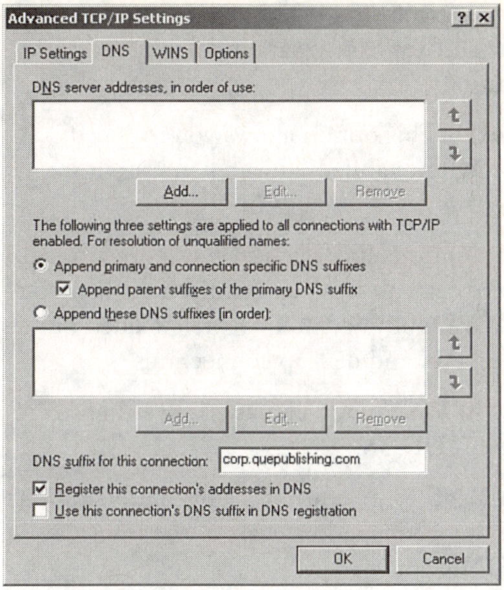

FIGURE 3.42 The DNS tab of the Advanced TCP/IP Settings dialog box is where you can control how the client will interact with the Windows Server 2003 DNS server(s).

6. In the Advanced TCP/IP Settings dialog box, you can configure several DNS client computer settings. In this case, leave the default settings. By default, Windows XP Professional is configured to register with DNS. You control this setting by selecting or deselecting the Register This Connection's Addresses in DNS option. You can also select Use This Connection's DNS Suffix in DNS Registration, but this option is useful only if your system is part of a different domain than the one in which you are registering. You might use this option if you travel frequently and want to ensure that your system's DNS registration name is consistent.
7. Click OK to return to the Internet Protocol (TCP/IP) Properties dialog box, and then click OK to return to the Local Area Connection Properties dialog box. Last, click OK to close the Local Area Connection Properties dialog box and put unapplied changes into effect.

A number of advanced TCP/IP options can be configured in the Advanced TCP/IP Settings dialog box in conjunction with the DNS client computer. They include the following:

- DNS server addresses, in order of use.
- Parameters for resolving unqualified domain names. An unqualified domain name is one is that is simply supplied as "host", such as `fileserver042`, and not fully qualified, such as `fileserver042.corp.quepublishing.com`. The options include the following:
  - **Append Primary and Connection-Specific DNS Suffixes**—This option appends the domain suffixes configured in the System Properties dialog box to any unqualified domain names sent for resolution.

- **Append Parent Suffixes of the Primary DNS Suffix**—This option adds not only the specified domain suffixes, but also the suffixes of any parent domains to any unqualified domain names sent for resolution.
- **Append These DNS Suffixes (In Order)**—This option allows you to specify specific DNS suffixes to be appended to any unqualified domain names sent for resolution.
- **DNS Suffix for This Connection**—This option allows you to configure a specific DNS suffix for this connection in the Network and Dial-up Connections list. You can specify different suffixes in case you have multiple LAN adapters loaded or you want to use different suffixes between the LAN and dial-up connections.
- **Register This Connection's Addresses in DNS**—You can use this setting to configure the computer to take advantage of DDNS.
- **Use This Connection's DNS Suffix in DNS Registration**—This option allows you to use the DNS suffix specified with this connection as part of the information used when the host is registered with DDNS.

NOTE

What If I'm Using Windows 2000 Professional? The steps for configuring DNS registration on a client system have not changed in Windows XP—they are the same steps used in Windows 2000. If you know these steps in one operating system, you know them for both.

NOTE

Append These DNS Suffixes Although you can enter in additional DNS suffixes manually on the Advanced TCP/IP Settings DNS tab, it's worth noting that this configuration is usually best made by using Group Policy.

To modify the DNS settings in the System Properties dialog box, follow the procedure outlined in Step by Step 3.8.

STEP BY STEP

3.8 Modifying the DNS Settings for Active Directory Integration

1. Right-click the My Computer icon on the desktop. From the context menu, select Properties.
2. Select the Computer Name tab, as seen in Figure 3.43.

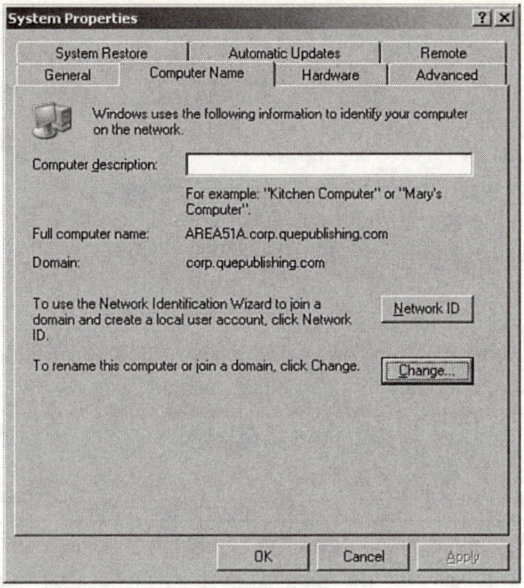

FIGURE 3.43 The Computer Name tab of the System Properties dialog box can be used to configure not only the computer name, but also a description and domain or workgroup membership.

3. From the Computer Name tab, click the Change button. The Computer Name Changes dialog box appears, as seen in Figure 3.44.

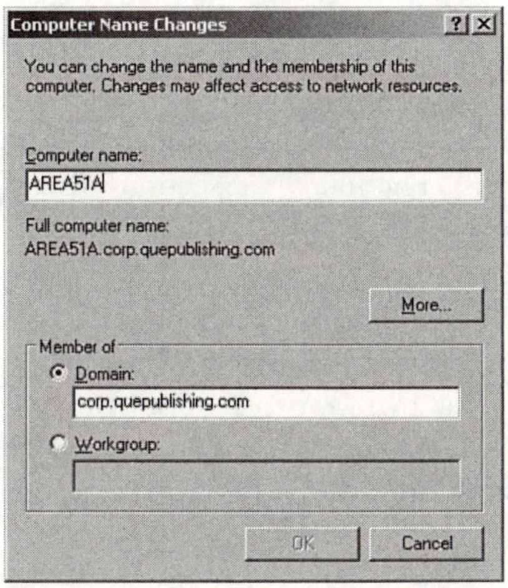

FIGURE 3.44 From this screen, you can change the name and domain membership of the computer.

4. Click More, and the DNS Suffix and NetBIOS Computer Name dialog box appears as seen in Figure 3.45. Change the DNS domain name if needed (for example, `corp.quepublishing.com`). Checking the Change Primary DNS Suffix When Domain Membership Changes option ensures that the host's DNS domain matches its Active Directory domain.

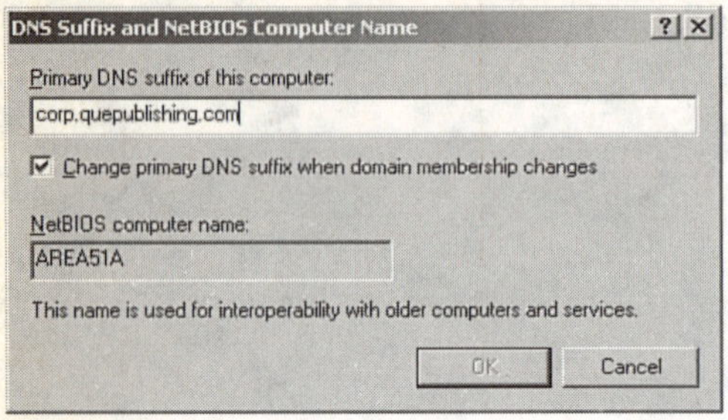

FIGURE 3.45 This dialog box allows you to set a DNS domain to append to the computer name as well as to configure how the DNS settings should behave when the computer logs in to Active Directory.

5. Click OK to save the changes. Click OK to return to the System Properties dialog box. Click OK twice to close the System Properties dialog box. When you are prompted to reboot the computer, do so.

NOTE

Default DNS Suffix By default, you should never need to change the primary DNS suffix of a Windows XP or 2000 Professional computer in an Active Directory domain. You will not need to change it because the default primary DNS suffix is the local primary DNS suffix, which is the DNS name of the Active Directory domain to which the computer is joined. Configuring the DNS suffix as seen in Step by Step 3.8 is an advanced configuration action. It's worth noting that the primary DNS suffix can also be controlled through Group Policy.

Testing the DNS Service

How can you test to make sure DNS is working? Several methods (`ping`, `nslookup`, or a Web browser) allow you to quickly check whether DNS is working. The following sections discuss them in order of complexity.

Using `ping` to Test the DNS Service

The first application for testing DNS is the `ping` utility. `ping`, as discussed in detail in Chapter 1, "Configuring and Troubleshooting TCP/IP Addressing," allows you to send an Internet Control Message Protocol (ICMP) message to a TCP/IP host. If you use the correct flag with it, `ping` can also perform name resolution as part of its testing procedure. The correct syntax for the `ping` command is the following:

```
ping <destination address>
```

A sample `ping` session might look like this:

```
ping ptgdc01.corp.quepublishing.com
Pinging ptgdc01.corp.quepublishing.com [192.168.0.155] with 32 bytes of data:
Reply from 192.168.0.155: bytes=32 time<1ms TTL=128
```

```
Reply from 192.168.0.155: bytes=32 time<1ms TTL=128
Reply from 192.168.0.155: bytes=32 time<1ms TTL=128
Reply from 192.168.0.155: bytes=32 time<1ms TTL=128
Ping statistics for 192.168.0.155:
      Packets: Sent = 4, Received = 4, Lost = 0 (0% loss),
Approximate round trip times in milli-seconds:
      Minimum = 0ms, Maximum = 0ms, Average = 0ms
```

A number of other switches can be used with the `ping` utility, as described in Chapter 1.

From the earlier example, you can see several things. First, because your `ping` returns the IP address 192.168.0.155, you know that DNS is functional. The rest of the information has to do with network latency and has little application for this chapter.

Using `nslookup` to Test the DNS Service

The next utility we need to look at is `nslookup`. `nslookup` is a standard command-line tool that is provided in most DNS server implementations, including Windows Server 2003. `nslookup` offers the capability to perform query testing of DNS servers and obtain detailed responses at the command prompt. This information can be useful for diagnosing and solving name resolution problems, for verifying that resource records are added or updated correctly in a zone, and for debugging other server-related problems.

You can use `nslookup` by typing **`nslookup`** at a command prompt and pressing Enter. You can run `nslookup` with the options listed in Table 3.3. In the table, identifiers are shown in uppercase and each [ ] indicates an optional parameter.

> **NOTE**
>
> **Displaying `nslookup` Options** You can display these options by typing **`nslookup`** at a command prompt, typing **?** at the interactive prompt, and then pressing Enter.

TABLE 3.3 Interactive `nslookup` Options

Option	Description
NAME	Prints information about the host/domain name using the default server.
NAME1 NAME2	Like NAME, but uses NAME2 as the server.
`help or ?`	Prints information on common commands.
`set` *OPTION*	Sets an option.
`all`	Prints options for the current server and host.
`[no]debug`	Prints debugging information.
`[no]d2`	Prints exhaustive debugging information.
`[no]defname`	Appends the domain name to each query.

(continues)

TABLE 3.3 Continued

Option	Description
`[no]recurse`	Asks for a recursive answer to a query.
`[no]search`	Uses a domain search list.
`[no]vc`	Specifies to always use a virtual circuit.
`domain=`*NAME*	Sets the default domain name to NAME.
`srchlist=`*N1*`[`*/N2/.../N6*`]`	Sets the domain to N1 and search list to N1, N2, and so on.
`root=`*NAME*	Sets the root server to NAME.
`retry=`*X*	Sets the number of retries to X.
`timeout=`*X*	Sets the initial timeout interval to X seconds.
`type=`*X*	Sets the query type (for example, A, ANY, CNAME, MX, NS, PTR, SOA, or SRV).
`querytype=`*X*	Sets the query type (for example, A, ANY, CNAME, MX, NS, PTR, SOA, or SRV).
`class=`*X*	Sets the query class (for example, `IN [Internet]`, ANY).
`[no]msxfr`	Uses Microsoft fast zone transfer.
`ixfrver=`*X*	Specifies the current version to use in `IXFR` transfer request.
`server` *NAME*	Sets the default server to NAME, using the current default server.
`lserver` *NAME*	Sets the default server to NAME, using the initial server.
`finger [`*USER*`]`	Fingers the optional NAME at the current default host.
`root`	Sets the current default server to the root.
`ls [opt]` *DOMAIN* `[>` *FILE*`]`	Lists addresses in `DOMAIN` (optional: output to `FILE`).
`-a`	Lists canonical names and aliases.
`-d`	Lists all records.
`-t` *TYPE*	Lists records of the given type (for example, A, CNAME, MX, NS, or PTR).
`view` *FILE*	Sorts an `ls` output file and views it with pg.
`exit`	Exits the program.

EXAM ALERT

Knowing `nslookup` **Because `nslookup` is the standard tool for troubleshooting DNS, you should be familiar with its capabilities and options for the exam. Also, be sure to remember that `nslookup` will not function correctly without properly configured and operating reverse lookup zones.**

NOTE

Knowing the `nslookup` Modes You should be familiar with the fact that `nslookup` functions in both interactive and noninteractive modes. You use noninteractive mode when you need only a single piece of information.

If you are not familiar with `nslookup`, the options just described are probably clear as mud. The best way to get a thorough understanding of the `nslookup` options and flags is to try them out. However, for a simple test of DNS using `nslookup`, select a hostname you know is in DNS and type the following:

```
nslookup ptgdc01.corp.quepublishing.com
```

This command returns the following:

```
Server:    ptgdc01.corp.quepublishing.com
Address:    192.168.0.155
Name:       ptgdc01.corp.quepublishing.com
Address:    192.168.0.155
```

In this example, you used the name of the DNS server for the test. You can use any host in the DNS table. The first name and address returned are the name and address for the DNS server you are querying. If this server does not have a PTR record in a reverse lookup zone, the server name is returned, along with the following message:

```
***Can't find server name for address (address of configured DNS server): Timed out
```

This does not mean anything is broken; it just means there is no reverse lookup zone configured or no reverse lookup zone entry for this server. If you still get name resolution in the Name/Address section of the response, the DNS server is working.

NOTE

`nslookup` Is Now on the Menu If you right-click the server in the DNS console, you'll see that Launch `nslookup` is now one of the options. This helps you identify and use available management/testing tools.

Using a Web Browser to Test the DNS Service

A final method for testing a DNS server is to use a Web browser such as Internet Explorer. You type the FQDN you want to reach into the Address box and press Enter. If DNS is working correctly, the IP address is displayed in the lower-left corner of the application. This occurs even if the host in question is not a Web server. The browser may not connect successfully, but you should see that resolution if DNS is configured correctly.

Challenge

You are the network administrator for NR Widgets, Inc., a multinational conglomerate, and you are based in the conglomerate's corporate headquarters. NR Widgets, Inc., is made up of three companies: NR Manufacturing, NR Consulting, and NR Telecommunications. Each company has its own IT department and maintains its own network infrastructure. Each company also has its own DNS domain.

You have been asked to prepare the network for a complete Windows Server 2003 rollout, which includes both client computers and servers, with the goal of having a purely Windows Server 2003 and Windows XP Professional network. The first thing on your list is to implement a Windows Server 2003–capable DNS infrastructure.

Through your discussions with the key stakeholders in this project, you've determined the following requirements for the deployment:

- Each IT department controls its own domain.
- Each company's users must have the fastest possible resolution for other companies' hosts.
- The users in the headquarters facility need fast DNS resolution for each of the company's hosts.
- Headquarters is a not a computing center, so it will not maintain any primary DNS servers.

Your task is to implement the required DNS solution for NR Widgets, Inc.

Try to complete this exercise on your own, listing your conclusions on a sheet of paper. After you have completed the exercise, compare your results to those given here.

Answers

Obviously, you need to install the required DNS servers in the required locations. As well, you would have been best off to implement this solution concurrently with the Active Directory implementation for the network, since you should strive to use Active Directory–integrated zones as much as possible. However, because that was not part of the problem definition you received, you should plan to proceed using standard DNS zones, which can be converted to Active Directory–integrated zones later.

You should roll out the new Windows Server 2003 DNS servers in the following manner:

- First, each company gets the primary DNS server for its own domain. This gives it control of its DNS domain. For redundancy, each company should also have a secondary master server.
- To allow each company to quickly resolve addresses for the other companies, each company's DNS servers should also be configured with stub zones pointing to the other company's DNS servers. This will allow users in either company to quickly get name resolution without the burden of managing additional secondary zones.
- Corporate headquarters needs a caching-only server that is configured to receive cache updates from the other DNS servers on the network. Another possibility is to set up a DNS server that acts as a secondary master to the three company domains.
- Finally, all DNS servers should be set to accept dynamic updates. This is a requirement in the environment that was detailed to you.

Integrating Active Directory and DNS

Throughout this chapter, we've been working with standard DNS zones on a Windows Server 2003 member server—a server that is not a Domain Controller. While there is nothing wrong (at a basic level) with this configuration and implementation of the Windows Server 2003 DNS service, to fully utilize the power and flexibility, you should use Active Directory–integrated DNS. Active Directory–integrated DNS offers several performance enhancements and is inherently more secure. Recall that the Security tab in the server Properties dialog box is unavailable for standard DNS servers; it is available only when DNS is running on a Domain Controller. Likewise, the Security tab in the zone Properties dialog box is available only when a zone is configured as Active Directory–integrated and running on a Domain Controller. Additionally, only when using Active Directory–integrated zones will you be able to configure Secure dynamic updates.

EXAM ALERT

Securely Implementing DNS Using Windows Server 2003 Active Directory is more secure than a flat file, and updates and zone transfers occur as part of Active Directory replication activities, which are encrypted. As a result, an Active Directory–integrated zone is the most secure DNS implementation possible.

Configuring Existing Zones for Active Directory Integration

If you have DNS running on your Domain Controller and have zones created, but have not created any Active Directory–integrated zones, then it is fairly painless to make the integration occur. Step by Step 3.9 presents the process you should follow.

NOTE

Getting into the Zone If you completed Step by Steps 3.2, 3.5, and 3.6 on a DNS server that was running on a Domain Controller and did not integrate the zones into Active Directory, then you can proceed directly into Step by Step 3.9. If you need to create a new standard primary zone on your DNS server that is running on a Domain Controller, then repeat Step by Step 3.5 and create a primary zone named `development.quepublishing.com`. In Step by Step 3.9, we use that zone, although you can use the previous `publishing.quepublishing.com` zone if it meets the requirements discussed.

STEP BY STEP

3.9 Changing Zone Replication and Dynamic Update Configuration

1. Log on to Windows Server 2003 using the Administrator account or another account that has administrator privileges.

2. Open the DNS console by selecting Start, Control Panel, Administrative Tools, DNS.

3. Select the zone to be configured, right-click it, and select Properties from the context menu. The zone Properties dialog box opens to the General tab, as seen in Figure 3.46.

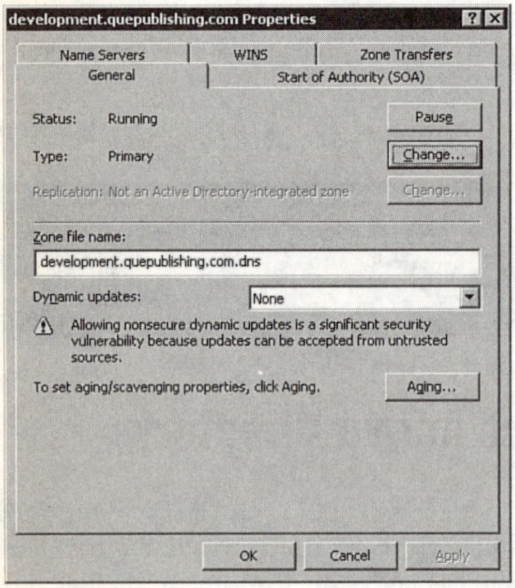

FIGURE 3.46 You will change the zone replication and dynamic update configuration from the General tab of the zone Properties dialog.

4. Click the Change button in the Type area of the General tab to open the Change Zone Type dialog box, as seen in Figure 3.47.

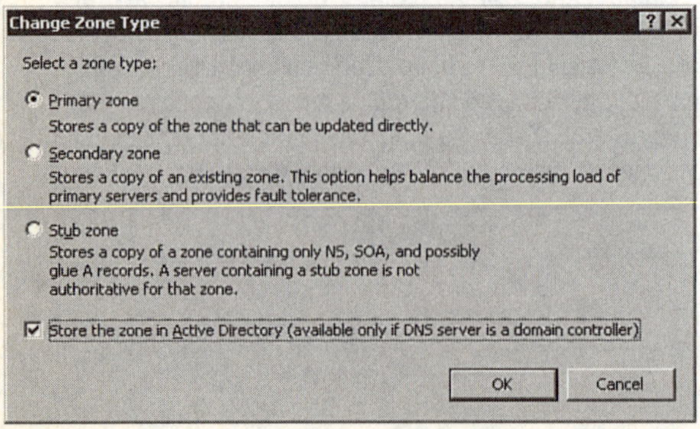

FIGURE 3.47 The configuration change to Active Directory–integrated requires only one check box to be clicked.

5. Click the Store the Zone in Active Directory check box and click OK to accept the configuration change. You will be prompted to confirm that you really want to make the change; click Yes to make the change.
6. The General tab of the zone Properties dialog box will now reflect the change you've made and allow you to configure the replication scope of the zone, as seen in Figure 3.48.

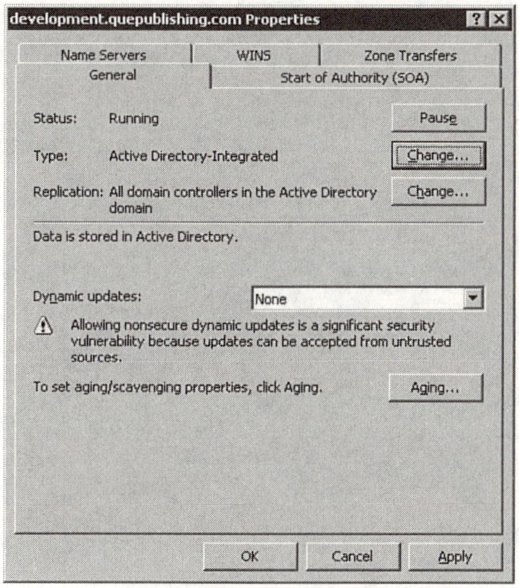

FIGURE 3.48 Note the changes to the General tab of the zone Properties after changing the zone to Active Directory–integrated.

7. To change the replication scope of the zone, click the Change button in the Replication section of the General tab. The Change Zone Replication Scope dialog box opens, as seen in Figure 3.49.

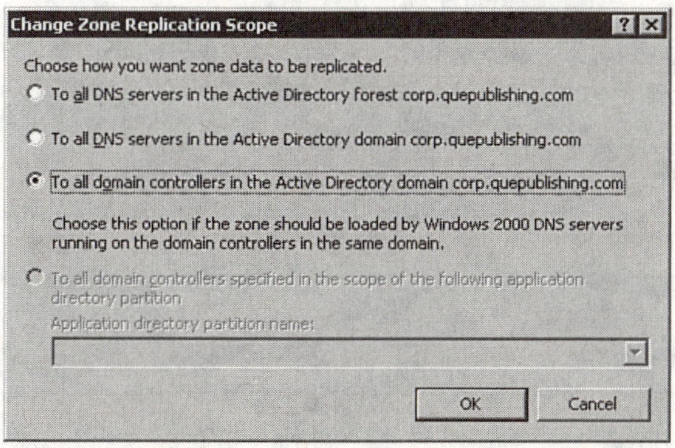

FIGURE 3.49 You can configure how the zone is replicated in your Active Directory environment.

8. The option to replicate the zone to all Domain Controllers in the domain is usually the best option. Click OK to close the Change Zone Replication Scope dialog box.

9. The last configuration you need to make is to configure to allow only Secure dynamic updates from the Dynamic updates drop-down list. After this has been completed and applied, your zone settings should look like those seen in Figure 3.50.

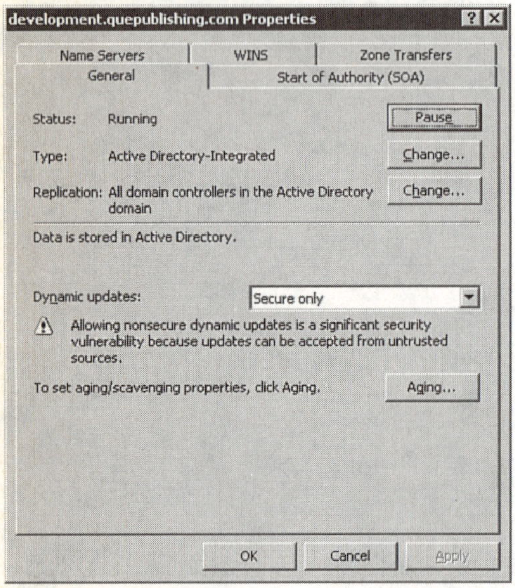

Figure 3.50 This zone is now configured for optimal operation.

EXAM ALERT

About Secure Dynamic Updates When you enable Secure dynamic updates on a DNS zone, this results in a situation where there can be only one owner for a resource record, and only that one owner can update that resource record. Obviously this is an unacceptable and impossible condition when you may have multiple DHCP servers that are trying to register host (A) records on behalf of clients that cannot perform the action themselves since the DHCP server registering the record becomes the owner of that record.

Without some other provision in place, only the DHCP server that originally registered the record could update the record in the future; thus, problems would soon ensue in your DNS zones. To avoid this problem, all authorized DHCP servers should be added to the `DnsUpdateProxy` security group. The servers that are a member of this special security group are blocked from recording ownership on any resource records they create or update in DNS. Since no ownership information is recorded on the record, any other DHCP server on your network can then make changes to that record as required.

You should realize, however, that this solution does decrease the security offered by enforcing only secure dynamic updates because there is no owner specified for these records. Windows 2000 and Windows XP client computers will not cause this problem because they can register their own A records without any assistance from the DHCP server. As a new feature, you should expect to see a question relating to the `DnsUpdateProxy` security group on your 70-291 exam.

Creating New Active Directory–Integrated Zones

If you want to create a brand new Active Directory–integrated zone, you can do that easily enough. To complete that process, follow the steps outlined in Step by Step 3.10, which is very similar to the steps you completed previously in Step by Step 3.5.

STEP BY STEP

3.10 Creating and Configuring a New Active Directory–Integrated Zone

1. Log on to Windows Server 2003 using the Administrator account or another account that has administrator privileges.
2. Open the DNS console by selecting Start, Control Panel, Administrative Tools, DNS. Right-click the Forward Lookup Zones container and select New Zone from the context menu. The Welcome to the New Zone Wizard appears. Click Next to dismiss the Wizard's opening page and continue to the Zone Type screen, which was shown in Figure 3.23.
3. Select Primary zone to make this DNS server authoritative for the zone you are creating. Also ensure that you select the check box to make the zone Active Directory–integrated. Click Next to continue to the Active Directory Zone Replication Scope page, as seen in Figure 3.51.

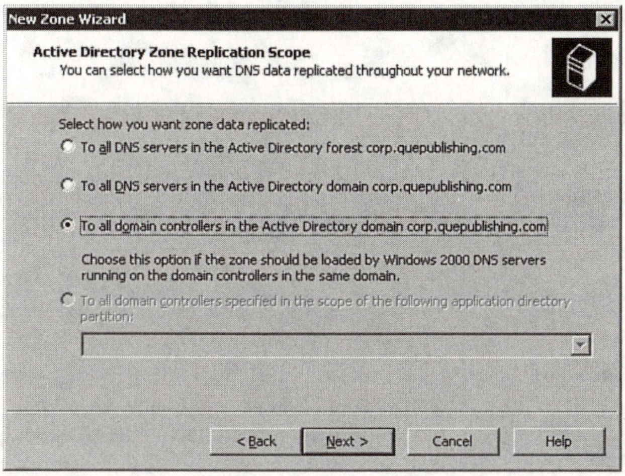

FIGURE 3.51 You'll get to configure how the zone is replicated this time.

4. Typically, you'll be fine selecting the To All Domain Controllers in the Domain option. Make your selection and click Next to continue to the Zone Name screen, as was shown in Figure 3.24.
5. Enter the name of the domain for which you will be resolving names into the Zone Name field. In this example, I'm using marketing.quepublishing.com, but you can use something else if you like. Click Next and the Dynamic Update screen appears, as seen in Figure 3.52.

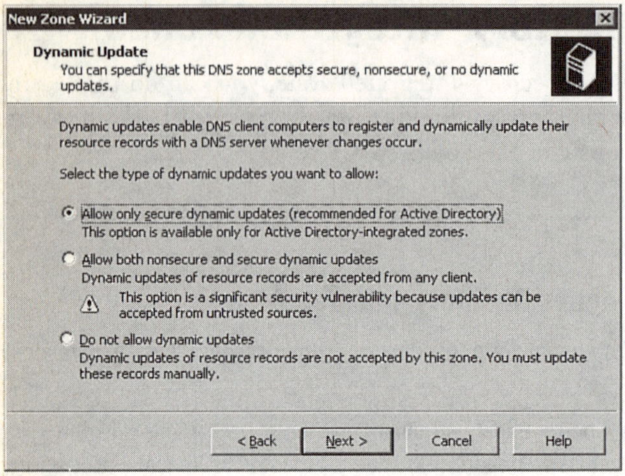

FIGURE 3.52 You'll also get to configure how dynamic updates to the zone are handled.

6. On the Dynamic Update screen, select Only Allow Secure Dynamic Updates. After making your selection, click Next. The Completing the New Zone Wizard dialog box appears, as seen in Figure 3.53. This screen allows you to review the configurations you selected and either go back to correct mistakes or cancel the wizard before the changes are committed.

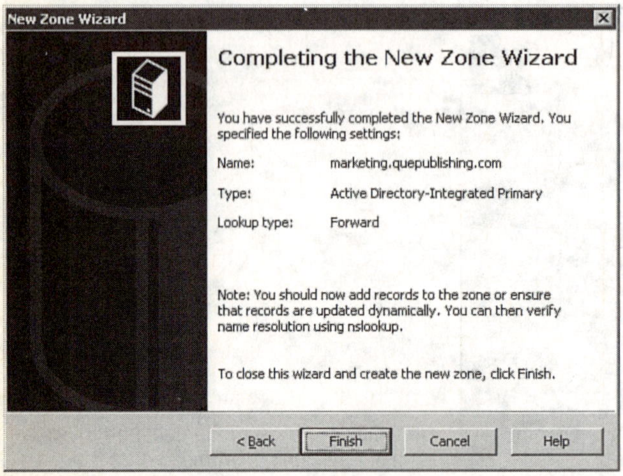

FIGURE 3.53 You need to double-check your information before committing the changes you just made.

7. Click Finish to complete the configuration. Notice that the zone that was configured by the wizard now appears in the DNS console.

The DNS and Active Directory Relationship

To this point, we've discussed DNS in detail, including how to integrate DNS into Active Directory. As you've no doubt noticed, DNS is an important network service. Active Directory, as you've also likely noticed by now, is the heart and soul of a Windows Server 2003 network infrastructure. Thus, it only stands to reason that Active Directory cannot function without a reliable and functional DNS implementation in place.

Here are some key points that emphasize the importance of DNS to Active Directory:

- Without a properly working DNS infrastructure, Domain Controllers will not be able to replicate information about the domain among themselves.
- Without a properly working DNS infrastructure, Windows 2000 and Windows XP client computers will experience long logon times or possibly the inability to log on at all.
- Without a properly working DNS infrastructure, Exchange Server 2003 and Exchange 2000 Server will not be able to work, and servers will likely fail to start critical services properly.

Of course, the list goes on, but the failures mentioned are some of the more important ones—ones that will likely bring your Active Directory domain to its knees. In short, without DNS, you won't have an Active Directory implementation.

Managing and Monitoring DNS

Objective:

Install and configure the DNS Server service.

- Configure DNS server options.
- Configure DNS zone options.

Manage DNS.

- Manage DNS record settings.

Monitor DNS. Tools might include System Monitor, Event Viewer, Replication Monitor, and DNS debug logs.

Now that you know how to install, configure, and create entries for zones, you need to understand how to manage and monitor the DNS server. If your job is typical of most, you will spend a great deal more time managing DNS servers than installing them.

Although the DNS server doesn't include any specific monitoring capabilities, you should be aware of a number of additional options as you manage your DNS server over the long term. One utility that is very useful for managing the DNS server is the DNS snap-in to the MMC, which is listed as DNS in the Administrative Tools menu.

Capabilities of the DNS Console

To take a closer look at the capabilities of the DNS console, open the DNS console. Then, select the DNS server and select the Action menu to see these available actions:

- **Set Aging/Scavenging for All Zones**—Opens the Server Aging/Scavenging Properties dialog box.
- **Scavenge Stale Resource Records Manually**—Allows the manual removal of outdated or incorrect DNS entries.
- **All Tasks**—Includes tasks such as starting, stopping, pausing, resuming, and restarting the DNS server service.
- **Delete**—Deletes the DNS server.
- **Refresh**—Causes all the displayed information to be refreshed for the current status.
- **Export List**—Exports the information from the DNS server to a tab- or comma-delimited text or Unicode text file.
- **Properties**—Opens the Properties dialog box for the selected DNS server, as discussed earlier in this chapter.

The following sections take a closer look at several of these actions.

Configuring Aging/Scavenging

Aging and scavenging of resource records will be important to you if you have clients that come and go from your network or have clients that have IP address changes. In reality, that statement describes almost 100 percent of all networks that use DNS today, so aging and scavenging are useful for almost every DNS implementation to help keep records clean and up to date. By default, aging and scavenging are not enabled or configured on a newly installed Windows Server 2003 DNS server, so you'll need to perform those tasks yourself or run the risk of slowly poisoning your DNS information with outdated and conflicting resource records.

In terms of DNS, *aging* is the process of placing a timestamp on a dynamically created resource record and then tracking the age of that record. *Scavenging*, in DNS, is the process of deleting any resource records that have timestamps on them that are found to be outdated. As a result, scavenging can occur only when aging has also been enabled and properly configured. In order for aging and scavenging to work correctly, they must be configured on the DNS server and also on any zones residing on that DNS server for which you want aging and scavenging to occur.

NOTE

Not Backwards Compatible Once you enable and configure aging and scavenging on a zone, only Windows Server 2003 and Windows 2000 Server DNS servers will be able to read the zone.

To enable aging and scavenging for a server, complete the steps outlined in Step by Step 3.11.

STEP BY STEP

3.11 Configuring a Server for Aging and Scavenging

1. Log on to Windows Server 2003 using the Administrator account or another account that has administrator privileges.
2. Open the DNS console by selecting Start, Control Panel, Administrative Tools, DNS.
3. Right-click the DNS server for which you want to configure aging and scavenging and select Set Aging/Scavenging for All Zones to open the Server Aging/Scavenging Properties dialog box, as seen in Figure 3.54.

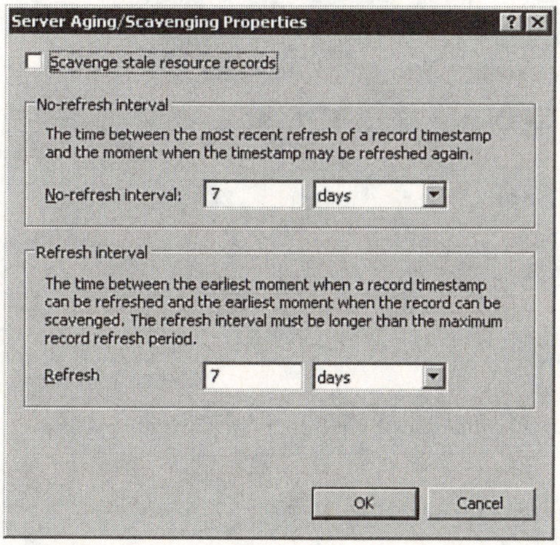

FIGURE 3.54 By default, aging and scavenging are disabled in Windows Server 2003 DNS.

4. Enable aging and scavenging by selecting the Scavenge stale resource records option. If desired, you can change the No-refresh and Refresh intervals (explained in the list below), although the defaults will work fine in most cases. After making your selection, click OK to confirm it.

   - **No-refresh Interval**—This option controls the time between the most recent refresh of a record's time stamp and when the time stamp can be refreshed again. In a very busy network where computers come on and leave frequently, you might want to lower this from the default, which is 7 days.

   - **Refresh Interval**—This option sets the time between the earliest moment that a record time stamp can be refreshed and the earliest moment a record can be scavenged.

5. The Server Aging/Scavenging Confirmation dialog box appears as seen in Figure 3.55. If you want to enable the same configuration on all of your Active Directory–integrated zones, which is usually the best choice, then select the Apply These Settings option and click OK to apply your settings at the server and zone level.

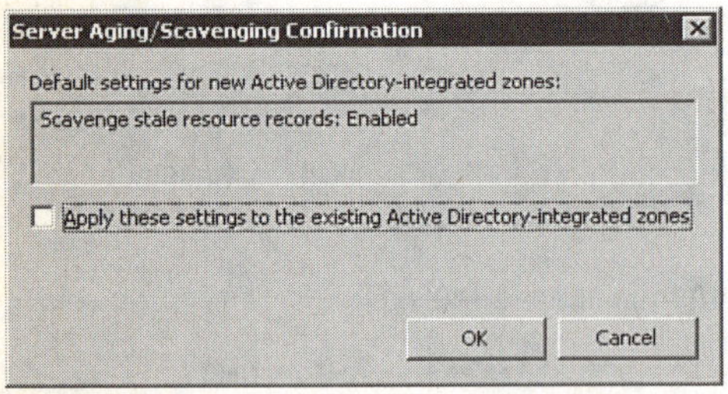

Figure 3.55 You can quickly and easily apply your aging and scavenging settings to all Active Directory–integrated zones.

If the server on which you configured aging and scavenging contains any standard zones, you will now need to configure aging and scavenging on them manually. Likewise, if you did not allow the configuration to be applied to your existing Active Directory–integrated zones, as seen in Figure 3.55, then you'll need to configure aging and scavenging manually on them as well. Step by Step 3.12 presents this process.

STEP BY STEP

3.12 Configuring a Zone for Aging and Scavenging

1. Log on to Windows Server 2003 using the Administrator account or another account that has administrator privileges.

2. Open the DNS console by selecting Start, Control Panel, Administrative Tools, DNS.

3. Right-click the DNS zone for which you want to configure aging and scavenging and select Set Properties from the context menu to open the zone Properties dialog box, which was seen in Figure 3.50.

4. Click the Aging…button to open the Zone Aging/Scavenging Properties dialog box, as seen in Figure 3.56.

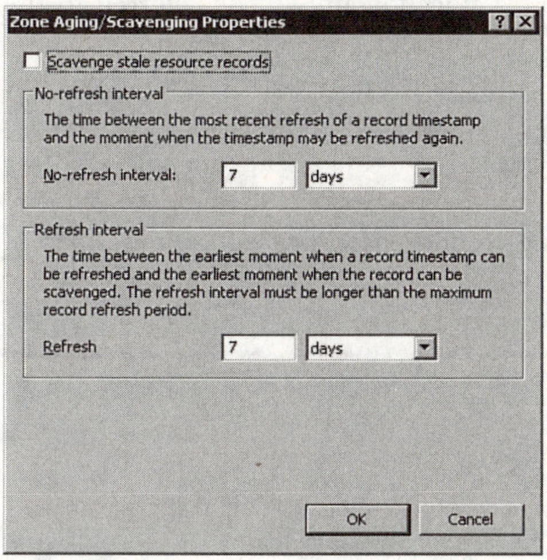

FIGURE 3.56 Aging and scavenging are configured manually for standard DNS zones.

5. Enable aging and scavenging by selecting the Scavenge Stale Resource Records option. If desired, you can change the No-refresh and Refresh intervals, although the defaults will work fine in most cases. After making your selection, click OK to confirm it.
6. You will now be warned about the fact that making these changes to your zone will render it incompatible with older DNS servers, as previously mentioned. Click Yes to apply the aging and scavenging configuration to the zone.

Scavenging Stale Resource Records Manually

You can force scavenging of stale resource records by right-clicking a server and selecting the Scavenge Stale Resource Records Manually option from the context menu. Selecting this option manually removes any out-of-date resource records. When you choose this option, the Update Server Data Files option writes to the server's hard drive any changes to the table that are in RAM. To clear the server cache manually, you will need to right-click the DNS server and select Clear Cache from the context menu.

Implementing Delegated Zones for DNS

You can create a delegated zone for DNS, whereby you assign responsibility for a specific subdomain within the DNS namespace to another entity. Typically, this translates into your delegating responsibility for one or more child subdomains in your DNS namespace (which are usually mapped directly to your Active Directory organization) to another group or branch within your organization.

When you delegate a domain, DNS queries on the existing domain will be referred to the name server in the delegated domain for resolution. You can delegate only down the hierarchy, so the delegated domain must be a subdomain of the domain doing the delegation. For example, the domain `marketing.quepublishing.com` can delegate resolution for the domain `it.marketing.quepublishing.com` to another server, but `it.marketing.quepublishing.com` cannot delegate up the DNS hierarchy by delegating for the `marketing.quepublishing.com` domain. This might be a little confusing, but the configuration procedure, described in Step by Step 3.13, should make it a little clearer.

STEP BY STEP

3.13 Creating a Delegated Zone

1. Log on to Windows Server 2003 using the Administrator account or another account that has administrator privileges.
2. Open the DNS console by selecting Start, Control Panel, Administrative Tools, DNS.
3. Right-click the DNS zone in which you would like to create a delegated domain, and from the context menu, select New Delegation. The New Delegation Wizard appears; click Next to dismiss the opening page and continue. The Delegated Domain Name dialog box appears, as seen in Figure 3.57.

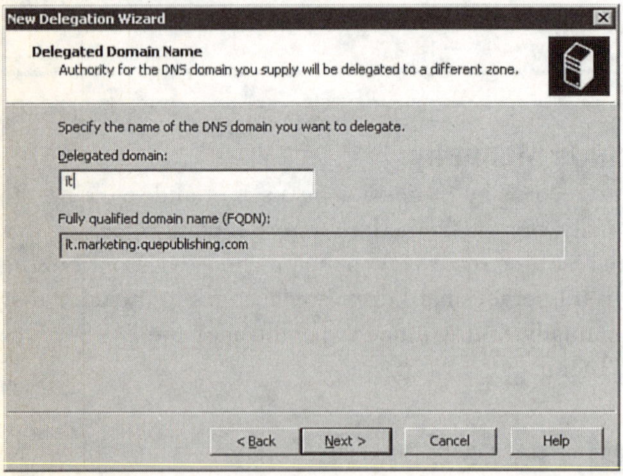

FIGURE 3.57 The Delegated Domain Name screen lets you name and create the subdomain for which you are creating the delegation.

4. In the Delegated Domain Name screen, enter the unqualified name for the domain to which you want to delegate (that is, the name of the subdomain you want to create) in the Delegated Domain field. For example, you can use `IT` for the domain name. Notice that it is carried into the Fully Qualified Domain

Name (FQDN) field. Click Next to continue. The Name Servers dialog box appears, as seen in Figure 3.58.

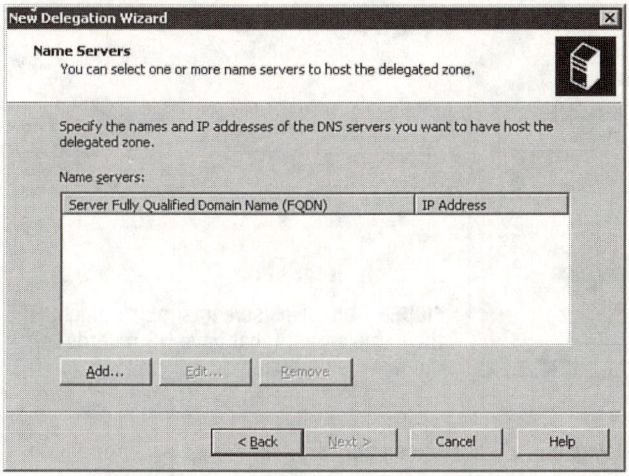

FIGURE 3.58 The name server or servers to which you are delegating the domain can exist in any domain but are typically located in the domain in which the subdomain is being created.

5. In the Name Servers dialog box, click Add, and the New Resource Record dialog box appears, as seen in Figure 3.59. When you delegate a zone, you must first configure the Name Server (NS) record for the new domain. You can do this either by browsing to the name server in Active Directory or specifying it by name or IP address. After you have filled in the IP address field, click Add to add the server to your NS record list. Click OK to return to the Name Servers dialog box, as seen in Figure 3.60. Note that your new DNS server appears on the list.

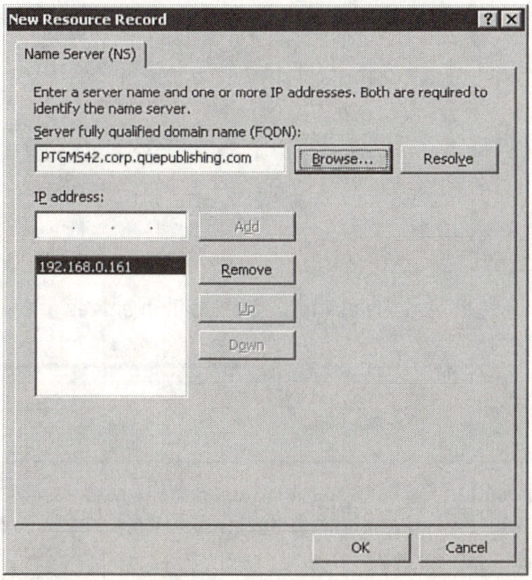

FIGURE 3.59 You need to test to be sure that the new name server's name can be resolved if you enter it manually.

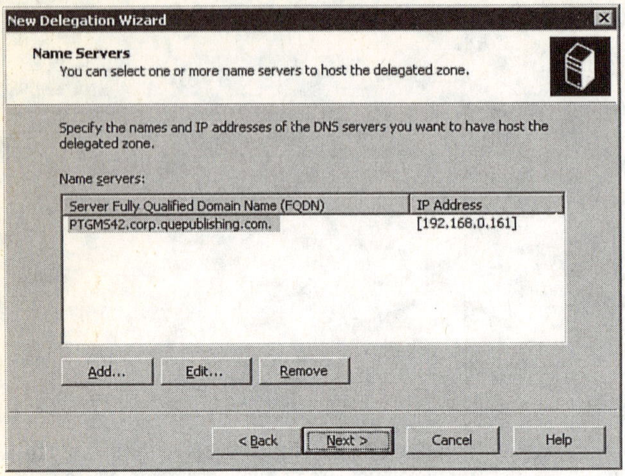

FIGURE 3.60 This screen should contain all the name servers that have NS records for the new subdomain you are creating.

6. Click Next, and the Completing the New Delegation Wizard screen appears. Verify that the information shown on this screen is correct. To complete the wizard and create the new domain, click Finish. You should see the newly created subdomain listed under the existing domain in the DNS console, as seen in Figure 3.61.

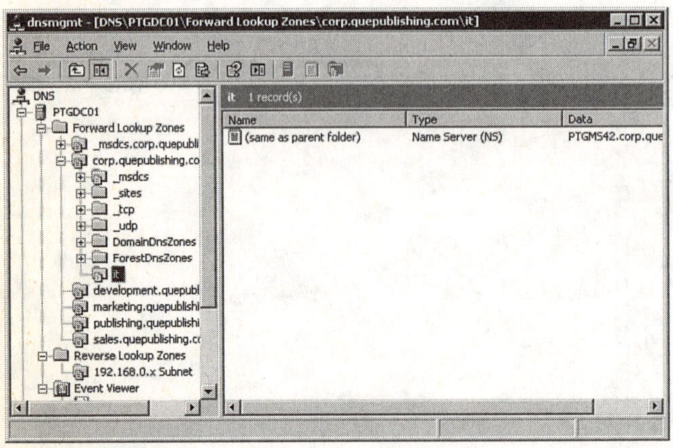

FIGURE 3.61 You need to visually ensure that the domain you create and the associated delegation entries are installed correctly.

NOTE

Names for a Record When you create a record, you can use the FQDN or just the hostname. If you use just the hostname, the rest of the FQDN for the domain in which you are creating the entry will automatically be appended.

Manually Creating DNS Resource Records

We've spent most of this chapter looking at the dynamic methods for creating entries in the DNS zone. Now let's look at how to manually create an entry. You might use this method for non-Windows Server 2003 hosts, table entry types that are not supported by DDNS, or hosts that you just want to configure with a static entry. For example, if your company's server naming convention is based on server location and purpose, a Web server for Que Publishing located in New York City might be named `nycweb001`, which would make its dynamic entry `nycweb001.publishing.quepublishing.com`. If you wanted people to be able to go to www.quepublishing.com, you would create a manual entry in DNS to allow users to access the server using the more common naming convention. When you manually create a DNS entry, you have these four options:

- **New Host**—This creates an A record.
- **New Alias**—This creates a CNAME record.
- **New Mail Exchanger**—This creates an MX record.
- **Other New Records**—This allows you to select the other record types.

Next you will create a new host record. To manually create a DNS entry, follow the procedure outlined in Step by Step 3.14.

STEP BY STEP

3.14 Manually Creating a DNS Entry

1. Log on to Windows Server 2003 using the Administrator account or another account that has administrator privileges.
2. Open the DNS console by selecting Start, Control Panel, Administrative Tools, DNS.
3. Right-click the zone in which you want to add an entry and select New Host (A). The New Host dialog box, as seen in Figure 3.62, opens.
4. In the Name field, enter the hostname. Enter the IP address in the IP Address box. If you want to create an entry in the reverse lookup zone for that network, you can select the Create Associated Pointer (PTR) Record option. Click Add Host to create the entry. Click Done when you have finished adding A records to the zone.

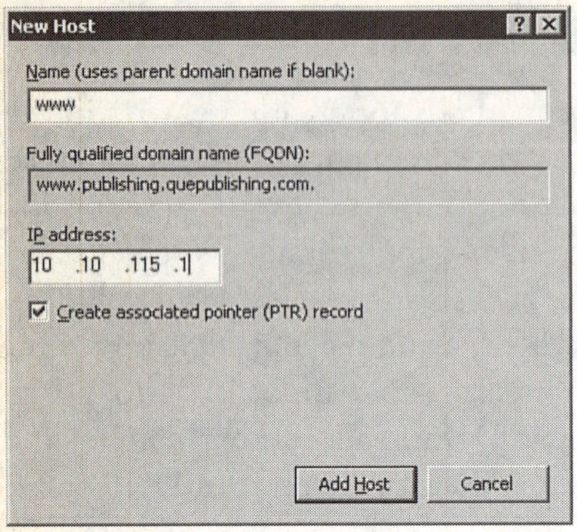

FIGURE 3.62 You need to know the correct DNS name and IP address of the host you are adding.

NOTE

Record Types Refer back to Table 3.1 for a complete listing of record types.

Monitoring the DNS Service

There are a number of ways to monitor different components of the DNS service, including using the Monitoring tab of the server Properties dialog box, the System Monitor, the Event Viewer, the DNS debug logs, and the Replication Monitor. Let's look at using the Monitoring tab options of the server Properties dialog box first.

The Server Properties Monitoring Tab

The simplest method for monitoring the DNS server service is to use the monitoring capabilities that are built in to the DNS console application. As discussed earlier in this chapter, the Monitoring tab of the DNS server Properties dialog box can be used to configure monitoring of the Windows Server 2003 DNS service.

To set up testing and monitoring, follow the procedure outlined in Step by Step 3.15.

STEP BY STEP

3.15 Testing the DNS Service

1. Open the DNS console by selecting Start, Control Panel, Administrative Tools, DNS.
2. Right-click the DNS server and select Properties. The DNS server Properties dialog box appears. Select the Monitoring tab as seen in Figure 3.63. You can configure a simple query or a recursive query or even automatic testing of the DNS service from this tab.

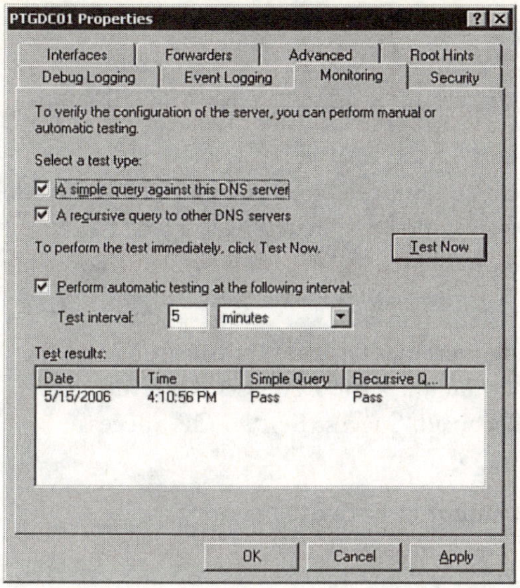

Figure 3.63 The Monitoring tab of the DNS server Properties dialog box allows you to perform simple DNS resolution testing to ensure that the DNS service is working properly.

3. Click Test Now to perform the selected tests.
4. Click OK to return to the DNS console.

This test allows you to perform two types of queries:

- **Simple (iterative) query**—A simple query, also called an iterative query, is one in which the name server provides the best response based on what that server knows from local zone files or from caching. If a name server doesn't have any information to answer the query, it simply sends a negative response.
- **Recursive query**—A recursive query forces a DNS server to respond to a request with either a failure response or a success response. With a recursive query, the DNS server must contact any other DNS servers it needs to contact to resolve the request. This is a much more resource-intensive query mechanism than the simple query.

If the test fails, you see an error message in the DNS console, and an alert icon appears on the DNS server.

System Monitor

The following groups of counters are available for the DNS object:

- **AXFR**—These counters are associated with the full zone transfer requests received by the master DNS server. This group includes the Requests Received, Requests Sent, Response Received, Success Received, and Success Sent counters.

- **Caching Memory**—This counter tracks the amount of memory used by the DNS server.
- **Database Node Memory**—This counter tracks the amount of database node memory used by the DNS server.
- **Dynamic Update**—These counters are associated with the dynamic updating of DNS. This group includes the NoOperation, NoOperation/sec, Queued, Received, Received/sec, Rejected, Timeouts, Written to Database, and Written to Database/sec counters.
- **IXFR**—These counters are associated with the incremental zone transfer requests received by the master DNS server. This group includes the Requests Received, Requests Sent, Response Received, Success Received, Success Sent, TCP Success Received, and UDP Success Received counters.
- **Nbtstat Memory**—This counter tracks the amount of `nbtstat` memory in use by the server.
- **Notify Received/Sent**—These counters track the notifications sent and received by the secondary DNS server.
- **Record Flow Memory**—This counter tracks the amount of record flow memory used by the DNS server.
- **Recursive**—These counters are associated with the recursive queries the DNS server must make. This group includes the Queries, Queries/sec, Query Failure, Query Failure/sec, Send TimeOuts, and TimeOut/sec counters.
- **Secure Update**—These counters are associated with the number of secure updates sent and received. This group includes the Failure, Received, and Received/sec counters.
- **TCP/UDP**—These counters track the respective TCP and UDP queries and responses. This group includes the Message Memory, Query Received, Query Received/sec, Response Sent, and Response Sent/sec counters.
- **Total**—These counters total the respective categories of requests and responses. This group includes the Query Received, Query Received/sec, Response Sent, and Response Sent/sec counters.
- **WINS**—Because DNS under Windows Server 2003 can be used for WINS lookups, the DNS counters include the following WINS-specific counters: Lookup Received, Lookup Received/sec, Response Sent, Response Sent/sec, Reverse Lookup Received, Reverse Lookup Received/sec, Reverse Response Sent, and Reverse Response Sent/sec.

- **Zone Transfer**—These counters are associated with the process of transferring copies of the DNS table between DNS servers. This group includes the Failure, Request Received, SOA Request Sent, and Success counters.

To configure DNS performance monitoring, follow the procedure outlined in Step by Step 3.16.

NOTE

Identifying a Counter If you need to know what a counter means and you have left your copy of this book at home under your pillow, fear not. Microsoft provides an option that does an excellent job of defining the counters: You select the counter you want to know more about and then click the Explain button.

STEP BY STEP

3.16 Configuring DNS Performance Monitoring

1. Open the Performance console by selecting Programs, Administrative Tools, Performance.
2. In the left pane of the Performance console, select System Monitor.
3. To create an entry in System Monitor, click the + icon. The Add Counters window appears, as shown in Figure 3.64. By default it opens to the Processor performance object.

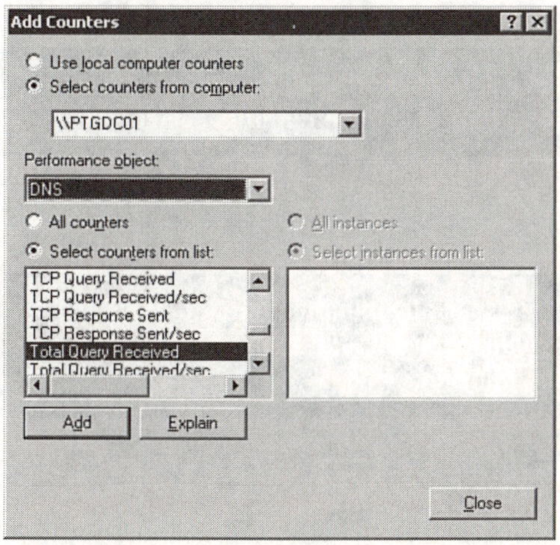

FIGURE 3.64 The DNS performance object offers a number of parameters to monitor.

4. Select the DNS performance object. The list of counters that are available for DNS is displayed. If you aren't sure what a counter does, select it and click the Explain button.

5. After you have decided what counter you want to monitor, click Add. (Total Query Received is usually a good monitor for seeing what the Performance console can do for you.) You can add multiple counters either by selecting each counter and clicking Add or by using the standard Windows multiple-item-select method of holding down the Ctrl key while you select all the counters you want to monitor and clicking Add. Click Close when you are done. You should see your counters being graphed, similar to those shown in Figure 3.65.

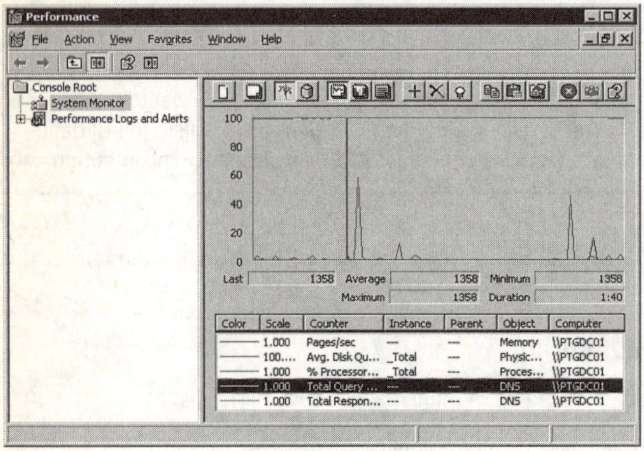

FIGURE 3.65 The graphing capabilities of the Performance console are great for giving you orders-of-magnitude reporting on activities.

EXAM ALERT

Don't Memorize All the Counters Microsoft does not expect you to memorize all these counters. You should, however, be familiar with the different types and know how to use the Performance console.

EXAM ALERT

The AXFR and IXFR Counters Two types of counters that are especially important are the AXFR and IXFR counters. Remember that AXFR counters are used in conjunction with full zone transfers, and IXFR counters are used in conjunction with incremental zone transfers.

Event Viewer

The Event Viewer is where the DNS event logs can be viewed and any informational, warning, or error messages can be reviewed to ensure that DNS is working as it should. To check the DNS event log, follow the procedure outlined in Step by Step 3.17.

STEP BY STEP

3.17 Reviewing an Error in the DNS Event Log

1. Open the Event Viewer by selecting Start, Administrative Tools, Event Viewer. The Event Viewer console opens.
2. Select the DNS Server log. The list of events for that log appears in the right pane of the Event Viewer, as seen in Figure 3.66.

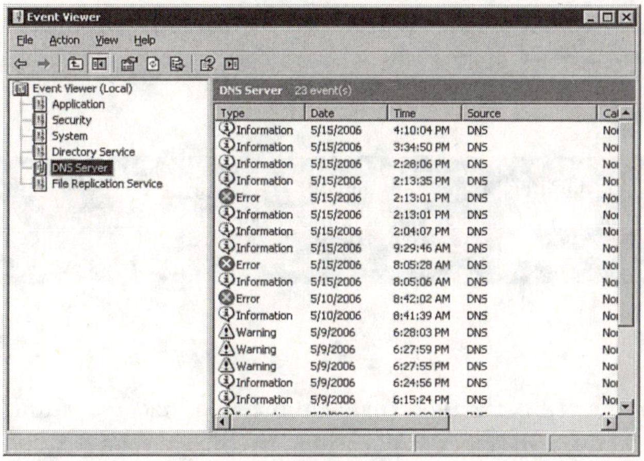

FIGURE 3.66 If you configured the DNS service to log all events, you should see a list of events in the DNS Server log.

3. Double-click an entry from the right pane. The Event Properties window opens, as seen in Figure 3.67.

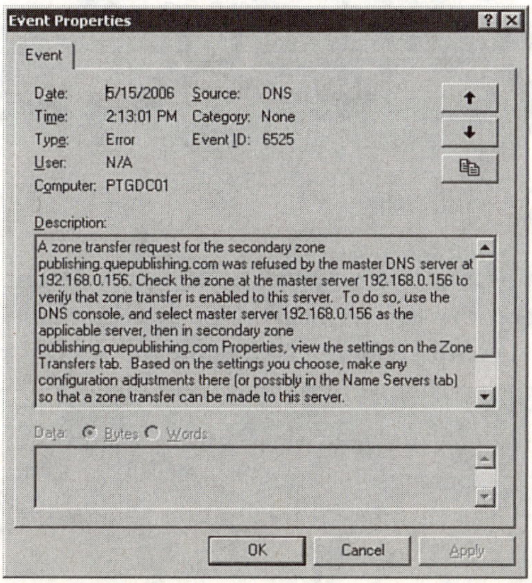

FIGURE 3.67 The Event Properties window gives you very detailed information about the event that was logged.

4. After you have reviewed the event, click OK to return to the Event Viewer. You should try to look at several other types of events before you close the Event Viewer.

The DNS Debug Log

The DNS debug log captures detailed information about each packet that is sent or received by the DNS server. This log can be read with any text editor (Notepad for example) and is geared toward users with very in-depth knowledge of DNS and DNS packet data. Figure 3.60 shows sample DNS debug log output. By default, the DNS debug log can be found in the `%systemroot%\system32\dns` directory. You can also specify a location for this file on the Debug Logging tab of the DNS server Properties dialog box.

EXAM ALERT

Reading DNS Debug Logs You might be wondering if you're going to have to read a DNS debug log for the exam. Definitely not. For the exam, you should know how to enable the DNS debug log and how to view it. Interpreting the data is beyond the scope of Exam 70-291.

Replication Monitor

The Replication Monitor (`replmon.exe`) is a utility that is available in the *Windows Server 2003 Resource Kit*, and it is used to monitor Active Directory replication. If you are using Active Directory to store and replicate DNS information, you might want to use the Replication Monitor to verify that Active Directory is replicating DNS information accurately.

EXAM ALERT

`replmon.exe` It's not likely that you'll see the `replmon.exe` utility on your 70-291 exam, but you should be aware of its existence and its basic purpose.

Securing DNS

Although Active Directory–integrated zones with Secure dynamic updates are fairly secure, there are some more advanced configuration changes that can be made in the interest of further securing the server. While not a complete listing of items by any means, the following list presents some of the more common items that you can work with to increase security:

- **Network interfaces**—If your DNS server has multiple network interfaces, the DNS service will by default listen for and respond to name resolution queries on all of them. You can add some security to your DNS server installation by configuring it so that it listens only on the IP address that DNS clients use to contact it.

- **Disabling recursion**—Recursion is enabled by default in Windows Server 2003 DNS, which allows the DNS server to perform recursive queries to other DNS servers on behalf of its DNS clients and other DNS servers that have forwarded queries to it for resolution. If a DNS server is not intended to perform recursive queries, you should disable them to prevent recursion from being used as an attack vector on the DNS server.
- **Securing the cache against pollution**—This advanced server option is enabled by default to aid in ensuring that server's DNS cache is secured against pollution. Cache pollution can result when a DNS query response returns incorrect nonauthoritative or malicious data. By keeping this option enabled, the DNS server will not accept resource records in a query response that were not requested in the original query. You should not disable this protection.
- **Removing root hints**—If you have configured an internal DNS root in your DNS infrastructure, configure the root hints on all of your other internal DNS servers to point only to your internal DNS root server. By removing the ability for the other DNS servers to contact root servers on the Internet, you remove the capability to accidentally disclose your private internal information on the Internet.
- **Use a private DNS namespace**—If your network clients will never need to communicate with the Internet, you can use a private DNS namespace, such as `quepublishing.corp`, along with an internal root DNS server and applicable firewall configuration to prevent DNS-related traffic from ever leaving your organization. You should note that simply by using a private DNS namespace, you have not eliminated the ability to communicate with the Internet.
- **Use a split DNS namespace**—If your network clients will need to communicate with the Internet, consider using a split DNS namespace. In this model, the internet namespace may be something such as `quepublishing.com`, while the internal namespace may be `corp.quepublishing.com`. Each section of the DNS namespace should be hosted on separate DNS servers located on the applicable side of your corporate firewall. Requests made by clients internally should be forwarded to your external DNS servers if the internal DNS servers cannot provide the requested query answer. This would be accomplished by configuring your internal DNS servers to forward requests only to your external DNS servers. Additionally, you should configure your external DNS servers to forward requests only to your ISP's trusted DNS servers.
- **Use firewall rules**—You can configure and implement a firewall rule on your packet-filtering firewall to separate your internal network from the Internet. This would allow TCP and UDP traffic on port 53 between your internal and external DNS servers.
- **Harden servers**—You can get detailed information and assistance on hardening Windows Server 2003 servers from the "Windows Server 2003 Security Guide."

Chapter Summary

This chapter discussed all the key components of using a Windows Server 2003 DNS server in a Windows Server 2003 environment. It first covered the history and function of DNS, and then it discussed reverse lookups, in which an IP address can be resolved to a hostname, and the different types of records. It also looked at the naming conventions for both standard DNS and the DNS service included with Windows Server 2003.

This chapter also discussed installing and configuring the Windows Server 2003 DNS server service, including all the major configuration activities from the initial installation to the manual creation of DNS records. This chapter also covered configuring a DNS client computer and configuring a zone for dynamic updates.

Finally, the chapter concluded with a discussion of managing and monitoring the DNS service.

Key Terms

- Aging
- Caching
- Caching-only server
- Conditional forwarding
- DHCP
- Domain
- DNS
- DNS server
- DNS client computer
- Exclusion
- Forward lookup
- FQDN
- Hierarchy
- Leaf
- Lease
- MIB

- Node
- Primary master
- Record types
- Reverse lookup
- RFC
- Scavenging
- Secondary master
- SOA
- Suffix
- TCP/IP
- TLD
- Tree
- Zone

Apply Your Knowledge

In this chapter, you learned what DNS is and how it works to make name resolution easier, quicker and more accurate. In the following exercises, you will practice some of the concepts and methods discussed in this chapter.

Exercises

3.1 Creating a Stub DNS Zone

In this exercise, you will use the DNS console to create a forward lookup zone.

Estimated time: 10 minutes

1. Open the DNS console by selecting Start, Control Panel, Administrative Tools, DNS. Right-click the DNS server and select New Zone.
2. Click Next, and the Zone Type dialog box appears. Select Stub Zone for the type of zone to create. Click Next. The Active Directory Zone Replication Scope dialog box appears. (Note that this dialog box will appear only if your DNS server is also a DC; if you are configuring this on a member server, skip Step 3.)

3. Select the To All Domain Controllers in the Active Directory Domain *<your domain name>* option and click Next. The Forward or Reverse Lookup Zone dialog box appears.
4. Select Forward Lookup Zone. Click Next. The Zone Name dialog box appears.
5. In the Name field of the Zone Name dialog box, enter the name **`Stub`**. Click Next. The Zone File dialog box appears.
6. Accept the default to create a new zone file. Click Next. The Completing the Configure DNS Server Wizard dialog box appears.
7. Click Finish to complete the configuration. The new domain appears in the DNS console.

3.2 Manually Create a DNS Record

In this exercise, you will manually create a DNS record.

Estimated time: 5 minutes

1. Open the DNS console by selecting Start, Control Panel, Administrative Tools, DNS. Right-click the zone you want to add an entry in and then select the type of entry you want to create.
2. Select New Alias because for this procedure, you will create a new alias (CNAME) record. The New Alias dialog box appears.
3. In the Alias Name field, enter the alias name. You can use the FQDN or just the hostname. If you use just the hostname, the rest of the FQDN for the domain in which you are creating the entry will automatically be appended.
4. Enter the FQDN for the host you are aliasing in the Fully Qualified Name for Target Host box.
5. Click OK to create the entry.

3.3 Monitoring DNS Server Performance by Using the Performance Console

This exercise walks you through adding a counter to the Performance console so that you can create a baseline for or troubleshoot a DNS server.

Estimated time: 15 minutes

1. Open the Performance console by selecting Programs, Administrative Tools, Performance.
2. In the Performance console, select System Monitor.
3. To create an entry in System Monitor, click the + icon. The Add Counters window appears. Notice that by default it opens to the Processor performance object.
4. Select the DNS performance object.
5. Select the counter you want to monitor and click Add. You can add multiple counters either by selecting each counter and clicking Add or by using the standard Windows multiple-item-select

method of holding down the Ctrl key while you select all the counters you want to monitor and then clicking Add. Click Close when you are done.

Exam Questions

1. You are the systems administrator for Wild Widgets, Inc. You are training a new employee on the use of the DNS service in Windows Server 2003. She asks you how a DNS request is resolved, assuming that the name is not cached and is for someone else's domain. What do you tell her?

   ❍ **A.** The client computer makes a request to the local DNS server. The DNS server looks in a local memory cache for names it has recently resolved. The name server looks in the DNS server's host tables to see if there is a static or dynamic entry for the hostname to an IP address lookup. The name server refers the request to a root name server. The root name server refers the request to a name server for the TLD in the hostname. The TLD name server refers the request to a name server for the second-level domain in the hostname, and so on, until a name server is encountered that can resolve the complete hostname.

   ❍ **B.** The client computer makes a request to the local DNS server. The name server looks in the DNS server's host tables to see if there is a static or dynamic entry for the hostname to an IP address lookup. The DNS server looks in a local memory cache for names it has recently resolved. The name server refers the request to a root name server. The root name server refers the request to a name server for the TLD in the hostname. The TLD name server refers the request to a name server for the second-level domain in the hostname, and so on, until a name server is encountered that can resolve the complete hostname.

   ❍ **C.** The client computer makes a request to the local DNS server. The name server looks in the DNS server's host tables to see if there is a static or dynamic entry for the hostname to an IP address lookup. The name server refers the request to a root name server. The root name server refers the request to a name server for the TLD in the hostname. The TLD name server refers the request to a name server for the second-level domain in the hostname, and so on, until a name server is encountered that can resolve the complete hostname.

   ❍ **D.** The client computer makes a request to the local DNS server. The DNS server looks in a local memory cache for names it has recently resolved. The name server looks in the DNS server's host tables to see if there is a static or dynamic entry for the hostname to an IP address lookup. The name server refers the request to a name server for the TLD in the hostname. The TLD name server refers the request to a name server for the second-level domain in the hostname, and so on, until a name server is encountered that can resolve the complete hostname.

2. You are the systems administrator for Phil's Phill-up Stations, a chain of gas stations. As part of the network, you maintain a Windows Server 2003 DNS server to receive DDNS updates. Because you have a mixed network, you want the server to accept both secure and nonsecure updates. The server is installed and running but doesn't receive dynamic updates at this time. How do you set up the DNS server to receive dynamic updates?

- ❍ **A.** Open DNS Administrator. Select the DNS server and right-click. Select Receive Dynamic Updates. The Dynamic Updates Wizard starts. Follow the prompts to complete the configuration of dynamic updates.
- ❍ **B.** Open the DNS console by selecting Start, Control Panel, Administrative Tools, DNS. Open the properties of the zone you want to configure to receive dynamic updates. On the General tab, set the Dynamic Updates pull-down menu to Nonsecure and Secure. Click OK.
- ❍ **C.** Open the DNS console by selecting Start, Control Panel, Administrative Tools, DNS. Open the properties of the zone you want to configure to receive dynamic updates. On the Updates tab, set the Allow Dynamic Updates pull-down menu to Yes. Click OK.
- ❍ **D.** Open the DNS console by selecting Start, Control Panel, Administrative Tools, DNS. Open the properties of the zone you want to configure to receive dynamic updates. On the Updates tab, set the Allow Dynamic Updates pull-down menu to Yes. Click OK.

3. You are the systems administrator for the Oui Find-em detective agency. Your boss has asked you to register a DNS domain name for the company. Which of the following is not a legal top-level domain name?

- ❍ **A.** `findem.art`
- ❍ **B.** `findem.net`
- ❍ **C.** `findem.org`
- ❍ **D.** `findem.cc`

4. You are the systems administrator for Little Faith Enterprises Meat Packing. You run a pure Windows Server 2003 network, with six Windows Server 2003 DNS servers for your domain. One of the secondary servers doesn't seem to be getting updates. How can you check to verify that the server is receiving updates?

- ❍ **A.** Open Performance Manager. Click the Add Counter icon. Select the DNS server object and then select the Zone Transfer Success counter. Click Add to add the counter and monitor the zone transfers.
- ❍ **B.** Open the Performance console. Click the Add Counter icon. Select the DNS server object and then select the AXFR Successes counter. Click Add to add the counter and monitor the zone transfers.
- ❍ **C.** Open the DNS console. Right-click the zone with which you are having problems. Select Statistics from the context menu and verify that zone transfers are being received.

- ❍ **D.** Open the Performance console. Click the Add Counter icon. Select the DNS server object and then select the Zone Transfer Success counter. Click Add to add the counter and monitor the zone transfers.

5. You are the systems administrator for Mad Hatter Top Hats, Inc. You are responsible for the company's Windows Server 2003 network, including DNS. You have been asked to create a reverse lookup entry for each workstation on the network. How do you accomplish this task in the most efficient and accurate manner possible?

- ❍ **A.** Use the DNS console to create a reverse lookup zone. Manually add each workstation to the reverse lookup zone.
- ❍ **B.** Use the DNS console to create a reverse lookup zone. Configure the forward lookup zone to accept dynamic updates. The reverse lookup zone will be automatically updated.
- ❍ **C.** Use the DNS console to create a reverse lookup zone. Configure the DNS server to accept dynamic updates. The reverse lookup zone will be automatically updated.
- ❍ **D.** Use the DNS console to create a reverse lookup zone. Configure the reverse lookup zone to accept dynamic updates.

6. You are the systems administrator for the Hittem Boxing Glove Corporation, which is running a routed network with a centrally located Windows Server 2003 DNS server. You need to create a record in DNS to allow Internet mail to be sent to your domain. What kind of domain record do you need?

- ❍ **A.** A CNAME record
- ❍ **B.** An A record
- ❍ **C.** A PTR record
- ❍ **D.** An MX record

7. You manage the Windows Server 2003 DNS servers for the Bang Bang Hammer Corporation. You are running in a purely Windows Server 2003 environment, and you need to make sure workstations are registered properly in DNS for Active Directory integration. How should you configure DNS integration?

- ❍ **A.** Configure the appropriate zones to accept dynamic updates.
- ❍ **B.** Configure the DNS server to accept dynamic updates.
- ❍ **C.** Configure the DHCP server to be sure to send dynamic updates.
- ❍ **D.** Install the Windows Server 2003 DNS client on the workstations.

8. You are the systems administrator for UR Write Publishing. You are responsible for maintaining the Windows Server 2003 network for the company, including the Windows Server 2003 DNS servers. You have one remote office that is located across a slow WAN link. What is the best way to set up DNS to resolve internal hostnames?

   ❍ **A.** Create a delegated zone for the remote office and have all the DNS client computers in that office resolve from that zone.

   ❍ **B.** Configure a caching-only server and have all the DNS client computers resolve from that server.

   ❍ **C.** Use a centralized DNS server and configure it for incremental updates.

   ❍ **D.** Configure the DNS client computers to autodiscover the closest DNS server.

9. You are the collaborative computing administrator for the Call-Me Telephone Company. You have a single DNS server resolving names for your internal domain, and you have an Internet connection. You need to configure DNS on the client computers to resolve Internet addresses. How will you make this configuration?

   ❍ **A.** On each client computer, install the Microsoft DNS client. Configure the client computer to resolve to the DNS server. Configure the root hints on the server to point at the Internet root servers.

   ❍ **B.** On each client computer, configure the DNS settings under the Internet Protocol (TCP/IP) Properties dialog box of the LAN connection to resolve to the DNS server. Configure the root hints on the server to point at the Internet root servers.

   ❍ **C.** Install a new DNS server to resolve Internet domain names. On each client computer, configure the DNS settings under the Internet Protocol (TCP/IP) Properties dialog box of the LAN connection to resolve to the DNS server.

   ❍ **D.** On each client computer, configure the DNS settings under the Internet Protocol (TCP/IP) Properties dialog box of the LAN connection to resolve to the DNS server.

10. Which of the following is the FQDN for the host `home` in the `sales` domain for the UR write company if the company's domain is `urwrite.net`?

   ❍ **A.** `home`

   ❍ **B.** `home.sales.net`

   ❍ **C.** `home.urwrite.net`

   ❍ **D.** `home.sales.urwrite.net`

11. You are the systems administrator for Blue Sky Airlines. Your company has a mixed Windows Server 2003 and Windows NT 4.0 Server network and you are running a Windows NT 4.0 DNS server, as well as a Windows NT 4.0 DHCP server. There are 10 Windows 98 computers in the Sales Department that need to use DDNS updates for identification purposes. How will you enable this?

❍ **A.** Upgrade your DNS server to Windows Server 2003. Configure it to accept dynamic updates. Configure the Windows 98 client computers to send dynamic updates.

❍ **B.** Upgrade your DNS server to Windows Server 2003. Configure it to accept dynamic updates. Upgrade your Windows 98 computers to Windows 98 Second Edition to get the DDNS capability. Configure the Windows 98 client computers to send dynamic updates.

❍ **C.** Upgrade your Windows 98 computers to Windows XP Professional to get the DDNS capability. Configure the Windows XP client computers to send dynamic updates.

❍ **D.** Upgrade your DNS server to Windows Server 2003. Configure it to accept dynamic updates. Upgrade your Windows 98 computers to Windows XP Professional to get the DDNS capability.

12. You are the systems administrator for Little Big Men Clothiers. You have installed a Windows Server 2003 DNS server, but people are unable to resolve names. You need to test the DNS server. Where should you start in your troubleshooting efforts?

❍ **A.** From the command prompt of a Windows XP Professional host, run the `nslookup` utility to check the functionality of the DNS service.

❍ **B.** From the command prompt of a Windows XP Professional host, run the `ipconfig` utility to check the functionality of the DNS service.

❍ **C.** From the Windows Server 2003 DNS server, type **`ping -a`** and the address of the DNS server. Examine the results to see if the server is working.

❍ **D.** From the Windows Server 2003 DNS server, type **`ping -R`** and the address of the DNS server. Examine the results to see if the server is working.

Answers to Exam Questions

1. **A**. The correct order is cache, local DNS server table, root server, TLD server, and then any additional subdomain servers; thus Answers B, C, and D are incorrect. For more information, see the section "DNS Domains Defined."

2. **B**. Dynamic updates are set by using the Dynamic Updates pull-down menu on the General tab of the zone properties; thus Answers A, C, and D are incorrect. For more information, see the section "Configuring Zones."

3. **A**. `art` is a proposed TLD. `org`, `net`, and `cc` are actual production TLDs; thus Answers B, C, and D are incorrect. For more information, see the section "The History of DNS."

4. **D**. Performance Manager is the name of the Windows NT application; thus Answer A is incorrect. In Windows Server 2003 the Performance console runs as part of the MMC. There are no statistics available for the DNS server; thus Answer C is incorrect. The correct counter is Zone Transfer Success; thus Answer B is incorrect. For more information, see the section "Managing and Monitoring DNS."

5. **D**. You must create a reverse lookup zone and configure it to accept dynamic updates. If you manually configure each PTR record, you are likely to make mistakes and are not taking advantage of dynamic updates to do the work for you; thus Answer A is incorrect. By configuring a forward lookup zone to accept dynamic updates, you have not configured the reverse lookup zone; thus Answer B is incorrect. Dynamic updates are configured at the zone level, not the server level; thus Answer C is incorrect. For more information, see the section "Reverse Lookups."

6. **D**. An MX (mail exchanger) record is used to identify the mail server(s) for a domain. A CNAME record is an alias; thus Answer A is incorrect. An A record is used for name-to-address resolution; thus Answer B is incorrect. A PTR record is used for reverse lookups; thus Answer C is incorrect. For more information, see the section "DNS Record Types."

7. **A**. You need to configure the appropriate zones to accept dynamic updates. Each zone needs to be configured individually to accept dynamic updates. Dynamic updates are configured at the zone level, not the server level; thus Answer B is incorrect. The configuration to allow or disallow dynamic updates is performed on DNS zones, not on the DHCP server; thus Answer C is incorrect. There is no "client" piece of DNS that needs to be installed; thus Answer D is incorrect. For more information, see the section "Configuring Zones."

8. **B**. You need to configure a caching-only server and have all the remote DNS client computers resolve from that server. A delegated zone will not help with resolution across the slow link; thus Answer A is incorrect. Using a centrally located server will not help with the issue of the slow link; thus Answer C is incorrect. There is no setting to DNS server auto discovery; thus Answer D is incorrect. For more information, see the section "Configuring Caching-Only Servers."

9. **D**. You just need to configure the workstations to use the existing DNS server to resolve names. This is done under the Internet Protocol (TCP/IP) Properties dialog box of the network connection. The server automatically forwards any requests for unknown domains to the appropriate servers; thus Answer B is incorrect. There is no "client" piece of DNS that needs to be installed; thus Answer A is incorrect. An additional DNS server is not required for Internet name resolution; thus Answer C is incorrect. For more information, see the section "Configuring DNS Client Computers."

10. **D**. `home.sales.urwrite.net` is the correct answer. `home` is the server, `sales` is a department subdomain, `urwrite` is the secondary domain, and `net` is the TLD; thus Answers A, B, and C are all incorrect. For more information, see the section "DNS Domains Defined."

11. **D**. You need a Windows Server 2003 DNS server and a Windows XP (or Windows 2000) client computer to use DDNS without needing to reconfigure DHCP. Windows 98 computers do not support dynamic updates; thus Answers A and B are incorrect. There is no configuring needed on the client side for dynamic updates, as long as the client supports them (Windows XP and Windows 2000); thus Answer C is incorrect. For more information, see the section "Configuring Zones."

12. A. Running `nslookup` from the command prompt is a good way to test DNS, and should be your first step for DNS-related issues. The `ipconfig` command is a very useful TCP/IP troubleshooting tool, but it not going to be as typically useful for DNS-related issues as the `nslookup` command; thus Answer B is incorrect. The `ping` command is useful for basic connectivity testing between two computers, but would not likely be the best first step in troubleshooting a name resolution issue; thus Answers C and D are incorrect. For more information, see the section "Testing the DNS Service."

Suggested Reading and Resources

1. Albitz, Paul, and Liu, Cricket. *DNS and BIND*, 4th Edition. O'Reilly & Associates, 2001.
2. Langfeldt, Nicolai. *The Concise Guide to DNS and BIND*. Que Publishing, 2000.
3. Parker, Tim. *Teach Yourself TCP/IP in 14 Days*, 2nd Edition. Que Publishing, 2001.
4. Davies, Joseph, and Lee, Thomas. *Microsoft Windows Server 2003 TCP/IP Protocols and Services Technical Reference*. Microsoft Press, 2003.
5. Stevens, W. Richard. TCP/IP Illustrated, Volume 1: The Protocols. Addison-Wesley, 1994.
6. "Deploying Network Services," http://technet2.microsoft.com/WindowsServer/en/Library/119050c9-7c4d-4cbf-8f38-97c45e4d01ef1033.mspx.
7. "Technical Overview of Windows Server 2003 Networking and Communications," www.microsoft.com/windowsserver2003/techinfo/overview/netcomm.mspx.
8. "Windows Server 2003 Reviewer's Guide," www.microsoft.com/windowsserver2003/techinfo/overview/reviewersguide.mspx.
9. Windows Server 2003 Online documentation: "Network Services," www.microsoft.com/technet/prodtechnol/windowsserver2003/proddocs/entserver/sag_NPStopnode.asp.
10. "Windows Server 2003 Security Guide," http://www.microsoft.com/technet/security/prodtech/windowsserver2003/W2003HG/SGCH00.mspx.

4

CHAPTER FOUR

Implementing and Managing WINS

Although there has been a clear shift in Microsoft's focus on name resolution toward DNS-based name resolution, there is still a lot of NetBIOS name resolution heritage in Windows Server 2003. Since the introduction of networking in Microsoft Windows, NetBIOS and NetBIOS name resolution have been standard. From `lmhosts` files to broadcasts to WINS servers, Windows has always relied on NetBIOS name resolution mechanisms.

In many organizations, you will still have legacy clients in your environment. As a result, it's entirely possible that you will need to understand how WINS works, what it does, and how to configure and manage it. Sadly enough, there are still some fairly new applications that are DNS-ignorant and understand only how to perform NetBIOS name resolution. It is for these two reasons that Microsoft still considers NetBIOS name resolution to be important enough to retain in Windows Server 2003. It is a fair assumption, however, that we can expect to see support for WINS phased out of the next version of the Windows Server operating system or perhaps even the version after that.

Although there are no exam objectives directly addressed in this chapter, we felt the material presented here was still relevant enough to warrant coverage. Additionally, it's not out of the realm of possibilities that you will need to understand the information presented here on test day (and after) as you carry out your day-to-day administrative activities. Please do take the time to read through this chapter as you stand a good chance of having at least one question on your exam that deals directly or indirectly with WINS.

Outline

Introduction

If you are familiar with Windows NT 4.0 networks, you are undoubtedly familiar with the intricacies of a WINS infrastructure. You might also be wondering why Microsoft didn't get rid of WINS with Windows 2000 when DNS was crowned the king of name resolution. Well, the good news is that with Windows Server 2003, WINS is intended and needed only for backward compatibility. Windows Server 2003 running in native mode does not need to use WINS at all. The Active Directory (AD) and Domain Name Service (DNS) are used to provide the WINS-like functionality of resolving names into IP addresses.

So, that means we don't need to talk about WINS, right? Sorry, but you don't get off that easily. Until your network is 100 percent Windows Server 2003 (or higher) and no applications on the network require NetBIOS name resolution, you will still need WINS to provide backward compatibility for legacy Windows operating systems, particularly with any NT domains. With that in mind, let's talk about what WINS is and how it works.

Introduction to WINS

In today's Internet-centric environment, the Transmission Control Protocol/Internet Protocol (TCP/IP) has become the ubiquitous networking protocol. For long-time Unix users, the re-emergence of TCP/IP is a good thing. TCP/IP came out of the Unix arena and has been the native protocol for Unix systems since the late 1980s.

Microsoft, on the other hand, opted to not use TCP/IP as the native networking protocol in early versions of Windows. Instead of TCP/IP, these early versions of Windows used NetBEUI as the native networking protocol. NetBEUI was a pretty good protocol for small networks; it required no configuration and didn't require complex addressing as TCP/IP does. However, NetBEUI can't handle routing and does not perform well in large environments. Therefore, Microsoft needed to add TCP/IP support.

When Microsoft began to add TCP/IP support to its LAN server products, the company ran into a little problem. The naming system used on Microsoft networks at that time would not function on routed TCP/IP networks. Microsoft LAN Manager computers used the computer's NetBIOS names for identification. Although this makes maintaining the network very simple for an administrator because servers are automatically located on the network by name, this naming system was a problem with the TCP/IP protocol.

NetBIOS has a design limitation that shows up in routed networks because NetBIOS relies heavily on broadcast messages to locate servers. *Broadcast messages* are messages that are processed by every computer on a network segment, rather than by a specific computer. This paradigm is usable on smaller networks but can add overwhelming amounts of broadcast traffic on an enterprise network. To confine the impact of broadcast messages on a TCP/IP network, IP routers do not forward broadcast messages. Therefore, Microsoft had to find a way to make NetBIOS naming work in a standard TCP/IP network.

Broadcasts Are Evil

In most corporate networks today, Ethernet switches are in use to help route and reduce traffic. Switches work by forwarding packets to only the hardware or MAC addresses for which they are intended. By doing this, it effectively improves the maximum speed of the network. However, broadcast traffic isn't sent to a single address; it's sent to every address and thus must be sent to every machine connected to the Ethernet switch. The end result is that the switch can't perform its function.

The more broadcast traffic that occurs on a network, the less effective an Ethernet switch is. Thus, in switched environments, as in most environments these days, reducing the number of broadcasts is critical.

Microsoft's first -solution, introduced in its older operating system called LAN Manager server, was to use a LAN Manager `hosts` (`lmhosts`) file on each computer on the network. Similar to the `hosts` file used before DNS was available, an `lmhosts` file consists of records matching NetBIOS names to IP addresses. When a computer couldn't find a particular NetBIOS computer on the local network, it would consult its `lmhosts` file to see whether the computer could be found elsewhere.

An `lmhosts` file is a text file that must be edited manually. After creating a master `lmhosts` file, an administrator must copy the file to every computer on the network. Every time a computer is installed or removed, the master `lmhosts` file must be updated and redistributed. Doesn't that sound like fun? (This might sound familiar—the architects of TCP/IP faced a similar issue with `hosts` files before the DNS specification was written.)

Microsoft also needed a dynamic name -service that would maintain a list of computers on the network—a name service that could work in routed TCP/IP environments. Microsoft's answer was the Windows Internet Name Service (WINS), which functioned as a NetBIOS server. Four elements can be found in a WINS network:

- **WINS servers**—When WINS client computers enter the network, they contact a WINS server using a directed message. The client computer registers its name with the WINS server and uses the WINS server to resolve NetBIOS names to IP addresses.
- **WINS client computers**—WINS client computers use directed messages to communicate with WINS servers. All versions of Windows since Windows for Workgroups can be WINS client computers.
- **Non-WINS client computers**—Older Microsoft network client computers that can't use direct WINS communications can still benefit from WINS. Their broadcast

messages are intercepted by WINS proxy computers that act as intermediaries between clients that must broadcast and WINS servers. MS-DOS and Windows 3.1 client computers function as non-WINS clients.

- **WINS proxies**—All versions of Windows client computers since Windows for Workgroups can function as WINS proxies. They intercept broadcasts on their local subnets and communicate with a WINS server on behalf of the broadcasting client computer.

NOTE

Configuring the WINS Proxy Should you have a need to configure a WINS proxy within your environment, the task is an easy one. Simply open the Registry Editor on the Windows XP Professional or Windows Server 2003 computer to be configured as the WINS proxy and change the following key value to 1 (REG_DWORD):

```
HKEY_LOCAL_MACHINE\System\CurrentControlSet\Services\NetBT\Parameters\
EnableProxy
```

After making this change, you will need to restart the TCP/IP NetBIOS Helper service on the computer.

As is discussed in the "Configuring WINS Replication" section later in this chapter, WINS servers can replicate their databases so that each WINS server can provide name resolution for the entire network. Whenever possible, it is desirable to have at least two WINS servers. This lets name resolution take place when one name server is down. It also lets administrators distribute WINS activity across multiple servers to balance the processing loads. WINS server addresses are one of the configuration settings that can be issued -with DHCP.

Installing and Configuring WINS

Installing the WINS -service on your Windows Server 2003 computer is just as simple and straightforward as the two network services (DHCP and DNS) you have previously installed.

To install the WINS service, follow the instructions provided in Step by Step 4.1.

EXAM ALERT

Managing Windows Server 2003 Services The Step by Step examples use a utility called the WINS console. It is important to note that this manager is nothing more than the Microsoft Management Console with the WINS management snap-in installed. Microsoft creates these versions of the Microsoft Management Console to enable new users of Windows Server 2003 to more easily manage their systems. Thus, don't be confused if you see references to the Microsoft Management Console in the exam. That's all the WINS manager is.

STEP BY STEP

4.1 Installing the Windows Internet Naming Service (WINS)

1. Log on to Windows Server 2003 using the Administrator account or another account that has administrator privileges.

2. Open the Control Panel and then open the Add/Remove Programs applet. The Add or Remove Programs dialog box appears, as seen in Figure 4.1.

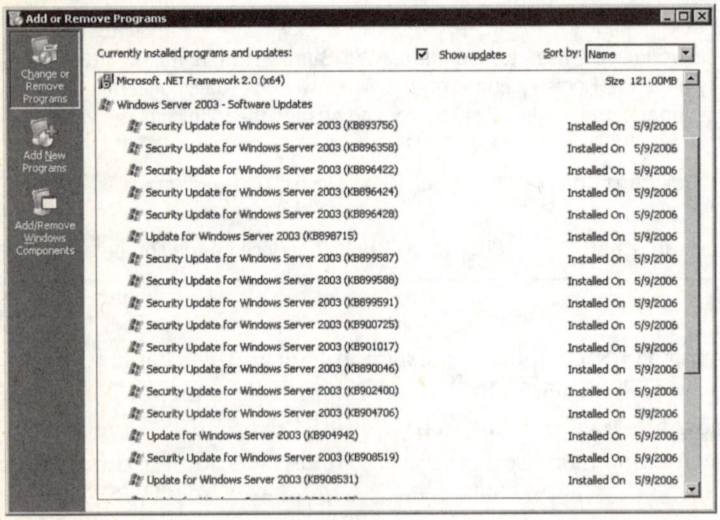

FIGURE 4.1 The Add or Remove Programs dialog box provides useful information about installed applications, including application size and, in some cases, the frequency of use of an installed application.

3. Click Add/Remove Windows Components on the left side of the Add or Remove Programs dialog box. The Windows Components Wizard -dialog box appears, as seen in Figure 4.2.

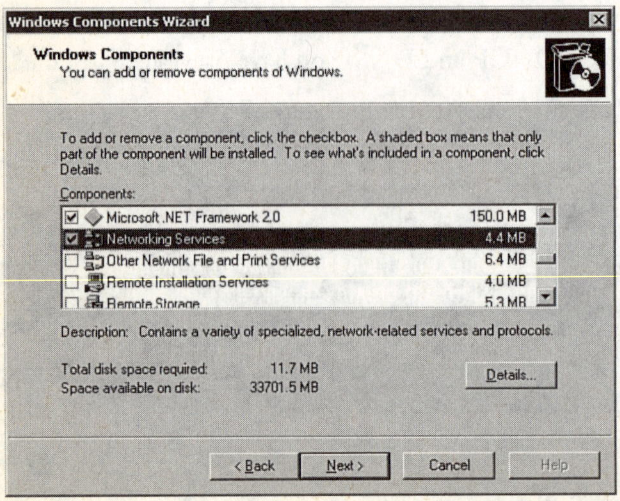

FIGURE 4.2 The Windows Components Wizard allows you to install, remove, or configure the various components of Windows Server 2003.

4. Select Networking Services and click Details. The Networking Services dialog box, shown in Figure 4.3, appears. Select Windows Internet Naming Service (WINS) and then click OK.

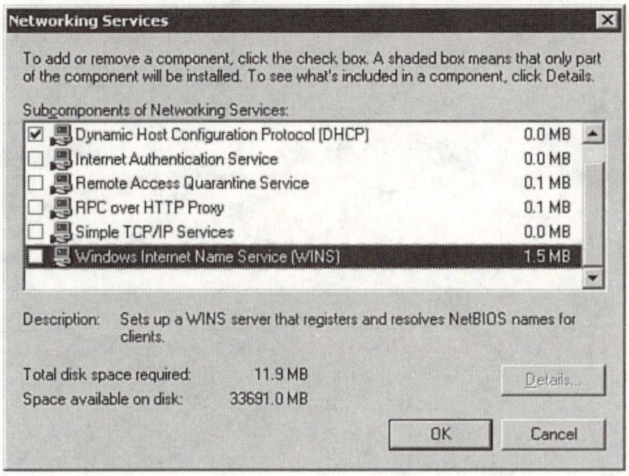

FIGURE 4.3 On the Networking Services screen, you need to select WINS and click OK.

5. On the next screen that appears, click Next to complete the installation. The Windows Component Wizard prompts you for the Windows Server 2003 CD-ROM if it needs to copy files.
6. When the wizard is finished, it displays a summary of the changes to be made. Click Finish to complete the installation.

NOTE

DHCP and the WINS Service If, for some reason, you have your Windows Server 2003 computer configured to use DHCP addressing, you will receive a message from the installation process indicating that the WINS service should be installed only on a server with a static address. The Local Area Connection Properties dialog box will open to enable you to correct the issue. Microsoft includes this message because it is actually a very bad idea to put WINS (or any other network service) on a dynamically addressed server.

You shouldn't let your WINS server use a dynamic address, because the address might change one day. If that occurs, all your users will lose access to the server because the addresses used to point at the WINS server are configured statically. The same is true for a DNS server, a DHCP server, a domain controller, and so on, as we discussed earlier in Chapter 1, "Configuring and Troubleshooting TCP/IP Addressing."

Congratulations—you just installed WINS. Keep in mind that you still need to configure your client computers to use the new server, but the server portion of the install is complete.

Now that WINS is installed, let's look at configuring it.

Configuring WINS

Several properties can be configured in the Windows Internet Naming Service. They can be accessed by opening the WINS console, as seen in Figure 4.4.

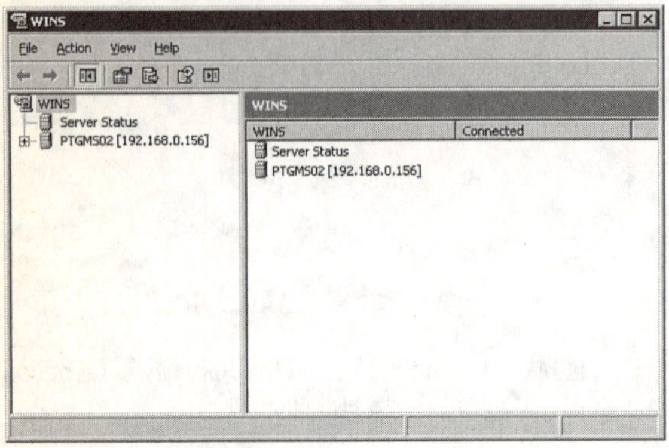

FIGURE 4.4 The WINS console is used for all configurations for the WINS service.

You can open the WINS console by clicking Start, Programs, Administrative Tools, WINS. To access a WINS server's Properties dialog box, simply select it, right-click it, and select Properties from the context menu. The WINS server Properties dialog box will open to the General tab, as discussed next.

The General Tab

The General tab, shown in Figure 4.5, is used to configure statistics and backups for the WINS server. You can use this tab to configure the automatic update of WINS statistics and the interval at which they update from this tab. You also can configure the default backup path for the WINS database and enable the automatic backup of the database when the server is shut down; the latter is an administrative task that is highly recommended.

NOTE

Should I Back Up? You should configure the WINS backup paths to a network share; this configuration ensures the maximum fault tolerance for the WINS database in case the server doesn't come back up.

The Intervals Tab

The Intervals tab, shown in Figure 4.6, is used to set the WINS database records renewal, deletion, and verification intervals.

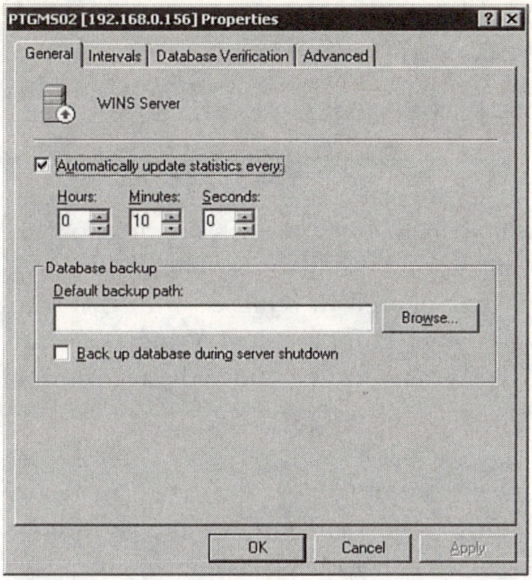

FIGURE 4.5 The General tab is used for configuring statistics and backups for the WINS database.

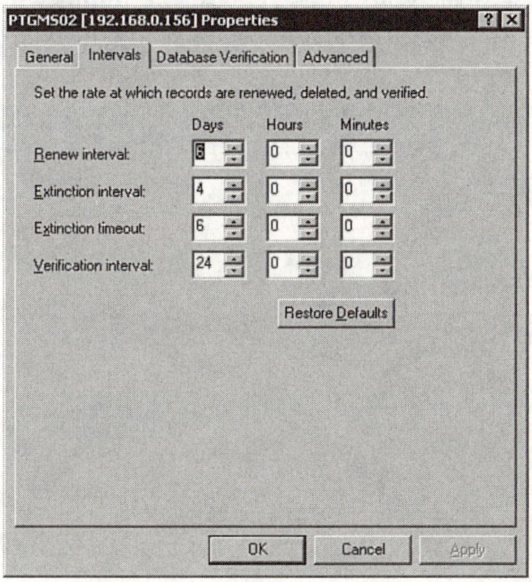

FIGURE 4.6 In most networks, the default intervals are usually adequate for a stable WINS environment.

You can set the following intervals:

- **Renew Interval**—Determines the frequency of record renewal.
- **Extinction Interval**— Determines the length of time before a released record is considered extinct.

- **Extinction Timeout**— Determines the length of time after a record has been marked as extinct before it is removed from the database.
- **Verification Interval**—Determines the frequency at which database records are verified for accuracy.

When a record is deleted from WINS, the server will actually Tombstone it, which is to mark it locally as extinct and release it from active use by that local WINS server. The Tombstoned record is then replicated to all other WINS servers configured to replicate with that local WINS server, thus applying that Tombstoned status to other WINS servers. When the verification interval has passed, the WINS servers can then automatically remove the record from the WINS database.

The Database Verification Tab

The Database Verification tab, seen in Figure 4.7, enables you to configure the verification parameters associated with the WINS database. You can enable database verification for a specific interval. The default interval is 24 hours; thus, if enabled, the database consistency will be verified once a day. You also specify the time to begin the consistency check, the number of database records to check for each period, as well as the source against which to verify the database. You can verify database consistency against owner servers (these are the servers from which the record being verified was replicated) or randomly selected partner servers. Although disabled by default, it is highly recommended that you configure database verification for your WINS databases.

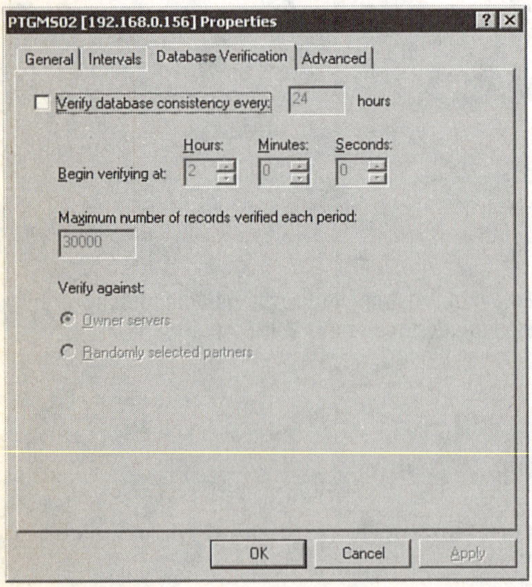

FIGURE 4.7 Ensuring the consistency of the WINS database is critical to a stable WINS environment.

The Advanced Tab

The Advanced tab, shown in Figure 4.8, is used to configure the remaining WINS parameters, including the following:

- **Logging**—You can enable detailed event logging for troubleshooting WINS when there are problems. The entries are written to the System log and, if left on too long, can cause this log to fill up and become less useful in troubleshooting and monitoring.
- **Burst handling**—You can configure the load that can be put on the server by specifying the number of WINS requests that the server will accept before returning a retry message. This can be set to Low, Medium, High, or Custom, which enables you to specify several connections.
- **Database path**—This is the path for the WINS database. If you have fault-tolerant drives in your server, be sure that the WINS database is located on one of them.
- **Database version number**—You should not need to modify this parameter, but the starting version number is used for consistency purposes. By giving each version of the database an incrementing version number, Windows Server 2003 is capable of comparing two WINS databases and determining which one is the most recent. DNS uses a similar mechanism for synchronizing its tables.
- **LAN Manager compatibility**—You can also set WINS to use LAN Manager–compatible computer names so that any legacy LAN Manager installations can still use WINS for name resolution.

EXAM ALERT

Burst Mode First introduced to WINS in Windows 2000 Server, burst mode provides a means to allow many clients to simultaneously attempt to register their records. Changing the setting seen in Figure 4.8 changes the size of the burst queue, which determines how many name registration and refresh requests are received by the WINS server before burst mode is initiated.

When burst mode is in effect, additional client requests are answered with a positive response by the WINS server immediately. This immediate response also includes a variable TTL (time to live) value, which then forces the clients to contact the WINS server again at a more controlled rate.

That covers the basic installation and configuration of a WINS server. Let's look at configuring WINS replication between two WINS servers.

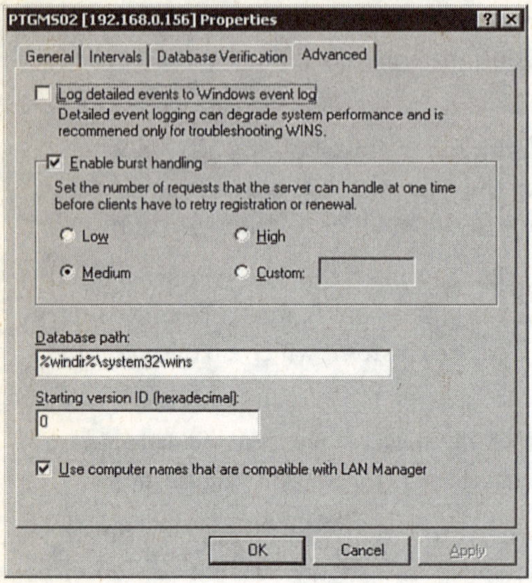

FIGURE 4.8 The Advanced tab is the catchall for the remaining WINS parameters and contains some important parameters for troubleshooting and load regulating.

Enabling and Configuring WINS Replication

In most environments that rely on WINS for name resolution for legacy systems, it is important to ensure that more than one WINS server exists so that you provide redundancy and availability. To ensure that each server has a current copy of the database, it is important to configure replication between your WINS servers. Let's take a quick look at the types of replication you can configure for the WINS service:

- **Pull replication**—In pull replication, your server pulls the database from the replication partner. A pull replication is time-based and occurs at the time you have configured. You can decide whether to establish a persistent connection for replication, and you can set the start time and interval for replication.
- **Push replication**—In push replication, your server pushes its database to the replication partner. A push replication is event-driven, and the number of database updates determines when the event occurs. You can decide whether to use a persistent connection for push activities, and you can set the number of changes in the version ID before replication.
- **Replication partner type**—The partner type can be push, pull, or push/pull, depending on your requirements. (In push/pull replication, database replication can occur using either method: push or pull.)

NOTE

WINS Replication One new feature of WINS since Windows NT 4.0 is the ability of Windows Server 2003 (and Windows 2000 Server) WINS servers to maintain a persistent connection with one or more of the replication partners, enabling real-time replication.

To enable WINS replication, complete Step by Step 4.2.

STEP BY STEP

4.2 Enabling WINS Replication

1. Open the WINS manager by selecting Start, Programs, Administrative Tools, WINS.
2. In the right pane, right-click Replication Partners and select New Replication Partner. The New Replication Partner dialog box opens and asks you to enter the address of another WINS server, as seen in Figure 4.9. This can be either the server name or IP address. If the server name can't be resolved, you will be prompted to enter the address of the server.

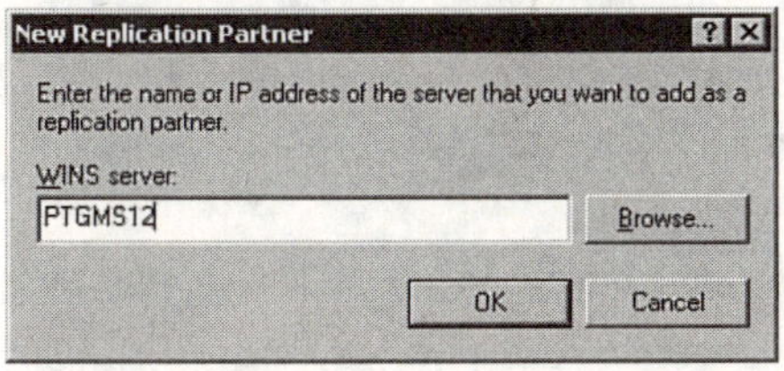

FIGURE 4.9 The replication partner can be listed by name or address.

3. Enter the name of the server and click OK.
4. Click Replication Partners in the left pane. You should see your new replication partner in the right pane, as seen in Figure 4.10.

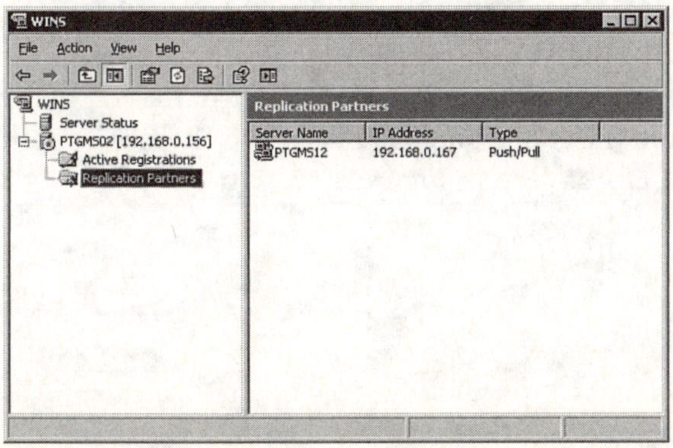

FIGURE 4.10 After the replication partner has been created, it is listed in the Replication Partners pane of WINS manager.

5. Right-click the newly created replication partner and select Properties. This opens the Replication Partner Properties dialog box, which shows only the name and address of the replication partner.
6. Click the Advanced tab, as seen in Figure 4.11. On this tab, you can configure the replication properties for the replication partner. Select the appropriate type for your environment.

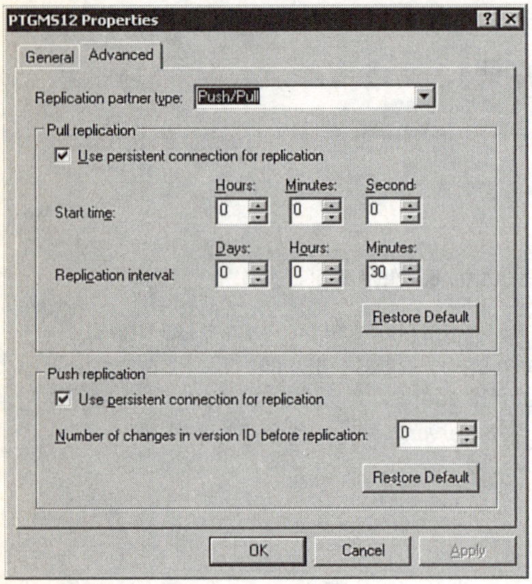

FIGURE 4.11 The Advanced tab enables you to customize the WINS replication setting to meet your network's requirements.

7. Click OK when the settings meet your requirements; however, more often than not, no changes will be needed here.

You have now configured replication with a WINS replication partner. Now let's look at the global replication properties.

Configuring WINS Replication

To review the global replication properties, open the WINS manager application as described in the first part of Step By Step 4.2 and select the Replication Partners folder in the left pane. Right-click the folder and select Properties from the context menu. This opens the Replication Partners Properties dialog box to the General tab, as seen in Figure 4.12.

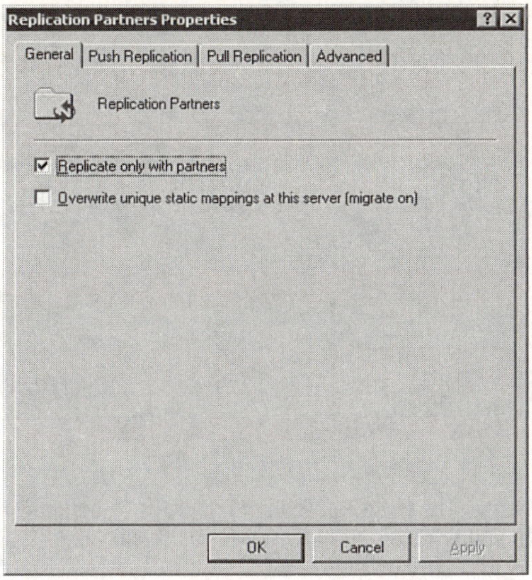

FIGURE 4.12 The General tab provides basic replication configuration options.

The General Tab

The options on the General tab are pretty basic in nature compared to many others. To prevent replication from occurring with WINS servers that you've not already configured replication for, you need only leave the default selection of Replicate only with partners checked. In addition, you can enable the Overwrite unique static mappings option to enable the WINS server to overwrite existing static mappings in the database with dynamic mappings during WINS replication. Static WINS mappings, like static IP addresses and static DNS records, can become a burden to manage efficiently and accurately and are thus to be avoided in most cases.

The Push Replication Tab

The Push Replication tab, seen in Figure 4.13, provides configurable options that govern how push replication behaves for your WINS server.

Options available for configuration include those to start a push replication at server startup or when an address changes in a mapping in the database. By configuring a value in the Number of changes in version ID field, you are specifying how many updates can be made in the WINS database before push partners are informed of the changes. The last option on the Push Replication tab allows you to enable persistent connections, which is typically advisable as long as the replication partners support them.

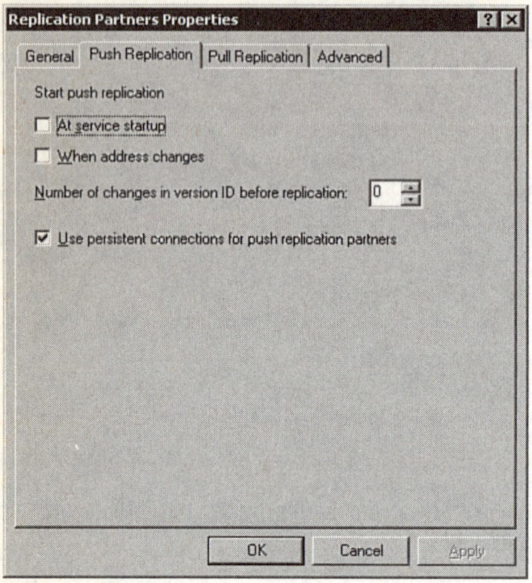

FIGURE 4.13 The Push Replication tab provides options allowing you to configure how WINS push replication behaves.

The Pull Replication Tab

The Pull Replication tab, seen in Figure 4.14, provides configurable options that govern how pull replication behaves for your WINS server.

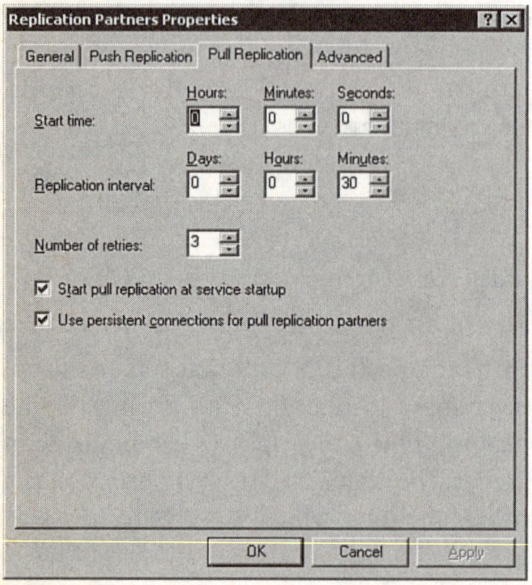

FIGURE 4.14 The Pull Replication tab provides options that allow you to configure how WINS pull replication behaves.

The options on the Pull Replication tab are fairly straightforward and pertain to how the pull replication should occur for this server. You can, in most cases, leave the default entries for Start time and Replication interval as is—doing so will result in a replication schedule that starts push replication every 30 minutes. The Number of Retries option allows you to specify how many failed attempts the server will make to replicate with a partner before giving up. Additionally, you can configure the server to push replicate at startup and use persistent connections with replication partners; both of these options are defaults and should typically stay selected.

The Advanced Tab

The Advanced tab, seen in Figure 4.15, provides configurable options that govern how pull replication behaves for your WINS server.

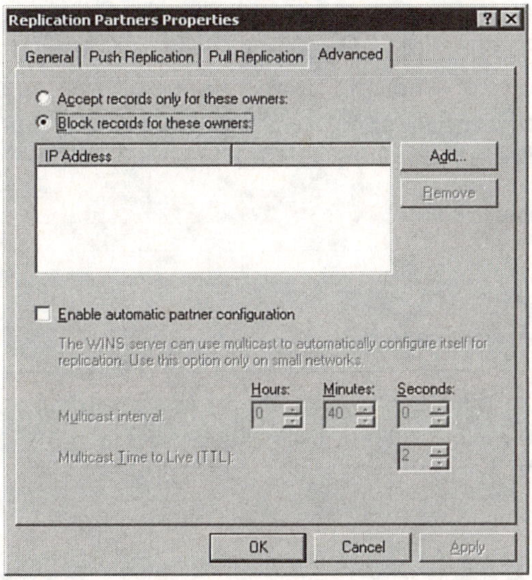

FIGURE 4.15 The Advanced tab provides you with the rest of the replication options.

The options found on the Advanced tab are a collection of what didn't fit anywhere else. For instance, you have the option to configure a list of servers that will be the only ones from which you accept new WINS records. You also have the option to configure a list of servers from which you will block acceptance of new records. This can be helpful in larger enterprises where there may be unknown WINS servers and you want to limit replication to only those servers you know.

Conversely, you have the option to allow the WINS server to automatically discover and configure replication partners through a scheduled multicast message. Typically, you'll not want to configure the auto discovery settings; doing so will lead to loss of administrative control over how replication is configured and how it occurs for your WINS servers.

EXAM ALERT

Global Replication Settings Because we just finished discussing configuring replication partners, these parameters should look familiar. However, in this section, the changes apply to any replication partners created after the modifications are made. They will not be applied to existing replication partners.

You have now successfully configured all the possible Windows replication partner parameters. Let's take a quick look at identifying WINS issues.

Troubleshooting WINS Issues

The majority of WINS issues you encounter will be related to connectivity, so the first item you will need to examine is testing TCP/IP connectivity. The first application for testing IP connectivity is the `ping` utility. `ping` enables you to send an Internet Control Message Protocol (ICMP) to a TCP/IP host. By using the correct flag, `ping` can also perform name resolution as part of its testing procedure. The correct format for this command is this:

```
ping -a <destination address>
```

Used in this way, the `-a` switches provide host name resolution.

NOTE

`ping` Rides Again You should be familiar enough by now with the options available for using the `ping` command, but if you need a refresher, refer to Chapter 1 and look them over again.

A sample `ping` session might look like this:

```
ping -a ptgms02
Pinging PTGMS02.corp.quepublishing.com [192.168.0.156] with 32 bytes of data:
Reply from 192.168.0.156: bytes=32 time<1ms TTL=128
Reply from 192.168.0.156: bytes=32 time<1ms TTL=128
Reply from 192.168.0.156: bytes=32 time<1ms TTL=128
Reply from 192.168.0.156: bytes=32 time<1ms TTL=128
Ping statistics for 192.168.0.156:
    Packets: Sent = 4, Received = 4, Lost = 0 (0% loss),
Approximate round trip times in milli-seconds:
    Minimum = 0ms, Maximum = 0ms, Average = 0ms
```

Because the number of sent packets equals the number of received packets, the connection between the workstation and the WINS server is good. If you do not get any packets returned, you should investigate the network issues further.

The next piece of the WINS puzzle is the client computer WINS configuration. To check whether the WINS configuration of your Windows XP or Windows 2000 client computers is correct, perform Step by Step 4.3.

STEP BY STEP

4.3 Checking the WINS Settings in a Windows XP Client Computer

1. Open a command prompt by selecting Start, Programs, Accessories, Command Prompt.
2. At the command prompt, type **`ipconfig/all`**. You will get a result similar to the one shown in Figure 4.16.

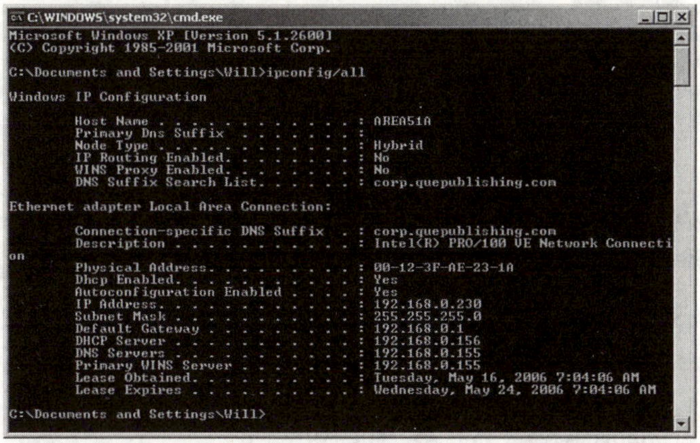

FIGURE 4.16 The `ipconfig` utility gives you all the information on the IP configuration of any of your adapters.

3. Check for the entry `Primary WINS Server`; it will be toward the end of the list of parameters. Verify that a WINS server is configured and that it is the correct server. If no server exists or if the server is incorrect, you will need to set the correct server in one of two places. If you use DHCP, you must update your DHCP settings. If you are using static addresses, the WINS server can be configured by using the Network applet in the Control Panel and setting the correct server in the TCP/IP Properties.

The final piece of the WINS puzzle is verifying that the server is functioning. You should check several things, including the following:

- **Is the WINS service running?**—You can determine this by opening the Task Manager (press Ctrl+Alt+Del and select Task Manager) and, on the Processes tab, verifying that the WINS service (`wins.exe`) is running, as seen in Figure 4.17. If the service is not running, you should probably reboot the server to ensure that no other issues exist.

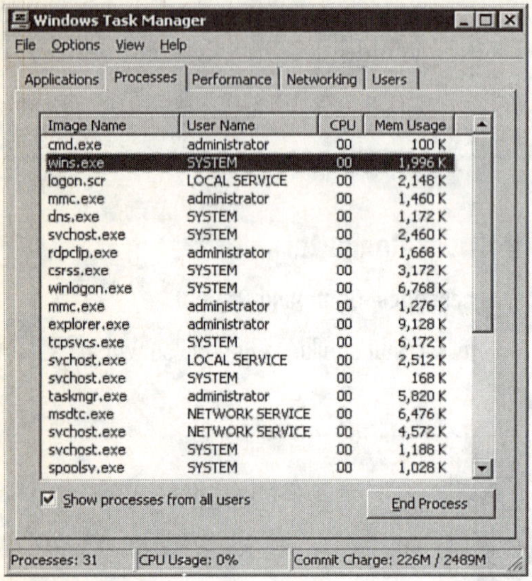

FIGURE 4.17 Task Manager is one of the fastest ways to verify that a service is running.

- **Is the WINS service responding to requests?**—The best way to answer this question is to check the server statistics. (You can also use the Performance console to get some of this information. The use of this console is discussed in depth in the "Managing and Monitoring WINS" section later in this chapter.) To check the server statistics, right-click the server in the WINS Manager and select WINS Server Statistics, as seen in Figure 4.18. If you check these statistics over a 15-minute period and they don't increment, you probably have a WINS issue somewhere.

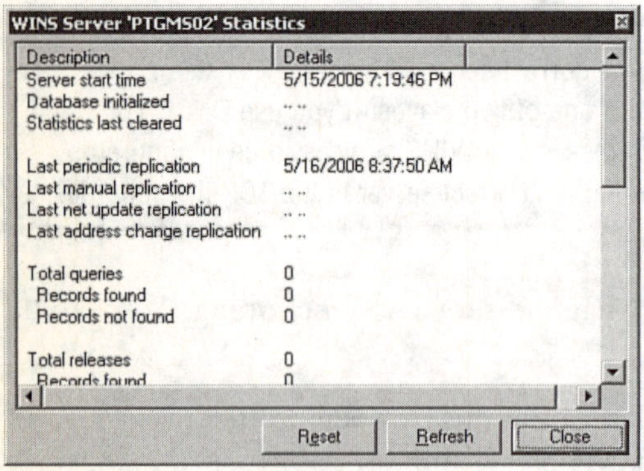

FIGURE 4.18 The WINS Server Statistics dialog box provides an excellent snapshot of the WINS service.

We have covered the basic steps in troubleshooting WINS. As with any equipment-down situation, every situation is unique and might require unique troubleshooting steps.

Challenge

You are the systems administrator for LFE Incorporated, which is a lawn furniture manufacturing company. You have a five-site network, and each site has its own IP subnet. You are presently running several Windows NT 4.0 workstations and servers and are in the process of upgrading to Windows Server 2003 servers for the first time.

You have been using `lmhosts` files for NetBIOS name resolution thus far, but you would like to move to a centralized name resolution solution as part of the Windows Server 2003 migration that still allows you to support legacy applications. You need to ensure that name resolution is available for all computers on all subnets and that they resolve all hosts on the network.

Through your discussions with the key stakeholders in this project, you've determined the following key points for the deployment:

- You have a five-site network, each site with its own IP subnet.
- You need a centralized NetBIOS name resolution service to allow users to resolve names.

Your task is to implement the required WINS solution for LFE Incorporated.

Try to complete this exercise on your own, listing your conclusions on a sheet of paper. After you have completed the exercise, compare your results to those given here.

Answers

This is an excellent example of a small Microsoft network desperately in need of a WINS infrastructure. A good WINS design requires that a WINS server be at each location for both local and remote resolution. To make it work, you need to do the following:

1. Install the Windows Server 2003 WINS service on at least one Windows Server 2003 server in each location.
2. Configure the WINS servers as replication partners, and make sure they replicate their databases appropriately.
3. Configure each of the client computers to use WINS resolution with the local WINS server as the primary server.
4. If you are using DHCP, be sure to update the DHCP setting to reflect the new WINS servers.

Configuring NetBIOS Name Resolution

Microsoft TCP/IP uses NetBIOS over TCP/IP (NetBT) as specified in RFCs 1001 and 1002 to support the NetBIOS client and server programs in the LAN and WAN environments. Before we discuss the specifics of NetBIOS name resolution, let's briefly review how computers communicate on the network. This should help in understanding how the various NetBIOS modes work and why some are preferable to others.

Computers can communicate on a network in two ways:

- Through broadcast messages, which every computer receives.
- Through directed messages, which are sent to a specific computer.

Whenever possible, it was preferable to communicate through directed messages. This cut down on the amount of network traffic and ensured that only the affected hosts received the message. This also ensured that the messages propagated across routers. Because of this, Microsoft needed to ensure that WINS communicated primarily with directed messages. The company accomplished this by allowing several types of NetBIOS naming methods. These naming methods are commonly called *node types*. A *node* is simply a device on a network. Every computer running a Microsoft OS is configured to use one of four node types. The node type determines whether the computer will register and resolve names through broadcast messages, directed messages, or some combination of broadcast and directed messages.

EXAM ALERT

Microsoft Does Test on Backward Compatibility Don't be fooled. Just because WINS is a legacy technology doesn't mean you won't be tested on it on the exam. Microsoft recognizes the importance of backward compatibility, and as a result, you can expect to see questions about WINS on this exam. If you have not worked with it in a legacy environment, take the necessary steps to make sure you understand how WINS works.

Before you can work with WINS, you need to know what the node types are and when they are used:

- **b-node (broadcast node)**—Relies exclusively on broadcast messages and is the oldest NetBIOS name registration and resolution mode. A host needing to resolve a name request sends a message to every host within earshot, requesting the address associated with a host name. b-node has two shortcomings: broadcast traffic is undesirable and becomes a significant user of network bandwidths, and TCP/IP routers don't forward broadcast messages, which restricts b-node operation to a single network segment.
- **p-node (point-to-point node)**—Relies on WINS servers for NetBIOS name registration and resolution. Client computers register themselves with a WINS server when they come on the network. They then contact the WINS server with NetBIOS name resolution requests. WINS servers communicate using directed messages, which can cross routers, so p-node can operate on large networks. Unfortunately, if the WINS

server is unavailable or if a node isn't configured to contact a WINS server, p-node name resolution fails.

- **m-node (modified node)**—A hybrid mode that first attempts to register and resolve NetBIOS names using the b-node mechanism. If that fails, an attempt is made to use p-node name resolution. m-node was the first hybrid mode put into operation, but it has the disadvantage of favoring b-node operation, which is associated with high levels of broadcast traffic.
- **h-node (hybrid node)**—A hybrid mode that favors the use of WINS for NetBIOS name registration and resolution. When a computer needs to resolve a NetBIOS name, it first attempts to use p-node resolution to resolve a name via WINS. Only if WINS resolution fails does the host resort to b-node to resolve the name via broadcasts. Because it typically results in the best network utilization, h-node is the default mode of operation for Microsoft TCP/IP client computers configured to use WINS for name resolution. Microsoft recommends leaving TCP/IP client computers in the default h-node configuration.

EXAM ALERT

Configuring the Node Type If you're using DHCP to provide TCP/IP configuration information to your clients, you can use DHCP Option 46 "WINS/NBT Node Type" to configure the node type in use. Additionally, DHCP Option 44 is used to configure WINS servers to be used by your clients.

The Method WINS Uses to Resolve a Name

The time might come when you need to understand exactly how WINS registers and resolves a name. (Because h-node is not only the default but also the recommended configuration, we will restrict our discussion to the h-node name resolution.) When a WINS client computer configured for h-node needs to resolve a host name, it goes through the following steps:

1. It checks its NetBIOS name cache. If the name is found, it returns it.
2. It queries the WINS server. If the name is found, it returns it.
3. It issues a broadcast to find the host on the local network. If the name is found, it returns it.
4. It looks for the `lmhosts` file to check for an entry. If the name is found, it returns it.
5. It looks for the `hosts` file to check for an entry. If the name is found, it returns it.
6. It queries the DNS server for the entry. If the name is found, it returns it.
7. If all these methods fail, the WINS client computer issues an error message saying that it can't communicate with the host.

Although networks can be organized using a mixture of node types, Microsoft recommends against it. b-node client computers do not receive p-node directed messages, and p-node client computers ignore b-node broadcasts. Therefore, it is conceivable that two client computers could be established with the same NetBIOS name.

If WINS is enabled on a Windows XP or Windows 2000 computer, the system uses h-node by default. Without WINS, the system uses b-node by default. Non-WINS client computers can access WINS through a WINS proxy, which is a WINS-enabled computer that listens to name query broadcasts and then queries the WINS server on behalf of the requesting client computer.

EXAM ALERT

Registering with WINS When your Windows client computer enters the network, it registers with WINS so that other Microsoft client computers can resolve its name to an address. For the exam, you should be aware that although a WINS proxy server can be used to resolve names for hosts that have registered with WINS, it can't be used to register with WINS. You need access to the WINS server to successfully register.

To see which node type is configured on a Windows XP computer, follow the steps outlined in Step by Step 4.4.

STEP BY STEP

4.4 Identifying the NetBIOS Node Type

1. Open a command prompt by selecting Start, Programs, Accessories, Command Prompt.
2. At the command prompt, type **`ipconfig/all`**. You will get a result similar to the one shown in Figure 4.16. The node type is indicated to the right of the heading Node Type. In this example, the machine is running in h-node, the default for Windows XP and Windows 2000.

Next, let's look at the best way to manage and monitor WINS and manage your new WINS server.

Managing and Monitoring WINS

We have looked at installing and configuring the Windows Server 2003 WINS Server service. Next, we need to look at managing and monitoring the server now that it is running. If your job is typical of most, you will spend a great deal more time managing WINS servers than installing them.

Although the WINS server includes limited monitoring capabilities, you do have access to the WINS statistics referenced in the "Troubleshooting" section of the chapter. To get the server statistics, just open WINS Manager and right-click the server in question. From the context menu, select Display Server Statistics, and a snapshot of the server statistics is displayed, as seen previously in Figure 4.18. The WINS statistics display should be a starting point for you when you are unsure of what the problem might be or just want to get a quick snapshot of what is going on with your WINS server.

The WINS manager application has additional capabilities. From the open WINS manager application, you can select the WINS server and then use the Action menu to access these actions:

- **Display Server Statistics**—This option displays statistics discussed in a previous section of this chapter.
- **Scavenge Database**—This option enables you to manually clean unused entries from the WINS database.
- **Verify Database Consistency**—This option causes the server to go out to the network hosts and verify the entries in the WINS database. This process can be very processor and network intensive, so be sure to run it after hours.
- **Verify Version ID Consistency**—This option forces the WINS server to go to all the other WINS servers on the network and then check the database version numbers to ensure that they are consistent. This is potentially another long operation, so it should be run after hours—or at least not when everyone in the office is trying to read email.
- **Start Push Replication**—This option manually performs a push replication.
- **Start Pull Replication**—This option manually performs a pull replication.
- **Back Up Database**—This option enables you to make a backup copy of the WINS database. Always be sure you have a copy of this database, just in case. If you specify the backup directory, the server will automatically back up the database every 24 hours.
- **Restore the Database**—This option enables you to restore a backup copy of the database.
- **Tasks**—This option leads to a menu consisting of the following commands:
    - **Start**—Starts the WINS Server service. This option is available only if the service is stopped or paused.
    - **Stop**—Stops the WINS Server service. Available when the service is running or paused. This option causes the server statistics to be reset.
    - **Pause**—Pauses the WINS Server service. This option does not reset the statistics.

  - **Resume**—Resumes the WINS Server service when paused. This option is available only when the service is paused.
  - **Restart**—Restarts the WINS Server service. This option is available unless the server is stopped.
- **Delete**—This option deletes a WINS server from the WINS manager.
- **Refresh**—This option causes all the displayed information to be refreshed with a current status.
- **Export List**—This option enables you to export the information from the WINS server to a tab- or comma-delimited text or Unicode text file.
- **Properties**—This option opens the server properties, as discussed in a previous section of this chapter.

The Windows Server 2003 WINS service also includes some new functionality for managing the WINS database. If you open the WINS manager and click Active Registrations, you will see a list of all the dynamically added entries in the WINS database. Although this is useful, it would be nice to be able to search for a specific entry, or even to filter on specific record types. The good news is that you can. If you right-click the Active Registration folder and select Find by Name or Find by Owner, you can search the WINS database for specific entries. Under Find by Owner, you can even filter which WINS record types should be shown. If you are working in a large environment (500 computers or more), you will find these capabilities invaluable because computers can often enter 10–12 entries each into the WINS database. You probably won't relish reading through 5,000–6,000 WINS records looking for a specific machine.

The Windows Server 2003 WINS service enables you to delete not only static records, but also dynamic records. This is a major improvement over previous versions of WINS, in which you couldn't delete dynamic entries.

Now that we have examined the options for managing the WINS server, let's take a look at some of the ways to monitor the service. Before you do Step by Step 4.5, you should look at which counters you can use to monitor WINS. The WINS object has the following counters associated with it:

- **Failed Queries/Sec**—Gives you the number of failed WINS queries per second. If this number is very high or suddenly spikes, you might have an issue with WINS resolution.
- **Failed Releases/Sec**—Gives you the number of failed WINS released per second. If this number is very high or suddenly spikes, you might have an issue with WINS resolution.

- **Group Conflicts/Sec**—The rate at which group registrations by the WINS server resulted in conflicts with the database.
- **Group Registrations/Sec**—The rate at which group registrations are being received.
- **Group Renewals/Sec**—The rate at which group registrations are being renewed.
- **Queries/Sec**—The rate at which queries are being received.
- **Releases/Sec**—The rate at which releases are being received.
- **Successful Queries/Sec**—The number of successful queries per second. This is useful if you are trending your WINS usage.
- **Successful Releases/Sec**—The number of successful releases per second. This is useful if you are trending your WINS usage.
- **Total Number of Conflicts/Sec**—This is the sum of the unique and group conflicts per second.
- **Total Number of Registrations/Sec**—This is the sum of the unique and group registrations per second.
- **Total Number of Renewals/Sec**—This is the sum of the unique and group renewals per second.
- **Unique Conflicts/Sec**—The rate at which unique registrations and renewals causes conflicts with the database.
- **Unique Registrations/Sec**—The rate at which unique registrations are received by the server.
- **Unique Renewals/Sec**—The rate at which unique renewals are received by the server.

To configure WINS performance monitoring, follow Step by Step 4.5.

STEP BY STEP

4.5 Monitoring WINS Performance

1. Open the Performance application by selecting Start, Programs, Administrative Tools, Performance.
2. In the Performance console, select System Monitor node, as seen in Figure 4.19.
3. To create an entry in System Monitor, click the Add (+) icon. The Add Counters windows opens. By default, it opens to the Processor performance object.
4. Select the WINS Server performance object. You will see the list of counters that are available for the WINS service, as seen in Figure 4.20.

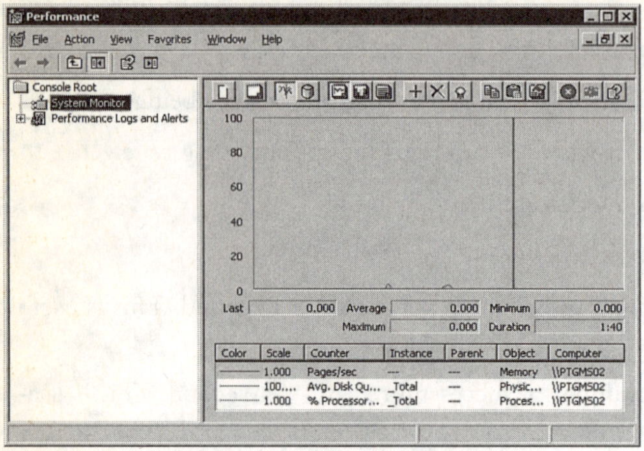

FIGURE 4.19 The System Monitor enables you to monitor the performance of your server's statistics in real-time.

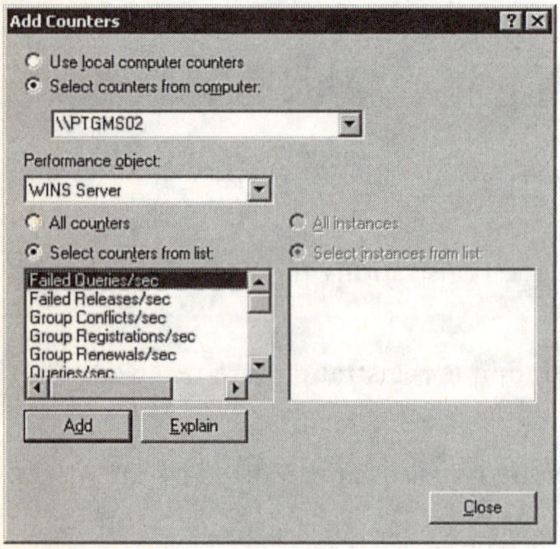

FIGURE 4.20 The counters associated with WINS enable you to comprehensively examine the WINS server's activities.

5. After you have decided which counter you want to monitor, click Add. You can add multiple counters either by selecting each counter and clicking Add or by holding down the Ctrl key while you select all the counters you want to monitor and clicking Add. Click Close when you are done. You will see your counters being graphed in a manner similar to those shown in Figure 4.21.

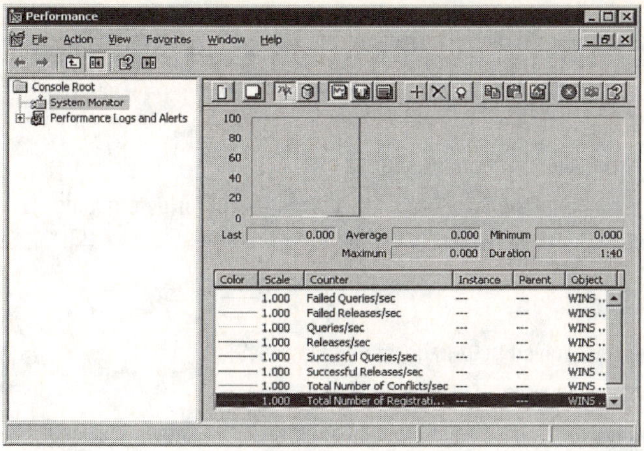

FIGURE 4.21 Once you've added counters, you can view the performance of the server.

We've looked at the management options available in the WINS manager application, and we've discussed how to monitor the performance of the various WINS counters using the Performance console. At this point, you should have a good understanding of the Windows Server 2003 WINS Server service and WINS in general.

Client Tools

A thorough understanding of WINS and server-based resolutions is great, but it won't help diagnose problems on a client. The tools discussed in the following sections—`nbtstat`, `ipconfig`, and `netdiag`—are helpful in resolving name resolution problems.

nbtstat

NBT stands for NetBIOS over TCP/IP. Thus, `nbtstat` gives you statistics for NetBIOS over TCP/IP. The utility is used to determine which NetBIOS names the machine has cached and to which IP addresses those names resolved. You need to be aware of the options for using the `nbtstat`, as outlined in Table 4.1.

TABLE 4.1 The `nbtstat` Command Switches

Switch	Description
-a	Displays the name table of a remote machine given its name. Figure 4.22 shows the results of nbtstat -a.
-A	Displays the name table of a remote machine given its IP address.
-c	Displays the cache of NetBIOS names held by the local machine. This is useful for determining which names the local client has requested recently and how they were resolved. Figure 4.23 shows the results of NBTSTAT -c.
-n	Displays a list of local NetBIOS names.
-r	Displays a list of names that have been resolved by broadcast and via WINS.
-R	Purges and reloads the remote cache name table.
-s	Displays a sessions table, showing the names of remote machines. Figure 4.24 shows the results of NBTSTAT -s.
-S	Displays a sessions table, showing only IP addresses for remote machines.
-RR	Performs a release and refresh by sending Name Release packets to the WINS and then starting a Refresh.

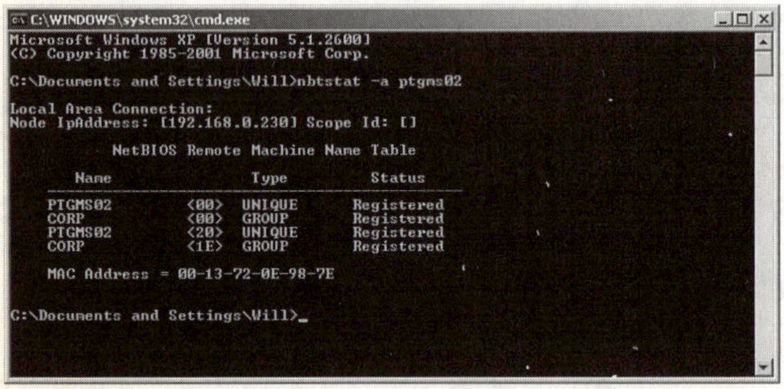

FIGURE 4.22 `nbtstat -a` shows the machine's NetBIOS table.

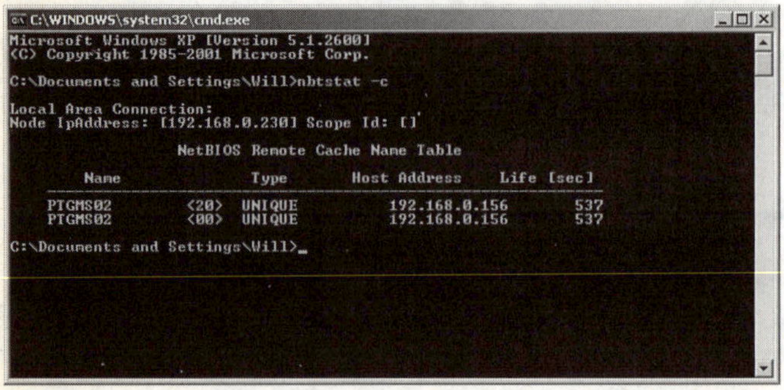

FIGURE 4.23 `nbtstat -c` shows the local NetBIOS cache.

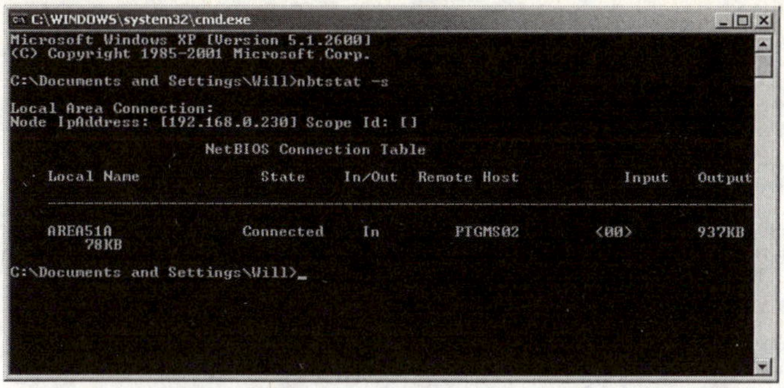

FIGURE 4.24 `nbtstat -s` shows the current NetBIOS sessions.

ipconfig

Perhaps the most widely used TCP/IP utility is the `ipconfig` utility. It is the only way to display all the dynamic information retrieved from a DHCP server. It also allows you to update DHCP and name resolution information. `ipconfig` is the primary utility you will use when attempting to diagnose and fix IP configuration problems, and it was discussed in depth in Chapter 1.

EXAM ALERT

`ipconfig` **Know the options for the `ipconfig` utility, and, more importantly, know what they do. You'll be expected to know which option to use in a given situation.**

netdiag

Unlike the other tools discussed in this chapter, `netdiag` is not included as a part of the standard Windows Server 2003 installation. To install `netdiag`, you must install the Windows Server 2003 Support tools or download it as a separate update. The `netdiag` utility is available from the Microsoft Web site for free.

For the exam, you need to know that the `netdiag` tool is used to diagnose all types of connectivity problems. It automatically runs a series of tests to help you determine where your connectivity problems lay.

NOTE

netdiag You can get more information about the Windows Server 2003 SP1 Support Tools by visiting the following Knowledge Base article: http://support.microsoft.com/kb/892777. This article also provides a link to the download. Alternatively, you can find the Windows Server 2003 Support Tools on your Windows Server 2003 product CD; it's the file named `suptools.msi` located in the "\SUPPORT\TOOLS" folder.

File-Based Name Resolution

One of the easiest ways to ensure that name resolution is working is to hardcode it into the local files that Windows first looks to for information. By entering the information in the local files, you can ensure that the computer does not attempt to resolve the name and will use the address you've specified. Two files are used for name resolution. The first file, the `hosts` file, resolves IP names into IP addresses and can be thought of as an alternative to DNS. The second file, the `lmhosts` file, resolves NetBIOS names into IP addresses and can be thought of as an alternative to WINS. In the following sections, we examine these files and how you can use them to troubleshoot.

hosts

In the last chapter, you learned that the first name resolution solution on the Internet used a host file and that DNS was added later. On a Windows Server 2003 computer, the `hosts` file is located in the `%windir%\system32\drivers\etc` folder. This is the file you must modify to change the hard-coded host resolution. Entries in the `hosts` file are simple; they begin with the IP address and are followed by the host name. If you open the `hosts` file on your system, you will see that it already contains the special localhost name, which you can use as a template for adding new names.

After you make your changes, you do not need to reboot the system. Windows Server 2003 will detect the change to the file and will automatically use it, although it's never a bad idea to run the `ipconfig /flushdns` command after making modifications to the file.

lmhosts

`lmhosts` is short for LAN Manager Hosts. It's one of the few places in which Windows Server 2003 truly shows its OS/2 LAN Manager heritage. The format of the `lmhosts` file is different from the `hosts` file, but it is located in the same `%windir%\system32\drivers\etc` directory as the `hosts` file. Unlike the `hosts` file, no default `lmhosts` file is created when you install Windows Server 2003. However, Windows Server 2003 includes an `lmhosts.sam` file that is a sample file that you can rename to `lmhosts` and use as a starting point.

The `lmhosts` file is similar to the `hosts` file, except that it has these additional options:

- **#PRE**—Placed after an entry, it causes the entry to be preloaded. The effect of this is that the entry is permanently loaded into memory. This is a good idea for hosts that will be accessed frequently.

- **#DOM:*<domain>***—Associates an entry with the domain given. Helps the computer locate a domain controller for the network.
- **#INCLUDE *<filename>***—Includes the named file as if it were located in the `lmhosts` file. This is infrequently used because there is additional overhead to process the file.

In general, you must know that the `lmhosts` file is used for NetBIOS name resolution and that the `hosts` file is used for IP name resolution.

Chapter Summary

In this chapter, you learned the intricacies of NetBIOS name resolution, which is heavily focused on the use of WINS servers but also uses broadcasts to resolve names when WINS servers are not available.

WINS is important because it allows for NetBIOS name resolution across router boundaries and reduces or eliminates the need for computers to broadcast to register and resolve machine names. Preventing broadcasts is important to maintain performance on today's networks that use Ethernet switches to improve overall network performance.

Next, you learned how to configure NetBIOS name resolution, as well as how to configure WINS replication partners. Then, we discussed the various mechanisms available for managing and monitoring your WINS servers.

You then learned the basic troubleshooting commands and how they are used to diagnose and fix IP configuration problems. The use of the `ipconfig` utility in particular is important for troubleshooting and resolving basic problems.

Finally, you learned the basics of the Windows Server 2003 name resolution files. These files, `hosts` and `lmhosts`, resolve IP names and NetBIOS names, respectively.

Key Terms

- Active Directory
- b-node
- Domain Name System (DNS)
- Dynamic Host Control Protocol (DHCP)
- h-node
- `hosts` file
- Internet Control Message Protocol (ICMP)
- `lmhosts` file
- m-node
- NetBIOS
- p-node
- Pull replication
- Push/pull replication

- Push replication
- Replication partner
- Request for Comment (RFC) documents
- Transmission Control Protocol/Internet Protocol (TCP/IP)
- Windows Internet Naming Service (WINS)

Apply Your Knowledge

In this chapter, you have learned what WINS is and how it works. In the following exercises, you will practice some of the concepts and methods discussed in this chapter.

Exercises

4.1 Installing WINS

In this exercise, you will install WINS on your Windows Server 2003 server.

Estimated Time: 10 minutes

1. Log on to Windows Server 2003 using the Administrator account or another account that has administrator privileges.
2. Open the Control Panel and then open the Add/Remove Programs applet. The Add or Remove Programs dialog box appears.
3. Click Add/Remove Windows Components on the left side of the Add or Remove Programs dialog box. The Windows Components Wizard dialog box appears.
4. Select Networking Services and click Details. The Networking Services dialog box appears. Select Windows Internet Naming Service (WINS) and then click OK.
5. On the next screen that appears, click Next to complete the installation. The Windows Component Wizard prompts you for the Windows Server 2003 CD-ROM if it needs to copy files.
6. When the wizard is finished, it displays a summary window of the changes to be made. Click Finish to complete the installation.

4.2 Configuring a Replication Partner

In this exercise, you will configure a replication partner.

Estimated Time: 5 minutes

1. Open the WINS manager by selecting Start, Programs, Administrative Tools, WINS.
2. Right-click Replication Partners and select New Replication Partner from the context menu.
3. Enter the server name **`winstest`**. You will be prompted to enter the address of the server because it cannot be found on your network.
4. Enter **`10.10.10.254`** and click OK. You will be returned to the WINS Manager.
5. Click Replication Partners in the left pane. You should see your new replication partner in the right pane.

4.3 Performing a Manual Push Replication

In this exercise, you will manually perform a push replication.

Estimated Time: 5 minutes

1. Open the WINS manager by selecting Start, Programs, Administrative Tools, WINS.
2. Right-click WINS server and select Start Push Replication.
3. Enter the server name or IP address of the other WINS server and click OK.
4. Select Start for This Partner Only as the replication method. You can select Propagate to All Partners as the other method. Click OK; you will receive a message that the replication request has been queued.
5. Check the event log for a status of the request and to see when it has completed.

4.4 Performing a Manual Pull Replication

In this exercise, you will manually perform a pull replication.

Estimated Time: 5 minutes

1. Open the WINS manager by selecting Start, Programs, Administrative Tools, WINS.
2. Right-click WINS server and select Start Pull Replication.
3. Enter the server name or IP address of the other WINS server and click OK.
4. When asked to confirm the request, click Yes. You will receive a message stating that the replication request has been queued.
5. Check the event log for a status of the request and to see when it has completed.

Exam Questions

1. You are the WINS administrator for LFE Incorporated. You want to be sure to have a reliable backup of your WINS database available in case of problems, but you don't want to manually back up the database every day. What is the best way to automatically back up your WINS database?

   ❍ **A.** Purchase a third-party backup utility and schedule nightly backups of the entire server.

   ❍ **B.** Use the Windows Scheduler service and configure a WINS Database Backup task.

   ❍ **C.** In the WINS manager, specify the backup directory and backup interval.

   ❍ **D.** In the WINS manager, specify the backup directory.

2. You are the systems administrator for Lost in the Woods Guide Service. You have a Windows Server 2003 server running WINS in your corporate headquarters and another in a branch office. You want the server in the branch office to get a replica of the corporate server's database every two hours. How do you do it?

   ❍ **A.** Configure the branch WINS server as a push replication partner with a two-hour interval.

   ❍ **B.** Configure the branch WINS server as a pull replication server with a two-hour interval.

   ❍ **C.** Configure the corporate WINS server as a push replication partner with a two-hour interval.

   ❍ **D.** Configure the corporate WINS server as a pull replication server with a two-hour interval.

3. You are the systems administrator for a five-location pet food manufacturer. You have a WINS server at all five locations, and you would like them to replicate with each other automatically. How do you do it?

   ❍ **A.** Configure each WINS server as a replication partner. In the Replication Partner Properties, select Replicate with All Partners.

   ❍ **B.** Configure each WINS server as a replication partner. In the Replication Partner Properties, select Replicate Only with Partners.

   ❍ **C.** In the Replication Partner Properties, deselect Replicate Only with Partners. The server will automatically replicate with any WINS servers.

   ❍ **D.** Install WINS. Any WINS servers on the network will automatically replicate.

4. You are the systems administrator for LFE Inc., a novelty manufacturing company. You have a large population of Windows NT 4.0 Workstation client computers on your Windows Server 2003 network. You have a new administrator who is trying to learn how WINS works. You want to explain it. By default, which WINS server will a client computer use for resolution?

❍ **A.** The WINS server that responds first to the broadcast request

❍ **B.** The default WINS server the client receives from DHCP or that is configured in TCP/IP properties

❍ **C.** The primary WINS server the client receives from DHCP or that is configured in TCP/IP properties

❍ **D.** The WINS server that is the least number of network hops away

5. You are the systems administrator for BT Machines, a heavy equipment manufacturing company. You have a large population of Windows NT 4 Workstation client computers on your Windows Server 2003 network. You are concerned that there are computers coming on the network that have the same NetBIOS name. Which WINS statistic should you check to see if this is the case?

❍ **A.** Unique Conflicts/Sec

❍ **B.** Total Number of Conflicts/Sec

❍ **C.** Group Conflicts/Sec

❍ **D.** Failed Releases/Sec

6. You are the systems administrator for BT Machines, a heavy equipment manufacturing company. You have a large population of Windows NT 4 Workstation client computers on your Windows Server 2003 network. You want to quickly check the total number of client computers adding updates to the WINS database. Which parameter should you check?

❍ **A.** Unique Registrations/Sec

❍ **B.** Total Number of Registrations/Sec

❍ **C.** Total Number of Renewals/Sec

❍ **D.** Total Number of Registrations/Sec and Total Number of Renewals/Sec

7. You are the systems administrator for Blue Sky Air, and you are training another administrator to assist with maintaining the network. She is having a hard time understanding the different NetBIOS node types and knowing which type of node the new Windows XP Professional computers use. What is the default node type for Windows XP?

❍ **A.** h-node

❍ **B.** m-node

❍ **C.** p-node

❍ **D.** b-node

8. Now that your new assistant understands the node type used by Windows XP Professional by default, she would like you to help her differentiate the node types. Which of the following statements about node types is accurate?

   ❍ **A.** h-node and m-node favor WINS servers, but m-node does not have the capability to use broadcasts if the WINS server is down.

   ❍ **B.** h-node and b-node favor WINS servers, but b-node does not have the capability to use broadcasts if the WINS server is down.

   ❍ **C.** b-node and m-node both favor broadcast resolution first, but b-node can resolve using a WINS server if the host is on another subnet.

   ❍ **D.** h-node and p-node both favor WINS servers, but h-node can use a broadcast for name resolution if the WINS server is not available.

9. You are the systems administrator for Little Faith Enterprises, a publishing company. You use Windows Server 2003 servers for the corporate headquarters but have a mix of Windows 2000 Professional and Windows NT 4 client computers on the network. You have deployed WINS for backward compatibility, but you are unsure whether WINS is working. What is the best way to find out?

   ❍ **A.** Using the Performance console, select the WINS server object and the Successful Resolutions/Sec counter. Verify that the counter value is greater than 0.

   ❍ **B.** Using the Performance console, select the WINS server object and the Queries/Sec counter. Verify that the counter value is greater than 0.

   ❍ **C.** Open the WINS manager, select the server in question, and from the Action menu, select Server Statistics. Verify that the number of Total Queries is increasing. Click Refresh to update the statistics.

   ❍ **D.** Open the WINS manager, select the server in question, and from the Action menu, select Server Statistics. Verify that the number of Records Found Under Total Queries is increasing. Click Refresh to update the statistics.

10. You are the systems administrator for New Riders Harley Davidson and are installing a WINS server on your Windows Server 2003 server. Your end users are all using DHCP. What is the best way to configure the workstations to use the WINS server?

   ❍ **A.** Make sure the WINS server is installed on a domain controller. WINS resolution will occur automatically.

   ❍ **B.** Modify the DHCP scope options for the WINS server to include the address of the new WINS server.

   ❍ **C.** Open the Network applet and open the TCP/IP properties. On the WINS tab, modify the TCP/IP properties to point at the WINS server. Repeat this for each machine.

   ❍ **D.** Update the `lmhosts` file to include the address of the new WINS server.

11. You are the systems administrator for a three-location car dealership. One location is the headquarters, and the other two are dealerships. You are migrating from a workgroup-based Windows NT 4 network to a Windows Server 2003 network. Each site is connected to the other two using a frame relay connection and a bridge. As part of the migration, you have decided to deploy WINS for the legacy client computers; however, management would like to spend as little as possible. What is the least expensive way to roll out WINS in this environment?

❍ **A.** Install one WINS server on the headquarters network.

❍ **B.** Install one WINS server on each network.

❍ **C.** Install a WINS server at headquarters and another for redundancy at one of the dealerships.

❍ **D.** Install one server on each dealership network and two in the headquarters network for redundancy.

12. The WINS service was created to replace which of the following?

❍ **A.** The Domain Name Service

❍ **B.** The `hosts` file

❍ **C.** The `lmhosts` file

❍ **D.** The WINS file

13. You are the overworked systems administrator for a single-site direct-marketing company. You have two network segments in your building, with servers on both networks, and a Windows Server 2003 server is being used to route between segments. You have a mixture of MS-DOS, Windows 95/98, Windows NT 4.0 Workstation, and Windows 2000 Professional computers as client computers in this network. You install WINS on the server, and your DOS client computers are incapable of seeing the servers on the other side of the router. Why can't the DOS client computers see computers across the router?

❍ **A.** DOS does not use a dynamic routing protocol, so it can't see across the router.

❍ **B.** DOS can't interpret WINS names for resolution.

❍ **C.** DOS requires a WINS client computer before being capable of interfacing with the WINS server.

❍ **D.** DOS uses b-node resolution of NetBIOS names.

14. You are the systems administrator for the Women's Place clothing store. You have six satellite locations all connected with low-bandwidth WAN links. Each location has its own WINS server for name resolution and will need to be replicated to. What is the best configuration for the WINS replication from the corporate WINS server to those in the field?

❍ **A.** Configure a pull replication from the remote servers to the central server and schedule it to occur whenever 100 entries have been added to the table.

❍ **B.** Configure a push replication from the remote servers to the central server and schedule it to occur whenever 100 entries have been added to the table.

❍ **C.** Configure a pull replication from the central server to the remote servers and schedule it to occur whenever 100 entries have been added to the table.

❍ **D.** Configure a push replication from the central server to the remote servers and schedule it to occur whenever 100 entries have been added to the table.

Answers to Exam Questions

1. **D.** If you specify the backup directory, the server will automatically back up the WINS database every 24 hours. While you'll likely be using a third-party backup solution for your network, one is not required specifically to back up the WINS database; thus Answer A is incorrect. WINS database backups cannot be scheduled outside of the WINS console; thus Answer B is incorrect. Since WINS will back up the database daily, there is no need to specify the internal; thus Answer C is incorrect. For more information, see the section "Managing and Monitoring WINS."

2. **B.** Pull replications are triggered by a time interval. For the branch WINS server to get a replica of the corporate WINS database, it would need to be scheduled to pull the information at a two-hour interval. Push replication is not time based, but instead is change based; thus Answers A and C are incorrect. Configuring the corporate office WINS server as a pull partner; would cause WINS replication to occur in the opposite direction than desired; thus Answer D is incorrect. For more information, see the section "Configuring WINS Replication."

3. **B.** After the WINS servers have been configured as replication partners, they replicate with each other based on the replication configuration. There is no "Replicate with All Partners" option; thus Answers A and C are incorrect. Without performing any additional configuration, you'll get no replication; thus Answer D is incorrect. For more information, see the section "Configuring WINS Replication."

4. **C.** Because no default WINS server exists (don't confuse it with the default gateway), the answer is C, the primary WINS server. Therefore, Answers A, B, and D are incorrect. For more information, see the section "Configuring NetBIOS Name Resolution."

5. **A.** The conflicts per second would show you whether you have computers with name conflicts. The Total Number of Conflicts/Sec counter is the sum of the unique and group conflicts per second; thus Answer B is incorrect. The Group Conflicts/Sec counter is the the rate at which group

registrations by the WINS server resulted in conflicts with the database. The Failed Releases/Sec counter is the number of failed WINS releases per second. For more information, see the section "Managing and Monitoring WINS."

6. **D.** If you want to capture all the client computers that are registering with the server and not just new registrations, you need to look at the total for both the Total Number of Registrations/Sec and Total Number of Renewals/Sec; thus Answers A, B, and C are incorrect. For more information, see the section "Managing and Monitoring WINS."
7. **A.** Windows XP Professional computers use h-node (hybrid) for NetBIOS name resolution; thus Answers B, C, and D are incorrect. This node type favors the WINS server for name resolution but will attempt to resolve the name by broadcast if the WINS server is unavailable. For more information, see the section "Configuring NetBIOS Name Resolution."
8. **D.** h-node (Hybrid) is the preferred method because it relies on the WINS server before resorting to a broadcast. p-node uses a WINS server but can't use broadcasts for NetBIOS name resolution. m-node tries a broadcast first; thus Answer A is incorrect. b-node uses broadcasts exclusively, which don't cross routers to other subnets; thus Answers B and C are incorrect. For more information, see the section "Configuring NetBIOS Name Resolution."
9. **D.** Although Answer C is almost a correct answer, the Total Queries includes records not found; thus Answers A, B, and C are incorrect. If all the queries are returning a Records Not Found result, the server probably has a problem. You should make sure that the number of records found (successful queries) is increasing. For more information, see the section "Managing and Monitoring WINS."
10. **B.** Because this is a DHCP environment, just add/update the WINS option for the DHCP scope. Answer C might work, but it is much more labor intensive than the one-time scope update. Installing WINS on a Domain Controller is certainly possible, but is not going to accomplish anything in this scenario; thus Answer A is incorrect. On a network with a functioning WINS server, there is no reason to use an `lmhosts` file; thus Answer D is incorrect. For more information, see the section "Installing and Configuring WINS."
11. **A.** Because this is a bridged network, you need just a single server to provide WINS for each location. A bridged network has only one logical segment. This means that broadcasts will propagate across the WAN connections; thus Answers B, C, and D are incorrect. Although this is not a typical configuration, it may still exist on smaller legacy networks. Although using a single server is not recommended, it would work in this environment, although with no redundancy in the event of a failure. For more information, see the section "Installing and Configuring WINS."
12. **C.** WINS is a dynamic replacement for the `lmhosts` file. DNS replaced the `hosts` file; thus Answers A and B are incorrect. There is no such thing as the WINS file; thus Answer D is incorrect. For more information, see the section "Introduction to WINS."
13. **D.** DOS can't use WINS because it is limited to a b-node resolution. b-node is a broadcast-only resolution method, and the broadcasts can't cross the router; thus Answers A, B, and C are incorrect. For more information, see the section "Configuring NetBIOS Name Resolution."

14. **D.** For this question, keep two components in mind. The first is the trigger, which occurs when a certain number of entries are added. It is the least bandwidth-intensive mechanism. The second is the direction the information must travel. Answer D is the only one with the correct combination of these factors; thus Answers A, B, and C are all incorrect. For more information, see the section "Configuring WINS Replication."

Suggested Reading and Resources

1. Davies, Joseph, and Lee, Thomas. *Microsoft Windows Server 2003 TCP/IP Protocols and Services Technical Reference*. Microsoft Press, 2003.
2. "Deploying Network Services," http://technet2.microsoft.com/WindowsServer/en/Library/119050c9-7c4d-4cbf-8f38-97c45e4d01ef1033.mspx.
3. "Technical Overview of Windows Server 2003 Networking and Communications," www.microsoft.com/windowsserver2003/techinfo/overview/netcomm.mspx.
4. "Windows Server 2003 Reviewer's Guide," www.microsoft.com/windowsserver2003/techinfo/overview/reviewersguide.mspx.
5. Windows Server 2003 Online documentation: "Network Services," www.microsoft.com/technet/prodtechnol/windowsserver2003/proddocs/entserver/sag_NPStopnode.asp.

CHAPTER FIVE

Implementing, Managing, and Maintaining Network Security

Implementing and maintaining security of a Windows Server 2003 network is a big job—certainly not one to be taken lightly. Although an MCP exam (Exam 70-298, "Designing Security for a Microsoft Windows Server 2003 Network") is devoted entirely to the design and implementation of security solutions in a Windows Server 2003 network, there are a few basic things about baseline network security that you need to know to pass Exam 70-291, "Implementing, Managing, and Maintaining a Microsoft Windows Server 2003 Network Infrastructure."

Microsoft lists the following objectives for the baseline security portion of the "Implementing, Managing, and Maintaining Network Security" section of Exam 70-291:

Objectives

Implement secure network administration procedures.

- **Implement security baseline settings and audit security settings by using security templates.**
- **Implement the principle of least privilege.**
- Every plan needs a starting point. When it comes to securing a Windows Server 2003 network, a good starting point is to implement baseline settings with one of the many preconfigured security templates included with Windows Server 2003. In addition, you need to understand and live by the principle of least privilege, whereby users (and administrators) have only the minimum permissions required to reasonably perform their jobs. This helps prevent security problems due to account misuse or compromise.

Install and configure software update infrastructure.

- **Install and configure software update services.**
- **Install and configure automatic client update settings.**
- **Configure software updates on earlier operating systems.**
- In a perfect world, you would be able to install your server or client operating system and have it be perfectly secure right out of the box. Although Microsoft has made great progress toward meeting that ideal in Windows Server 2003, it's not quite a reality yet. Part of keeping an operating system secure involves identifying and applying updates as required. Windows Server 2003 makes this easy for you, however, by providing support for Windows Server Update Services (WSUS).

Outline

Study Strategies

- Practice configuring and implementing the built-in security templates as much as you can, which can be a bit of a challenge to fully understand if you've never worked with them before. You should also practice using auditing; practice is the best way to gain an understanding of the topics being presented here.
- Get your hands dirty. The Step by Step exercises throughout this book provide plenty of directions and exercises, but you should go beyond those examples and create some of your own. If you can, experiment with each of the topics we discuss in this chapter to see how they work and why you would use each one.

Introduction

This chapter presents a wide cross-section of basic information that you will be expected to know for Exam 70-291, "Implementing, Managing, and Maintaining a Microsoft Windows Server 2003 Network Infrastructure," in regard to keeping your Windows Server 2003 servers and the network as a whole secure. Although the topic of Windows Server 2003 security is bigger than this chapter, and even this book, this chapter examines some of the starting points and easiest configuration changes that you can do to begin a security plan. Maintaining a secure network is not a one-step or one-day event; it is a daily, ongoing event that requires you to not only implement an initial solution but also to monitor it and massage it over time to ensure that new threats and required changes are taken into account. Too many times in the past, administrators have tried to treat server and network security as a "set it and forget it" type of item—but that's just not possible today. After you've completed this chapter, however, you should be well on your way to understanding the basic foundation of security in Windows Server 2003 and be ready to move forward into more advanced topics.

Understanding the Principle of Least Privilege

Objective:

Implement secure network administration procedures.

- Implement the principle of least privilege.

Windows Server 2003 is inherently more secure right out of the box than any previous version of Windows. Although Windows Server 2003 is more secure than its predecessors, that fact does not relieve you of the responsibility to evaluate, implement, and audit security measures for Windows Server 2003 servers. In addition, you still need to be aware of the security problems that can affect Windows 2000, Windows XP, and legacy clients.

The use of security templates, which is discussed in the next section, combined with careful planning and attentive administration of the network, can enforce the *principle of least privilege* on a network. This principle means that users are given only the minimum privileges required to perform the specific set of tasks that they have been assigned.

If you use the principle of least privilege, a compromised user account has a smaller impact on the overall security of the network than a compromised account that contains permissions that the user did not need. Ideally, all normal user operations should be carried out in the context of a regular user account. If additional privileges are required for a specific reason, the administrator can either log in to the network with a special account for the purpose of performing those actions or use the Run As command to perform those actions within the context of the account that has the additional privileges.

Working with Security Templates

Windows Server 2003, just like Windows 2000 and Windows XP, comes with a complete set of preconfigured security templates that you can use to quickly apply standardized security settings to a single computer, an organizational unit (OU), or a domain, if desired. Whereas enforcing the principle of least privilege is mainly a matter of policy, making use of and customizing security templates is a hands-on activity. These preconfigured templates can be thought of as great starting points from which to make your own customized security templates; they can also be thought of as ready-made solutions. Neither strategy is more correct than the other.

In simple terms, a *security template* is little more than a specially formatted flat-text file that can be read by the Security Configuration Manager tools. These preconfigured templates have the extension `.inf` and are located in the `%systemroot%\security\templates` folder on a Windows Server 2003 computer. You can use the Security Configuration and Analysis snap-in, the `secedit.exe` tool, or the Local Security Policy console to apply these templates to a local computer. You can apply templates to an OU or domain by importing them into the Security Settings section of the applicable Group Policy by using the Group Policy Editor. In addition, you can use these preconfigured templates to create a baseline for an unknown system that you can compare against a known set of configuration settings by using the Security Configuration and Analysis snap-in or the `secedit.exe` tool.

The following sections examine the preconfigured security templates provided with Windows Server 2003 and how they are used, customized, and implemented.

The Windows Server 2003 Security Templates

Objective:

Implement secure network administration procedures.

- Implement security baseline settings and audit security settings by using security templates.

Table 5.1 details the preconfigured security templates that are available in Windows Server 2003.

TABLE 5.1 The Preconfigured Security Templates in Windows Server 2003

Template (Filename)	Description
Default (`Setup security.inf`)	This template is created during the installation of Windows on the computer. This template varies from one computer to the next, depending on whether the installation was performed as a clean installation or an upgrade. `Setup security.inf` represents the default security settings that a computer started out with and thus can be used to reset portions of security as required. This template can be applied to both workstations and member servers, but not to domain controllers (DCs), and it should never be applied via Group Policy due to the large amount of data it contains. Doing so could result in performance degradations.
Default DC (`DC security.inf`)	This template is automatically created when a member server is promoted to a DC. It represents the file, registry, and system service default security settings for that DC and can be used later to reset those areas to their default configurations.
Compatible (`compatws.inf`)	The Compatible workstation/member server template provides a means to allow members of the Users group to run applications that do not conform to the Windows Logo Program for Windows 2000 and above. Applications that were written for Windows NT 4.0 do not use the same security model that Windows 2000 and above applications use. Applications that do conform to the Windows Logo Program can be, in the majority of cases, successfully run by members of the Users group without any further modifications required. For applications that do not conform, there are two basic choices: You can make the users members of the Power Users group or relax the default permissions of the Users group. The Compatible template solves this problem by changing the default file and registry permissions that are granted to the Users group to allow them to run most applications that are not part of the Windows Logo Program. As a side effect of applying this template, all users are removed from the Power Users group because the basic assumption is that the template is being applied in an effort to prevent the need for that group. This template should not be applied to DCs, so you need to be sure not to import it into the Default Domain Policy or the Default Domain Controller Policy.

TABLE 5.1 Continued

Template (Filename)	Description
Secure (`securews.inf` and `securedc.inf`)	The Secure templates are the first ones to actually begin the process of locking down the computer to which they are applied. There are two different Secure templates: `securews.inf`, which is for workstations and member servers, and `securedc.inf`, which is for DCs only. The Secure templates prevent the usage of the LAN Manager (LM) authentication protocol. Windows 9x clients need to have Active Directory Client Extensions installed to enable NT LAN Manager version 2 (NTLMv2). Only when NTLMv2 is enabled on these legacy clients can they communicate with Windows 2000 and above clients and servers using these templates. These templates also impose additional restrictions on anonymous users. Such restrictions include preventing them from enumerating account and share information. The secure templates also enable Server Message Block (SMB) signing on the server side. By default, SMB signing is enabled on client computers. If you apply this template, SMB packet signing will always be negotiated between clients and servers.
Highly Secure (`hisecws.inf` and `hisecdc.inf`)	The Highly Secure templates impose further restrictions on the computers to which they are applied to. Whereas the Secure templates require at least NTLM authentication, the Highly Secure templates require NTLMv2 authentication. The Secure templates enable SMB packet signing, and the Highly Secure templates also require SMB packet signing. In addition to the various extra security restrictions that are imposed by the Highly Secure templates, these templates also make several changes to group membership and the login process. All members of the Power Users group are removed from this group. In addition, only members of the Domain Admins group and the local administrative account will be allowed to be members of the local Administrators group.

(continues)

TABLE 5.1 Continued

Template (Filename)	Description
	When the Highly Secure templates are used, it is assumed that only Windows Logo Program–compliant applications are in use. Therefore, there is no provision in place for users to use noncompliant applications because the Compatible template is not needed and the Power Users group has no members. Members of the Users group are able to use applications that are compliant with the Windows Logo Program compliant. In addition, members of the Administrators group can use any application they want.
System Root (`rootsec.inf`)	This template defines the root permissions for the root of the system volume. If these permissions are changed, they can be reapplied by using this template. In addition, you can modify this template to apply the same permissions to other volumes. Explicitly configured permissions are not overwritten on child objects when you use this template.
No Terminal Server Use SID (`notssid.inf`)	This template is used on servers that are not running Terminal Services to remove all unnecessary Terminal Services security identifiers (SIDs) from the file system and registry. This, however, does not increase the security of the server.
Internet Explorer SACL (`iesacls.inf`)	This template is used to enable auditing on registry keys that are used by Internet Explorer. By default, the keys in question are set to allow the built-in Everyone group Full Control. By enabling this auditing, changes can be tracked should users (or the applications they use within Internet Explorer) attempt to modify the settings of any of these keys.

NOTE

Working with Templates If you should find yourself working with one of the preconfigured security templates and wanting to make changes, stop! Before making any changes to any of the preconfigured templates, be sure to save a copy of the template using a different name and then make your changes to the copy. By following this process, you'll always be sure to have your pristine preconfigured templates intact and available for later usage.

CAUTION

Templates Are Incremental All the preconfigured security templates are incremental, meaning that they have been designed to be applied to computers that are using the default security settings. These templates do not implement the default security settings before they apply their security settings.

Security Configuration Manager Tools

Objective:

Implement secure network administration procedures.

- Implement security baseline settings and audit security settings by using security templates.

Now that you've seen the security templates that are available for use, let's take a brief look at the tools that are available for the design, testing, and application of these (and other) security templates. The Security Configuration Manager is not one console or tool per se; it is actually a collection of tools and utilities that you can use to implement security solutions across a network.

The following are the components of the Security Configuration Manager:

- The Security Configuration and Analysis snap-in
- The Security Templates snap-in
- Group Policy security extensions
- The `secedit.exe` command

NOTE

Security Configuration Wizard We discuss Microsoft's latest security tool, the Security Configuration Wizard (SCW), later in this chapter in the section "The Security Configuration Wizard." The SCW goes beyond the basic security implementation we're examining here that relies only on security templates. When you use the SCW to configure and implement security, you can take an overall approach to mitigating security vulnerabilities on your Windows Server 2003 SP1 and Windows Server 2003 R2 servers.

Each of these tools is examined in the following sections. In these sections, we explain how they relate to implementing security solutions using the preconfigured security templates that are supplied in Windows Server 2003. At this point, you need to construct a customized MMC console, as outlined in Step by Step 5.1.

STEP BY STEP

5.1 Creating a Customized Security Console

1. Open an empty MMC shell by selecting Start, Run and entering **mmc** in the Open field. Click OK. An empty MMC shell appears, as shown in Figure 5.1.

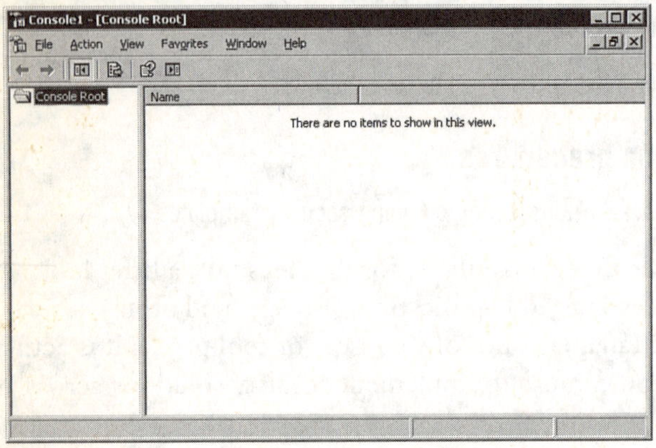

FIGURE 5.1 Starting with an empty MMC shell, you can build any number of customized configuration and management consoles.

2. Select File, Add/Remove Snap-in to open the Add/Remove Snap-in dialog box. Click Add to open the Add Standalone Snap-in dialog box, as shown in Figure 5.2.

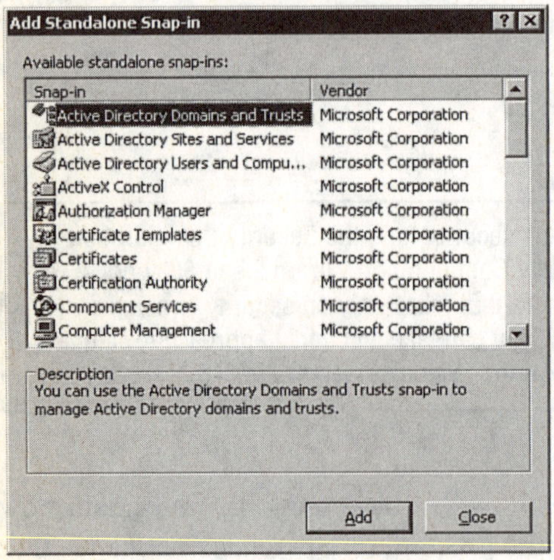

FIGURE 5.2 You can add a number of snap-ins from here.

3. Scroll down the Snap-in list and select the Security Configuration and Analysis and Security Templates snap-ins by double-clicking each of them.

4. Click Close and then click OK to return to the MMC console (see Figure 5.3).

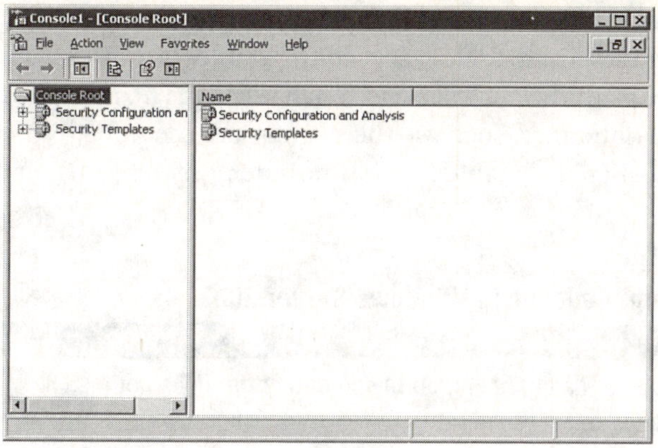

FIGURE 5.3 The customized console is not as empty as it was.

5. Save the console by selecting File, Save. A standard Save dialog box appears. Specify the filename and location to save the console to. By default, the console will be saved into the Administrative Tools folder of the currently logged in user.

Armed with a custom security console, let's move forward and examine how the tools are put to work.

The Security Configuration and Analysis Snap-in

The Security Configuration and Analysis snap-in is an important tool in an administrator's security template toolbox. By using the Security Configuration and Analysis snap-in, you can create, configure, test, and implement security template settings for a local computer. Therein lies its one real weakness: It can be used to work only with the settings of a local computer. You can, however, find ways to get around this limitation by using the other tools that are at your disposal, including `secedit.exe` and the security extensions to Group Policy, both of which are discussed later in this chapter.

The Security Configuration and Analysis snap-in can be used in two basic modes—configuration and analysis—although not necessarily in that order. When you're using the Security Configuration and Analysis snap-in to analyze the current system security configuration, no changes are ever made to the computer being analyzed. The administrator simply selects a security template to compare the computer against (either a preconfigured template or a custom-created template). The settings from the template are loaded into a database and then compared to the settings currently implemented on the computer. It is possible to import multiple templates into this database, thus merging their settings into one conglomerate database. In addition, you can specify that existing database settings are to be cleared before another template is imported into the database. When the desired security templates have been loaded into the database, any number of analysis actions can be performed, both by the Security Configuration and Analysis snap-in and by the `secedit.exe` command, as discussed later in this chapter.

After the database has been populated and an analysis scan has been initiated, the Security Configuration and Analysis snap-in examines each and every configurable Group Policy option and then reports back to you the results of the analysis scan. Each setting is marked with an icon that denotes one of several possible outcomes, such as "the settings are the same," "the settings are different," or "the settings do not apply." Table 5.2 outlines the possible icons that you might see and what they indicate.

TABLE 5.2 The Preconfigured Security Template Icons in Windows Server 2003

Icon	Description
Red X	The item is defined in the analysis database and on the computer but does not match the currently configured setting.
Green check mark	The item is defined in the analysis database and on the computer and matches the currently configured setting.
Question mark	The item is not defined in the analysis database and was not examined on the computer.
Exclamation point	The item is defined in the analysis database but not on the computer.
No special icon	The item is not defined in the analysis database or the computer.

The best way to understand the Security Configuration and Analysis snap-in is to work with it. Step by Step 5.2 presents the process of comparing the security configuration of a Windows Server 2003 member server to that of the `securews.inf` template.

NOTE

Not All Computers Are Created Equal Not every computer has the same security settings initially. Your results when performing this process may vary depending on the initial state of the computer being used for the analysis.

STEP BY STEP

5.2 Using the Security Configuration and Analysis Snap-in to Analyze Settings

1. From the customized security console you created in Step by Step 5.1, select the Security Configuration and Analysis node. Notice that the Security Configuration and Analysis snap-in actually provides you with some instructions as to how to proceed.

2. Right-click the Security Configuration and Analysis node and select Open Database from the context menu. The Open Database window appears, as shown in Figure 5.4.

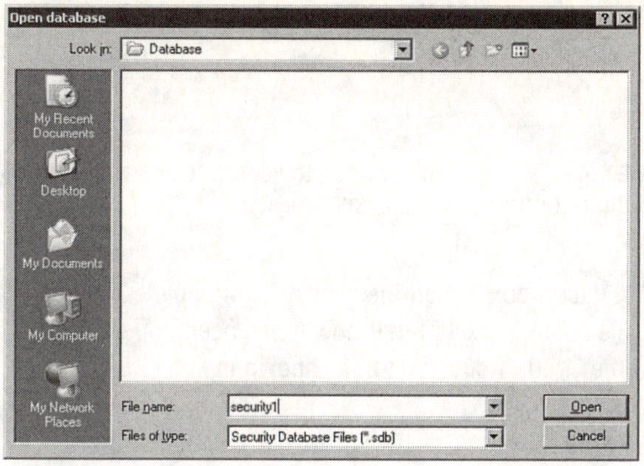

FIGURE 5.4 You can either load an existing database or create a new one.

3. Because you do not have an existing database, create a new one by entering the name **`security1`** into the File Name field and clicking Open to open it.

4. On the Import Template dialog box, shown in Figure 5.5, select the security template you are loading into the database. In this exercise, you should use the `securews.inf` template. If this is an existing database that you want to clear out, be sure to select the Clear This Database Before Importing option. Click Open after you make your selections. The Security Configuration and Analysis snap-in appears again.

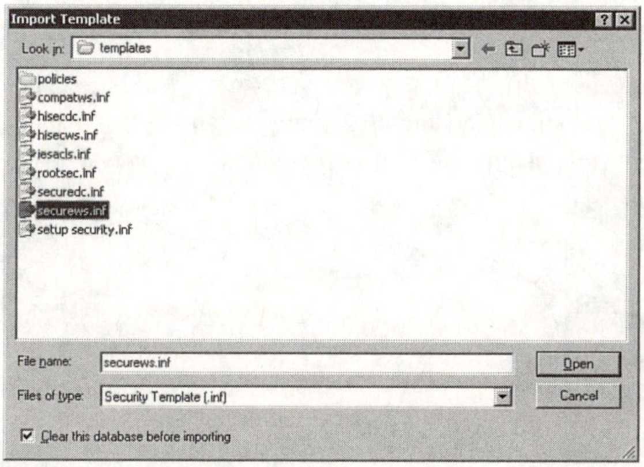

FIGURE 5.5 You need to select a template to load into the database.

5. To perform the analysis operation, right-click the Security Configuration and Analysis node and select Analyze Computer Now to start the analysis. The Perform Analysis dialog box appears.

6. Provide a pathname and a filename for an error log. In most cases, the default pathname and filename, as shown in Figure 5.6, are suitable, but you can change this as required. Click OK to start the analysis process.

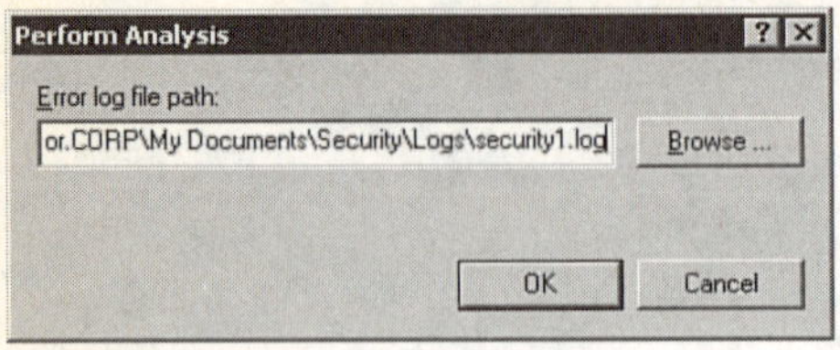

FIGURE 5.6 The error log is used to keep track of any errors encountered during the analysis process.

7. You will briefly see the Analyzing System Security dialog box. When the analysis is complete, you are returned to the Security Configuration and Analysis snap-in, except that now it has been populated and looks similar to what you might expect to see in the Group Policy Editor, as shown in Figure 5.7.

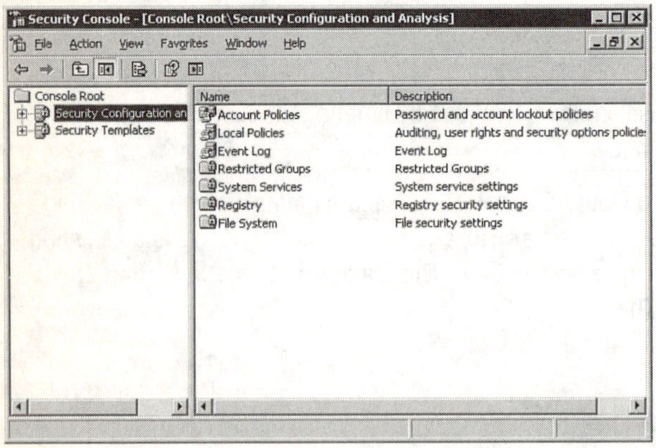

FIGURE 5.7 The analysis output resembles the information shown in the Group Policy Editor.

8. Open the Account Policies, Password Policy node, as shown in Figure 5.8, and you can see that some items are not in agreement between the database settings and the computer settings.

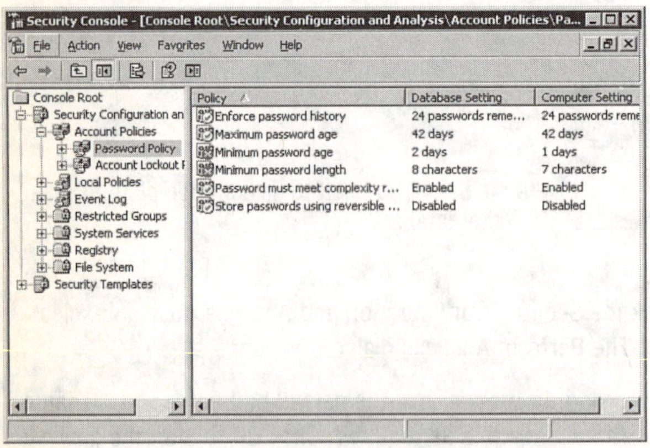

FIGURE 5.8 You can quickly determine the status of the computer against the settings of the security template.

As seen in Figure 5.7, you can analyze and configure several areas by using the Security Configuration and Analysis snap-in:

- **Account Policies**—This node contains items that control user accounts. In Windows NT 4.0, these items are managed from the User Manager for Domains. There are two subnodes of this node: the Password Policy node and the Account Lockout Policy node. The Password Policy node deals with account password–related items, such as minimum length and maximum age. The Account Lockout Policy node contains options for configuring account lockout durations and lockout reset options.
- **Local Policies**—This node contains policies that are applied to the local machine. There are three subnodes of this node: Audit Policy, User Rights Assignment, and Security Options. The Audit Policy node is pretty self-explanatory; it offers options for configuring and implementing various auditing options. The User Rights Assignment node contains miscellaneous options that deal with user rights, such as the ability to log in to a computer across the network. The Security Options node contains many other options—such as the option to set a login banner or to allow the system to be shut down without being logged in first—that previously could be edited only in the Windows NT 4.0 registry or by using System Policies.
- **Event Log**—This node contains options that allow you to configure the behavior and security of the event log. In this node, for example, you can include maximum log sizes and disallow guest access to the event logs.
- **Restricted Groups**—This node allows you to permanently configure which users are allowed to be members of specific groups. For example, company policy may provide the ability to perform server backups to a specific group of administrators. If another user who is not otherwise authorized with these privileges is added to this group and not removed after he or she has performed the intended function, you have created a security problem because the user has more rights than normally authorized. By using the Restricted Groups node, you can reset group membership to the intended membership.
- **System Services**—This node allows you to configure the behavior and security assignments associated with all system services running on the computer. Options include defining that a service is to start automatically or be disabled. In addition, you can configure the user accounts that are to have access to each service.
- **Registry**—This node allows you to configure access restrictions that specify who is allowed to configure or change individual registry keys or entire hives. This option does not give you the means to create or modify registry keys, however; you must still do that by using the Registry Editor.
- **File System**—This node allows you to set folder and file NTFS permissions. This is especially handy if you need to reset the permissions on a large number of folders or files.

After a security settings analysis is completed and you have examined the results, you can begin the process of determining what changes need to be made. You can configure your changes directly into the database by using the Security Configuration and Analysis snap-in, or you can create or edit a security template by using the Security Templates snap-in, as discussed in the next section. When you use the Security Configuration and Analysis snap-in to make changes, your changes reside only in the database until you do one of two things: export the database to a security template file or apply the database settings to the computer. When you work with the Security Templates snap-in, you actually make changes to the template directly and need to save it when you're finished. The end result is the same no matter which way you go about it.

The second part of the Security Configuration and Analysis snap-in is the configuration, which is the application of settings contained in the database to the local computer. Before you apply the settings to the computer, you should have first completed the analysis as detailed in Step by Step 5.2. After this is done and you are happy with the configuration (or have edited the configuration to suit your needs), you can apply the settings by right-clicking the Security Configuration and Analysis node and selecting Configure Computer Now from the context menu. You are again asked for the pathname and filename of the error log. After you provide this information, the settings in the database are applied to the computer. Running the analysis again confirms this by showing that all items are now in agreement.

EXAM ALERT

For the Local Computer Only Remember that the Security Configuration and Analysis snap-in can be used to apply the settings to the local computer only. You need to export the database to a security template if you want to apply the settings to another computer or to a larger scope of computers, such as a domain or an OU.

As mentioned, if you need to get the database settings out and into the form of a security template, you need to right-click the Security Configuration and Analysis node and select Export Template from the context menu. The Export Template To window appears, as shown in Figure 5.9, prompting you to enter the path and filename of the security template. You should be sure to use a unique name—in other words, do not save over one of the preconfigured security templates because you might need it again in the future.

The Security Templates Snap-in

The Security Templates snap-in, shown in Figure 5.10, might at first seem to have no real purpose. However, this is not the case at all. You can use this snap-in to modify existing templates or create new ones from scratch without the danger or possibility of accidentally applying the template to the computer or Group Policy object (GPO).

To customize an existing template, you should first save a new copy of it and then you can begin making changes to it to suit your requirements. When you are done, be sure to save it again and you'll be ready to start using your new, customized, security template.

To start out with a completely empty template—in which no settings are preconfigured—right-click the template location node (where the template file system path is displayed on the left side of the console) and select New Template from the context menu.

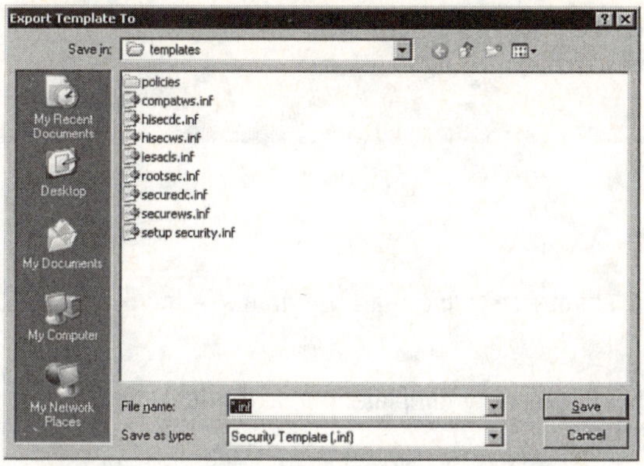

FIGURE 5.9 You need to be sure to specify a unique name for an exported template to avoid overwriting a preconfigured security template.

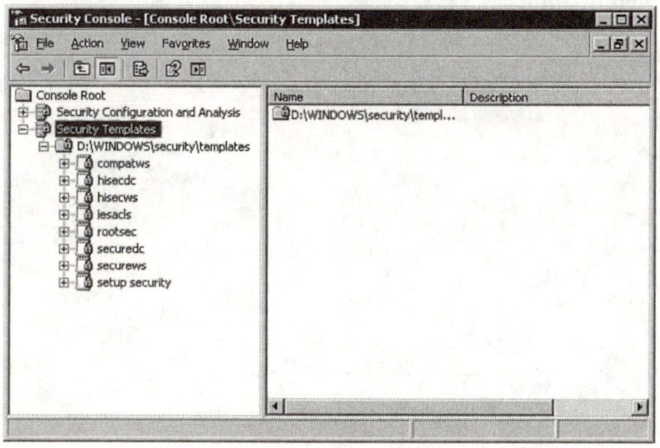

FIGURE 5.10 The Security Templates snap-in allows you to work with existing and new templates.

Group Policy Security Extensions

Applying a security template to a local computer by using the Security Configuration and Analysis snap-in is not the only way to apply a security template. Imagine the amount of time and effort involved in applying a security template locally at each computer using the Security Configuration and Analysis snap-in. As difficult and time consuming as it would be, imagine doing it to several different types of computers, such as DCs, member servers, and client workstations. You would have the added hassle of trying to remember which template goes on what computer.

NOTE

Editing Group Policy Objects In this chapter, we show you how Group Policy Objects are accessed and edited using the default configuration of Windows Server 2003. For all practical purposes, it's recommended that you download and install the Group Policy Management Console (GPMC) for enhanced Group Policy control and visibility. You can find out more information about the GPMC at the following location: http://www.microsoft.com/windowsserver2003/gpmc/gpmcintro.mspx.

Fortunately, you can easily and quickly import security templates into GPOs by using the Group Policy Editor. Step by Step 5.3 outlines this process.

STEP BY STEP

5.3 Importing a Security Template into a GPO

1. Open the Active Directory Users and Computers console by selecting Start, Programs, Administrative Tools, Active Directory Users and Computers.
2. Locate the domain or OU to which you want to apply the security template. In this example, we will be applying the `securews.inf` template to the CORP OU.
3. Right-click the CORP OU and select Properties from the context menu. The Sales Properties dialog box appears. Switch to the Group Policy tab, as shown in Figure 5.11.

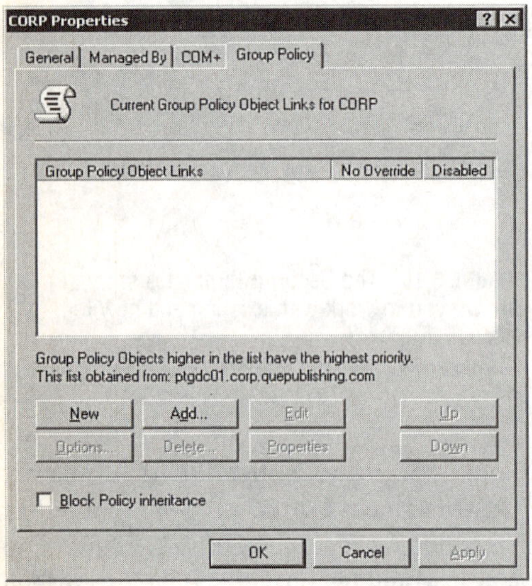

FIGURE 5.11 You need to create a new GPO if no GPOs exist.

4. To create a new GPO, click the New button. Supply a name for the new GPO and press Enter.
5. Click the Edit button to open the Group Policy Editor for the selected GPO.
6. Expand the nodes as follows: Computer Configuration, Windows Settings, Security Settings. You screen should now resemble Figure 5.12.
7. Right-click the Security Settings node and select Import Policy from the context menu. The Import Policy From dialog box shown in Figure 5.13 appears, providing a list of the preconfigured security templates. You can navigate to another location if required to use a custom-created security template.

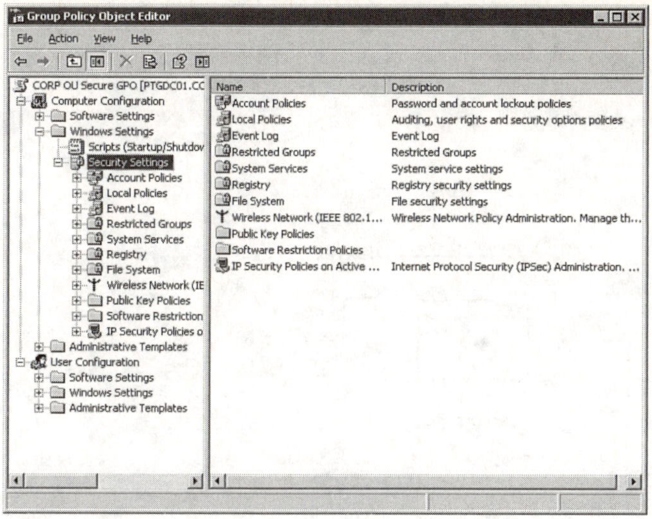

FIGURE 5.12 You'll be able to import a security template from the Security Settings node.

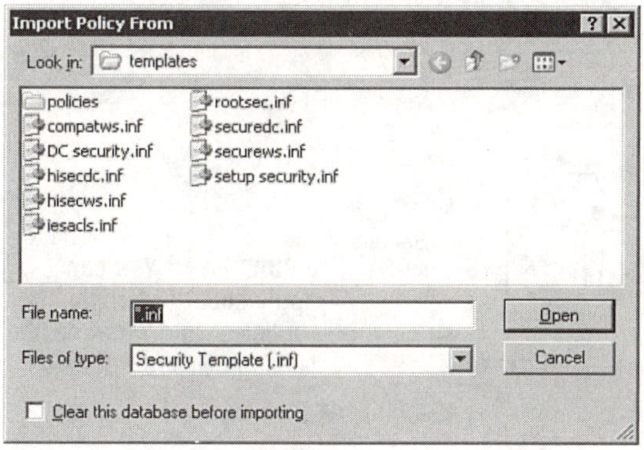

FIGURE 5.13 You need to select the security template that you want to import into the GPO.

8. Select the desired policy and click the Open button. The settings configured in the template are now applied to the GPO and will be applied during the next Group Policy refresh cycle.

Note that you can also perform this evolution at the domain level to apply security settings to all computers within the domain. As a general rule, you should apply the most generic settings at the domain level. Then, at the OU level, you should apply specific settings that pertain to the computers in that OU. Figure 5.14 provides an example of how this might work for an organization that consists of several OUs.

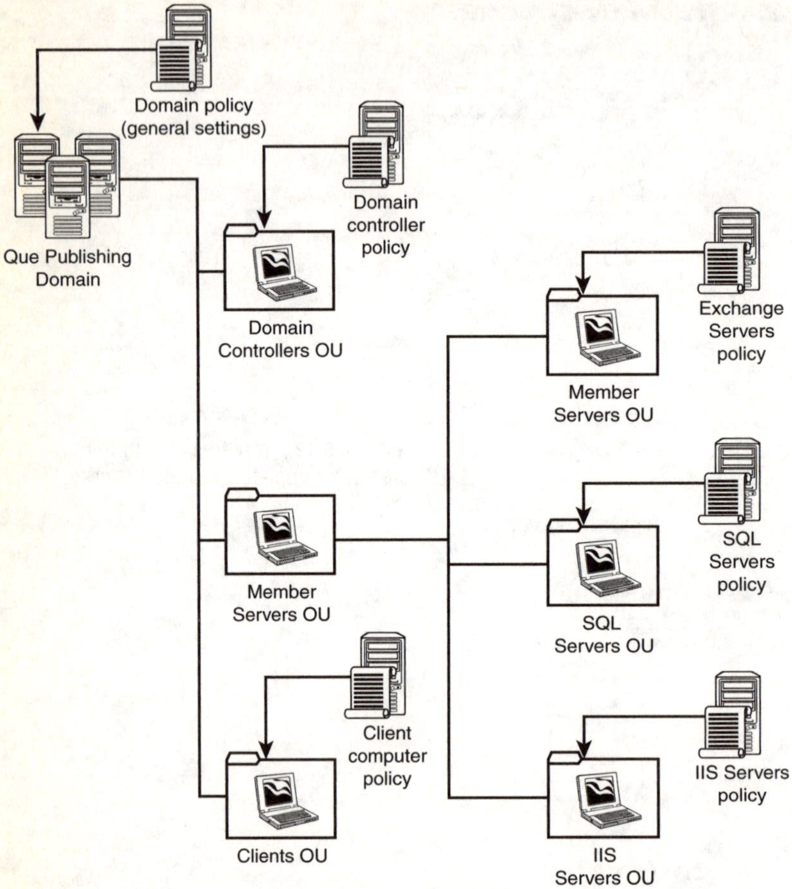

FIGURE 5.14 You can apply security templates (policies) at several nested levels in Group Policy.

`secedit.exe`

We have spent a good amount of time in this chapter examining the ways you can work with security templates by using the Windows GUI. What about configuring security from the command line? As you might have guessed, there is a command-line alternative to the Security Configuration and Analysis snap-in, and it comes in the form of the `secedit.exe` command.

You can use `secedit.exe` to perform the same functions as the Security Configuration and Analysis snap-in, plus a couple additional functions not found in the snap-in. The `secedit.exe` command has various top-level options available for use, as detailed in Table 5.3.

TABLE 5.3 The `secedit.exe` Options

Option	Description
`/analyze`	Allows you to analyze the security settings of a computer by comparing them against the baseline settings in a database.

TABLE 5.3 Continued

Option	Description
`/configure`	Allows you to configure the security settings of the local computer by applying the settings contained in a database.
`/export`	Allows you to export the settings configured in a database to a security template .inf file.
`/import`	Allows you import the settings configured in a security template .inf file into a database. If you will be applying multiple security templates to a database, you should use this option before performing the analysis or configuration.
`/validate`	Validates the syntax of a security template to ensure that it is correct before you import the template into a database for analysis or configuration.
`/GenerateRollback`	Allows you to create a rollback template that can be used to reset the security configuration to the values it had before the security template was applied.

Of the available options, you will most often make use of `/analyze` and `/configure`. Examples and explanations of their usage are provided here.

To analyze the current security configuration of the local computer, you would issue the `secedit.exe` command with the following syntax:

```
secedit /analyze /db FileName /cfg FileName /overwrite /log FileName
 /quiet
```

EXAM ALERT

Viewing the Results of a Security Analysis You need to view the results of a security analysis in the Security Configuration and Analysis snap-in by opening the database created during the analysis. At first it might seem like running the analysis from the command line and then viewing the results in the GUI is counter-productive. In reality, the opposite is the case. Say you run `secedit.exe` from a script on multiple computers. You can then view the databases, one for each computer, in the GUI at your leisure to determine what changes need to be made to the security settings on the computers. You can use the `%computername%` variable when creating the database and log files to create one set of results for each computer being scanned.

The `secedit /analyze` parameters are explained in detail in Table 5.4.

TABLE 5.4 The `secedit /analyze` Parameters

Parameter	Description
`/db FileName`	Specifies the pathname and filename of the database to be used to perform the analysis.
`/cfg FileName`	Specifies the pathname and filename of the security template that is to be imported into the database before the analysis is performed.

(continues)

TABLE 5.4 Continued

Parameter	Description
`/overwrite`	Specifies that the database is to be emptied before the security template is imported.
`/log FileName`	Specifies the pathname and filename of the file that is used to log the status of the analysis process. By default, a log named `scesrv.log` is created in the `%windir%\security\logs` directory.
`/quiet`	Specifies that the analysis process should take place without further onscreen comments.

For example, suppose that you wanted to analyze the settings on a computer and compare the settings to those contained in the `securews.inf` template. You could issue the following command to perform this function:

```
secedit /analyze /db d:\sectest\test1.sdb
/cfg d:\WINDOWS\security\templates\securews.inf /log d:\sectest\test1.log
```

If all goes well, you should see something like what is shown in Figure 5.15.

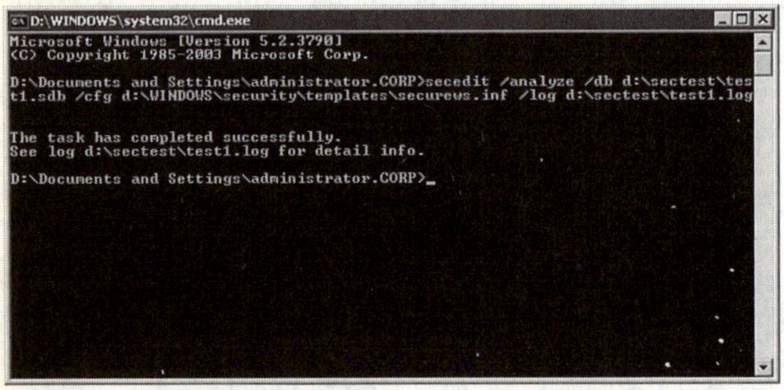

FIGURE 5.15 You can quickly perform an analysis from the command line by using the `secedit.exe` command.

To configure the current security configuration of the local computer, you would issue the `secedit.exe` command with the following syntax:

```
secedit /configure /db FileName /cfg FileName /overwrite
/areas Area1 Area2 ... /log FileName /quiet
```

The `secedit /configure` parameters are explained in detail in Table 5.5.

TABLE 5.5 The `secedit /configure` Parameters

Parameter	Description
`/db FileName`	Specifies the pathname and filename of the database to be used to perform the configuration.
`/cfg FileName`	Specifies the pathname and filename of the security template that is to be imported into the database before the configuration is performed.

TABLE 5.5 Continued

Parameter	Description
`/overwrite`	Specifies that the database is to be emptied before the security template is imported.
`/areas`	Specifies the security areas that are to be applied to the system. By default, when this parameter is not specified, all security areas are applied to the computer. These are the available options: ▶ **SECURITYPOLICY**—This area includes account policies, audit policies, settings for the event logs, and other security options. ▶ **GROUP_MGMT**—This area is the Restricted Group settings. ▶ **USER_RIGHTS**—This area is the User Rights Assignment settings. ▶ **REGKEYS**—This area is the Registry permissions settings. ▶ **FILESTORE**—This area is the File System permissions settings. ▶ **SERVICES**—This area is the System Service settings.
`/log FileName`	Specifies the pathname and filename of the file that is used to log the status of the analysis process. By default, a log named `scesrv.log` is created in the `%windir%\security\logs` directory.
`/quiet`	Specifies that the configuration process should take place without further onscreen comments.

For example, suppose that you wanted to configure the settings on a computer with the settings in the `securews.inf` template. If you wanted the database and log files to be located in the `d:\sectest\` directory and your Windows installation was located on volume D, you could issue the following command to perform this function:

```
secedit /configure /db d:\sectest\test1.sdb
/cfg D:\WINDOWS\security\templates\securews.inf /log d:\sectest\test1.log
```

Auditing Server and Network Security

Objective:

Implement secure network administration procedures.

- Implement security baseline settings and audit security settings by using security templates.

Implementing a baseline security solution is only the first step in implementing security on servers and a network. After you've implemented security templates, you need to audit the servers and network to determine what is happening.

Auditing in Windows Server 2003 can be a one- or two-part process, depending on what you are auditing. If you want to audit only system events such as user logins and privilege use, then you need to configure the appropriate auditing categories. If you also want to audit object access, you need to first enable this setting and then configure auditing specifically on the object. The following sections examine both types of auditing.

Before we get into configuring auditing, however, it is important that you understand that auditing can be configured at more than one level. That is, you can configure auditing at the same levels to which you can apply Group Policy. These levels include a local computer, a domain, and a specific OU. You should keep this point in mind when you're implementing an organization's auditing plan.

Configuring Auditing

To start auditing, you need to begin by enabling it in Group Policy. You can do this by configuring the applicable GPO directly or by making your changes in a security template. For the purposes of this chapter, you can make the changes in a security template and then import that template into specific GPOs to implement the auditing solution. After auditing is configured, audit events are written into the security log of the event viewer. In this section, you will learn about some of the events that you are likely to encounter.

Windows Server 2003 provides the following areas in which you can enable auditing:

- **Audit Account Logon Events**—This option configures auditing to occur for user logons and logoffs. A success audit generates an audit entry when a user successfully logs in, and a failure audit generates an entry when a user unsuccessfully attempts to log in.
- **Audit Account Management**—This option configures auditing to occur for each event of account management on a computer. Typical account management events include creating a user, creating a group, renaming a user, disabling a user account, and setting or changing a password. A success audit generates an audit entry when any account management event is successful, and a failure audit generates an entry when any account management event fails.
- **Audit Directory Service Access**—This option configures auditing to occur when a user accesses an Active Directory object that has its own system access control list (SACL). This setting is only for Active Directory objects, such as GPOs, not for file system and registry objects. A success audit generates an audit entry when a user successfully accesses an Active Directory object that has an SACL specified, and a failure audit generates an entry when an unsuccessful access attempt occurs.
- **Audit Logon Events**—This option configures auditing to occur upon each instance of a user logging on or off a computer. The audit events are generated on DCs for domain account activity and on local computers for local account activity. When both the Audit Logon Events and the Audit Account Logon Events options are configured, logons and logoffs that use a domain account generate logon or logoff audit events on the local computer as well as the DC. A success audit generates an audit entry when a logon attempt succeeds, and a failure audit generates an audit entry when a logon attempt fails.
- **Audit Object Access**—This option configures auditing to occur upon each user access of an object, such as a file, folder, printer, or registry key that has its own SACL configured. To configure auditing for object access, you also need to configure auditing for

each object on which you want to perform auditing. A success audit generates an audit entry when a user successfully accesses an object, and a failure audit generates an audit entry when a user unsuccessfully attempts to access an object.

- **Audit Policy Change**—This option configures auditing to occur upon every occurrence of changing user rights assignment policies, audit policies, or trust policies. A success audit generates an audit entry when a change to one of these policies is successful, and a failure audit generates an audit entry when a change to one of these policies fails.
- **Audit Privilege Use**—This option configures auditing to occur upon every occurrence of a user exercising a user right. A success audit generates an audit entry when the exercise of a user right succeeds, and a failure audit generates an audit entry when the exercise of a user right fails.
- **Audit Process Tracking**—This option configures auditing to occur for events such as program activation, process exit, handle duplication, and indirect object access. A success audit generates an audit entry when the process being tracked succeeds, and a failure audit generates an audit entry when the process being tracked fails.
- **Audit System Events**—This option configures auditing to occur when certain system events, such as computer restarts and shutdowns, occur. A success audit generates an audit entry when a system event is executed successfully, and a failure audit generates an audit entry when a system event is executed unsuccessfully.

For the purposes of auditing, you might want to create a new security template. However, if you want to make the configuration in an existing security template, you can do that as well. Step by Step 5.4 outlines the process of configuring and implementing auditing settings.

STEP BY STEP

5.4 Configuring and Implementing Auditing

1. Open the custom security console you created in Step by Step 5.1.
2. Create a new security template by right-clicking the storage location node and selecting New Template.
3. Enter the template name and description as shown in Figure 5.16.
4. In the new template, navigate to the Audit Policy node, as shown in Figure 5.17.
5. Double-click the items for which you want to configure auditing. For example, to configure the Audit Account Logon Events option, open its properties and select the Define These Policy Settings in the Template option and the Success and Failure options, as shown in Figure 5.18. Click OK to accept your configuration.

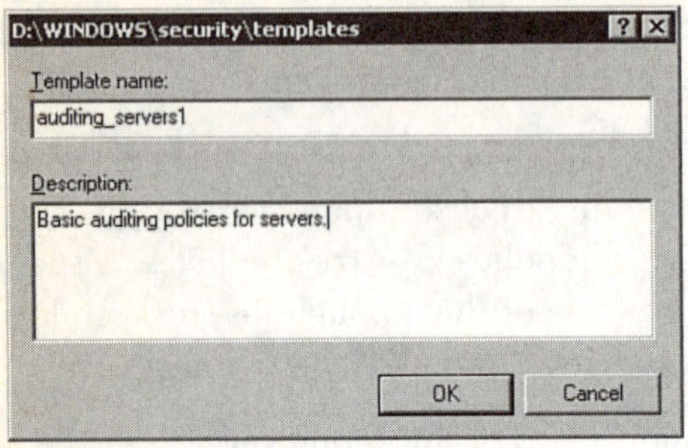

FIGURE 5.16 Be sure to provide a helpful name and description in case you need to later figure out what the template does.

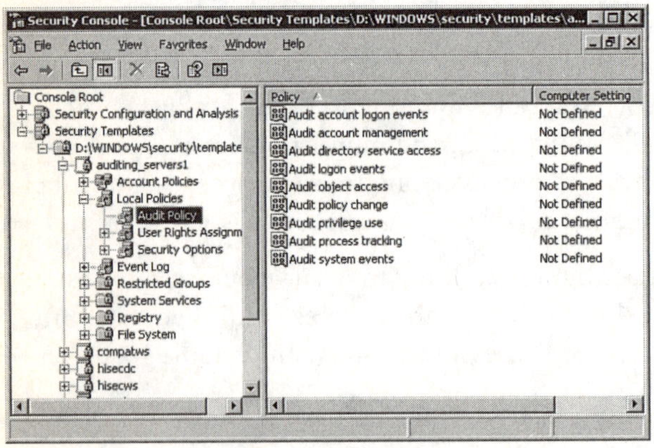

FIGURE 5.17 After the template has been created, you need to locate the auditing settings.

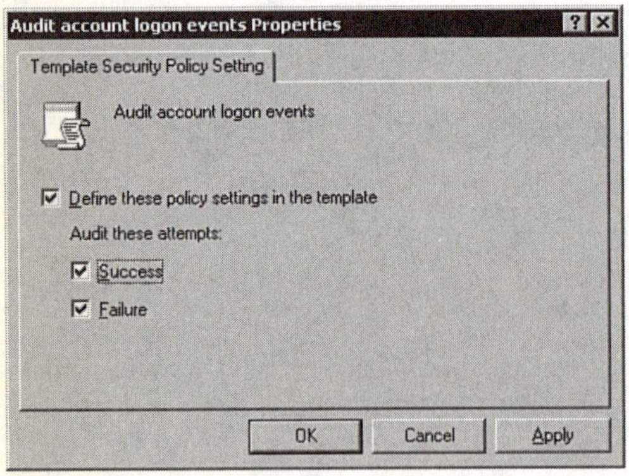

FIGURE 5.18 You can configure Success, Failure, or both for auditing.

6. Configure Success and Failure auditing for the Audit Object Access option.
7. After you configure your desired auditing options, save the template by right-clicking it in the left pane and selecting Save from the context menu.
8. Open the Active Directory Users and Computers console.
9. Open the Group Policy Editor for the Sales OU by creating a new GPO or editing an existing GPO.

10. Import the security template that contains your auditing settings, as discussed in Step by Step 5.3.

11. Configure auditing options for the objects (files, folders, printers, and so on) for which you want to audit access. For example, to configure some auditing options for a Word document named `July Executive Schedule.doc`, right-click the document and select Properties from the context menu.

12. Switch to the Security tab and click the Advanced button to open the Advanced Security Settings dialog box. Switch to the Auditing tab, which is shown in Figure 5.19.

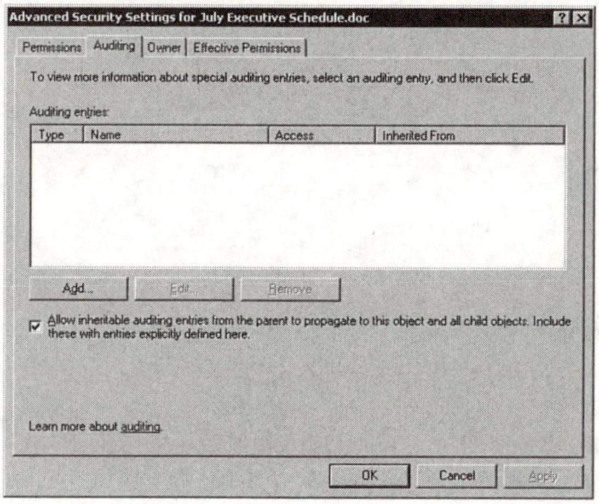

FIGURE 5.19 You need to select the Auditing tab of the Advanced Security Settings dialog box.

13. Click the Add button to open the Select User or Group dialog box, as shown in Figure 5.20. From here you need to select the users or groups to which the auditing entries will be applied. Keep in mind that if you are going to audit multiple users or groups, it is most efficient (in terms of system usage) to have them in as few auditing entries as possible. Also, if you need to audit the actions of all users, you should use the Everyone group. If you do not know the names of the users or groups that you want to add to this auditing entry, click Advanced, Find Now to open a list from which you can choose. After you have configured the desired users and groups, click OK to continue. The Auditing Entry dialog box appears.

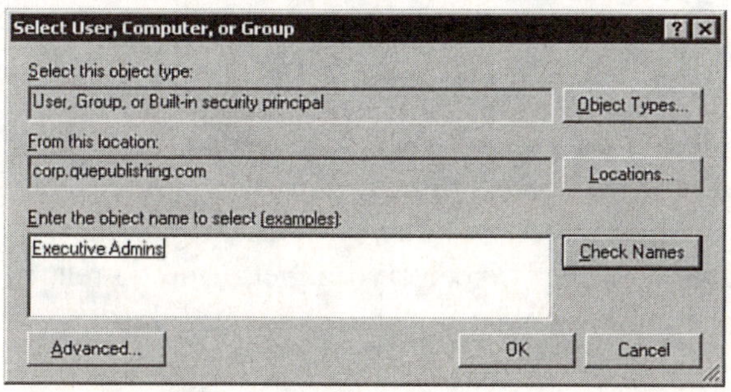

FIGURE 5.20 You need to select the users and groups for which you want to configure auditing before you can select what is to be audited.

14. On the Auditing Entry dialog box, which is shown in Figure 5.21, you can select what success or failure events you want to audit for on the selected object. Make your selections and then click OK to confirm them.

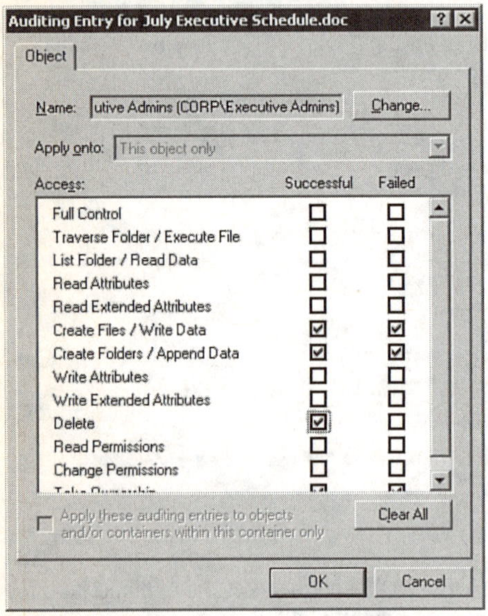

FIGURE 5.21 You have several items that you can select for object auditing.

15. Close the remaining dialog boxes; you are done configuring auditing.

With auditing configured, you might want to test it and see how it works. Recall that audit entries are written into the security log, so you need to go there to examine them. You can find the event logs by selecting Start, Programs, Administrative Tools, Event Viewer. If you open the security log, you can see the audit entries. A closed lock next to an item indicates a failure audit, and a key next to an item indicates a success audit, as seen in Figure 5.22.

Of course, there is more to successful auditing than just configuring it and checking the security log from time to time. The following are some of Microsoft's recommended practices for successfully implementing and maintaining a security auditing solution:

- **Create an audit plan before you implement auditing**—You need to determine what you are auditing. Are you trying to audit for user access to unauthorized resources, or are you trying to audit for attempts to access the network illicitly? Perhaps you have in mind another entirely different reason for auditing. Like everything else you do related to managing a network, proper prior planning ensures the success of your solution.

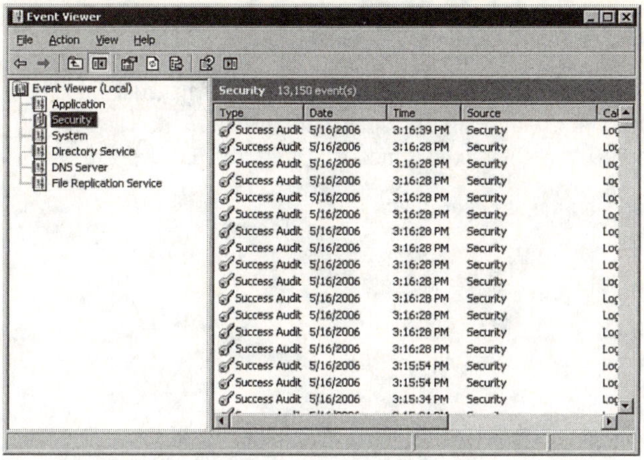

FIGURE 5.22 The security log can quickly fill up if you are auditing many items.

- **Collect and archive logs across the entire organization**—Visiting each computer and examining its local security log is not a viable solution for any but the smallest of organizations. To make the log collection process easier and more accurate, you should consider using a Microsoft product such as DumpEL, EventCombMT, or Log Parser. You can find the links to these tools in the "Suggested Reading and Resources" section at the end of this chapter.
- **Audit system events for success and failure events**—By auditing system events, you can monitor unusual activity that could indicate when an attacker is trying to gain access or compromise systems.
- **Audit policy change events for success events**—Auditing of successful policy change events can indicate that someone is changing items to which he or she should not have access.
- **Audit account management events for success events**—Auditing of successful account management events can help you verify that changes are successful. You might be tempted to audit failure events, but that can lead to an overwhelming number of entries that can degrade system performance over time. Failure auditing should be done only for short periods, and it should look for specific activity only.
- **Audit account logon events for success events on DCs**—Auditing of successful account logon events enables you to determine when users are logging on and off the network. This can be useful for tracking down activity occurring outside normal working hours.
- **Configure specific object access auditing**—You should configure only the object auditing that you need. In other words, if all you want to audit is users attempting to read a document, you don't need to configure auditing for full control. By limiting the object access auditing you configure, you can cut down on extraneous log entries through which you would otherwise have to sift.

Challenge

You are the systems administrator for Kelly's Jelly, Inc. You have been tasked by the IS manager with developing and implementing a customized security solution for the company's new network. The network will consist of Windows Server 2003 server computers and Windows XP Professional workstations.

Kelly's business structure consists of the following major departments:

- Accounting
- Administration
- Design
- Engineering
- Maintenance
- Production
- Stock control

The user and computer accounts for each department are to be placed in an OU bearing the same name as the department. The member servers are to be placed in OUs by function: File and Print, Exchange, SQL, and RRAS. In addition, all Domain Controllers will remain in their default container.

Your task is to create the required OU structure and security policies to implement custom security policies for the company.

Try to complete this exercise on your own, listing your conclusions on a sheet of paper. After you have completed the exercise, compare your results to those given here.

Answers

Because each department is to have its own OU for user and computers, you will need to first create those seven organizational units. Additionally, you have four different types of member servers that will each require an OU to be created to house them. The default Domain Controllers OU will be used to hold all Domain Controllers in the company.

Once you have created the 11 new OUs, you can then go about the task of creating and implementing security policies for the company. Typically you will apply the most general policies at the domain level. These policies should be common to all OUs under the domain root. Beyond that, you can create and implement the security policies for each of the organizational units as required. It's likely that the department OUs will get the same security policy via a linked group policy object, thus making your organizational units more organizational than they appeared at first.

The Security Configuration Wizard

The Security Configuration Wizard (SCW) is a new, more advanced, security hardening tool for Windows Server 2003 SP1 and Windows Server 2003 R2. If you have servers running these latest versions of Windows Server 2003, the SCW is worth taking a look at.

By default, the SCW is not installed on your Windows Server 2003 computer. Before we can work with it, you'll need to install it as detailed in Step by Step 5.5.

STEP BY STEP

5.5 Installing the Security Configuration Wizard

1. Log on to Windows Server 2003 using the Administrator account or another account that has administrator privileges.

2. Open the Control Panel and then open the Add/Remove Programs applet. The Add or Remove Programs dialog box appears, as seen in Figure 5.23.

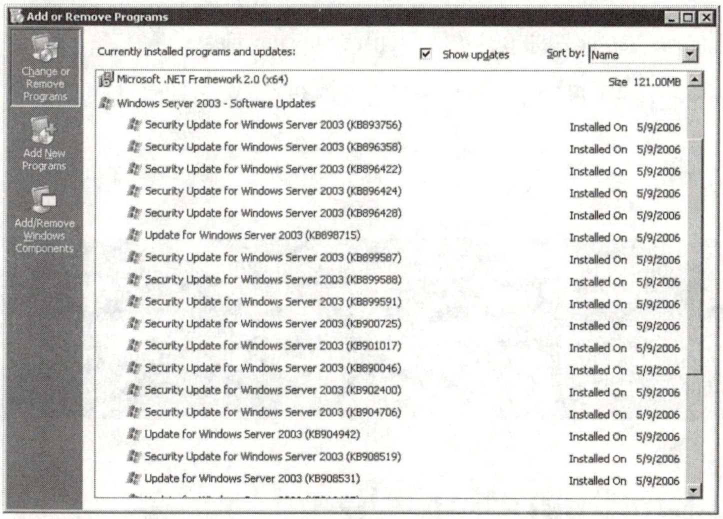

FIGURE 5.23 The Add or Remove Programs dialog box provides useful information about installed applications, including application size and, in some cases, the frequency of use of an installed application.

3. Click Add/Remove Windows Components on the left side of the Add or Remove Programs dialog box. The Windows Components Wizard dialog box appears, as seen in Figure 5.24.

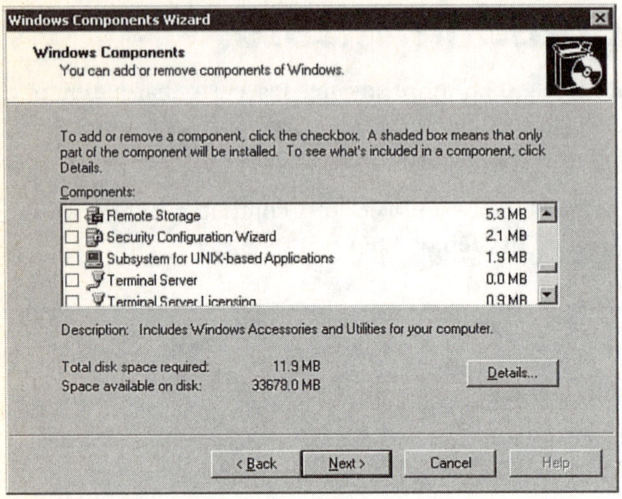

FIGURE 5.24 The Windows Components Wizard allows you to install, remove, or configure the various components of Windows Server 2003.

4. Select the Security Configuration Wizard option and then click OK.
5. On)the next dialog box that appears, click Next to complete the installation. The Windows Component Wizard prompts you for the Windows Server 2003 CD-ROM if it needs to copy files.
6. When the wizard is finished, it displays a summary of the changes to be made. Click Finish to complete the installation.

EXAM ALERT

The Security Configuration Wizard The Security Configuration Wizard is a new tool added to Windows Server 2003 with SP1. If your servers are Windows Server 2003 SP1 or Windows Server 2003 R2, then the SCW is available for you. As a new tool, and a security-related one at that, you should expect that it will likely make an appearance on your 70-291 exam, although it's not likely that you will need to have expert-level experience in using the SCW.

Using the Security Configuration Wizard

Now that the Security Configuration Wizard has been installed on your server, we'll examine its usage in this section. Step by Step 5.6 details the steps to be followed to use the SCW to create a new policy.

STEP BY STEP

5.6 Using the Security Configuration Wizard to Create a Policy

1. Select Start, Control Panel, Administrative Tools, Security Configuration Wizard. The Welcome to the Security Configuration Wizard dialog box appears as seen in Figure 5.25. After)reading the information presented, click Next to continue.

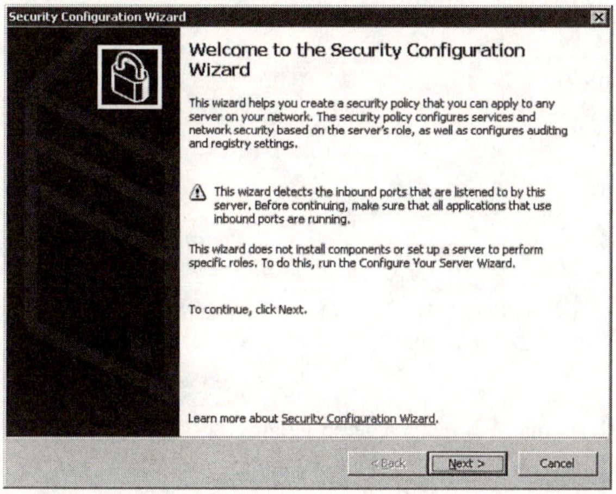

FIGURE 5.25 This Welcome screen presents some important and useful information.

2. On the Configuration Action dialog box, as seen in Figure 5.26, you will need to tell the SCW what to do. For this exercise, we want to Create a New Security Policy. After making your selection, click Next to continue.

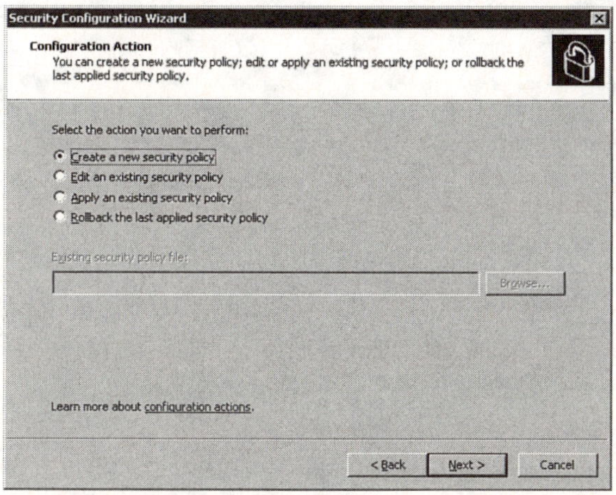

FIGURE 5.26 The Configure Action dialog box allows you to tell the SCW what to do.

3. On the Select Server page, as seen in Figure 5.27, you will select a server that will serve as the baseline by which the security policy is created. By default, the server the SCW is being run on will be populated for you. After making your selection, click Next to continue.

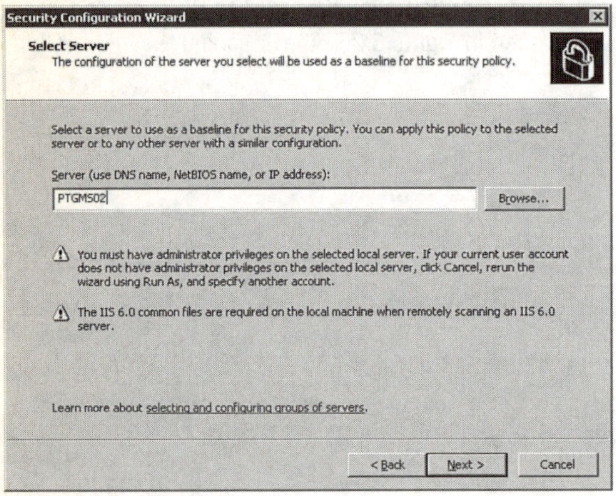

FIGURE 5.27 You'll need to specify a server to act as the baseline.

4. On the Processing Security Configuration Database dialog box, as seen in Figure 5.28, the configuration will be processed briefly before you will be able to click Next to continue. When the processing is complete, click Next to continue. If you want to examine the Security Configuration Database first, you can click the View Configuration Database button before clicking Next.

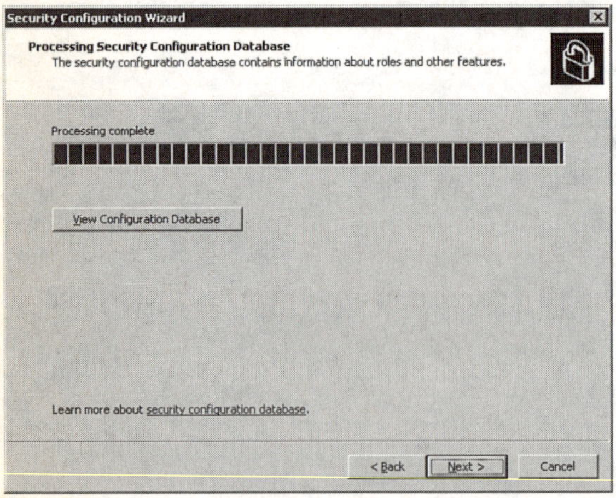

FIGURE 5.28 The security configuration will be analyzed and processed by SCW.

5. The SCW now moves to the next phase of the configuration process. On the Role-Based Service Configuration dialog box, as seen in Figure 5.29, you will again be presented with critical information. After reading the information, click next to continue on with the Security Configuration Wizard.

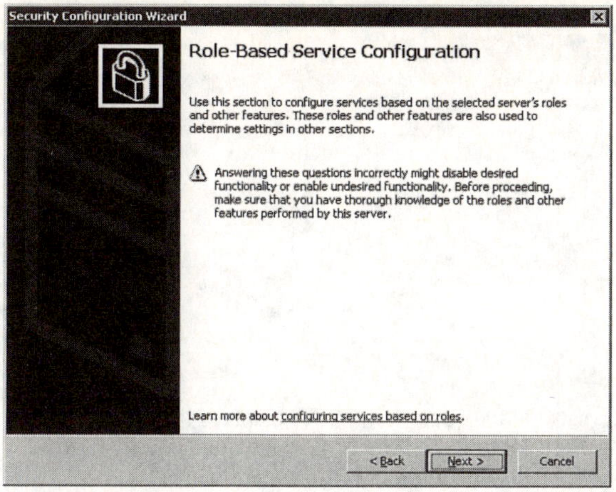

FIGURE 5.29 More critical information is presented to you before continuing.

6. On the Select Server Roles dialog box, as seen in Figure 5.30, you view the currently installed and roles the server has. Clicking the View drop-down arrow changes the view, allowing you to examine all roles, uninstalled roles, installed roles (but not necessarily active roles), and selected roles (both installed and active). Clicking the arrow next to a role opens a small informational box below the role. If you want to add or remove a role, which only configures the ports and services but does actually install any required files, you can do so. Click Next to continue after making any changes (typically none if the server is already configured correctly beforehand).

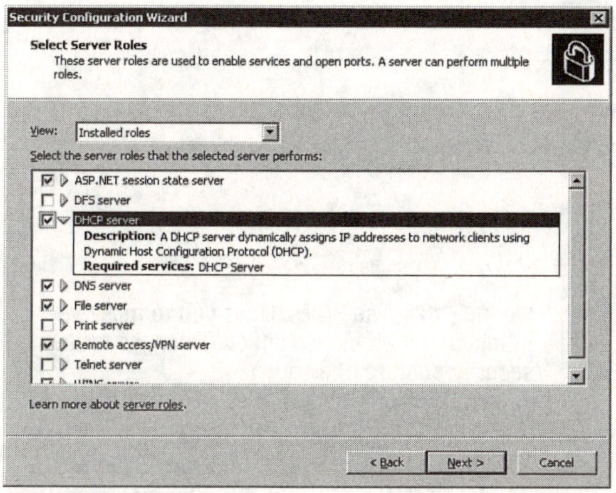

FIGURE 5.30 The SCW displays the current roles the server is fulfilling and allows you to change them.

7. On the Select Client Features dialog) box, as seen in Figure 5.31, you can view the server's currently installed client features. The View drop-down arrow works the same as on the Select Server Roles page to change the features list. Click Next to continue after making any changes (typically none if the server is already configured correctly beforehand).

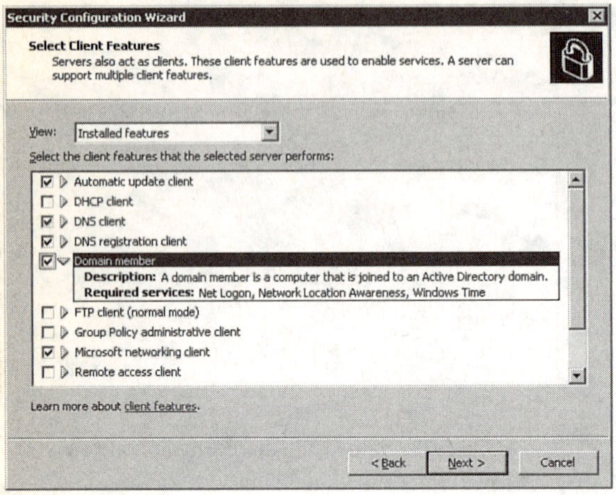

FIGURE 5.31 The SCW displays the current client features the server is using and allows you to change them.

8. On the Select Administration and Other Options dialog box, as seen in Figure 5.32, you can get granular (and thus dangerous) with the configuration changes you make on a server. Note the option selected in Figure 5.32. If you need to make any changes, do so, but be sure to understand the implications that the changes may have. Click Next to continue.

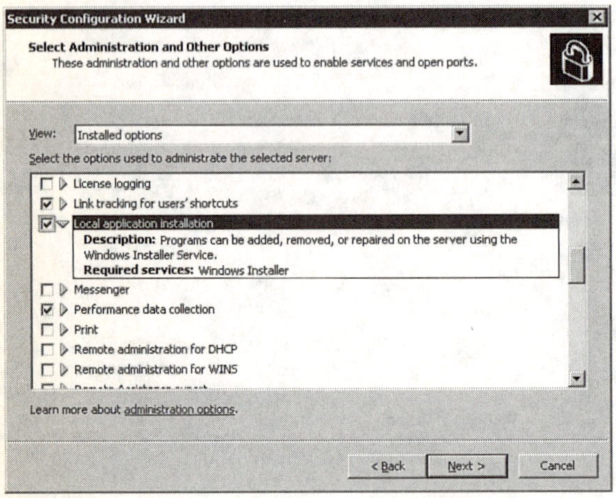

FIGURE 5.32 The SCW allows you to make very granular and otherwise difficult changes to the security posture of a server.

9. On the Select Additional Services dialog box, as seen in Figure 5.33, you will be presented with any additional services the SCW encountered during its analysis. Click Next to continue after making any changes (typically none if the server is already configured correctly beforehand).

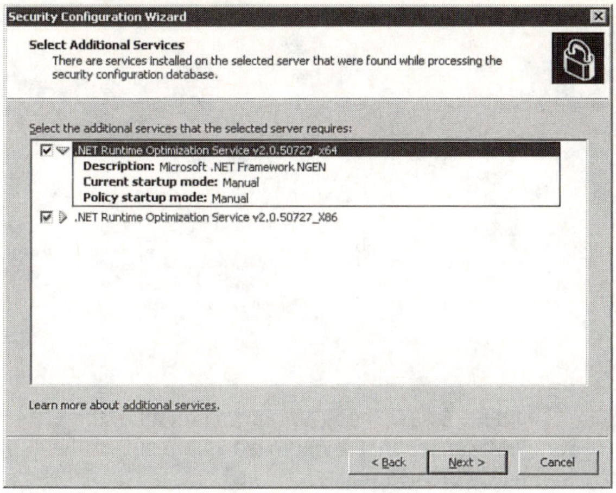

FIGURE 5.33 The SCW alerts you to any other services it found during the analysis.

10. On the Handling Unspecified Services dialog box, as seen in Figure 5.34, the SCW asks you what to do if it finds services on the target server that were not on the baseline server. In most cases, it's usually safer to leave the default selection of Do Not Change the Startup Mode of the Service as your selection. If you know for a fact that you want to have unspecified services disabled, and you are willing to take that risk, select that option. After making your choice, click Next to continue.

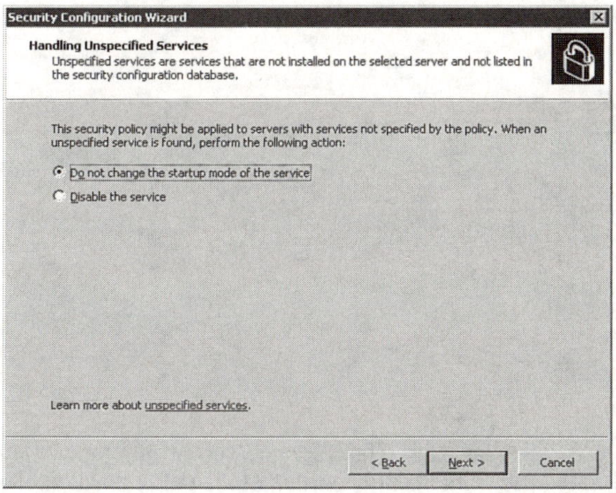

FIGURE 5.34 The SCW wants to know what to do about unspecified services it finds.

11. On the Confirm Service Changes) dialog box, as seen in Figure 5.35, you are given a last look at how the server services will be modified by the creation and implementation of the policy. If you need to make changes, you'll need to go back to the applicable page of the Wizard. Once you're ready to continue, click Next.

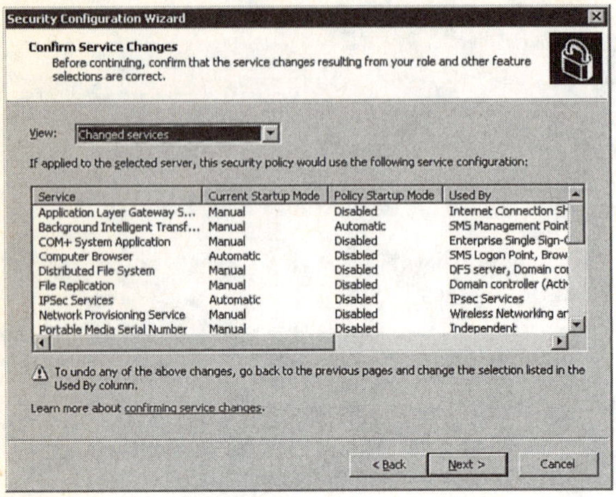

FIGURE 5.35 The SCW shows you all of the service changes that it will make as a result of the newly created policy.

12. The SCW now moves to the next phase of the configuration process. On the Network Security dialog box, as seen in Figure 5.36, you are once again given important information to read. You can opt to skip the Network Security portion of the Wizard by leaving the Skip This Section option selected and clicking Next. If you want to continue on to the Network Security portion of the SCW, unselect the Skip option and click Next.

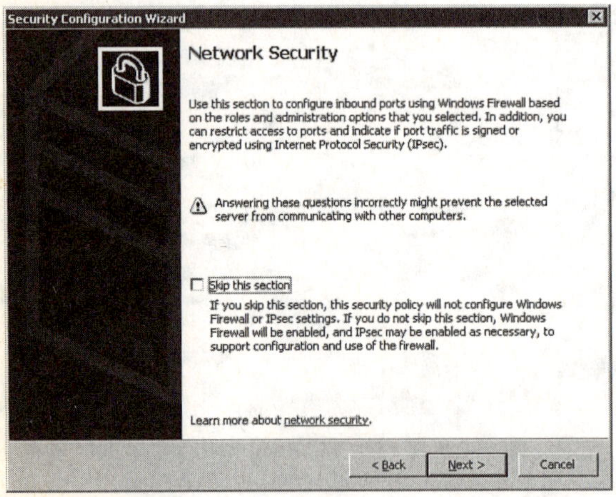

FIGURE 5.36 The SCW now moves into the Network Security portion of the policy creation.

NOTE

No Security for RRAS and VPN Servers The Security Configuration Wizard will not process the Network Security section on servers that are configured with Routing and Remote Access. You will be forced to skip ahead to the next section of the Wizard, the Registry Settings section.

13. On the Open Ports and Approve Applications dialog box, as seen in Figure 5.37, you are given the option to open or close ports in the policy. Click Next to continue after making any changes (typically none if the server is already configured correctly beforehand).

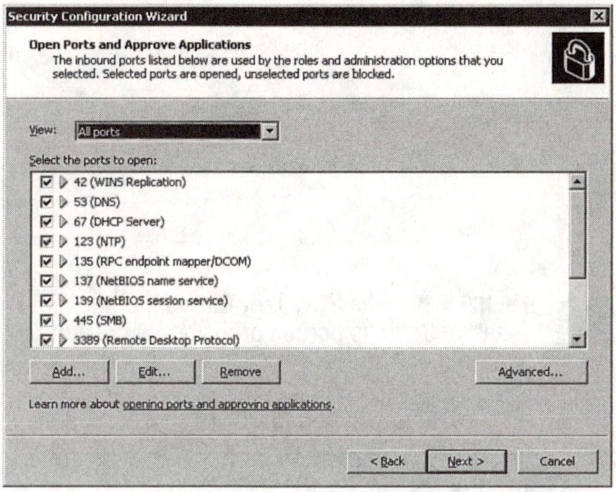

FIGURE 5.37 The SCW allows you to configure which ports will and will not be opened as part of the policy; this is another area that can get you into trouble if you are not careful.

14. On the Confirm Port Configuration dialog box, as seen in Figure 5.38, you are presented with a summary of what the SCW will do to the ports on the server as part of the policy. If you need to make a change, click Back; otherwise, click Next to continue to the next part of the Wizard.

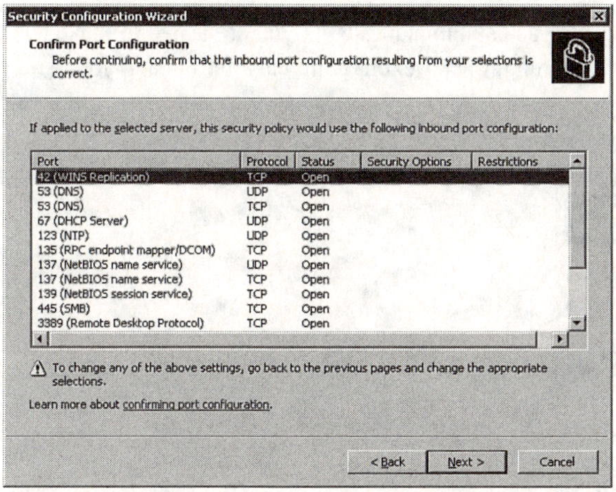

FIGURE 5.38 The SCW summarizes the port changes that it will make as part of the policy.

15. The SCW now moves to the next) phase of the configuration process. On the Registry Settings dialog box, as seen in Figure 5.39, you are once again given important information to read. You can opt to skip the Registry Settings portion of the Wizard by leaving the Skip This Section option selected and clicking Next. If you want to continue on to the Registry Settings portion of the SCW, unselect the Skip option and click Next.

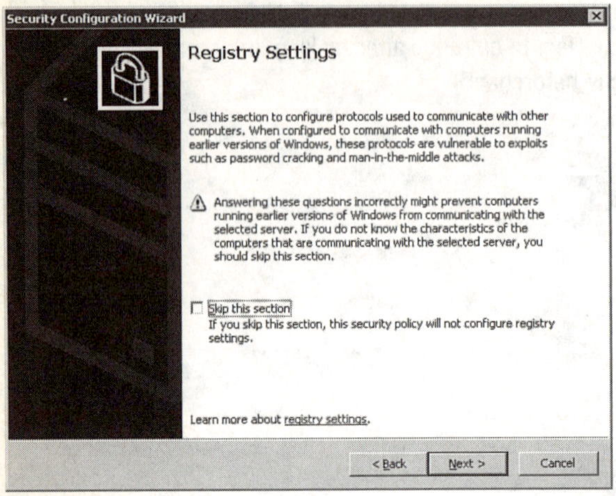

FIGURE 5.39 The SCW now moves into the Registry Settings portion of the policy creation.

CAUTION

Beware the Registry The upcoming Registry Settings section of the Security Configuration Wizard is easy to misunderstand. As such, it can be difficult to make sound decisions about the options presented. Tread carefully and make sure you understand the options presented before you move on to the next dialog box. Of course, the SCW is always ready to help you understand what you're about to configure. It helps you by providing an informational link on each page.

16. On the Require SMB Security Signatures dialog box, as seen in Figure 5.40, you are asked to make two choices about how to enable and configure SMB signing. Click Next to continue after making your choices.

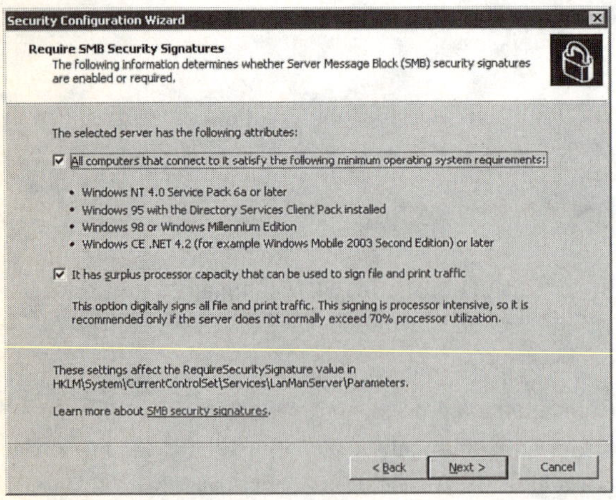

FIGURE 5.40 SMB signing will strengthen network communications security on your network.

17. On the Outbound Authentication Methods dialog box, as seen in Figure 5.41, you are asked to make choices about how the server to be configured with the policy will be allowed to authenticate with remote servers. Note the default selection of Domain Accounts provides the highest level of authentication security. Click Next to continue after making your choices.

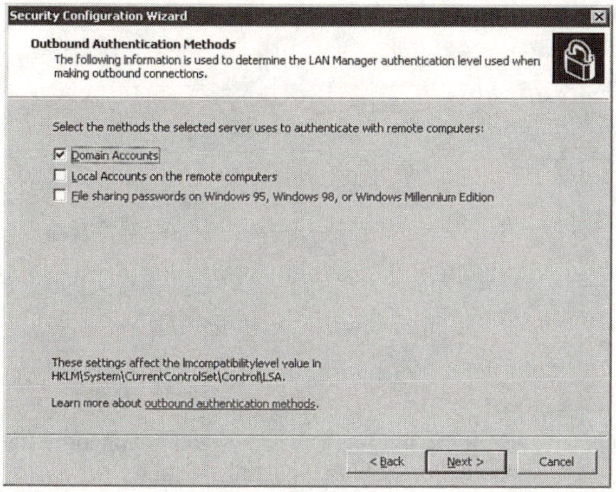

FIGURE 5.41 Typically, for maximum security, you should allow only Domain Accounts authentication for the server.

18. On the Outbound)Authentication Using Domain Accounts dialog box, as seen in Figure 5.42, you are presented with two options that describe the Domain Controllers in your environment. By default, only the first option is selected. However, the second option should be selected in an Active Directory domain because time synchronization from the server configured as the time master should keep all computers within five minutes of each other. Click Next to continue after making your choices.

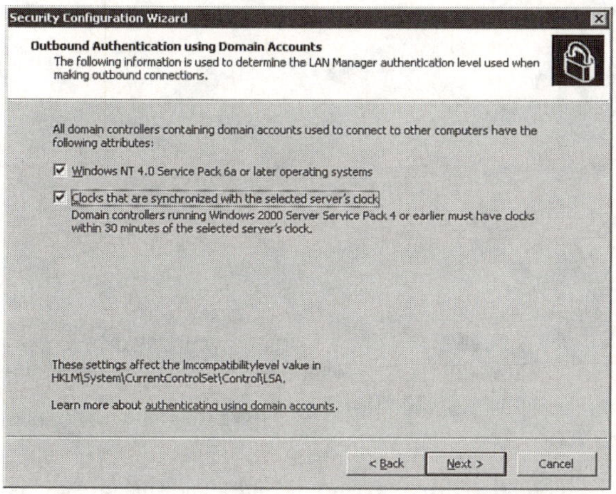

FIGURE 5.42 For maximum security, make sure that all computers are in synchronization with the server's clock.

19. On the Inbound Authentication Methods dialog box, as seen in Figure 5.43, both options are selected by default. For maximum security, you will want to unselect both options. However, before implementing this policy on a server, make sure you understand the implications of requiring NTLMv2 authentication. Click Next to continue after making your choices.

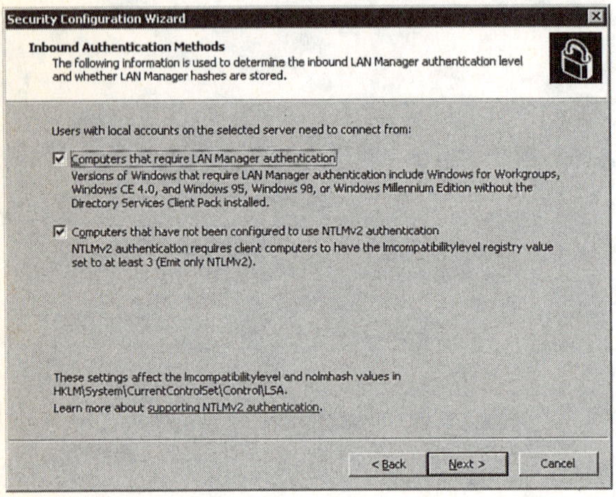

FIGURE 5.43 The SCW allows you to configure the security level of inbound authentication.

20. On the Registry Settings Summary dialog box, as seen in Figure 5.44, you are presented with a summary of what the SCW will do to the registry on the server as part of the policy. If you need to make a change, click Back; otherwise, click Next to continue to the next part of the Wizard.

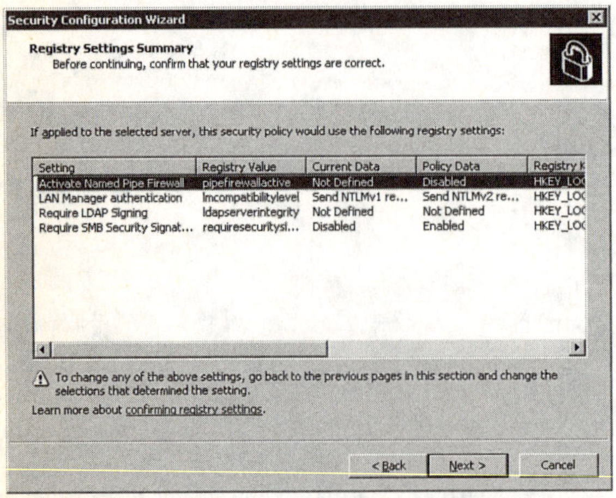

FIGURE 5.44 The SCW gives you a chance to see how the registry will be modified as a result of the policy being created.

21. The SCW now moves to the next phase of the configuration process. On the Audit Policy dialog box, as seen in Figure 5.45, you are once again given important information to read. You can opt to skip the Audit Policy portion of the Wizard by leaving the Skip This Section option selected and clicking Next. If you want to continue on to the Audit Policy portion of the SCW, unselect the Skip option and click Next.

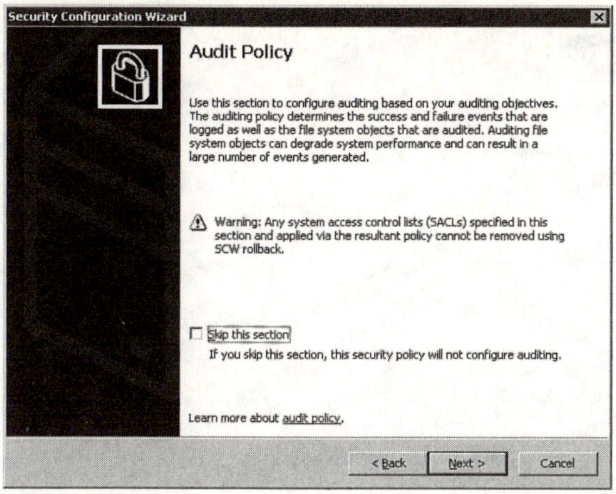

FIGURE 5.45 The SCW now moves into the Audit Policy portion of the policy creation.

22. On the System Audit Policy dialog box, as seen in Figure 5.46, you are asked to decide what type of auditing you will configure. The default setting is to Audit Successful Activities; however, for maximum auditing (which will fill your security log up even faster), you can opt for the Audit Successful and Unsuccessful Activities option. Click Next to continue after making your choice.

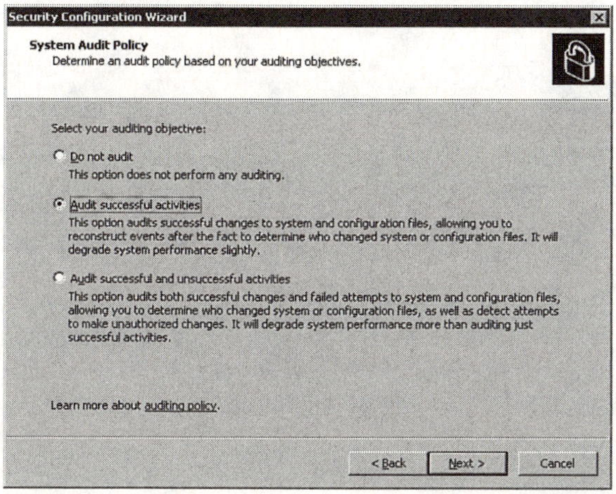

FIGURE 5.46 The SCW will help you to configure auditing via the policy being created.

23. On the Audit Policy)Summary dialog box, as seen in Figure 5.47, you are presented with a summary of your auditing choices. Note that even though we selected to audit success events on the previous page only, the SCW has implemented a best practice for us and enabled both success and failure auditing for key security events. If you need to make a change, click Back; otherwise, click Next to continue to the next part of the Wizard.

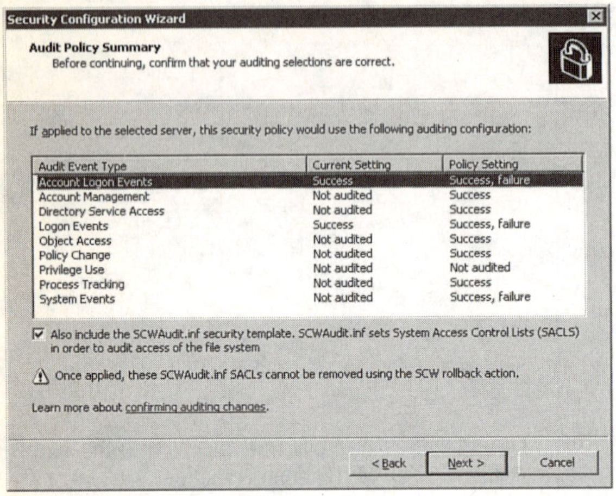

FIGURE 5.47 The SCW shows you what the auditing policy will be like after the policy is applied.

24. The Save Security Policy dialog box now appears. There are no configuration choices to make on this page. Click Next to dismiss it and continue.

25. On the Security Policy File Name dialog box, as seen in Figure 5.48, you are asked to enter a file name for the policy and also a useful description. Note that path is provided by default; however, in a larger environment, you might consider saving the policies to a central share so that they can be used by multiple administrators.

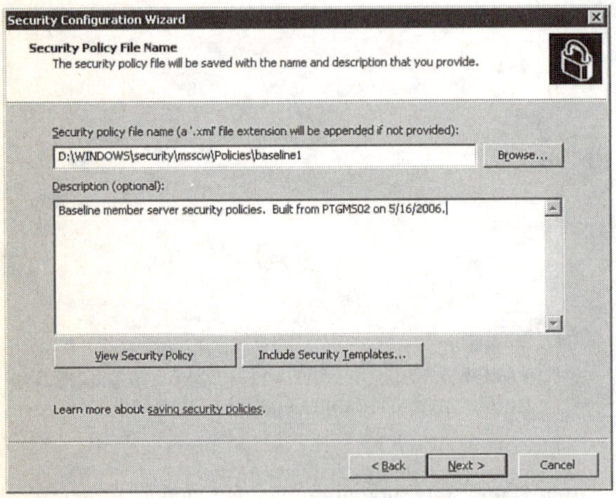

FIGURE 5.48 Finally…you get to save the policy.

26. If you want to examine the complete policy and its settings, click the View Security Policy button to SCW Viewer, as seen in Figure 5.49. Otherwise, click Next to continue.

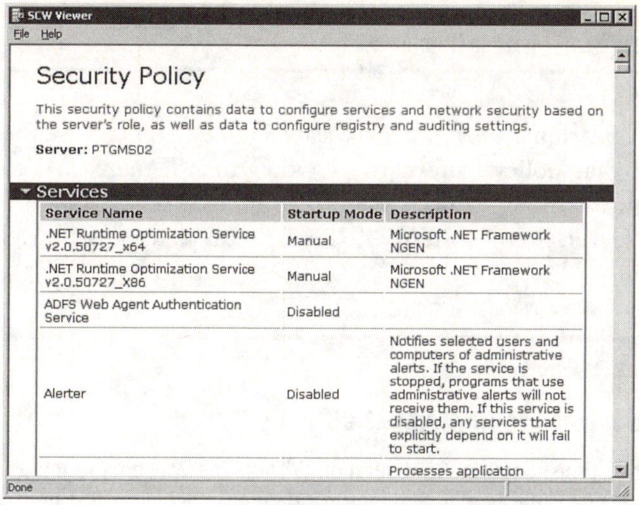

FIGURE 5.49 The SCW Viewer allows you to get an all-at-once look at the policy you've just created.

27. You will be prompted with a warning dialog, as seen in Figure 5.50. Click OK to acknowledge the warning and continue.

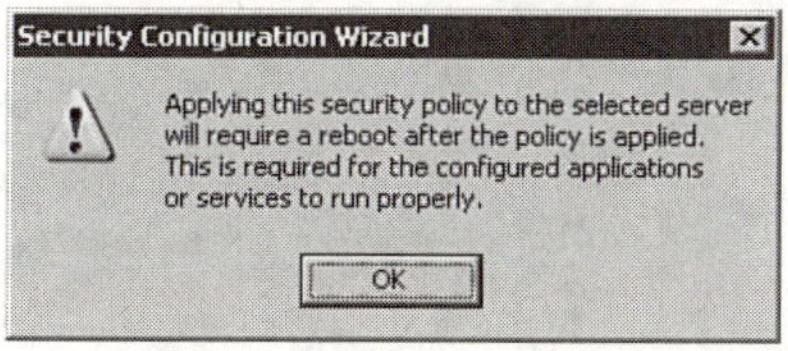

FIGURE 5.50 The server will need to be restarted after you apply the settings in an SCW policy.

28. On the Apply Security Policy dialog box, as seen in Figure 5.51, you will be asked to make one last decision. Select the Apply Later option and click Next.

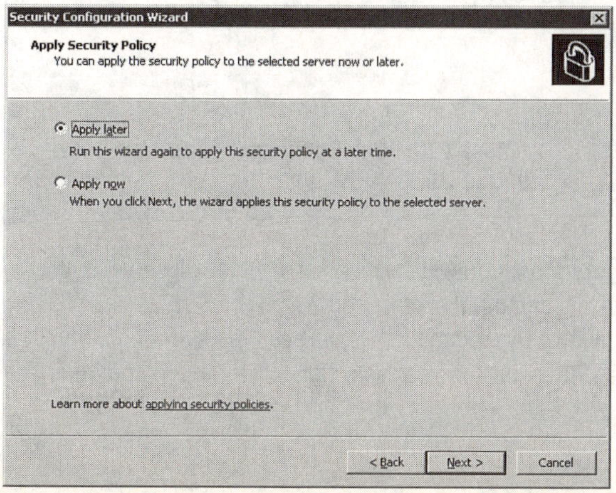

FIGURE 5.51 Save the policy for application later.

29. The Completing the Security Configuration Wizard dialog box appears, signaling the end of the policy creation process. Click Finish to close the Security Configuration Wizard.

Now that the Security Configuration) Wizard has been used to create a policy, you can use the SCW on other servers to implement that policy. Alternatively, you can use the SCW to implement policies on remote servers if the SCW is already installed on that server and you have administrative credentials to that server. Step by Step 5.7 details the steps to be followed to use the SCW to create a new policy.

STEP BY STEP

5.7 Using the Security Configuration Wizard to Implement a Policy

1. Select Start, Control Panel, Administrative Tools, Security Configuration Wizard. The Welcome to the Security Configuration Wizard screen appears. After reading the information presented, click Next to continue.
2. On the Configuration Action dialog box, as seen in Figure 5.52, you will need to tell the SCW what to do. For this exercise, we want to Apply an Existing Security Policy. If you need to locate the policy, click the Browse button to open the Open dialog box seen in Figure 5.53. After making your selection, click Next to continue.

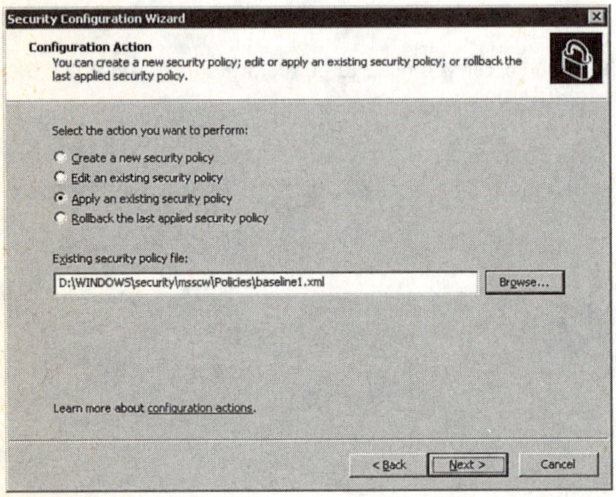

FIGURE 5.52 The Configure Action page allows you to tell the SCW what to do.

3. On the Select Server dialog box, as seen in Figure 5.54, you will select a server that will serve as the baseline by which the security policy is created. By default, the server on which the SCW is being run will be populated for you. Enter the server name and server credentials, as seen in Figure 5.55, if you are implementing the policy on a remote server. After making your selection, click Next to continue.

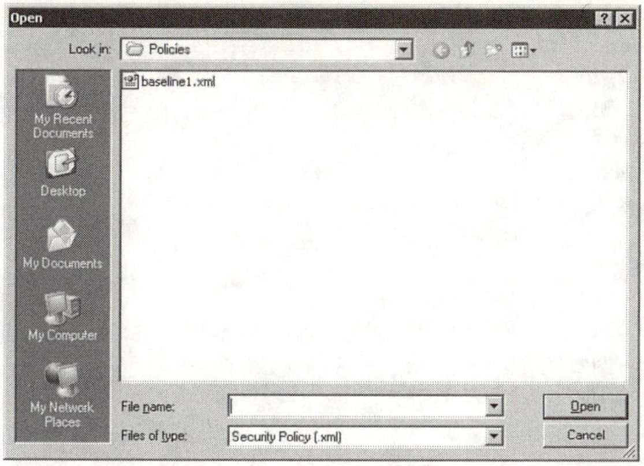

FIGURE 5.53 The Open dialog box helps you find the policy to be applied.

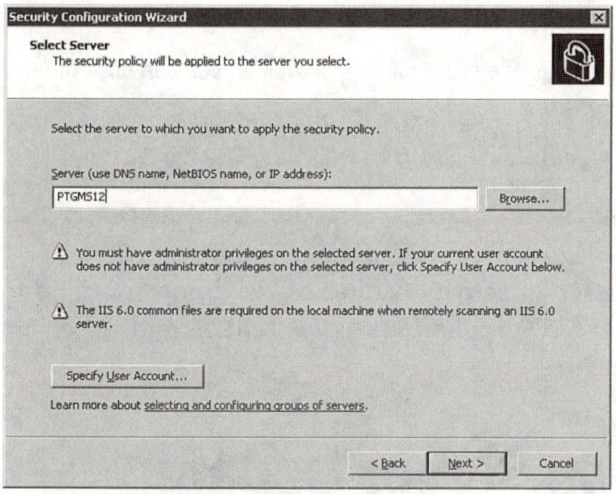

FIGURE 5.54 You need to tell the SCW the server on which to implement the policy.

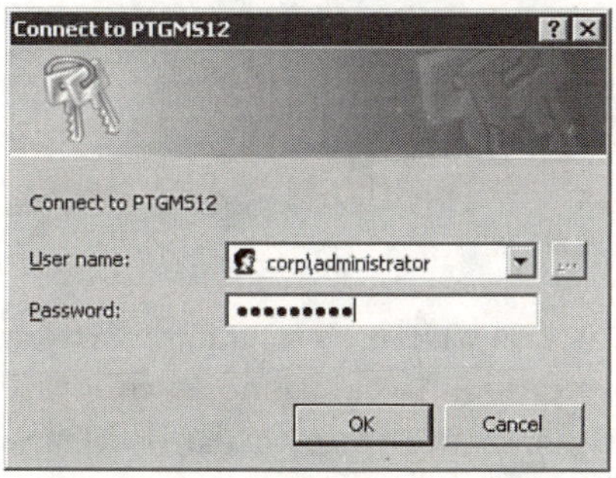

FIGURE 5.55 For remote servers, you'll need to provide credentials.

4. On the Apply Security) Policy dialog box, as seen in Figure 5.56, you will be given a final chance to review the policy being applied by clicking the View Security Policy button (seen previously in Figure 5.49). When you are ready to implement the policy, click Next.

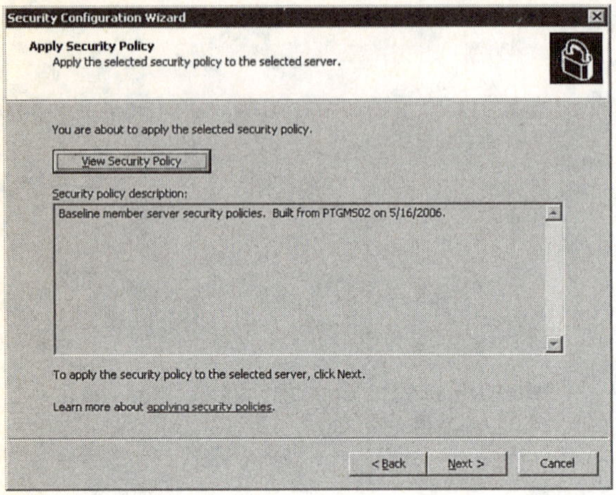

FIGURE 5.56 You have one last chance to avoid implementing the policy.

5. The Applying Security Policy dialog box appears. After the processing is complete, you can click the Next button to continue.
6. On the Completing the Security Configuration Wizard dialog box, click Finish to close the Security Configuration Wizard.

With our discussion of securing and auditing server activity behind us, we'll now move on to using the Windows Server Update Services (WSUS) application to keep clients and servers up to date with required patches and security updates.

Implementing Windows Server Update Services (WSUS)

Objective:

Install and configure software update infrastructure.

- Install and configure software update services.

So far in this chapter, we have examined how you can implement a baseline server and network security program through the use of security templates and auditing. To keep a network secure as time goes by, you need to keep your servers and client workstations up-to-date with the latest patches and hot fixes. WSUS can handle this for you in an easy-to-use and easy-to-manage format.

Although Windows Server 2003 provides native support for the Windows Server Update Service (WSUS) and the older Server Update Service (SUS), it does not by default include WSUS. It's easy enough, however, to acquire the WSUS installation package and get to work configuring and implementing WSUS on a network. But what, really, is WSUS? WSUS is nothing more than a locally controlled and managed Windows Update server. Instead of allowing the Automatic Updates client on your client workstations and servers to download updates directly from the Microsoft Windows Update servers, you can install and configure one or more WSUS servers on your internal network and point your client workstations and servers toward those WSUS servers.

As you might imagine, the ability to have your client workstations use an internal server for Windows Update can be a tremendous benefit to you because it means decreased bandwidth usage. As important as bandwidth savings might be, there is actually a larger benefit to be realized by implementing a WSUS solution on your internal network: the ability to approve specific updates that are to be installed on your clients. When you use Windows Update, your client computers install any available update that matches their needs, but with WSUS, you can specify which of the available updates are authorized to be pushed to the clients after you are satisfied that the update will pose no problems for your clients. This is a tremendous benefit that often goes unrealized.

The requirements to install WSUS on a Windows Server 2003 computer are as follows:

- The system partition of the server must be formatted with the NTFS file system.
- The partition on which you install WSUS must be formatted with the NTFS file system.
- The system partition must have at least 1GB of free space available.
- The partition where you install WSUS must have a minimum of 6GB of free space available; however, it is recommended that it have at least 30GB of free space available.
- The partition where WSUS setup installs the Windows SQL Server 2000 Desktop Engine (WMSDE) must have at least 2GB of free available.
- The server must have Internet Information Services (IIS) 6.0 installed.
- The server must have the Microsoft .NET Framework 1.1 Service Pack 1 for Windows Server 2003 software installed.
- The server must have the Background Intelligent Transfer Service (BITS) 2.0 update installed.
- The server must have Windows SQL Server 2000 Desktop Engine (WMSDE), which will be installed by the WSUS setup.

NOTE

.NET Framework 1.1 Even though the .NET Framework is currently in version 2.0 for Windows Server 2003, WSUS installs only when using the .NET Framework 1.1 SP1 for Windows Server 2003. As of the time of this writing, WSUS did not support the .NET Framework 2.0, but that will likely change in the future. You can download the .NET Framework 1.1 and .NET Framework 1.1 SP1 for Windows Server 2003 from MSDN at the following location: http://msdn.microsoft.com/netframework/downloads/updates/version1/default.aspx.

Clients to be updated by WSUS must meet one of the following requirements:

- Microsoft Windows 2000 Professional with SP3 or SP4.
- Windows 2000 Server with SP3 or SP4 or Windows 2000 Advanced Server with SP3 or SP4.
- Microsoft Windows XP Professional, with or without SP1 or SP2.
- Microsoft Windows Server 2003, Standard Edition; Windows Server 2003, Enterprise Edition; Windows Server 2003, Datacenter Edition; or Windows Server 2003, Web Edition.

With the formalities out of the way, we can now get down to the business of installing and configuring a WSUS server. After that, we examine how you can take care of the client end of your business.

Installing the WSUS Server

To begin the process of installing and configuring WSUS, you need to first ensure that you have met the guidelines presented in the previous section. After that, you need to download the WSUS installation package from http://www.microsoft.com/windowsserversystem/updateservices/default.mspx. Step by Step 5.8 outlines the process you follow to get WSUS installed on a server.

NOTE

Installing IIS 6.0 Exam 70-291 covers the basic installation and configuration of IIS 6.0 on a Windows Server 2003 computer; thus we will not duplicate that coverage here. You will be expected to perform the installation of IIS that is required in order to install WSUS on your server. If you need a review, see this Web site for more information: http://www.microsoft.com/WindowsServer2003/iis/default.mspx.

STEP BY STEP

5.8 Installing a WSUS Server

1. Double-click the WSUS installation file to begin the installation on your new WSUS server. If prompted with a security warning, click Run to start the installer.

2. If you haven't met the requirements to install WSUS, you'll be presented with an error dialog like the one seen in Figure 5.57. After installing the required components, start the installation again.

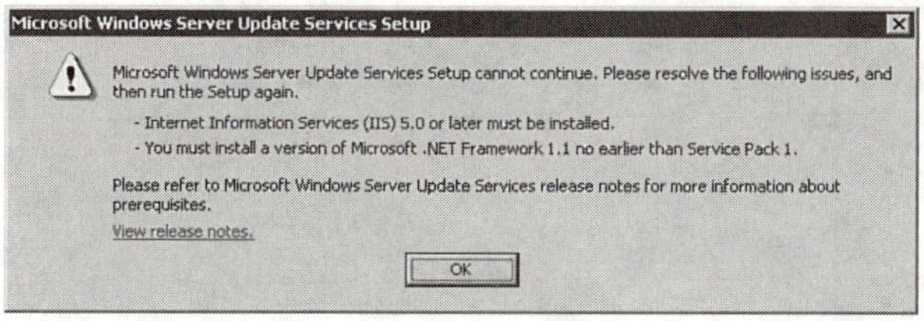

FIGURE 5.57 It looks like we didn't meet all of the requirements to install WSUS on the server.

3. If your server is ready for an installation of WSUS, you will be presented with the Welcome to the Microsoft Windows Server Updates Services Wizard dialog box. Click Next to dismiss the opening page wizard.

4. On the License Agreement dialog box, click the I Accept the Terms of the License Agreement radio button and click Next to continue. You will not be able to continue the installation of WSUS without accepting the EULA.

5. On the Select Update Source dialog box, as seen in Figure 5.58, WSUS will provide you with a default storage location for the update files. Recall that this location must be NFTS formatted and should not be the same volume as your system partition. If you want, you can change the location, but bear in mind the requirements that WSUS presents. You can also turn off the storing of updates locally if you like, although it is recommended that you leave it in the default configuration. Click Next to continue after making your selection.

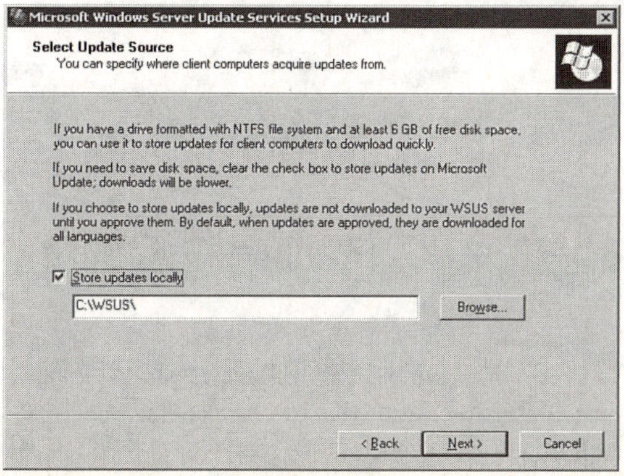

FIGURE 5.58 WSUS will provide you with a default location to store files.

6. On the Database Options dialog box, shown in Figure 5.59, WSUS will provide you with a default path for the SQL Server desktop engine installation. If you want, you can change the location, but bear in mind the requirements that WSUS presents. If an existing SQL Server database was detected on the server, WSUS would allow you configure that for use. Click Next to continue after making your selection.

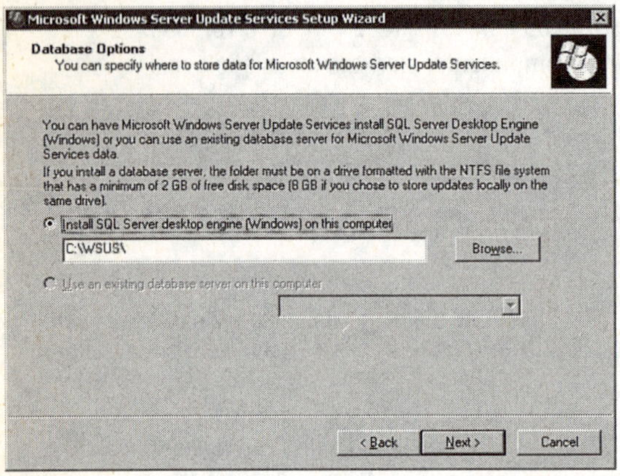

FIGURE 5.59 WSUS will need a location to install the SQL Server desktop engine.

7. On the Web Site Selection dialog box, which is shown in Figure 5.60, you will need to tell WSUS what IIS Web site to use. The default selection is the existing default IIS Web site, which will work fine in most cases, especially if this server will have no other user-facing Web sites. Note that the configuration you pick will change the connection information provided in the bottom half of the page. Click Next to continue after making your selection.

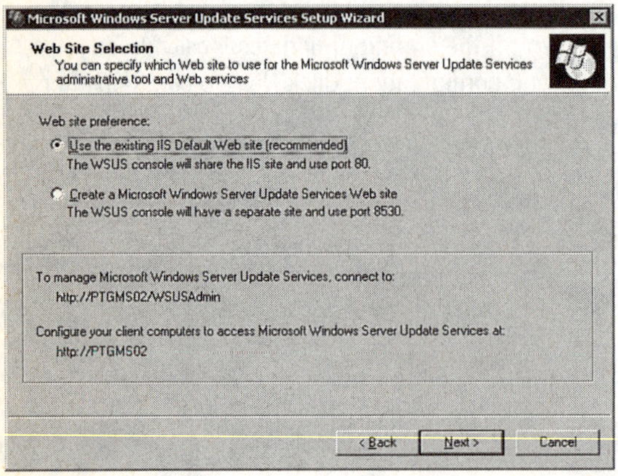

FIGURE 5.60 The WSUS will need an IIS Web site made available to it.

8. On the Mirror Update Settings dialog box, which is shown in Figure 5.61, WSUS allows you to configure this new WSUS server to inherit update approval information from. This can be useful if you are creating a hierarchy of WSUS servers, such as in a headquarters-branch office scenario, or if you have

another WSUS server from which you want to get approved update information. After you make your selection, click Next to continue.

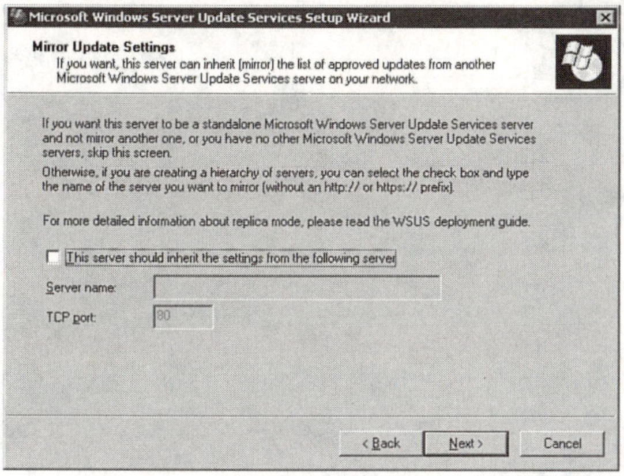

FIGURE 5.61 WSUS allows your new server to inherit information about approved updates from another WSUS server.

9. On the Ready to Install Microsoft Windows Server Update Services dialog box, shown in Figure 5.62, make a note of the URL that is specified. This is the URL you will need to use later when configuring the Group Policy for WSUS and Automatic Updates to point your Automatic Updates to the WSUS server. When you are ready to complete the installation phase, click Next. The wizard installs WSUS on your server.

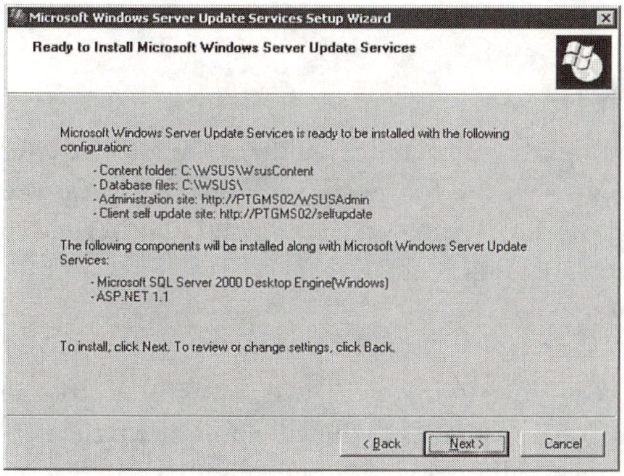

FIGURE 5.62 You should make a note of the URL to which you will be pointing your Automatic Updates clients.

10. When the wizard has completed, click Finish to close the wizard. You can now administer your WSUS server from http://*servername*/WSUSAdmin.

11. In most cases, the WSUS server administration page automatically appears at this time. If it does not, you can open your WSUS server administration page by entering **`http://`*`servername`*`/WSUSAdmin`** or by clicking the Microsoft Software Update Services item in the Administrative Tools folder. Either way, the WSUS administration page appears, as shown in Figure 5.63.

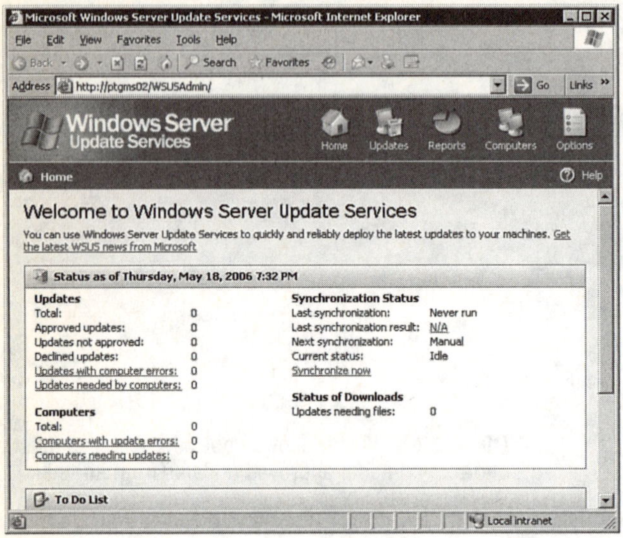

FIGURE 5.63 All administration of WSUS takes place from within a Web browser.

Congratulations, you've just installed a WSUS server—but your job is not done yet. Before you can start pushing updates to clients in need, you've got some more configuration work to do. We'll now move on to examining the different configuration areas you will need to work with in order to get the WSUS server up to speed.

Configuring the WSUS Server

The process of configuring a WSUS is fairly straightforward and shouldn't take all that long to complete. We'll examine each configuration area in the following sections. To access the WSUS server options page, simply click the Options link located in the top-right corner of the main window. This opens the Options page, shown in Figure 5.64.

Synchronization Options

Clicking the Synchronization Options link seen in Figure 5.64 will bring you to the Synchronization Options page, as seen in Figure 5.65. From here you will configure basic networking information and synchronization schedules—all important items if your WSUS server is to work properly.

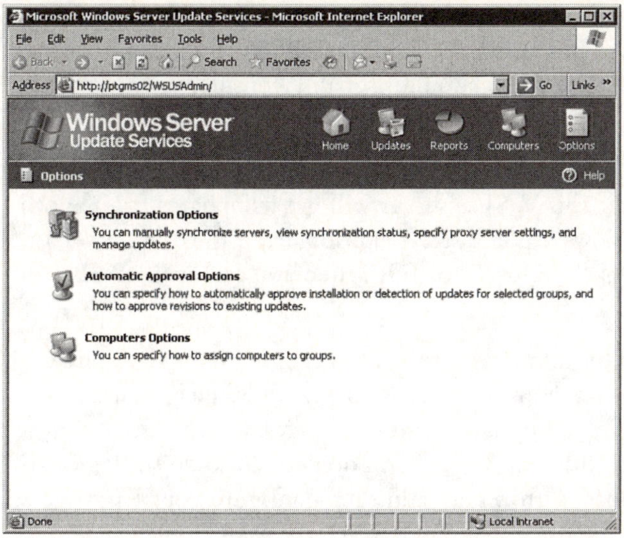

FIGURE 5.64 You will need to spend a little time ensuring that all options are set and configured as required.

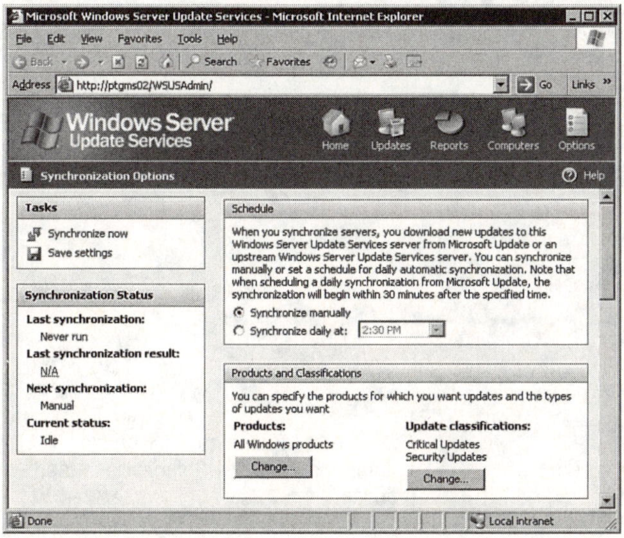

FIGURE 5.65 The Synchronization Options page allows you to get your server connected to the Internet and tell it how to process the downloading of updates.

Starting at the top of the page, you will need to configure the WSUS server with the correct information in the following areas:

- **Schedule**—Specifies how often you want to download new updates.
- **Products and Classifications**—Specifies for what versions of Windows—such as Windows 2000 or Windows XP—the WSUS should provide updates. Additionally, you can specify what classification (severity level) of updates should be downloaded. These classifications include Critical Updates and Security Updates.

- **Proxy Server**—If your network requires all Internet-bound traffic to pass through a proxy server, you can enter in the required information including credentials to allow your WSUS server to download updates. You should probably consider creating a special, dedicated user account under which the WSUS server should access the Internet—this will allow you to track Internet usage more accurately.
- **Update Source**—Specifies whether this WSUS server will get its updates from another WSUS server or from the Windows Update site. Additionally, if the WSUS server, and its source for WSUS updates is configured for SSL, then you can enable SSL from this location.
- **Update Files and Languages**—This allows you to configure how the updates are stored, and most importantly, it allows you to configure in which languages updates are downloaded. The default is to download updates in all languages, which can be a large waste of disk space, network bandwidth, and time if you don't need to do so. It's worth taking the time to click the Advanced button here and then configure your language options, as seen in Figure 5.66.

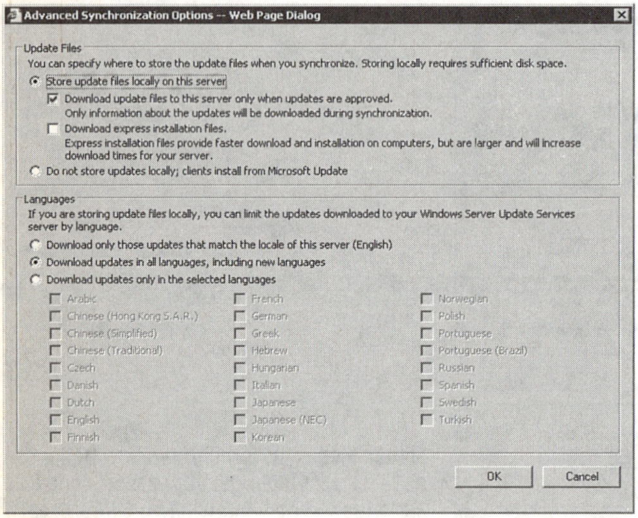

FIGURE 5.66 Changing the language options for your WSUS server is a good practice.

After you're done making changes on the Synchronization Options page, be sure to click the Save Settings link at the top of the page. After that, click the Options button to get back to the main Options page.

Automatic Approval Options

By clicking the Automatic Approval Options link seen previously in Figure 5.64, you will be brought to the Synchronization Options page, as seen in Figure 5.67. From here you will configure how the WSUS server will handle updates.

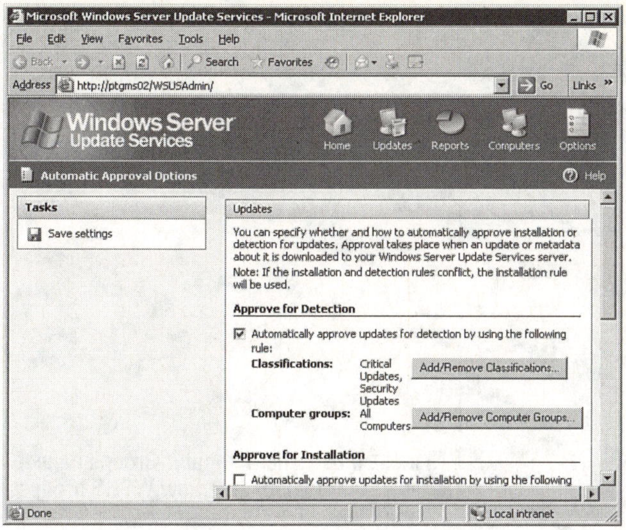

FIGURE 5.67 The Automatic Approval Options page allows you to configure how your WSUS server will handle updates.

Starting at the top of the page, you will need to configure the WSUS server in the following areas:

- **Updates**—By default, WSUS will detect that computers need updates, but it will not automatically approve them for installation. In most cases, this is the recommended configuration. You can also change what types of updates are detected and/or automatically approved and also for what computer groups they will be detected and/or approved.
- **Revisions to Updates**—By default, WSUS will automatically approve revisions to updates that have been previously approved. For maximum control, you'll likely want to change this setting.
- **Windows Server Update Services Updates**— By default, WSUS will automatically approve updates to the WSUS server itself. You can opt to disable this behavior, but it may have an adverse impact on the functionality of the WSUS server in some rare instances.

After you're done making changes on the Automatic Approval Options page, be sure to click the Save Settings link at the top of the page. After that, click the Options button to get back to the main Options page.

Computers Options

If you click the Computers Options link seen previously in Figure 5.64, you will be brought to the Computers Options page, as seen in Figure 5.68. From here you will configure how the WSUS server groups computers.

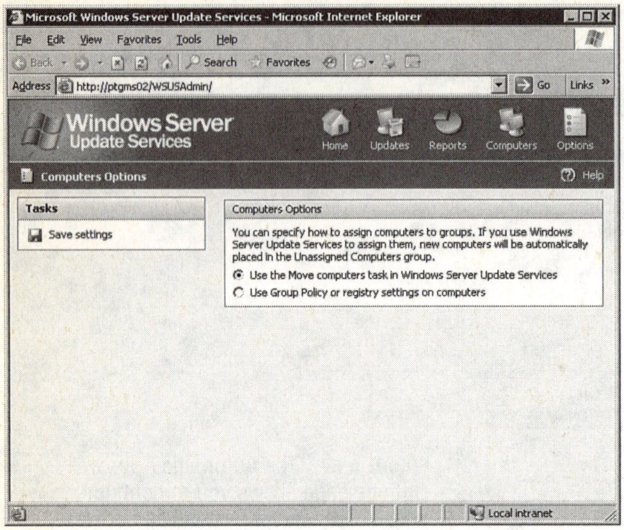

FIGURE 5.68 The Computer Groups page allows you to configure how WSUS groups computers.

You can opt to group computers within WSUS, or you can group computers by using Group Policy. To group them by Group Policy, click the Help icon and follow the instructions in the help document. After you're done making changes on the Automatic Approval Options page, be sure to click the Save Settings link at the top of the page. After that, click the Home button to get back to the main WSUS page.

The Computers Page

By clicking the Computers link at the top of any WSUS page, you will be brought to the Computers page, as seen in Figure 5.69.

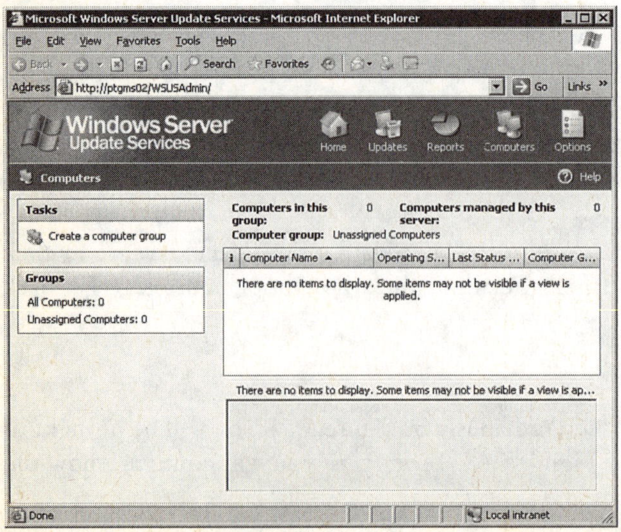

FIGURE 5.69 The Computers page allows you to configure computer groups within WSUS.

The Computers page is the management location from which all computer grouping is done. Only computers that have been configured to receive updates from this WSUS server will be shown on this page; that is there are no computers listed (yet) in Figure 5.69. We'll examine this page in more detail after Group Policy has been configured for WSUS. If you want to, you can create new computer groups at this time by clicking the Create a Computer Group link to open the dialog box seen in Figure 5.70.

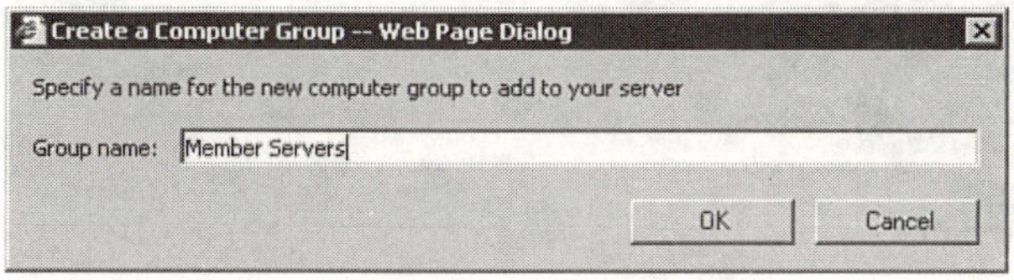

FIGURE 5.70 The creation of computer groups is fairly easy in WSUS.

The Reports Page

By clicking the Reports link at the top of any WSUS page, you will be brought to the Reports page, as seen in Figure 5.71.

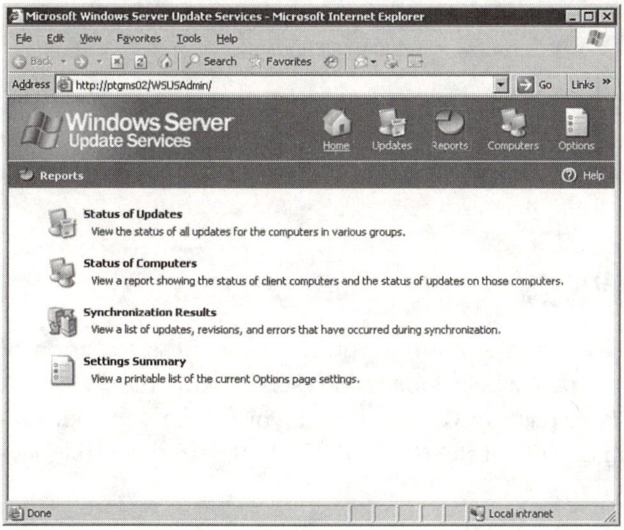

FIGURE 5.71 The Reports page is your central location for WSUS reporting.

Once you've synchronized the WSUS server and started updating clients with it, you can come back to the Reports page to run reports that will help you keep tabs on what the WSUS server is doing.

The Updates Page

By clicking the Updates link at the top of any WSUS page, you will be brought to the Updates page, as seen in Figure 5.72.

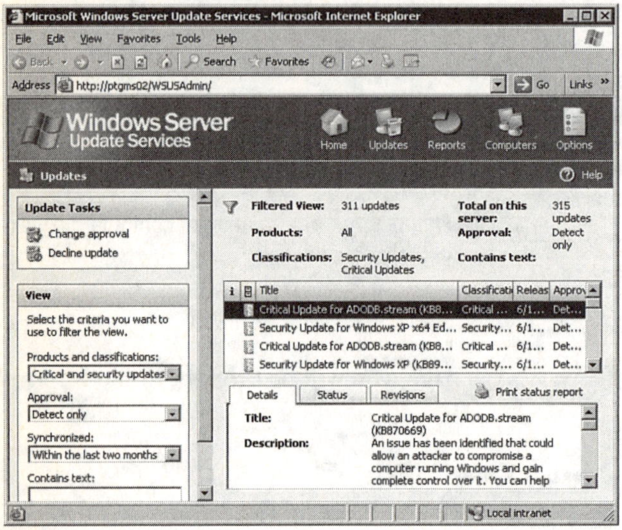

FIGURE 5.72 The Updates page details the status of all updates.

Once you've synchronized the WSUS server and started approving updates, you can come back to the Updates page to see the status of each update. Notice the fairly granular filtering options available to you on the left side of the page.

Updating Clients with WSUS

Now that you've performed all of the basic configuration required after the installation of WSUS, you're ready to take the next steps—synchronizing the server with the Windows Update servers, configuring Group Policy to push WSUS settings to your clients, and approving updates and having client computers download them. We explore these tasks in this section.

Synchronizing the WSUS Server

To get your initial WSUS server synchronization accomplished, you'll want to use the Synchronization Options page, as seen previously in 5.65, and click the Synchronize Now link in the top-left corner of the page. Note how the page changes after you start synchronization, as seen in Figure 5.73.

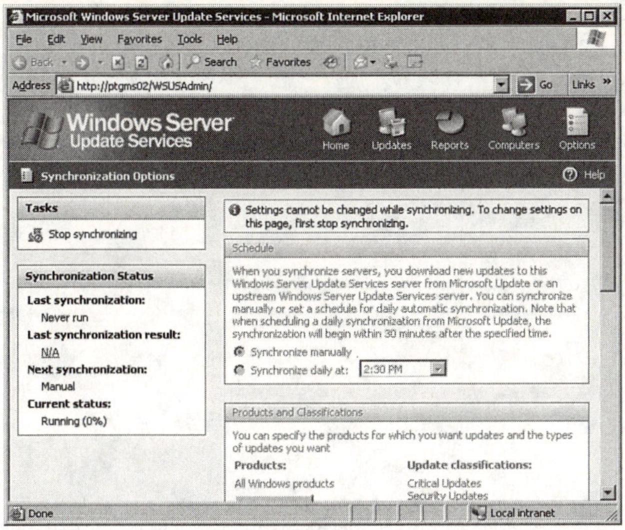

FIGURE 5.73 Once you start a synchronization event, you'll need to wait for it to finish before doing anything else.

If you go back to the Home page, you will be able to see the percent complete progress on the synchronization event.

> **NOTE**
>
> **Sit Back and Relax** Once you start the initial synchronization event, you may be waiting for several hours (depending on how many languages you've selected) for all available updates to be downloaded. Of course, this is a good time to get your Group Policy Object created and in place.

Configuring Group Policy for WSUS

Once you've gotten WSUS installed and configured to your liking on your server, you need to configure Automatic Updates on your client workstations. Windows Server 2003 includes the administrative templates that allow you to start managing Automatic Updates from within Group Policy. In addition, in smaller organizations where Active Directory may not be in use, you can configure Automatic Updates directly on each local computer.

Step by Step 5.9 examines the process of configuring Automatic Updates through Group Policy in Windows Server 2003.

STEP BY STEP

5.9 Configuring the Automatic Updates via Group Policy

1. Open the Active Directory Users and Computers console by selecting Start, Programs, Administrative Tools, Active Directory Users and Computers.

2. Navigate to the node for which you want to apply Automatic Updates settings, such as a specific OU or perhaps the domain. For this example, we'll apply the settings to the CORP OU, as shown in Figure 5.74.

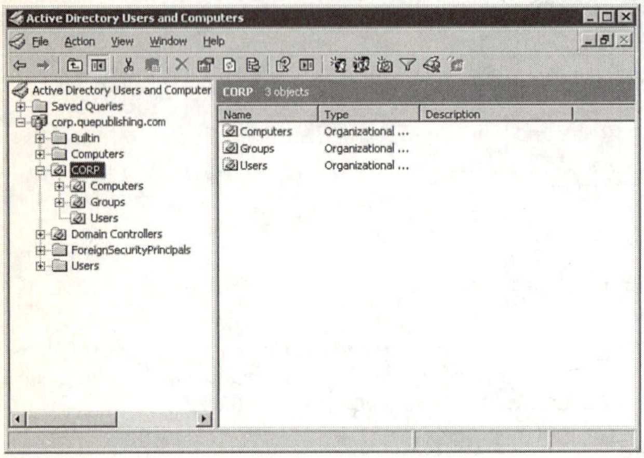

FIGURE 5.74 You can apply your Automatic Updates client settings to any OU or domain of your choosing.

3. Right-click the CORP OU and select Properties from the context menu. The Sales Properties dialog box appears. Select the Group Policy tab, as seen previously in Figure 5.11.

4. To create a new GPO, click the New button. Supply a name for the new GPO, such as `WSUS Settings` and press Enter.

5. Click the Edit button to open the Group Policy Editor for the selected GPO.

6. In the Group Policy Editor, expand the following nodes: Computer Configuration, Administrative Templates, Windows Components, and Windows Update, as seen in Figure 5.75.

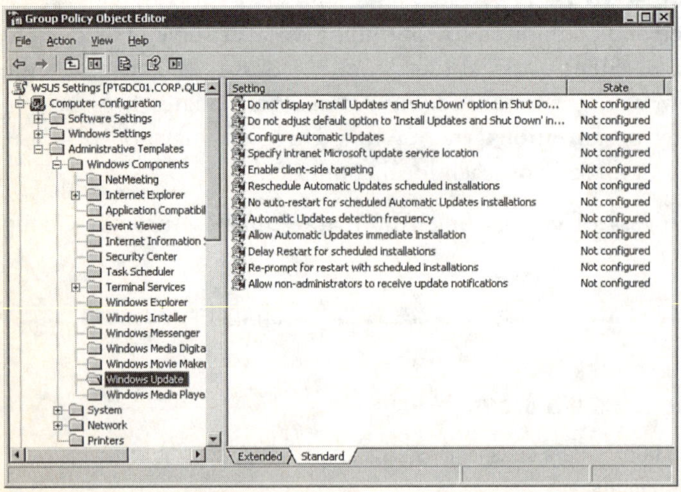

FIGURE 5.75 You can configure Automatic Updates client options from Group Policy, if desired.

7. To configure an option from this node, double-click it.
8. Configure the Configure Automatic Updates option by opening it and selecting the Enabled option, as shown in Figure 5.76. Click OK to close the dialog box when complete. You have four options available for installing updates:
   - **2**—Notify for download and notify for install
   - **3**—Auto download and notify for install
   - **4**—Auto download and schedule the install
   - **5**—Allow local admin to choose setting

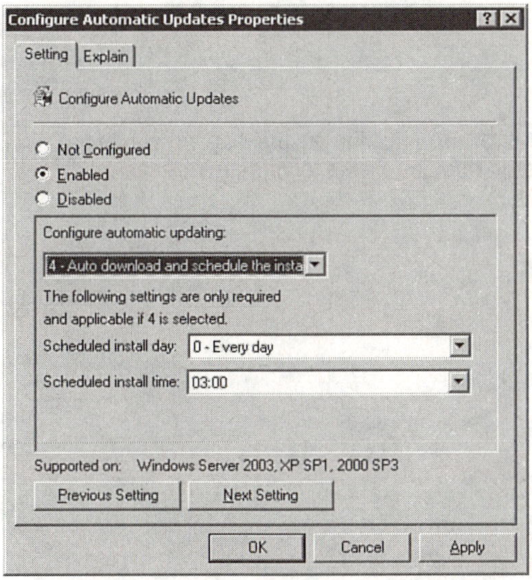

FIGURE 5.76 The Configure Automatic Updates option must be set to Enabled to allow WSUS to function.

9. Configure the Specify Intranet Microsoft Update Service Location option by opening it and selecting the Enabled option. Provide the URL to your WSUS server, as shown in Figure 5.77. You can use the same IIS server for both WSUS and statistics, as shown.
10. Configure the Reschedule Automatic Updates Scheduled Installations option by opening it and selecting the Enabled option. Configure the amount of time after which Automatic Updates should try again after a failed installation, as shown in Figure 5.78.
11. Configure the No Auto-Restart for Scheduled Automatic Updates Installations option by opening it and selecting the Enabled option to prevent the computer from automatically restarting after Automatic Updates has installed new updates or by selecting Disabled to allow the computer to be restarted, as shown in Figure 5.79.

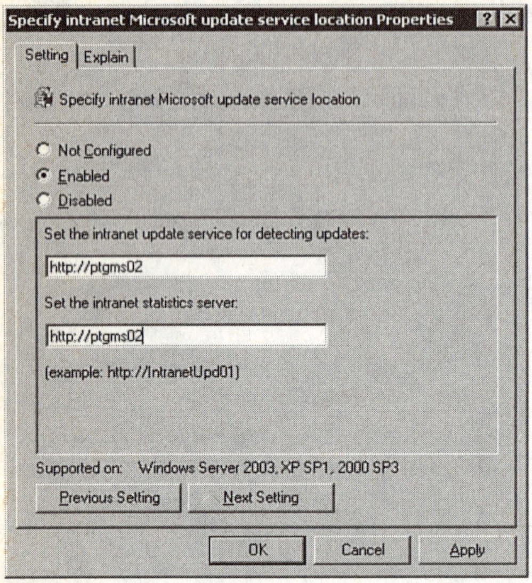

FIGURE 5.77 You need to ensure that you point your Automatic Updates clients to your internal servers.

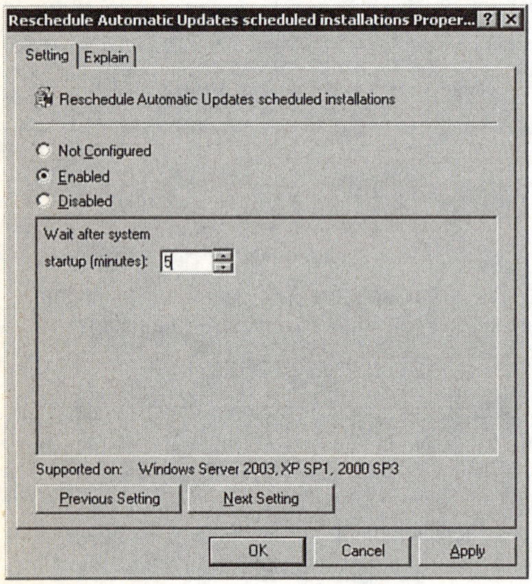

FIGURE 5.78 You can configure Automatic Updates to retry failed installations.

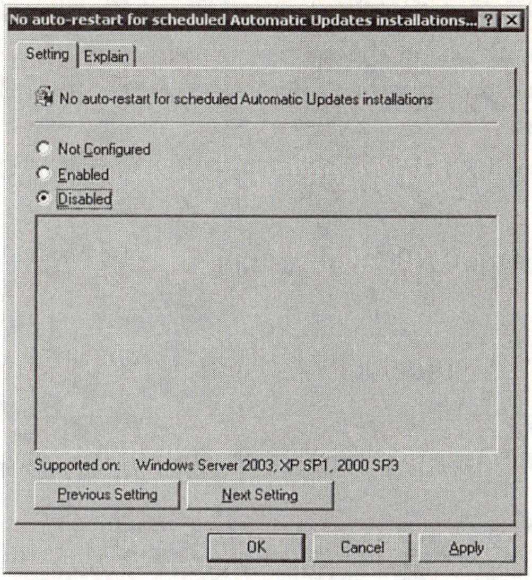

FIGURE 5.79 You should, in most cases, allow client computers to be restarted after the updates have been installed.

Configuring Local Group Policy for WSUS

In organizations where Active Directory is not in use, you can still easily configure the Automatic Updates client to download and install available updates from the Microsoft Windows Update Web servers. The options are available from either the Automatic Updates tab of the System applet or from the Automatic Updates applet, both of which are located in the Control Panel.

Alternatively, you can configure the local group policy on these computers to point towards an installed and configured WSUS server. To open the Local Computer Policy console, simply click Start, Run, enter **`gpedit.msc`**, and click OK. The Automatic Updates settings will be found in the same location as seen previously in Figure 5.75: Computer Configuration, Administrative Templates, Windows Components, Windows Update.

Approving WSUS Updates and Updating Client Computers

After you've completed all of the WSUS installation and configuration steps up to this point, only one basic task remains—actually getting the updates onto your client computers in need. This task encompasses three steps: having Group Policy apply to the clients, approving updates for download and/or installation, and verifying that the updates have been applied.

You can verify that Group Policy has taken effect on the server or workstation by examining the Automatic Updates applet or Automatic Updates tab in the System applet. Figure 5.80 shows that all options have been grayed out, thus indicating that some policy is configuring them and you cannot make changes to them directly.

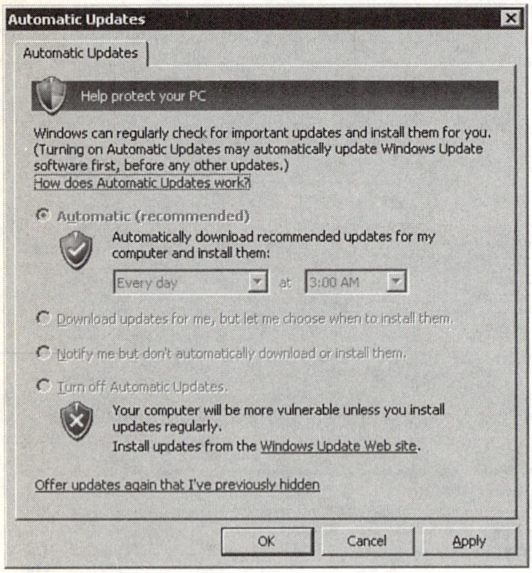

FIGURE 5.80 Automatic Updates on this computer has been set by a policy and cannot be changed directly.

To approve an update, you need only select it in the listing on the Updates page, as seen previously in Figure 5.72, and click the Change approval link found in the top-right corner of the page. You should not typically approve updates until you've conducted enough testing to verify that the update will not cause any problems in your environment under most conditions (because you can never, unfortunately, plan for *everything*). Clicking the Change Approval link will cause the Approve Updates page to open as seen in Figure 5.81, which allows you to change the approval status of the update. Note that you can select multiple updates to approve at a single time if desired.

If you ever need a reminder of what you should be doing next when it comes to administering your WSUS implementation, look no further than the bottom of the Home page. The To Do List, as seen in Figure 5.82, will keep you on top of your WSUS game.

You can verify update installation by checking the Add or Remove Programs applet on client computers or by examining the logs within WSUS.

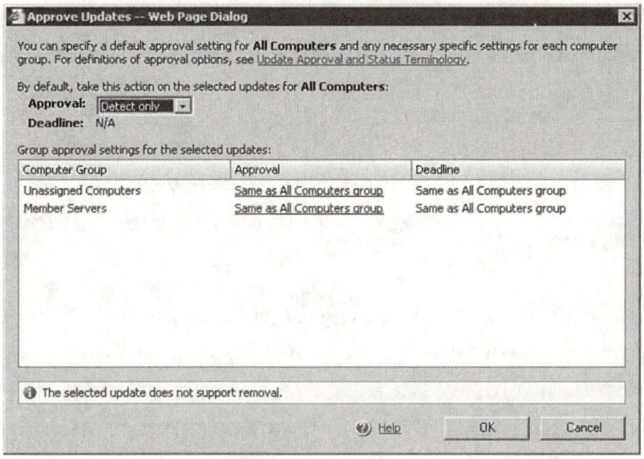

FIGURE 5.81 You will need to approve updates to install after you've tested them.

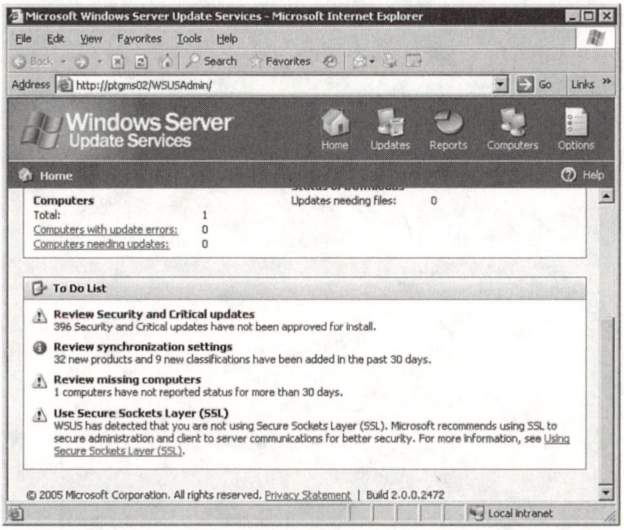

FIGURE 5.82 The WSUS To Do List helps keep you on top of required management tasks.

Managing Updates for Legacy Operating Systems

Objective:

Install and configure software update infrastructure.

- Configure software updates on earlier operating systems.

The reality of your network may dictate that you provide support for legacy desktop clients such as Windows 98 clients. These older operating systems cannot participate in a WSUS server environment for multiple reasons, one of which is their inability to receive GPO settings. For clients such as these, you have a few options available when it comes to keeping them up-to-date.

Microsoft offers the old standby Windows Update that any of these legacy computers can use, regardless of their network status. Anyone who has used any version of Windows past Windows 95 is most likely familiar with Windows Update. You can connect to the Windows Update Web site at http://windowsupdate.microsoft.com.

Another Microsoft-provided option is to implement and use the Systems Management Server (SMS) application, which you can use to manage and monitor legacy versions of Windows, including rolling out updates and patches. A recent addition to the SMS package provides support for more easily determining and installing required updates on client computers; in addition, SMS provides some of the same support that WSUS does. You can find more information about SMS, currently in version 2003, at www.microsoft.com/smserver. A new version is coming shortly that promises even more powerful management features for administrators; you can find out more about it at http://www.microsoft.com/smserver/evaluation/2003/smsv4.mspx.

Chapter Summary

This chapter examines three basic parts of keeping Windows Server 2003 computers and the entire network secure:

- **Applying baseline security**—Every security plan must have a starting point. By making use of the preconfigured security templates supplied with Windows Server 2003, you can quickly and effortlessly implement varying levels of security within an organization at the levels that are appropriate. You can take this a step further by creating customized security templates that specifically meet your needs and security requirements. By configuring and testing security templates in the Security Configuration and Analysis snap-in, you can avoid mistakenly applying them to a large group of computers via Group Policy until you are ready to do so.
- **Performing auditing**—Even the best planned and implemented security solution can be circumvented. Auditing on a network can help you to detect unauthorized or abnormal network activities early, before they have a chance to become a successful attack that could have catastrophic effects on your network and your organization as a whole. Like many things, there is, however, a fine line between too much auditing and too little auditing; you need to find the perfect balance that satisfies your organizational requirements without affecting performance too adversely.
- **Keeping computers up-to-date**—As network administrators, you must absolutely, at all times, keep servers and network clients updated with the latest security patches and updates. In many cases, WSUS can be used to perform this task for you. In cases in which WSUS cannot be used, administrators should be judicious in their use of Windows Update or other solutions such as SMS to ensure that all clients are up-to-date and protected.

Additionally, we examined the Security Configuration Wizard, new in Windows Server 2003 Service Pack 1 and Windows Server 2003 R2. This Wizard allows you to create and implement advanced security policies that can be all encompassing and include every part of a server's configuration.

EXAM ALERT

SCW Revisited You will likely not be required to demonstrate any advanced knowledge of the SCW on your 70-291 exam, but don't let that stop you from getting to know what it is and how it works.

Key Terms

- Auditing
- Automatic Updates
- Compatible security template
- Default DC security template
- Default security template
- Failure event
- Group Policy Editor
- GPO
- Highly Secure security template
- Principle of least privilege
- Security Configuration and Analysis snap-in
- secedit.exe
- Secure security template
- Security Configuration Wizard
- Security template
- Security Templates snap-in
- Success event
- WSUS

Apply Your Knowledge

In this chapter, you have learned about getting and keeping your Windows Server 2003 computer secure. In the following exercises, you will practice some of the concepts and methods discussed in this chapter.

Exercises

5.1 Analyzing a Local Computer's Security Settings

In this exercise, you will use the Security Configuration and Analysis snap-in to perform an analysis of the local computer's security.

Estimated Time: 15 minutes

1. Open your custom security console or create one that contains the Security Configuration and Analysis snap-in.
2. Right-click the Security Configuration and Analysis node and select Open Database from the context menu.
3. Create a new database by entering the name **`securitydb`**.
4. Select the security template you are loading into the database for this exercise.
5. Right-click the Security Configuration and Analysis node and select Analyze Computer Now to start the analysis.
6. Provide an error log name and pathname and click OK to start the analysis process. After the analysis is complete, you are returned to the Security Configuration and Analysis snap-in.
7. Compare the database settings to those of the local computer. How are they different? How are they the same? What do you need to change to implement the required security?

5.2 Importing a Security Template into Group Policy

In this exercise, you will import a security template into a Group Policy object.

Estimated Time: 15 minutes

1. Open the Active Directory Users and Computers console.
2. Locate the domain or OU to which you want to apply the security template.
3. Right-click the appropriate OU or domain and select Properties from the context menu. The Properties dialog box appears. Select the Group Policy tab.
4. To create a new GPO, click the New button. Supply a name for the new GPO and press Enter.
5. Click the Edit button to open the Group Policy Editor for the selected GPO.
6. Expand the nodes as follows: Computer Configuration, Windows Settings, Security Settings. Right-click the Security Settings node and select Import Policy from the context menu.
7. Select the template to be imported.

5.3 Implementing Auditing

In this exercise, you will implement auditing of a file object.

Estimated Time: 15 minutes

1. Open the Active Directory Users and Computers console.
2. Locate the domain or OU for which you want to perform auditing.
3. Right-click the appropriate OU or domain and select Properties from the context menu. The Properties dialog box appears. Select the Group Policy tab. To create a new GPO, click the New button. Supply a name for the new GPO and press Enter.
4. Navigate to the Audit Policies node.
5. Configure success and failure auditing for the Audit Object Access option.
6. Close the Group Policy Editor and the Active Directory Users and Computers console.
7. Locate the file for which you want to configure auditing in Windows Explorer. Right-click the file and select Properties from the context menu. The Properties dialog box appears.
8. Select the Security tab and click the Advanced button to open the Advanced Security Settings dialog box. Select the Auditing tab.
9. Click the Add button to open the Select User or Group dialog box. After you have configured the desired users and groups, click OK to continue.
10. In the Auditing Entry dialog box, you can select what success or failure events you want to audit for on the selected object. After you make your selections, click OK to confirm them.
11. Close the remaining dialog boxes, and you are done configuring auditing.

Exam Questions

1. You are the systems administrator of a Windows Server 2003 Active Directory network. Your network consists of 1,500 Windows XP Professional client computers spread out over 15 OUs with approximately 100 computers each. You have just finished creating a customized security template that specifies the Account Policy and auditing settings that are required by your organization's corporate policy for specific departments. What is the best way for you to apply this template to only the Sales, Marketing, Production, and Engineering OUs?

   ❍ **A.** Import the security template at the domain level into a GPO.

   ❍ **B.** Import the security template into each required OU by using a GPO.

   ❍ **C.** Script the `secedit.exe` command to apply the security template to the required computers.

   ❍ **D.** Manually apply the security template to each of the computers.

2. You are the systems administrator for Just Right Tops, LLC. Your network consists of three geographically distant sites that function as three different domains. No site has a direct link to any other site. You have recently completed the creation of two custom security templates that are to be applied to all computers in all three sites of your company network. How can you most easily deploy these security templates at all three sites?

   ❍ **A.** Create and configure a new DC for each remote site. Apply the security templates to the DCs. Place a new DC in each site and allow Active Directory to replicate.

   ❍ **B.** Export the security templates into `.inf` files by using the Security Configuration and Analysis snap-in. Deliver the security templates to the remote location and import them into the appropriate GPOs.

   ❍ **C.** Establish connectivity between all sites and force the remote site DCs to perform replication with the local site DCs after implementing the new security templates.

   ❍ **D.** Re-create the security templates at each remote site and then import them into the appropriate GPOs.

3. You are the systems administrator of the corporate network for Gidget's Widgets, LLC. You have instructed Andrea, your assistant administrator, to configure file access auditing for all files in the `CorpDocs` folder on your file server. In which node of the Group Policy Editor will Andrea find the auditing options?

   ❍ **A.** Account Policies

   ❍ **B.** Local Policies

   ❍ **C.** Restricted Groups

   ❍ **D.** File System

4. You are the systems administrator for Sunbrew Dairy Farms, Inc. You are currently interviewing a candidate for the position of assistant systems administrator. You have asked Christopher, the candidate, for what the `secedit.exe` command can be used. Which of the following answers that Christopher gives you is correct? (Choose all that apply.)

   ❍ **A.** `secedit.exe` can be used to analyze the current security settings.

   ❍ **B.** `secedit.exe` can be used to apply new security settings to a computer.

   ❍ **C.** `secedit.exe` can be used to apply new security settings to a GPO.

   ❍ **D.** `secedit.exe` can be scripted, allowing it to be run on many computers across the entire network.

5. You are the systems administrator for Good Faith Enterprises, LLC. You want to increase the security of your client workstations, which are all Windows 2000 Professional computers, without causing any adverse effect on network communications between computers. Which security template should you use to accomplish your goal?

- ❍ **A.** `securews.inf`
- ❍ **B.** `securedc.inf`
- ❍ **C.** `compatws.inf`
- ❍ **D.** `hisecws.inf`

6. You are an assistant systems administrator for the Nimbus Flying Broom corporation. You are responsible for 75 Windows XP Professional workstations and 5 Windows Server 2003 member server computers. You have been directed to perform a security analysis on each computer, comparing its settings to those contained in the `hisecws.inf` template. How can you accomplish your assigned task with the least amount of administrative effort and trips to remote computers?

- ❍ **A.** The only way to perform this analysis is to physically visit each computer and use the Security Configuration and Analysis snap-in.
- ❍ **B.** You can create a script that runs the Security Configuration and Analysis snap-in on each computer and collects the results in a central location for later viewing.
- ❍ **C.** You can create a script that runs the `secedit /analyze` command on each computer and collects the results in a central location for later viewing.
- ❍ **D.** You can analyze remote computers from the Security Configuration and Analysis snap-in by targeting it at the desired computer.

7. Austin is the systems administrator for the Eternal Light Group, LLC. He is attempting to perform an analysis of a computer by using the Security Configuration and Analysis snap-in. What is the correct order of performance of the following steps? (Ignore any steps that are not needed.)

1. Select the security template to be used in the analysis.
2. Right-click Security Configuration and Analysis and then select Analyze Computer Now.
3. Select the log file to be used in the analysis.
4. Right-click Security Configuration and Analysis and then select Open Database.
5. Right-click Security Configuration and Analysis and then select Configure Computer Now.
6. Select the database to be used in the analysis.

- ❍ **A.** 2, 1, 3, 4, 6, 5
- ❍ **B.** 4, 1, 6, 2, 5, 3
- ❍ **C.** 4, 6, 1, 2, 3
- ❍ **D.** 2, 6, 1, 3, 4

8. You have just completed an analysis of a computer by using the Security Configuration and Analysis snap-in. When you examine the results, you notice several items that have red X icons next to them. What does this indicate?

❍ **A.** The item is not defined in the analysis database and was not examined on the computer.

❍ **B.** The item is defined in the analysis database and on the computer, and it matches the currently configured setting.

❍ **C.** The item is defined in the analysis database but not on the computer.

❍ **D.** The item is defined in the analysis database and on the computer, but it does not match the currently configured setting.

9. You are the systems administrator for Gidget's Widgets, LLC. You are trying to explain to one of your assistant administrators, Hannah, how the `secedit.exe` command can be used to apply security templates to computers. Which of the following additional switches do you need to make sure she uses with the `secedit /configure` command? (Choose all that apply.)

❍ **A.** `/analyze`

❍ **B.** `/db`

❍ **C.** `/log`

❍ **D.** `/cfg`

10. You are the systems administrator for Fast Sloth Enterprises. You need to increase the security of your Windows XP Professional client computers and Windows Server 2003 servers. Which security template should you apply to your workstations to ensure that they have the most secure configuration?

❍ **A.** `securews.inf`

❍ **B.** `hisecdc.inf`

❍ **C.** `hisecws.inf`

❍ **D.** `rootsec.inf`

11. You are the systems administrator for Fast Sloth Enterprises. After increasing the security of your network client computers, you need to implement an auditing system to keep track of when computers are restarted and shut down. Which of the following options should you configure to track these events?

❍ **A.** Audit Process Tracking

❍ **B.** Audit System Events

❍ **C.** Audit Object Access

❍ **D.** Audit Privilege Use

12. Allison is the systems administrator for the Never Crash Software Company. She is attempting to configure auditing for access to files in the `SecretDocs` folder on her file server. She has configured the Audit Object Access option for both success and failure audit events in the domain GPO, but after two weeks, she doesn't see in the security log any audit entries related to her auditing. What is the most likely reason for this occurrence?

❍ **A.** Allison does not have the correct domain privileges to configure auditing of this type.

❍ **B.** Allison has not forced her modifications to the domain GPO to replicate to the rest of the DCs.

❍ **C.** The file server on which the `SecretDocs` folder is located is offline.

❍ **D.** Allison has not configured auditing actions on the `SecretDocs` folder on the file server.

13. Andrea is the systems administrator for the Think Pink Bike Company. She has recently finished implementing an auditing solution for her Windows Server 2003 network. Andrea wants to track unauthorized access attempts to the company network. After two weeks, she has not found any authorized access attempts, even though she tried password guessing several users' accounts just this morning. What is the most likely reason for the problem that Andrea is experiencing?

❍ **A.** Andrea has not configured success audits for the Audit Account Logon Events option.

❍ **B.** Andrea has not configured failure audits for the Audit Account Management option.

❍ **C.** Andrea has not configured failure audits for the Audit Logon Events option.

❍ **D.** Andrea has not configured success audits for the Audit Policy Change option.

14. You are the systems administrator for the Sunbrew Dairy Farms, Inc. corporate network. You have just completed the installation and configuration of WSUS for your network. Your client computers are all running Windows 2000 Professional SP2, and your servers are all Windows Server 2003 computers. After a week has passed, you notice that none of your clients have received any updates that are available from your WSUS server. What is the most likely reason for this problem?

❍ **A.** Your WSUS server has lost network connectivity to the Internet and has not downloaded any updates from the Windows Update Web servers.

❍ **B.** You have not correctly configured the Group Policy options for Automatic Updates.

❍ **C.** The GPO in which you configured the Automatic Updates changes has not been replicated to the rest of the network.

❍ **D.** Your client computers are not using the correct version of the Automatic Updates client software.

15. You are the systems administrator for the Wing Walkers, Inc. corporate network. You are configuring WSUS for your network's client computers, which are all running Windows XP Professional SP1. You want all client computers to automatically download from your WSUS server and install any required updates each night at 11:30 p.m. After the updates have been installed, you want the client computers to restart so that the updates can fully install and the computers will be ready for work the next morning. What must you do to ensure that updates will be installed each night and the computers will be restarted after the updates are installed? (Choose all that apply.)

   ❍ **A.** You must configure the Automatic Updates client options on each of your Windows XP Professional SP1 client computers to download and install updates nightly.

   ❍ **B.** You must set the Configure Automatic Updates option in Group Policy to Enabled and set option 4. You then need to configure a schedule for nightly updates at 11:30 p.m.

   ❍ **C.** You must set the No Auto-Restart for Scheduled Automatic Updates Installations option in Group Policy to Disabled.

   ❍ **D.** You must set the Specify Intranet Microsoft Update Server Location option in Group Policy to Enabled and enter the URL of your WSUS server.

Answers to Exam Questions

1. **B**. The best way to apply the settings to only those computers that require them is to import the template into a GPO associated with each OU that requires the settings. Importing the security template into the domain-level GPO would apply the settings to all computers in the domain, most likely with unwanted side effects; thus Answer A is incorrect. Applying the template via the `secedit.exe` command or manually using the Security Configuration and Analysis snap-in is possible, but is not efficient; thus Answers C and D are incorrect. For more information, see the section "Group Policy Security Extensions."

2. **B**. Because you created custom security templates using the Security Configuration and Analysis snap-in, you can simply export them into `.inf` files and transfer them to the remote sites via any available means. When they are at the remote sites, the security templates can be imported to the appropriate GPOs, thus placing them into effect. There is no need to create a new Domain Controller based on the information presented; thus Answer A is incorrect. Security templates are replicated as part of Active Directory replication; thus Answer C is not correct. Re-creating the security templates is not efficient and is error prone; thus Answer D is incorrect. For more information, see the section "The Security Configuration and Analysis Snap-in."

3. **B**. The Local Policies node of the Group Policy Editor contains three subnodes: Audit Policy, User Rights Assignment, and Security Options. The Audit Policy subnode is where Andrea will find the auditing items she will need to configure. The Account Policies node contains items that control user accounts; thus Answer A is incorrect. The Restricted Groups node allows you to permanently configure which users are allowed to be members of specific groups; thus Answer C is incorrect. The File System node allows you to set folder and file NTFS permissions; thus Answer D is incorrect. For more information, see the section "The Security Configuration and Analysis Snap-in."

4. **A**, **B**, **D**. The `secedit.exe` command can be used to analyze a computer, configure a computer, export a computer's security settings to a template, import the settings from a template, validate the context of a template, and create a rollback template. Because `secedit.exe` is a command-line tool, you can script it and use it on many computers across an entire network, but you cannot use it to apply settings directly to a GPO; thus Answer C is incorrect. For more information, see the section "`secedit.exe`."

5. **A**. By applying the Secure template, `securews.inf`, you can increase the security of the client workstations without adversely affecting network communications. The `securedc.inf` template is to be used only for Domain Controllers; thus Answer B is incorrect. The `compatws.inf` template will actually lower security on the computer it applied to; thus Answer C is incorrect. The `hisecws.inf` template will likely cause problems for client communications after it has been applied; thus Answer D is incorrect. For more information, see the section "The Windows Server 2003 Security Templates."

6. **C**. The easiest way to accomplish this task is to create a script that runs the `secedit /analyze` command on the computers and collects the results in a central network location. There is no need to visit each computer; thus Answer A is incorrect. The Security Configuration and Analysis snap-in cannot be scripted. Thus you would use `secedit`; therefore Answer B is incorrect. You cannot target remote computers using the Security Configuration and Analysis snap-in; thus Answer D is incorrect. For more information, see the section "`secedit.exe`."

7. **C**. The correct steps to be used to perform an analysis of a computer with the Security Configuration and Analysis snap-in are as follows: Select Open Database, select the database, select the security template, select Analyze Computer, and select the log file. Since no configuration is needed, only an analysis, Answers A and B are incorrect. Answer D presents the required actions in the wrong order. For more information, see the section "The Security Configuration and Analysis Snap-in."

8. **D**. A red X icon next to an item in the Security Configuration and Analysis snap-in results indicates that the item is present in both the database and the computer, but does not match the currently configured setting. A question mark indicates that the item is not defined in the analysis database and was not examined on the computer; thus Answer A is incorrect. A green check mark indicates that the item is defined in the analysis database and on the computer and matches the currently configured setting; thus Answer B is incorrect. An exclamation point indicates that the item is defined in the analysis database but not on the computer; thus Answer C is incorrect. For more information, see the section "The Security Configuration and Analysis Snap-in."

9. **B**, **C**, **D**. The `/db` switch specifies the pathname and filename of the database to be used, the `/log` switch specifies the pathname and filename of the error log to be used during the process, and the `/cfg` switch specifies the pathname and filename of the security template to be loaded into the database. The `/analyze` switch would only be used if you were analyzing the computer; thus Answer A is incorrect. For more information, see the section "`secedit.exe`."

10. C. Of the given choices, the `hisecws.inf` template provides the most secure configuration to Windows XP Professional clients. The `securews.inf` template would not provide the most secure workstation; thus Answer A is incorrect. The `hisecdc.inf` template is to be used only for Domain Controllers; thus Answer B is incorrect. The `rootsec.inf` template defines the root permissions for the root of the system volume, and is not appropriate for this scenario; thus Answer D is incorrect. For more information, see the section "The Windows Server 2003 Security Templates."

11. B. The Audit System Events option configures auditing for certain system events, such as computer restarts and shutdowns. The Audit Process Tracking option configures auditing to occur for events such as program activation, process exit, handle duplication, and indirect object access; thus Answer A is incorrect. The Audit Object Access option configures auditing to occur upon each user access of an object, such as a file, folder, printer, or registry key that has its own SACL configured; thus Answer C is incorrect. The Audit Privilege Use option configures auditing to occur upon every occurrence of a user exercising a user right; thus Answer D is incorrect. For more information, see the section "Configuring Auditing."

12. D. The most likely cause of the problems that Allison is having is that she had not yet configured auditing actions on the folder itself. If Allison did not have the required permissions, she would not have been able to configure the auditing in the first place; thus Answer A is incorrect. Replication is nearly instantaneous within a site and occurs four times per hour, by default, between sites, so after two weeks this is likely not a problem unless Active Directory has larger issues; thus Answer B is incorrect. While a server being offline would definitely preventing auditing on its contents from occurring, this is certainly not the most likely cause of the problem; thus Answer C is incorrect. For more information, see the section "Configuring Auditing."

13. C. In order to track failed logon attempts, Andrea needs to configure failure auditing to occur for the Audit Logon Events option. Auditing for successful account logons is not going to help with monitoring failed attempts to login; thus Answer A is incorrect. Auditing for account management or policy change will not help in tracking failed logins; thus Answers B and D are incorrect. For more information, see the section "Configuring Auditing."

14. D. In order to participate in WSUS, the Windows 2000 computers will need to be updated to at least SP3, although you should update them fully to SP4. While it is possible that your WSUS has lost Internet connectivity, it's not the most likely problem in this scenario; thus Answer A is incorrect. If you've followed the configuration process for WSUS, then you've configured group policy; thus Answer B is not likely the cause of your problem. When using WSUS, as opposed to using SUS previously, there is no need to download and install a special Automatic Updates client—you only need to ensure that clients to be updated meet the required operating system and service pack levels listed; thus Answer C is incorrect. For more information, see the section "Implementing Windows Server Update Services (WSUS)."

15. B, C, D. In order for WSUS to operate, the WSUS server must be provided to the Automatic Updates client computers via the Specify Intranet Microsoft Update Server Location option. In addition, you need to configure the schedule by using the Configure Automatic Updates option and configure for restarting by using the No Auto-Restart for Scheduled Automatic Updates Installations option. When you're using WSUS with group policy, you won't be able to configure the options locally on each client computer; thus Answer A is incorrect. For more information, see the section "Implementing Windows Server Update Services (WSUS)."

Suggested Reading and Resources

1. WSUS home page, http://www.microsoft.com/windowsserversystem/updateservices/default.mspx.

2. Windows Server 2003 online help, "Auditing Security Events," www.microsoft.com/technet/prodtechnol/windowsserver2003/proddocs/entserver/AuditTN.asp.

3. Windows Server 2003 online help, "Security Configuration Manager," www.microsoft.com/technet/prodtechnol/windowsserver2003/proddocs/entserver/SEconcepts_SCM.asp.

4. Security Configuration Wizard for Windows Server 2003, http://www.microsoft.com/windowsserver2003/technologies/security/configwiz/default.mspx.

5. DumpEL and EventCombMT, located in the Microsoft Download Center, http://www.microsoft.com/downloads.

6

CHAPTER 6

Implementing, Managing, and Troubleshooting Network Access

It is difficult to work in today's network environment without encountering some form of remote access. Whether it's dialing in from a hotel room while on a business trip or using a virtual private network (VPN) to connect to the office from home, or even connecting a branch office by using the Internet and a VPN to connect a branch office, companies rely on remote access. With Windows Server 2003, Microsoft provides an extensive suite of remote access capabilities. This chapter covers the remote access portion of the "Implementing, Managing, and Maintaining Routing and Remote Access" objectives for Exam 70-291, "Implementing, Managing, and Maintaining a Microsoft Windows Server 2003 Network Infrastructure."

Microsoft lists the following objectives for the remote access portion of the "Implementing, Managing, and Maintaining Routing and Remote Access" section of Exam 70-291:

Objectives

Configure Routing and Remote Access user authentication.

- **Configure remote access authentication protocols.**
- **Configure Internet Authentication Service (IAS) to provide authentication for Routing and Remote Access clients.**
- **Configure Routing and Remote Access policies to permit or deny access.**
- If you are going to install and configure a remote access server, you need to understand the Windows Server 2003 remote access authentication process, including the remote access protocols used and how to leverage centralized authentication and the associated Routing and Remote Access Service (RRAS) policies. You need to know how to configure policies in conjunction with the authentication protocols to control your remote access environment. You also need a thorough understanding of IAS, which allows you to provide centralized authentication for RRAS.

Manage remote access.

- **Manage packet filters.**
- **Manage Routing and Remote Access routing interfaces.**

- **Manage devices and ports.**
- **Manage routing protocols.**
- **Manage Routing and Remote Access clients.**
- After you have installed a Windows Server 2003 remote access server, you need to understand how to manage the remote access environment, from the implementation of packet filters to the configuration and management of remote access clients. With the tremendous focus on secure remote access in the corporate world, a thorough understanding of all the facets of remote access management is required not only for the exam but also for the administration of a Windows Server 2003 environment.

Implement secure access between private networks.

- Windows Server 2003 helps you establish network-to-network VPN connections for connecting private networks (such as a branch office and a headquarters building) by using a public network such as the Internet. Due to the comparatively low cost of this solution, it is becoming increasingly popular as an inexpensive way to connect locations. This objective requires that you understand how to configure two Windows Server 2003 servers to permit network-to-network connections.

Troubleshoot user access to remote access services.

- **Diagnose and resolve issues related to remote access VPNs.**
- **Diagnose and resolve issues related to establishing a remote access connection.**
- **Diagnose and resolve user access to resources beyond the remote access server.**
- In a production remote access implementation, the ability to identify, diagnose, and resolve problems is critical. For this objective, Microsoft requires that you understand how to resolve problems with VPN access, dial-in access, and access to resources on the network after you have successfully connected.

Troubleshoot Routing and Remote Access routing.

- **Troubleshoot demand-dial routing.**
- **Troubleshoot router-to-router VPNs.**
- Because Windows Server 2003 can be used to connect remote networks, either via demand-dial routing or a router-to-router VPN, the ability to identify, diagnose, and resolve issues with these connections is very important. For this objective, Microsoft requires that you understand how to resolve problems with demand-dial routing and router-to-router VPNs.

Outline

Study Strategies

- Understand the features and functions of Windows Server 2003 RRAS-supported authentication protocols.
- Understand the VPN protocols supported by Windows Server 2003 RRAS.
- Understand the security capabilities of all the different remote access mechanisms. With the focus on security in the industry today, Microsoft considers security to be one of the cornerstones of the Windows Server 2003 operating system.
- Review the different types of encryption available for authenticating and securing your information through remote access.
- Understand the capabilities of remote access policies, especially in conjunction with IAS. Windows Server 2003 includes a number of policy-based management capabilities, and understanding the policies associated with remote access is important for this exam.
- Be sure to complete the exercises at the end of the chapter. Microsoft continues to strive to make certification exams more rigorous. Familiarity with the theory and also with the hands-on portion of the configuration and troubleshooting of remote access is important for this exam.
- Take the next step: Experiment with the system. The exercises in this chapter provide good guidelines, but you should see what happens when you select other settings, delete entries or entire servers, and try anything else you can think of. If you have an Internet connection and a lab setup in your house, see if you can set up a VPN connection that you (or a friend) can access remotely. It is better to make mistakes in a lab environment than in a live one, and it helps you prepare for the exam.

Introduction

One of the key differences between today's work environment and the same environment a decade ago is the need for access. A decade ago you might have gone on a trip and, unless your pager went off, you weren't likely to haul out your portable computer to check your mail. Today, email, corporate intranets, customer resource management applications, and a variety of other network-based resources need to be available to employees from virtually anywhere. The days when your users reported to work every morning at one of the corporate offices are rapidly becoming a thing of the past—users are no longer tied to corporate networks. In fact, at some companies, more employees work in home offices and connect to the corporate network by using the Internet and remote access technologies than sit in corporate offices connected to a LAN. This has resulted in the blurring of the lines of what is considered the corporate network and what your duties are as a Windows Server 2003 network administrator. In fact, it could be your responsibility to implement and support the technology to provide employees secure local and remote access to their resources.

The good news is that the technology has come a long way in a decade, and the Microsoft Windows Server operating system capabilities have improved as well. In 1993, you probably connected to a network by dialing in using a 14,400bps modem, connecting to either a standalone modem or a modem bank on the other end. Not only have connection speeds increased dramatically since then, but with the adoption of high-speed Internet connections in many venues, there are now a multitude of options for connecting to a remote network. Windows Server 2003 supports a wide variety of solutions for providing this connectivity, ranging from supporting the same basic dial-in architecture used a decade ago to interconnecting offices over the Internet by using VPN connections.

Configuring RRAS User Authentication

The first step in understanding how to set up a Windows Server 2003–based remote access server is to understand how Windows Server 2003 RRAS user authentication works, beginning with the remote access authentication protocols.

Configuring Remote Access Authentication Protocols

Objective:

Configure Routing and Remote Access user authentication.

- Configure remote access authentication protocols.

Before we discuss the remote access authentication methods available within Windows Server 2003 RRAS, we should briefly discuss the underlying access protocols:

- **Serial Line Interface Protocol (SLIP)**—The granddaddy of serial line protocols, SLIP is supported for legacy applications and is almost never used. Windows Server 2003 supports SLIP as a client-only protocol; it does not support it as a server protocol. A Windows Server 2003 server can dial into another server by using SLIP, but it cannot receive SLIP-based connections.
- **Point-to-Point Protocol (PPP)**—PPP provides a standard transport method for point-to-point links, commonly called dial-up connections. *Dial-up connections* usually refer to either asynchronous modem connections or Integrated Services Digital Network (ISDN) connections. In addition to a transport method, PPP also defines the authentication protocols that can be used to negotiate a connection before allowing network-layer protocols such as TCP/IP or IPX to be transmitted over the connection.

The authentication protocols used in conjunction with Windows Server 2003 RRAS include the following:

- **Password Authentication Protocol (PAP)**—PAP uses unencrypted (plain text) passwords for authenticating users on a PPP link. PAP is generally considered to be an obsolete protocol due to the password encryption issues, rendering it the least secure PPP authentication protocol available. Although PAP does provide a simple method for establishing a PPP connection, the only time you might encounter it would be if you needed to connect a legacy, non-Windows host to your RRAS server.
- **Challenge Handshake Authentication Protocol (CHAP)**—CHAP provides a more secure PPP authentication mechanism than PAP by negotiating encrypted authentication with Message Digest 5 (MD5). MD5 is an industry-standard hashing scheme that allows connection authentication without actually transmitting the password over the network. You generally see CHAP used to allow Windows Server 2003 to securely connect to third-party PPP servers, leveraging the fact that CHAP is an industry-standard protocol.

NOTE

Introduction to Hashes Hashes, when discussed in the context of authentication and encryption, are, in their simplest form, numbers generated from a string of text. In the context of authentication, a user's password is stored on the system as a hash value, created by applying a specific hashing algorithm to derive the value. When the user attempts to authenticate to the system, he or she enters his or her password, and the system applies the same specific hashing algorithm to the password. That value is then passed across the connection, and it is compared to the stored hash on the host system. If the hashes agree, the password is valid, and the connection is established.

For example, let's say Alice has a password of `Dogface`. The hashing algorithm states that each letter of the password is supposed to be converted to a number by doubling the numeric value of each letter in the alphabet. After the number is converted, all 0s are removed, and the result is the hash. In our example, the initial conversion for `Dogface` would be `830142610`. Remove the 0s, and the hash becomes `8314261`. There is no easy way to retrieve the password from that hash, and by comparing that number to the stored value, you can verify the user's password without ever transmitting it across the network.

- **Shiva PAP (SPAP)**—SPAP is used specifically to allow Shiva client computers to connect to a Windows Server 2003 server and to allow Windows 2000 client computers to connect to Shiva servers.
- **Microsoft CHAP (MS-CHAP)**—MS-CHAP is an extension of CHAP that increases CHAP's capabilities by integrating the encryption and hashing algorithms used on Windows networks. MS-CHAP supports LAN Manager authentication, as well as the ability to change passwords as part of the authentication process. Like CHAP, MS-CHAP uses a challenge-response mechanism. In this case, the mechanism is called *password hashing*, and it keeps the password from being sent across the connection. Although Microsoft has kept MS-CHAP as consistent with standard CHAP as possible, the MS-CHAP protocol is designed specifically for use by Windows computers.
- **MS-CHAP version 2 (MS-CHAPv2)**—MS-CHAPv2 corrects several problems with the original version of MS-CHAP, including removing the support for the notoriously weak LAN Manager authentication, adding the ability for two-way authentication (which allows the client to authenticate the PPP host to which it is connecting), and adding support for much stronger cryptographic keys for the authentication process. MS-CHAP uses the Message Digest 4 (MD4) hashing algorithm and the Data Encryption Standard (DES) encryption algorithm to generate the challenge and the response. It also allows for mutual authentication, the generation of stronger initial data encryption keys for Microsoft Point-to-Point Encryption (MPPE), and different encryption keys for sent and received data.

NOTE

Which Protocol Should You Use? In a purely Microsoft environment, MS-CHAPv2 is the most secure PPP authentication protocol that uses a user ID and password to authenticate a user.

- **Extensible Authentication Protocol (EAP)**—EAP was developed in response to an increasing need for stronger authentication mechanisms for remote user access services such as remote access servers and VPNs. The number of mobile users has increased and the technical sophistication of attackers has also increased, and today user ID/password authentication is not secure enough for many organizations. EAP provides a standard mechanism for support of additional authentication methods within PPP, such as token cards, one-time passwords, and public key authentication using smart cards or certificates. Unlike the user ID/password capabilities of the other PPP authentication protocols, EAP, in conjunction with external authenticators such as a smart card or token card, is not vulnerable to brute-force or dictionary password attacks.

  Windows Server 2003 leverages the EAP-MD5 CHAP and EAP–Transport-Level Security (EAP-TLS) authentication methods as part of its remote access and VPN services, as follows:

  - **EAP-MD5 CHAP**—EAP-MD5 CHAP is an EAP type that uses the same challenge handshake protocol as PPP-based CHAP, but the challenges and responses are sent as EAP messages. In other words, EAP-MD5 allows for the use of external authentication that utilizes external hosts while still allowing the use of a user ID and password. An example of this is using EAP in conjunction with an external Remote Authentication Dial-in User Service (RADIUS) server for storing the database of user accounts and passwords that could authenticate to a RAS server. Windows Server 2003 includes RADIUS authentication capabilities as part of IAS.

    It is important to note that although this form of EAP does add additional capabilities for PPP authentication, because the underlying authentication is still based on a user ID/password combination, this type of EAP is still vulnerable to brute-force and dictionary password attacks.

  - **EAP-TLS**—EAP-TLS is a mutual authentication method that is similar to MS-CHAPv2. With EAP-TLS, not only can the server authenticate the client as part of the authentication process, but also the client can verify the identity of the server. EAP-TLS is also the EAP type that is used in certificate-based or token-based security environments. As a result, EAP-TLS provides the most secure authentication method.

- **RADIUS**—RADIUS is an authentication and accounting system that is used by many Internet service providers and is available in Windows Server 2003. When you connect to a Windows Server 2003 remote access server, you need to enter your username and password. This information is passed to a RADIUS server, which checks that the information is correct and then authorizes access. When used in conjunction with Windows Server 2003 RRAS, RADIUS allows centralized storage of remote access authentication, allowing multiple Windows Server 2003 remote access servers to authenticate to the same credentials.

Table 6.1 lists the RFCs related to the Windows Server 2003 authentication protocols.

TABLE 6.1 RFCs Related to Windows Communication and Authentication Protocols

Protocol	RFC Number	Title and Date
PPP	2484	"PPP LCP Internationalization Configuration Option," January 1999
PAP	1334	"PPP Authentication Protocols," August 1996
CHAP	1994	"PPP Challenge Handshake Authentication Protocol (CHAP)," August 1996
MS-CHAP	2433	"Microsoft PPP CHAP Extensions," October 1998
MS-CHAPv2	2759	"Microsoft PPP CHAP Extensions, Version 2," January 2000
EAP	2284	"PPP Extensible Authentication Protocol (EAP)," March 1998
RADIUS support for EAP	2869	"RADIUS Extensions," June 2000
EAP-TLS	2716	"PPP EAP TLS Authentication Protocol," October 1999
RADIUS	2865	"Remote Authentication Dial In User Service (RADIUS)," June 2000

Before you can configure authentication with Windows Server 2003, you need to enable Windows Server 2003 to accept connections. Step by Step 6.1 demonstrates how to configure Windows Server 2003 RRAS to accept dial-in and VPN connections. You need two network interface cards (NICs) installed in your server to support VPN remote access connections properly.

STEP BY STEP

6.1 Setting Up Windows Server 2003 RRAS for Dial-in and VPN Access

1. Log on to Windows Server 2003 by using the Administrator account or another account that has administrator privileges.
2. Open the Routing and Remote Access console by selecting Start, Control Panel, Administrative Tools, Routing and Remote Access. By default, the local computer is listed as a server as seen in Figure 6.1. Notice the red arrow. It indicates that RRAS is not presently enabled.
3. Right-click the server you want to configure and select Configure and Enable Routing and Remote Access. The Routing and Remote Access Server Setup Wizard starts.
4. Click Next to start configuring RRAS. The Configuration dialog box of the wizard appears, as seen in Figure 6.2.

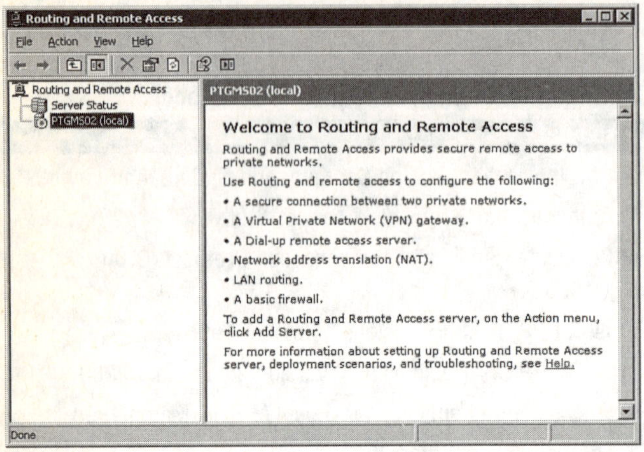

FIGURE 6.1 The Routing and Remote Access console is used to configure RRAS for a variety of functions, including enabling dial-in and VPN access.

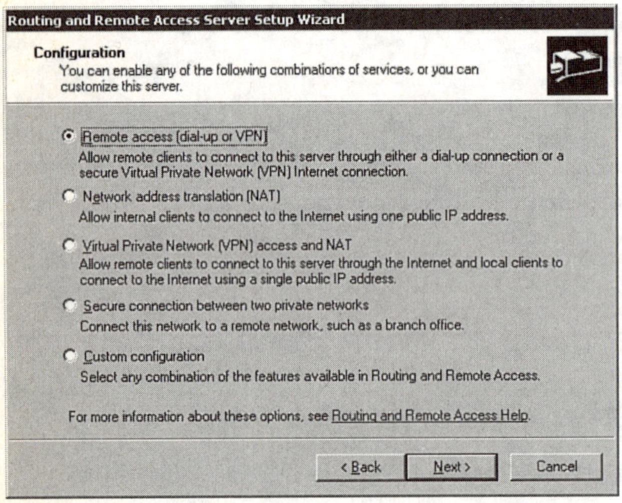

FIGURE 6.2 The Routing and Remote Access Server Setup Wizard includes the most common configuration options to make the configuration process as easy as possible.

5. Select the Remote access (dial-up or VPN) option and click Next to continue. The Remote Access dialog box of the wizard appears, as seen in Figure 6.3.
6. In the Remote Access dialog box, select VPN and Dial-up and click Next to continue. The VPN Connection dialog box of the wizard appears, as seen in Figure 6.4.

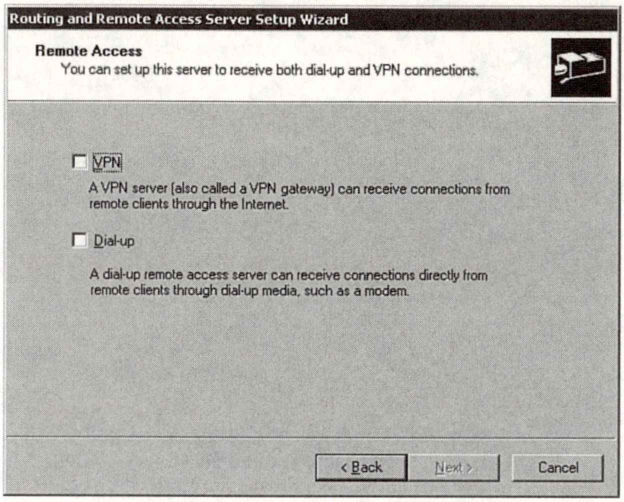

FIGURE 6.3 The Remote Access dialog box allows you to set up dial-in connections, VPN connections, or both types of connections.

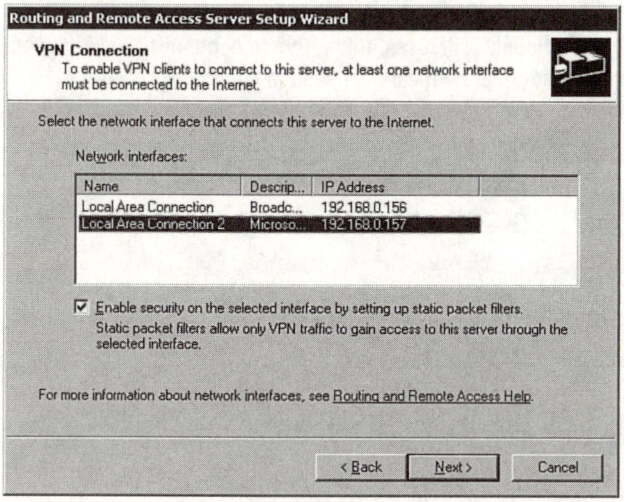

FIGURE 6.4 The VPN Connection dialog box allows you to select the external network interface to be used for VPN connections.

7. Select the network connection you plan on using as the external server NIC for the VPN. This is the connection that is used by remote access VPN clients to connect to the server. Leave the Enable Security on the Selected Network Interface by Setting Up Static Packet Filters check box checked. This provides additional security on that network adapter. Click Next to continue. The IP Address Assignment dialog box of the wizard appears, as seen in Figure 6.5.

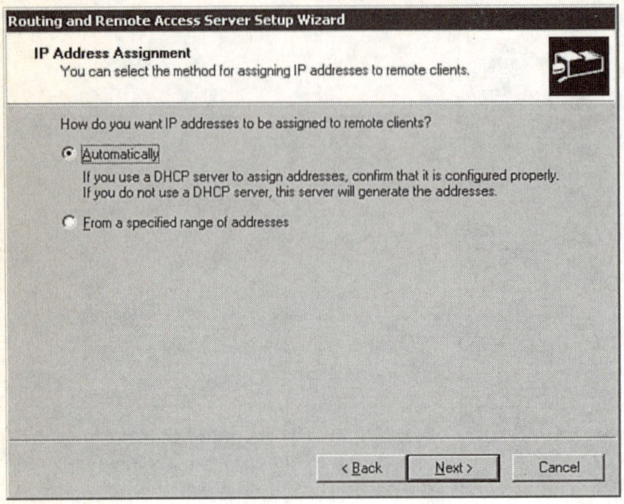

FIGURE 6.5 The IP Address Assignment dialog box allows you to select how IP addresses will be assigned to remote access clients.

8. Select Automatically to allow the server to use a network DHCP server for issuing addresses or to automatically assign addresses by using the server default addresses. Click Next to continue. The Managing Multiple Remote Access Servers dialog box of the wizard appears, as seen in Figure 6.6.

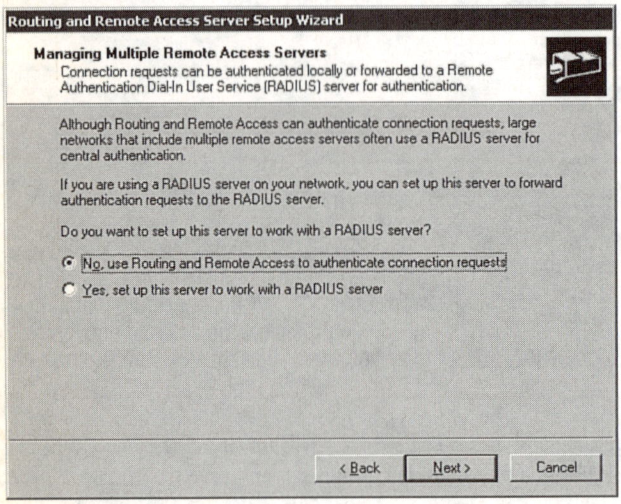

FIGURE 6.6 The Managing Multiple Remote Access Servers dialog box is used to determine whether the server will authenticate users locally or use a central RADIUS server for authentication.

9. Select No, Use Routing and Remote Access to Authenticate Connection Requests and click Next. The Completing the Routing and Remote Access Server Setup Wizard dialog box appears, as seen in Figure 6.7. Click Next to complete the installation.

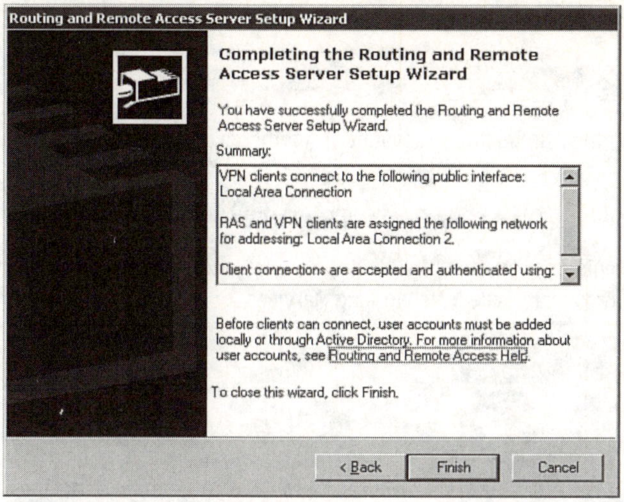

FIGURE 6.7 The Completing the Routing and Remote Access Server Setup Wizard allows you to double check your settings before you commit the changes permanently.

Configuring IAS to Provide Authentication for RRAS Clients

Objective:

Configure Routing and Remote Access user authentication.

- Configure Internet Authentication Service (IAS) to provide authentication for Routing and Remote Access clients.

IAS is included as part of the Microsoft Windows Server 2003, Standard Edition, Enterprise Edition, and Datacenter Edition. IAS is not included with the Web Edition of Windows Server 2003. IAS is the Microsoft implementation of the RADIUS server and proxy. Acting as a RADIUS server, IAS is commonly used to provide centralized authentication, authorization, and accounting for remote access and VPN connections. IAS can also provide authentication and accounting for additional network services, including authenticated DHCP (in which case a user cannot get an IP address without authenticating successfully), network and wireless connectivity, and switch, router, and firewall management authentication, to name a few. When acting as a RADIUS proxy, IAS can be used to forward authentication and accounting messages to other RADIUS servers, such as a central RADIUS server.

Step by Step 6.2 guides you through the process of installing IAS on a Windows Server 2003 server.

STEP BY STEP

6.2 Installing Windows Server 2003 IAS

1. Log on to Windows Server 2003 by using the Administrator account or another account that has administrator privileges.
2. Open the Add or Remove Programs applet by selecting Start, Control Panel, Add or Remove Programs.
3. Click the Add/Remove Windows Components icon on the left side of the applet, and when the Windows Components dialog box seen in Figure 6.8 appears, select Networking Services.

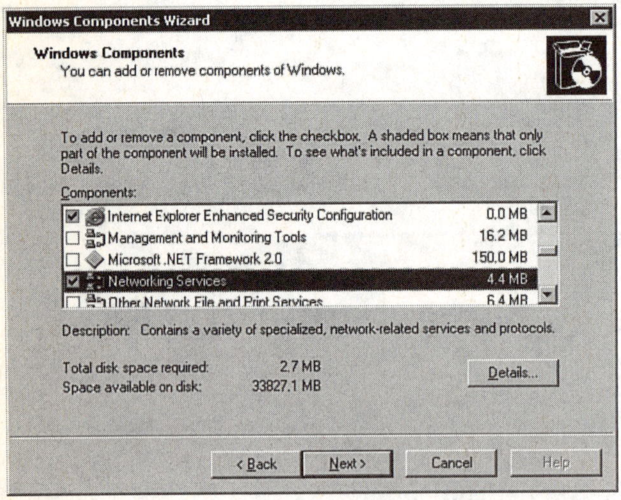

FIGURE 6.8 The Add or Remove Programs applet can be used to add or remove system components such as IAS.

4. Click Details to open the Networking Services dialog box, as seen in Figure 6.9, and select Internet Authentication Service. Click OK to return to the Windows Components dialog box.

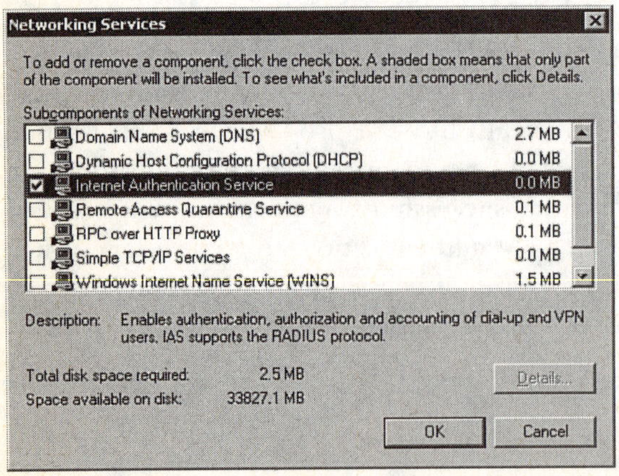

FIGURE 6.9 The Networking Services dialog box allows you to add or remove any of the available Windows Server 2003 networking services.

5. Click Next to continue the installation. When the installation progress is complete, the Completing the Windows Components Wizard dialog box appears. Click Finish to complete the installation.

Now that IAS is installed, you need to look at how to enable RRAS so that you can use the service for authentication and accounting. Step by Step 6.3 details this process.

STEP BY STEP

6.3 Configuring RRAS to Use RADIUS Authentication and Accounting

1. Log on to Windows Server 2003 by using the Administrator account or another account that has administrator privileges.
2. Open the Routing and Remote Access console by selecting Start, Administrative Tools, Routing and Remote Access.
3. Right-click the server located in the left pane of the Routing and Remote Access console and select Properties. The server Properties dialog box appears. Select the Security tab, as seen in Figure 6.10.

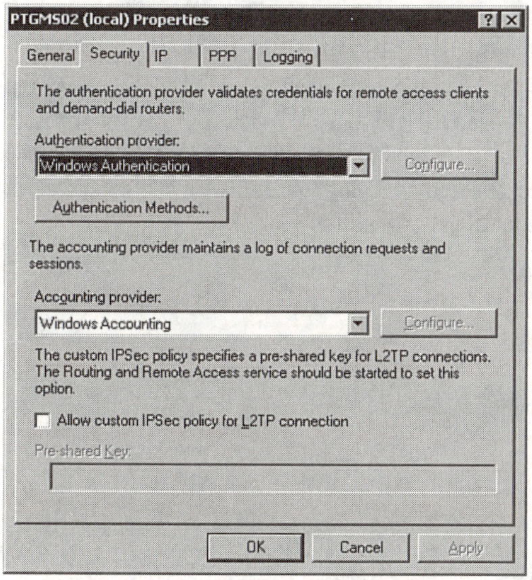

FIGURE 6.10 The Security tab is used to configure the authentication and accounting providers and the authentication method used to authenticate client systems.

4. On the Security tab, under the Authentication provider drop-down menu, select RADIUS Authentication (the default is Windows Authentication). Then click Configure to the right of this drop-down menu to configure the authentication provider. The RADIUS Authentication dialog box, as seen in Figure 6.11, appears.

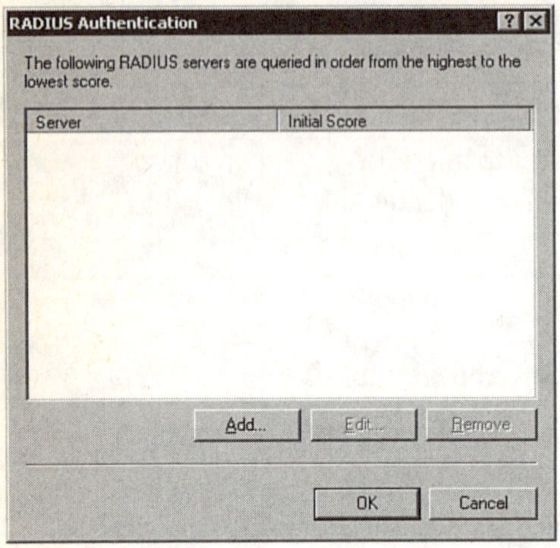

FIGURE 6.11 If there are RADIUS servers available on your network for authentication, they appear in the RADIUS Authentication dialog box.

5. Click Add to add a RADIUS server for authentication. The Add RADIUS Server dialog box, as seen in Figure 6.12, appears. You need to enter the name or IP address of the server and a secret to authenticate the server (optional but recommended). Then, if needed, you can also set a timeout value (the length of time to wait for a response from the RADIUS server) and an initial score. (The initial score determines the initial responsiveness score of the RADIUS server. This score increases or decreases based on the ongoing responsiveness of the RADIUS server and can be used to rank RADIUS servers in a multiserver environment. The default is 30.) You also need to set the port, which is the TCP port used to communicate with the RADIUS server. (The default is 1812, which is the RFC port for RADIUS communications.) You can also require the use of the message authenticator, which uses a shared secret to provide an additional level of security through the use of digital signatures.

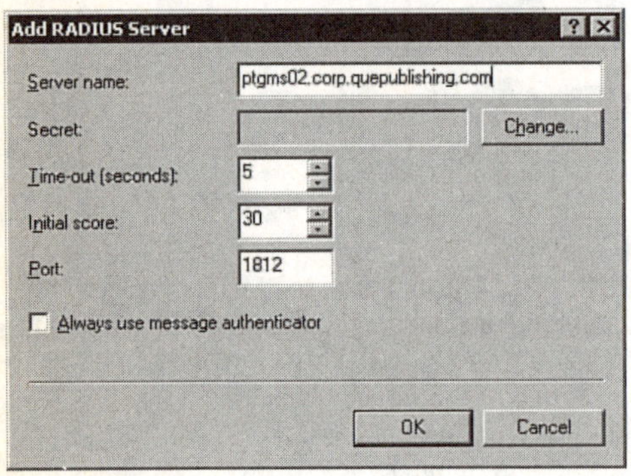

FIGURE 6.12 The Add RADIUS Server dialog box allows you to configure the RADIUS server(s) to be used for remote access authentication.

6. Click Change to set the shared secret for RADIUS authentication. The Change Secret dialog box, as seen in Figure 6.13, appears. Enter the same secret (the longer, the better) in both fields and click OK to save the secret.

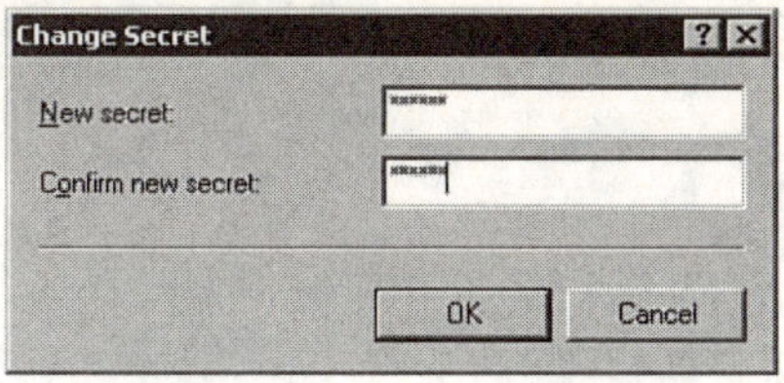

FIGURE 6.13 The shared secret is used to authenticate the RADIUS client (the RRAS server) and the RADIUS server (the server running IAS).

7. Click OK to add the RADIUS server. Figure 6.14 shows the server successfully added. Click OK again to return to the Security tab.

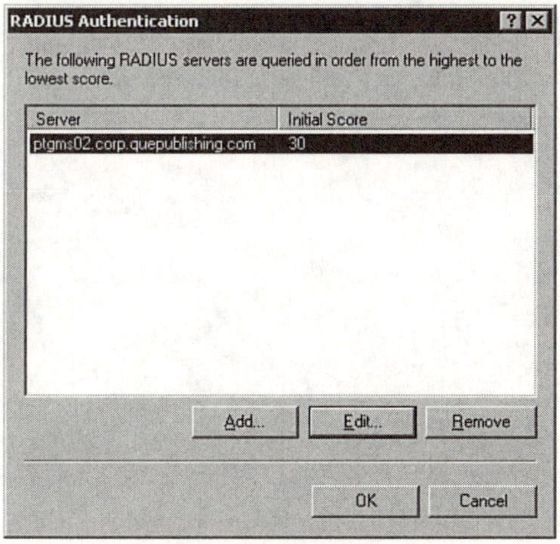

FIGURE 6.14 A new RADIUS server entry shows up in the RADIUS Authentication dialog box.

8. On the Security tab, under the Accounting Provider drop-down menu, select RADIUS Accounting to allow accounting information to be stored on a central RADIUS server. (The default is Windows Accounting, which stores accounting information locally.) Then click Configure to the right of this drop-down menu to configure the authentication provider. The RADIUS Accounting dialog box, as seen in Figure 6.15, appears.

9. Click Add to add a RADIUS server for accounting. The Add RADIUS Server dialog box, as seen in Figure 6.16, appears. You need to enter the name or IP address of the server and a secret to authenticate the server. Then, if needed, you can also set a timeout value and an initial score. You also need to set the port, which is the TCP port used to communicate with the RADIUS server. (The default is 1813, which is the RFC port for RADIUS accounting communications.)

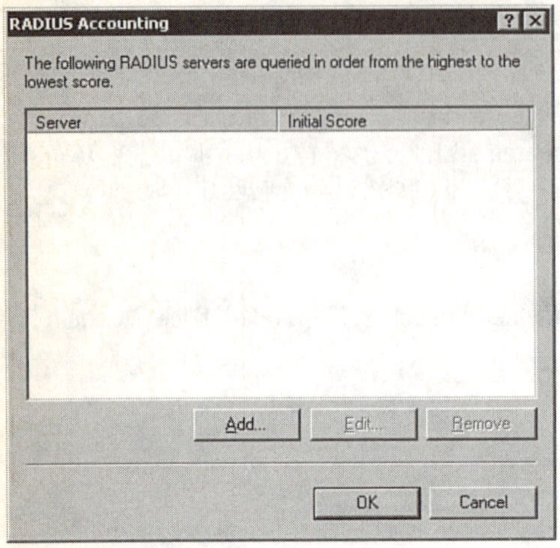

FIGURE 6.15 If there are RADIUS servers available on your network for accounting, they appear in the RADIUS Accounting dialog box.

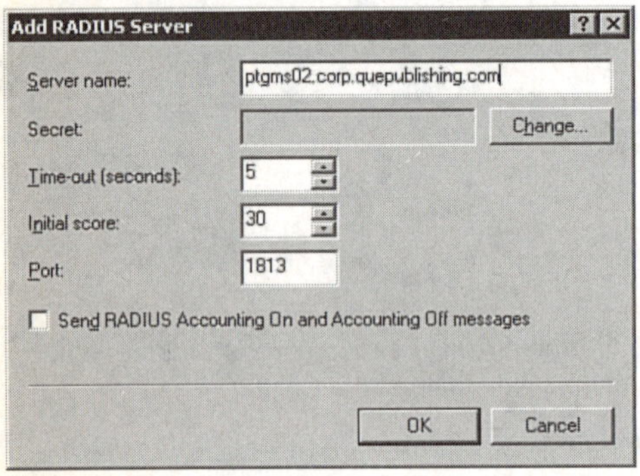

FIGURE 6.16 The Add RADIUS Server dialog box allows you to configure the RADIUS server(s) to be used for remote access accounting.

10. Click Change to set the shared secret for RADIUS authentication. The Change Secret dialog box appears. Enter the same secret (the longer, the better) in both fields and click OK to save the secret. The secret you enter here needs to be the same secret used for RADIUS authentication.

11. Click OK to add the RADIUS server. You should see the server successfully added to the RADIUS Accounting dialog box, similar to Figure 6.14. Click OK again to return to the Security tab, and click OK to close the server Properties dialog box.

EXAM ALERT

RADIUS Ports For the exam, you should remember the default RADIUS ports and their purpose. Port 1812 is used for authentication, and port 1813 is used for accounting.

EXAM ALERT

Shared Secret If you are going to use the same RADIUS server for authentication and for accounting, you need to be sure that you set the same shared secret for both options in the RRAS server Properties dialog box. There can be only one relationship between a RADIUS server and a RADIUS client, and it can have only one shared secret.

You have now installed IAS and configured Windows Server 2003 RRAS to use IAS for authentication and accounting. The final configuration for this architecture is to configure IAS to permit your Windows Server 2003 server to use IAS for authentication and accounting. Step by Step 6.4 details how to complete this process.

STEP BY STEP

6.4 Configuring IAS to support a RADIUS Authentication and Accounting Client

1. Log on to Windows Server 2003 by using the Administrator account or another account that has administrator privileges.
2. Open the Internet Authentication Service console by selecting Start, Administrative Tools, Internet Authentication Service, as seen in Figure 6.17.

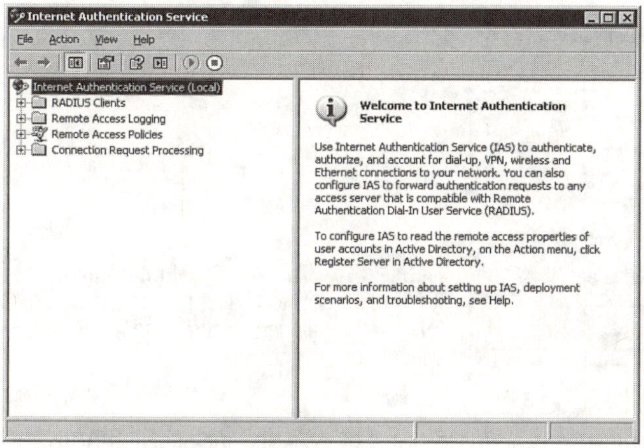

FIGURE 6.17 The Internet Authentication Service console is used to configure RADIUS clients.

3. Right-click the RADIUS Clients folder in the left pane and select New RADIUS Client. The New RADIUS Client dialog box appears, as seen in Figure 6.18.

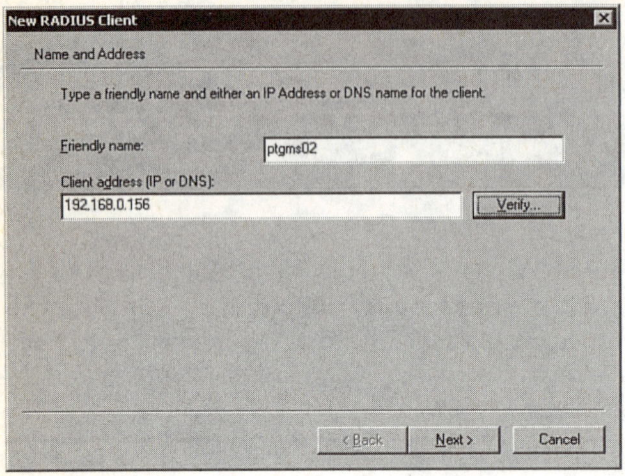

FIGURE 6.18 To start configuring a RADIUS client, you need a friendly name and the IP address of the client.

4. Enter a friendly name for the RADIUS client and an IP address or DNS name and click Next to continue. The Additional Information dialog box appears, as seen in Figure 6.19.

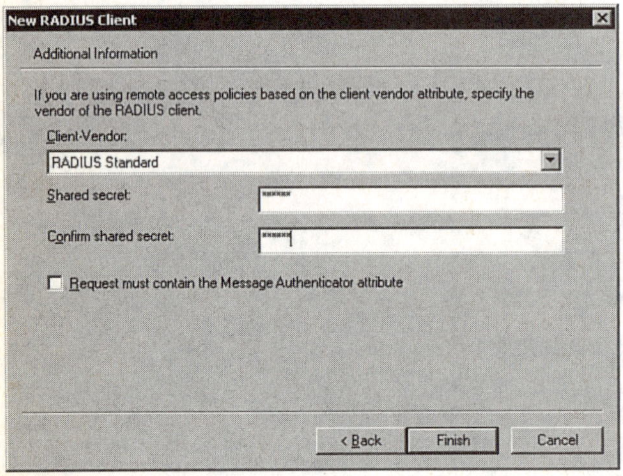

FIGURE 6.19 The Additional Information dialog box is used to collect the remaining information needed to complete the RADIUS client setup.

5. Select a type from the Client-Vendor pull-down menu (for this Step by Step, use the default, RADIUS Standard). If you don't know what the RADIUS client is, use RADIUS Standard, which will work in many cases. Next type the same shared secret used in the configuration of the RADIUS client setup in Step by Step 6.3. Do not select the Request Must Contain the Message Authenticator attribute check box. Click Next to continue. You are returned to the Internet Authentication Service console, and your new RADIUS client should appear under the RADIUS Clients folder, as seen in Figure 6.20.

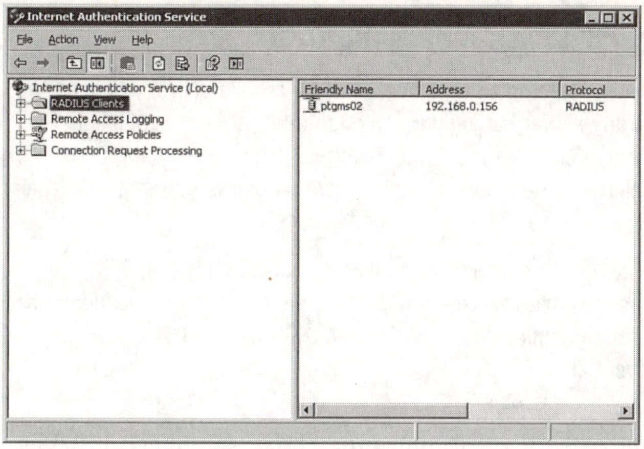

FIGURE 6.20 When a RADIUS client has been added, it should appear in the RADIUS Clients folder.

Configuring RRAS Policies to Permit or Deny Access

Objective:

Configure Routing and Remote Access user authentication.

- Configure Routing and Remote Access policies to permit or deny access.

Remote access policies are a set of conditions and connection settings that give network administrators flexibility in authorizing connection attempts. They provide both granular and flexible configuration settings for both dial-in and VPN connections. This granularity and flexibility unfortunately comes at the expense of ease of use; remote access policies can be very complex, and you need an in-depth understanding of them to successfully provide secure remote access to users. With remote access policies, you can grant remote access by individual user account or through the configuration of specific remote access policies. Windows Server 2003 uses three types of remote access policies to control access:

- **Group**—Access can be controlled by group policies created on each Windows Server 2003 RRAS server. This is the simplest method for authenticating users, as long as you use a single server for remote access.
- **Local IAS**—These local policies are derived from RADIUS and can be used to define access permissions based on a number of client attributes. This mechanism requires that IAS be installed on the Windows Server 2003 remote access server. This is typically the best solution if you are planning on adding additional Windows Server 2003 remote access servers and don't want to have to replicate the policies to each new server.

Issues to Consider in Configuring Systems for Mobile Users

If you deploy Windows Server 2003 as your dial-in remote access solution for mobile users, you need to keep a couple things in mind. First, because any server has only a limited number of communication ports, you will probably need a multiport modem card. Various manufacturers offer these types of products, but you should be sure to check the Microsoft Hardware Compatibility List before you make any purchases.

You should also avoid installing this capability on any Domain Controllers or application servers. Although the overhead associated with supporting dial-in users is fairly low, the security ramifications of connecting a modem or modems to a production application server, or even worse, to a DC, are significant. You should try to avoid that architecture if at all possible.

Windows Server 2003 supports two methods for creating a remote access policy: utilizing a wizard to create commonly used remote access policies and using a custom method that allows you to create less common remote access policies. However, before we look at creating a policy, we need to discuss how Windows Server 2003 determines whether to accept a remote access connection.

The first step in establishing a remote access connection is for the client to successfully authenticate to the server. *Authentication* is the verification of user credentials used in the connection attempt. This is typically a user ID and password (unless EAP is used in conjunction with a token or smart card). The client sends its credentials to the server, where they are validated.

After the client has been successfully authenticated, it needs to be authorized to connect. A client that can authenticate, but that is not authorized, will have its connection attempt denied.

Three mechanisms are used by the Windows Server 2003 RRAS to authorize a connection, depending on the server's authentication configuration:

- **Windows authentication**—If the server uses Windows authentication, the connection is authenticated using the local server's security configuration, and then the dial-in properties of the user account and locally stored remote access policies are used to authorize the connection.
- **Non-IAS RADIUS authentication**—If the server uses non-IAS RADIUS authentication, the credentials of the connection attempt are passed to the RADIUS server for both authentication and authorization. If the connection attempt is both authenticated and authorized, the RADIUS server sends an accept message to the server, and the connection attempt is accepted. If the connection attempt fails to be authenticated or authorized, the RADIUS server sends a reject message to the server, and the connection attempt is rejected.

- **IAS authentication**—If the server is configured to use an IAS server, the IAS server performs authentication through the selected Windows authentication mechanisms and then performs the authorization through the dial-in properties of the user account and remote access policies stored on the IAS server.

In versions of Windows before Windows 2000 Server, remote access authorization was based on individual configurations made in the User Manager or the Remote Access utility. In Windows Server 2003 (and Windows 2000 Server), remote access policies can also be used in addition to the per-user configuration of grant or deny access to grant or deny access to the network. A remote access policy is a collection of one or more ordered rule sets (conditions) that define whether or not a connection can be authorized or rejected. Each rule set contains one or more conditions that a remote access connection is evaluated against, a group of profile settings, and also a remote access permission (grant or deny access) setting. When a remote access connection is authorized, the remote access policy profile then specifies a set of conditions on the connection. Dial-in properties, if any, that have been configured on the user's account also provide a set of restrictions. The net result is that any properties configured on a user's account directly override those configured in the remote access policy—thus the sum is the total of the most restrictive conditions with NTFS file and folder permissions.

By default, a new implemention of RRAS on a Windows Server 2003 computer contains two remote access policies: Connections to Microsoft Routing and Remote Access Server and Connections to Other Access Servers. The first policy has a single condition specified, MS-RAD-Vendor Matches "^311$", which signifies Microsoft RRAS implementations. This policy is set to deny access if this condition is met, which only Microsoft RRAS server would meet—all other devices accessing the RRAS server would fail to meet this condition and thus would move onto the second policy for evaluation. The second policy also has only one condition, a date and time window that covers all 24-hour periods in all seven days of the week—thus any remote access connection that is evaluated against this remote access policy will meet the condition and the connection will be denied since this policy also denies all connections that meet its policy condition.

The net result of these default remote access policies is that no clients will be able to connect to your remote access server by default. You, can, however delete or modify either or both of these remote access policies to allow the RRAS server to grant access to users who meet the policy conditions that you specify. It's also worth noting that you do not have to have any remote access policies in place. In that case, you'll have to control remote access via the configuration on the Dial-in tab of the user's account Properties dialog box, as seen in Figure 6.21. In a Windows 2000 mixed or Windows Server 2003 interim domain functional level domain, you will only have the option to Allow Access or Deny Access, with the default selection being Allow Access. In a Windows 2000 native or Windows Server 2003 domain functional level, the Control Access Through Remote Access Policy option becomes available for selection and is the default option for newly created user objects.

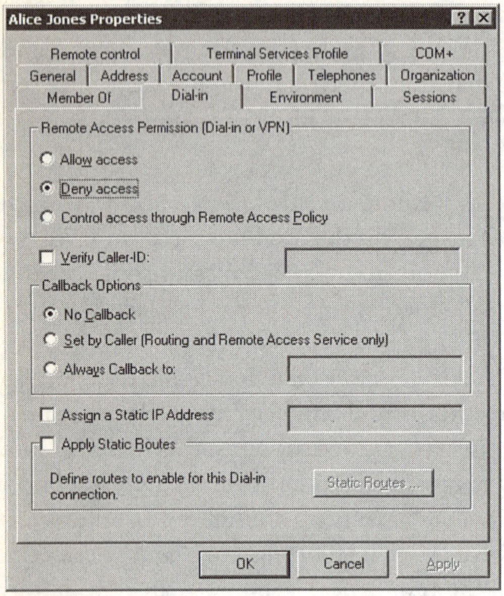

FIGURE 6.21 The Dial-in tab of the user account Properties dialog box.

EXAM ALERT

The Default RRAS Remote Access Policies Be sure that you understand that the default remote access policies will deny all connection attempts made to a RRAS server, thus preventing the RRAS server from functioning in its intended role. You must modify or delete the first default remote access policy, "Connections to Microsoft Routing and Remote Access Server" to enable RRAS to allow remote access connections to be made.

Step by Step 6.5 walks you through the creation of a new remote access policy to allow VPN access to anyone in the Domain Users group by using the wizard.

- What about the user settings of Allow Access or Deny Access in the user properties?
- Do you need a policy?
- What if you don't have one?
- What are the three components that make up a policy?
- What are the default policies that already exist? Can I modify them? Can I delete them? And what happens?

NOTE

Using Local Authentication for the Rest of the Step by Steps To ensure the success of the following Step by Steps, make sure that the authentication method set on the server Properties dialog box Security tab is set to Windows Authentication. Setting up a remote access policy under IAS for centralized policy management works in exactly the same way as setting up the policy locally, but it complicates any testing you might want to do.

STEP BY STEP

6.5 Using the New Remote Access Policy Wizard to Create a VPN Access Policy

1. Log on to Windows Server 2003 by using the Administrator account or another account that has administrator privileges.
2. Open the Routing and Remote Access console by selecting Start, Administrative Tools, Routing and Remote Access.
3. Right-click the Remote Access Policies node in the left pane of the Routing and Remote Access console and select New Remote Access Policy from the menu. The New Remote Access Policy Wizard appears.
4. Click Next to continue. The Policy Configuration Method dialog box of the wizard, as seen in Figure 6.22, appears. Select the Use the Wizard to Set Up a Typical Policy for a Common Scenario option. In the Policy name field, type **`Allow Remote Access to Remote Users`**. If you are in a complex environment where there are many remote access policies, you might even need a naming convention for these policies to keep them straight.

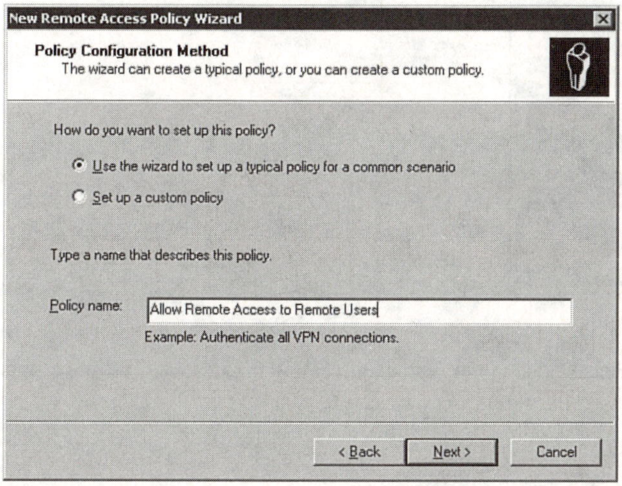

FIGURE 6.22 The Policy Configuration Method dialog box allows you to decide whether to use the wizard or manual configuration to create a remote access policy.

5. Click Next to continue. The Access Method dialog box of the wizard appears, as seen in Figure 6.23. In this case, select VPN. Be aware of the additional options for your information—it is good to know what can be done with this wizard.

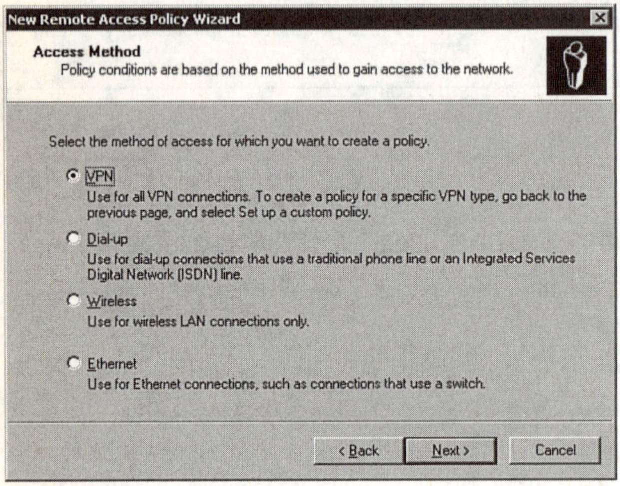

FIGURE 6.23 The Access Method dialog box allows you to select how users will be connecting to the Windows Server 2003 remote access server.

6. Click Next to continue to the User or Group Access dialog box of the wizard. Select the Group option and Click Add to open the Select Groups dialog box, as seen in Figure 6.24. Type **`Domain Users`** in the Enter the Object Names to Select field. If you click Check Names, the console confirms that the object exists in Active Directory.

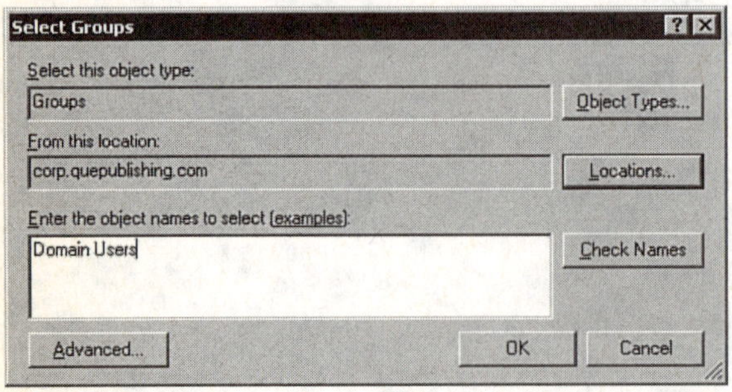

FIGURE 6.24 The Select Groups dialog box allows you to populate the list of groups that will be affected by this policy.

7. Click OK to return to the User or Group Access dialog box, as seen in Figure 6.25. Notice that the group you entered in Step 6 now appears in the list of groups.

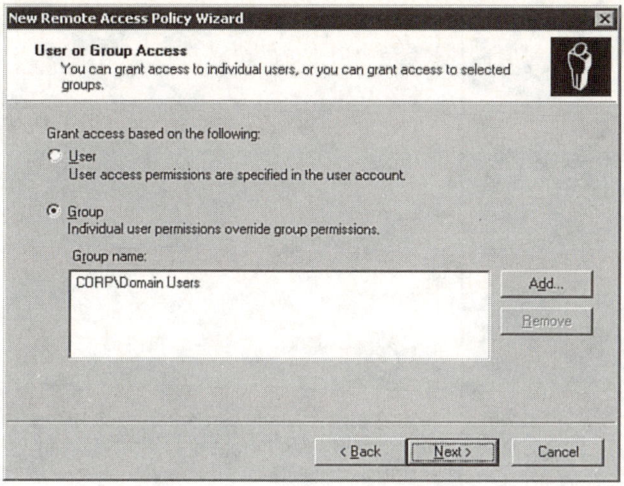

FIGURE 6.25 Any groups added appear in the Group name field of the User or Group Access dialog box.

8. Click Next to continue. The Authentication Methods dialog box of the wizard appears, as seen in Figure 6.26. Notice that the only authentication types allowed are EAP, MS-CHAPv2, and MS-CHAP. To use other authentication types, you need to use a custom remote access policy. Make sure MS-CHAPv2 is selected.

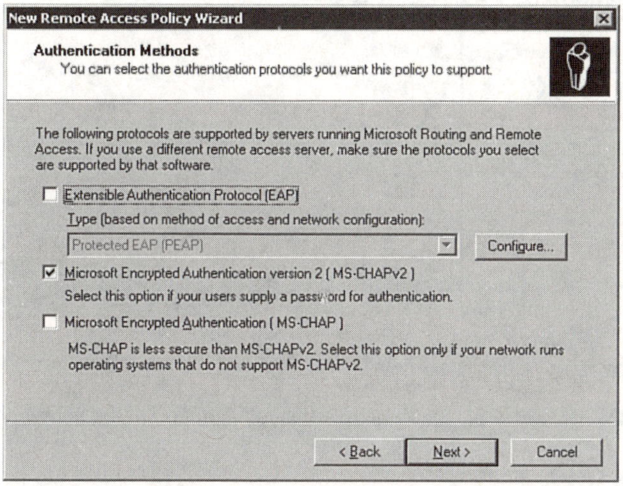

FIGURE 6.26 The Authentication Methods dialog box is used to select which authentication methods will be permitted for accessing the Windows Server 2003 RRAS server by using this remote access policy.

9. Click OK to continue. The Policy Encryption Level dialog box of the wizard appears, as seen in Figure 6.27. Because you are dealing with a VPN connection, select Strongest Encryption. If this were a dial-up connection, you would have an additional option—no encryption.

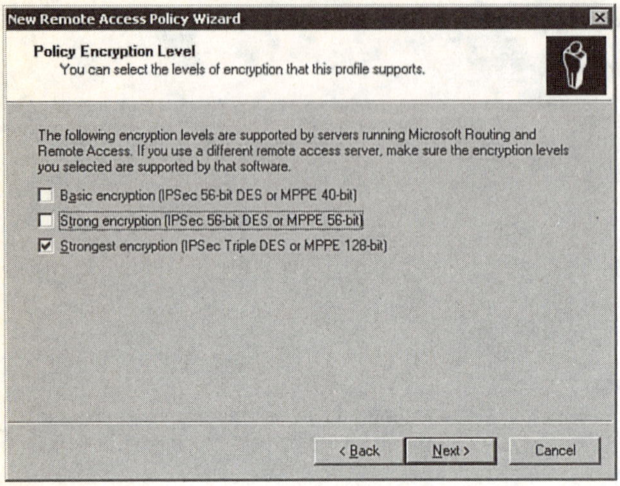

FIGURE 6.27 Windows Server 2003 RRAS supports three different encryption strengths for VPN connections.

10. Click Next to continue. The Completing the New Remote Access Policy Wizard dialog box appears, as seen in Figure 6.28.

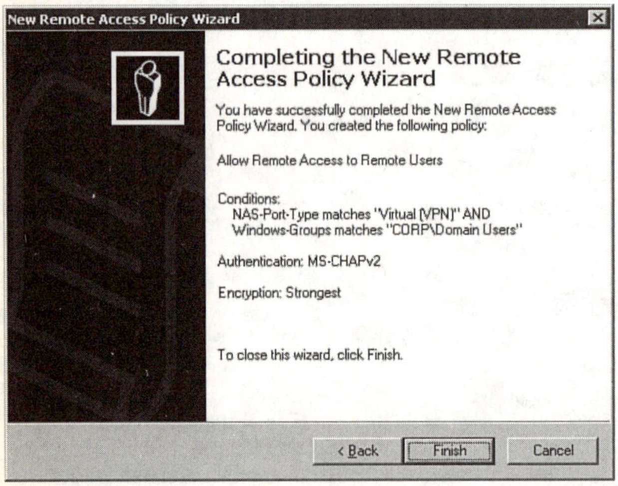

FIGURE 6.28 The Completing the New Remote Access Policy Wizard dialog box summarizes the configuration of the policy.

11. Click Finish to complete the policy creation. Figure 6.29 shows the newly created remote access policy.

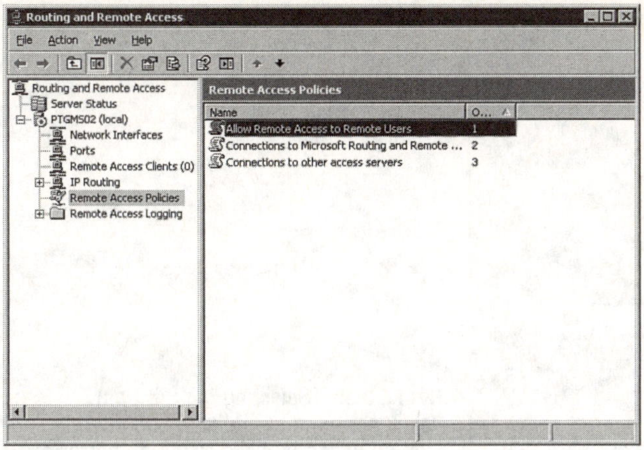

FIGURE 6.29 The Remote Access Policies folder shows all the policies that are in effect on the local server.

Step by Step 6.6 takes you through the process of creating a custom remote access policy that restricts access based on the day of the week and the time of day.

STEP BY STEP

6.6 Using the Routing and Remote Access Console to Create a Custom RRAS Policy to Restrict the Times When Users Are Able to Connect Remotely

1. Log on to Windows Server 2003 by using the Administrator account or another account that has administrator privileges.
2. Open the Routing and Remote Access console by selecting Start, Administrative Tools, Routing and Remote Access.
3. Right-click Remote Access Policies in the left pane and select New Remote Access Policy from the menu. The New Remote Access Policy Wizard appears.
4. Click Next to continue. The Policy Configuration Method dialog box appears. Select the Set Up a Custom Policy option, as seen in Figure 6.30. In the Policy name field, type **`Deny Access Based on Time of Day`**.
5. Click Next to continue. The Policy Conditions dialog box of the wizard appears, as seen in Figure 6.31. You can use this dialog box to add the conditions that need to be matched for the policy to take effect. You have the option to configure multiple conditions, but in this case, select a single condition.

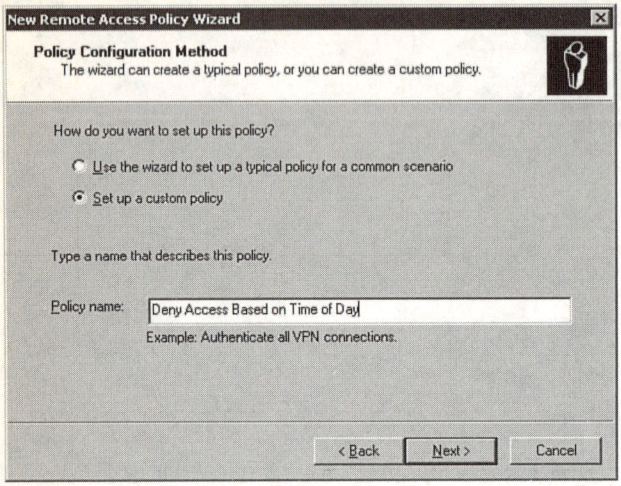

FIGURE 6.30 Selecting the Set Up a Custom Policy option in the Policy Configuration Method dialog box allows you to perform advanced policy creation.

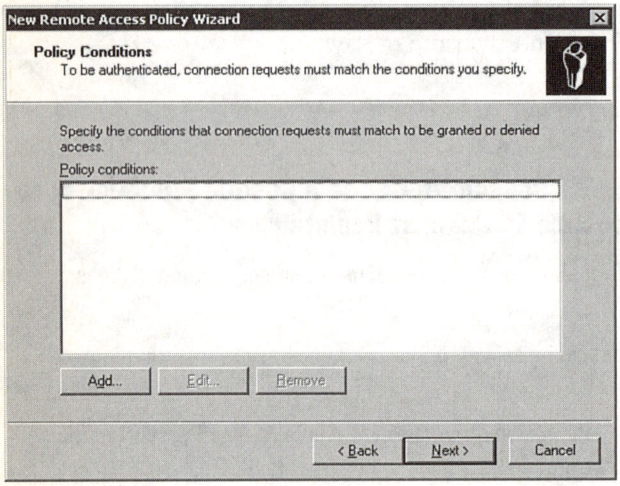

FIGURE 6.31 The Policy Conditions dialog box allows you to select conditions from an extensive list of options.

6. Click the Add button to open the Select Attribute dialog box, as seen in Figure 6.32.
7. Because you are working on setting time restrictions for remote users, select Day-and-Time Restrictions from the list of conditions. (Later on, you should explore the rest of these conditions so that you are familiar with them.) Click the Add button to select this attribute. The Time of Day Constraints screen appears. It is initially blank because the default setting is Denied. Changing the setting to Permitted changes the screen to entirely blue, which indicates Permit Access. Select the times from 5:00 a.m. until 8:00 p.m. for all days of the week and click the Permit Access radio button. The selected region should turn blue to indicate that access is permitted during that time. The result should look like Figure 6.33.

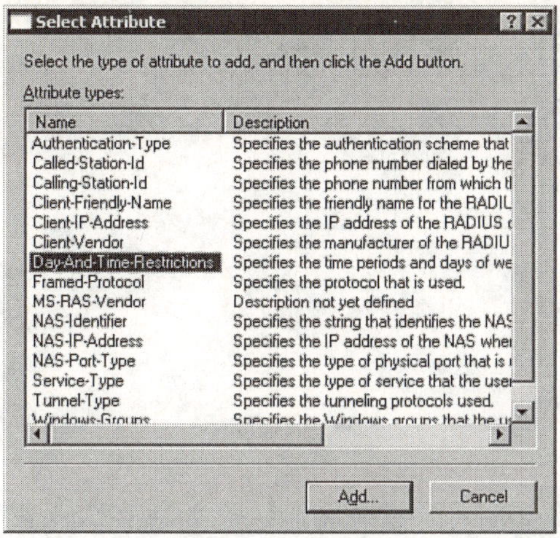

FIGURE 6.32 Windows Server 2003 offers an extensive list of options for setting conditions on a remote access policy.

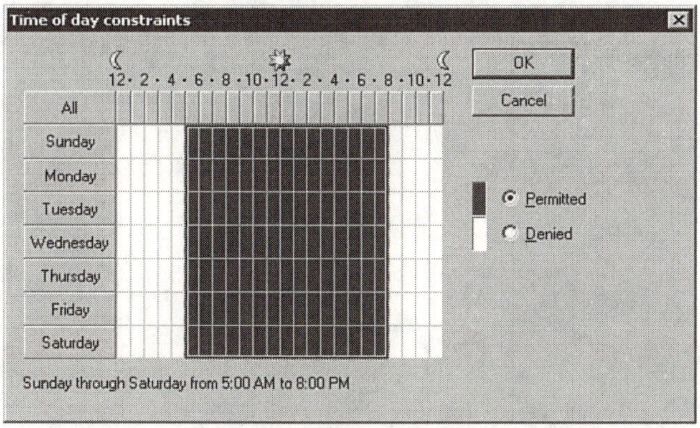

FIGURE 6.33 The time-of-day constraints are some of the most common conditions to be set in a remote access policy.

8. Click OK to continue. The time-of-day restriction appears in the Policy conditions field of the Policy Conditions dialog box, as seen in Figure 6.34. Note that a connection attempt must meet all policy conditions in order for the policy to be enforced. That is to say that a connection attempt must meet all policy conditions in order for that policy to allow or deny the connection attempt depending on how the policy has been configured.

9. Click Next to continue. The Permissions dialog box of the wizard appears, as seen in Figure 6.35. Select Grant Remote Access Permission. This allows users to connect to the Windows Server 2003 RRAS server during the permitted times.

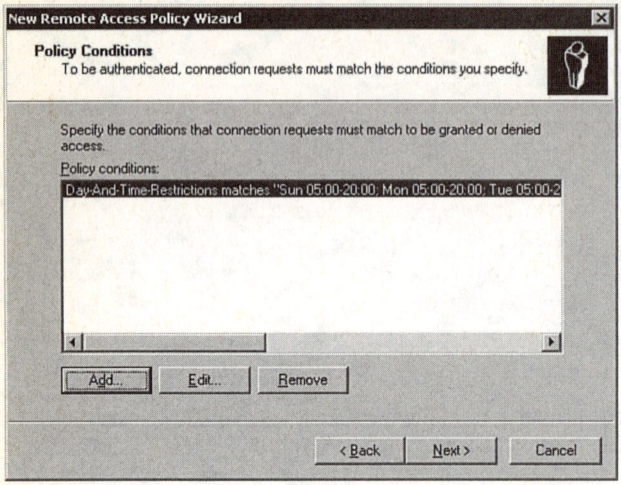

FIGURE 6.34 Any conditions that you set appear in the Policy Conditions field.

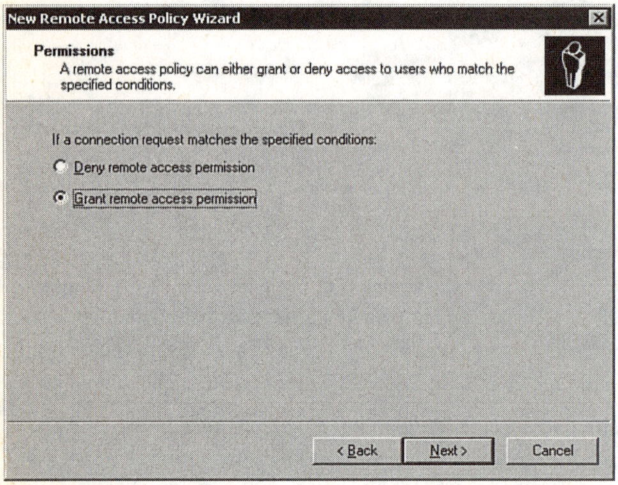

FIGURE 6.35 The Permissions dialog box allows you to configure a policy to accept connections that meet the conditions of the policy or deny them if needed.

10. Click Next to continue. The Profile dialog box of the wizard appears, as seen in Figure 6.36.
11. Click Edit Profile. The Edit Dial-in Profile dialog box appears, as seen in Figure 6.37. Dial-in profiles are discussed in detail in the next section of this chapter. Note that profile settings are cumulative and all will be enforced on clients.
12. Click OK to return to the Profile dialog box and click Next to continue. The Completing the New Remote Access Policy Wizard dialog box appears.
13. Click Finish to complete the creation of the new remote access policy.

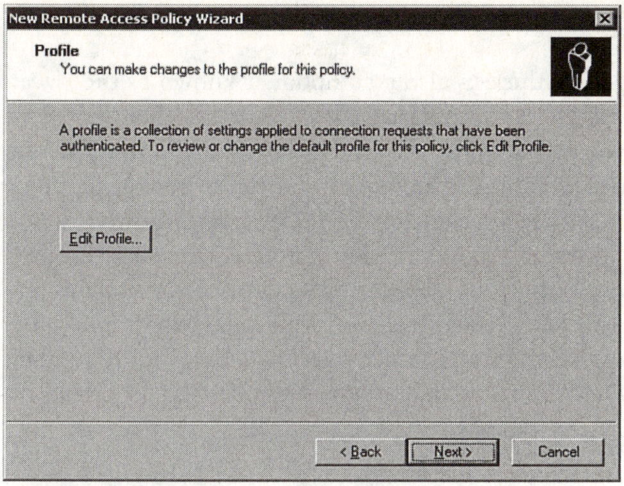

FIGURE 6.36 The Profile dialog box gives you access to the remote access profile, which allows you to further refine the configuration of the remote access policy.

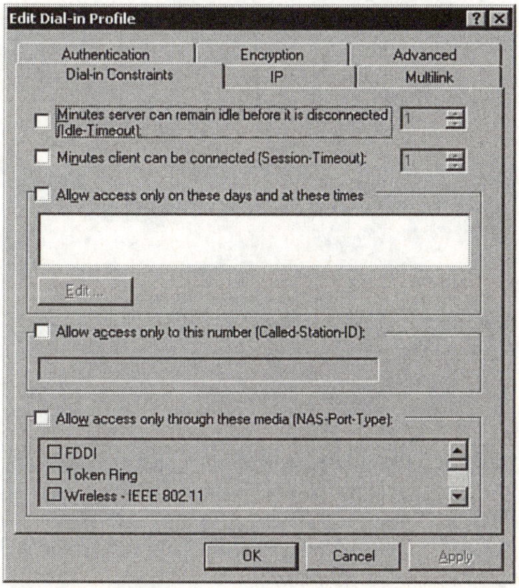

FIGURE 6.37 The Edit Dial-in Profile dialog box allows you to configure a number of parameters that are used to authenticate users.

EXAM ALERT

Order Matters Remote access policies are applied in the order in which they appear in the remote access policy list. This can sometimes lead to conflicting policies or unintended results, so it is important to understand not only how remote access policies work, but also how the order in which they are applied can affect their results. Keep this in mind when dealing with remote access policies on your 70-291 exam.

Remote Access Profiles

In conjunction with the remote access policy, there is also a component known as the *remote access profile*. This profile contains a number of variables that allow you to further refine the parameters of the remote access policy. You can modify a remote access profile during the creation of a remote access policy, as is done in Step by Step 6.6, or you can review or modify a profile for an existing remote access policy by right-clicking the policy in either the Routing and Remote Access console or the Internet Authentication Service console, selecting Properties, and then clicking the Edit Profile button. The Settings tab of the Properties dialog box appears, as seen in Figure 6.38, and you can use it to add additional conditions to the policy, edit the profile, or review or change the grant and deny access settings on the policy. There are six tabs available in the Edit Dial-in Profile dialog box; the following sections look at them one at a time.

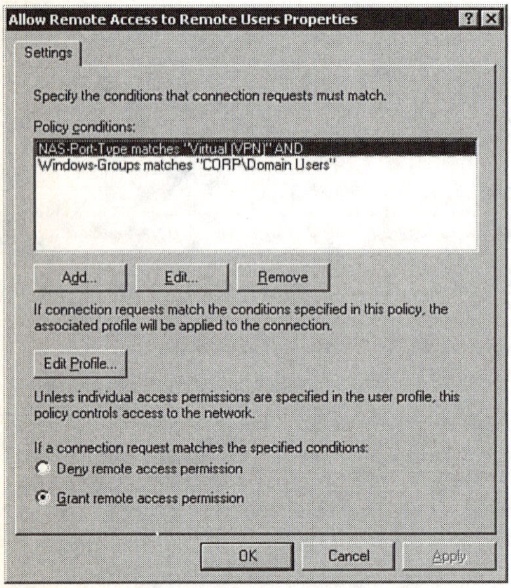

FIGURE 6.38 The Settings tab of the Properties dialog box allows you to refine the configuration of a remote access policy.

The Dial-in Constraints Tab

You'll configure the parameters on the Dial-in Constraints tab when you want to control idle and session timeout setting, certain day and time windows, a specific dial-in number, or port type. The parameters that can be configured on the Dial-in Constraints tab of the Edit Dial-in Profile dialog box, as seen in Figure 6.39, include the following:

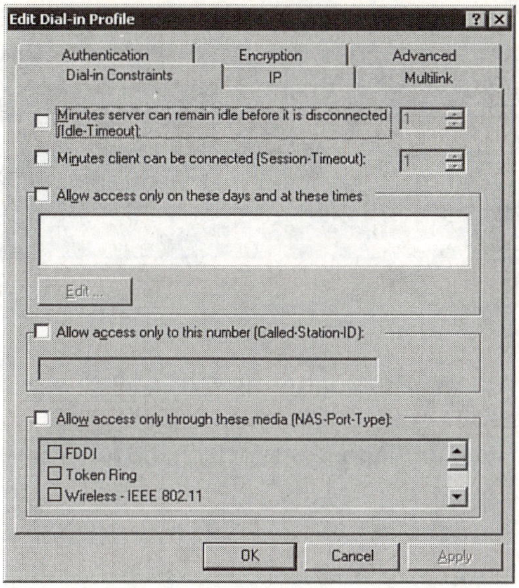

FIGURE 6.39 The Dial-in Constraints tab can be used to restrict how dial-in access can be used.

- **Minutes server can remain idle before it is disconnected (Idle-Timeout)**—This setting allows you to set the number of minutes of inactivity a user has before the system disconnects the user. This setting can be used to limit toll charges being incurred by an idle system or to protect a network from the vulnerability a connected but idle system presents. This setting can also be used to maximize the availability of ports if the server has a limited number of ports. This prevents idle users from tying up ports that might be needed by other users.
- **Minutes client can be connected (Session-Timeout)**—This setting allows you to set the total number of minutes a session can last. This can be used to limit toll charges for users who may leave themselves connected for extended periods of time.
- **Allow access only on these days and at these times**—This setting allows you to place day and time limits on any remote access policy, without needing to make that a condition of the policy.
- **Allow access only to this number (Called-Station-ID)**—This setting is typically used in conjunction with a branch office connection to ensure that the connection is originating from the appropriate number. This field can contain a phone number or an IP address, so it can be used in conjunction with a site-to-site VPN as well as a branch demand-dial connection.
- **Allow access only through these media (NAS-Port-Type)**—This parameter allows you to control the types of network media that can be used to connect by using this profile. You might use this to ensure that a VPN connection can be established only by using LAN media and not dial-in lines.

EXAM ALERT

Changing Parameters: New Wording in Windows Server 2003 Don't get confused with Windows 2000 parameters—the parameters in the Edit Dial-in Profile dialog box have changed subtly in Windows Server 2003. Microsoft has changed the language from "Restrict to" to "Allow Only" terminology. For example, in Windows 2000, the parameter Restrict Dial-in to This Number Only is now Allow Access Only to This Number (Called-Station-ID) in Windows Server 2003. The Called-Station-ID field is the remote access policy condition used to set this parameter.

The IP Tab

You'll configure the parameters on IP tab when you want to control how IP addresses are assigned or what types of IP filters should be used. The parameters that can be configured on the IP tab of the Edit Dial-in Profile dialog box, as seen in Figure 6.40, include the following:

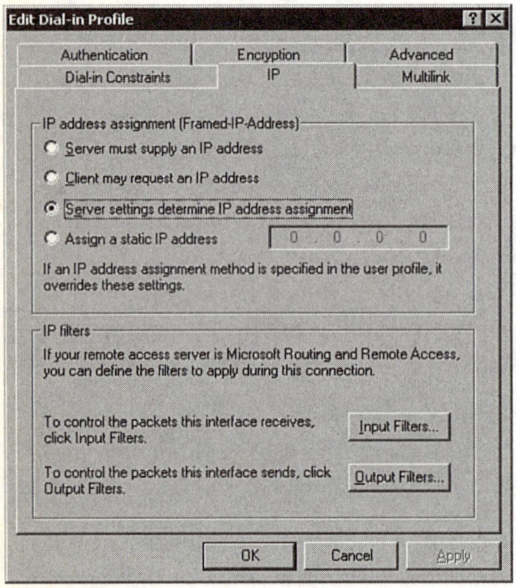

FIGURE 6.40 The IP tab can be used to configure the characteristics of IP for a remote access policy.

- **IP address assignment (Framed-IP-Address)**—The options in this section define how users being authorized by this policy will get their IP addresses. This is typically left at the default setting, but you can change the setting to restrict how IP addresses are assigned.
- **IP filters**—This section allows you to set IP packet filters on the connection. For example, if this connection were being used only for getting Web access to your intranet server, you might set an inbound filter for port 80 (HTTP) to access only the intranet server. IP packet filters are discussed in detail later in this chapter in the section "Managing Packet Filters."

The Multilink Tab

You'll configure the parameters on the Multilink tab when you want to control how multilink connections are handled. A multilink connection is one that makes use of more than one port at a time, such as more than one modem or VPN port at a time. The parameters that can be configured on the Multilink tab of the Edit Dial-in Profile dialog box, as seen in Figure 6.41, include the following:

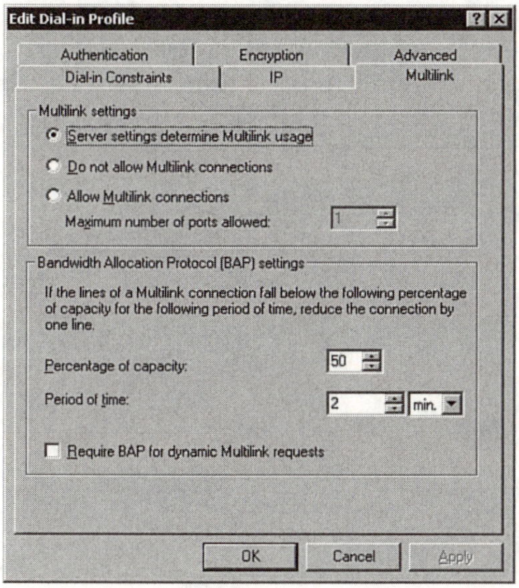

FIGURE 6.41 The Multilink tab can be used to configure the Multilink capabilities (aggregation of multiple physical connections into a single logical connection) of Windows Server 2003 RRAS.

- **Multilink settings**—The settings in this section control how the Multilink protocol can be used with the remote access policy:
  - **Server settings determine Multilink usage**—When this option is selected, the RRAS server settings are used to determine whether Multilink is permitted.
  - **Do not allow Multilink connections**—This setting disables the use of Multilink.
  - **Allow Multilink connections**—This setting allows a client computer to connect by using multiple ports and can also be used to set the maximum number of ports that can be used.

Although it can improve performance, Multilink can be a very resource-intensive solution. Not only does it tie up multiple ports per user at the server end of the connection, but it also requires multiple modems and phone lines on the user's end. This has largely been phased out as multiple modem lines are replaced by high-speed Internet connections such as cable modem lines and Digital Subscriber Line (DSL).

- **Bandwidth Allocation Protocol (BAP) settings**—BAP monitors the utilization on a Multilink connection and dynamically reduces the number of connected lines if the user's utilization drops below a certain amount. You use this section to set the utilization percentage and time before dropping one line of the Multilink connection. You can (and should) require the use of BAP with any Multilink connection. BAP can also be configured to request additional bandwidth when utilization reaches a threshold.

The Authentication Tab

The parameters that can be configured on the Authentication tab of the Edit Dial-in Profile dialog box allow you to configure what authentication methods will be used, as seen in Figure 6.42, and include the following:

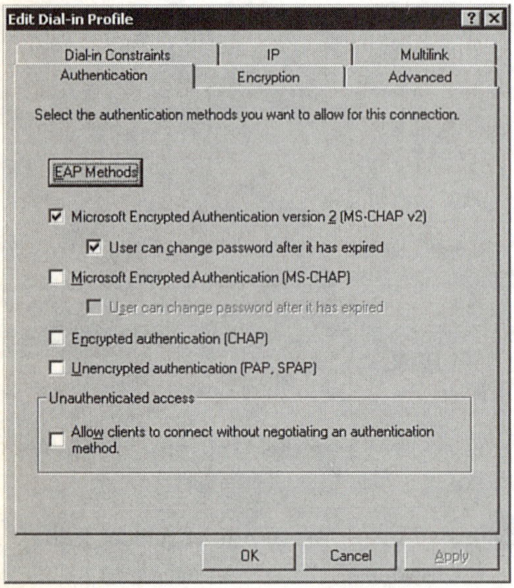

FIGURE 6.42 The Authentication tab allows you to configure the authentication protocols that can be used with this profile.

- **Authentication methods**—You can select what protocols can be used to authenticate a user connecting via this remote access policy. Whenever possible, you should use MS-CHAPv2 or EAP, each of which provides the most secure authentication.
- **Unauthenticated access**—You should never enable unauthenticated access. It essentially allows clients to connect without authenticating first and should never be used as

a production option because it bypasses all authentication security. Allowing unauthenticated access can be very useful when you're troubleshooting problems because it allows the elimination of authentication as a source of the problems. You just need to be sure to reenable authentication when the problem is resolved.

The Encryption Tab

The Encryption tab of the Edit Dial-in Profile dialog box, as seen in Figure 6.43, enables you to select how strong the encryption used by this connection must be. If you are running an entirely Windows 2000 or greater client population, you should permit only the strongest level of encryption. If you have older clients, you might need to permit less strong encryption levels.

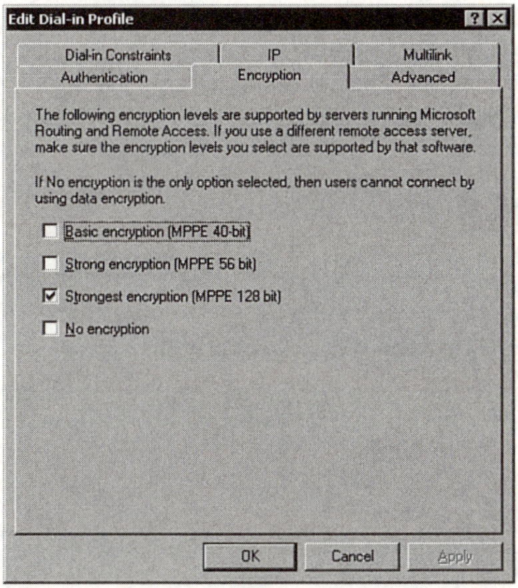

FIGURE 6.43 The Encryption tab is used to specify the permitted encryption strengths for a connection.

The Advanced Tab

The Advanced tab of the Edit Dial-in Profile dialog box, as seen in Figure 6.44, allows you to specify additional connection attributes, typically related to RADIUS requirements for a connection. This tab is generally used only for very complex implementations involving centralized RADIUS servers for remote access policy storage.

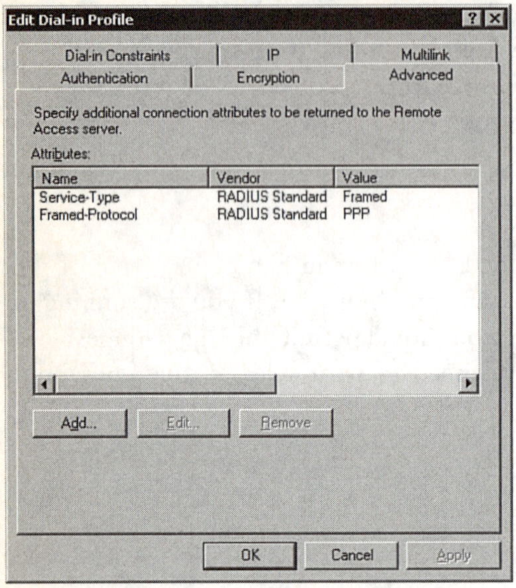

FIGURE 6.44 The Advanced tab is used to specify additional connection attributes to be returned to the remote access server.

Managing Remote Access

After you have successfully installed and configured a Windows Server 2003 remote access server and worked your way through the Routing and Remote Access console so that you understand the options, you face the hard part: managing the server with remote access configured. To successfully maintain the remote access server, you need to understand how packet filters work; how to handle routing interfaces, devices, ports, and protocols; and how to manage the remote access clients.

Managing Packet Filters

Objective:

Manage remote access.

- Manage packet filters.

One of the most interesting features of Windows Server 2003 is the ability to implement packet filters. A *packet* is a portion of a message that is transferred across a network. For example, when you download Windows Server 2003 Service Pack 1, the file is broken into many smaller packets to be transmitted to your computer, and then it is reassembled after all the packets have been delivered. A packet filter acts as a crude form of firewall, permitting or denying traffic based on rules set in the filter. Packet filters work by looking at the makeup of each packet, comparing that composition to the list of filters, and then making a decision about whether to forward or drop the packet based on those rules.

Step by Step 6.7 walks you through the creation of a packet filter by using the Windows Server 2003 Routing and Remote Access console. Note that inbound packets are those being sent to the server and outbound packets are those being sent from the server.

STEP BY STEP

6.7 Using the Routing and Remote Access Console to Create a Packet Filter

1. Log on to Windows Server 2003 by using the Administrator account or another account that has administrator privileges.
2. Open the Routing and Remote Access console by selecting Start, Administrative Tools, Routing and Remote Access.
3. Select Remote Access Policies in the left pane and then right-click the remote access policy created in Step by Step 6.5. Select Properties from the menu. The Remote Access Policy Settings dialog box appears.
4. Click the Edit Profile button. The Edit Remote Access Profile dialog box appears. In the IP Filters section of the IP tab (refer back to Figure 6.40), click Input Filters. The Inbound Filters dialog box appears, as seen in Figure 6.45.

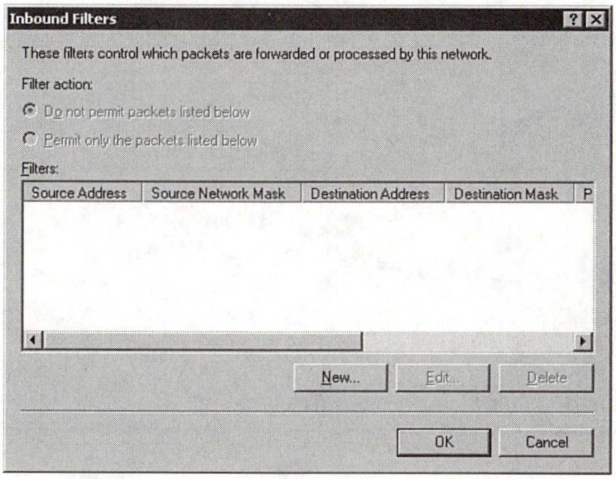

FIGURE 6.45 Inbound filters can be set on a variety of packet-based conditions.

5. Click New to create a new packet filter. The Add IP Filter dialog box appears, as seen in Figure 6.46.

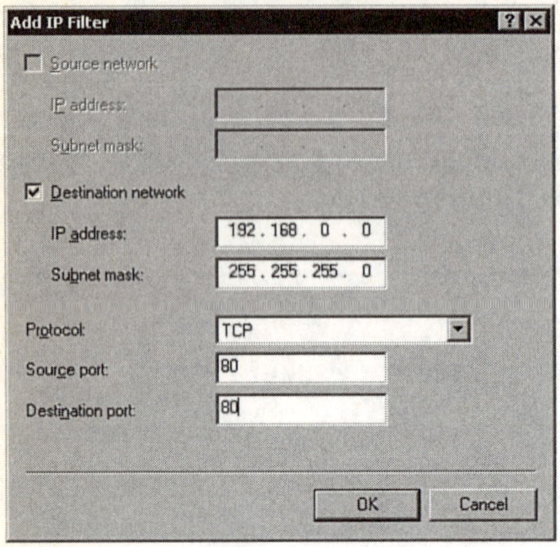

FIGURE 6.46 To create an input filter, you need to know the source IP address or network, subnet mask, and protocol type to be filtered.

6. Complete the fields as shown in Figure 6.46, prohibiting a single Class C network from sending packets to the Windows Server 2003 host. Click OK to create the filter. Figure 6.47 shows the newly created filter. Click OK to return to the Routing and Remote Access console.

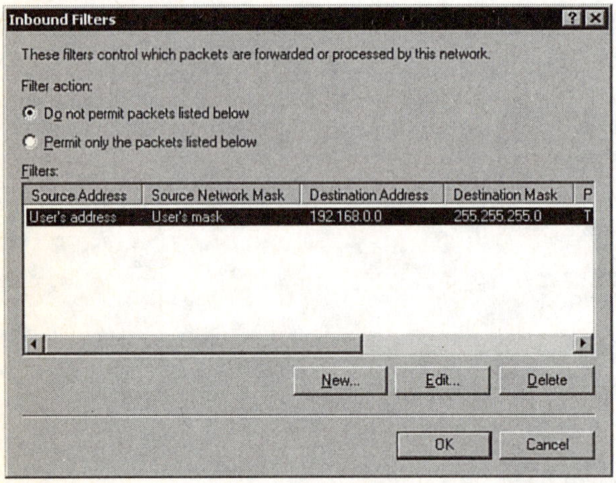

FIGURE 6.47 Any packet filters you have created appear on the Inbound Filters dialog box.

EXAM ALERT

Don't Confuse Input and Output Filters An input filter configured by using the Windows Server 2003 Routing and Remote Access console deals with the packets that the Windows Server 2003 host receives. These filters act only on packets that are received by the router, either allowing or dropping the packets based on the filter configuration. A packet that is not permitted by a receive filter will be dropped before it can be received by the router. Output filters determine whether packets will be sent by the router. The router will receive the packet, and if the packet is permitted by the filter, it is sent. If the filters do not permit the packet to be sent, it is dropped.

Managing RRAS Routing Interfaces

Objective:

Manage remote access.

- Manage Routing and Remote Access routing interfaces.

Another important component with which you need to be familiar is the routing interfaces used by Windows Server 2003 RRAS. A *routing interface* is a physical or logical interface over which unicast or multicast packets can be forwarded. Windows Server 2003 supports three types of routing interfaces:

- **LAN**—A LAN interface is a physical interface to a LAN connection such as Ethernet or Token Ring. These interfaces are identified by the NIC and are always active. They do not typically require authentication to permit connectivity.
- **Demand-dial**—A demand-dial interface is a logical interface that represents a point-to-point connection. The point-to-point connection can be either a physical connection (a modem-to-modem connection using an ISDN line) or a logical connection (an Internet-based router-to-router VPN connection). Demand-dial connections can be persistent (that is, established and then staying connected) or on-demand (that is, connected as needed and then disconnected when the need is gone). Demand-dial interfaces typically require authentication as part of the connection process.
- **IP-in-IP tunnel**—An IP-in-IP tunnel interface is a logical interface that represents a tunneled point-to-point connection. IP-in-IP tunnel interfaces do not require an authentication process for connection to occur. This type of interface sends IP packets through the tunnel by encapsulating them with an additional IP header. This allows IP packets that would not ordinarily traverse a network to be routed from one part of the network to another.

To effectively manage the routing interfaces of a Windows Server 2003 RRAS, you need to be familiar with how to get additional information on an interface and how to manage the interface configuration. Step by Step 6.8 walks you through how to get additional information on an interface and where to find the configuration settings.

STEP BY STEP

6.8 Reviewing the Management Information and Configuration Settings of a LAN Routing Interface

1. Log on to Windows Server 2003 by using the Administrator account or another account that has administrator privileges.
2. Open the Routing and Remote Access console by selecting Start, Administrative Tools, Routing and Remote Access.
3. In the left pane, select General. A list of all the interfaces appears in the right pane, as seen in Figure 6.48.

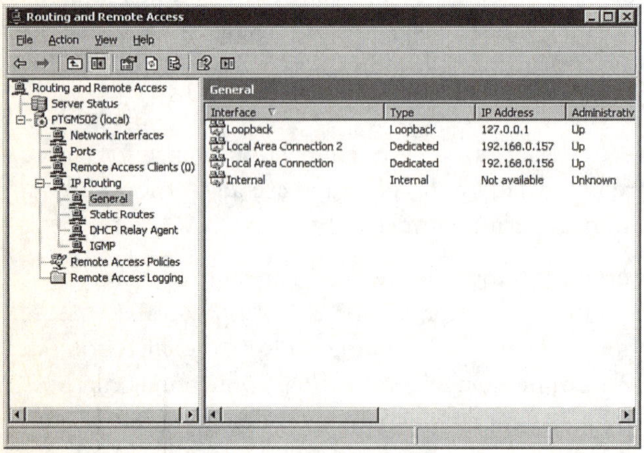

FIGURE 6.48 The General folder shows all the interfaces available to RRAS, along with their types, addresses, and statuses.

4. Right-click the Local Area Connection 2 interface. (If you have more than one LAN adapter, select any of them.) From the context menu that appears, you can update routes, show the TCP/IP information for the interface, show any IP address translations, and show the routing table, TCP connections, and UDP listeners. You can also obtain this information by using a variety of command-line tools. Select Properties to open the Local Area Connection 2 Properties dialog box, as seen in Figure 6.49.
5. The General tab of the Local Area Connection 2 Properties dialog box allows you to configure the use of the IP Manager, enable IP router discovery advertisements, configure packet filters, and set the router to check for fragmentation. Click the Configuration tab, as seen in Figure 6.50, to continue.

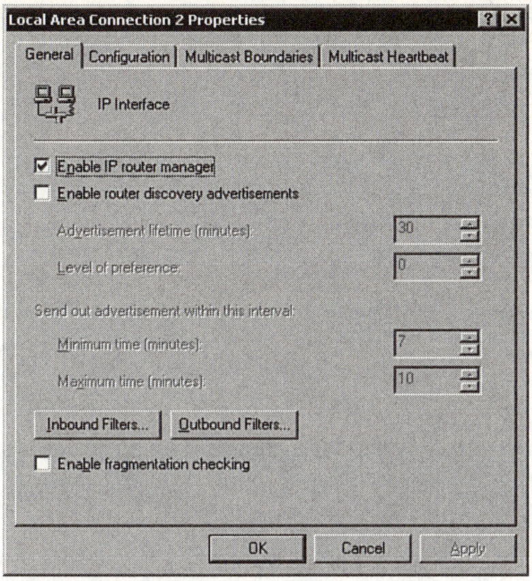

FIGURE 6.49 The Local Area Connection 2 Properties dialog box allows you to manage the configuration of a LAN routing interface.

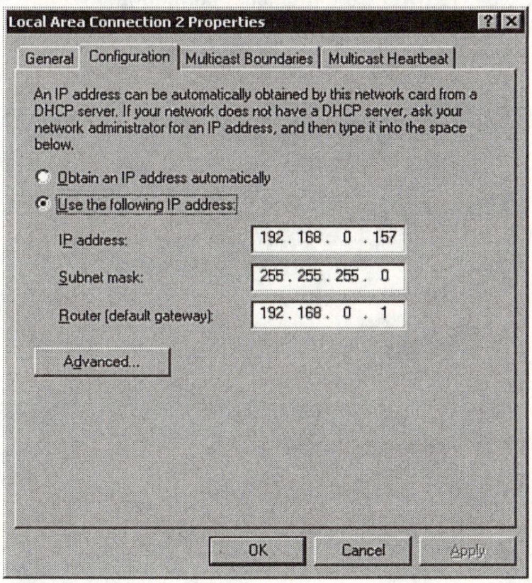

FIGURE 6.50 The Configuration tab of the Local Area Connection 2 Properties dialog box allows you to set the IP address characteristics of the interface.

6. The Configuration tab allows you to configure the interface to use DHCP to obtain an address or to set a static IP address and router gateway on the address. Click Advanced to see the Advanced IP Addressing dialog box, as shown in Figure 6.51.

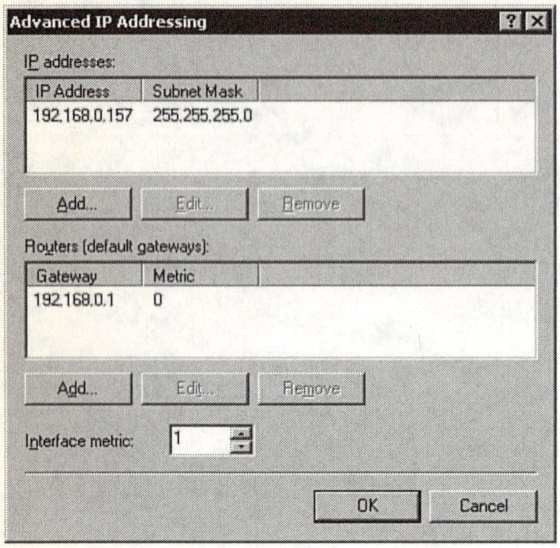

FIGURE 6.51 The Advanced IP Addressing dialog box allows you to perform more complex IP address configurations.

7. The Advanced IP Addressing dialog box allows you to set multiple IP addresses and routers (default gateways) on a single interface. Click OK to return to the Local Area Connection 2 Properties dialog box. Select the Multicast Boundaries tab, as seen in Figure 6.52, to review the multicast configuration options.

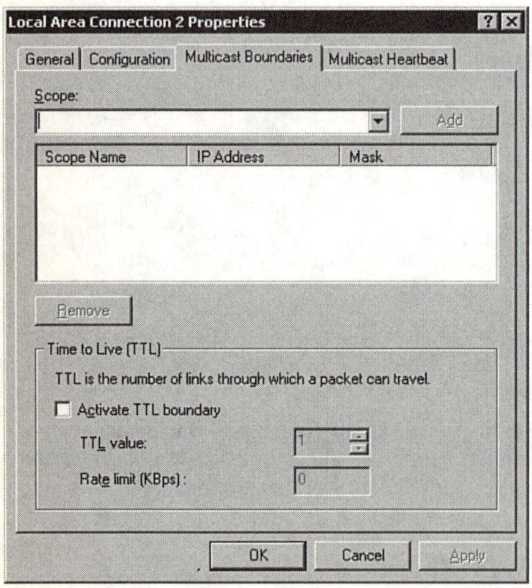

FIGURE 6.52 The Multicast Boundaries tab is useful only in a network that supports multicast routing.

8. From the Multicast Boundaries tab, you can set a multicast scope and a time-to-live (TTL) boundary. You should configure these options only if you have a thorough understanding of the multicast routing in use on the network. Select the Multicast Heartbeat tab, as seen in Figure 6.53, to review additional multicast options.

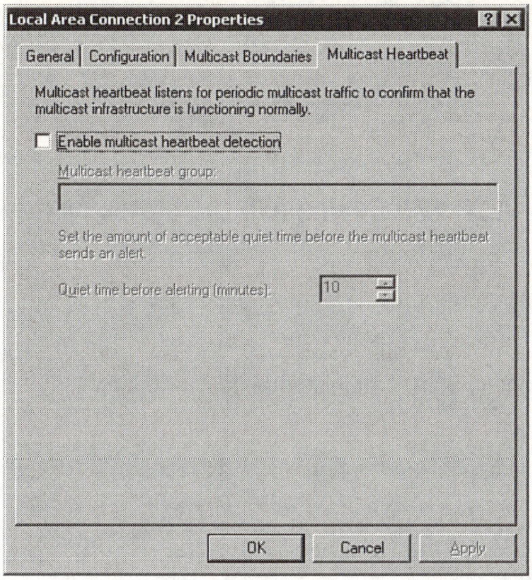

FIGURE 6.53 The Multicast Heartbeat tab has options that are useful only in a network that supports multicast routing.

9. On the Multicast Heartbeat tab, you have the ability to configure a multicast heartbeat, so if your server ever loses connection to the multicast traffic on the network, the server sends an alert. Click OK to return to the Routing and Remote Access console.

Managing Devices and Ports

Objective:

Manage remote access.

- Manage devices and ports.

The next piece of the remote access puzzle is working with the devices and ports that need to be managed. A *device* is hardware or software that Windows Server 2003 RRAS uses to provide ports for demand-dial and remote access connections. A device can be a physical unit, such as a modem, or a virtual connection, such as a VPN connection. A *port* is defined in RRAS as a channel of a device that is used to support remote access connections.

EXAM ALERT

Devices and Ports For the exam, be sure to remember that the *device* is typically the hardware and the *port* is the software used to access the hardware. The only exception to this rule is in a VPN connection, where both the device and port are software.

Step by Step 6.9 reviews the configuration and status of a Layer 2 Tunneling Protocol (L2TP) VPN port by using the Routing and Remote Access console.

STEP BY STEP

6.9 Reviewing the Configuration Settings of an L2TP VPN Device and the Status of the Associated L2TP Port

1. Log on to Windows Server 2003 by using the Administrator account or another account that has administrator privileges.
2. Open the Routing and Remote Access console by selecting Start, Administrative Tools, Routing and Remote Access.
3. In the left pane, select Ports. A list of all available ports appears in the right pane, as seen in Figure 6.54.

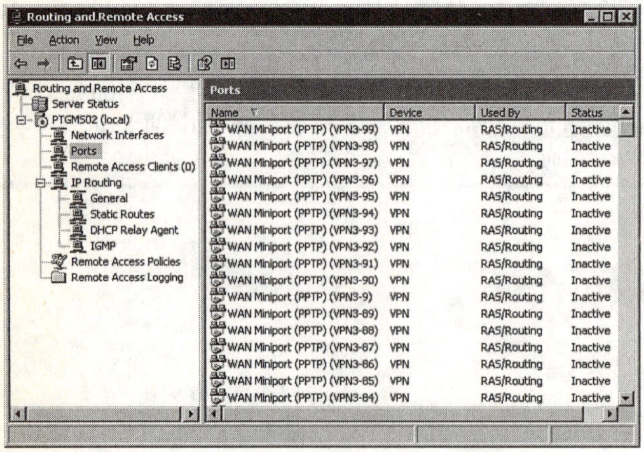

FIGURE 6.54 The Ports folder contains all the ports available to Windows Server 2003 RRAS.

4. Right-click the Ports folder and select Properties. The Ports Properties dialog box, as seen in Figure 6.55, appears.
5. Select the WAN Miniport (L2TP) device and click Configure. The Configure Device dialog box, as seen in Figure 6.56, appears.
6. Review the configuration settings and then click OK and then click OK again to return to the Routing and Remote Access console. In the console, right-click one of the Point-to-Point Tunneling Protocol (PPTP) ports and select Status from the context menu. The Port Status dialog box, as seen in Figure 6.57, appears.

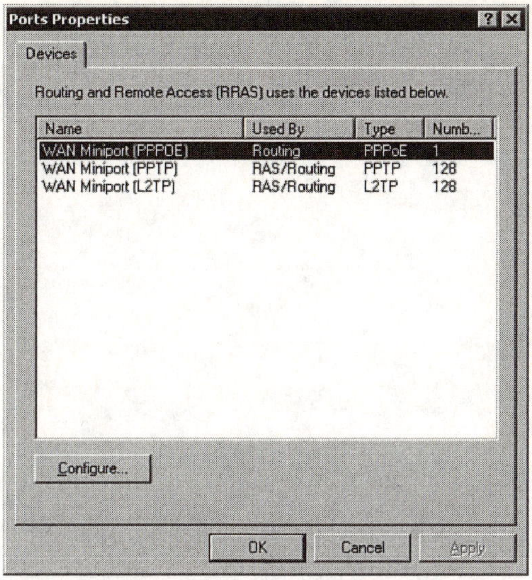

FIGURE 6.55 The Ports Properties dialog box shows all the devices configured in Windows Server 2003 RRAS.

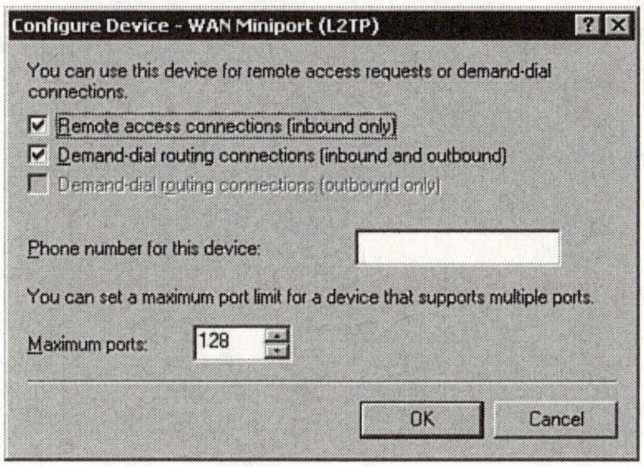

FIGURE 6.56 The Configure Device dialog box allows you to control how a device can be used and how many ports are associated with it.

7. The Port Status dialog box gives you valuable information about the line condition, speed, connection duration, connection statistics, errors, and network registration information. Click OK to close the Port Status dialog box and return to the Routing and Remote Access console.

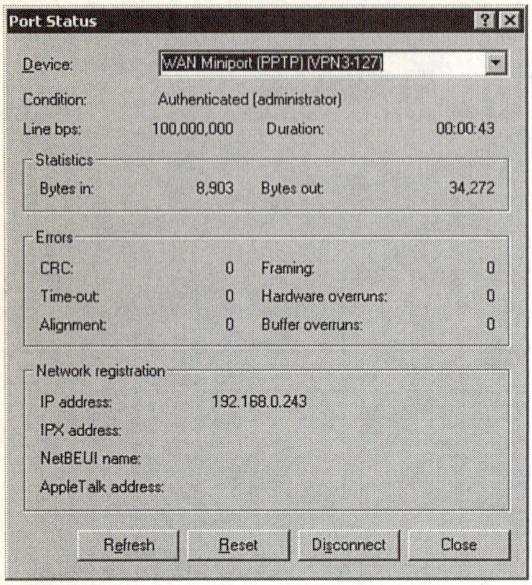

FIGURE 6.57 The Port Status dialog box provides extensive information about the actual status of a port.

Generally you will be asked to check on the status of a port rather than actually manage it. When a remote access server is in production, you spend almost all your time reviewing logs and checking port status to troubleshoot remote access issues.

Managing Routing Protocols

Objective:

Manage remote access.

- Manage routing protocols.

The installation and management of TCP/IP routing protocols is covered in detail in Chapter 7, "Implementing, Managing, and Troubleshooting Routing." This chapter takes a look at how to install and manage non-TCP/IP routing protocols on the Windows Server 2003 RRAS.

Windows Server 2003 supports the following non-TCP/IP routing protocols:

- **AppleTalk**—This protocol provides routing information for Apple/Macintosh computers.
- **Microsoft TCP/IP version 6**—For companies that are working to be early adopters of the latest generation of IP addressing, Windows Server 2003 supports IP version 6.
- **NWLink**—NWLink is typically used when there are legacy IPX/SPX systems on the network. NWLink was originally created by Novell as part of their server operating system, and support for NWLink is still required in many environments.

Step by Step 6.10 looks at how to implement the AppleTalk protocol and its associated routing. You need to have the AppleTalk protocol installed on the server prior to trying Step by Step 6.10.

EXAM ALERT

On Which Protocol Should You Concentrate? Given the prevalence of TCP/IP on almost all networks, the material in Chapter 7 is more applicable to a production environment than is the information in this chapter. For the purposes of the exam, you need to be familiar with the high-level information on installing, managing, and supporting all the routing protocols, including, but not limited to, TCP/IP.

STEP BY STEP

6.10 Managing AppleTalk Routing Interfaces

1. Log on to Windows Server 2003 by using the Administrator account or another account that has administrator privileges.

2. Open the Routing and Remote Access console by selecting Start, Administrative Tools, Routing and Remote Access.

3. In the left pane, select AppleTalk Routing. (If the protocol was installed with the RRAS console open, you need to restart the console to get the new protocol to appear.) A list of interfaces available for AppleTalk routing appears in the right pane, as seen in Figure 6.58.

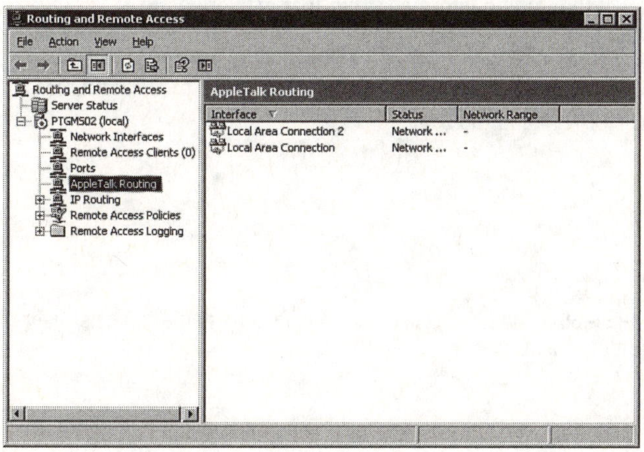

FIGURE 6.58 After the AppleTalk protocol has been installed on a local area connection, the AppleTalk Routing option is available in the Routing and Remote Access console.

4. Before configuring the network adapters, you will need to enable AppleTalk routing. Right-click the AppleTalk Routing node and select Enable AppleTalk Routing from the context menu.

5. Right-click Local Area Connection 2 in the right pane and select Properties. The Local Area Connection 2 Properties dialog box, as seen in Figure 6.59, appears.

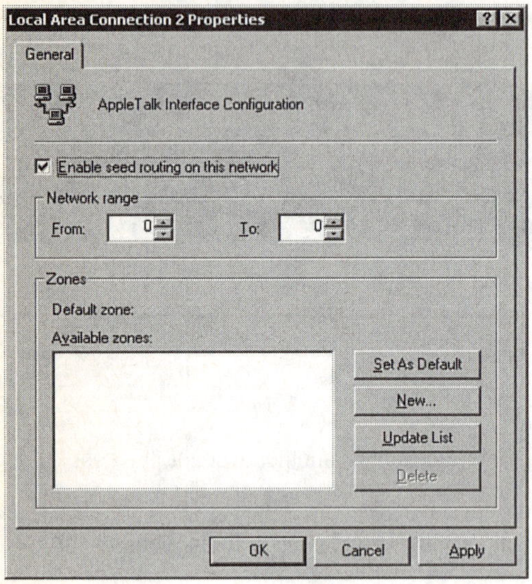

FIGURE 6.59 AppleTalk routing is easy to configure, requiring only an address range and zone name.

6. Select Enable Seed Routing on This Network to make the server an AppleTalk seed router. A seed router initializes and broadcasts routing information about any directly connected networks. A seed router tells other routers where to send packets destined for the attached network(s). Each physical network must have one or more seed routers to broadcast the routing information for that network.

7. In the Zones section, click New to create a zone to be broadcast. The New Zone dialog box, as seen in Figure 6.60, appears. A *zone* is a logical grouping of nodes used to simplify network browsing. Enter a zone name in the Zone Name field and click OK to add the zone.

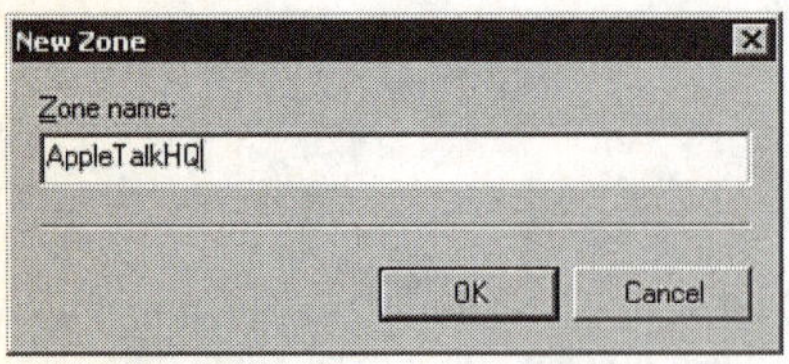

FIGURE 6.60 You should use an intuitive zone name to assist users in finding resources.

8. The Local Area Connection 2 Properties dialog box now shows the new zone, as seen in Figure 6.61. Click OK to complete the configuration and return to the Routing and Remote Access console.

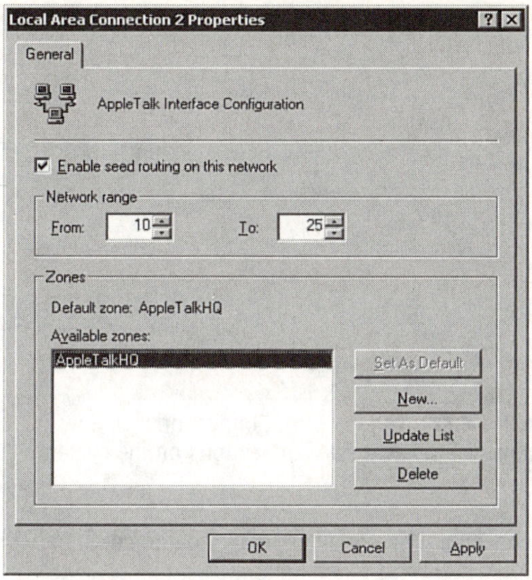

FIGURE 6.61 The Available zones list shows all the configured zones being broadcast by the server.

Managing RRAS Clients

Objective:

Manage remote access.

- Manage Routing and Remote Access clients.

Now that you have set up a remote access server, you need to take a look at the other side of the equation—setting up a client to connect to the server. Step by Step 6.11 demonstrates how to set up a Windows XP client to use a PPTP VPN connection to connect to a Windows Server 2003 server configured for remote access VPN connections. You need to make sure that your remote access policy permits connections to complete this exercise.

STEP BY STEP

6.11 Configuring a Windows XP Professional Host to Connect to a Windows Server 2003 Server Running RRAS and Using a PPTP VPN

1. Right-click the My Network Places icon on the desktop and select Properties. The Network Connections window, as seen in Figure 6.62, appears.

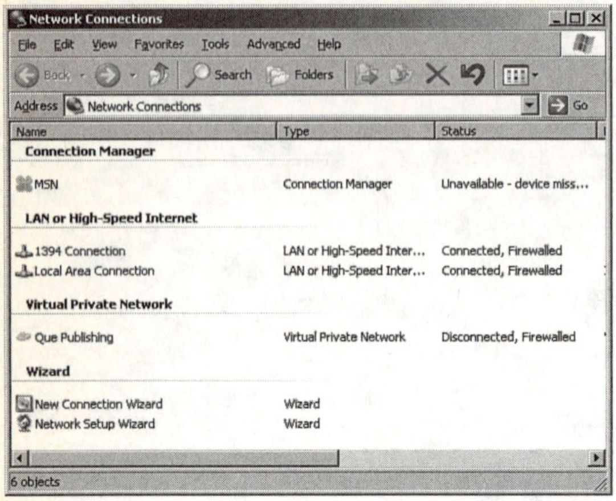

FIGURE 6.62 The Network Connections window shows all the available connections on the system.

2. Double-click the New Connection Wizard. The New Connection Wizard opens. Click Next to continue.
3. The Network Connection Type dialog box of the wizard, as seen in Figure 6.63, appears.

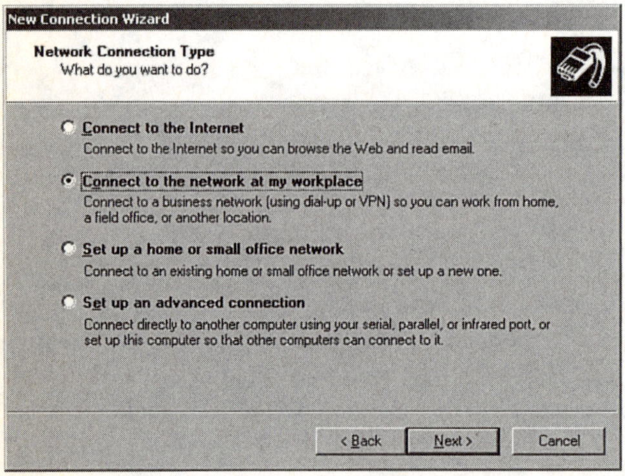

FIGURE 6.63 The Network Connection Type dialog box offers four options for setting up connections.

4. Select Connect to the Network at My Workplace and click Next. The Network Connection dialog box of the wizard, as seen in Figure 6.64, appears.
5. Select Virtual Private Network connection and click Next. The Connection Name dialog box of the wizard, as seen in Figure 6.65, appears.

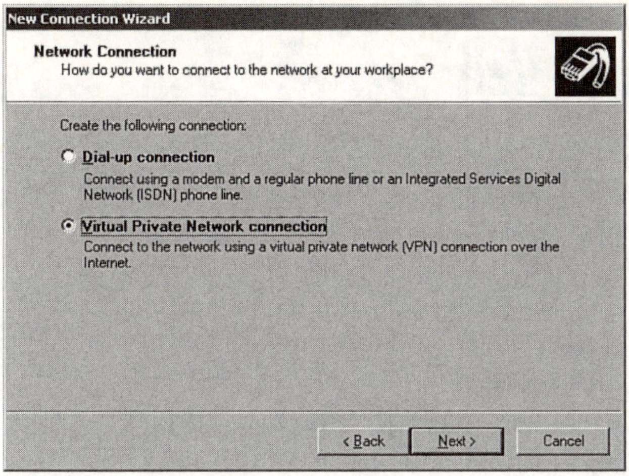

FIGURE 6.64 The Network Connection dialog box allows you to select the transport type for a new connection.

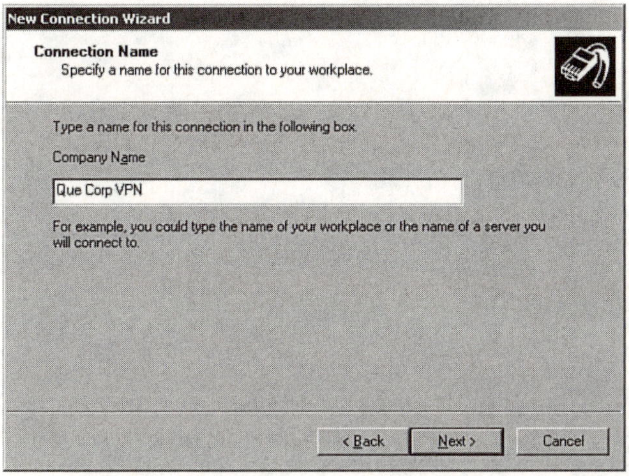

FIGURE 6.65 You should choose an intuitive name for a VPN connection.

6. Type a name for the connection in the Company Name field and click Next to continue. The Public Network dialog box of the wizard, as seen in Figure 6.66, appears.
7. In the Public Network dialog box, you have the option to have the VPN connection make the initial public network connection for you. Select Do Not Dial the Initial Connection and click Next to continue. The VPN Server Selection dialog box of the wizard, as seen in Figure 6.67, appears.

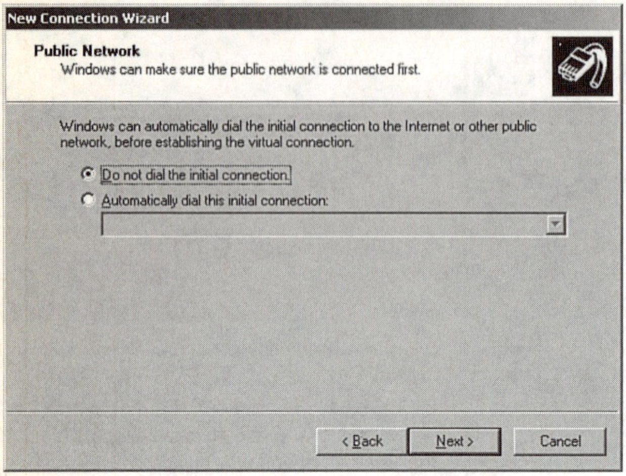

FIGURE 6.66 You can automate a VPN connection by having the VPN connection also dial your ISP.

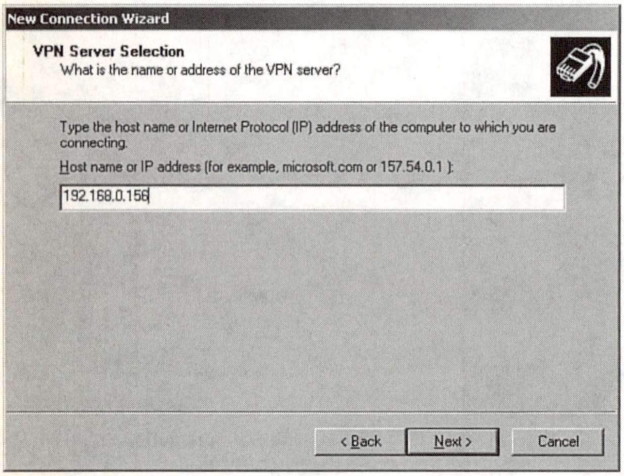

FIGURE 6.67 The VPN Server Selection dialog box is used to identify the remote VPN server, either by IP address or DNS name.

8. On the VPN Server Selection screen, enter the DNS name or IP address of the VPN server to which you are trying to connect. Click Next to continue. The Completing the New Connection Wizard dialog box, as seen in Figure 6.68, appears.

9. Click Finish to complete the configuration. The Connect dialog box, as seen in Figure 6.69, appears automatically.

10. Enter the username and password for an account that is authorized to connect via remote access and click Connect to open the connection. Under no circumstances should you ever select Save This Username and Password for a Connection of This Type. Not only is the storage of the password weak, but if your system is ever compromised, this would give the attacker an open invitation to attack your internal network.

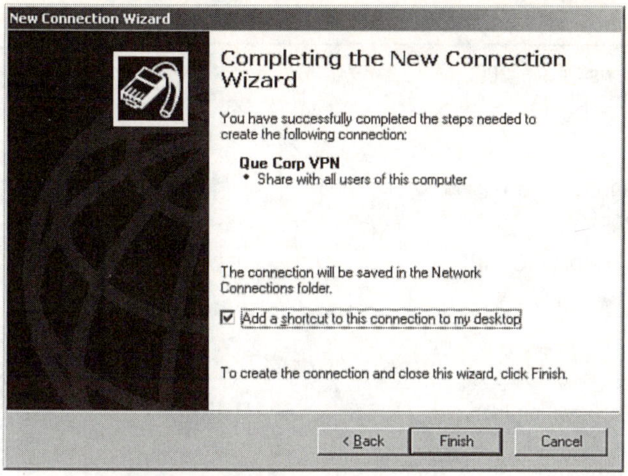

FIGURE 6.68 The Completing the New Connection Wizard dialog box allows you to create a desktop icon for the new connection.

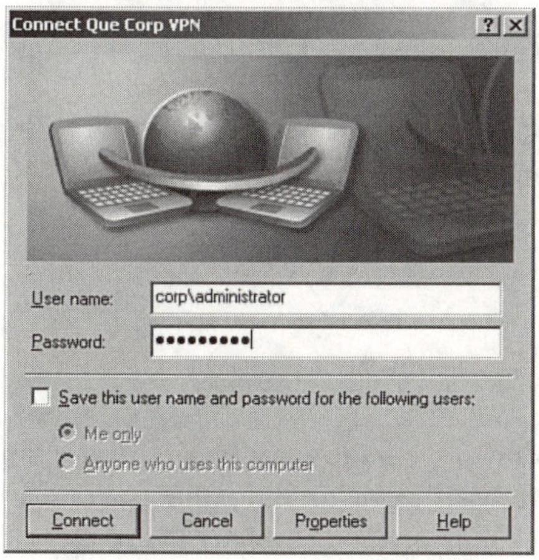

FIGURE 6.69 The Connect screen allows you to log in to the remote VPN server.

11. If your connection is successful, a taskbar pop-up appears. If you do not successfully connect, you should see the section "Troubleshooting User Access to Remote Access Services" later in this chapter to work out why the connection failed.
12. Click the Connection Complete taskbar pop-up to open the connection status window, which gives you a snapshot of what is happening with the connection. Click the Details tab to get specific information about the connection.

The steps for installing a remote access client in the Windows 2000 Professional operating system are virtually identical to those used in Step by Step 6.11. If you want to install a client on an older Microsoft operating system, you need to download the client from the Microsoft website.

NOTE

Remote access protocols supported by Windows Server 2003:

- Serial Line Interface Protocol (SLIP)
- Point-to-Point Protocol (PPP)

Remote access authentication protocols supported by Windows Server 2003:

- Password Authentication Protocol (PAP)
- Challenge Handshake Authentication Protocol (CHAP)
- Shiva PAP (SPAP)
- Microsoft CHAP (MS-CHAP)
- MS-CHAP version 2 (MS-CHAPv2)
- Extensible Authentication Protocol (EAP), which includes:
  - EAP-MD5 CHAP
  - EAP-TLS
- RADIUS

Implementing Secure Access Between Private Networks

Objective:

Implement secure access between private networks.

You have learned how to connect a remote user to a production Windows Server 2003 system by using RRAS. RRAS can also provide features that are used to securely connect networks together. Windows Server 2003 RRAS provides two mechanisms for securely connecting private networks: VPN and demand-dial routing.

Windows Server 2003 VPNs

A VPN creates a logical private network across an existing public network infrastructure such as the Internet. You've already seen this from a client-server perspective in Step by Step 6.11, but now we're going to examine this from a server-to-server or network-to-network point of view. This connection is called *virtual* because the logical connection is built independently of the underlying physical network. In other words, the VPN connection is not aware of the physical route the packets take across the network—it is aware only of the endpoints of the virtual connection.

The purpose of a VPN is to securely extend a private internal network to users and external networks. When a VPN is configured correctly, a user should be unable to differentiate a VPN connection from a LAN connection. More importantly, the user's applications should not be able to differentiate between the two types of connections either. Therefore, using a VPN is a seamless method for integrating remote users or locations into a private network.

There are two common types of VPNs that you are likely to encounter:

- **Remote access VPN**—A remote access VPN is typically used to allow remote users to connect to a private corporate network securely. Remote access VPNs were one of the major drivers of the VPN technology because they allow users to connect to a corporate network without requiring the extensive modem cards and lines needed for large remote access server implementations.
- **Site-to-site VPN**—Also known as a network-to-network VPN, a site-to-site VPN is typically used to replace expensive private WAN links with lower-cost VPN connections, utilizing the Internet as the underlying public network. When implemented correctly, site-to-site VPNs can provide a cost-effective, reliable option to replace the more traditional WAN connections. An additional use for site-to-site VPNs that is becoming more common has to do with the growing requirement for companies to interconnect with business partners, vendors, and customers. Not only do VPNs provide a secure mechanism for these interconnections, but they can be created much more quickly than installing a WAN connection, which typically takes from 45 to 60 days.

One other type of VPN connection that is less common but growing in popularity is a VPN connection across a private network. This is a variant of the site-to-site connection, but instead of replacing a private WAN connection, it is used to enhance the security of the WAN. This type of connection is typically used in environments where different sections of the internal network require different levels of security. For example, a VPN might be required to access the Research and Development network within a company to ensure secure connections between corporate offices that exchange sensitive data, or to secure top-secret data within government files traversing the internal network.

All three of these VPN types are easily supported with the Windows Server 2003 RRAS.

Supported VPN Protocols

Windows Server 2003 supports two VPN protocols: PPTP and L2TP.

PPTP

PPTP is a proprietary VPN protocol originally developed by the PPTP Forum, a group of vendors that included Ascend Communications, Microsoft Corporation, 3Com, ECI Telematics, and U.S. Robotics. PPTP was designed as an extension of PPP to allow PPP to be tunneled through an IP network. One of the main differentiators of PPTP versus IPSec is that PPTP supports the encapsulation of not only IP, but also IPX or NetBEUI. This is particularly useful in Windows and Novell environments that have not migrated to TCP/IP.

PPTP uses the proprietary MPPE protocol to encrypt the link between the VPN client and server, and it uses the Generic Routing Encapsulation (GRE) protocol for the encapsulation of the encrypted PPTP data in the PPP frame, which can be an IP datagram, an IPX datagram, or a NetBEUI frame.

One of the key benefits of PPTP is that because Microsoft helped develop it, it has been bundled with all current versions of Microsoft's operating systems. This caused some problems because some security experts felt that PPTP was not secure enough to be used for Internet-based VPN connections, but Windows Server 2003 contains an updated version of PPTP that is secure.

At one time, PPTP was the most widely used VPN protocol, but the release of IPSec has had a significant impact on PPTP's use. Although PPTP is still popular with Microsoft shops and when Windows Server 2003 is being used as the VPN server, IPSec is enjoying increasing popularity with companies that are using hardware-based VPN servers. PPTP is steadily being replaced by L2TP and will likely not be widely used for much longer or in future versions of Windows.

For more details on PPTP, see RFC 2637, "Point-to-Point Tunneling Protocol" (July 1999). It is important to note that this is an informational RFC and was never adopted as a standard. This is a key difference between PPTP and IPSec.

L2TP

L2TP is a combination of the best features of PPTP and the Layer 2 Forwarding (L2F) protocol. The L2F protocol was an early competing protocol for PPTP that was developed by Cisco Systems. Like PPTP, L2TP was designed as an extension of PPP to allow PPP to be tunneled through an IP network. However, L2TP defines its own tunneling protocol, based on L2F. L2TP support was first included in a Microsoft server product with the release of Windows 2000 Server, and it continues to be supported in Windows Server 2003. Prior to Windows 2000, PPTP was the only supported VPN protocol in the Windows operating system family.

L2TP uses one of the IPSec protocols, Encapsulating Security Payload (ESP), for encryption. For this reason, L2TP under Windows Server 2003 is also known as L2TP/IPSec. The use of IPSec as the encryption mechanism allows L2TP/IPSec to utilize third-party encryption hardware to offload the encryption functions of the VPN connections from the VPN server. Also, the standard implementation of L2TP/IPSec requires the use of machine Public Key

Infrastructure (PKI) certificates. This ensures a more secure connection, but at the cost of a more complex implementation—you must have access to a Certificate Authority (CA) to implement an L2TP/IPSec VPN connection.

As mentioned in the previous paragraph, L2TP uses IPSec for encryption. We examine IPSec in more detail in the next section.

IPSec

IPSec is a set of protocols developed by the Internet Engineering Task Force (IETF) to allow for the secure exchange of data via the IP. As a result, IPSec is used by many vendors to deliver VPN services. One of the major limitations of IPSec is that the IETF guidelines do not allow IPSec to support the traversal of networks by using Network Address Translation (NAT). Microsoft has addressed this issue in the latest version of its IPSec VPN.

Two encryption modes are supported by standard IPSec: transport and tunnel. Transport-mode IPSec encrypts only the data portion of a packet. The packet's header information is left intact. For a more secure connection, tunnel-mode IPSec encrypts not only the data portion of a packet, but also the header.

The protocols used by IPSec include the following:

- **Internet Security Association and Key Management Protocol/Oakley (ISAKMP/Oakley)**—The ISAKMP/Oakley protocol is used to share a public key between the sender and receiver of a secure connection. This protocol allows the receiving system to retrieve a public key and then authenticate the sender by using digital certificates.
- **Internet Key Exchange (IKE)**—The IKE protocol is used to authenticate the endpoints of an IPSec connection, negotiate the exchange of IPSec keys, and negotiate IPSec security associations (SAs). An SA is used by the IPSec endpoints to define how data will be encrypted and decrypted. IKE also uses the Diffie-Hellman public-key cryptography protocol to exchange the session keys used to create the initial secure connection.
- **Authentication Header (AH)**—The AH protocol authenticates the data packet and ensures the integrity of the data being sent. This protocol uses hashing algorithms to ensure packet and data integrity by signing the packets with a hash. The hash is then decoded at the other end of the connection to verify the data. The algorithms used by AH include MD5 and Secure Hash Algorithm (SHA).
- **ESP**—The ESP protocol encrypts the data contents of a packet. In conjunction with ESP, IPSec can use a number of encryption algorithms, including DES and Triple DES (3DES).

NOTE

Network Interfaces and a Windows Server 2003 VPN You need two NICs installed in a server to set up a Windows Server 2003 VPN (and to complete Step by Step 6.12 in the following section). With Windows Server 2003, you must have an external (Internet) interface and an internal (local LAN) interface to install a VPN connection. However, if you want the server to act as the endpoint of a VPN connection and do not need to route traffic to the internal network, you can use a single-interface server.

Configuring a VPN Connection

Now that you are familiar with some of the underlying protocols involved in creating a VPN connection, Step by Step 6.12 demonstrates the creation of a VPN demand-dial connection.

STEP BY STEP

6.12 Enabling VPN Demand-Dial Routing on a Windows Server 2003 Server

1. Log on to Windows Server 2003 by using the Administrator account or another account that has administrator privileges.
2. Open the Routing and Remote Access console by selecting Start, Administrative Tools, Routing and Remote Access.
3. In the left pane, right-click the server and select Properties from the context menu. The server (local) Properties dialog box, as seen in Figure 6.70, appears.

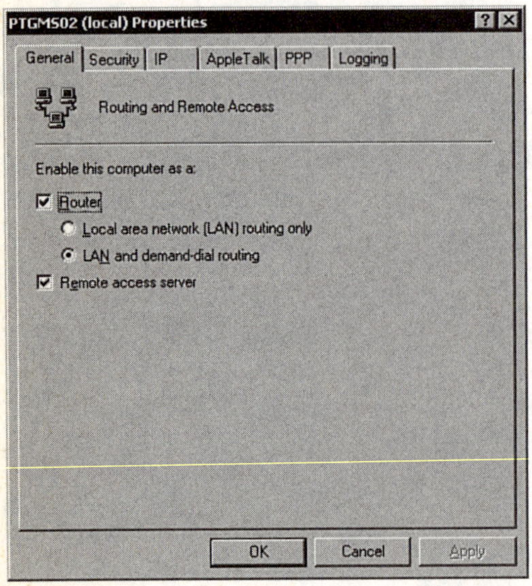

FIGURE 6.70 Before you can configure demand dial routing, it must be enabled on the server.

4. On the General tab, select LAN and demand-dial routing. Click OK to return to the Routing and Remote Access console.
5. Right-click Network Interfaces within the console tree and select New Demand-Dial Interface from the context menu. The Demand-Dial Interface Wizard appears.
6. Click Next to proceed. The Interface Name dialog box appears.
7. In the Interface Name field, type a name for this connection interface. Click Next to continue. The Connection Type dialog box of the wizard, as seen in Figure 6.71, appears. Note that if your server does not have a modem installed, the first option displayed in Figure 6.71 will be unavailable to you.

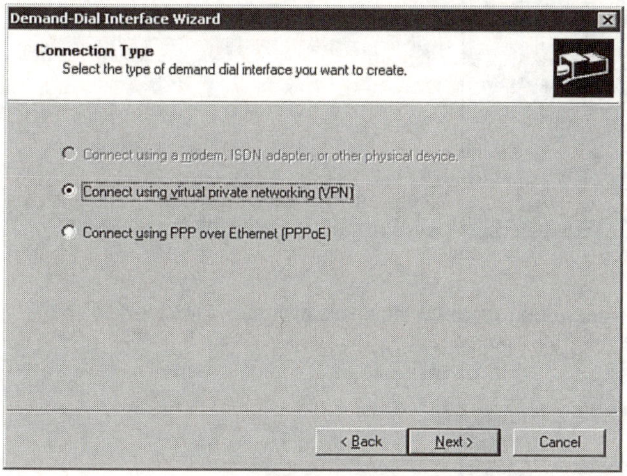

FIGURE 6.71 The Connection Type dialog box offers three alternatives for a demand-dial connection.

8. In the Connection Type dialog box, select Connect Using Virtual Private Networking (VPN) and click Next to continue. The VPN Type dialog box of the wizard, as seen in Figure 6.72, appears.

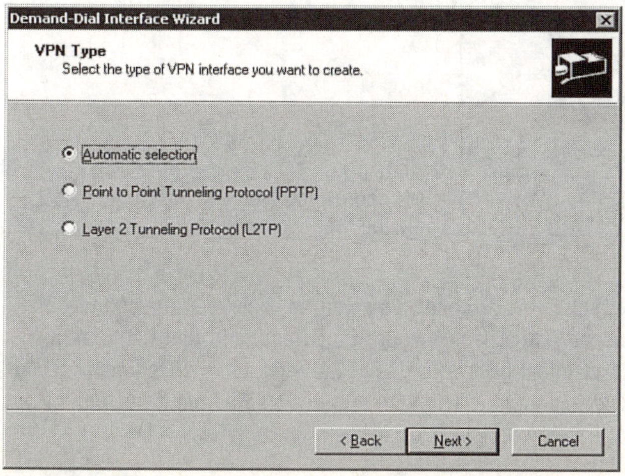

FIGURE 6.72 If you aren't sure which VPN type to use, the server automatically selects a VPN type when it tries to connect.

9. Select Automatic Selection and click Next. The Destination Address dialog box of the wizard, as seen in Figure 6.73, appears.

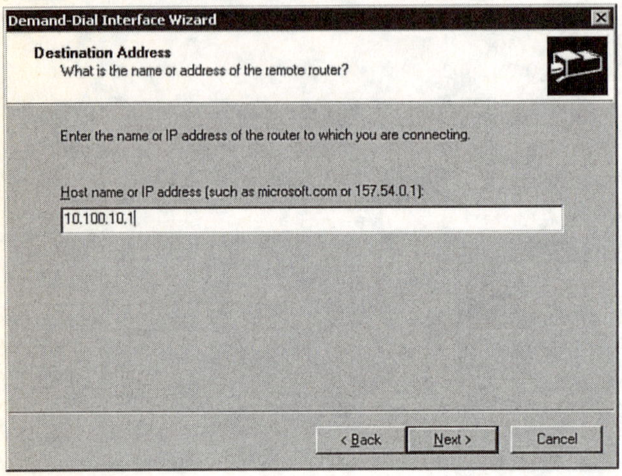

FIGURE 6.73 You can use an IP address or a DNS name to identify the remote router.

10. Enter the IP address or DNS name of the answering router in the space provided. Click Next to continue. The Protocols and Security dialog box, as seen in Figure 6.74, appears.

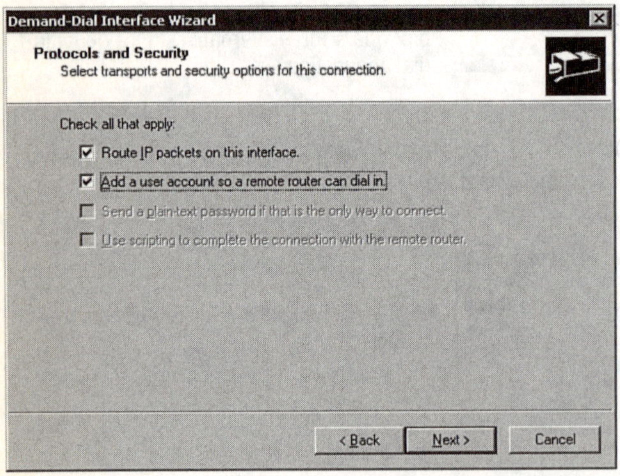

FIGURE 6.74 Because you are creating a VPN connection, you will be able to select only the first two options.

11. On the Protocols and Security dialog box, select the protocols you want to route over the connection. Select Route IP Packets on This Interface and Add a User Account So a Remote Router Can Dial In. You cannot select the option of sending a plaintext password due to the security ramifications associated with unencrypted passwords. Click Next to continue. The Static Routes for Remote Networks dialog box, as seen in Figure 6.75, appears.

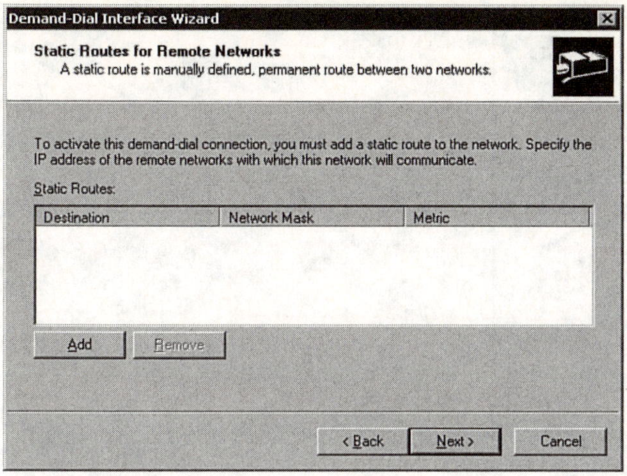

FIGURE 6.75 You will need to define at least one static route.

12. Click Add to open the Static Route dialog box, as seen in Figure 6.76.

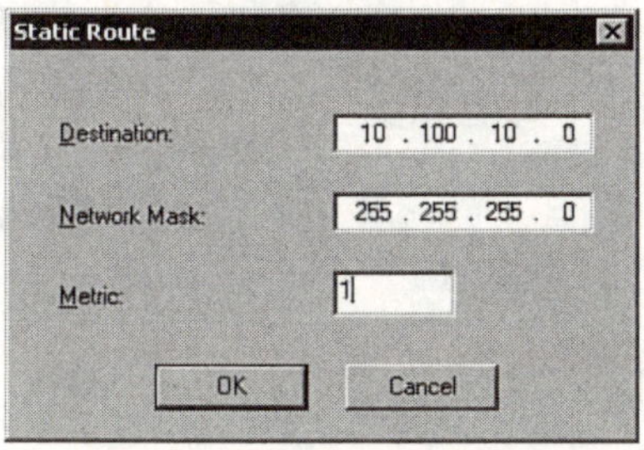

FIGURE 6.76 Enter your static route configuration information.

13. Enter the network and the subnet mask and click OK to add the new route. You can see the new route in the Static Routes for Remote Networks dialog box, as seen in Figure 6.77. Click Next to continue. The Dial In Credentials dialog box, as seen in Figure 6.78, appears.

14. As a result of selecting the Add a User Account So a Remote Router Can Dial In option in Step 9, you need to create a user ID and password for the remote router to authenticate with when it dials in. Enter a username and password and then click Next to continue. The Dial Out Credentials dialog box, as seen in Figure 6.79, appears.

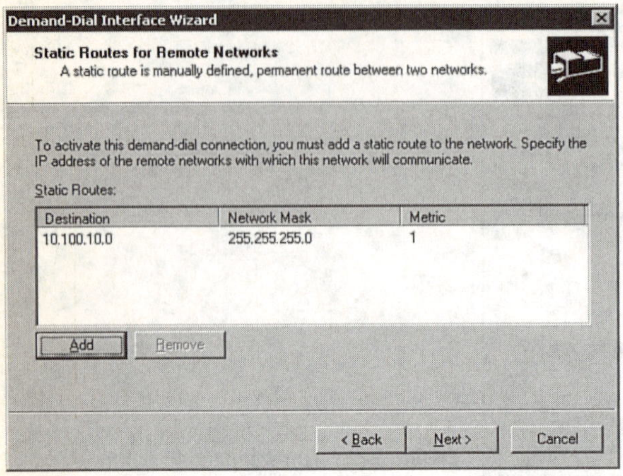

FIGURE 6.77 The static route has been added.

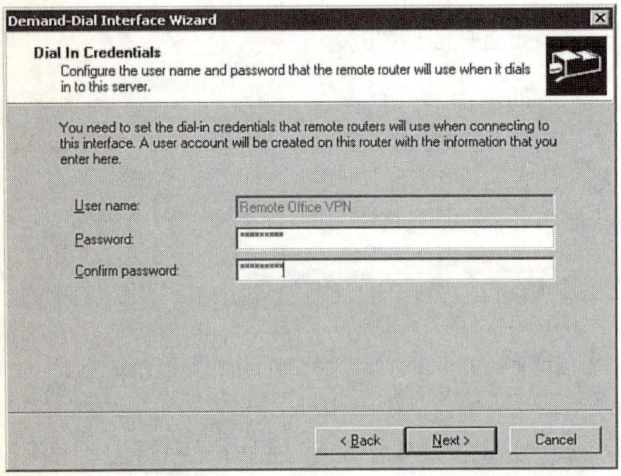

FIGURE 6.78 You need to supply the credentials the remote router will be using to connect to this server.

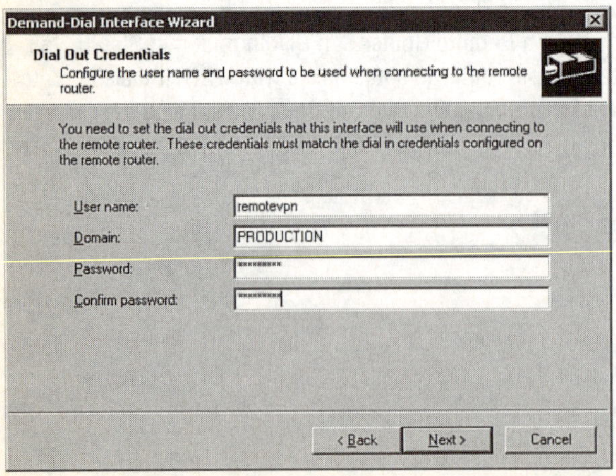

FIGURE 6.79 You need to supply the credentials that this router will be using to connect to the remote server.

15. In the Dial Out Credentials dialog box, enter the security credential information that will allow you to connect to the answering router, including the username, domain, and password. Click Next to continue. The Completing the Demand-Dial Interface Wizard dialog box appears.
16. Click Finish to return to the Routing and Remote Access console. You should see your new demand-dial interface in the right pane of the Routing and Remote Access console when Network Interfaces is selected in the left pane.

EXAM ALERT

Using VPNs with Network Address Translation For the exam, be sure you know that unlike in previous versions of Windows, the IPSec VPN client included with Windows Server 2003 can traverse a firewall or network by using NAT. In previous versions of Windows, PPTP was needed if NAT was used in any portion of the connection, due to the limitations of the existing IPSec protocol suite specifications.

In previous versions of the Windows Server operating system, access across a network using NAT with an IPSec tunnel wasn't possible. NAT can still present some problems, so we need to talk about what exactly NAT is. As you are undoubtedly aware, the Internet relies on TCP/IP for communications. In addition, for two systems to communicate by using TCP/IP, each system must have a unique IP address. Without a unique address, the network cannot deliver the packet to a system. This sounds like a straightforward process until you consider the size of the Internet.

In the early days of the Internet, when IP addressing was being developed, the 32-bit addressing scheme (known as IP version 4 [IPv4]) was considered more than adequate for any potential network growth. Theoretically, there were 4,294,967,296 unique addresses available by using 32-bit addressing, and even discounting the reserved ranges, there are still more than 3 billion possible addresses. At the time, that was enough addresses to provide an address for every person on the planet, including children.

Unfortunately, the designers of the IPv4 addressing scheme dramatically underestimated the explosive growth of the Internet and the popularity of TCP/IP in business and home networks. There are no longer enough addresses to go around. As a result, a new addressing scheme is being developed. IPv6 is an addressing scheme that allows for a dramatically larger pool of addresses, but it is enjoying very limited deployment on the Internet today. This is in large part due to the use of NAT. (For more information on NAT, see RFC 3022, "Traditional IP Network Address Translator [Traditional NAT].")

NAT is a standard that allows you to use one set of IP addresses on your internal LAN and a second set of IP addresses for the Internet connection. There is a device (usually a router or firewall) between the two connections, and it provides NAT services and manages the translation of internal addresses to external addresses. This allows companies to use large numbers of unregistered internal addresses while only needing a fraction of that number of addresses on the Internet, thus conserving the addresses.

There are two main types of NAT:

- **Static NAT**—Static NAT maps an unregistered IP address on a private network to a registered IP address on a public network, on a one-to-one basis. Static NAT is typically used when the translated device needs to be accessible from the public network. For example, a Web server on your private network might have the unregistered address 10.100.100.100 but be using the NAT address 12.2.2.123. A user trying to connect to that Web site can enter 12.2.2.123, and the router or firewall at the other end translates that address to 10.10.10.10 when the packet reaches it, allowing the remote user to access the Web site.
- **Dynamic NAT**—Dynamic NAT maps an unregistered IP address to a registered IP address from a group of registered IP addresses. Dynamic NAT is most commonly used when large pools of systems on the internal network need to access the Internet and don't have a requirement for a static address. When a workstation initiates a connection to the public network, its unregistered address is translated to the next available registered address. You commonly see this used in corporate networks and in some ISP networks (with DSL and cable modem connections, for example).

NOTE

Which NAT Will You Encounter? What sort of NAT might you run into in the corporate world? The answer is both. Dynamic NAT is most common, as it allows for better utilization of registered addresses, but static NAT is used in circumstances in which the translated address must remain the same—as in for a Web server, for example.

The most critical thing to remember about NAT is that due to limitations in the first version of the IPSec standard, IPSec cannot traverse a translated network. IPSec requires that both the VPN client and the VPN server have static, untranslated addresses on the public network for connection to occur. What this means from a practical perspective is that if you are trying to connect and there is NAT in the network architecture anywhere, you need the latest Microsoft IPSec client to connect successfully.

Demand-Dial Routing

In this chapter, we have already discussed in detail the most common method for connecting two private networks: VPN. Now we need to discuss the use of demand-dial routing connection for connecting private networks.

A demand-dial network consists of a calling router and an answering router. When you're using Windows Server 2003, both the calling and answering routers must have RRAS installed. You typically see demand-dial routing used in two instances:

- **Redundant network links**—Demand-dial routing is a good solution for providing redundant network links. In the event that a primary, always-connected network connection is unavailable, a Windows Server 2003 server with demand-dial routing can initiate a backup dial connection until the primary connection is available again.
- **Small office connections**—Demand-dial routing is also used in small office environments or remote offices where the expense of maintaining a constant connection is too high. A demand-dial connection can be established when access to external network resources is needed, and then the connection can be terminated when the connection is no longer needed.

NOTE

Demand-Dial Routing Is Not Just for Modems Anymore Although this service is still called demand-dial, it can also refer to connections made by using a VPN connection across a public network. This is becoming more common as Internet access becomes more ubiquitous. Windows Server 2003 also introduced support for PPP over Ethernet (PPPoE) connections. PPPoE is based on PPP and Ethernet and provides a specification for connecting hosts on an Ethernet network to the Internet through a broadband medium (DSL, cable modem, or wireless). PPPoE combines Ethernet's ability to support multiple hosts on a LAN with PPP's serial connection capabilities.

To enable demand-dial routing on an existing Windows Server 2003 server, complete Step by Step 6.13.

NOTE

Modem Required You will need to have a modem installed in your server to complete Step by Step 6.13.

STEP BY STEP

6.13 Enabling Demand-Dial Routing on a Windows Server 2003 Server

1. Log on to Windows Server 2003 by using the Administrator account or another account that has administrator privileges.
2. Open the Routing and Remote Access console by selecting Start, Administrative Tools, Routing and Remote Access.

3. Right-click Network Interfaces within the console tree and select New Demand-Dial Interface from the context menu. The Demand-Dial Interface Wizard appears.
4. Click Next to proceed. The Interface Name dialog box of the wizard appears.
5. In the Interface Name field, type a name for the connection interface. Click Next to continue. The Connection Type dialog box of the wizard appears.
6. In the Connection Type dialog box, select Connect Using a Modem, ISDN Adapter, or Other Physical Device and then click Next to continue. The Select a Device dialog box of the wizard appears.
7. Select the physical device you want to use and click Next. The Phone Number dialog box of the wizard appears.
8. Enter the phone number of the answering router in the space provided. Click Next to continue. The Protocols and Security dialog box of the wizard appears.
9. In the Protocols and Security dialog box, you can select the protocols you want to route over this connection. Select Route IP Packets on This Interface and Add a User Account So a Remote Router Can Dial In. You should avoid enabling the sending of a plaintext password whenever possible, due to the security ramifications associated with unencrypted passwords. Click Next to continue. The Static Routes for Remote Networks dialog box of the wizard appears.
10. Click Add to open the Static Route dialog box. Enter the destination, the network mask, and the metric and then click OK to add the new route. Click Next to continue. The Dial In Credentials dialog box of the wizard appears.
11. As a result of selecting the Add a User Account So a Remote Router Can Dial In option in step 9, you need to create a user ID and password for the remote router to authenticate with when it dials in. In the Dial In Credentials dialog box, enter a username and password and then click Next to continue. The Dial Out Credentials dialog box of the wizard appears.
12. Enter the security credential information that will allow you to connect to the answering router, including the username, domain, and password. Click Next to continue. The Completing the Demand-Dial Interface Wizard dialog box appears.
13. Click Finish to return to the Routing and Remote Access console. You should see the new demand-dial interface in the right pane of the Routing and Remote Access console when Network Interfaces is selected in the left pane.

When a calling router receives a packet over the network, the router determines the best route to use to forward the packet. If the route chosen is a demand-dial route, a connection is initiated with the other side. A connection can be initiated over either a physical connection such as an analog or ISDN line or over a logical connection known as a *tunnel*. Such tunnels are established by using either PPTP or L2TP.

After the demand-dial router determines that a connection needs to be established, the demand-dial router determines whether a connection currently exists. If the status is connected, the packet is forwarded to the destination host. If no connection is in place, the calling router must establish a connection.

To establish a connection from the calling router to the answering router, the calling router checks the dial-out hours and demand-dial filters configured on the interface. If dial-out hours or demand-dial filters prohibit establishing a connection, the connection attempt fails, and the host that originated the packets is notified that the destination host is unreachable. If, after the router checks, the connection is able to proceed, the router retrieves the configuration of the demand-dial interface and then, based on the configuration, a connection is established with the answering router. The Windows Server 2003 demand-dial router supports several types of connections, including the following:

- **Modem or ISDN**—With this type of configuration, the configured phone number is dialed.
- **VPN**—With this type of configuration, the configured host or IP address is used to establish either a PPTP or IP Security (IPSec) connection.
- **Direct serial or direct parallel port**—With this type of configuration, a direct connection is made between the calling router and the answering router over the serial port or parallel port. (This is almost never used outside a lab/test environment.)

After a connection has been made, it is necessary for the calling router to negotiate a PPP connection with the answering router. Part of the negotiation is to send the credentials of the calling router. The answering router then checks the credentials against a local accounts database and/or remote policies or forwards the connection attributes to a RADIUS server, where the credentials are checked.

In addition to authenticating the users' credentials, PPP negotiates parameters for the connection, such as the IP addresses of both routers, the name servers to be used, and any static routes that may have been put in place by the user.

Finally, the answering router looks up the user initiating the connection to find a matching interface. If a matching demand-dial interface is located, the connection state is changed to a connected state, and the routing connection is established. If a matching interface is not found, the calling entity is identified as a remote access client computer, and a routing connection is not established.

Types of Demand-Dial Connections

Two types of connections are available with demand-dial routing: on-demand connections and persistent connections.

An on-demand connection is initiated when a packet is received by the calling router. When the calling router receives information for the answering router, it initiates the connection. After the information has been transmitted to the answering router and the connection has remained idle for a period of time, the connection is dropped. You can configure the demand-dial timeout on the Options tab of the demand-dial interface Properties dialog box.

In a demand-dial environment, one router can be configured to initiate the connection, or both routers can be configured to initiate connections. Having only one router configured to initiate the connection is known as a *one-way connection*. Having both routers configured to initiate connections is known as a *two-way connection*.

In a one-way initiated connection, the calling router is configured with a username that is used to connect to the answering router. Associated with this user account are static routes that define which packets are to be routed to the other side. When the connection is initiated and the username is authenticated by the answering router, the static routes associated with the username are added to the routing table of the answering router.

A two-way initiated connection is very similar to a one-way initiated connection, except that both routers must be configured with the necessary information to allow each to establish the connection. In addition, the calling and answering routers must both be configured.

In both a one-way initiated connection and a two-way initiated connection, the router initiating the call must be configured with a username that matches the username on a demand-dial interface on the answering router.

An on-demand connection can introduce problems for time-sensitive applications because the application must be able to tolerate a delay while the calling router initiates the connection with the answering router and the static routes configured on both routers are propagated throughout the internetworks on both sides. The length of this delay varies, depending on the type of physical or logical connection being established.

With a persistent connection, there is no delay while the calling router initiates a connection with the answering router. The connection is available on a permanent basis. This type of connection is generally found in WAN environments where the connection is over a leased line, X.25 connection, or ISDN connection. With a persistent connection, the calling router can be configured to reestablish the connection automatically if the connection is lost.

The choice of connection provides insight into the type of routing that should be configured over the connection. If the connection is persistent, one of the dynamic routing protocols, such as RIP or OSPF, may be used with special configuration to take into consideration the use of a demand-dial connection.

In an on-demand connection scenario, the use of a dynamic routing protocol might not be the most appropriate choice. Dynamic protocols need to periodically exchange information between routers to keep their routing tables up-to-date. This is a function of how dynamic routing protocols work. The requirement to periodically exchange information with other routers in the environment can cause a connection to be made each time the update process takes place, or in some cases, it can keep the connection up permanently, depending on how often the update process takes place. This may not be what is desired in an environment where you are trying to minimize costs.

In an on-demand connection, the preferred way of enabling routing is to use either static routes or autostatic updates. Step by Step 6.12 looked at using the static routes method, and the following section describes autostatic updates. When you're configuring static routes, you need to consider using a default route (0.0.0.0). The default route is used to specify what should be done with network traffic when none of the existing routes provide a path for it. If no route exists, the router forwards the traffic through the default route. If all the IP traffic needs to traverse the demand-dial connection, a default route should be the only route that needs to be configured. For more information on static routes, see Chapter 7, "Implementing, Managing, and Troubleshooting Routing."

Autostatic Updates

An *autostatic update* is a request from a router for all known routes or services from the router on the other side of the connection. After the request is received, the router adds the requested routes to its routing table. An autostatic update is a one-time, one-way exchange of routing information. Autostatic updates do not occur automatically on initiation of a demand-dial connection. Rather, the autostatic update must be manually initiated, or a schedule must be put in place to update routes. After the routes have been sent, the two routers do not exchange updates of routing information unless a manual request to update is made or a scheduled request occurs, depending on how autostatic updates are configured within the environment. Autostatic updates are useful for environments where there are too many routes for static routing to be manageable.

Challenge

You are the network administrator for NR Widgets, Inc., a multinational conglomerate, and you are based in the conglomerate's corporate headquarters. NR Widgets has a mobile population of about 200 people who need access to the network for submitting expense reports.

About 100 of the users live and work within your local area code, and the rest are scattered throughout the country. Your management does not want to pay for long-distance calls for remote access.

Your mobile users consist of three groups. The first group is the highly technical telecommuters, who need access to everything. They are also very security conscious and want to make sure their information is as secure as possible. The second group is the local users who need access but are not too concerned about the security of the connection. The third group consists of about 35 users who work from home and have high-speed Internet connections.

(continues)

(continued)

Your manager has tasked you to accomplish the following goals:

- You must ensure that each group has access to the network.
- You must ensure that each group of users has the information security it needs.
- You must ensure that long-distance or toll-free numbers are not used.

Through your discussions with the key stakeholders in this project, you've determined the following additional information:

- The management of your company is reluctant to make a major investment in toll charges for a dial-based remote access solution.
- Your company has three main populations of users, each with different remote access requirements.
- Each team needs to have a particular level of security.

Your task is to implement the required remote access solution for NR Widgets, Inc.

Try to complete this exercise on your own, listing your conclusions on a sheet of paper. After you have completed the exercise, compare your results to those given here.

Answers

As you have discovered in this chapter, you can meet the requirements of this case by configuring Windows Server 2003 RRAS. However, by now, you probably realize that it is a bit more complicated than just running the Routing and Remote Access Server Setup Wizard. First, you need to take a close look at each population of users. The technical telecommuters, who have access to confidential information, need to have a configuration that leverages the robust security and encryption mechanisms of Windows Server 2003 RRAS. You might need their profile configured for dial-back, and you might also need to use smart cards for authentication.

You probably need to limit the access of the second group of users so that these users can't get sensitive information on the network because these users are using a less secure, more user-friendly authentication policy.

Finally, although it is easy to configure a network—for example, an Internet-based VPN—you still need to make decisions. You need to examine the amount of bandwidth you have to the Internet to support these users. You need to consider where the server is placed. Should it be behind a firewall or directly on the Internet? You need to consider which VPN protocol is best suited for the environment. You might even find that your remote users who are not in the local area code want to utilize a local ISP in conjunction with the VPN solution, allowing you to further save on toll charges. All this is very dependent on the environment and the circumstances and requires effective planning. Here's what you need:

- You need to have one server that is running Windows Server 2003 server and RRAS.
- The server needs to have modems installed and configured for dial-in users.
- Users who do not have the ability to dial locally to the server need to leverage the Windows Server 2003 VPN service; therefore, the server needs an Internet connection.
- The server needs remote access profiles to control the session security for each group.

Troubleshooting User Access to Remote Access Services

You've got your Windows Server 2003 server installed and configured, and it is supporting all your remote users as a remote access server and as a VPN server. The clients are installed, and you are ready for a long vacation. Don't book that flight just yet, though. What are you going to do when something breaks? To further complicate things, you are now dealing with a remote user or location, and potentially Internet connection issues, firewall conflicts, misconfigured workstations, and a number of other issues that you will need to identify and correct.

To make matters worse, because your users are now scattered around the country or even around the world, troubleshooting their situations can be a real problem—you can't walk to their desks to see what's going on. And if the CFO is in Europe, you might find yourself troubleshooting issues at some pretty odd hours, due to the time difference. The CFO gets up in the morning and wants to check his email. It's breakfast time, and he's planning on eating and catching up on mail. Of course it's 2:00 a.m. at your house, but you might get a call when the CFO can't connect to the VPN server. To help you work your way through these types of issues, the rest of this chapter discusses troubleshooting remote access problems.

Troubleshooting 101

One of the challenges that network and server administrators face is dealing with interruptions in service. This is a particularly large issue for administrators who are responsible for remote access or VPN-related problems. When a server is down, it is relatively easy to start troubleshooting it; it is almost always located in one of the company's offices. But how do you deal with a problem when it's the company CEO sitting in a hotel room in Hong Kong and she needs to get her email now? There are two generally accepted troubleshooting methods used by new administrators during their first encounter with a remote access outage: They either panic or they start trying things until the problem goes away. Neither of these is a recommended strategy for addressing problems in general, and they can be particularly problematic when dealing with remote access issues.

Whenever you run into a problem, you need to use a structured approach to troubleshooting. There are several benefits to doing so. First, if you have a plan, you generally won't panic. You know what to do. Second, a consistent approach allows you to correct problems more efficiently than just trying things until the problem is corrected. Finally, if you use a consistent approach and document your results, you will be able correct a problem that recurs by using a known solution. In fact, if your documentation is good, someone else will be able to apply your solution if the problem crops up again. This is very useful if you are on vacation; the last thing you want to be working on during Mardi Gras in New Orleans is the server-down situation at the office, especially if it's the same problem you found and fixed three months ago.

Now wouldn't it be nice if this book included the perfect troubleshooting process, so all you would need to do is follow a flowchart, and by the time you got to the end of the chart, the problem would be solved? If it were that easy, companies wouldn't need IT departments—we would all be replaced by the sales team. This book provides a generic troubleshooting methodology. You are encouraged to use the process described here, change it to fit your needs/ troubleshooting style, or even develop your own. The point is not to use one specific method, but to make sure you use a consistent process that works for you in your environment.

Here is a generic process that you can use as a basis for a troubleshooting process:

1. **Identify the symptoms**—You can't fix a problem until you are sure what it is. Far too often you will hear things like "The Internet is down" or "Mail is down." What exactly does that mean? "The Internet is down" might mean that people can get to Web sites but not FTP. Or people might be able to get to some Web sites but not others. Or one person may not be able to get to her favorite quilting Web site. Until you have specific symptoms, you cannot correct a problem.

2. **Determine the problem scope**—How big is this problem? Is it 1 user, 100 users, or the entire company? Is it the secretary's cube, the entire floor, or the entire building? Knowing how big the problem is helps you get a handle on the urgency of the issue, and it gives you valuable clues about what the problem might be. If the sixth floor is down, you might look at the network infrastructure that supports that floor. In many cases, "the Internet is down" really means your boss can't get to her stock ticker. Although that may be an important issue, you can probably finish your lunch before you run to the boss's office.

3. **Look for changes**—A remarkably large number of problems in a complex computing environment are related to changes. If a single user is having a problem, did he install a cool new game that he received in an email message from his buddy? If you just lost access to the Internet, did anyone upgrade router code or install a new firewall rule? The toughest part about troubleshooting a change-related problem is identifying what changed. Unfortunately, identifying who made the change can be an even bigger challenge.

4. **Try the most likely solution**—When you have completed your information gathering, try the solution you think is the most likely.

5. **Determine whether the problem is fixed**—You've tried to fix the problem. Did it work? If not, repeat Step 4 with the next most-likely fix. Repeat until the problem is solved.

6. **See if you broke anything else**—This is a critical step because changes to the environment, even if it's change that occurs when you are trying to fix something, can have unpredictable side effects. You need to look for them. The last thing you want to find out as you are headed home for the day is that the fix you put in for Sales at lunch

broke Accounting—you could be in for a long night. Always test your solutions after you implement them.

7. **Document it**—Documenting your solution is probably the most important part of the troubleshooting process. In six months, when you see the same problem, you don't want to rely on memory to come up with the solution again. Make sure you have something to which to refer.

Diagnosing and Resolving Problems Related to Remote Access VPNs

Objective:

Troubleshoot user access to remote access services.

- Diagnose and resolve issues related to remote access VPNs.

Remote access VPN problems typically fall into the following categories:

- Unable to connect to the VPN server
- Unable to authenticate to the VPN server

Unable to Connect to the VPN Server

When troubleshooting the inability of a remote user to connect to the VPN server, you should start at the network layer. Assuming that the remote user is connecting to the VPN server across the Internet (the most common architecture), you can try the following:

1. Determine whether this is a problem with one user or many users. If it's a problem with a single user, the problem is most likely on that person's end. If it's a problem with a single user, proceed through this list. If it's a problem with many users, you should start looking at the server side. Is the server up? Is the Internet connection up?

2. Verify that the remote user has Internet access. You can have the remote user test this by having her connect to an Internet Web site such as www.microsoft.com. If she cannot access a generic Web site, you need to look further into the user's local network connection.

3. If the user can access an Internet Web site, see if she can access the Internet connection that the VPN server is on. The user should try to access a Web site on the same segment (if there is one) or by using IP troubleshooting tools such as `ping` and `tracert`. If the user cannot access devices on the VPN server's Internet connection, you should look further into problems on the VPN server Internet connection.

4. If the connectivity is working but the tunnel still won't come up, has the user successfully connected before? If she has, see if anything has changed with the user's connection or her system. Has she upgraded a modem, installed a firewall, or made any changes that could prevent a VPN connection from being established? Is she connecting from her usual Internet connection, or is she traveling? If there have been no changes, check with the user's ISP to ensure that there haven't been any changes on the ISP's network that could affect the VPN connection. If the user has never connected successfully in the past, you should review her local network configuration; a firewall might be preventing the connection from working. When in doubt, you should have the user remove any extraneous network components (firewall, wireless routers, and so on) and connect as directly as possible. You should try to eliminate as many variables as possible.
5. If the user is using NAT on the network connection, make sure that the VPN is using PPTP, or if PPTP is not available, make sure the NAT-compatible VPN client is being used.
6. If Steps 1–5 don't identify the cause of the problem, you might need to have the user use a modem and dial in by using a direct ISP connection. If the VPN server still can't be reached, you might need to reinstall the VPN client or potentially re-image the client to ensure that the configuration is correct.

Unable to Authenticate to the VPN Server

If the remote user can contact the VPN server but cannot authenticate, you can try the following:

1. Determine whether this is a single-user problem or whether it affects a larger population of users. If it affects more that one user, check to make sure Windows Server 2003 RRAS is running and that the authentication infrastructure (Active Directory, IAS, or a third-party RADIUS server) is functioning correctly. For a single-user issue, continue with the following steps. If it's a problem with many users, you should start looking at the server side.
2. Ensure that the user account, domain name, and password are correct. Sometimes a client connection problem can be as simple as a stuck Caps Lock key.
3. Ensure that the user account of the VPN client is not locked out, expired, or disabled.
4. Ensure that the user account has permission to connect by using remote access.
5. Verify that there are enough PPTP or L2TP ports enabled. You can enable more ports if needed or check to ensure that the ports are not hung or otherwise unavailable.
6. Ensure that the connection components (client, server, and remote access policy) use at least one common authentication method.

7. Ensure that the client and remote access policy use at least one common encryption method.
8. Ensure that the client and server are using a common tunneling protocol.
9. If you are using an L2TP/IPSec VPN, ensure that the certificate configuration is correct. The client must have a valid machine certificate, and the CA must be available to authenticate the validity of the certificate.
10. When you are using a remote access policy, you can try setting the policy to use no authentication. Just be sure to reenable it when you have completed your troubleshooting.

EXAM ALERT

Common Encryption Methods One of the most common problems in real-world authentication troubleshooting is not having the client and remote access policy share a common encryption method. Because this is something that administrators see fairly often, you might also see this on the exam.

If you get through this list and are still unable to identify the problem, it is probably time to have the user bring her computer by the office (or mail it in) so that you can take a closer look at the configuration and do some more intensive testing.

Diagnosing and Resolving Problems Related to Establishing a Remote Access Connection

Objective:

Troubleshoot user access to remote access services.

- Diagnose and resolve issues related to establishing a remote access connection.

There is a lot of overlap in the problems with remote access connections and the problems with remote access VPN connections, due to the fact that they share many of the same components.

Remote access connection problems typically fall into the following categories:

- Unable to connect to the remote access server
- Unable to authenticate to the remote access server

Unable to Connect to the Remote Access Server

When troubleshooting the inability of a remote user to connect to the remote access server, start with the phone lines. Then you can try these steps:

1. Determine whether this is a problem with one user or many users. If it's a problem with a single user, the problem is most likely on that person's end. If it's a problem with a single user, proceed through this list. If it's a problem with many users, you should start looking at the server side. Is the server up? Is the Internet connection up?
2. Verify that the remote user has the correct phone number. This is a quick check and saves you some embarrassment. You don't want to spend a lot of time troubleshooting the problem, only to find out the user had the wrong area code set.
3. Ensure that there is a dial tone. Have the user verify that he gets a dial tone when he tries to connect. You might need to have him turn up the modem volume to verify this. If the user has a dial tone, have him try configuring the modem to dial a phone line, and see if the phone rings successfully. If it does, you know the user's line is working, and you probably need to look elsewhere for the cause of the problem.
4. If the user can get a dial tone and successfully dial a phone number, have him listen to the modem dialing. Does it just ring and ring? Get a busy signal? Does the user get a modem tone, but the modems are unable to negotiate a connection?
5. If the connectivity is working, but the connection still won't come up, has the user successfully connected before? If he has, see if anything has changed with his connection or his system. Has the user upgraded a modem, installed a firewall, or made any changes that could prevent a connection from being established? Is he connecting from his usual phone line, or is he traveling? If he has never connected successfully in the past, you should review the configuration of his remote access client.
6. If Steps 1–5 don't identify the cause of the problem, you might need to reinstall the dial connection or potentially re-image the client to ensure that the configuration is correct.

Unable to Authenticate to the Remote Access Server

If the remote user can connect to the modem but cannot authenticate to the remote access server, you can try the following:

1. Determine whether this is a single-user problem or whether it affects a larger population of users. If it affects more that one user, check to make sure Windows Server 2003 RRAS is running and that the authentication infrastructure (Active Directory, IAS, or a third-party RADIUS server) is functioning correctly. For a single-user issue, continue with the following steps. If it's a problem with many users, you should start looking at the server side.

2. Ensure that the user account, domain name, and password are correct. Sometimes a client connection problem can be as simple as a stuck Caps Lock key.
3. Ensure that the user account is not locked out, expired, or disabled.
4. Ensure that the user account has permission to connect by using remote access.
5. Verify that there are enough modem ports. You can add additional modems if needed or check to ensure that the ports are not hung or otherwise unavailable.
6. Ensure that the connection components (client, server, and remote access policy) use at least one common authentication method.
7. Ensure that the client and remote access policy use at least one common encryption strength.
8. Ensure that the policies are ordered as you expect, thus ensuring they are processing and allowing or denying connections as you expect.

If you get through this list and are still unable to identify the problem, it is probably time to have the user bring his computer by the office (or mail it in) so that you can take a closer look at the configuration and do some more intensive testing.

Diagnosing and Resolving Problems with User Access to Resources Beyond the Remote Access Server

Objective:

Troubleshoot user access to remote access services.

- Diagnose and resolve user access to resources beyond the remote access server.

On some occasions, you might find that a user can connect to the Windows Server 2003 remote access server but is unable to access resources on the internal network. This is generally due to one of the following issues:

- The protocol the client is using is not enabled for routing. In this case, you should verify the protocol at both ends to ensure that it is configured appropriately.
- Clients are not allowed to access the entire network.
- If the server is using static IP routing, the network/resources that the user is trying to connect to are not in the routing table. If the routes are not present, remote access VPN clients cannot access locations on the intranet.

- The internal network may not have a route back to the remote access server client addresses. In this case, you should verify that the network the user is trying to access has a route back to the client addresses.
- There might be packet filters that are interfering with the access. You should verify that there are no packet filters on the profile properties of the remote access policy that correspond to the connection the client is using to connect.

You will find that these types of issues generally affect groups of users because the problem is typically on the intranet side of the connection. Looking for changes is especially important when you're troubleshooting these types of issues.

Troubleshooting RRAS Routing

We have looked at some of the problems that affect a remote access connection. You might encounter similar problems with RRAS routing, either with demand-dial routing or router-to-router VPNs. There are also some unique issues to be aware of, as described in the following sections.

Troubleshooting Demand-Dial Routing

Objective:

Troubleshoot Routing and Remote Access routing.

- Troubleshoot demand-dial routing.

When you experience a demand-dial routing problem, you should check the following for possible sources of the problem:

- Ensure that the transport medium (modem, ISDN, and so on) is working correctly. It's important that you don't overlook the physical issues. A loose wire or bad modem can prevent a connection from working.
- Ensure that RRAS is running on both the local and remote routers.
- Ensure that the demand-dial interface on each router is enabled.
- Ensure that demand-dial routing is enabled on both routers.
- Make sure there is an available port on each of the involved routers.
- Ensure that the static routes are configured appropriately. Also check to make sure the static route has the Use This Route to Initiate Demand-Dial Connections option enabled.

- Ensure that the dial-out hours are not preventing the connection. Something as simple as having the hours set to p.m. instead of a.m. can cause serious connectivity problems.
- Check when the demand-dial filters on both routers. You might be accidentally blocking the connection because of the filters.
- Ensure that the calling router, the answering router, and the applicable remote access policy are using at least one common authentication method.
- Ensure that the calling router, the answering router, and the applicable remote access policy are using at least one common encryption method.
- Check the credentials on both routers. The username, password, and domain information should be verified and must match on both routers. You should also make sure that the account is not disabled or locked.
- Ensure that there is an applicable remote access policy that allows the connection.
- Make sure the authentication infrastructure (Active Directory, IAS, or a third-party RADIUS server) is functioning correctly.

Troubleshooting Router-to-Router VPNs

Objective:

Troubleshoot Routing and Remote Access routing.

- Troubleshoot router-to-router VPNs.

There are some commonalities between troubleshooting remote access VPNs and troubleshooting demand-dial routing. There are a large number of overlapping functions with those services. When troubleshooting router-to-router problems, you should consider the following:

- Ensure that the transport medium is working correctly. If the two routers cannot reach each other, they cannot connect. This troubleshooting can be done with the `ping` command or the `tracert` command.
- Ensure that RRAS is running on both the local and remote routers.
- Ensure that the user account for the connection is not locked out, expired, or disabled.
- Ensure that the VPN ports are enabled for inbound and outbound demand-dial routing connections.
- Verify that there are enough VPN ports. You can add additional modems if needed or check to ensure that the ports are not hung or otherwise unavailable.

- Ensure that the routers and remote access policy use at least one common authentication method.
- Ensure that the routers and remote access policy use at least one common encryption strength.
- Ensure that the routers are using a common tunneling protocol.
- Ensure that the VPN connection has the appropriate permissions through dial-in properties of the user account and remote access policies.
- Ensure that there are no conflicts between the remote access profiles on the calling and answering routers.
- Ensure that the authentication infrastructure (Active Directory, IAS, or a third-party RADIUS server) is functioning correctly.

Troubleshooting Tools

A variety of tools can also be used to troubleshoot remote access connections, including `ping`, `tracert`, `pathping`, `ipconfig`, Event Viewer, Network Monitor, the `netsh` command, and Performance console. You will recognize these tools from other chapters because troubleshooting remote access can be very similar to troubleshooting problems on a network.

ping

The `ping` command is practically as old as TCP/IP networking itself. You can use the `ping` command to test basic network connectivity between two computers, over local and remote networks. The basic syntax of the `ping` command is `ping` *`computerIP`*. This command causes Windows to send four special Internet Control Message Protocol (ICMP) packets to the remote computer, and those packets are then returned to the local computer. For more information on the `ping` command, see Chapter 1, "Configuring and Troubleshooting TCP/IP Addressing."

tracert

The `tracert` (short for *trace route*) command traces the route between two hosts by using ICMP echo packets to report back at every hop between the hosts. The `tracert` command provides a lot of useful information, including the IP address of every router connection it passes through and, in many cases, the name of the router (depending on the use of DNS for router names). The `tracert` command also reports the round-trip time (in milliseconds) for the packet to travel from the source host to each router and back. This information can tell you a lot about where network congestion or breaks are. For more information on the `tracert` command, see Chapter 9, "Maintaining and Troubleshooting a Network Infrastructure."

pathping

The pathping command acts as the equivalent of the tracert command by allowing you to identify which routers are in the path the packets are taking. It also acts as the equivalent of the ping command by sending ping requests to all the routers over a specified time period and then computing statistics based on the packets returned from each router. pathping displays the amount of packet loss at each router or link, allowing you to determine which routers and links (subnets) might be causes of connectivity troubles. For more information on the pathping command see Chapter 7.

ipconfig

The ipconfig command can be used to quickly determine the settings that have been configured for the network adapters in computers. In addition, you can use this command to release and renew DHCP-assigned IP addresses and flush the local DNS cache. For more information on the ipconfig command, see Chapter 1.

Event Viewer

The Event Viewer is used to view system, application, security, and a variety of other event logs, allowing you to gather information about hardware, software, and system problems. RRAS logs information about routing, connections, and errors to the system log in Windows Server 2003. This is a good place to look for specific errors when troubleshooting RRAS problems.

Network Monitor

Network Monitor is a tool you can use to capture network traffic. It can be used to diagnose problems when two computers do not communicate with one another or when a computer has trouble functioning in a network environment. For instance, a computer may have problems resolving names or finding a path to another computer (that is, it might be having routing problems).

Network Monitor can be configured to capture network traffic in several ways. It can be configured to capture all network traffic that it receives, to respond to events on the network, or to monitor only a subset of the traffic (for instance, a particular protocol, such as HTTP traffic only). After the network data has been captured, Network Monitor analyzes the data and translates it into its logical frame structure to make the protocol information readable to the person capturing the information.

netsh

netsh is a command-line and scripting utility for networking components that can be used with local or remote computers. The netsh utility can also be used to save a configuration script that can be used for configuring other servers. In the context of troubleshooting, the `netsh` command can be used to gather additional information about RAS or VPN connections. Due to the complexity of the tool, the specific commands are beyond the scope of this book, but you should be aware that the tool exists. If you are interested in the full information on the tool, search www.microsoft.com for the string "Netsh commands for remote access"; note that the the TechNet page changes location frequently.

Performance Console

The Performance console can provide a number of types of information. It is generally the best tool for monitoring specifics about Windows Server 2003 services. The Performance console offers the following counters for the RAS object:

- **Alignment Errors**—This counter helps you determine whether the size of the packet received is different from the size expected.
- **Buffer Overrun Errors**—This counter helps you determine whether the software is unable to handle the rate at which data is being received.
- **Bytes Received**—This counter helps you determine the total number of bytes received by the service.
- **Bytes Received/Sec**—This counter helps you determine the number of bytes received by the service in a second.
- **Bytes Transmitted**—This counter helps you determine the total number of bytes transmitted by the service.
- **Bytes Transmitted/Sec**—This counter helps you determine the number of bytes transmitted by the service in a second.
- **CRC Errors**—This counter helps you determine whether a frame received contains erroneous data and the packet did not pass the cyclic redundancy check (CRC).
- **Frames Received**—This counter helps you determine the total number of frames received by the service.
- **Frames Received/Sec**—This counter helps you determine the number of frames received by the service per second.
- **Frames Transmitted**—This counter helps you determine the total number of frames transmitted by the service.
- **Frames Transmitted/Sec**—This counter helps you determine the number of frames transmitted by the service per second.
- **Percent Compression In**—This counter tells how well inbound traffic is being compressed.

- **Percent Compression Out**—This counter tells how well outbound traffic is being compressed.
- **Errors—Serial Overrun Errors, Timeout Errors, Total Errors, and Total Errors/Sec**—These objects handle all the error information for RRAS.

We will look at configuring the Performance console in an exercise at the end of this chapter.

NOTE

What Are We Measuring—Port Level or Aggregate? The Performance console allows you to monitor counters on either a port–by–port level or an aggregate (entire server) level. You can select RAS Ports to look at a single port or RAS Total to see the stats for the entire server.

Advanced Network Access Configuration: The Network Access Quarantine Control

As you have seen earlier in this chapter, the normal remote access connections with which you have worked have validated only the credentials of the user. However, with the ever-growing threat to computer networks from viruses, spyware, and other unwanted applications, it only makes sense that a truly secure network would be one that controls which computers can remotely connect to it as well. Once a user has made a remote access connection to your network with his or her computer, that computer becomes part of the network (if only temporarily) and thus can spread unwanted malware.

EXAM ALERT

Network Access Quarantine Control This is an advanced topic and not likely to be found on your 70-291 exam, as evidenced by its omission from the exam objectives. It's anticipated that you will likely not have the required environment to implement Network Access Quarantine Control; thus, we will not be examining it in great enough detail in this book to warrant Step by Step exercises. Our coverage here will be limited to an introduction so that you'll at least be familiar with what it does and how it works.

Network Access Quarantine Control, a new feature introduced with Windows Server 2003, is a means to prevent users who possess valid credentials, but who are using computers that do not meet the required corporate configuration, from making remote access connections. As an example, you might not necessarily want a valid user to connect with an incorrectly configured computer that is missing one of the following:

- A required service pack
- A required security update
- Up-to-date, and active, antivirus software
- A software firewall (such as the Windows Firewall) that is operational on the network adapter

If all of your company's computers are internal and never leave the building, your job would be easier and you would not need remote access or Network Access Quarantine Control. However, it is more common now than ever for valid network users to connect back to the corporate network from any number of locations, such as from home, from a hotel room via a portable computer, or even from an Internet café. To combat the out-of-control problem that keeping all of these computers up to corporate specifications would be, the Network Access Quarantine Control delays remote access by your users to your corporate network until the configuration of the computer they are using has been examined and approved. A special script is provided by an administrator to be used in this examination.

When Network Access Quarantine Control is enabled and configured, a remote access user who successfully authenticates is not just dumped onto the network as he normally would be. Instead, after the user has been authenticated, the computer is granted IP address (as it normally would be) and then the connection is placed into a quarantine, in which network access is substantially limited. The script that was provided for Network Access Quarantine Control is then run on the remote computer to check its configuration. If the script determines that the remote computer is compliant with the policies in effect, then that computer is removed from the quarantine and is provided with normal remote access—as if Network Access Quarantine Control was not in effect. While the computer is in the quarantine, its network access can be restricted by using packet filters to control traffic to or from the computer. Additionally, a time limit can be configured for the quarantine such that the remote computer is automatically disconnected after a set amount of time. If the script determines that the remote computer is not compliant, the script then directs the user to an internal Web page that provides instructions on how to install the required items.

Although Network Access Quarantine Control does appear to be a security solution, it is not that in the most typical sense. While it will increase your overall network security, it does not replace all of the other security considerations you must give to your network. Network Access Quarantine Control was designed not to stop unauthorized users from making remote connections to your network, but instead to stop otherwise authorized users with non-compliant computers from making remote connections to your network.

To learn more about this advanced remote access topic, visit http://www.microsoft.com/technet/itsolutions/network/vpn/quarantine.mspx.

Chapter Summary

This chapter discusses all the key components of using Windows Server 2003 to implement and maintain a remote access solution. It first introduced you to Routing and Remote Access and then moved on to the configuration and management of RRAS for remote user access and secure network-to-network communications. Virtual Private Networks (VPNs) were discussed at length, including the three types of VPNs that Windows Server 2003 supports.

The chapter concludes with a discussion of troubleshooting remote access and demand-dial connections as well as a brief introduction to the newest feature of RRAS, the Network Access Quarantine Control.

Key Terms

- 3DES
- AH
- Authentication
- Autostatic update
- CA
- CHAP
- Demand-dial routing
- DES
- Encryption
- ESP
- IAS
- IKE
- IPSec
- ISAKMP/Oakley
- L2F
- Modem
- MS-CHAP
- MS-CHAPv2

- Multilink
- `netsh`
- PAP
- PPTP
- RADIUS
- Remote access policy
- Remote access profile
- RRAS
- SPAP
- VPN

Apply Your Knowledge

In this chapter, you have learned how remote access is configured and managed. In the following exercises, you will practice some of the concepts and methods discussed in this chapter.

Exercises

6.1 Creating a Remote Access Policy

In this exercise, you will use the Routing and Remote Access console to create a remote access policy. In this exercise, you will create a policy for users connecting by using PPP.

Estimated Time: 10 minutes

1. Open the Routing and Remote Access console.
2. Expand the application tree in the left pane by double-clicking the server. Right-click Remote Access Policy and select New Remote Access Policy.
3. Enter the name **`Exercise 1`** and click Next to continue.
4. Click Add to add a condition. Select the Framed Protocol attribute from the list of attributes and click Add.

5. Select PPP from the list of protocols. Click Add.
6. Click OK to add the condition. Click Next.
7. Select the Grant Remote Access Permission option. Click Next.
8. Click Finish to complete the creation of the profile.

6.2 Configuring an Idle Timeout for an RRAS Server

This exercise walks you through modifying a profile to add an idle timeout for a remote access policy.

Estimated Time: 15 minutes

1. Open the Routing and Remote Access console.
2. Right-click the Exercise 1 remote access policy that you created in Exercise 6.1. Select Properties from the context menu.
3. Click the Edit Profile button.
4. Go to the Dial-Constraints tab. Select the Disconnect If Idle option and set the timeout value to 30 minutes.
5. Click OK to commit the changes. Click OK to return to the Routing and Remote Access console.

6.3 Monitoring Routing and Remote Access by Using the Performance Console

This exercise walks you through adding a counter to the Performance console so that you can see how many errors the RRAS ports are experiencing.

Estimated Time: 15 minutes

1. Open the Performance console.
2. Under Performance, select System Monitor.
3. Click the + icon to add the counter.
4. Select the RAS Total performance object.
5. Select the Total Errors counter and click Add.
6. Click Close to complete the exercise.

Exam Questions

1. What feature of RRAS can be used to aggregate bandwidth across multiple modem connections?

   ❍ **A.** Multinet

   ❍ **B.** Multilink

   ❍ **C.** X.25

   ❍ **D.** VPN

2. You are the systems administrator for Phil's Phill-up Stations, a chain of gas stations. As part of the network, you maintain a Windows Server 2003 RRAS server to provide remote access services as part of a VPN. What VPN protocols will the server support? (Choose three.)

   ❍ **A.** PPTP

   ❍ **B.** IPSec

   ❍ **C.** PPP

   ❍ **D.** EAP

   ❍ **E.** L2TP

3. You are the systems administrator for Little Faith Enterprises Meat Packing. As part of the troubleshooting of a support problem, you need to check to see whether a user is connected to the RRAS server. How can you do this?

   ❍ **A.** Open Performance Manager, click the Add Counter icon, select the RAS object, choose the Connected Users counter, click OK, and check the resulting statistic.

   ❍ **B.** Open the Performance console, click the Add Counter icon, select the RAS object, choose the Connected Users counter, click OK, and check the resulting statistic.

   ❍ **C.** Open the Routing and Remote Access console, right-click the RAS server, choose Connected Users, and check for the user in the Connected Users dialog box.

   ❍ **D.** Open the Routing and Remote Access console, and under the server in the tree view, select Remote Access Clients. Check for the user in the Remote Access Clients list.

4. You need to configure strong authentication for a Windows Server 2003 RRAS server. Which protocols should you use? (Choose three.)

   ❍ **A.** IPSec

   ❍ **B.** PAP

   ❍ **C.** EAP

   ❍ **D.** CHAP

   ❍ **E.** MS-CHAP

5. You manage a Windows Server 2003 RRAS server that is used for remote dial-in access. You have an end user who is trying to connect to the RRAS server but keeps getting the message that he is not an authorized user. He is able to connect to the network and log in from his office across the LAN. What might be causing the problem?

❍ **A.** The user is not using the correct password.

❍ **B.** The user is not using an ID that is authorized to use the dial-in server.

❍ **C.** The user is trying to use his LAN account instead of his dial-in account.

❍ **D.** One of the modems on the server is probably down.

6. You manage a Windows Server 2003 RRAS server that is used for remote dial-in access. You have an end user who is trying to connect to the RRAS server but keeps getting the message that he is not an authorized user. He is able to connect to the network and log in from his office across the LAN. After doing some research, you find that the user ID was not authorized for remote access. How would you fix this situation?

❍ **A.** Using the Routing and Remote Access console, open the user's ID and under the Remote Access tab, grant him access.

❍ **B.** Using the Routing and Remote Access console, create a remote access policy. Then use the Windows-Groups criteria and add the user to an authorized group.

❍ **C.** Using the Routing and Remote Access console, create a remote access profile. Then use the Windows-Groups criteria and add the user to an authorized group.

❍ **D.** Using the Routing and Remote Access console, create a remote access profile. Then configure that profile to grant remote access permission.

7. You are the systems administrator for Runaway Travel, and you have just installed a new Windows Server 2003 RRAS server to replace a hardware RAS server. Your users are using a third-party PPP dialer that was used for the old system. What is the most secure authentication protocol that can be used for this connection?

❍ **A.** PAP

❍ **B.** EAP

❍ **C.** CHAP

❍ **D.** IPSec

8. You are the systems administrator for Runaway Travel, and you have just installed a new Windows Server 2003 RRAS server to replace a hardware RAS server. Your users are using the Windows 2000 Professional dialer. What is the most secure authentication protocol available for this situation?

❍ **A.** CHAP

❍ **B.** MS-CHAP

❍ **C.** PPP

❍ **D.** IPSec

9. You are the systems administrator for Runaway Travel, and you have just installed a new Windows Server 2003 RRAS server to replace a hardware RAS server. Your users are using a variety of client computer operating systems and PPP dialers. What is the most secure way to ensure that all the users have access?

❍ **A.** In the dial-in profile for the users, select MS-CHAP and MS-CHAPv2.

❍ **B.** In the dial-in profile for the users, select Encrypted Authentication (CHAP).

❍ **C.** Use IPSec in conjunction with RAS.

❍ **D.** Allow remote PPP client computers, and computers using all the other protocols, to connect without negotiating any authentication method.

10. You are the systems administrator for the Go to Philly Bus Company, and you have a requirement for a Windows Server 2003 RRAS server to replace a hardware solution. How do you install and configure the service?

❍ **A.** Using the Networking and Dial-up Connections Wizard, install RRAS.

❍ **B.** Using the Networking and Dial-up Connections Wizard, install Remote Access Service.

❍ **C.** Use RRAS to configure the service. Configure it with Windows Server 2003 Administration.

❍ **D.** Use Add or Remove Programs to add RRAS to the server. Configure the application by using RRAS.

11. You are the security administrator for Barb's House of Pancakes. You have been asked to implement smart cards for remote access authentication, using the Windows Server 2003 RRAS. What protocol do you need?

❍ **A.** IPSec

❍ **B.** PPTP

❍ **C.** MS-CHAPv2

❍ **D.** EAP

12. You are the Internet administrator for the Go to Philly Bus Company, and you are using a Windows Server 2003 server as a VPN server. You need to configure additional IPSec VPN ports. How do you accomplish this?

❍ **A.** Run the VPN Wizard and configure the additional ports.

❍ **B.** Go to the Network Connections window and double-click Create a New Connection. When the New Connection Wizard starts, select New Inbound VPN and follow the prompts.

❍ **C.** In the Routing and Remote Access console, edit the properties of the L2TP ports and add the additional connections.

❍ **D.** In the Routing and Remote Access console, edit the properties of the IPSec ports and add the additional connections.

13. What is the strongest encryption protocol supported by Windows Server 2003?

❍ **A.** DES

❍ **B.** IPSec

❍ **C.** MS-CHAPv2

❍ **D.** 3DES

14. You are the security administrator for Jolly Snowmen Ice Cream. Your manager has asked you to explain the use of encryption on your Windows Server 2003 server. You know you are running 3DES. What service does 3DES provide to your installation?

❍ **A.** 3DES encrypts dial-in traffic over the phone lines.

❍ **B.** 3DES encrypts L2TP VPN traffic.

❍ **C.** 3DES provides encrypted authentication.

❍ **D.** 3DES provides encrypted address information in conjunction with PPTP.

Answers to Exam Questions

1. **B**. The correct term for this feature is Multilink. Multilink allows for the use of multiple connections to a single server, which are then aggregated to provide additional bandwidth. Multinet does not relate to RRAS; thus Answer A is incorrect. X.25 is a type of WAN connection; thus Answer C is incorrect. A VPN is used to provide secure remote access over an insecure network; thus Answer D is incorrect. For more information, see the section "The IP Tab."

2. **A**, **E**. Windows Server 2003 RRAS supports the following VPN protocols: PPTP and L2TP. IPSec is an encryption protocol; thus Answer B is incorrect. PPP is a remote access protocol; thus Answer C is incorrect. EAP is an authentication protocol; thus Answer D is incorrect. For more information, see the section "Supported VPN Protocols."

3. **D**. You can see this information in the right pane of the Routing and Remote Access console by clicking the Remote Access Clients entry. The Routing and Remote Access console will show any connected users in this folder; thus Answer C is incorrect. Double-clicking the connection will provide additional information. The Performance Manager was used in Windows NT 3.51 and 4.0; thus Answer A is incorrect. The Performance console will not provide the required information you need; thus Answer B is incorrect. For more information, see the section "Managing RRAS Clients."

4. **C**, **D**, **E**. IPSec is not an authentication protocol; thus Answer A is incorrect. PAP sends the authentication information as clear text; thus Answer B is incorrect. EAP, CHAP, and MS-CHAP are all secure authentication protocols. For more information, see the section "Configuring Remote Access Authentication Protocols."

5. **B**. The user is not using an ID that is authorized to use the dial-in server. You must be authorized in a remote access policy before you can connect via dial-in. Since the user can connect via the LAN, using the wrong password or user ID is not likely the problem; thus Answers A and D are incorrect. Remote access uses the same credentials as normal LAN access; thus Answer C is incorrect. For more information, see the section "Troubleshooting User Access to Remote Access Services."

6. **B**. Using the Routing and Remote Access console, you create a remote access policy. Then you use the Windows-Groups criteria and add the user to an authorized group. Remote access is not configured for users directly through the RRAS console; thus Answer A is incorrect. You want to create a policy, which contains a profile; thus Answers C and D are incorrect. For more information, see the section "Configuring RRAS Policies to Permit or Deny Access."

7. **C**. With a third-party dialer, the best you will be able to manage for authentication is CHAP. CHAP is an industry-standard protocol that is supported by virtually all PPP dialers. PAP would also work, but it offers no security whatsoever; thus Answer A is incorrect. IPSec is not an authentication protocol; thus Answer D is incorrect. EAP is a protocol that is used for devices such as smart cards; thus Answer B is incorrect. For more information, see the section "Configuring Remote Access Authentication Protocols."

8. **B**. For communication between Windows PPP client computers, MS-CHAP is the most secure protocol of those listed because it integrates encryption and hashing algorithms. CHAP is an industry-standard protocol that is supported by virtually all PPP dialers, but is less secure than MS-CHAP; thus Answer A is incorrect. PPP is a remote access protocol, not an authentication protocol; thus Answer C is incorrect. IPSec is not an authentication protocol; thus Answer D is incorrect. For more information, see the section "Configuring Remote Access Authentication Protocols."

9. **D**. The trick here is to understand that the "connect without negotiating any authentication method" configuration is the lowest common denominator for connections. Using this configuration is the only way to ensure that all the users can get to the network by using your RAS solution. Users can still connect by using greater security; thus Answers A, B, and C are incorrect. For more information, see the section "Diagnosing and Resolving Problems Related to Establishing a Remote Access Connection."

10. **C**. RRAS is installed with the operating system. You need to use the Routing and Remote Access console to make sure everything is configured correctly; thus Answers A, B, and D are incorrect. For more information, see the section "Configuring RRAS Policies to Permit or Deny Access."

11. **D**. EAP is the protocol needed to support smart cards. IPSec is not an authentication protocol; thus Answer A is incorrect. PPTP is a VPN protocol; thus Answer B is incorrect. MS-CHAPv2 is an authentication protocol, but does not support smart cards; thus Answer C is incorrect. For more information, see the section "Configuring Remote Access Authentication Protocols."

12. **C**. You can just edit the properties of the L2TP ports, which are installed and configured when RRAS is installed; thus Answers A and B are incorrect. Because by default IPSec uses L2TP as a transport under Windows Server 2003, the ports are L2TP ports, not IPSec ports; thus Answer D is incorrect. For more information, see the section "Managing Devices and Ports."

13. **D**. 3DES is the strongest encryption protocol used by Windows Server 2003; thus Answers A, B, and C are all incorrect. For more information, see the section "Windows Server 2003 VPNs."

14. **B**. 3DES is used in conjunction with IPSec. Because IPSec is used with L2TP, Answers A, C, and D are all incorrect. For more information, see the section "Windows Server 2003 VPNs."

Suggested Readings and Resources

1. Jones, Don, and Rouse, Mark. *Microsoft Windows Server 2003 Delta Guide*. Que Publishing, 2003.

2. Habraken, Joe. *Sams Teach Yourself Microsoft Windows Server 2003 in 24 Hours*. Sams Publishing, 2003.

3. Doyle, Jeff. *Routing TCP/IP*, Volume I (CCIE Professional Development). Cisco Press, 1998.

4. "Network Access Quarantine Control," http://www.microsoft.com/technet/itsolutions/network/vpn/quarantine.mspx.

5. Davies, Joseph, and Lee, Thomas. *Microsoft Windows Server 2003 TCP/IP Protocols and Services Technical Reference*. Microsoft Press, 2003.

CHAPTER 7

Implementing, Managing, and Troubleshooting Routing

On an IP network, routing provides the map of the network, giving directions to data on how to go from one host to another. Routing can come into play whether you are trying to connect to a system on the other side of your building or on the other side of the Internet. This chapter covers one objective from the unit "Implementing, Managing, and Maintaining Routing and Remote Access" for Exam 70-291, "Implementing, Managing, and Maintaining a Microsoft Windows Server 2003 Network Infrastructure." Given the critical nature of TCP/IP as the predominant underlying protocol for the majority of internetworks, including the largest of them all, the Internet, understanding how IP routing works as it relates to Windows Server 2003 is particularly important for this exam.

Microsoft defines the objective as follows:

Objectives

Manage TCP/IP routing.

- **Manage routing protocols.**
- **Manage routing tables.**
- **Manage routing ports.**
- You need to be able to maintain your IP routing infrastructure after it is installed, configured, and successfully passing traffic. Given the critical nature of TCP/IP, both in a Windows Server 2003 network and in mixed network environments, being able to manage and monitor the routing environment is an important part of your job if you are doing routing with Windows Server 2003. Because Microsoft wants to be sure you are ready for any eventuality, you need to understand this subject even if you're implementing demand-dial routing, and supporting routing protocols on your Windows Server 2003 servers is not part of your job description at the moment.

Outline

Study Strategies

- Be prepared to answer a number of questions related to routing protocols and their operation. Many of these questions will be in scenario format, in which the implementation of a particular protocol will be based on a network topology design. Therefore, you need to have a firm understanding of the way the protocol works in small, medium, and large network designs and understand where each protocol best fits within these network scenarios. When you have a solid understanding of the theory presented in this chapter, you should try to gain some practical experience by using Windows Server 2003 Advanced Server as much as possible. You should implement the various protocols to see how they work and how they are configured within a network environment.
- Expect to answer scenario questions on implementing and configuring specific protocols based on the advantages and disadvantages of each routing protocol.

Introduction

This chapter explains how TCP/IP routing protocols in Windows Server 2003 work and how to implement and configure them on a Windows Server 2003 network. The underlying theory of routing is discussed so that you have a firm foundation for the later discussion on routing protocols, such as Open Shortest Path First (OSPF) and Routing Information Protocol (RIP).

This chapter also explains some of the problems you may encounter within a routing environment, and it discusses tools that can be used to help diagnose problems.

Introduction to IP Routing

Routing is the process of forwarding a packet based on the packet's destination address. Routing can occur at the sending host, which is known as *host routing*, and at a router, which is known as *router routing*. In both cases—at a sending host and at a router—a decision has to be made about to where the packet is to be forwarded.

To make these decisions, the IP layer consults a routing table stored in the memory of the routing device. Routing table entries are created by default when TCP/IP initializes, and additional entries are added either manually by a system administrator or automatically through communication with routers.

But what exactly is a router? In its simplest form, a *router* is any device that forwards packets from one interface to another. This is a simple description for a complex process, as you will see as you get further into routing later in this chapter.

Routers come in two basic types: software and hardware.

A *software router* is a computer running an operating system (for this discussion, that operating system is Windows Server 2003) and multiple services, including a routing service. Some benefits of software routers include the following:

- **Tight integration with the operating system**—The routing service is frequently integrated with the operating system and other services.
- **Consistent/easy-to-use user interface**—No retraining is required on a new interface/operating system because the routing functions are configured through the standard user interface.
- **Low cost**—Typically software routing is done on multipurpose systems and does not utilize dedicated hardware. This reduces the overall cost, although if you were to dedicate a software router for just routing, any cost savings would be negligible.

- **Flexibility**—Software routers allow you to configure and run multiple services on a single platform.

NOTE

When Do You Use a Software Router? Typically you find software routers in small offices that are looking for an inexpensive, easy-to-manage solution. Although there are a number of benefits to software-based routers, the drawbacks frequently outweigh them during the selection process. A hardware router is not typically affected by viruses or prone to performance problems due to runaway processes.

Although there are benefits to using software routers, there are also some pretty significant drawbacks compared to using hardware routers. They include the following:

- **Slower**—Due to the additional overhead associated with the operating system and any additional services that are running, software routers are typically slower than hardware routers.
- **Less reliable**—Due to the potential for server problems with the operating system and other running services, as well as the greater number of hardware components compared to in a hardware router, software routers are typically less reliable than hardware routers.
- **Limited scalability**—Scaling a software router to multiple high-speed interfaces (Gigabit Ethernet, for example) is subject to the limitations of the computer hardware. Because most PC-based servers are not designed to route multiple high-speed network interface cards (NICs), software routers generally do not scale as easily or as well as hardware routers. Also, adding additional services, such as access control lists or firewall services, affects a software router's performance to a greater degree than it would the performance of a comparable hardware router.
- **Limited protocol support**—Software routers typically do not support anywhere near the number of routing protocols hardware routers do. Windows Server 2003 is limited to using the IP routing protocols RIPv2 and OSPF, and it does not presently support any of the more advanced IP-based routing protocols, such as Border Gateway Protocol (BGP) version 4.

In years past, a *hardware router* was a dedicated hardware device whose main function was to route packets. Many of today's hardware routers are multifunction devices, having additional functionality such as DHCP, firewall, caching, and in some cases, even intrusion detection services. The benefits of hardware routers include the following:

- **Higher performance than software routers**—Hardware routers run on custom-built, single-purpose hardware platforms, with highly optimized operating systems.

- **Highly reliable**—Hardware routers are typically more reliable than their software counterparts, due in large part to the limited software capabilities and dedicated hardware. A hardware router typically has higher modularity than a software router.
- **Wide protocol support**—You can typically configure hardware routers to route any routable protocol from AppleTalk to XNS, as long as you buy the proper software. They also support a greater number of routing algorithms than do software routers. In a large network environment, this can be critical.

Although there are benefits to using hardware routers, there are also some drawbacks to using them compared to using software routers. They include the following:

- **Higher cost**—Hardware routers are typically dedicated platforms, which tends to make them more expensive than software routers that are also providing other services. This line is blurring, however, as additional features continue to become available on hardware routers.
- **Less user friendly**—Hardware routers are typically configured using a `telnet` or serial-based command line. There is typically a completely new operating system for each new hardware router, and all new commands are involved in installing and maintaining hardware routers.
- **More complex**—Although an individual router may not be more complex than its software-based counterpart, as you scale to large networks and begin running multiple protocols and routing algorithms, a hardware router environment can rapidly become very complex.

The hardware versus software router argument is typically more clear-cut in the real world than it is in a book or on a Microsoft exam. In most network environments, hardware routers are used almost exclusively, with software routers being reserved for only the smallest networks or locations, or used in conjunction with demand-dial network connections (discussed later in this chapter, in the section "Windows Server 2003 Routing Interfaces").

Host Routing

Now that you have an idea of what routers do and the types of routers you might run into, let's talk about the simplest form of routing—host routing.

For a host (known as the *sending host*) to successfully communicate across a shared network to another host (known as the *destination host*), it needs to have the address of the remote host. For a more real-life example of this mechanism, think about the last time you wanted to call your manager to tell her you were too sick to come in to work. You (the sending host) wanted to communicate with your manager (the destination host) to tell her you were going to be out sick (the data). Before you could call your manager, you needed to have a phone number (address) and access to the public phone network (the shared network). To send the data across the network, you needed the address of your manager's phone for the transaction to be completed. Sending data across a data network works according to the same basic principles.

On an IP-based network, the IP address of the remote host is the address you need to communicate successfully. As you learned in Chapter 1, "Configuring and Troubleshooting TCP/IP Addressing," an *IP address* is a series of numbers that act as a computer's address on the network. An example of an IP address is 172.16.68.4; this is actually a decimal representation of the actual binary address, which is made up of 4 octets of binary data. An octet is an 8-bit binary number. For ease of use, octets are typically represented in what is known as "dotted-decimal notation," as in 172.16.68.4.

To understand how IP routing works, you also need to understand the two components of an IP address. Each IP address is made up of two components—the network address and the host address. The network address identifies what network the host is on, and the host address is the specific address of the host itself. To expand on our earlier addressing example, you can think of the network address as the area code (it lets you know what part of the network the host is on) and the host address as the seven-digit local phone number. This is a high-level explanation of IP addressing, which is covered in detail in Chapter 1.

NOTE

Do I Really Need to Remember All Those IP Addresses? A computer host needs to use IP addresses to find another computer on the network, but a typical user finds remembering all those addresses to be a bit problematic. For that reason, a number of services exist to make this process easier for the computer user. On most of today's networks, there are address resolution mechanisms such as Domain Name System (DNS) that can be used to translate an easy-to-remember host name, such as www.quepublishing.com, to the host IP address. (See Chapter 3, "Implementing and Managing DNS," for more information.)

After the sending host has determined the IP address of the destination host, the next step is to determine whether the sending host can send directly to the destination or whether it needs to forward the data to a router that can deliver the data to the destination host. The sending host makes this decision by comparing the network address of the source with the network address of the destination. If the two network addresses are the same, the sending host knows that the destination host is on the same network segment and addresses the packet to the destination's address directly. In Figure 7.1, you can see an example of a small routed network that we'll use to help explain this concept a little more clearly.

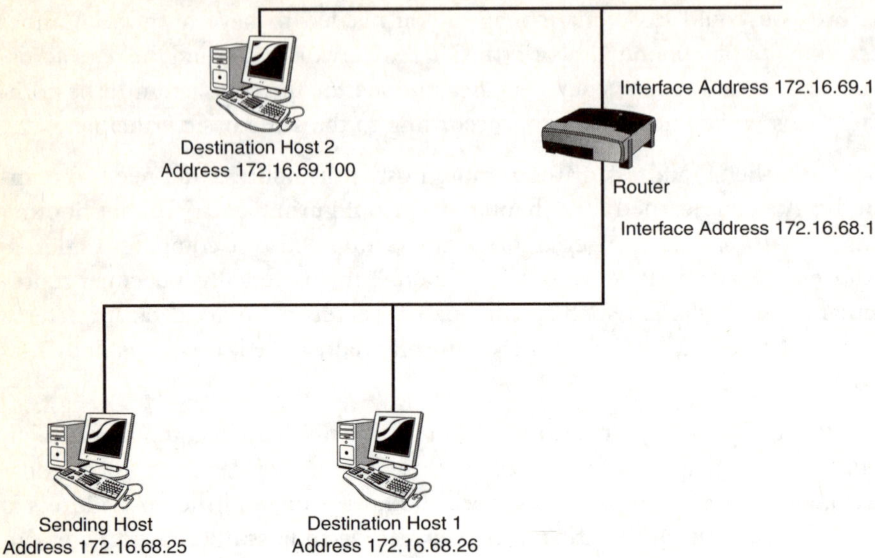

FIGURE 7.1 This is an example of a small routed network.

If the sending host in Figure 7.1 needs to send data to destination host 1, it does the following:

1. The sending host looks at its IP address, 172.16.68.25, to determine the network address. For this example, the network address is 172.16.68.
2. The sending host looks at the network address of destination host 1, 172.16.68, to determine whether the destination host is on the same subnet.
3. Because the network addresses are the same for the sending and destination hosts, the sending host and destination host 1 are on the same network, so the sending host sends the packet directly to the host at 172.16.68.26.

If the two network addresses do not match, the host must forward the message on to a router so that it can try to send the packet to the destination on the sending host's behalf. Based on the destination address, the router then uses its routing table to determine the best interface for sending the packet out to reach its destination. Each router along the path repeats this process until the destination host finally receives the packet. If routers determine that the destination host is unreachable, a destination unreachable packet is sent back to the host. For example, if the sending host in Figure 7.1 were to send data to destination host 2, the process would go like this:

1. The sending host looks at its IP address, 172.16.68.25, to determine the network address. For this example, the network address is 172.16.68.
2. The sending host looks at the network address of destination host 2, 172.16.69, to determine which network the data needs to be sent to.

3. Because the network addresses of the sending and destination hosts are not the same, the sending host and destination host 2 are not on the same network. Therefore, the sending host sends the packet to the router on the interface that has the same network address as the sending host: 172.16.68.1.
4. The router looks at the destination address on the packet and consults its routing table to determine the best interface to which to forward the packet. In this simple network, the router has an interface on the destination network (172.16.69).
5. Because the router knows it has an interface on the 172.16.69 network, it forwards the data to destination host 2 through the 172.16.69.1 interface.

NOTE

Numbering Conventions Wherever possible, you should address router interfaces by using a standard numbering convention. This not only makes finding a router on a subnet much easier, but also assists in troubleshooting. One fairly common convention is to reserve addresses at the top or the bottom of the subnet. Thus, on a network segment with one router, you know the address will be 172.16.74.1 (or .254). You can number segments with multiple routers upward (or downward) in sequential order.

Another useful convention (where possible) is to use the same host address on each interface of a router. For example, in Figure 7.1, each router interface has a host address of .1.

These examples are highly simplified, for clarity's sake. The rest of this chapter looks at the underlying principles involved with this process in great detail.

NOTE

The Real System Address The IP address is not actually the address used on the local network to deliver data. When the data reaches the destination network, the router looks to the Address Resolution Protocol (ARP) cache to translate the IP address to a Media Access Control (MAC) address for the system. The MAC address is the physical address of the NIC in the host, and it allows for the actual delivery of the data.

How does a sending host know where the router is to use it to forward data to a destination host on another network? This can be accomplished using one of the following methods:

- The default gateway address is configured (either statically or via DHCP), and the host's local ARP cache is queried to identify the physical address of the router interface.
- An Internet Control Message Protocol (ICMP) redirect message is sent by an IP router to the sending host, informing it of a better route to a destination host. The better route becomes a host route in the routing table.

- A TCP/IP host can "listen" to the routing protocol traffic used by routers. This is known as *RIP listening* or *passive RIP*. A RIP listening host has the same information in its local routing table as the RIP routers on the network, but it does not broadcast any routing updates. Windows Server 2003 implements eavesdropping through a feature called *silent RIP*.

EXAM ALERT

RIP Listening and Windows Server 2003 You cannot configure RIP listening on Windows Server 2003 because all routing on Windows Server 2003 is done using Routing and Remote Access Service (RRAS).

In Step by Step 7.1, we look at how to enable RIP listening on a Windows XP Professional host. We enable this on a Windows XP system to illustrate how you might configure a workstation to take advantage of local routing information. In a production environment, you might do this to ensure that workstations on a network have the ability to continue to function in the event of a network outage—this would require that at least two routers be available on that network.

STEP BY STEP

7.1 Enabling RIP Listening on a Windows XP Professional Computer

1. Open the Add or Remove Programs applet by selecting Start, Control Panel, Add or Remove Programs.
2. Click Add/Remove Windows Components. The Windows Components Wizard dialog box opens, as seen in Figure 7.2.

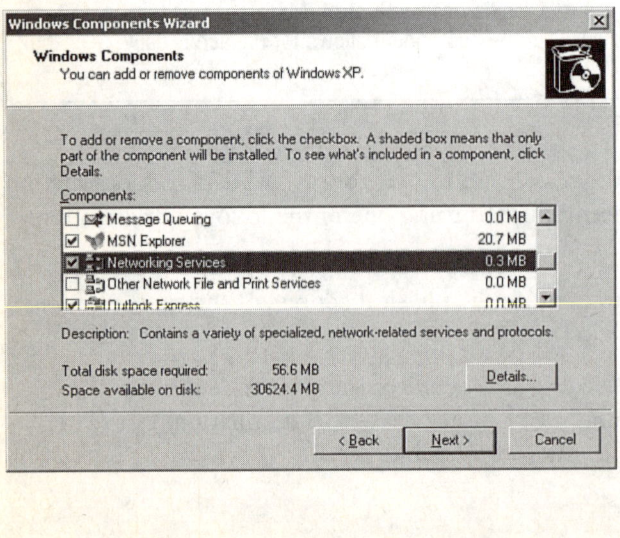

FIGURE 7.2 The Windows Components Wizard is used to add, remove, or modify the application components of Windows XP Professional.

3. In the Windows Components dialog box, highlight Networking Services and then click Details. The Networking Services dialog box, seen in Figure 7.3, appears.

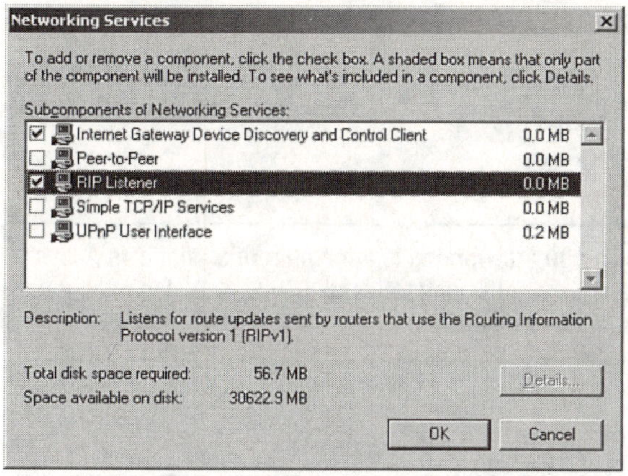

FIGURE 7.3 The Networking Services dialog box allows you to add, remove, or configure networking components such as RIP Listener.

4. Select the RIP Listener option and then click OK.
5. Click Next and then follow the instructions in the wizard. You might need your original Windows XP Professional installation media to continue this installation.

Router Routing

So far in this chapter, we have discussed what is commonly considered the easy piece of the routing puzzle—getting the data off the host and onto the network. In this section, we look at how the data moves from router to router and is ultimately delivered to its destination.

When a router receives a packet that must be forwarded to a destination host, the router has to make a decision. It needs to determine whether it can deliver the packet directly to the destination host or whether it needs to forward the packet to another router. To make this decision, the router examines the destination network address. If the router has an interface that is connected to the same network as the destination host, it can deliver the packet directly. This process gets interesting when the router is not connected to the same network as the destination host and it needs to determine the best route to the destination host so that it can forward the packet correctly. As mentioned earlier in this chapter, this is known as *router routing*.

EXAM ALERT

What's in a Name? You will not typically hear the phrase router routing outside a textbook or an exam guide such as this one. The reason is that the phrase router routing is used only to differentiate between routing that is done by the host and routing that is done by the router. You need to be familiar with this terminology for the exam, but in the real world, you will generally use the term routing to refer to the process of getting a packet from a sending host to a destination host.

When a router needs to forward a packet to another router, it uses the information in its routing tables to choose the best path for forwarding the packet. The decision about the router to which to forward the packet is determined by a number of variables related to each of the network paths to the destination host, including the number of hops and the cost of each hop.

Windows Server 2003 supports routing using RRAS. To enable RRAS within Windows Server 2003, follow the procedure described in Step by Step 7.2.

NOTE

You Must Have Permissions If the server with which you are working is a member of a Windows Active Directory domain, you need to have domain administrator permissions to install RRAS. You also need the server to be added to the domain's RAS and IAS Servers security group.

EXAM ALERT

Installing RRAS If you run across a question on the exam that deals with installing RRAS, it's a trick question. RRAS is installed with the Windows Server 2003 operating system, and it needs to be configured only if you are going to use it. It is not active on the system until it is configured, but it does not need to be installed.

STEP BY STEP

7.2 Enabling RRAS

1. Open the Routing and Remote Access console by selecting Start, Control Panel, Administrative Tools, Routing and Remote Access. By default, the local computer is listed as a server, as seen in Figure 7.4. Notice the arrow; it indicates that RRAS is not presently enabled.

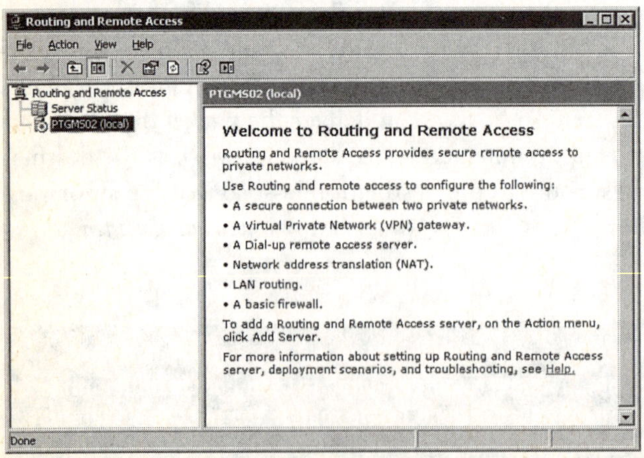

FIGURE 7.4 The Routing and Remote Access console is used to configure RRAS for a variety of functions, including acting as a router.

2. Right-click the name of the server you want to configure and select Configure and Enable Routing and Remote Access. The Routing and Remote Access Server Setup Wizard starts.

3. Click Next to start configuring RRAS. The Configuration page of the wizard appears, as seen in Figure 7.5.

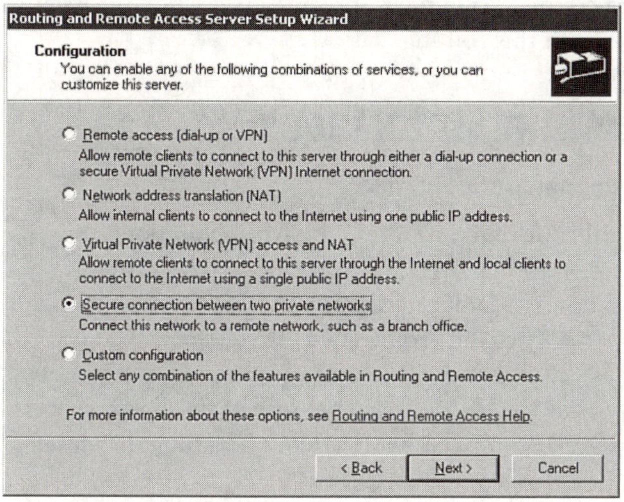

FIGURE 7.5 The Configuration page of the Routing and Remote Access Server Setup Wizard includes the most common configuration options to make the configuration process as easy as possible.

4. Select the Secure connection between two private networks option and click Next to continue. The Demand-Dial Connections dialog box opens, as seen in Figure 7.6.

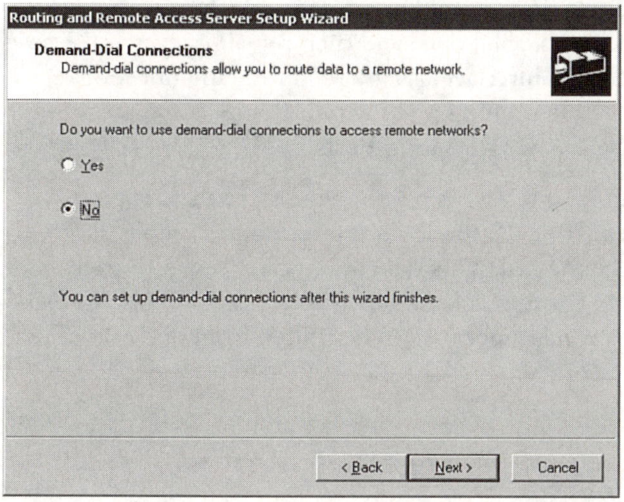

FIGURE 7.6 Demand-dial routing allows you to open connections between routers when traffic needs to pass through the router and to disconnect when the router is not needed.

5. In the Demand-Dial Connections dialog box, select No and click Next to continue. The Completing the Routing and Remote Access Server Setup Wizard dialog box opens.
6. Click Finish to complete the enabling of routing services.

Now that you have enabled routing services on a Windows Server 2003 system, we need to discuss what interfaces can be used to perform this routing.

Windows Server 2003 Routing Interfaces

Windows Server 2003 supports three types of routing interfaces:

- **LAN**—A LAN interface is a physical connection to the LAN. Most commonly an Ethernet connection (although there are other LAN media, such as Token Ring, 100VGAnyLAN, and ARCNet still in use in older networks), the LAN interface is the router's connection to a constantly active network connection. If you are using a Windows Server 2003 host as a WAN router with a Frame Relay adapter, the Frame Relay interface will commonly appear as a LAN interface because of its always-active nature. LAN interfaces generally do not require authentication, as do the other interface types.
- **Demand-dial**—The demand-dial connection is a WAN connection that is more commonly supported in Windows Server 2003 than in LAN connections. The interface for this connection is a logical interface representing the point-to-point path of two routing devices across an analog phone line or point-to-point VPN connection. Unlike LAN connections, demand-dial connections are either on-demand (that is, established when needed) or persistent (that is, established once and then remaining active). Also unlike LAN connections, a demand-dial interface usually requires authentication. Demand-dial interfaces are supported by routing ports within RRAS. We discuss these later in this chapter in the section "Managing Routing Ports."
- **IP-in-IP tunnel**—An IP-in-IP tunnel interface is a logical interface that represents a tunneled point-to-point connection. IP-in-IP tunnel interfaces do not require an authentication process to become connected. This type of interface sends IP packets through the tunnel by encapsulating them with an additional IP header. This allows IP packets that would not ordinarily traverse a network to be routed from one part of the network to another.

The Routing Process

When a router needs to forward a packet to another router for delivery to a remote network, it consults a database of information known as the *routing table*. This database is stored in the router's random access memory (RAM) to ensure that this lookup process can be performed quickly. As the packet travels across the network toward its destination, each router along the way makes a decision about where to forward the packet by consulting its routing table. When a destination host sends a reply packet, it is possible that the same path may not be used to reach the original sender. This depends on the metrics of each path along the route. In other words, the way to the destination host may not be the best path back. The following sections discuss the two types of routing: static and dynamic.

Static Routing

Objective:

Manage TCP/IP routing.

- Manage routing tables.

Manually configuring the routing table of a host with the routes for each destination network is known as *static routing*. Static routing is best suited to small environments where the amount of information to configure is small and the overhead of generating the routing information is unacceptable. Static routers do not scale well to large or frequently changing internetworks because of their manual administration.

Using the `route` Command to Configure Static Routes

The `route` command is primarily used to configure static routes within a network. It can also be used to troubleshoot by listing all the routes that the computer knows about.

The syntax of the `route` command is as follows:

```
ROUTE [-f] [-p] [command [destination] [MASK netmask] [gateway] [METRIC metric] [IF interface]
```

Table 7.1 describes the parameters that can be used with the `route` command.

TABLE 7.1 Parameters of the `route` Command

Parameter	Description
`-f`	Clears the routing tables of all gateway entries. If this is used in conjunction with one of the commands, the tables are cleared before the command is run.
`-p`	When this parameter is used with the `add` command, it makes a route persistent across boots of the system. By default, routes are not preserved when the system is restarted. This parameter is ignored for all other commands, which always affect the appropriate persistent routes. This option is not supported in Windows 95.
`PRINT`	Prints a route.
`ADD`	Adds a route.
`DELETE`	Deletes a route.

(continues)

TABLE 7.1 Continued

Parameter	Description
CHANGE	Modifies an existing route.
destination	Specifies the destination. The *destination* parameter can contain a host address, subnet address, network address, or default gateway.
MASK	Specifies that the next parameter is the *netmask* value.
netmask	Specifies a subnet mask value for this route entry. If not specified, it defaults to 255.255.255.255.
gateway	Specifies the gateway.
METRIC	Specifies that the next parameter is the *metric* value.
metric	Specifies the metric—for example, cost for the destination.
IF	Specifies that the next parameter is the *interface* value.
interface	Specifies the interface number for the route.

NOTE

The mask Parameter The mask parameter defines what portion of the destination address must match for the route to be used. When the mask is written in binary, a 1 is significant (that is, must match), and a 0 need not match. For example, say that a 255.255.255.255 mask is used for a host entry. The mask of all 255s (that is, all 1s) means that the destination address of the packet to be routed must exactly match the network address for this route to be used. As another example, say the network address 157.57.8.0 has a netmask of 255.255.248.0. This netmask means that both of the first two octets must match, the first 5 bits of the third octet must match (that is, 248 must equal 11111000), and the last octet does not matter. Thus, any address of 157.57 and the third octet of 8 through 15 (that is, 15=00001111) will use this route.

The *gateway* parameter specifies where the packet needs to be sent. This can be the local NIC or a router on the local subnet.

The *metric* parameter specifies a cost that is to be associated with the route. This cost is used in the decision about how packets should be routed. Packets are routed through the route that has the lowest cost.

Step by Step 7.3 shows how to add a static route for the network 10.100.10.0.

STEP BY STEP

7.3 Adding a Static Route to Windows Server 2003

1. Open the command prompt by selecting Start, Programs, Accessories, Command Prompt. The Command Prompt window opens.

2. Display the system's existing routing table by typing **route print** and pressing Enter. Make note of the routes listed so that you can check them against the routes listed after you add the static route. You should see information similar to the following (which will vary from computer to computer, based on your computer's interfaces, network addresses, and existing routes):

```
IPv4 Route Table
===========================================================================
Interface List
0x1 ........................... MS TCP Loopback interface
0x10003 ...00 13 72 0e 98 7e ...... Broadcom NetXtreme Gigabit Ethernet
===========================================================================
===========================================================================
Active Routes:
Network Destination        Netmask          Gateway       Interface  Metric
          0.0.0.0          0.0.0.0      192.168.0.1   192.168.0.156     20
        127.0.0.0        255.0.0.0        127.0.0.1       127.0.0.1      1
      192.168.0.0    255.255.255.0    192.168.0.156   192.168.0.156     20
    192.168.0.156  255.255.255.255        127.0.0.1       127.0.0.1     20
    192.168.0.255  255.255.255.255    192.168.0.156   192.168.0.156     20
        224.0.0.0        240.0.0.0    192.168.0.156   192.168.0.156     20
  255.255.255.255  255.255.255.255    192.168.0.156   192.168.0.156      1
Default Gateway:       192.168.0.1
===========================================================================
Persistent Routes:
  None
```

3. In the Command Prompt window, type the following command and then press Enter: **route add 10.100.10.0 mask 255.255.255.0** ***192.168.0.156*** **metric 2**.

   A successful entry returns you to the command prompt, with no message. If the entry addition is unsuccessful, you receive an error message. The gateway value (in italics in this example entry) must match an interface IP address on the server for this to be successful.

4. To display the system's routing table with the newly added route, type **route print** and press Enter. This displays information similar to the following (note the newly added route, in bold in the text shown):

```
IPv4 Route Table
===========================================================================
Interface List
0x1 ........................... MS TCP Loopback interface
0x10003 ...00 13 72 0e 98 7e ...... Broadcom NetXtreme Gigabit Ethernet
===========================================================================
===========================================================================
Active Routes:
Network Destination        Netmask          Gateway       Interface  Metric
          0.0.0.0          0.0.0.0      192.168.0.1   192.168.0.156     20
      10.100.10.0    255.255.255.0    192.168.0.156   192.168.0.156      2
        127.0.0.0        255.0.0.0        127.0.0.1       127.0.0.1      1
      192.168.0.0    255.255.255.0    192.168.0.156   192.168.0.156     20
```

```
     192.168.0.156  255.255.255.255        127.0.0.1        127.0.0.1    20
     192.168.0.255  255.255.255.255    192.168.0.156    192.168.0.156    20
         224.0.0.0        240.0.0.0    192.168.0.156    192.168.0.156    20
   255.255.255.255  255.255.255.255    192.168.0.156    192.168.0.156     1
Default Gateway:        192.168.0.1
===========================================================================
Persistent Routes:
  None
```

Dynamic Routing

Generating routing table information by learning the routes from information on the network is called *dynamic routing*. This is done by using a dynamic routing protocol such as RIP or OSPF. Let's examine what a routing protocol is: A general definition of *protocol* is "an agreed-on method for exchanging data between two devices." A routing protocol defines the method for exchanging routing information between two routing devices. A *dynamic routing protocol* is used to exchange routing information that is built and maintained automatically. When you are using a dynamic routing protocol, routing information is exchanged between routers to update the information kept in their routing tables. This can be done either periodically (at scheduled intervals) or on demand. If they are set up correctly at the outset, dynamic routers require little administration after they have been configured. Because they learn routing information dynamically, and have the ability to route around failures when the network architecture will support it, dynamic routers are generally used in large network environments where it would not be practical to use static routing. The two dynamic routing protocols that are supported by Windows Server 2003 are RIP and OSPF.

Routing Protocols

Objective:

Manage TCP/IP routing.

- Manage routing protocols.

A routing protocol is based either on a distance-vector or link-state algorithm. The differences between the two algorithms include when routing information is exchanged, what information is sent when the routing information is exchanged, and how quickly the protocol can route around outages (when the network topology will support it).

Distance-Vector Routing

Distance-vector routing protocols require that each router tell its neighbors what is in its routing table. This is done by sending the entire routing table when the router boots and then sending it again at scheduled intervals. Each router uses updates from its neighboring routers to update its own routing table based on the information it receives. Using the information from these updates, a router can build a network map in its routing table and determine hop counts (that is, the distance to any network) for each network entry in the routing table. Routing updates sent using a distance-vector routing protocol are unacknowledged and unsynchronized, which is one of the drawbacks of distance-vector protocols. Some other drawbacks of this type of routing protocol include the following:

- **High overhead**—Because every router on the network sends its entire routing table when it sends an update, distance-vector protocols produce very large routing tables. This adds overhead to the router memory needed to store these tables and the router processing power needed to maintain these tables. Large routing tables can also cause problems for an administrator who is trying to determine the source of a problem.
- **Not scalable**—Distance-vector networks are limited to 15 hops for any given route. In a large network (such as the Internet), it is easy to have network segments that are greater than 15 hops away; these would be unreachable in a distance-vector network.
- **Network bandwidth intensive**—Distance-vector networks require that routers exchange their entire routing tables whenever they do updates. On a large network with large routing tables, these routing updates can utilize significant amounts of bandwidth, especially across small WAN connections or demand-dial links.
- **Long convergence time**—*Convergence* is the amount of time it takes a routing algorithm to detect and route around a network failure. Distance-vector protocols typically have longer convergence times than link-state protocols.
- **Routing loops**—Distance-vector protocols can suffer from routing loop problems when there are multiple paths to a network. A routing loop occurs when the routing table creates a routing path that loops between routers. The packet is sent from router to router until its TTL is exceeded. Routing loops typically occur in poorly designed networks.
- **Count-to-infinity problems**—Count-to-infinity problems occur when there is a network outage and the routing algorithm cannot calculate a new router. One router broadcasts a route and increments the hop count for the router, and then a second router broadcasts the same route to the first router, also incrementing the hop count, and so on, until the route metric (that is, the hop count) reaches 16 and the route is discarded.

Distance-vector routing protocols have additional mechanisms that allow them to avoid the count-to-infinity problems and to improve convergence. They include the following:

- **Split horizon**—The split-horizon mechanism prevents routes from being broadcast out the interface from which they were received. Split horizon eliminates count-to-infinity problems and routing loops during convergence in single-path internetworks and reduces the chances of count-to-infinity problems occurring in multipath internetworks.
- **Split horizon with poison reverse**—The split horizon with poison reverse mechanism allows routes to be broadcast back to the interface from which they were received, but they are announced with a hop count of 16, which indicates that the network is unreachable (in other words, the route has been poisoned and is unusable through that interface). In a single-path internetwork, split horizon with poison reverse has no benefits in addition to those of split horizon. However, in a multipath internetwork, split horizon with poison reverse greatly reduces routing loops and count-to-infinity problems, which can still occur in a multipath internetwork because routes to networks can be learned from multiple sources.
- **Triggered updates**—Triggered updates allow a router to announce changes in metric values almost immediately, rather than wait for the next periodic announcement. The trigger is a change to a metric in an entry in the routing table. For example, networks that become unavailable can be announced with a hop count of 16 through a triggered update. If triggered updates were sent by all routers immediately, each triggered update could cause a cascade of broadcast traffic across the IP internetwork. Triggered updates improve the convergence time of RIP internetworks, but at the expense of additional broadcast traffic as the triggered updates are propagated.

The main advantages of distance-vector routing are that it requires little maintenance and that it is easy to configure. Both of these advantages make it popular in small network environments.

Link-State Routing

Link-state routing was designed to overcome the disadvantages of distance-vector routing, and it does a decent job of this. Routers using link-state routing protocols learn about their network environment by "meeting" their neighboring routers. This is done through a hello packet, which tells the neighboring router what networks the first router can reach. When the introduction is complete, the neighboring router sends the new network information to each of its neighboring routers by using a link-state advertisement (LSA). The neighboring routers copy the contents of the packet and forward the LSA to each attached network except for the one on which the LSA was received. This process is known as *flooding*.

A router that uses a link-state routing protocol builds a tree, or map, of shortest paths, with itself as the root. The tree is based on all the LSAs seen. The tree contains the route to each destination in the network. After this tree has been built, routing information is sent only when changes to the network occur instead of periodically, as with distance-vector protocols.

There are a number of advantages to link-state protocols, especially when compared to the distance vector-based routing protocols. These advantages include the following:

- **Smaller routing tables**—Because the router maintains a table only of link states, rather than a copy of every route on the network, it is able to maintain much smaller routing tables.
- **Highly scalable**—Link-state protocols are not limited to 15 hops as distance vector-based protocols are, so they are able to scale to much larger networks.
- **More efficient use of network bandwidth**—Because link-state information is not exchanged after the network has converged, routing updates do not consume precious bandwidth, unless there is an outage that forces the network to reconverge.
- **Faster convergence**—Link-state routing protocols converge faster than distance-vector protocols because updates are sent as soon as a change to the network occurs, instead of having to wait for the periodic update used with the distance-vector protocols.

One disadvantage of link-state protocols is that they are more complex to understand and configure than distance-vector protocols. They also require additional processing power on the router due to the need to calculate the routing tree.

Configuring Routing Protocols in Windows Server 2003

Objective:

Manage TCP/IP routing.

- Manage routing protocols.

Up to this point, the chapter discusses the theory behind different routing protocol types, how they work, and some of the mechanisms that are used to resolve problems that arise with the different types of routing protocols. In the following sections, the discussion focuses on the actual routing protocols supported by Windows Server 2003: RIP and OSPF.

Working with RIP

RIP is a distance-vector protocol that uses hop count as its metric for measuring the number of routers that must be crossed to reach the desired network. RIP is widely used for routing traffic in the global Internet and is an interior gateway protocol (IGP), which means that it performs routing within a single autonomous system (AS). There are two versions of RIP: RIPv1 and RIPv2. Windows Server 2003 uses RIPv2, although it can be configured to communicate with RIPv1 if needed.

RIPv1

In RIPv1, all route announcements are addressed to the IP subnet (that is, all host bits are set to 1), and a MAC-level broadcast is initiated. As a result, non-RIP hosts and RIP hosts receive RIP announcements. For large or very large RIP internetworks, the amount of broadcast traffic on each subnet can become significant.

NOTE

RIP Storms If you are working on a network that uses RIP, you may encounter RIP storms. A RIP storm occurs when there are so many RIP broadcasts on a subnet that there is no room left on the network for data—all the network space is being used for RIP broadcasts. RIP storms occur more commonly with RIPv1 than with RIPv2, and they usually occur during a time when the network is changing.

NOTE

What's Wrong with RIPv1? One of the largest drawbacks of RIPv1 is the fact that it cannot support variable-length subnet masks (VLSMs). The concepts of IP routing and subnetting are covered in detail in Chapter 1, but at this point, it is important that you understand that RIPv1 is unable to understand any networks other than the standard Class A, Class B, or Class C networks defined by the TCP/IP RFCs. Supernetted or subnetted network routes are not broadcast by RIPv1.

To add RIP to a Windows Server 2003 host, follow the instructions in Step by Step 7.4.

STEP BY STEP

7.4 Adding RIP to RRAS

1. Open the Routing and Remote Access console by selecting Start, Control Panel, Administrative Tools, Routing and Remote Access.

2. In the left pane of the console, expand the list under IP Routing and right-click General. From the context menu, select New Routing Protocol. The New Routing Protocol dialog box, as seen in Figure 7.7, appears.

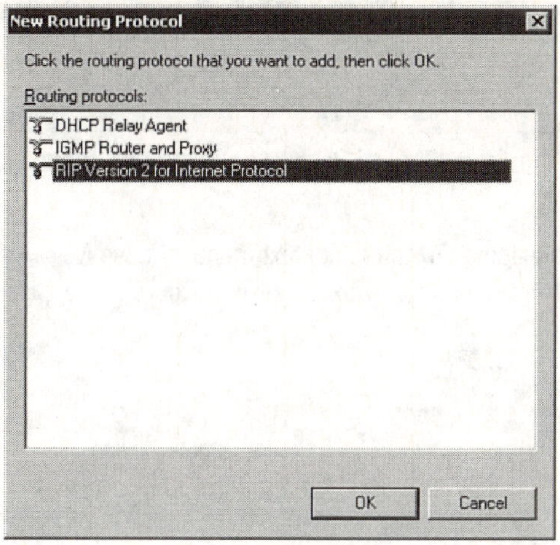

FIGURE 7.7 The New Routing Protocol dialog box can be used to add protocols to a Windows Server 2003 server.

3. Select RIP Version 2 for Internet Protocol and click OK. RIP then appears under the IP Routing entry, as seen in Figure 7.8, and is installed on the Windows Server 2003 server.

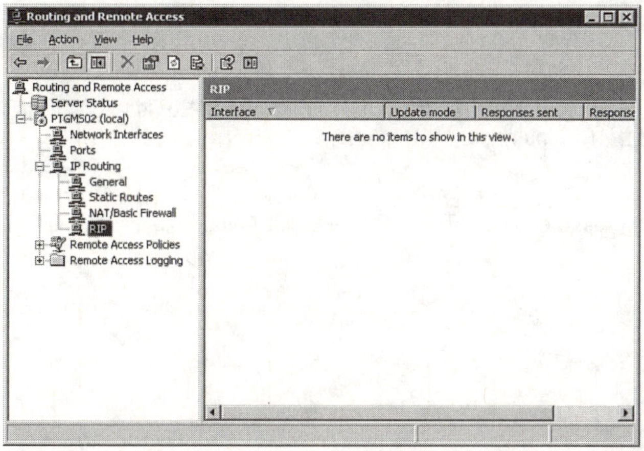

FIGURE 7.8 RIP appears under the IP Routing heading in the Routing and Remote Access console.

After RIPv2 is installed, you need to understand how to configure it to communicate with other routers on the network. To configure RIP on an RRAS server, follow the procedure outlined in Step by Step 7.5.

STEP BY STEP

7.5 Configuring RIP on Windows Server 2003

1. Open the Routing and Remote Access console by selecting Start, Control Panel, Administrative Tools, Routing and Remote Access.
2. Expand the IP Routing heading and right-click the RIP subheading. From the context menu, choose New Interface. The New Interface for RIP Version 2 for Internet Protocol dialog box, as seen in Figure 7.9, appears.

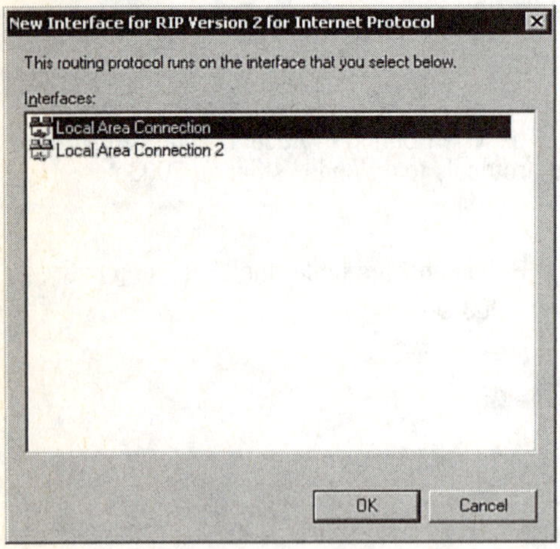

FIGURE 7.9 The first step in configuring RIP is to create an RIP interface.

3. Select the appropriate local area connection and click OK. The RIP Properties dialog box, as seen in Figure 7.10, appears.

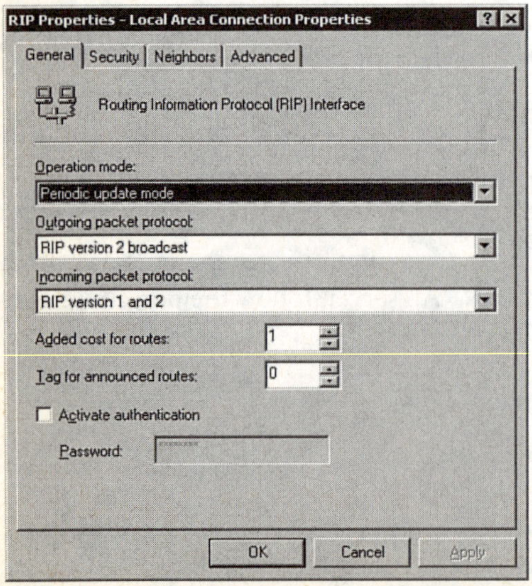

FIGURE 7.10 The RIP Properties dialog box allows you to configure RIP to work in a network environment.

4. On the General tab, under Outgoing Packet Protocol, select RIP Version 1 Broadcast. Under Incoming Packet Protocol, select RIP Version 1 and 2. Click OK to return to the Routing and Remote Access console. The changes are activated. You have now configured the server to work with any legacy RIPv1 routers that might still be on the network.

CAUTION

Don't Play with Routing on a Production Network Working with any protocols on a live network is a risky proposition; it should be avoided at all costs. At one company, an engineer was convinced he understood how routing worked, and he also believed he was a Windows expert.

During one of his experiments with routing on a Windows NT 4.0 server, this engineer bridged the corporate production network with a customer network in the same building. This was a large customer network, and due to the fact that this "expert" had routing enabled, he created a RIP storm that overwhelmed seven of the remote office routers, which promptly went into a constant reboot.

This is generally not considered an excellent career move in large companies. If you are going to experiment with routing, you should be sure to do it on an isolated network.

Earlier in the chapter we discussed configuring a host to support the RIP Listener service, which allows a host to build a routing table by listening to the RIP broadcasts on the network while not broadcasting any updates to the network. The equivalent service on a Windows Server 2003 server with routing enabled is known as silent RIP. A silent RIP router processes RIP announcements but does not announce its own routes.

To enable silent RIP on a Windows Server 2003 router, follow the procedure described in Step by Step 7.6.

STEP BY STEP

7.6 Enabling Silent RIP on Windows Server 2003

1. Open the Routing and Remote Access console by selecting Start, Control Panel, Administrative Tools, Routing and Remote Access.
2. Expand the console tree and select RIP. The list of available interfaces running RIP appears in the right pane of the console, as seen in Figure 7.11.
3. Right-click the interface that you want to configure for silent RIP mode, and from the context menu, select Properties. The Local Area Connection Properties dialog box, seen previously in Figure 7.10, appears.
4. On the General tab, in the Outgoing Packet Protocol drop-down list box, select Silent RIP. Click OK to return to the Routing and Remote Access console. The changes are applied.

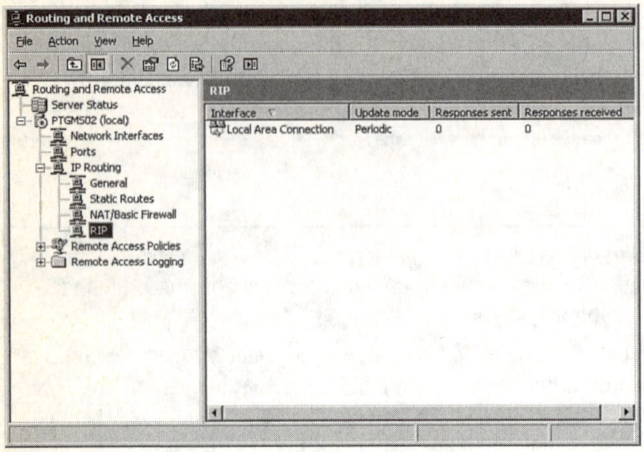

FIGURE 7.11 You can find the complete list of interfaces supporting a particular protocol by looking in the right pane of the console.

So far we have looked at two simple RIP configuration options. The following sections discuss some of the specific features of RIP.

RIPv1 Routing Characteristics

RIPv1 was designed for class-based IP internetworks in which the network ID can be determined from the values of the first three bits of the IP address in the RIP route. Because the subnet mask is not included or announced with the route, the RIP router must determine the network ID based on a limited set of information. For each route in a RIPv1 message, the RIPv1 router does one of the following:

- If the network ID fits the address class (Class A, Class B, or Class C), the default class-based subnet mask is assumed.
- If the network ID does not fit the address class and the network ID fits the subnet mask of the interface on which it is received, the subnet mask of the interface on which it was received is assumed. If the network ID does not fit the subnet mask of the interface on which it is received, the network ID is assumed to be a host route with the subnet mask 255.255.255.255.

The problem with this mechanism is that a supernetted route might be interpreted as a single network ID rather than as the range of network IDs that it is designed to represent. This means that subnet routes being advertised outside the network ID that is being supernetted might be interpreted as host routes.

RIPv1 routers do not advertise the subnets of a subnetted class-based network ID outside the subnetted region of the IP internetwork. However, because only the class-based network ID is being advertised outside the subnetted environment, subnets of a network ID in a RIPv1 environment must be contiguous. If subnets of an IP network ID are noncontiguous, known as *disjointed subnets*, the class-based network ID is announced by separate RIPv1 routers in different parts of the internetwork. As a result, IP traffic can be forwarded to the wrong network.

Finally, RIPv1 does not provide any protection from a rogue RIP router starting up on a network and announcing false or inaccurate routes. RIPv1 announcements are processed regardless of their source. A malicious user could use this lack of protection to overwhelm RIP routers with hundreds or thousands of false or inaccurate routes. That's why you should always try to use RIPv2 if you will be using RIP at all.

RIPv2 Routing Characteristics

RIPv2 seeks to address some of the problems associated with RIPv1. The goals in the development of RIPv2 were to minimize broadcast traffic, use variable-length subnetting to conserve IP addresses, and secure routing environments against misconfigured or malicious routers. To meet these goals, several new features were added to RIPv2, including the following:

- Rather than broadcasting RIP announcements, RIPv2 supports sending RIP announcements to the IP multicast address 224.0.0.9. Non-RIP nodes are not disturbed by RIP router announcement traffic. The disadvantage of this new feature is that silent RIP nodes must also be listening for multicast traffic sent to 224.0.0.9. If you use silent RIP, you should verify that the silent RIP nodes can listen for multicast RIPv2 announcements before you deploy multicast RIPv2. The use of multicast announcements is optional. The broadcasting of RIPv2 announcements is also supported.
- RIPv2 announcements send the subnet mask (also known as a *network mask*) along with the network ID. RIPv2 can be used in subnetted, supernetted, and VLSM environments. Subnets of a network ID do not have to be contiguous (that is, they can be disjointed subnets).
- RIPv2 supports the use of authentication mechanisms to verify the origin of incoming RIP announcements. Simple password authentication is defined in RFC 1723, but newer authentication mechanisms, such as Message Digest 5 (MD5), are available.

RIP Updates

RIP sends routing update messages at regular intervals and when the network topology changes. When a router receives a routing update that includes changes to an entry, it updates its routing table to reflect the new route. The metric value for the path is increased by 1, and the sender is told what the next hop is. A RIP router maintains only the best route (that is, the route with the lowest metric value) to a destination. After updating its routing table, the router immediately begins transmitting routing updates to inform other network routers of the change. These updates are sent independently of the regularly scheduled updates that RIP routers send. As discussed earlier in this chapter, these updates are sent in the form of the entire routing table.

When RIP is being used on a large network, the routing table can grow very large. Because only 25 routes can be sent in a single RIP packet, large routing tables have to be sent as multiple RIP packets.

RIP routers advertise the contents of their routing tables every 30 seconds on all attached networks through an IP subnet and a MAC-level broadcast. (RIPv2 routers can be configured to multicast RIP announcements.) In large networks, this can add significant overhead, which can be especially problematic on WAN links, where it is possible that significant portions of the WAN link bandwidth can end up being devoted to the passing of RIP traffic. As a result, RIP-based routing does not scale well to large internetworks or WAN implementations.

The RIP Routing Metric

RIP uses a single routing metric, hop count, to measure the distance between the source and a destination network. Each hop in a path from source to destination is assigned a hop count value, which is typically 1. (The hop count value can be configured on a Windows Server 2003 router.) When a router receives a routing update that contains a new or changed destination network entry, the router adds 1 to the metric value indicated in the update and enters the network in the routing table. The IP address of the sender is used as the next hop.

RIP prevents routing loops from continuing indefinitely by enforcing a limit on the number of hops allowed in a path from the source to a destination. The maximum number of hops in a path is 15; therefore, there can be only 15 routers between any two hosts. If a router receives a routing update that contains a new or changed entry, and if increasing the metric value by 1 causes the metric to be infinity (that is, 16), the network destination is considered unreachable.

Step by Step 7.7 shows you how to view some of the other RIP settings you might need to set.

STEP BY STEP

7.7 Viewing Additional RIP Configuration Options with Windows Server 2003

1. Open the Routing and Remote Access console by selecting Start, Control Panel, Administrative Tools, Routing and Remote Access.
2. Expand the console tree and select RIP. The list of available interfaces running RIP appears in the right pane of the console.
3. Right-click the name of the interface that you want to configure and from the context menu, select Properties. The Local Area Connection Properties dialog box opens.
4. Select the Security tab, as seen in Figure 7.12, to see how the RIP updates can be managed.

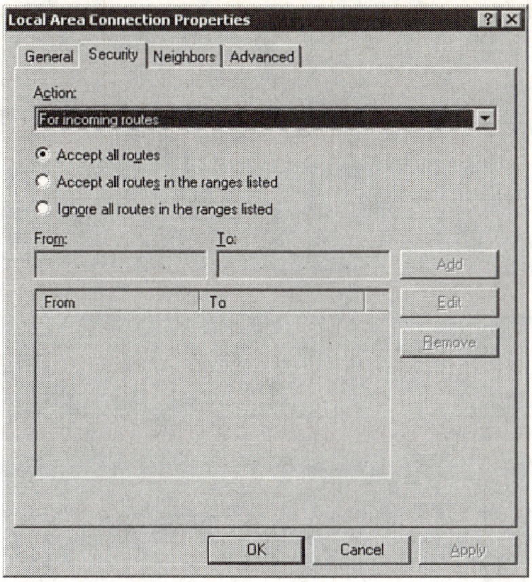

FIGURE 7.12 The Security tab allows you to restrict the networks that can send and receive RIP updates.

5. Select the Neighbors tab, as seen in Figure 7.13, to review the settings that can be configured pertaining to how the router interacts with its RIP neighbors.

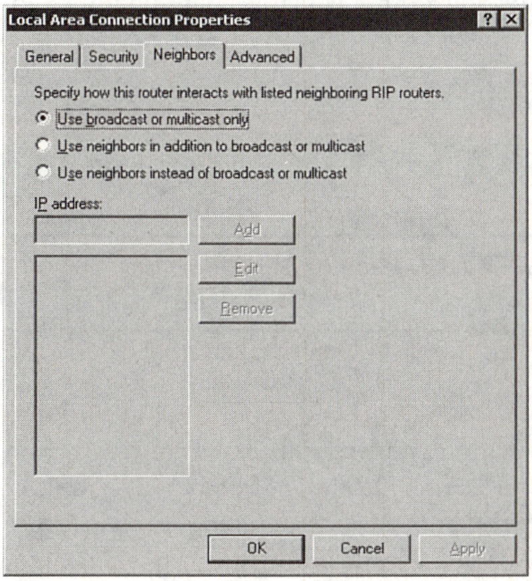

FIGURE 7.13 The Neighbors tab allows you to configure how RIP broadcasts are sent by a Windows Server 2003 router.

6. Select the Advanced tab, as seen in Figure 7.14, which allows you to configure the more complex settings associated with RIP and to see how Windows Server 2003 supports it.

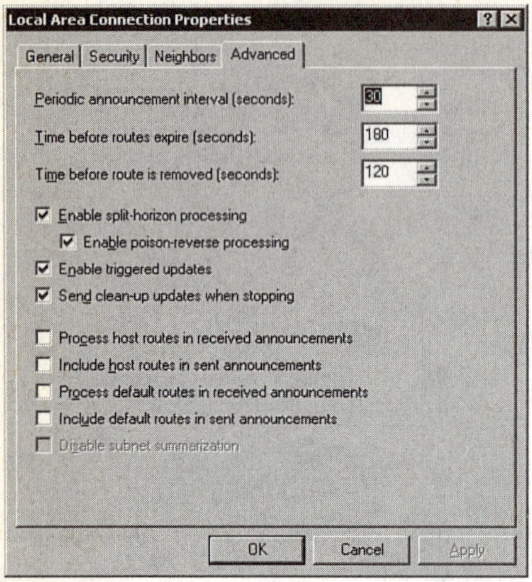

FIGURE 7.14 The Advanced tab allows you to configure advanced settings, such as using split horizon, poison reverse, and triggered updates.

7. Click OK to return to the Routing and Remote Access console.

We have dealt with RIP in some detail. Now let's look at OSPF, which is commonly thought of as RIP's successor in the IP routing arena.

Working with OSPF

NOTE

OSPF and 64-Bit Versions of Windows Server 2003 OSPF is not available on 64-bit versions of Windows Server 2003.

OSPF is a link-state routing protocol. It functions by sending LSAs to all the other routers within the same hierarchical area. (Don't worry if you don't understand what we mean by *hierarchical area*. It is discussed later in this chapter, in the section "Routing Hierarchies.") An LSA for a router consists of a router, its attached networks, and their configured costs. As OSPF routers accumulate link-state information into a database called the Link State Database (LSDB), they use the Shortest Path First (SPF) algorithm to calculate the shortest path to each node.

OSPF has the following benefits:

- Better convergence than RIP because routing changes are propagated immediately and do not have to wait for periodic updates.
- The routes OSPF calculates are always loop free. There is no possibility of loops occurring.
- Updates are sent only when routing changes rather than sending routing updates periodically. This ensures better use of bandwidth.
- Allows for logical definition of networks where routers can be divided into areas. This provides a mechanism for aggregating routes and cutting down on the unnecessary propagation of subnet information.
- It was designed to advertise the subnet mask with the network. OSPF supports VLSMs, disjointed subnets, and supernetting.
- It allows for routing authentication using different methods of password authentication.
- It routes outside an OSPF. ASs are advertised within the AS so that OSPF routers can calculate the least-cost route to external networks. This keeps track of external routes injected by exterior protocols.

To configure OSPF on an RRAS server, follow the procedure described in Step by Step 7.8.

STEP BY STEP

7.8 Installing and Configuring OSPF on Windows Server 2003

1. Open the Routing and Remote Access console by selecting Start, Control Panel, Administrative Tools, Routing and Remote Access.
2. Expand the console tree, and under IP Routing, right-click General. From the context menu, select New Routing Protocol. The New Routing Protocol dialog box appears, as seen in Figure 7.15.
3. Select Open Shortest Path First and click OK to install it. It now appears under IP Routing in the Routing and Remote Access console, as seen in Figure 7.16.
4. Right-click the newly installed OSPF protocol. From the context menu, select New Interface. The New Interface for Open Shortest Path First (OSPF) dialog box appears, as seen in Figure 7.17.

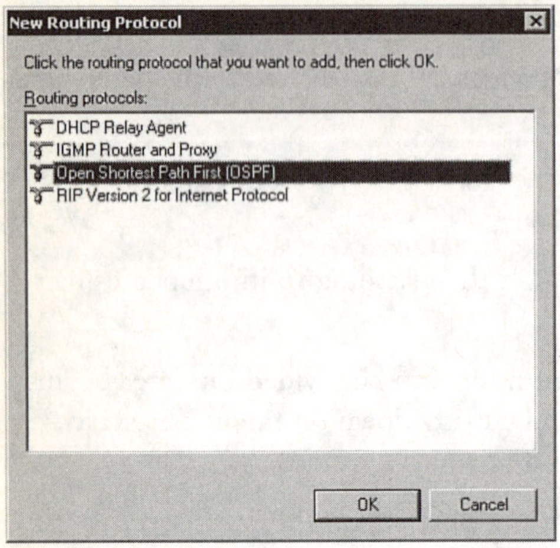

FIGURE 7.15 The New Routing Protocol dialog box can be used to add protocols to a Windows Server 2003 server.

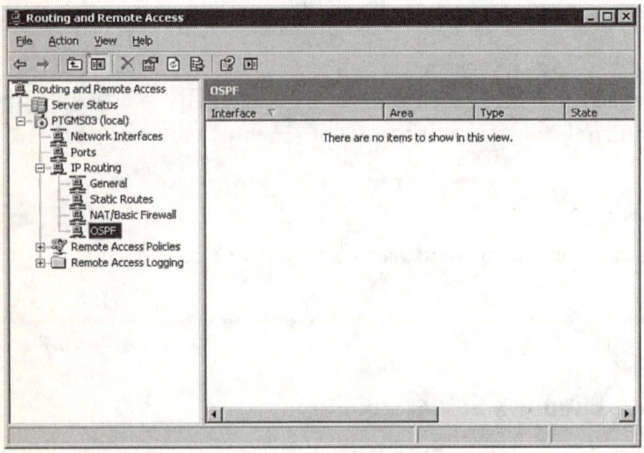

FIGURE 7.16 OSPF appears under IP Routing in the Routing and Remote Access console.

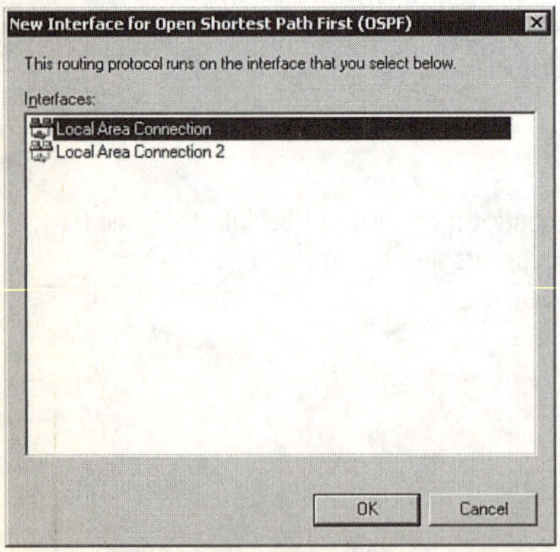

FIGURE 7.17 OSPF can be tied to a single interface or to multiple interfaces.

5. Select Local Area Connection and click OK. The OSPF Properties dialog box appears, as seen in Figure 7.18.

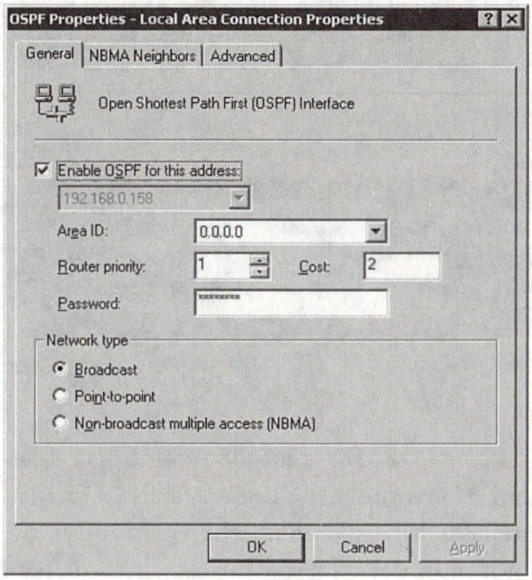

FIGURE 7.18 In the OSPF Properties dialog box, you can complete the configuration of the OSPF protocol.

6. On the General tab, select the Enable OSPF for This Address check box. In the Area ID drop-down list box, select the ID of the area to which the interface belongs (in this case, it should be 0.0.0.0, which is the default route since we have no other route to an external destination configured or available). In the Router Priority list box, click the arrows to set the priority of the router over the interface to 1 as there are no other OSPF routers configured yet. In the Cost field, set the cost of sending a packet over the interface to 2 (or any value) since you have only the default route available currently. If you have multiple OSPF routers in your environment supporting multiple routes, you would be able to configure these options accordingly to reflect your actual environment instead of a lab environment. In the Password field, type a password. In the Network Type group box, set the type of OSPF interface as Broadcast. Click OK to complete the installation of the interface. You are returned to the Routing and Remote Access console.

Now that you have successfully installed and configured OSPF, let's look a little more closely at how OSPF routing hierarchies work.

Routing Hierarchies

Unlike RIP, OSPF operates within a hierarchy. The basic structure of this hierarchy includes areas, ASs, and the OSPF backbone. The largest entity within the hierarchy is the AS. An AS is a collection of networks and routers that are under common administration and that share a common routing protocol.

EXAM ALERT

When Do I Need More Than One Area? A good rule of thumb for when to start creating a multiple-area OSPF network is when you reach 50 routers. If you have 50 routers on a network, the network is probably complex enough to warrant creating additional areas.

EXAM ALERT

OSPF Is a Complex Routing Protocol If it seems like OSPF is a really complex routing protocol, it's because it is. Engineers who architect OSPF networks for large companies usually have extensive training and experience. For the exam, you should have a general understanding of the concepts associated with OSPF. You will not be asked to design a complex OSPF network as part of the exam.

Areas

An AS can be divided into areas. Each area is identified by an area ID. This identifier has no relationship to an IP address or IP network ID, although it uses the same dotted-decimal format. Area IDs are not used to reflect routing data; they are actually convenient labels to simplify the management of the area. Although the area ID does not signify any IP routing information, if all the networks within an area correspond to a single subnetted network ID, the area ID can be set to the network ID. This can be convenient for administration of the areas. For example, if an area contains all the subnets of the IP network 10.1.0.0, the area ID can be set to 10.1.0.0. The reason for defining areas within an AS is to reduce the size of an LSDB.

NOTE

The LSDB The LSDB provides the overall picture of networks in relationship to routers within an area. The LSDB contains the collection of LSAs received from all routers in the same area. In an AS that has a large number of networks, each OSPF router must keep the LSA of every other router in its topological database.

To keep the size of LSDBs to a minimum, LSAs for an area's networks and routers are flooded within the area, but not to routers outside the area. Each area becomes its own link-state domain with its own topological database.

Routers with multiple interfaces can participate in multiple areas. These routers, which are called *area border routers*, maintain separate LSDBs for each area. The routing tables within these routers are a combination of the routing table entries of all the SPF trees for each topological database and static routes, Simple Network Management Protocol (SNMP) configured routes, and routes learned from other routing protocols. To reduce the number of entries in the routing table, the networks inside the area can be advertised outside the area by using summary route advertisements. By keeping area topologies separate, OSPF passes less routing traffic than it would if the AS were not partitioned.

The Default Route

Each area within an OSPF network can be configured with a default route. A default route has a destination address of 0.0.0.0 and a subnet mask of 0.0.0.0. The default route is used to route any packets that are destined for an address not explicitly listed in the routing table. Default routes are typically used to reduce the size of routing tables because they can be used to summarize all routes external to the area into a single route. Default routes typically point to the OSPF backbone.

OSPF Backbone

Every OSPF network must have at least one area. In an OSPF network that has more than one area, there must be a backbone area to interconnect all the other areas within the network. The backbone area will always have an area ID of 0.0.0.0, and it acts as the hub for all the other areas on the network. All other areas must communicate their routing information to the backbone area so that it can distribute the information to all other areas. Figure 7.19 shows an example of an internetwork that has several areas and a backbone.

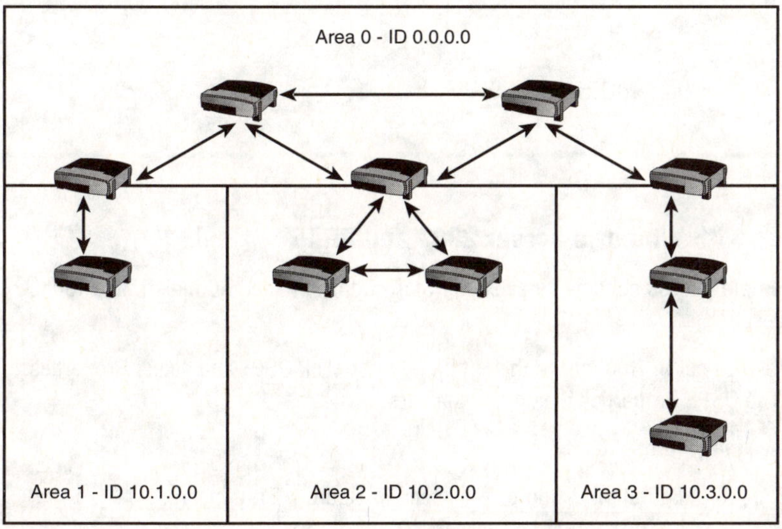

FIGURE 7.19 An OSPF network can have multiple areas.

Backbone routers not only route host traffic between areas, but also provide summary routes within areas to other routers on the backbone. These in turn provide summaries to the other routers within their areas. This ensures that any host within an area can reach any host in another area. This ensures that no area's routing tables contain detailed information about another area's topology, which minimizes the size of routing tables and ensures that the backbone handles all interarea traffic.

Area Routing

Area partitioning creates two types of OSPF routing, depending on whether the source and destination are in the same area or in different areas:

- **Intra-area routing**—Intra-area routing occurs when the source and destination are in the same area. With intra-area routing, the source routes the packet to its default gateway (an internal area router). The internal area router then makes use of the explicit routes (as calculated by the SPF algorithm) maintained in the area routers and routes the packet through the appropriate interface to the destination internal area router. The destination internal area router then forwards the packet to the destination host.
- **Interarea routing**—Interarea routing occurs when the source and destination are in different areas. When routing between areas, the source routes the packet to its default gateway (an internal area router), and the area router then forwards the packet to an area border router using the shortest path. The area border router then forwards the packets through backbone routers, using the shortest path to the area border router for the destination host. The area border router for the destination host then forwards the packets through internal area routers by using the shortest path, until the packets reach their destination.

Step by Step 7.9 shows how to create additional OSPF areas.

STEP BY STEP

7.9 Creating an OSPF Area with Windows Server 2003 and RRAS

1. Open the Routing and Remote Access console by selecting Start, Control Panel, Administrative Tools, Routing and Remote Access.
2. Expand the console tree and select IP Routing. In the left pane, right-click OSPF and select Properties from the context menu. The OSPF Properties dialog box appears.
3. Select the Areas tab, as seen in Figure 7.20.
4. Click Add, and the OSPF Area Configuration dialog box, as seen in Figure 7.21, appears.
5. In the Area ID field of the General tab, type a dotted-decimal number that identifies the area. To use a plaintext password, verify that the Enable Plaintext Password option is selected. To mark the area as a stub, select the Stub area option. In the Stub Metric field, click the arrows to set the stub metric. To import routes of other areas into the stub area, select the Import Summary Advertisements option. Click OK to apply the changes and then click OK again to return to the Routing and Remote Access console.

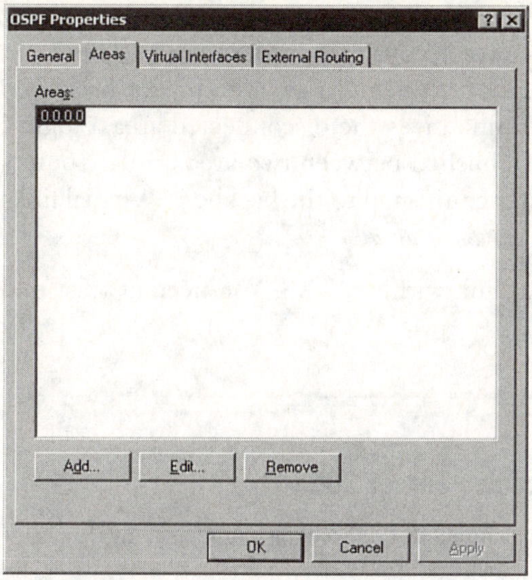

FIGURE 7.20 You can configure additional areas as needed.

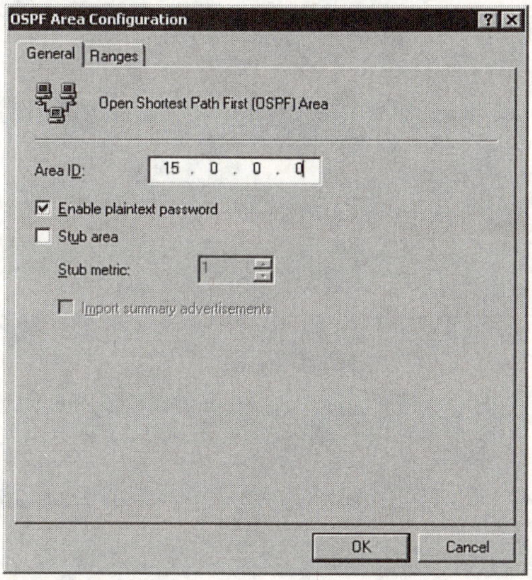

FIGURE 7.21 You need to know the network parameters and characteristics of an area before you add it to an OSPF network.

NOTE

Stub Areas A *stub area* is an OSPF area that doesn't advertise individual network routes from external areas. Instead, it relies on a default route (0.0.0.0, with a subnet mask of 0.0.0.0) to route all traffic out of the area. This is done to reduce the amount of memory required on the routers located in the stub area—they don't need to maintain a topology database.

Virtual Links

In rare cases it is possible that an area cannot have direct physical access to the backbone. In this instance, it is necessary to configure a connection from the new area to the backbone through a connection called a *virtual link*. A virtual link gives the disconnected area a logical path to the backbone. The virtual link has to be established between two area border routers that have a common area, with one area border router connected to the backbone. Virtual links are configured over a nonbackbone area known as a *transit area*.

Step by Step 7.10 shows how to configure a virtual link within RRAS. You need at least two OSPF areas in order to configure this interface.

STEP BY STEP

7.10 Configuring a Virtual Routing Link for Windows Server 2003

1. Open the Routing and Remote Access console by selecting Start, Control Panel, Administrative Tools, Routing and Remote Access.
2. Expand the console tree and select IP Routing. Right-click OSPF and select Properties from the context menu. The OSPF Properties dialog box, as seen in Figure 7.22, appears.

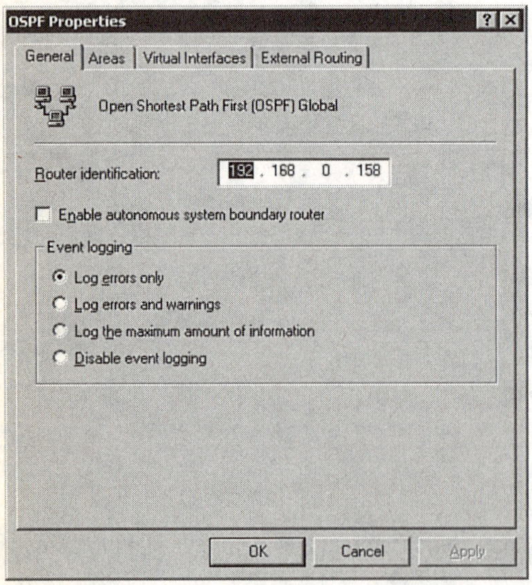

FIGURE 7.22 To set up a virtual routing link, you need to edit the OSPF properties.

3. On the Virtual Interfaces tab, click Add. The OSPF Virtual Interface Configuration dialog box, as seen in Figure 7.23, appears.

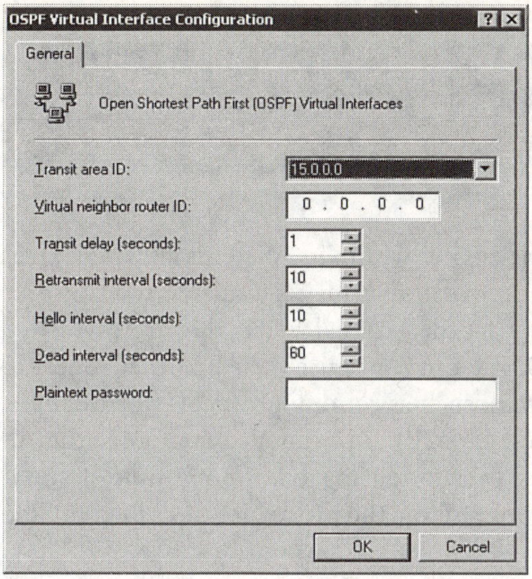

FIGURE 7.23 You need to know the network parameters and characteristics of a virtual link before you configure the virtual interface.

4. In the Transit Area ID pull-down menu, click the transit area over which you are connecting the virtual link.
5. In the Virtual Neighbor Router ID field, type the OSPF router ID of the router at the other endpoint of the virtual link.
6. In the Transit Delay (Seconds) field, click the arrows to set the transit delay, in seconds.
7. In the Retransmit Interval (Seconds) field, click the arrows to set the retransmit interval, in seconds.
8. In the Hello Interval (Seconds) field, click the arrows to set the hello interval, in seconds.
9. In the Dead Interval (Seconds) field, click the arrows to set the dead interval, in seconds.
10. Click OK to add the virtual interface, and click OK again to return to the Routing and Remote Access console.

AS Routing

Routing does not occur only within areas that use OSPF. When internetworks are connected to other internetworks that are under different administrative control, routing must be established. This type of routing between ASs is established by using external routes. AS border routers that run OSPF learn about exterior routes through other routing protocols, such as Interior Gateway Routing Protocol (IGRP), RIP, and BGP. AS border routers are similar to area border routers except that they route between different ASs.

EXAM ALERT

Supported Protocols Some of the most common border protocols, such as IGRP and BGP, are not supported by Windows Server 2003. They are important to know about because they are commonly used in production networks, but they will not be on the exam.

By default, an AS border router advertises all external routes within its AS. This allows all areas and networks within an area to reach destination networks that may lie outside the AS. As a network manager, you might find it necessary to restrict the external routes that are advertised within the AS. Using Windows Server 2003 RRAS, you can configure the AS border router to accept or ignore the routes of certain external sources, such as routing protocols (for example, RIPv2) or other sources (for example, static routes, SNMP). You can also configure the AS border router to accept or discard specific routes by configuring one or multiple destination/network mask pairs. To enable AS border routing, follow the procedure described in Step by Step 7.11.

STEP BY STEP

7.11 Configuring AS Border Routing in Windows Server 2003 RRAS

1. Open the Routing and Remote Access console by selecting Start, Control Panel, Administrative Tools, Routing and Remote Access.
2. Expand the console tree and select IP Routing. In the left pane, right-click OSPF and select Properties from the context menu. The OSPF Properties dialog box appears.
3. On the General tab, as seen previously in Figure 7.22, click Enable Autonomous System Boundary Router.
4. Select the External Routing tab, as seen in Figure 7.24, and click Accept Routes from All Route Sources Except Those Selected. If you want to exclude a specific route source, select it in the Route Sources dialog box. You can also select Ignore Routes from All Route Sources Except Those Selected if you want to accept routes from only one or two sources.
5. Click OK to return to the Routing and Remote Access console. OSPF boundary routing is enabled.

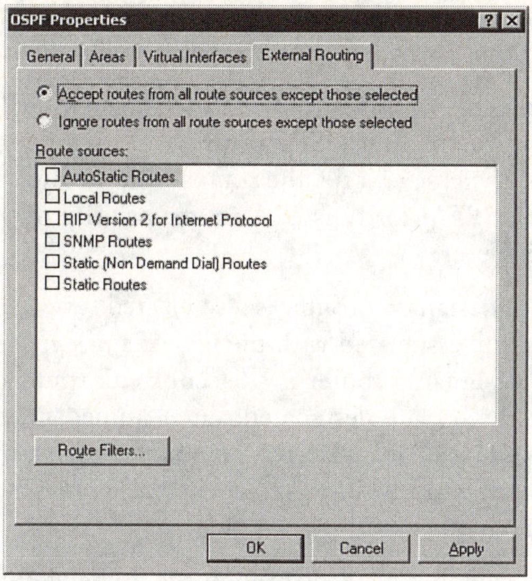

FIGURE 7.24 You have some flexibility in configuring the sources from which a router will accept updates.

OSPF Operation

The SPF routing algorithm is the basis for OSPF operations. When an SPF router is powered up, it initializes its routing protocol data structures and then waits for indications from lower-layer protocols that its interfaces are functional.

After a router has verified that its interfaces are functioning, it uses the OSPF Hello protocol to acquire neighbors. *Neighbors* are routers that have interfaces sharing a common network. The router sends hello packets to its neighbors and receives their hello packets. In addition to identifying neighboring routers, hello packets also act as keepalives to let routers know that other routers are still available.

Designated Routers

On multiaccess networks (that is, networks that support more than two routers), the Hello protocol elects a designated router and a backup designated router. Because the designated router is adjacent to all other routers, it acts as a hub for the distribution of link-state information, maintaining the synchronization of the topological database and controlling adjacencies between routers within the network. (The relationship between neighboring routers for the purposes of synchronizing the topological database is called an *adjacency*; adjacencies are discussed in more detail later in this chapter in the section “Adjacencies.”)

As an example of why a designated router is required, think about a broadcast network that has six OSPF routers. If you didn’t control the adjacency behavior, each router could establish an adjacency with each of the other routers, for a total of 15 adjacency relationships. On a broadcast network with n routers, a total of $n \times (n-1)/2$ adjacencies would be formed. This could result in unneeded flooding traffic as routers attempt to synchronize with all their adjacent routers. Designated routers allow a reduction in network traffic and in the size of the topological database.

The designated router is elected via the hello protocol. Hello packets are exchanged via IP multicast packets on each segment. The router with the highest OSPF priority on a segment becomes the designated router for that segment. In the case of a tie, the router with the highest router ID wins. The default for the interface OSPF priority is 1. A router priority of 0 means that the router cannot become a designated router.

In addition to electing a designated router, a backup designated router is also elected for each multiaccess network to prevent the loss in connectivity associated with the loss of a designated router. Like the designated router, the backup designated router is adjacent to all routers on the network. When the designated router fails, the backup designated router immediately becomes the designated router by sending LSAs to all its adjacent routers, announcing its new role. There is a short period of time when transit traffic can be impaired as the backup designated router takes over the role of the designated router.

Like the designated router, the backup designated router is elected through the exchange of hello packets. Each hello packet contains a field for the backup designated router of the network. If the backup designated router is not specified, the router with the highest router priority that is not already the designated router becomes the backup designated router. If multiple routers have the highest router priority, the router with the highest router ID is elected the backup designated router.

Adjacencies

When the topological databases of two neighboring routers are synchronized, the routers are said to be *adjacent*. On multiaccess networks, the designated router determines which routers should become adjacent. Topological databases are synchronized between pairs of adjacent routers. Adjacencies control the distribution of routing protocol packets, which are sent and received only on adjacencies.

Adjacencies are first developed when an OSPF router initializes; it sends out a periodic OSPF hello packet. The OSPF hello packet contains configuration information such as the router's router ID and the list of neighboring routers for which the router has received hello packets. Initially, the neighbor list in the OSPF hello packet does not contain any neighbors.

The initializing OSPF router also listens for neighboring routers' hello packets. From the incoming hello packets, the initializing router determines the specific router or routers with which an adjacency is to be established. Adjacencies are formed with the designated router and backup designated router, which are identified in the incoming hello packets. Designated routers and backup designated routers were discussed in more detail earlier in this chapter in the section "Designated Routers."

To begin the adjacency, the routers forming the adjacency describe the contents of their topological databases through a sequence of database description packets. This is known as the *database exchange process*, during which the two neighboring routers form a master/slave relationship. The contents of each router's topological database are acknowledged by its neighboring router.

Each router compares its LSAs with the LSAs of its neighbor and notes which LSAs need to be requested from the neighbor to synchronize the topological database. The missing or more recent LSAs are then requested through link-state request packets. Link-state update packets are sent in response to the link-state request packets, and their receipt is acknowledged. When all link-state requests of both routers have been satisfied, the topological databases of the neighboring routers are fully synchronized, and an adjacency is formed.

After an adjacency is formed, each neighboring router sends a periodic hello packet to inform its neighbor that the router is still active on the network. The lack of hello packets from a neighbor is used to detect a downed router.

If an event occurs, such as a downed link or router or the addition of a new network that changes the topological database of one router, the topological databases of adjacent routers are no longer synchronized. The router whose topological database has changed sends link-state update packets to its adjacent neighbor. The receipt of the link-state update packets is acknowledged. After the exchange, the topological databases of the adjacent routers are again synchronized.

NOTE

Distance-vector based routing protocols have the following drawbacks associated with them:

- High overhead
- Not scalable
- Network bandwidth intensive
- Long convergence time
- Routing loops
- Count-to-infinity problems

Distance-vector routing protocols have mechanisms that allow them to avoid the count-to-infinity problems as well as to improve convergence. They include the following:

- Split horizon
- Split horizon with poison reverse
- Triggered updates

There are a number of advantages to link-state protocols, especially when compared to the distance vector-based routing protocols. These advantages include the following:

- Smaller routing tables
- Highly scalable
- More efficient use of network bandwidth
- Faster convergence

One disadvantage of link-state protocols is that they are more complex to understand and configure than distance-vector protocols. They also require additional processing power on the router due to the need to calculate the routing tree.

Managing Routing Ports

Objective:

Manage TCP/IP routing.

- Manage routing ports.

The last piece of the Windows Server 2003 routing puzzle is the routing port. A *routing port* is a device or a channel of a device that supports a single point-to-point connection. For an example of a device that acts as a port, think of a modem. Integrated Services Digital Network (ISDN) is an example of a channelized connection (also known as a *multiport device*). A Primary Rate Interface (PRI) ISDN connection can support two data channels, known as B-channels (short for *bearer channels*). Each of these B-channels can act as the port for a point-to-point connection. There is an additional 16KB D-channel (short for *delta channel*) that is used for session control and error handling.

Step by Step 7.12 describes how to manage these ports. You need to have a modem configured on your test system to complete this exercise.

NOTE

Why Can't I Add a Port in the Routing and Remote Access Console? In the Windows Server 2003 operating system, ports are physical devices. As such, they are added either through the Modems applet in the Control Panel or through the Add/Remove Hardware applet for devices that are added as internal port adapters (for example, an ISDN adapter). RRAS is used to manage the ports after they have been installed on the operating system.

STEP BY STEP

7.12 Configuring RRAS Modem Ports

1. Open the Routing and Remote Access console by selecting Start, Control Panel, Administrative Tools, Routing and Remote Access.
2. Select Ports in the left pane of the console. The list of all available ports appears in the right pane, as seen in Figure 7.25.
3. Right-click Ports in the left pane and select Properties. The Ports Properties dialog box, as seen in Figure 7.26, appears. This screen displays all the types of ports presently configured for use by RRAS, but unlike the Ports window, it does not show the number of each type of port. Select the modem port and click Configure to continue. The Configure Device screen, as seen in Figure 7.27, appears.

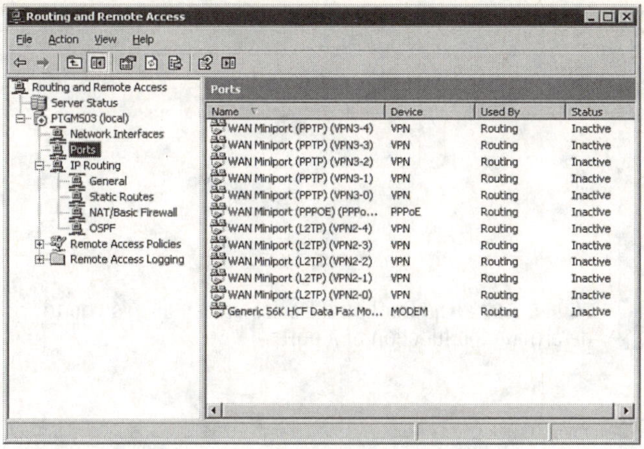

FIGURE 7.25 The Ports pane shows all the available ports on the system, including modem, VPN, Point-to-Point Protocol over Ethernet (PPPOE), and any other nonpermanent interface.

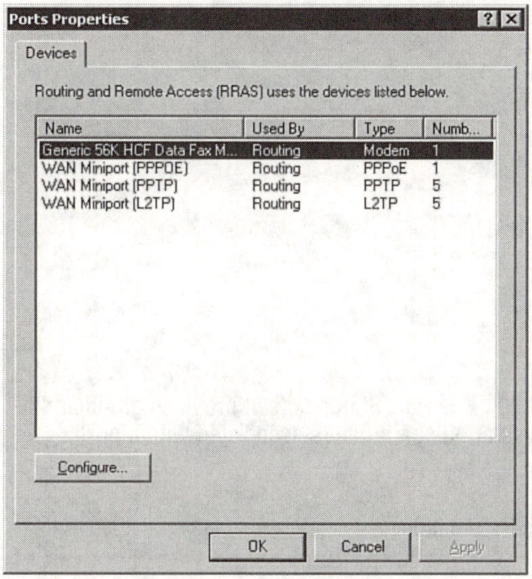

FIGURE 7.26 The Ports Properties screen shows the different types of ports installed on the system.

4. Select Demand-Dial Routing Connections (Inbound and Outbound). This makes the port available to participate in routing. You would use the other parameters on the Configure Device screen if the server were going to be used as a remote access server/dial-in server, which is beyond the scope for this exercise. Click OK to assign this port for use with demand-dial router connections. Click OK to return to the Routing and Remote Access console.

5. To check the status of the port, click the Ports icon in the Routing and Remote Access console. Each available port is displayed. Double-click the modem you configured in Steps 3 and 4. The Port Status screen appears, as seen in Figure 7.28. The Port Status screen displays a lot of useful statistics when a session is in progress, including how long the connection has been up, how much traffic has passed across the line, and the session addressing information.

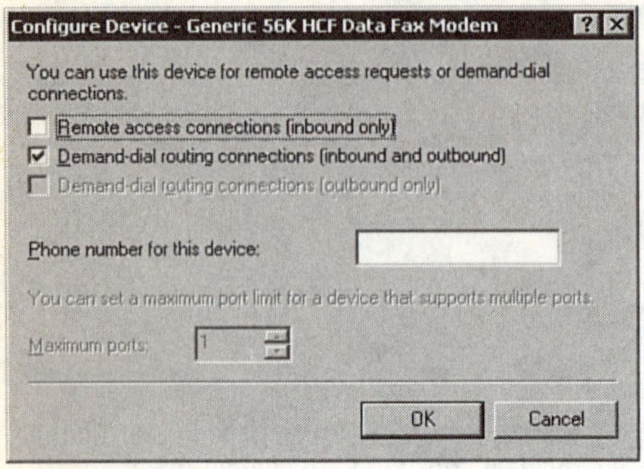

FIGURE 7.27 The Configure Device screen allows you to determine the function of a port.

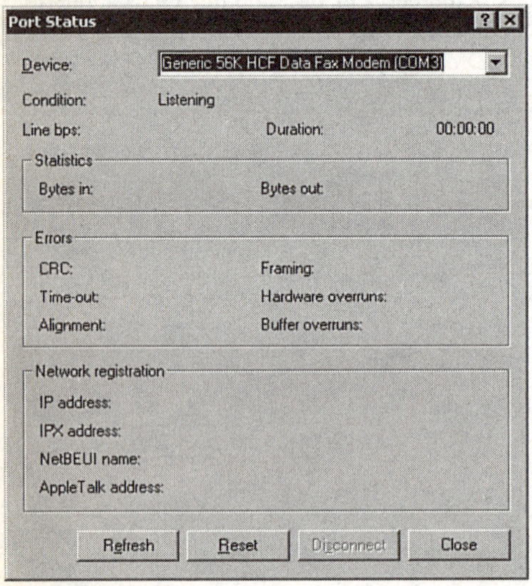

FIGURE 7.28 The Port Status screen provides granular status on the various parameters associated with a port.

6. Select Close to return to the Routing and Remote Access console.

Challenge

You are the system and network administrator of Nounsense Publishing, a small business that is interested in connecting offices and getting on the Internet. The main headquarters of the company is in Boston, and there is a two-employee sales office in San Francisco. You have been asked by the company owner to connect the offices as inexpensively as possible, as well as set up an Internet connection.

You would like to use a demand-dial connection for the small sales office and a dedicated Internet connection that will allow you to assign each of the workstations on the network a TCP/IP address that will identify it on the Internet. You currently have only one network segment in the corporate headquarters and a second in the San Francisco office. Your Internet connection must be online at all times, and you would like to minimize the management that is necessary on your part. You believe that the network will grow within the next year, and you would like to ensure that this can occur with a minimum of configuration.

Through your discussions with the key stakeholders in this project, you've determined the following additional information:

- There must be a dedicated connection to the Internet.
- There are two locations that need to be connected.
- The network may expand in the future, and that should occur with a minimum of configuration.
- At this time, there is only one segment on the network.

Your task is to implement the required routing solution for Nounsense Publishing.

Try to complete this exercise on your own, listing your conclusions on a sheet of paper. After you have completed the exercise, compare your results to those given here.

Answers

When you're configuring a small office network, you can connect the office to the Internet in several ways. For instance, you can connect a small office network to the Internet via a demand-dial connection, or you can configure a router with Network Address Translation. However, based on the requirements of the scenario, the most appropriate solution is to implement a dedicated connection.

You can connect the small office by using an ISDN or fractional T-1 line. Because you would like to minimize the configuration that is required, you should create a configuration based on either static routes or RIP. In this type of scenario, OSPF is much too complex a solution.

To determine whether to use static routes or RIP, you must look closely at the requirements. Because the network may expand in the future and it should occur with a minimum of configuration, it is best to use a dynamic routing protocol that can adapt to a change in the network topology. Therefore, you should use RIP rather than static routing.

Troubleshooting and Monitoring IP Routing

Up to this point, this chapter discusses the theory behind routing protocols and explores the individual routing protocols. The following sections focus on some of the other tools that can be used in a network environment to help configure routing and to troubleshoot routing problems, including some troubleshooting options for each of the routing protocols.

Using Network Monitor

Network Monitor is a tool you can use to capture network traffic. It can be used to diagnose problems when two computers do not communicate with one another or when a computer has trouble functioning in a network environment. For instance, a computer may have problems resolving names or finding a path to another computer (that is, it has routing problems).

Network Monitor can be configured to capture network traffic in several ways. It can be configured to capture all network traffic that it receives, to respond to events on the network, or to monitor only a subset of the traffic (for instance, a particular protocol, such as HTTP traffic only). After the network data has been captured, Network Monitor analyzes the data and translates it into its logical frame structure to make the protocol information readable to the person capturing the information. Each frame contains the following:

EXAM ALERT

Network Analysis Analyzing the traffic you see in Network Monitor is not only well beyond the scope of this book, but also cannot be tested on the exam. Network analysis is a science that takes a good deal of training and experience to master. For the exam, you should just be aware that Network Monitor gives you the capability to capture and analyze packets.

- The source address of the computer that is sending the frame
- The destination address of the computer that received the frame
- Headers from each protocol used to send the frame
- The data or a portion of the information being sent

After the data has been translated, the information is presented through the graphical display provided by Network Monitor. Figure 7.29 shows an example of what the data looks like after it has been captured.

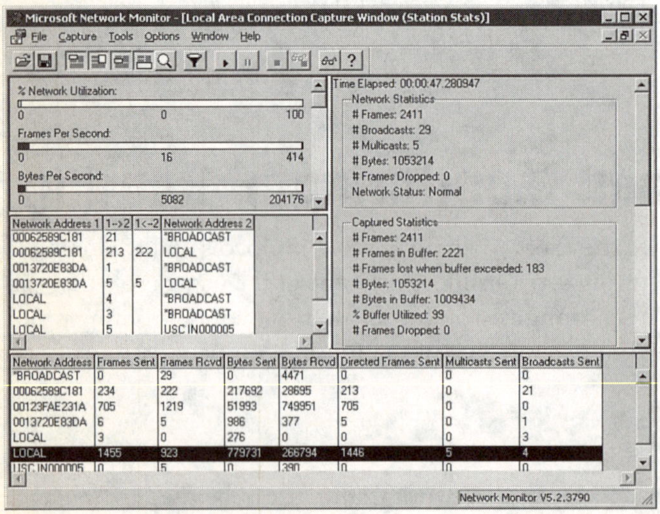

FIGURE 7.29 Network Monitor gives a lot of information about the traffic on a network.

Supporting Windows Server 2003 Routing

As a network administrator, you have the task of configuring and installing RRAS. After RRAS is configured and installed, you are then responsible for managing additional changes to the existing configuration, monitoring the installed configuration for problems, and troubleshooting problems when they arise.

RRAS Operation

After you have configured RRAS, you can perform several tasks to manage its ongoing operation. Some of the items you need to manage and monitor include the following:

- Administer a remote router.
- Check the status of existing interfaces.
- View existing routing tables and verify that routes are being received from routing protocols.
- Determine the status of RRAS services and reset the services, if required.

In most large companies, users, systems, and services can be located in multiple locations throughout the country (or even the world). Coupled with the centralization of information technology resources, this can present problems for managing remote installations. With RRAS, it is possible to remotely manage RRAS routers from a central location.

The RRAS console allows you to quickly determine whether the existing interfaces are active. In addition to monitoring the event logs for possible messages that indicate problems, you can also check the individual interfaces to see what their operational states are.

Even if you have determined that the interfaces for a particular server are operational, it's still possible that the existing interfaces are not receiving routes to update the routing tables. You, as an administrator, would like to determine whether the router is indeed receiving updates. Again, the RRAS console provided with Windows Server 2003 allows you to do this. To view the routing tables of a particular protocol, within the Routing and Remote Access console, select and expand the server and the IP Routing head, and then select Static Routes. Then right-click Static Routes and select the Show IP Routing Table option. You can then verify whether the router is receiving updates to its routing table from other routers in the network.

Finally, you might want to check the overall status of the services to determine whether they are running. If they are not running, you need to start them by choosing Computer Management, selecting Services and Applications, and then selecting Services. In the left pane of the Routing and Remote Access console, you need to verify that the Status column displays Started. If the service is not started, you should right-click Routing and Remote Access, and then click Start. If the router does not start, you should check the system event log for error messages.

Troubleshooting RIP Environments

After RIP is configured within your environment, you might be called on from time to time to troubleshoot problems that arise with routing. Although every problem is unique, Table 7.2 outlines some of the solutions that might help when you're responding to problems in a RIP environment.

TABLE 7.2 RIP Problems, Potential Causes, and Possible Solutions

Problem	Cause/Solution
Routing tables have improper routing information in a mixed RIP network.	RIPv2 routers are configured to multicast announcements. Multicast RIPv1 and RIPv2 announcements are never received by RIPv1 routers. If you have a mixed environment of RIPv1 and RIPv2, you need to ensure that the routers configured with RIPv2 use broadcast instead of multicast announcements.
Silent RIP hosts are not receiving routes.	RIPv2 routers are configured to multicast announcements. Multicast announcements are never received by silent RIP hosts. If silent RIP hosts on a network are not receiving routes from the local RIP router, you need to verify the version of RIP supported by the silent RIP hosts. If it is the listening service in Windows NT 4.0 Service Pack 4 or Windows Server 2003, you must configure the RIP routers for RIPv1 or RIPv2 broadcasting.
RIP routers are not being updated with valid routes.	You may be deploying variable- length subnetting, disjointed subnets, or supernetting in a RIPv1 or mixed RIPv1 and RIPv2 environment. You should not deploy variable-length subnetting, disjointed subnets, or supernetting in a RIPv1 or mixed RIPv1 and RIPv2 environment because it is not supported.
Host or default routes are not being propagated.	By default, RIP is not configured to propagate host or default routes. If these need to be propagated, you should change the default settings on the Advanced tab of the Properties dialog box of a RIP interface.

The problems described in Table 7.2 are only some of the ones that can arise in a RIP environment. For further troubleshooting information, refer to Microsoft TechNet or the Windows Server 2003 documentation.

Troubleshooting OSPF Environments

OSPF is a more complex protocol to understand than RIP. Therefore, there is more risk of problems arising because of the complexity of the protocol. The fact that OSPF is more hierarchical than other protocols offers an opportunity to help troubleshoot problems that may arise; you can isolate issues to a particular area or the interconnectivity between areas. Problems and their possible solutions include those shown in Table 7.3.

TABLE 7.3 OSPF Problems, Potential Causes, and Possible Solutions

Problem	Cause/Solution
OSPF adjacency is not forming between two neighbors.	OSPF is not enabled on the interface. You should verify that OSPF is enabled on the interface on the network segment where an adjacency should form. By default, when you add an interface to the OSPF routing protocol, OSPF is disabled for the interface and must be manually enabled. If OSPF is enabled, you should try to `ping` the neighboring router to ensure basic IP and network connectivity. You can use the `tracert` command to trace the route to the neighboring router. There should not be any routers between the neighboring routers.
A virtual link is not forming between two areas.	There may be a mismatched configuration of password, hello interval, or dead interval. You should verify that the virtual link neighbor routers are configured for the same password, hello interval, and dead interval. Another possible cause is that virtual link neighbors may be configured for the incorrect transit area ID. You should verify that both virtual link neighbors are configured for the same transit area ID and that they are configured to use the correct transit area.
Routing tables are not being updated with OSPF routes or improper OSPF routes are being received.	You may not be receiving summarized routes. If you are not receiving summarized OSPF routes for an area, you should verify that the area border routers for the area are configured with the proper destination/network mask pairs summarizing that area's routes. Another potential cause is that all area border routers are not connected to the backbone. You should verify that all area border routers are either physically connected to the backbone or logically connected to the backbone by using border routers, which are routers that connect two areas without going through the backbone.

Table 7.3 lists only some of the problems that can arise in an OSPF environment. For further troubleshooting information, refer to Microsoft Technet or the Windows Server 2003 documentation.

Chapter Summary

This chapter focuses on routing. It covers the underlying fundamentals of routing and covers such topics as distance-vector routing and link-state routing. It also discusses the two IP routing protocols supported by Windows Server 2003—RIP and OSPF—including their strengths and drawbacks. This chapter also covers some of the tools for working with routing and diagnosing problems with routing after it is set up and running.

Key Terms

- Adjacency
- Area
- Area border router
- ARP
- AS
- Default route
- Designated router
- Distance-vector routing
- IGP
- ISDN
- Link-state routing
- OSPF
- RIP
- Split horizon
- Split horizon with poison reverse
- `tracert`
- Triggered updates
- Virtual link

Apply Your Knowledge

In this chapter, you have learned about routing protocols and how routing is configured and managed using Windows Server 2003. In the following exercises, you will practice some of the concepts and methods discussed in this chapter.

Exercises

7.1 Adding a Static Route to the Existing Routing Table

This exercise explores using the `route` command to add a static route to an existing routing table on an RRAS server. This method provides a way for you to add static routes to routing configurations.

Estimated Time: 5 minutes

1. Select Start, Programs, Accessories, Command Prompt.
2. In the Command Prompt window, type the following:

   ```
   route ADD 157.0.0.0 MASK 255.0.0.0
   157.55.80.1 METRIC 3
   ```

3. Type **`route print`** in the Command Prompt window.
4. Type **`exit`** to leave the Command Prompt window.

7.2 Configuring an AS Border Router

This exercise explores using the Routing and Remote Access console to configure a border router for an AS within an OSPF network.

Estimated Time: 10 minutes

1. Open the Routing and Remote Access console by selecting Start, Control Panel, Administrative Tools, Routing and Remote Access.
2. In the console tree, select OSPF by using the plus (+) button to expand the Routing and Remote Access option, select the server, and highlight the IP Routing option.
3. Right-click OSPF and then click Properties.
4. On the General tab, click Enable Autonomous System Boundary Router.
5. On the External Routing tab, click either Accept Routes from All Route Sources Except Those Selected or Ignore Routes from All Route Sources Except Those Selected.
6. Select or clear the appropriate options next to the route sources.

7.3 Configuring an Interface of a Virtual Link

This exercise explores using the Routing and Remote Access console to configure a virtual interface for one side of an OSPF virtual link.

Estimated Time: 15 minutes

1. Open the Routing and Remote Access console by selecting Start, Control Panel, Administrative Tools, Routing and Remote Access.
2. In the console tree, select OSPF by using the plus (+) button to expand the Routing and Remote Access option, select the server, and highlight the IP routing option.
3. Right-click OSPF, and then click Properties.
4. On the Virtual Interfaces tab, click Add.
5. In the Transit Area ID field, select the transit area through which you are connecting the virtual link.
6. In the Virtual Neighbor Router ID field, type the OSPF router ID of the router at the other endpoint of the virtual link.
7. In the Transit Delay (Seconds) field, click the arrows to set the transit delay, in seconds.
8. In the Retransmit Interval (Seconds) field, click the arrows to set the retransmit interval, in seconds.
9. In the Hello Interval (Seconds) field, click the arrows to set the hello interval, in seconds.
10. In the Dead Interval (Seconds) field, click the arrows to set the dead interval, in seconds.
11. If the backbone area is configured to have a password, in the Plaintext Password field, type a password.

7.4 Adding an IP Routing Protocol to an RRAS Server

This exercise explores adding an IP routing protocol to your RRAS server.

Estimated Time: 5 minutes

1. Open the Routing and Remote Access console by selecting Start, Control Panel, Administrative Tools, Routing and Remote Access.
2. In the console tree, select General by using the plus (+) button to expand the Routing and Remote Access option, select the server, and then highlight the IP Routing option.
3. Right-click General and then click New Routing Protocol.
4. In the Routing Protocols dialog box, select the IP protocol and then click Add.

Exam Questions

1. You are a network engineer for Golden Eagle Airlines, a regional airline. You are in the process of migrating from a Novell NetWare network and have configured a Windows Server 2003 server as a router. One of the Novell NetWare servers had been acting as the building router previously. You have three LAN segments connected to the server. Each segment has a Class C IP address range associated with it, and you have configured the appropriate `route` commands to add the network entries to the routing table. You have set the subnet mask as 255.255.255.0, and you have not configured a default gateway for the router. What will happen when a packet arrives for a route that has not been configured on the router?

   ❍ **A.** The packet will be routed through the first segment that was configured on the router.

   ❍ **B.** The packet will be routed through all segments configured on the router.

   ❍ **C.** The router will use an ARP broadcast to resolve the address so that it knows how to route it.

   ❍ **D.** The packet will be dropped by the router.

2. You are the network administrator of Bombastic Publishing, a medium-sized publishing company. You are receiving calls from people at the help desk, indicating that they cannot get access to the server. You check into it and determine that you cannot `ping` the server across the router. You check the router, and the services seem as though they are started and running fine. You would now like to check the routing tables. Which utilities can you use to determine what the routing tables contain? (Choose all that apply.)

   ❍ **A.** The Routing and Remote Access console

   ❍ **B.** The `route` command

   ❍ **C.** The `tracert` command

   ❍ **D.** The `arp` command

3. You are the network administrator for Zanzibar Enterprises, a large manufacturing company. The company headquarters has a multioffice campus location with a large, complex network. The network uses RIP to provide routing information throughout the campus as well as to 30 remote sales offices, connected via T-1 WAN connections. The company just added four more buildings to the headquarters campus, resulting in a major expansion of the network. While you are in the process of adding the additional routers needed to connect the new network segments, users indicate that they cannot reach some segments on the network. A quick test of the new routers shows that they are routing, but a more in-depth review of the network shows that some of the routers do not have any information about other routers in the network. What could be the problem?

   ❍ **A.** RIP is not propagating information.

   ❍ **B.** RIP cannot support more than 15 hops.

   ❍ **C.** RIP is suffering from a count-to-infinity problem.

   ❍ **D.** The routers that are not reachable are not functioning properly.

4. You are a system administrator for Belmont Technical College, which has a campus network that is very large and growing. You are in the process of reengineering the network, and you remove some segments from the overall network topology. Your network makes use of RIP to route information throughout the infrastructure. Users indicate that they cannot reach some segments on the network. As you investigate the problem, you determine that some of the routers do not have any information about other routers in the network. What could be the problem? (Choose all that apply.)

   ❍ **A.** RIP is not propagating information.

   ❍ **B.** RIP cannot support more than 15 hops.

   ❍ **C.** RIP is suffering from a count-to-infinity problem.

   ❍ **D.** The routers that are not reachable are not functioning properly.

5. You are a technical architect for Little Faith Enterprises, a venture capital company. The headquarters office has a local network with several network segments. A host on one segment needs to send data to a host on the same segment. What methods will the host use to reach the other host? (Choose all that apply.)

   ❍ **A.** The host will query DNS for the address of the host and will use the address it obtains to reach the host.

   ❍ **B.** The host will use ARP to determine how to send to the other host on the network.

   ❍ **C.** The host will send the information to the router, which will, in turn, send it to the host.

   ❍ **D.** The routers will broadcast the information on the local segment to the destination host.

6. You are a help desk agent for Mount Abora Consulting, a managed services outsourcing company. You receive a call from a customer who is having a problem while trying to transfer information from her computer to another computer by using a custom-written application. The transfer keeps failing. You check into the problem and determine that the two hosts are on separate network segments. You check the configurations of each computer and find that each appears to be configured correctly. You do initial testing by `ping`ing between the systems, which works as it should. You need to do some more advanced troubleshooting, including examining the actual traffic between the two hosts. What tool can you use to do more detailed testing?

   ❍ **A.** Network Monitor

   ❍ **B.** Performance Monitor

   ❍ **C.** System Monitor

   ❍ **D.** SNMP

7. You are the lead technician for Dulcimer Music, a manufacturer of studio-quality recording equipment. The company has four locations connected by a WAN. There is one location in Toronto, there is one in New York, and there are two locations in Los Angeles—the headquarters and the main studio. The central Information Services department is located in Toronto, and the network is configured with high-speed T-3 connections from Toronto to all locations. The Los Angeles headquarters location also has a router set up with a connection to Toronto and another ISDN connection to the Los Angeles studio location. Your users in the headquarters communicate with application servers in the studio location on a regular basis. The company uses RIP. When routing traffic, which route will the traffic take, based on the information provided?

❍ **A.** The traffic will be routed through Toronto to the Los Angeles studio location.

❍ **B.** The traffic will be routed directly to the Los Angeles studio location.

❍ **C.** The traffic will be load balanced both through Toronto and directly to the Los Angeles studio location.

❍ **D.** The traffic will take the least congested route toward the Los Angeles studio location.

8. You are the network architect for Blue Moon Recordings, a small recording company. The company has four remote offices, and you have been asked to network the remote offices with the headquarters location. You have decided to use RIP as the routing protocol for the new network. Which of the following are benefits of using RIP in this environment? (Choose all that apply.)

❍ **A.** High overhead

❍ **B.** Low maintenance

❍ **C.** Fast convergence

❍ **D.** Ease of configuration

❍ **E.** Scalability

9. You are the network administrator of the Genie in a Bottle screensaver company. The company has a large corporate network that is using OSPF as the routing protocol. The company was just acquired by a competitor that is also using OSPF to route within its network. You are charged with bringing the two networks together, and you establish a virtual link with the other network. However, the virtual link is not forming. What could be the problem? (Choose all that apply.)

❍ **A.** The router on the other side has been set up to filter routes, and therefore the virtual link will take time to be established.

❍ **B.** The password for each of the two routers is different.

❍ **C.** The router interfaces on each router are set to different connection speeds.

❍ **D.** The router is configured with a hello interval that is different from the other router's.

10. You are an information technology manager with the Howl at the Moon Karaoke Company, the largest karaoke bar franchising company in the world. The company has a large corporate network that is using OSPF as the routing protocol within the environment. You have partitioned the network into several areas, with each area having a single router connected to the backbone. You are tuning performance and would like to ensure that as little routing traffic as possible is broadcast onto the network. What is the best method of doing this?

❍ **A.** Configure each area as a stub area and have each area router specify a default route.

❍ **B.** Configure each area router to distribute external routes only on startup.

❍ **C.** Configure each area as a transit area and have each area router specify a default route.

❍ **D.** Configure each area router to implement external route filters.

11. You are the network architect for the Really Big Soft Drink Company, a large beverage distribution company. The company has 74 remote offices, with offices on every continent except Antarctica, and you have been asked to network the remote offices with the headquarters location. You have decided to use OSPF as the routing protocol for the new network. Which of the following are benefits of using OSPF in this environment? (Choose all that apply.)

❍ **A.** High network overhead

❍ **B.** Low maintenance

❍ **C.** Fast convergence

❍ **D.** Ease of configuration

❍ **E.** Scalability

12. You are the information technology manager for Alph Construction. The company has four remote sites, and you are recommending to the CIO that the company use Windows Server 2003 servers as routers to connect the branch offices to the central office. Which of the following are reasons to use Windows Server 2003 servers as the routers for this implementation? (Choose all that apply.)

❍ **A.** Ease of use

❍ **B.** Broad protocol support

❍ **C.** Scalability

❍ **D.** Low cost

❍ **E.** Slower performance

13. You are the lead network engineer for White Clouds Airlines. The company has 55 offices, located throughout the United States, all connected to the corporate WAN with a mixture of hardware routers and Windows Server 2003 servers running RRAS for routing. The network is configured to use a mix of RIPv1 and RIPv2. You notice that routing tables have improper routing information. Which of the following is the most likely cause of this problem?

❍ **A.** RIPv2 routers are configured to multicast announcements. Multicast RIPv1 and RIPv2 announcements are never received by RIPv1 routers.

❍ **B.** RIPv2 routers are configured to multicast announcements. Multicast announcements are never received by RIPv1 hosts.

❍ **C.** By default, RIP is not configured to propagate host or default routes.

❍ **D.** On a network of this size, you must use OSPF to ensure that hardware and software routers have the correct routing table information.

Answers to Exam Questions

1. **D**. By default, if a default gateway is not configured, the router drops the packet and sends an ICMP message back to the host, indicating that the destination host is unreachable; therefore Answers A, B, and C are all incorrect. For more information, see the section "Introduction to IP Routing."
2. **A**, **B**. The two utilities that can be used to check routing tables are the RRAS administration tool and the `route` command. You use the `print` option to display the existing routes. The `tracert` command is used to determine reachability through the network; thus Answer C is incorrect. The `arp` command is used to display the IP-to-physical address table; thus Answer D is incorrect. For more information, see the section "Using the `route` Command to Configure Static Routes."
3. **B**. By default, the maximum number of hops between routers is 15. Given the scenario presented, this is the most likely cause of the problem because you tested the routers when you installed them; therefore Answers A and D are incorrect. The count-to-infinity problem occurs only when a segment is removed from the network; thus Answer C is incorrect. For more information, see the section "Routing Protocols."
4. **B**, **C**. In this scenario, segments are being removed from the overall network; nothing is noted about routers or segments being added. This indicates that the problem could indeed be a count-to-infinity problem; therefore, Answer C is correct. Because infinity is 15 hops, Answer B is also correct. Since some routers have correct information, it is not likely that RIP is not functioning, nor is it likely that the routers are not functioning; thus Answers A and D are incorrect. For more information, see the section "Routing Protocols."
5. **A**, **B**. To send to a destination host on the local segment, the sending host must first determine the network address from the hostname. To do this, it queries DNS to resolve the name to an IP address. The host then queries its local ARP table to see if it has a MAC address for the IP address. The host then sends a directed broadcast of the information to the destination host; thus Answers C and D are incorrect. For more information, see the section "Host Routing."

6. **A**. To further check what might be going on between the two machines, you need to use Network Monitor. Performance Monitor is used for gathering statistics about the performance of a machine; thus Answer B is incorrect. System Monitor is a tool that is available on Windows 95/98 and provides similar information to Performance Monitor for monitoring performance; thus Answer C is incorrect. SNMP is used for managing and configuring network devices; thus Answer D is incorrect. For more information, see the section "Using Network Monitor."
7. **B**. The traffic will be routed directly to the Los Angeles studio location. RIP routes traffic on a least-cost basis. Because there was no mention of costs being assigned to each of the segments, the cost will default to 1 for each segment. Routing through the Toronto location would incur a total cost of 2 hops, even though that is probably the fastest path to the Los Angeles studio location, given the line speed; thus Answers A, C, and D are incorrect. For more information, see the section "Working with RIP."
8. **B**, **D**. Benefits of RIP include low maintenance and easy configuration. High overhead is a characteristic of RIP, but it is not a benefit; therefore, Answer A is incorrect. Answers C and E are characteristics of OSPF, not of RIP. For more information, see the section "Dynamic Routing."
9. **B**, **D**. To establish a virtual link between the two organizations, it is necessary to ensure that the password, the hello interval, and the dead interval are configured to be the same. If they are not configured this way, the virtual link will have trouble being established; therefore answers A and C are incorrect. For more information, see the section "Working with OSPF."
10. **A**. A stub area contains a single entry and exit point. Routing to all-AS external networks in a stub area is done through a default route (destination 0.0.0.0, with network mask 0.0.0.0). To create the default route, the area border router of the stub area advertises a default route into the stub area. The default route is flooded to all the routers within the stub area but not outside the stub area. The routers within the area use the default route to route any addresses that are not reachable within the AS. There is no need for any of the other configuration options listed; thus Answers B, C, and D are all incorrect. For more information, see the section "Working with OSPF."
11. **C**, **E**. Benefits of OSPF include fast convergence and superior scalability. High overhead is a characteristic of OSPF, but it is not a benefit; therefore, Answer A is incorrect. Answers B and D are characteristics of RIP, not OSPF. For more information, see the section "Dynamic Routing."
12. **A**, **D**. Ease of use due to a consistent, familiar management interface and low cost are both benefits of using a Windows Server 2003 server as a router. Broad protocol support and scalability are both features of a hardware router, which is not limited by the hardware bus of the PC for interfaces, thus Answers B and C are incorrect. Although software routers are typically slower than hardware routers, that is not considered a benefit; thus Answer E is incorrect. For more information, see the section "Introduction to IP Routing."
13. **A.** Multicast announcements from RIPv2 routers will never be received by RIPv1 routers. If you have a mixed environment of RIPv1 and RIPv2, you need to ensure that the routers configured with RIPv2 are using broadcast instead of multicast announcements; thus Answers B, C, and D are incorrect. For more information, see the section "Troubleshooting RIP Environments."

Suggested Reading and Resources

1. Moy, John T. *OSPF Complete Implementation*. Addison-Wesley, 2000.
2. Doyle, Jeff. *Routing TCP/IP*, Volume I (CCIE Professional Development). Cisco Press, 1998.
3. Thomas, Tom M. *OSPF Network Design Solutions*. Cisco Press, 2003.
4. Charles, Kackie. *Windows 2000 Routing and Remote Access Service*. New Riders Publishing, 2000.
5. Davies, Joseph, and Lee, Thomas. *Microsoft Windows Server 2003 TCP/IP Protocols and Services Technical Reference*. Microsoft Press, 2003.
6. "Network Monitor," http://technet2.microsoft.com/WindowsServer/en/Library/ad2b59d1-0fb8-45e3-9055-a5aeba8817a91033.mspx.

8

CHAPTER 8

Implementing, Managing, and Troubleshooting IPSec to Secure Network Traffic

In today's competitive and security-focused business world, it's not surprising anymore to find companies that are concerned not only with the integrity and safety of data crossing in and out of the private network, but also with the data that is flowing internally between servers and hosts on the typically safe and secure internal network. To that end, Windows Server 2003 provides native support for the IP Security (IPSec) protocol, which can be configured and managed to provide secure data transfers across your network.

This chapter covers the IP Security (IPSec) portion of the unit "Implementing, Managing, and Maintaining Network Security" for Exam 70-291, "Implementing, Managing, and Maintaining a Microsoft Windows Server 2003 Network Infrastructure."

Objectives

Monitor network protocol security. Tools might include the IP Security Monitor Microsoft Management Console (MMC) snap-in and Kerberos support tools.

- After you've addressed the issue of securing the client and server operating systems, you should consider securing the traffic between them on the network. You can use the IPSec protocol to secure traffic between the computers on a network. After you have IPSec configured and placed in operation, you need to monitor it to ensure that communications are being secured as required.

Troubleshoot network protocol security. Tools might include the IP Security Monitor MMC snap-in, Event Viewer, and Network Monitor.

- As you might expect, intended results don't always work out perfectly—especially when you're dealing with IPSec, which can be a tough subject with which to come to terms. Fortunately, Microsoft provides several Windows Server 2003 tools that can be used to troubleshoot and correct IPSec-related problems.

Outline

Study Strategies

- Carefully work your way through the material discussing the component parts of an IPSec policy. Practice creating and implementing an IPSec policy between two computers on your network.
- Ensure that you are comfortable with creating IPSec policies before you try to monitor and troubleshoot IPSec. Although configuring and implementing IPSec is not covered in Exam 70-291, it's unlikely that you will be able to effectively monitor and troubleshoot IPSec if you cannot configure and implement it.
- Get your hands dirty. The Step by Step exercises throughout this book provide plenty of directions and exercises, but you should go beyond those examples and create some of your own. If you can, experiment with each of the topics we discuss in this chapter to see how they work and why you would use each one.

Introduction

Although we examined some of the basics of network security in Chapter 4, "Implementing and Managing WINS," we have much more to talk about when it comes to securing your network. This chapter, however, is not the end-all when it comes to security or securing your Windows Server 2003 network. Many volumes have been written on this topic, but we seek to examine only a small sampling of the overall subject area in this chapter that is directly related to the objectives for this exam.

Introduction to IP Security (IPSec)

IP Security (IPSec) is a framework of open standards for ensuring private, secure communications over IP networks. This protocol is rapidly becoming the underlying framework for secure communications using VPNs and will likely replace Point-to-Point Tunneling Protocol (PPTP) as Microsoft's VPN protocol of choice. IPSec takes advantage of many of the more popular encryption protocols in use today. IPSec is based on an end-to-end security model, which means that the only computers that must know about IPSec are the sending and receiving computers. The packets travel the network without being affected by any of the intervening network devices. Each IPSec device handles its own security and functions with the assumption that the transport medium is not secure. The Internet is an excellent example of a transport medium that is not secure.

The Microsoft Windows Server 2003 implementation of IPSec is based on standards developed by the Internet Engineering Task Force (IETF) IPSec working group. However, it is important to note that Microsoft uses two implementations of IPSec: the IETF version, also known as Pure IPSec Tunnel mode, or just tunnel mode; and the Microsoft variant on IPSec, which Microsoft calls L2TP/IPSec mode, or transport mode. An IPSec VPN configured to use transport mode secures an existing IP packet from source to destination, using the encryption and authentication methods discussed later in this section. Tunnel mode puts an existing IP packet inside a new IP packet that is sent to a tunnel endpoint in the IPSec format.

Both transport and tunnel mode can be encapsulated in Encapsulating Security Protocol (ESP) or Authentication Header (AH) headers. The original IETF Request for Comments (RFC 2401, http://www.ietf.org/rfc/rfc2401.txt) IPSec tunnel protocol specifications did not include mechanisms suitable for remote access VPN clients, instead focusing on site-to-site VPN implementations. For that reason, Microsoft's implementation of tunnel mode relies on the use of the L2TP protocol developed jointly with Cisco to provide this additional packet format. (An introduction to the components of IPSec comes later in this chapter.) It is worth noting that a newer RFC (RFC 3193, http://www.ietf.org/rfc/rfc3193.txt) introduced in late 2001 discusses using L2TP with IPSec.

NOTE

Protecting VPN Connections By default, client remote access VPN connections are protected using an automatically generated IPSec policy that uses IPSec transport mode (not tunnel mode) when the L2TP tunnel type is selected. You will probably see this configuration in almost every production implementation of a Windows Server 2003 IPSec solution. To enable this configuration, configure the Routing and Remote Access Service for L2TP VPN connectivity, as described previously in Chapter 6, "Implementing, Managing, and Troubleshooting Network Access."

EXAM ALERT

Understand IPSec The exam includes questions and scenarios on IPSec. Although you don't need to memorize the minutiae surrounding the encryption protocols used by IPSec, you should be familiar with what the components of IPSec are, how to implement an IPSec tunnel, and especially how to work with IPSec policies.

Understanding the Architecture and Components of IPSec

Let's look at the underlying architecture and components of the IPSec protocol. IPSec provides data integrity and identity protection services for each IP packet by adding a security protocol header to each IP packet. This header is made up of several components, each with its own function.

Authentication Header (AH)

The IPSec Authentication Header (AH) provides three services as part of the IPSec protocol. First (as its name might suggest), AH authenticates the entire packet. Second, it ensures data integrity. Third, it prevents any replaying of the packet by a third party who might try to penetrate the IPSec tunnel. One service AH doesn't provide is payload encryption. AH protects your data from modification, but an attacker who is snooping the network would still be able to read the data. To prevent the modification of the data, AH uses two hashing algorithms to "sign" the packet for integrity:

- The Message Digest 5 (MD5) algorithm applies the hashing function to the data in four passes.
- The Secure Hash Algorithm (SHA1) is closely modeled after MD5. SHA uses 79 32-bit constants during the computation of the hash value, which results in a 160-bit key. Because SHA has a longer key length, it is considered more secure than MD5.

AH uses an IP protocol decimal ID of 51 to identify itself in the IP header. The AH header contains the following fields:

- **Next Header**—This field identifies the next header that uses the IP protocol ID.
- **Length**—This field indicates the length of the AH header.
- **Security Parameters Index (SPI)**—Used in combination with the destination address and the security protocol (AH or ESP), the SPI is used by the receiver to identify the cryptographic keys and procedures to be used to decode the packet.
- **Sequence Number**—This field provides the anti-replay functionality of AH. The sequence number is an incrementally increasing number (starting from 0) that is never allowed to cycle and that indicates the packet number. The machine receiving the packet checks this field to verify that the packet has not been received already. If a packet with this number has already been received, the packet is rejected.
- **Authentication Data**—This field contains the Integrity Check Value (ICV) used to verify the integrity of the message. (This is the hash value mentioned previously.) The receiver calculates the hash value and checks it against the ICV to verify packet integrity.

An IP packet that has AH applied in transfer mode is modified with the AH header between the IP header and the TCP header, as shown in Figure 8.1.

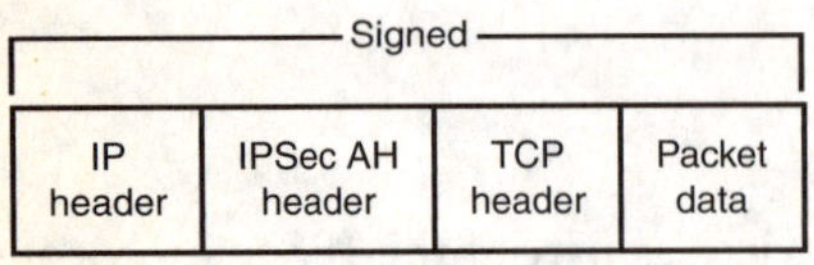

FIGURE 8.1 An IP packet with the AH header inserted in transfer mode.

AH can be used alone or in combination with the ESP protocol, which is discussed next.

Encapsulating Security Protocol (ESP)

Encapsulating Security Protocol (ESP) provides confidentiality in addition to authentication, integrity, and anti-replay. This portion of the IPSec protocol encrypts the data contents of the packet. The format of the ESP varies, depending on the type and mode of encryption being utilized. ESP can be used alone, in combination with AH, or using Microsoft's implementation, nested within the L2TP.

ESP appears in the IP header with an IP protocol decimal ID of 50. The ESP header contains the following fields:

- **SPI**—The receiver uses the SPI, in combination with the destination address and the security protocol (AH or ESP), to identify the cryptographic keys and procedures to be used to decode the packet.
- **Sequence Number**—This field provides the anti-replay functionality of ESP. The sequence number is an incrementally increasing number (starting from 0) that is never allowed to cycle and that indicates the packet number. The machine receiving the packet checks this field to verify that the packet has not been received already. If a packet with this number has already been received, the packet is rejected.

NOTE

Replaying: Why Is It Bad? You may have noticed that replaying has been included several times as part of the discussion of IPSec. Replaying is a somewhat obscure method for obtaining access to a system. A replay attack occurs when packets are intercepted by an unauthorized party, stored, and later retransmitted in an effort to trick one or both sides of the transmission into thinking that it is a valid communication. A replay attack becomes an issue because TCP/IP protocols such as Network File System (NFS) have no mechanisms to determine whether a packet is being replayed—even after several hours. Fortunately, the anti-replay mechanisms in IPSec make a replay attack a virtual impossibility.

The ESP trailer contains the following fields:

- **Padding**—Specifies 0 to 255 bytes used for 32-bit alignment and with the block size of the block cipher.
- **Padding Length**—Indicates the length of the Padding field in bytes.
- **Next Header**—Identifies the makeup of the payload, such as TCP or UDP.

The ESP authentication trailer contains one field: authentication data. This field contains the Integrity Check Value (ICV) and a media access control (MAC) used to verify the sender's identity and ensure message integrity.

ESP is inserted after the IP header and before an upper-layer protocol, such as TCP, UDP, or ICMP, or before any other IPSec headers (such as AH) that have already been inserted. Everything following ESP (the upper-layer protocol, the data, and the ESP trailer) is encrypted, as shown in Figure 8.2. The IP header is not signed and, therefore, not necessarily protected from modification unless tunneling mode is active, as shown in Figure 8.3.

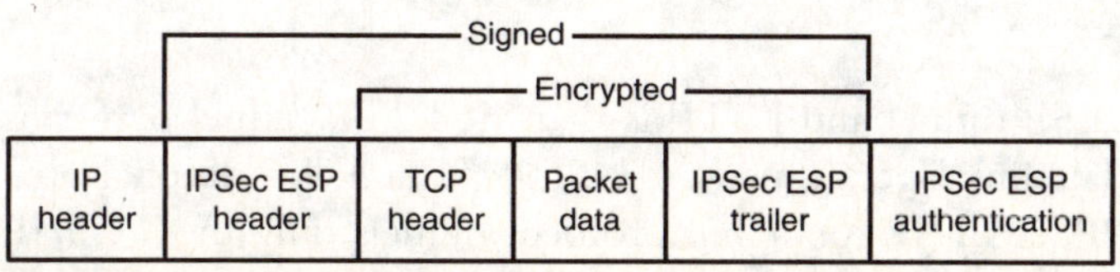

FIGURE 8.2 An IP packet with the ESP header inserted in transfer mode.

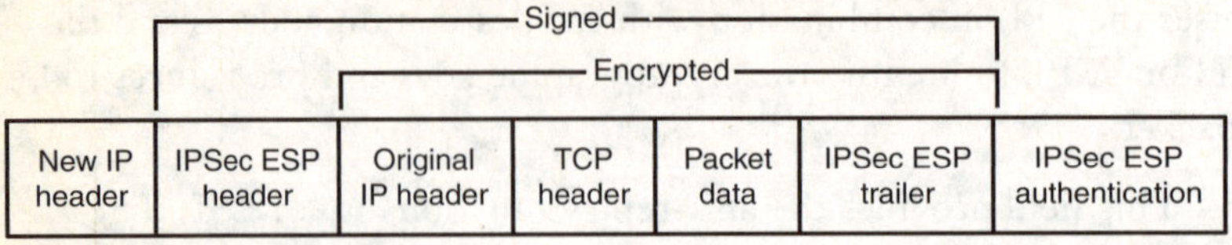

FIGURE 8.3 An IP packet with the ESP header inserted in tunnel mode; the original IP header is now encrypted.

The final piece of the IPSec protocol is the authentication and key exchange mechanism. Authentication and key exchange are accomplished using a pair of protocols.

Internet Security Key Association Key Management Protocol (ISAKMP/Oakley)

ISAKMP/Oakley (also known as ISAKMP/IKE, for Internet Key Exchange) provides the mechanism that allows disparate VPN servers to share encryption key information and make the IPSec protocol practical in today's environment. Before secured data can be exchanged between VPN servers, a contract between the two computers must be established. In this contract, called a Security Association (SA), both computers agree on how to exchange and protect information. In other words, the two servers (or the server and client computer) need to agree on how to encrypt and decrypt the data to be sent.

To enable this process, the IPSec protocol uses a standard process to build this contract between the two computers. This process combines the ISAKMP (Internet Security Association and Key Management Protocol) and Oakley key generation protocols. ISAKMP provides the centralized security association management, whereas Oakley actually generates and manages the encryption keys used to secure the information.

IKE actually performs a two-phase operation to establish the secure communication channel. In each phase, confidentiality and authentication are ensured by the use of encryption and authentication algorithms that are agreed upon by the computers negotiating. In the first phase (also known as main mode), the two computers establish a secure, authenticated channel called the Phase I (Main Mode) SA. The IKE provides identity protection during this phase. In the first phase (also known as quick mode), the two computers establish the rules for communication called the Phase II (Quick Mode) SA. During the second phase, a new shared key is created for use. After the Phase II SA is in place, IPSec secured communications can occur.

The final piece of this puzzle that needs to be covered is Microsoft's IPSec/L2TP implementation, which adds an additional tunneling protocol to the IPSec implementation.

L2TP and IPSec

The major difference between the ESP tunnel and L2TP is that the L2TP tunnel performs at Layer 2 of the OSI Model, the data link layer. This way, L2TP can tunnel additional protocols, such as IPX or NetBEUI. IPSec's ESP tunneling protocol tunnels only the TCP/IP protocol, based on the standard. When L2TP and IPSec are used in combination to provide a secured tunnel, the original packet header is used to carry the packet's source and final destination, whereas the tunnel packet's IP header might contain the address of an IPSec gateway. The L2TP header carries the information needed to route the packet over the network. The Point-to-Point Protocol (PPP) header within the encapsulated packet identifies the protocol of the original packet. In other words, when using L2TP to transfer data, IPSec is used to secure the tunnel. L2TP encapsulates the packet in a PPP frame. The PPP frame is then added to a UDP-type frame assigned to port 1701. UDP, which is part of the TCP/IP suite, qualifies for IPSec to secure the contents; thus, the contents of L2TP are secure, regardless of the originating protocol and/or data type.

One additional benefit of the L2TP method is that you have a choice of additional encryption algorithms for securing the data.

What's New with Windows Server 2003 IPSec

The following new features are supported in the Windows Server 2003 IPSec implementation:

- IPSec in Windows Server 2003 now supports the User Datagram Protocol (UDP) encapsulation of IPSec packets to allow Internet Key Exchange (IKE) and Encapsulating Security Protocol (ESP) traffic to pass through a Network Address Translation (NAT) device—something not possible in Windows 2000. It is now possible for Windows 2000 and Windows XP clients to establish IPSec connections with a Windows Server 2003 server that is located behind one or more NAT devices.

- The IP Security Monitor is now implemented as an MMC snap-in instead of as a standalone executable, as was the case in Windows 2000. Also, you can now monitor information about local and remote computers as well as several other enhancements.

- IPSec now supports the use of a 2048-bit Diffie-Hellman key exchange. As a result, the secret key resulting from the Diffie-Hellman exchange has greater strength. This results in a longer key length, which increases the difficulty an attacker faces when trying to determine a secret key.

- You can administer and control IPSec from the command line with new extensions to the `netsh` command. Using the `netsh ipsec` context, you can configure static or dynamic IPSec main mode settings, quick mode settings, rules, and configuration parameters. The `netsh ipsec` context replaces the `Ipsecpol.exe` tool that was provided with the Windows 2000 Server Resource Kit.

- IPSec now provides stateful filtering of network traffic during computer startup. Any outbound traffic initiated by the computer upon startup is permitted, as is any inbound reply traffic. Dynamic Host Configuration Protocol (DHCP) is exempt from this new protection provided by IPSec and is thus allowed during startup. You can also specify other types of traffic you want to exempt. Computer startup security can be configured only by using the `netsh` command with the `ipsec` context.

- Windows Server 2003 Enterprise Edition and Windows Server 2003 Datacenter Server Edition provide improved support for integration of IPSec with network load balancing. This allows a group of NLB servers to better provide highly available IPSec-based VPN services to clients. NLB can now accurately track IPSec-secured sessions, and the IPSec Internet Key Exchange (IKE) protocol can now detect when an IPSec-secured session is being established with a cluster server and quickly recover from a failover.
- IPSec provides an extension to the Resultant Set of Policy (RSoP) snap-in (another new addition to Windows Server 2003) that can be used to view IPSec policy assignments of computers or other Active Directory objects.

The following are the standard features of the Windows Server 2003 IPSec implementation:

- IPSec in Windows Server 2003 is policy based. It cannot be configured without an IPSec policy being in place, allowing an administrator to more easily apply settings to groups of objects such as computers or users.
- IPSec on Windows Server 2003 can use Kerberos v5, a digital certificate, or a shared secret (string) for user authentication.
- IPSec mutually authenticates computers prior to any data being exchanged.
- IPSec establishes a security association (SA) between the two host computers involved in the data transfer. An SA is the collection of a policy and keys, which define the rules for security settings.
- IPSec encrypts data using Data Encryption Standard (DES) or Triple DES (3DES).
- IPSec uses the MD5 or SHA1 algorithm for data hashing.
- IPSec is invisible to users. IPSec operates at the network level of the Open System Interface (OSI) model; therefore, users and applications do not directly interact with the protocol. After an IPSec tunnel has been created, users can connect to applications and services as if they were on the local network and not on the other side of a public network.

IPSec operates at the network layer; therefore, it is invisible to applications and computers. An understanding of the following features, however, will help you troubleshoot problems that may arise in connectivity:

- IPSec policies are part of Group Policy, both locally and within Active Directory. This built-in feature allows changes and management to be centralized. Settings for IPSec are enforced on the computer as the policy is enforced.

- The Internet Security Key Association Key Management Protocol (ISAKMP) monitors the negotiations between the hosts and provides the keys to use with security algorithms.
- The installed IPSec driver secures traffic between the two hosts.

Now that you have a basic introduction to the benefits and background of the IPSec protocol, you are ready to look at working with IPSec.

Configuring and Implementing IPSec

Before enabling IPSec on your local computer or domain, you should configure IPSec through policies. An IPSec policy is a set of rules that define how and when communication is secured between two endpoints. This is done through the configuration of various rules. Each rule contains a collection of actions and filters that begin when they encounter endpoints that match.

Policies allow you to quickly and easily configure IPSec based on the settings required within your organization. Windows Server 2003 comes with the following three preconfigured IPSec policies that may or may not meet your needs:

- **Client (Respond Only)**—This policy requires IPSec-provided security only when another computer requests it. This policy allows the computer to attempt unsecured communications first and switch to IPSec-secured communications if requested. This policy contains the default response rule, which creates dynamic IPSec filters for inbound and outbound traffic based on the requested protocol and port traffic for the communication that is being secured. This policy, which can be used on workstations and servers alike, provides the minimum amount of IPSec security.
- **Server (Request Security)**—This policy requests security from the other computer and allows unsecured communication with non IPSec-aware computers. The computer accepts inbound unsecured traffic but always attempts to secure further communications by requesting IPSec security from the sending computer. If the other computer is not IPSec-enabled, the entire communication is allowed to be unsecured. This policy, which can be used on workstations and servers alike, provides a medium level of IPSec security. If desired, you can opt to use this policy on a workstation computer as well.
- **Secure Server (Require Security)**—This policy is implemented on computers that require highly secure communications, such as servers transmitting sensitive data. The filters in this policy require all outbound communication to be secured, allowing only the initial inbound communication request to be unsecured. This policy has a rule to require security for all IP traffic, a rule to permit ICMP traffic, and the default response rule to respond to requests for security from other computers. This policy,

typically used only on servers, provides the highest level of IPSec security on a network. This policy can also be used on workstation computers if you want. Non IPSec-enabled computers cannot establish any communications with computers using this policy. If desired, you can opt to use this policy on a workstation computer as well.

You can opt to either use one of the preconfigured policies that comes with Windows Server 2003 or create your own policy. You can also modify the preconfigured policies to suit your needs if you want. Before we can go any further into our discussion about IPSec, we first need to create the tools that allow us to manage IPSec on a local computer. Step by Step 8.1 helps you to create your own IPSec management console.

STEP BY STEP

8.1 Creating the IPSec Management Console

1. Open a blank MMC by clicking Start, Run. Then type `mmc` to open a blank MMC, as shown in Figure 8.4.

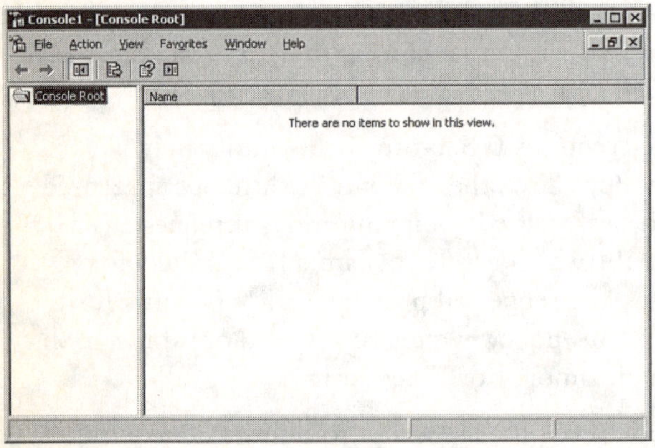

FIGURE 8.4 The MMC provides a powerful, flexible framework from which to manage Windows Server 2003.

2. In your new console, click the File menu and select Add/Remove Snap-in. The Add/Remove Snap-in dialog box opens, as shown in Figure 8.5.
3. Click the Add button to open the Add Standalone Snap-in dialog box, as shown in Figure 8.6.
4. Scroll down the list, select IP Security Monitor, and click the Add button.

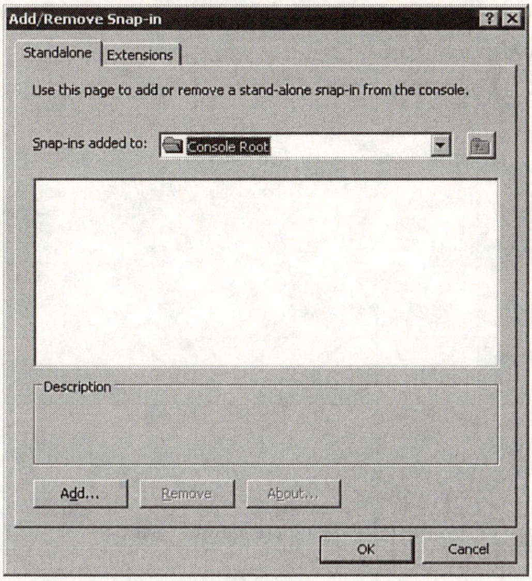

FIGURE 8.5 You can add snap-ins to your console to customize its management features.

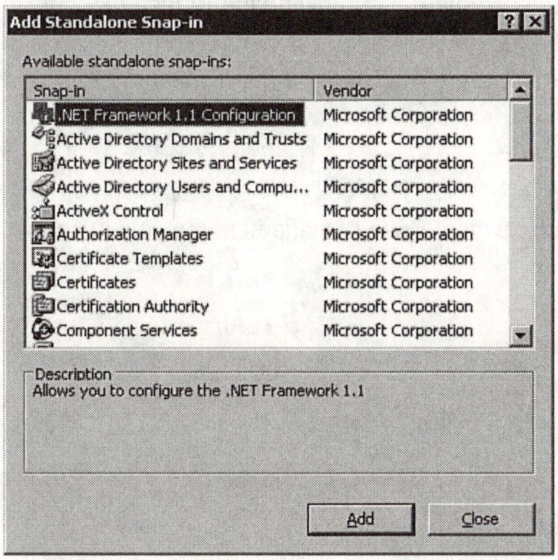

FIGURE 8.6 Windows Server 2003 comes with several dozen snap-ins from which you can choose.

5. Select IP Security Policy Management and click the Add button. You are prompted to choose the scope that the snap-in will manage, as shown in Figure 8.7.

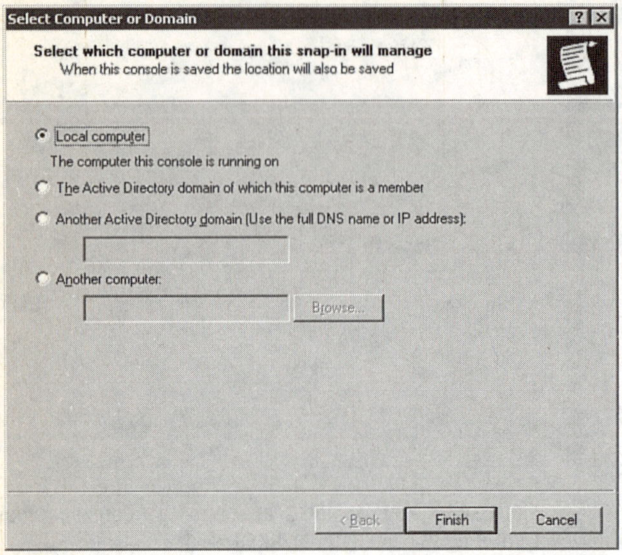

FIUGRE 8.7 Many MMC snap-ins can be targeted at several different levels of management.

6. For this example, choose Local Computer from the Select Computer or Domain page. Notice that you have the option to select the Active Directory domain of which this computer is part, another Active Directory domain, or another computer. Click Finish to complete the addition of the IP Security Policy Management snap-in to your console.
7. Click Close on the Add Standalone Snap-in dialog box.
8. Click OK on the Add/Remove Snap-in dialog box. Your completed IPSec management console is shown in Figure 8.8.

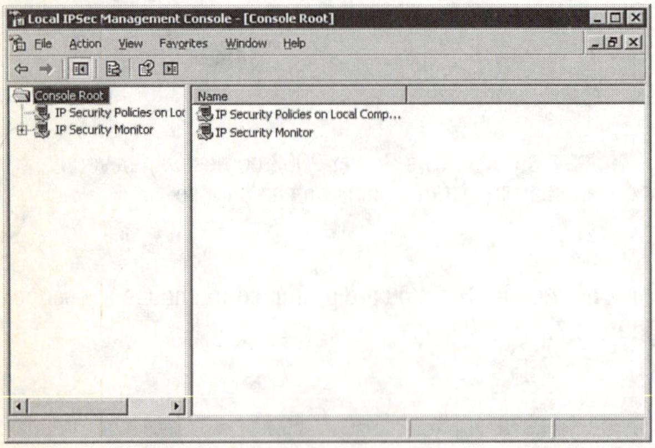

FIGURE 8.8 Your completed IPSec management console contains the tools you need to manage and monitor IP security.

9. Save your newly created console by clicking File, Save. Enter a suitable name, such as **`Local IPSec Management Console`**, and click Save. By default, the console is saved in the Administrative Tools folder of the currently logged-in user.

Armed with your newly created IPSec management console, you can now get down to work configuring and managing IPSec. At this point, you may want to do one of two things: implement a preconfigured IPSec policy or create one of your own. We explore the latter in the next Step by Step. You can accomplish the former by right-clicking the desired policy in the right pane of the console window, as seen in Figure 8.9, and selecting Assign from the context menu. Note that you can have only one IPSec policy assigned at a time.

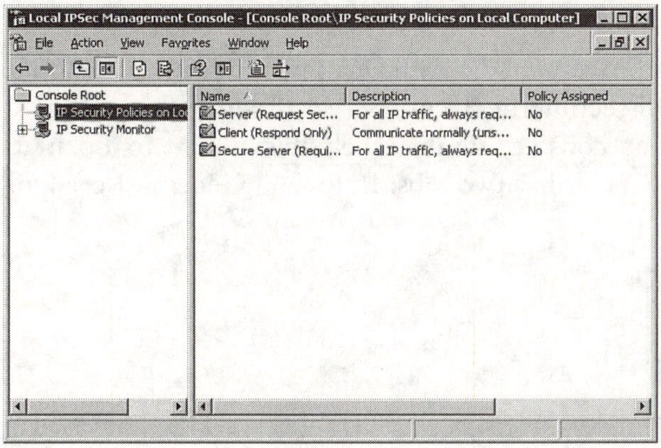

FIGURE 8.9 Assigning an IPSec policy to the local computer is a quick task.

You can verify that the policy is now assigned to the computer by examining the Active Policy node of the IP Security Monitor, as shown in Figure 8.10.

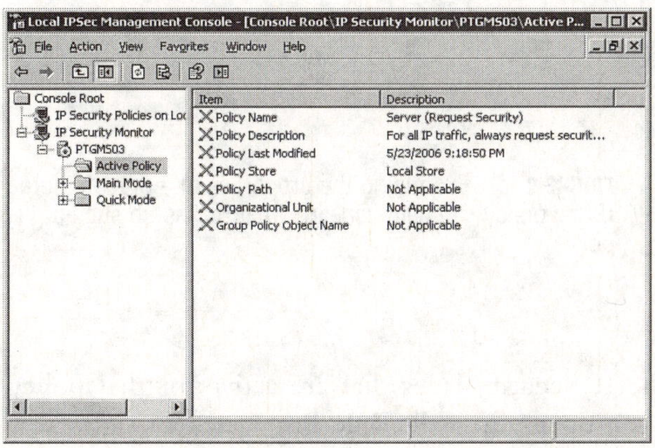

FIGURE 8.10 The IP Security Monitor can be used to display many bits of useful information about IPSec.

We examine the use of the IP Security Monitor console later in this chapter. For now, we need to look at the process to create a custom IPSec policy.

Understanding IPSec Policy Components

After you've decided to use IPSec on your network, you may realize that the preconfigured IPSec policies do not provide exactly the solution for which you are looking. You can opt to either customize an existing policy or create a new one from scratch. I prefer to create policies from scratch to ensure that I have complete control over every piece of the puzzle, and that's exactly what IPSec can turn out to be if not treated with caution and respect—one large puzzle that you are left to piece together.

Before we start to actually create our own IPSec policy, let's take a few moments to examine the parts that make up an IPSec policy by dissecting the Secure Server (Require Security) policy. From within your IPSec management console, double-click this policy to open its Properties dialog box, as shown in Figure 8.11. It has two tabs: Rules and General. Let's look at the Rules tab first.

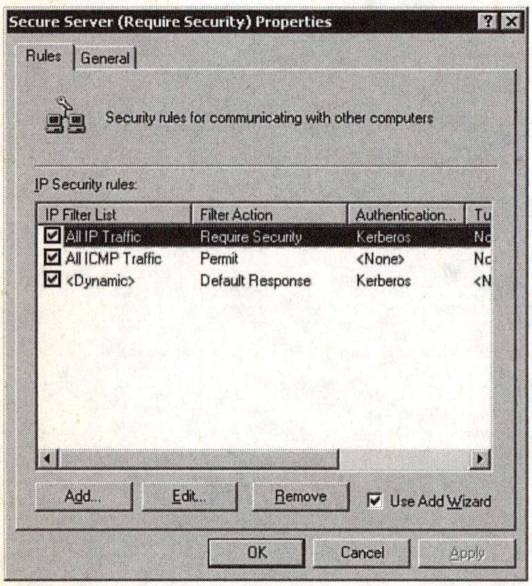

FIGURE 8.11 Examining the properties of a preconfigured IPSec policy can help us learn what makes up such a policy.

The Rules Tab

The IP Security Rules window lists all the IP security rules that are active for that policy. Selecting a rule and clicking the Edit button opens the Edit Rule Properties dialog box, as shown in Figure 8.12. The five tabs on the Edit Rule Properties dialog box contain the configuration settings for this particular rule.

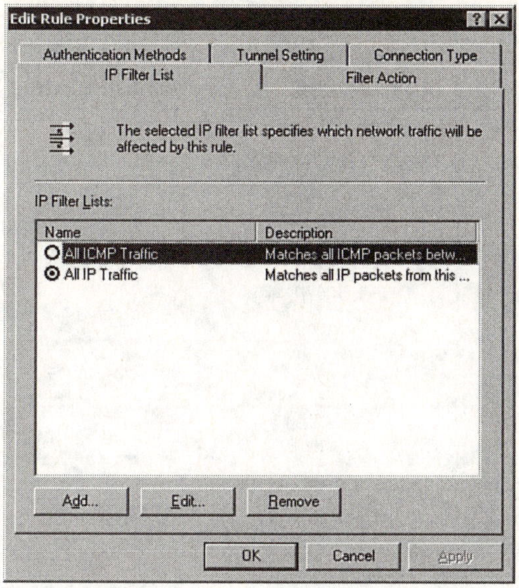

FIGURE 8.12 The IP Filter List tab of the Edit Rule Properties dialog box.

Edit Rule Properties—IP Filter List Tab

The IP Filter List tab shows all IP filters configured for the selected rule. An IP filter contains source and destination IP addresses that apply to this rule. Each IP address can be of an individual computer or of a network subnet. If this tab identifies a network communication that has a participant listed in an IP filter, a particular filter action that is specific for that connection is applied. Selecting the All IP Traffic filter for editing opens the dialog box shown in Figure 8.13. From here, you can specify many items, including the source and destination IP addresses to which this filter applies.

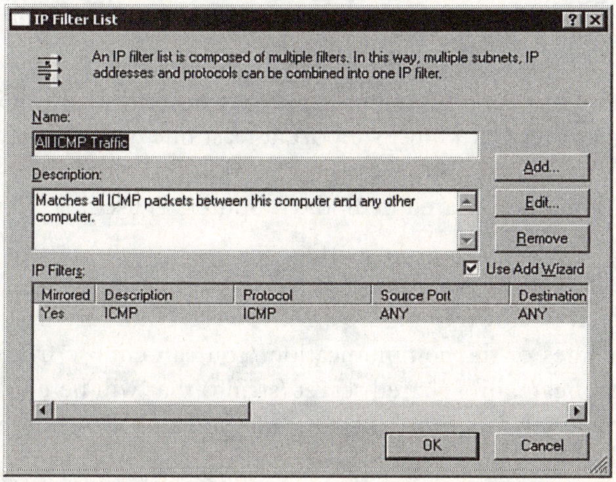

FIGURE 8.13 You can edit the filter properties to specify the source and destination computers to which they apply.

Edit Rule Properties—Filter Action Tab

The Filter Action tab of the Edit Rule Properties dialog box, which is shown in Figure 8.14, contains actions that specify the type of security and methods by which security is established.

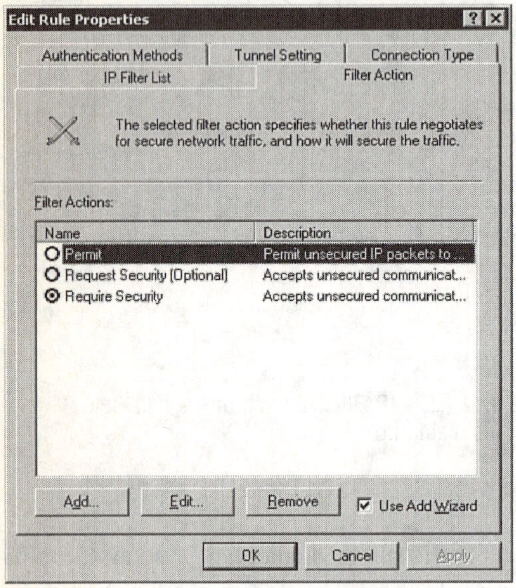

FIGURE 8.14 The Filter Action tab defines the types of security and methods by which security is established.

Filter actions, as seen in Figure 8.15, define the type of security and methods by which security is established. The default methods are Permit, Block, and Negotiate security. The Permit option passes the traffic without the requirement for security. This action is appropriate if you never want to secure traffic to which a rule applies. The Block action silently blocks all traffic from computers specified in the IP filter list. The Negotiate Security action specifies that the computer is to use a list of security methods to negotiate the appropriate security for the communication.

If the Negotiate security action is selected, both computers must make an agreement on the security parameters to be used, meaning that they both must support at least one common set of security parameters from those in the list. The list entries are processed in order of preference from top to bottom. The first security method shared by both computers is used.

Edit Rule Properties—Authentication Methods Tab

From the Authentication Methods tab, which is shown in Figure 8.16, you can configure what method will be used to authenticate both sides of the communication. You can choose from Kerberos (the default setting), a digital certificate, or a shared secret (string) that will be used to protect the key exchange process. You can configure more than one method and also choose the order of precedence for your configured methods. Using the shared secret is not recommended because this static entry can be compromised.

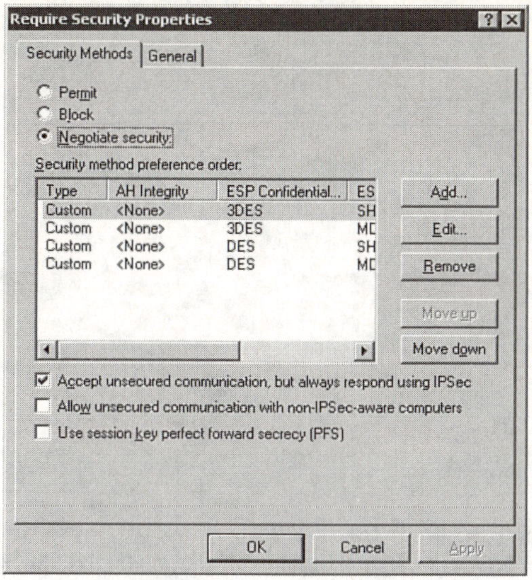

FIGURE 8.15 You can specify exactly what the computer will do when a filter action is processed.

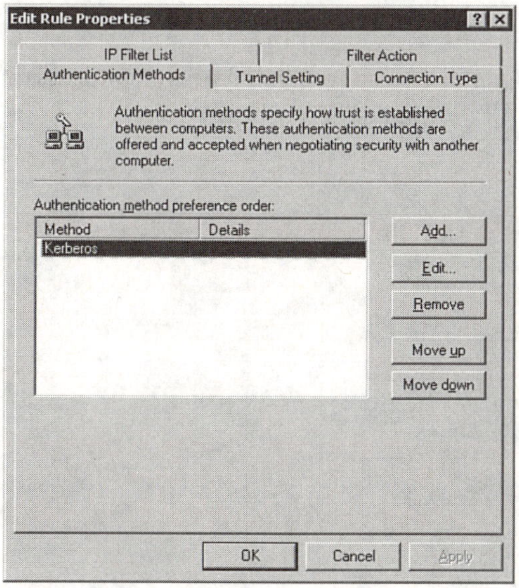

FIGURE 8.16 You can specify Kerberos, digital certificate, or shared secret as the authentication method.

Edit Rule Properties—Tunnel Setting Tab

From the Tunnel Setting tab, which is shown in Figure 8.17, you can have the rule apply to a tunnel by specifying an endpoint or not have it apply to a tunnel (transport mode) at all.

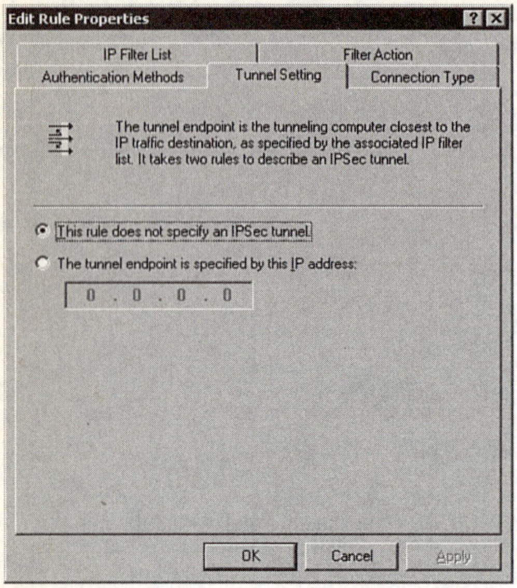

FIGURE 8.17 The Tunnel Setting tab allows you to configure a tunnel endpoint if required.

Edit Rule Properties—Connection Type Tab

The Connection Type tab, as shown in Figure 8.18, determines for which types of connections the rule will be applied: LAN, Remote Access, or All Network Connections.

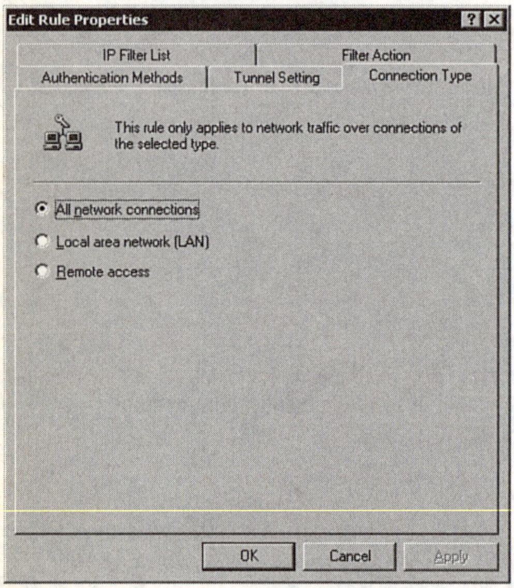

FIGURE 8.18 The Connection Type tab allows you to specify which connections are affected by the policy.

The General Tab

While the Rules tab contains all of the configuration settings that control how the policy behaves in regard to allowing or denying traffic to pass, the General tab contains the configuration settings that define how the IPSec policy, as a whole, behaves once it has been assigned (see Figure 8.19).

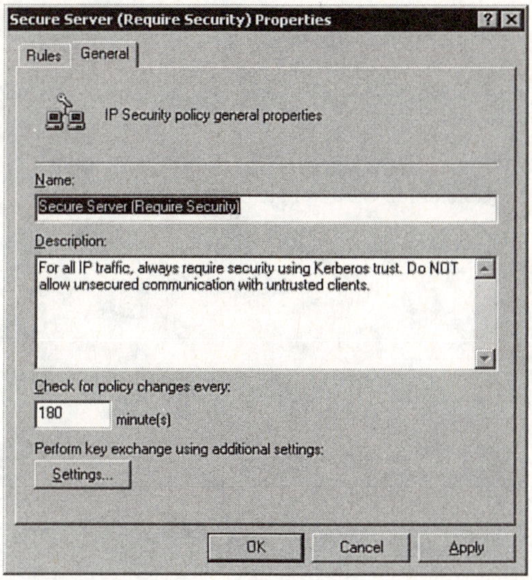

FIGURE 8.19 The General tab allows you to control the behavior of the IPSec policy itself.

On the General tab, you see some of the same basic items that you'll see on a lot of General tabs throughout Windows: the name and description of the policy. That's where the similarities end. You also have the options on the General tab to configure the interval at which the computer will check for updates and changes to the security policy. The default setting of 180 minutes is usually acceptable.

Clicking the Settings button at the bottom of the General tab opens the Key Exchange Settings dialog box, which is shown in Figure 8.20. In the Key Exchange Settings dialog box, you can configure for Master Key Perfect Forward Secrecy, which improves security of the keying process. Additionally, you can change the defaults provided for key generation.

Clicking the Methods button on the Key Exchange Settings dialog box opens the Key Exchange Security Methods dialog box, as seen in Figure 8.21. If you want to configure the methods used to protect the identities, you can accomplish that task from here. Note that by default the new 2048-bit Diffie-Hellman key exchange method is not used. You can select it by adding or editing a security method, as shown in Figure 8.22.

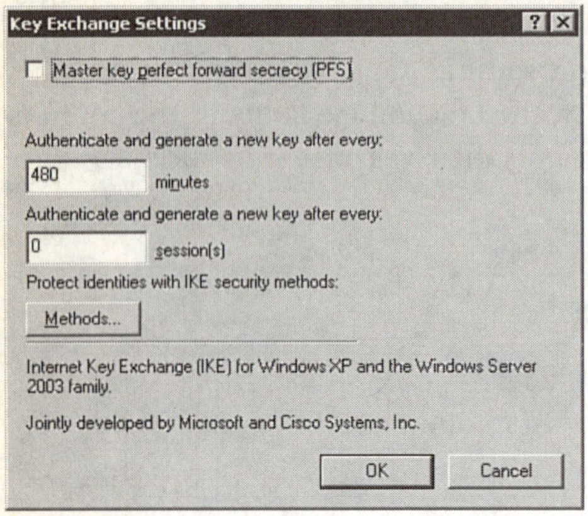

FIGURE 8.20 You can configure advanced IKE properties from the Key Exchange Settings dialog box.

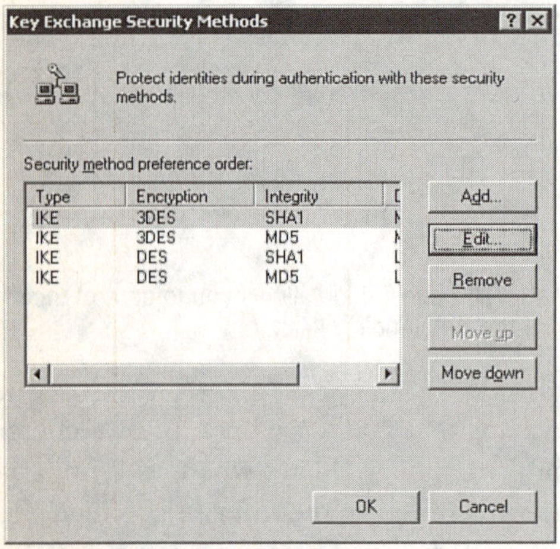

FIGURE 8.21 Customizing the key exchange security methods can increase security.

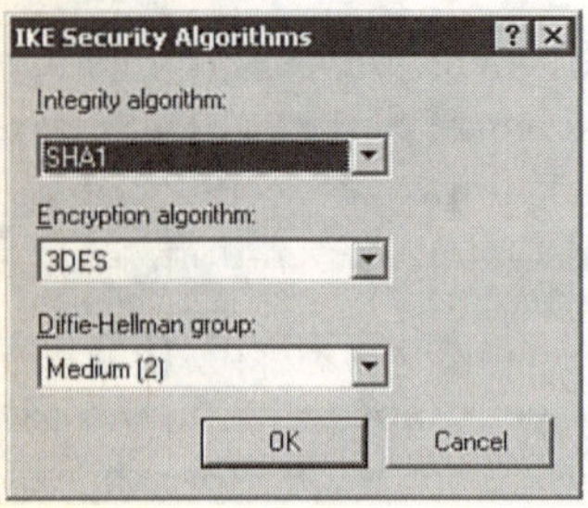

FIGURE 8.22 Using the new 2048-bit Diffie-Hellman key exchange method. Ironically, the General tab has options that are so advanced for configuring an IPSec policy that it should instead be called the Advanced tab. Don't take these configuration settings for granted when creating a custom IPSec policy.

Creating Customized IPSec Policies

You can create two basic types of IPSec policies: those that specify a tunnel and those that do not specify a tunnel. Tunneling is commonly used in the creation of a VPN and is called tunnel mode. Not using a tunnel, called transport mode, is commonly used between subnets or computers on an intranet. Step by Step 8.2 shows how to create a new IPSec policy that operates in transport mode between two subnets (192.160.11.0 and 192.168.12.0) in the same intranet of the company Que Publishing. These two subnets represent the Accounting and Payroll departments, respectively, and they need to pass only secured traffic between their subnets.

STEP BY STEP

8.2 Creating a Custom Transfer Mode IPSec Policy

1. Open the IPSec management console that you created in Step by Step 8.1.
2. Right-click IP Security Policies and select Create IP Security Policy from the context menu.
3. Dismiss the opening page of the IP Security Policy Wizard by clicking Next.
4. In the IP Security Policy Name dialog box, enter a descriptive name for the new policy. For this example, use **`Accounting to Payroll Security Policy`**, as shown in Figure 8.23. Optionally, you can enter the Description text as well. Click Next after entering the required information.

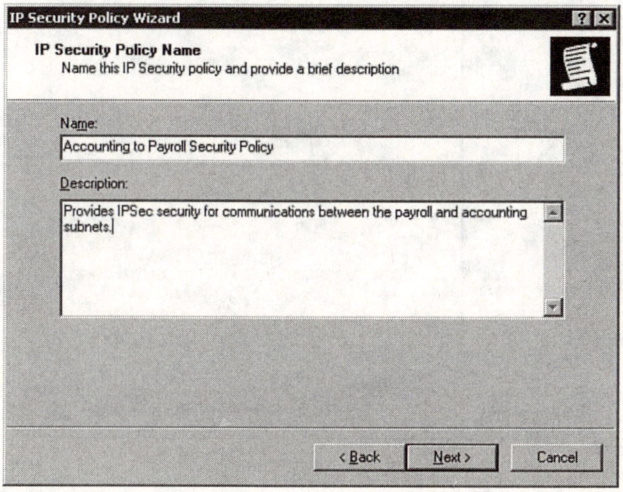

FIGURE 8.23 You should enter a policy name and description that will make sense later.

5. In the Requests for Secure Communication dialog box, as shown in Figure 8.24, deselect Activate the Default Response Rule option. You will configure this policy entirely by yourself. Click Next to continue.

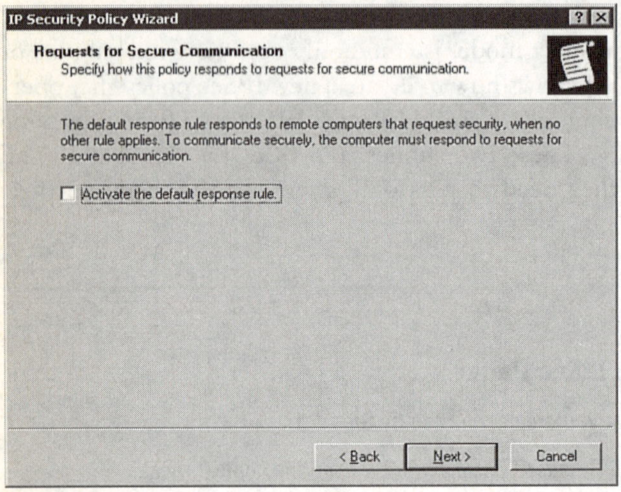

FIGURE 8.24 Removing the opportunity for unsecured communications to occur with the new rule.

6. You are now at the end of the wizard portion of the creation process. Ensure that the Edit Properties option is selected, as shown in Figure 8.25, and click Finish to begin editing the policy's properties.

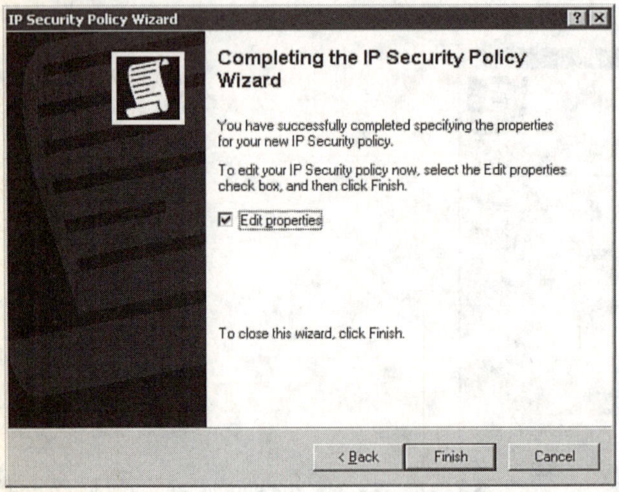

FIGURE 8.25 The completion of the wizard is not the completion of the policy creation process.

7. The Accounting to Payroll Security Policy Properties dialog box opens, as shown in Figure 8.26.

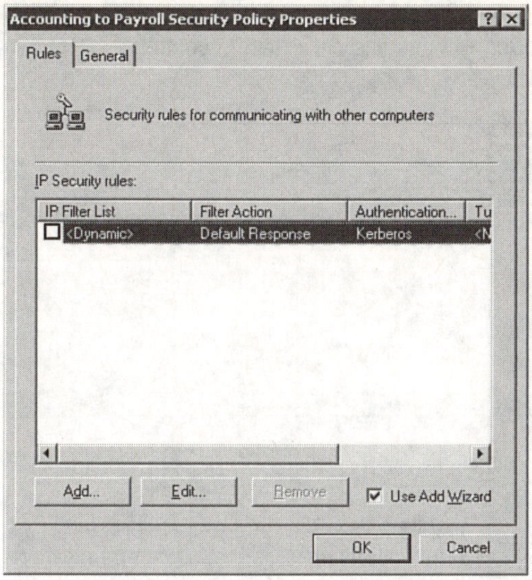

FIGURE 8.26 Your new IPSec policy requires some configuration to complete.

8. On the Rules tab, ensure that the Use Add Wizard option is selected; then click the Add button to start the Security Rule Wizard to create a new filter list and action.
9. Click Next to dismiss the opening page of the Security Rule Wizard.
10. In the Tunnel Endpoint dialog box, which is shown in Figure 8.27, select This Rule Does Not Specify a Tunnel (recall that this IPSec policy is being created to secure communications between two subnets on the same intranet). Click Next to continue.

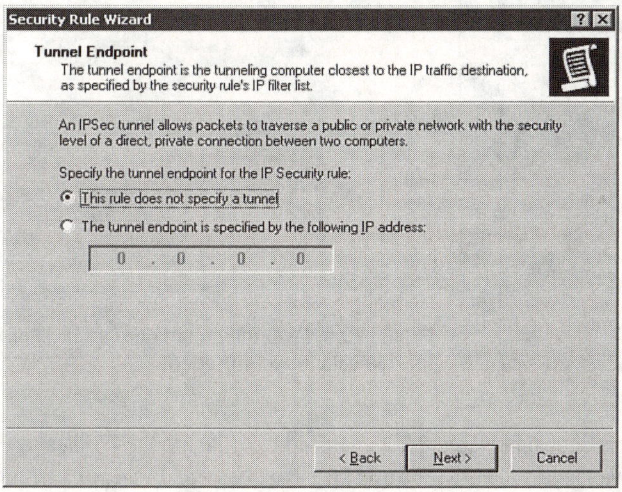

FIGURE 8.27 You can create a rule for either transport mode or tunnel mode.

11. In the Network Type dialog box, which is shown in Figure 8.28, select the network connections to which this rule applies. For this example, select All Network Connections and click Next to continue.

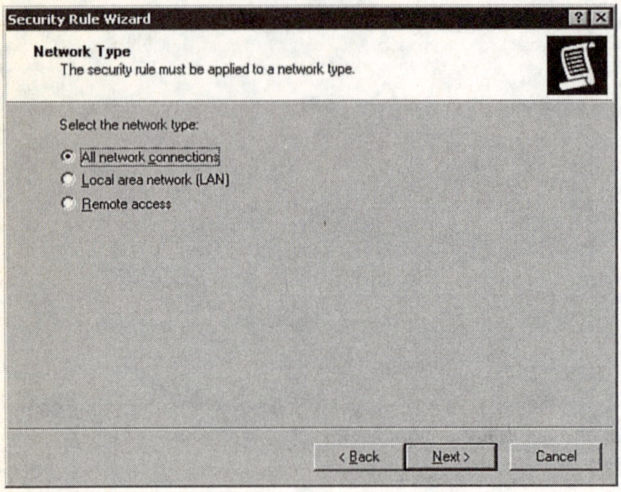

FIGURE 8.28 Selecting All Network Connections ensures that all communications by the server are secured using the new policy.

12. The IP Filter List dialog box, which is shown in Figure 8.29, shows that no IP filters are configured for this rule. Click the Add button to create a filter that meets your requirements.

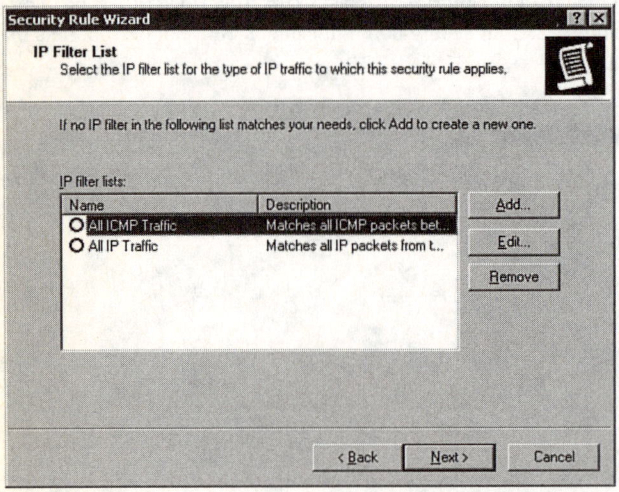

FIGURE 8.29 You must configure an IP filter for this rule to work properly.

13. From the IP Filter List dialog box, which is shown in Figure 8.30, you need to configure the IP filter properties for this rule. Enter a descriptive name such as **`Accounting to Payroll security`** in the name box and a description, if you like. Ensure that the Use Add Wizard option is selected and click the Add button.

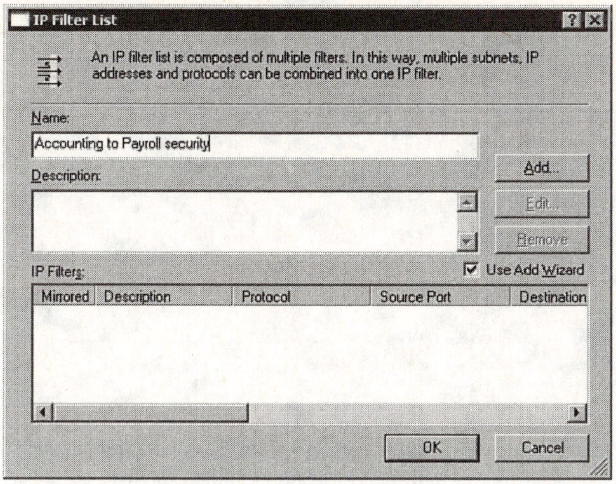

FIGURE 8.30 The process to configure an IP filter begins with the IP Filter List dialog box.

14. The IP Filter Wizard opens to start the process of configuring the IP filter. Click Next to dismiss the opening page of the wizard.

15. In the IP Filter Description and Mirrored property dialog box, which is shown in Figure 8.31, enter a description of the filter. Ensure that the mirrored option is selected. This option allows the rule to automatically match packets with the exact opposite source and destination addresses to ensure that machines from the destination subnet are also included in the incoming filter. Click Next to continue.

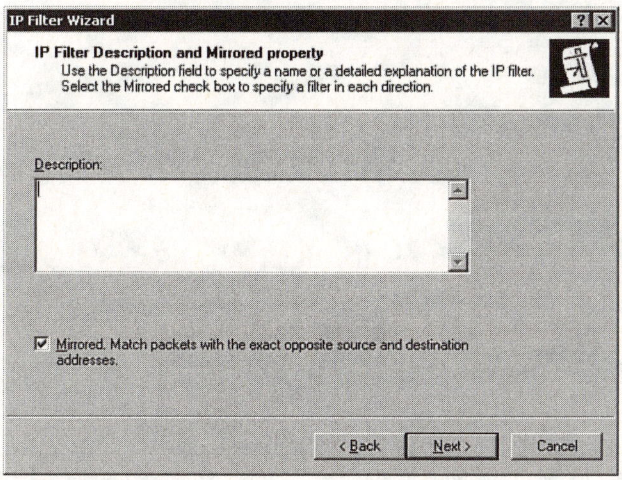

FIGURE 8.31 Allowing the IP filter to be mirrored saves you work.

16. In the IP Traffic Source dialog box, select the A Specific IP Subnet option and configure the IP Address and Subnet mask options as required. Recall that we are creating a policy between the 192.168.11.0 and 192.168.12.0 subnets. Enter **`192.168.11.0`** and the subnet mask of **`255.255.255.0`**, as shown in Figure 8.32, and click Next to continue.

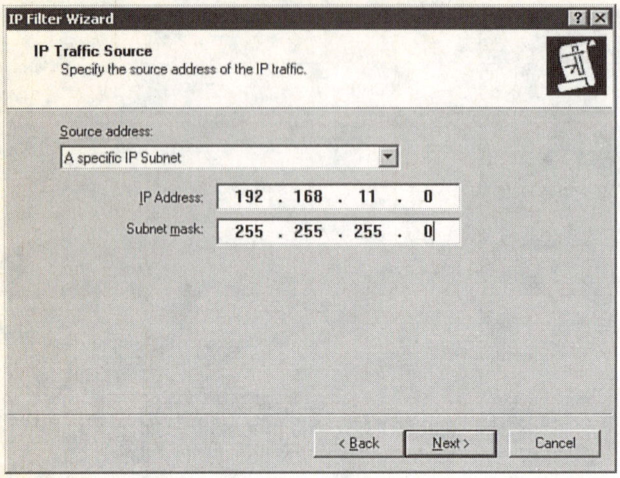

FIGURE 8.32 Be sure to specify the correct source address and subnet mask.

17. In the IP Traffic Destination dialog box, select the A Specific IP Subnet option and configure the IP address and Subnet mask options as required. Enter **`192.168.12.0`** and the subnet mask of **`255.255.255.0`**, as shown in Figure 8.33, and click Next to continue.

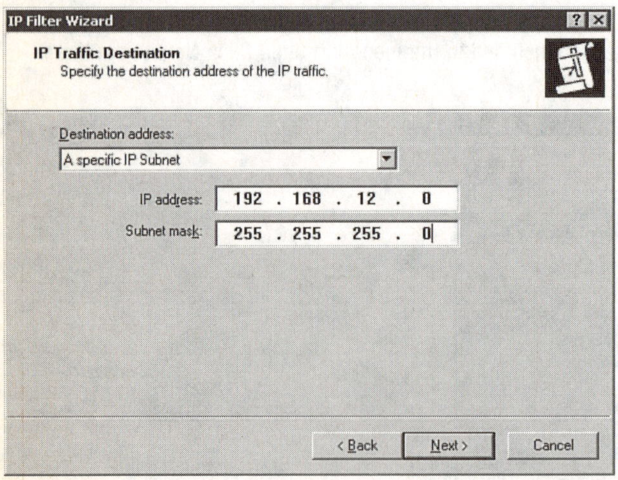

FIGURE 8.33 Be sure to specify the correct destination address and subnet mask.

18. In the IP Protocol Type dialog box, which is shown in Figure 8.34, you can configure which IP protocol types you want to be included in the filter. We want the filter to apply to all types, so leave the default selection of Any and click Next to continue.

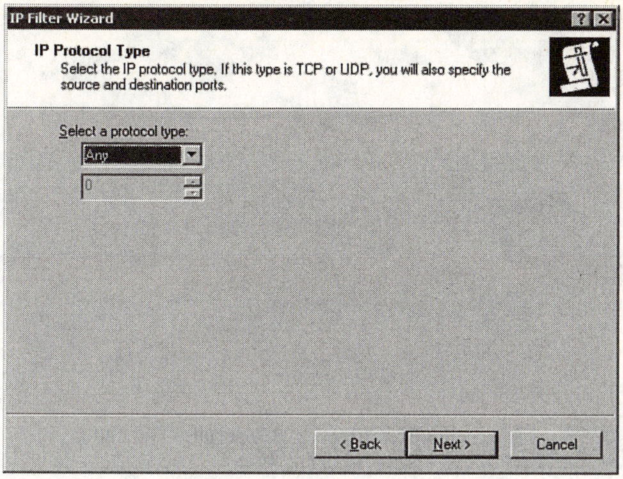

FIGURE 8.34 You can configure the filter to be very specific about the types of protocols to which it applies.

19. The Completing the IP Filter Wizard dialog box opens, as shown in Figure 8.35. Deselect the Edit properties option and click Finish.

FIGURE 8.35 The IP filter has been created, but much work still remains.

20. Back at the IP Filter List dialog box, as shown in Figure 8.36, you can see your newly created IP filter. Click OK to close the filter and complete the creation process. If you click Cancel, your newly created filter will be lost, so be careful.

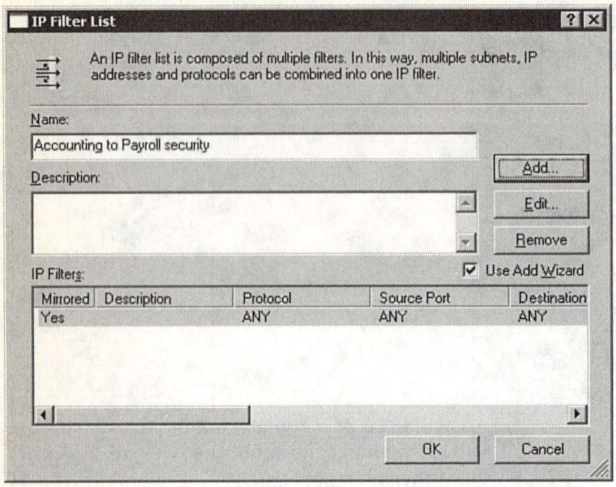

FIGURE 8.36 The new IP filter is listed on the IP Filter List dialog box.

21. Select the Accounting to Payroll security filter from the list on the IP Filter List dialog box, as shown in Figure 8.37, and click Next to continue with the Security Rule Wizard.

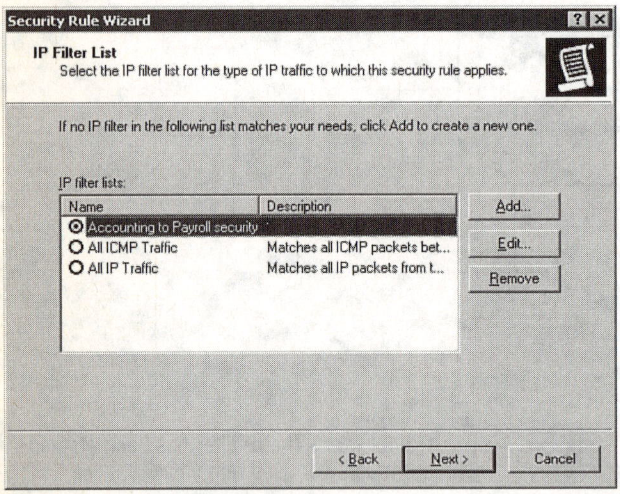

FIGURE 8.37 You need to select the filter for use after creating it.

22. In the Filter Action dialog box, which is shown in Figure 8.38, select a filter action. Ensure that the Use Add Wizard option is selected and click Add to start the Filter Action Wizard.
23. The Filter Action Wizard starts. Dismiss its opening dialog box by clicking Next.
24. In the Filter Action Name dialog box, enter a descriptive name and description for the filter. Click Next to continue.
25. In the Filter Action General Options dialog box, which is shown in Figure 8.39, select Negotiate Security and click Next to continue.

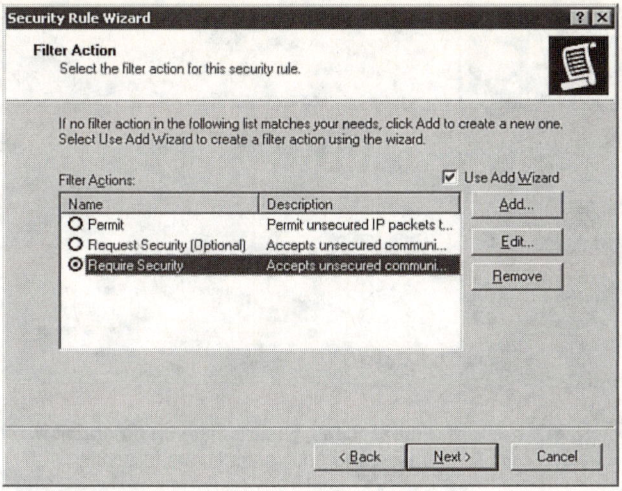

FIGURE 8.38 You now need to configure the action that the filter will take.

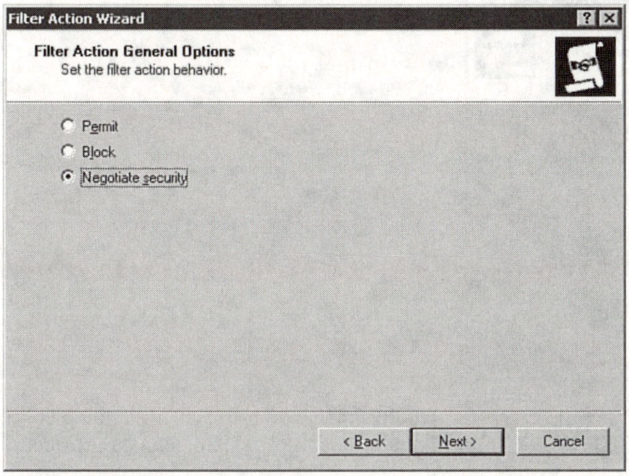

FIGURE 8.39 Instructing the filter action to negotiate security between communication computers.

26. In the Communicating with Computers That Do Not Support IPSec dialog box, which is shown in Figure 8.40, you are asked whether you want to allow unsecured communications. In this case, such communications are not allowed because all communications must be secured. Ensure that the Do Not Communicate with Computers That Do Not Support IPSec option is selected and click Next to continue.

27. In the IP Traffic Security dialog box, which is shown in Figure 8.41, select Custom to specify what security methods are to be used. Click Settings to edit the security settings.

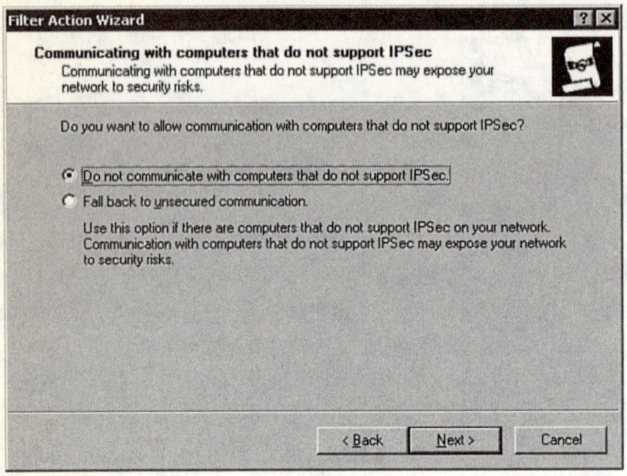

FIGURE 8.40 Ensure that you do not allow unsecured communications to occur.

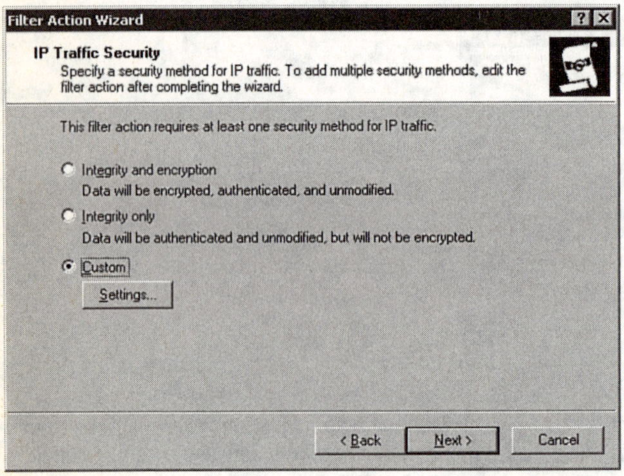

FIGURE 8.41 You can specify custom settings or use the standard settings provided.

28. The Custom Security Method Settings dialog box, which is shown in Figure 8.42, opens. From here, you can specify the settings you want. Ensure that both the AH and ESP check boxes are selected. Configure the desired integrity and encryption algorithms. Do not configure settings for the session key at this time. Click OK to accept your settings.
29. Back at the IP Traffic Security dialog box, click Next to continue.
30. In the Completing the IP Security Filter Action Wizard dialog box, which is shown in Figure 8.43, ensure the Edit Properties option is selected and click Finish.

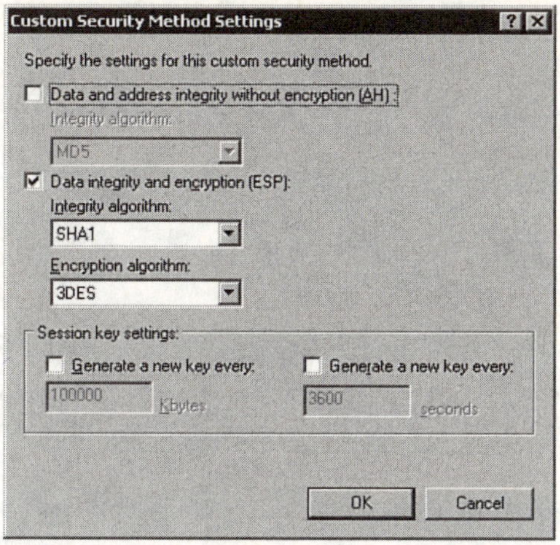

FIGURE 8.42 You can specify the encryption and integrity algorithms to be used in your filter action.

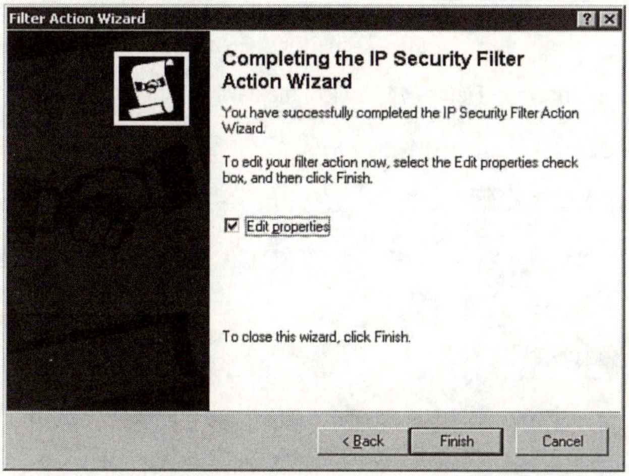

FIGURE 8.43 The Filter Action Wizard is completed, but the filter still requires a bit more configuration.

31. Back at the filter action Properties dialog box, which is shown in Figure 8.44, ensure the Use Session Key Perfect Forward Secrecy (PFS) option is selected and click OK. Selecting session key PFS ensures that the master key keying material cannot be used to generate more than one session key, which adds both security and overhead to the connection. Do not click Cancel unless you want to scrap your newly configured filter action. Click OK.

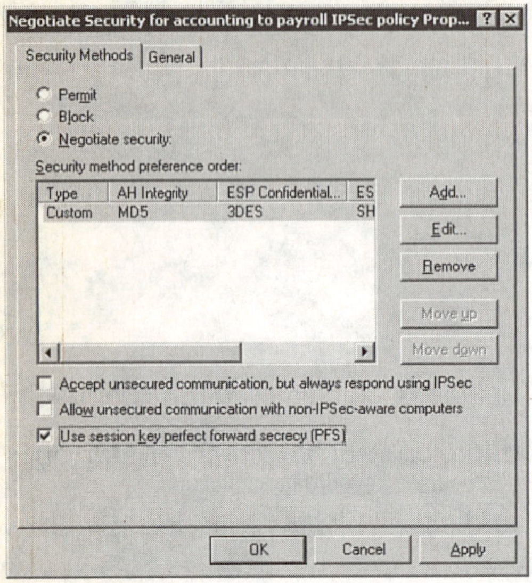

FIGURE 8.44 Selecting to use perfect forward secrecy to increase the security of the session key.

32. Back at the Filter Action dialog box, which is shown in Figure 8.45, select the newly created filter and click Next to continue.

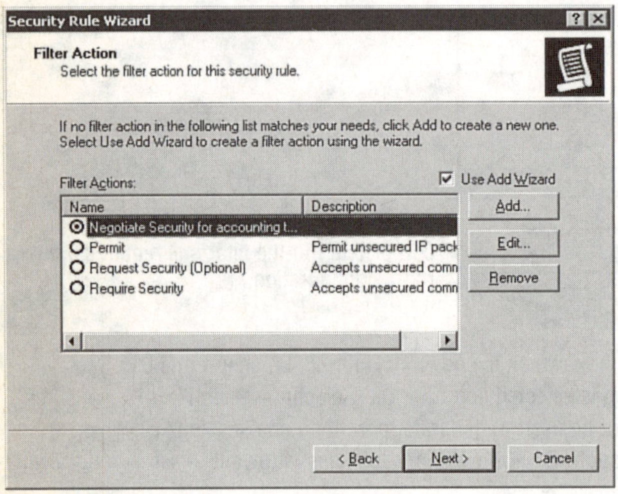

FIGURE 8.45 The filter action is configured, so it's time to move on.

33. In the Authentication Method dialog box, which is shown in Figure 8.46, select the primary authentication method this rule will use. The default selection of Kerberos v5 should be used in most cases. You can add additional authentication methods after the rule has been configured. Click Next to continue.

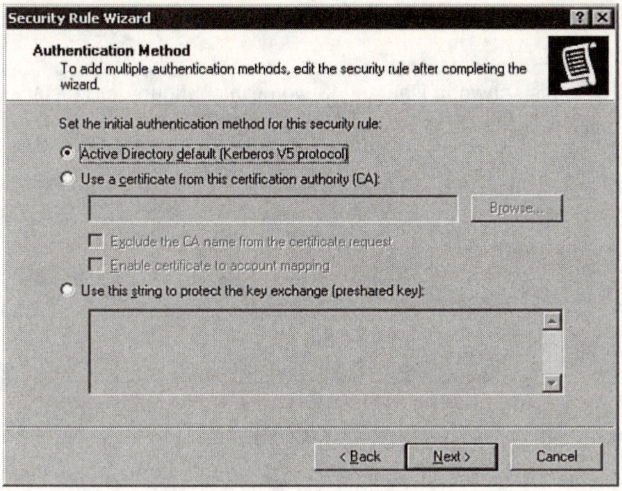

FIGURE 8.46 Specify the preferred authentication method; Kerberos v5 is preferred.

34. From the Completing the Security Rule Wizard dialog box, ensure that the Edit Properties option is deselected and click Finish to complete the rule creation process.

35. Finally, you are back to the policy Properties dialog box. You still have some additional configuration that you can complete, however. On the General tab, you can configure the interval at which the computer will check for updates and changes to the security policy, as shown in Figure 8.47. The default setting of 180 minutes is usually acceptable.

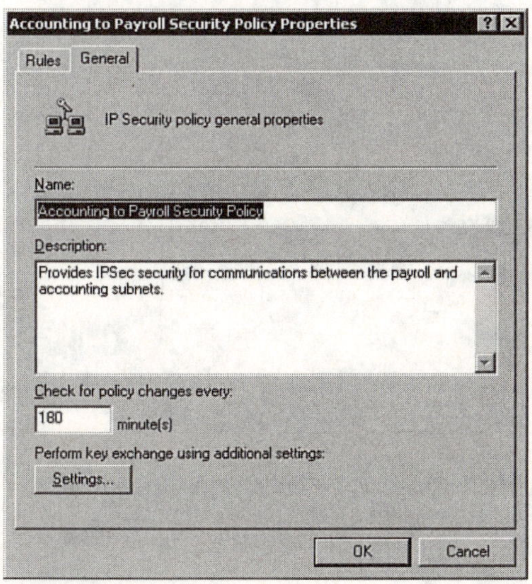

FIGURE 8.47 Configuring the policy update interval.

36. You can modify the settings used for the IKE process by clicking the Settings button at the bottom of the General tab.

37. In the Key Exchange Settings dialog box, which is shown in Figure 8.48, you can configure for Master Key Perfect Forward Secrecy, which improves security of the keying process. Additionally, you can change the defaults provided for key generation.

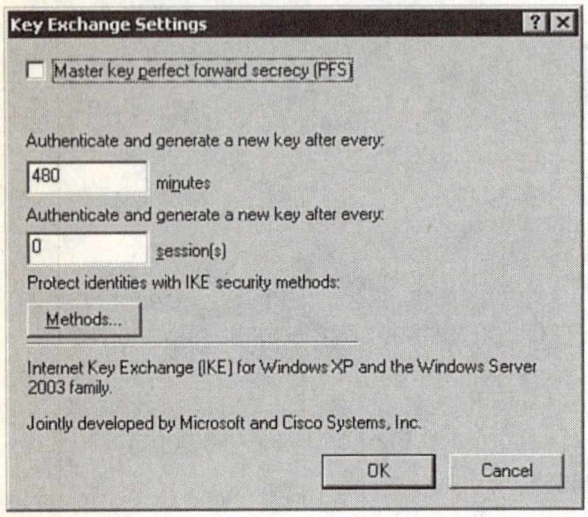

FIGURE 8.48 You can configure advanced IKE properties from the Key Exchange Settings dialog box.

38. If you want to configure the methods used to protect the identities, click the Methods button. The Key Exchange Security Methods dialog box opens, as shown in Figure 8.49. Note that by default the new 2048-bit Diffie-Hellman key exchange method is not used. You can select it by adding or editing a security method, as shown in Figure 8.50.

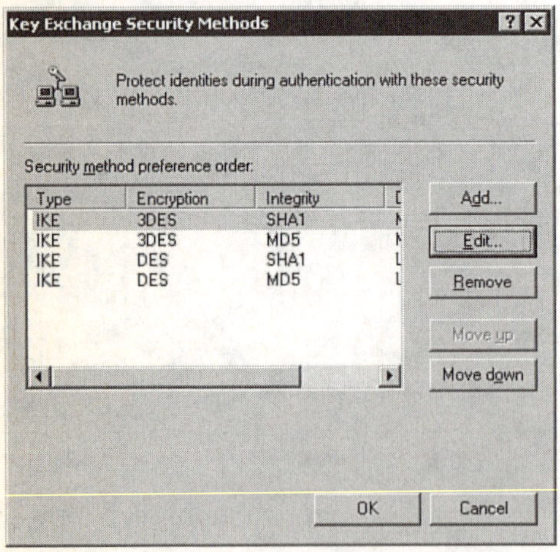

FIGURE 8.49 Customizing the key exchange security methods can increase security.

FIGURE 8.50 Using the new 2048-bit Diffie-Hellman key exchange method.

39. Click OK as required to return to the policy Properties dialog box.
40. Click OK to close the policy Properties dialog box. Your new IPSec policy is now configured and ready to use. Assign it as previously discussed at the end of the "Configuring and Implementing IPSec" section of this chapter.

IPSec can be deployed at any level within your organization. Thus far, we have examined it only from the point of view of a local computer. You can just as easily apply it via Group Policy using the Active Directory Users and Computers console, as shown in Figure 8.51.

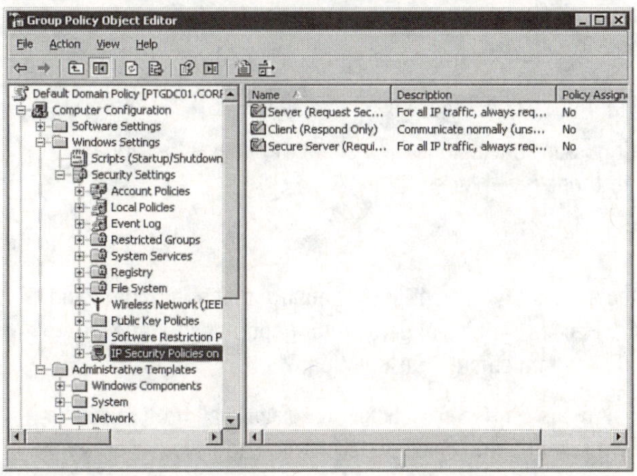

FIGURE 8.51 You can easily apply IPSec at the domain or OU level using Group Policy.

With the task of implementing IPSec out of the way, you are now left to monitor and troubleshoot it, as we examine in the next section.

Challenge

You are the system and network administrator of Axioms Publishing, a small publishing company. The company is located in a single building in Memphis, Tennessee, with each department on its own IP subnet. From time to time, the marketing and sales departments need to share confidential information about forthcoming books and promotions. This information needs to be protected from other users accessing the information while it is in transit across the network.

The information in question is stored on two different servers, a database server and a file server, both of which are running on Windows Server 2003. These two servers perform no other function but to store and serve up this confidential information. The servers are patched with the latest Service Pack and security updates and have been hardened to disable unneeded services. These servers are located on a separate IP subnet all by themselves and are physically secured inside the company's data center. The servers are also located in their own OU, named Confidential Servers, within Active Directory.

The workstations that the marketing and sales department use to access these servers, however, are not special purpose and are used by their users for day-to-day tasks, such as reading email, browsing the Internet, and accessing files and databases on other servers in your network. All marketing and sales department workstations are located in their own organizational units, named Marketing Computers and Sales Computers, respectively.

The CIO has asked you to ensure that these confidential resources be securely accessed only by users in the sales and marketing departments. All other users in the company must not be able to make a connection to either of these servers.

Your task is to implement the required IPSec solution for Axioms Publishing.

Try to complete this exercise on your own, listing your conclusions on a sheet of paper. After you have completed the exercise, compare your results to those given here.

Answers

When you're implementing a very specific IPSec solution, you want to first ensure that you understand the requirements and the scope for the solution. Because you've already got a good network and OU structure in place, you can simply build off of that to implement your solution.

At first, you might be tempted to create and assign custom IPSec policies that secure all traffic between these networks. If the workstations used by the marketing and sales departments had no other communications with the subnet on which the servers were located, then you could rightfully do just that. However, because the workstations are general-purpose computers and need to communicate securely (via IPSec) only when they are accessing the two servers in question, a different approach is required.

You should first create and link a new Group Policy Object to the Marketing Computers OU. In this new GPO, you should assign the Client (Respond Only) IPSec policy. This will cause all computers in the OU to attempt unsecured communications first and switch to IPSec-secured communications if requested, as will be the case when the servers require IPSec-secure communications. You should next link this GPO to the Sales Computers OU as well, thus making sure that those computers will behave the same way in regard to IPSec usage.

The next task for you to perform is to create and link a new GPO to the Confidential Servers OU. In this new GPO, you should assign the Secure Server (Require Security) policy. This will require that all communications to and from the server be IPSec secured.

Once these new Group Policy Objects are in place, you should start to see SAs forming and secure communications occurring between the servers and the workstations. The workstations should also be able to successfully communicate to non-IPSec-secured computers and servers, both inside and outside your network.

Monitoring and Troubleshooting Network Protocol Security

Objective:

Monitor network protocol security. Tools might include the IP Security Monitor Microsoft Management Console (MMC) snap-in and Kerberos support tools.

Troubleshoot network protocol security. Tools might include the IP Security Monitor MMC snap-in, Event Viewer, and Network Monitor.

With the discussion of creating and implementing IPSec policies behind us, although at a rather simple level, it's now time to move on and examine the monitoring and troubleshooting of IPSec on your network. Although the actual configuring and implementing of IPSec is beyond the scope of Exam 70-291, for the exam you are expected to be able to perform basic monitoring and troubleshooting. In addition, Kerberos is the default user authentication protocol in Windows Server 2003, and you will from time to time need to monitor and troubleshoot Kerberos as well.

EXAM ALERT

Know Your IPSec! For this exam, even though the objectives don't really lend themselves to it, you must have a solid understanding of IPSec, the three default IPSec policies, and basic IPSec policy components. Be sure you understand the background of IPSec before you take the exam.

Monitoring IPSec

Going back to the customized IPSec management console that you created earlier in Step by Step 8.1, let's spend some time now with the IP Security Monitor snap-in. The IP Security Monitor snap-in is divided into three major areas: the Active Policy node, the Main Mode node, and the Quick Mode node. The Active Policy node is shown in Figure 8.52. Table 8.1 explains each of the information items shown in the Active Policy node of the IP Security Monitor snap-in.

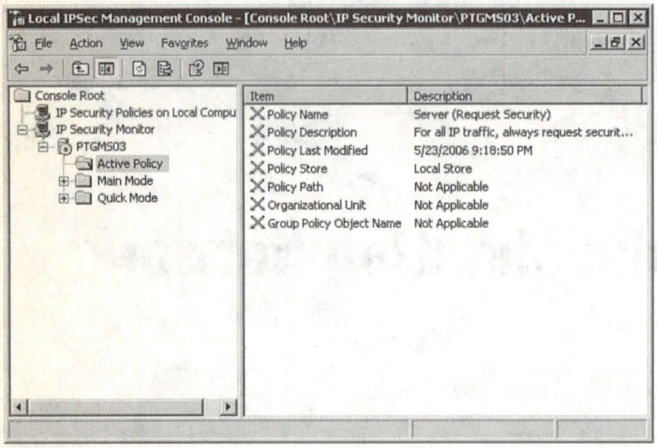

FIGURE 8.52 The Active Policy node statistics get you up to speed quickly on the currently assigned IPSec policy.

EXAM ALERT

Know the IPSec Monitoring Areas For this exam, make sure that you have a good understanding of what types of information you can find in each of the nodes of the IP Security Monitor.

TABLE 8.1 Active Policy Node Items

Item	Description
Policy Name	Specifies the name of the active IPSec policy.
Description	Describes the active IPSec policy.
Policy Last Modified	Provides the date and the time that the active IPSec policy was modified.
Policy Store	Provides the storage location for the active IPSec policy. For a local policy, it reads Local Store, and for a domain policy, it reads Domain Store.
Policy Path	Applies only to domain policies and provides the LDAP path to the active IPSec policy.
Organizational Unit	Applies only to domain policies and lists the organizational unit to which the group policy object (GPO) is applied.
Group Policy Object Name	Applies only to domain policies and lists the GPO to which the active IPSec policy is applied.

The Statistics folder in the Main Mode node, which is shown in Figure 8.53, provides information about the Phase I security associations (SAs), as detailed in Table 8.2. The remaining Main Mode folders all provide specific information about the IPSec policy currently in effect, and thus will be empty when no policy is in effect. The Main Mode SA, also known as the ISAKMP SA, is used to protect the IPSec security negotiations.

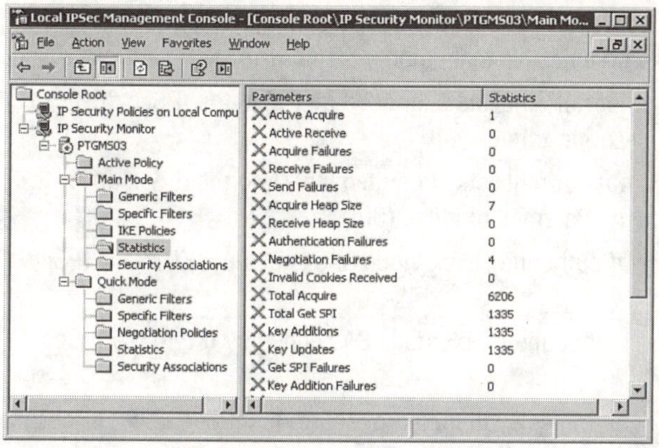

FIGURE 8.53 The Main Mode node Statistics folder displays information about the Phase I SAs.

TABLE 8.2 Main Mode (Internet Key Exchange) Statistics

Statistic	Description
Active Acquire	Specifies a request by the IPSec policy to have IKE perform a task. This number includes all outstanding and queued requests and is typically 1. Under heavy loading, this number increases.
Active Receive	Displays the number of IKE messages that have been received and are queued for processing.
Acquire Failures	Displays the number of times that an acquire has failed.
Receive Failures	Displays the number of times that errors have occurred in receiving IKE messages.
Send Failures	Displays the number of times that errors have occurred in sending IKE messages.
Acquire Heap Size	Displays the number of entries in the acquire heap, which stores active acquires. This number increases with heavy loading and decreases as the heap is cleared.
Receive Heap Size	Displays the number of entries in the IKE receive buffers for incoming IKE messages.
Authentication Failures	Displays the total number of identity authentication failures that have occurred during Main mode negotiation. This is a useful indicator to determine whether the authentication methods do not match between two computers attempting communications.
Negotiation Failures	Displays the total number of negotiation failures that occurred during Main Mode or Quick Mode negotiation. This is a useful statistic to determine whether security and/or authentication methods do not match between two computers attempting communications.

(continues)

TABLE 8.2 Continued

Statistic	Description
Invalid Cookies Received	Specifies a value contained in a received IKE message that is used by IKE to find the state of an active Main mode. If a cookie in a received IKE message cannot be matched with an active Main mode, then it is invalid.
Total Acquire	Displays the total number of requests submitted by IKE to the IPSec driver to establish an SA for securing traffic.
Total Get SPI	Displays the total number of requests submitted by IKE to the IPSec driver to obtain a unique Security Parameters Index (SPI).
Key Additions	Displays the number of outbound Quick mode SAs added by IKE to the IPSec driver.
Key Updates	Displays the number of inbound Quick mode SAs added by IKE to the IPSec driver.
Get SPI Failures	Displays the number of requests submitted by IKE to the IPSec driver to obtain a unique SPI that have failed.
Key Addition Failures	Displays the number of outbound Quick mode SA addition requests submitted by IKE to the IPSec driver that have failed.
Key Update Failures	Displays the number of inbound Quick mode SA addition requests submitted by IKE to the IPSec driver that have failed.
ISADB List Size	Displays the number of Main mode state entries, including negotiated Main modes, Main modes in progress, and Main modes that have failed and have not yet been deleted.
Connection List Size	Displays the number of Quick mode state entries. This number indicates the load placed on the computer.
IKE Main Mode	Displays the total number of successful SAs created during Main mode negotiations.
IKE Quick Mode	Displays the total number of successful SAs created during Quick mode negotiations. There are typically multiple Quick mode SAs created for each Main mode SA; thus, this value may not necessarily match that of the Main mode.
Soft Associations	Displays the total number of negotiations that resulted in the use of unsecured traffic (also known as *soft SAs*). Typically this is an indication of SAs formed with computers that do not support IPSec or were not able to negotiate successful IPSec connections. This can be an indication of mismatched security and authentication settings.
Invalid Packets Received	Displays the number of received IKE messages that were invalid. Most commonly, invalid IKE messages are a result of retransmitted IKE messages or unmatched shared keys between the communicating computers.

The Statistics folder in the Quick Mode node, which is shown in Figure 8.54, provides information about the Phase II SAs, as detailed in Table 8.3. The remaining Quick Mode folders all provide specific information about the IPSec policy currently in effect, and thus will be empty when no policy is in effect. The Quick Mode SAs, also known as the IPSec SAs, are those security associations that have been created to protect the data sent between computers communicating securely using IPSec.

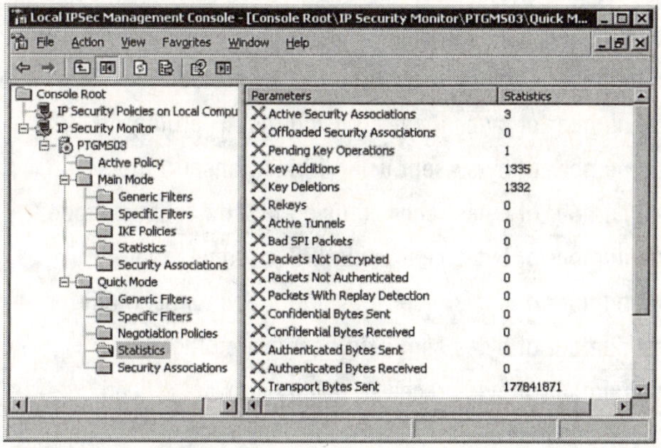

FIGURE 8.54 The Quick Mode node Statistics folder displays information about the Phase II SAs.

TABLE 8.3 Quick Mode (IPSec) Statistics

Statistic	Description
Active Security Associations	Displays the number of active IPSec SAs.
Offloaded Security Associations	Displays the number of active IPSec SAs that have been offloaded to hardware.
Pending Key Operations	Displays the number of IPSec key operations that are in progress.
Key Additions	Displays the total number of successful IPSec SA negotiations.
Key Deletions	Displays the number of key deletions for IPSec SAs.
Re-Keys	Displays the number of rekey operations for IPSec SAs.
Active Tunnels	Displays the number of active IPSec tunnels.
Bad SPI Packets	Displays the total number of packets for which the SPI was incorrect. SPIs are used to match inbound packets with SAs. If the SPI is incorrect, the inbound SA may have expired. If rekeying intervals are set very short, this number is likely to increase very rapidly. Under normal conditions, a bad SPI packet does not mean that IPSec is failing because SAs expire normally.
Packets Not Decrypted	Displays the total number of packets that were not decrypted successfully. This may indicate that a packet has arrived for which the SA has previously expired. When the SA expires, the session key used to decrypt packets is removed. By itself, this does not indicate that IPSec is failing.
Packets Not Authenticated	Displays the total number of packets for which data could not be verified, meaning that the integrity hash verification failed. Most commonly this is a result of an expired SA.

(continues)

TABLE 8.3 Continued

Statistic	Description
Packets with Replay Detection	Displays the total number of packets that contained a valid Sequence Number field.
Confidential Bytes Sent	Displays the total number of bytes sent using the ESP.
Confidential Bytes Received	Displays the total number of bytes received using the ESP.
Authenticated Bytes Sent	Displays the total number of bytes sent using the AH protocol.
Authenticated Bytes Received	Displays the total number of bytes received using the AH protocol.
Transport Bytes Sent	Displays the total number of bytes sent using IPSec transport mode.
Transport Bytes Received	Displays the total number of bytes received using IPSec transport mode.
Bytes Sent in Tunnels	Displays the total number of bytes sent using IPSec tunnel mode.
Bytes Received in Tunnels	Displays the total number of bytes received using IPSec tunnel mode.
Offloaded Bytes Sent	Displays the total number of bytes sent using hardware offload.
Offloaded Bytes Received	Displays the total number of bytes received using hardware offload.

Configuring the IP Security Monitor hasn't changed much since Windows 2000, except that the IP Security Monitor is now an MMC snap-in. You can open the IP Security Monitor properties for any server listed in the IP Security Monitor node by right-clicking it and selecting Properties from the context menu. The server Properties page opens, as shown in Figure 8.55. You have the option to change the refresh interval for the display of the IP Security Monitor statistics and to decide whether you want to enable DNS name resolution, which comes into play when you're examining the SAs that are formed.

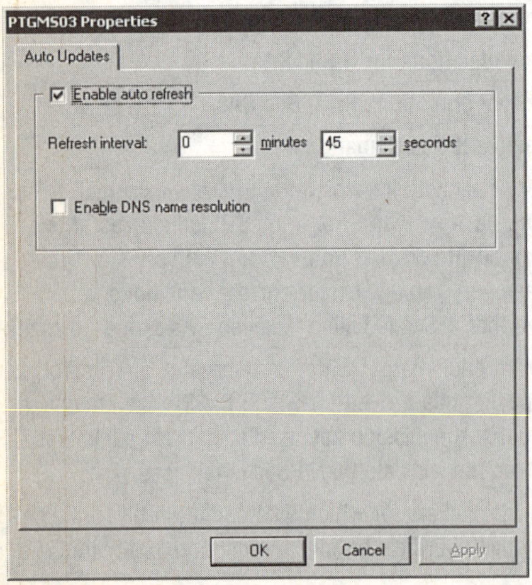

FIGURE 8.55 There's not much to configure for the IP Security Monitor's properties.

Troubleshooting IPSec

If you have problems with IPSec, you should first verify that any routers or firewalls that traffic may be passing through are configured to support IPSec traffic. You need to allow the following traffic:

- Protocol ID 50 and 51 or ESP and AH traffic
- UDP port 500 for IPSec negotiation traffic

Some other basic problems and troubleshooting tips for them are outlined here:

- **You are not able to establish any communications with a computer**—In this case, you should first verify that basic network connectivity exists between the computers in question by using the `ping` command. You should also ensure that all required network services, such as DHCP and DNS, are operating properly for both computers.
- **You are not able to establish any communications with a computer**—This may be a result of a computer having been removed from the domain. Whatever the cause, it causes IPSec communications to fail.
- **Communications are occurring, but not as expected**—You need to ensure that you have the correct (and compatible) IPSec policies assigned on both computers.
- **No hard associations are being formed**—If there are currently soft associations in place, a hard association will not be formed. You need to completely stop all communications between the computers for approximately 5–10 minutes to allow the soft associations to time out. The easiest way to do this is to disable the network connection. After you have allowed the soft association to time out, you should check to see that a hard association has been formed. If a hard association still has not been formed, you need to examine the IPSec policy to verify that unsecured communications are not allowed.
- **IPSec communications are failing after you configure a digital certificate for authentication**—You must make sure that the required digital certificate is installed on the computers that attempt to communicate by using that IPSec policy. This can also be a result of specifying an incorrect Certificate Authority (CA).
- **Some computers can create IPSec connections and some cannot**—This is most likely caused by not having the same IPSec policy applied to all the computers. If you intentionally use different policies, you need to ensure that they share at least one common authentication and security method.

You should also be aware that IPSec-related problems can be found in the security log. You can view IKE events (negotiation success and failure) by enabling success and/or failure auditing for the Audit Logon Events audit policy for the domain or the local computer. The IKE event category is also used for the auditing of user logon events in other services as well, but you can disable this by editing the registry. For more information on configuring and implementing auditing, refer back to Chapter 5, "Implementing, Managing, and Maintaining Network Security."

When success and/or failure auditing for the Audit Logon Events audit policy is enabled, IPSec records the success and/or failure of each Main mode and Quick mode negotiation. The establishment and termination of each negotiation is logged as a separate event for easier analysis and troubleshooting. Be aware, however, that when you enable audit logon events, the security log will likely quickly fill up with IKE events unless you opt to disable auditing of those events through registry editing.

The Network Monitor included in Windows Server 2003 can also be used to view IPSec traffic between the computer it is installed on and other network computers. Network Monitor includes parsers for the ISAKMP (IKE), AH, and ESP protocols. The parsers for ESP can parse inside the ESP packet only if null encryption is being used and the full ESP packet is captured. Network Monitor cannot parse the encrypted portions of IPSec-secured ESP traffic when the encryption is being performed in Windows. However, if the encryption is being performed by an IPSec hardware offload network adapter, the ESP packets have already been decrypted when Network Monitor captures them, and as a result, they can be parsed and interpreted into the upper-layer protocols. If you need to diagnose ESP Windows-encrypted communication (that is, software-encrypted communication), you must first disable ESP encryption and use ESP null encryption by changing the IPSec policy on each computer.

Monitoring and Troubleshooting Kerberos

Kerberos seems to pop up all over the place in Windows Server 2003. Kerberos is the default network authentication method for Windows Server 2003 networks. It can also be used as an IPSec authentication method. Although Kerberos is often thought of as a "set it and forget it" service, you might from time to time need to monitor and troubleshoot it.

Although there are no default tools provided in Windows Server 2003 that allow you to monitor and manipulate Kerberos tickets, two *Windows Server 2003 Resource Kit* tools are available that you can use:

- **`kerbtray.exe`**—You can use the `kerbtray.exe` utility to view cached Kerberos tickets for the current computer from within the Windows GUI.
- **`klist.exe`**—The `klist.exe` utility is a command-line tool that is similar to `kerbtray.exe`. `klist.exe` allows you to view and delete cached Kerberos tickets.

You can download the *Resource Kit* tools from the Microsoft Web site at www.microsoft.com/downloads by searching for "Windows Server 2003 Resource Kit Tools."

The following sections examine the function and usage of these two tools.

kerbtray.exe

The `kerbtray.exe` tool is used to display the cached ticket information for a computer running the Microsoft implementation of the Kerberos version 5 protocol. After `kerbtray.exe` has been installed and executed, it sits (appropriately enough) in the tray area of the taskbar, as shown in Figure 8.56.

FIGURE 8.56 The `kerbtray.exe` icon waits in the tray area of the taskbar.

By moving the cursor over the `kerbtray.exe` icon, you can quickly see a display that lets you know how much time is left before the ticket-granting ticket (TGT) expires. In addition, this icon changes during the last hour before the local security authority (LSA) renews the ticket. When you double-click the `kerbtray.exe` icon, the Kerberos Tickets dialog box opens, as shown in Figure 8.57, allowing you to quickly determine the cached ticket status.

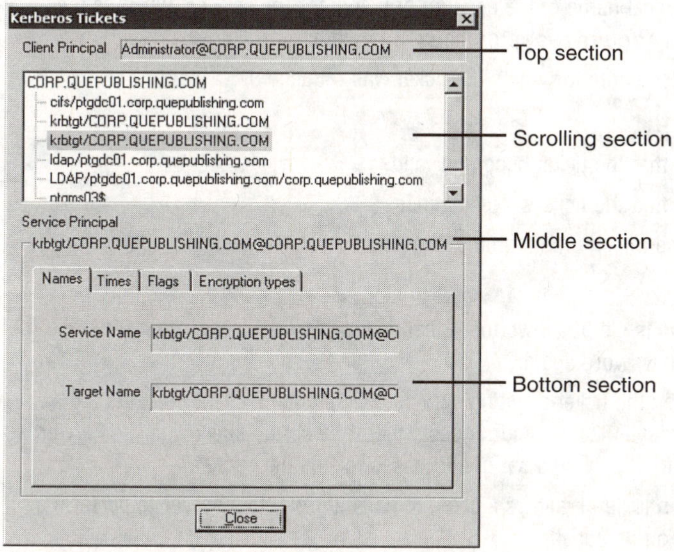

FIGURE 8.57 The Kerberos Tickets dialog box allows you to graphically view cached Kerberos tickets for the local computer.

The Kerberos Tickets dialog box consists of four informational areas:

- **Top section**—The top section provides the name of the Kerberos client principal that is associated with the Windows domain account.
- **Scrolling section**—The scrolling section lists the domains and tickets for all services that have been used since the user logon occurred. Selecting an item here causes its properties to display in the middle and bottom sections.
- **Middle section**—The middle section displays the service principal—the target principal for the selected ticket from the domain list.
- **Bottom section**—The bottom section provides a set of tabs (Names, Times, Flags, and Encryption Types) that provide attributes of the selected ticket in the scrolling section.

Table 8.4 details the information that you see on the tabs of the bottom section of the Kerberos Tickets dialog box.

TABLE 8.4 Options on the Kerberos Tickets Dialog Box Bottom Section Tabs

Option	Description
Names Tab	
Client Name	This is the requester of the ticket, which in most cases is the client's principal name.
Service Name	This is the canonical name of the account principal for the service, which is the same as the `samAccountName` property in the directory.
Target Name	This is the service name for which the ticket was requested.
Times Tab	
Start Time	This is the time that the ticket becomes valid.
End Time	This is the time that the ticket's validity ends.
Renew Until	This specifies the maximum lifetime of the ticket if it is renewable.
Flags Tab	
Forwardable	When this option is set, it allows for authentication forwarding without requiring the user to enter a password again.
Forwarded	This flag is set by the ticket-granting service (TGS) when a client presents a ticket with the Forwardable flag set and requests that it be set by specifying the Forwarded (KDC) option and supplying a set of addresses for the new ticket.
Proxiable	When this option is set, it allows a client to pass a proxy to a server to perform a remote request on its behalf.
Proxy	This flag is set on a ticket by the TGS when the service issues a proxy ticket.

TABLE 8.4 Continued

Option	Description
May Postdate	This flag can be set in a TGT to issue a postdated ticket based on the presented ticket.
Postdated	When this option is set, it indicates that a ticket has been postdated.
Invalid	When this option is set, it indicates that the ticket is not valid. For example, a postdated ticket is typically issued in this form.
Initial	When this option is set, it indicates that the ticket was issued by using the authentication server AS protocol and not issued based on a TGT.
Renewable	When this option is set, it allows the ticket holder to maintain a valid ticket for long periods of time.
HW Authenticated	This flag is used to provide additional information about the initial authentication, regardless of whether the current ticket was issued directly.
Preauthenticated	This flag is used to provide additional information about the initial authentication, regardless of whether the current ticket was issued directly.
OK as Delegate	When this option is set, it indicates that the server specified in the ticket has been determined by policy to be a suitable recipient of delegation.
Encryption Types Tab	
Ticket Encryption Type	This option specifies the encryption type that is used to encrypt the Kerberos ticket.
Key Encryption Type	This option specifies the encryption type that is used with the enclosed session key.

`klist.exe`

The `klist.exe` tool is run from the command line and provides similar functionality to that offered by `kerbtray.exe`. In addition, `klist.exe` allows you to purge cached tickets if desired. The basic syntax of the `klist.exe` command is this:

```
klist [tickets ¦ tgt ¦ purge]
```

The functions of the `klist.exe` options are detailed in Table 8.5.

TABLE 8.5 `klist.exe` Options

Option	Description
`tickets`	The `tickets` option lists information about the current cached tickets of services that you have authenticated to since logging on.
`tgt`	The `tgt` option lists information about the initial Kerberos TGT.
`purge`	The `purge` option allows you to delete a specific ticket.

The `tickets` and `tgt` switches are explained in more detail in Table 8.6.

CAUTION

Purging Tickets When you purge a ticket, you destroy all tickets that have been cached. You should do this with extreme caution. Purging tickets often prevents you from being able to successfully authenticate to network resources. If this occurs, you need to log off and log on again to obtain new tickets—and this can be disastrous if you have files open for editing across the network.

TABLE 8.6 The `klist.exe` `tickets` and `tgt`, Switches

Switch	Description
The `tickets` Switch	
`Server`	Lists the server and domain for the ticket.
`KerbTicket Encryption Type`	Lists the encryption type used to encrypt the Kerberos ticket.
`End Time`	Lists the time that the ticket becomes invalid.
`Renew Time`	Lists the maximum lifetime of the ticket, if it is renewable.
The `tgt` Switch	
`ServiceName`	Displays the service name for the TGT, which is `krbtgt`.
`TargetName`	Displays the name of the service for which the ticket was requested.
`FullServiceName`	Displays the canonical name of the account principal for the service.
`DomainName`	Displays the domain name of the service.
`TargetDomainName`	Displays the realm (domain) in which the ticket is good if the ticket is a cross-realm ticket.
`AltTargetDomainName`	Displays the name supplied to the `InitializeSecurityContext` that generated the ticket—which is typically a service principal name.
`TicketFlags`	Displays the ticket flags set on the current ticket in hexadecimal. The `kerbtray.exe` tool displays these flags on the Flags tab.
`KeyExpirationTime`	Displays the expiration time from the KDC reply.
`Start time`	Displays the time when the ticket becomes valid.
`End Time`	Displays the time when the ticket becomes invalid.
`RenewUntil`	Displays the maximum lifetime of the ticket, if the ticket is renewable.
`TimeSkew`	Displays the reported time difference between the client computer and the server computer for a ticket.

The `klist.exe` tool can be used to monitor and troubleshoot Kerberos from the command line. Figure 8.58 presents an example of what the `klist tickets` command might return.

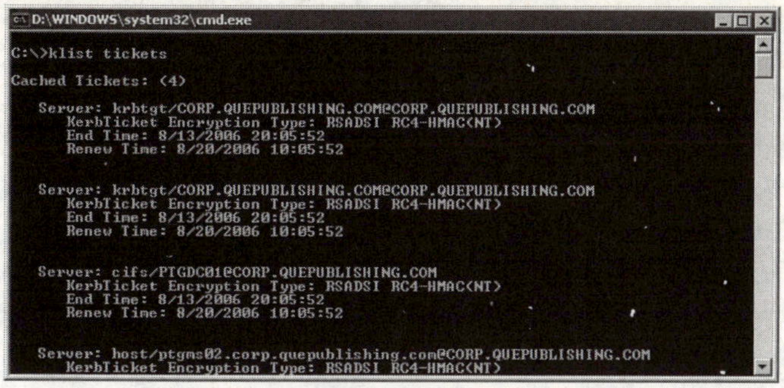

FIGURE 8.58 The `klist tickets` command displays information about all cached Kerberos tickets for the computer.

Chapter Summary

This chapter examines the usage and troubleshooting of IPSec on your network. IPSec can be used to secure communications both on your intranet and between endpoints over the Internet. VPNs can be created using IPSec and L2TP to ensure authenticity, integrity, and confidentiality of data in transit. The IPSec implementation in Windows Server 2003 has received several improvements since Windows 2000, most notably the capability to pass through NAT devices. Also, the Diffie-Hellman key exchange has been increased to a maximum of 2,048 bits to further increase the security of the secret key.

Key Terms

- IPSec
- Internet Key Exchange (IKE)
- `kerbtray.exe`
- `klist.exe`
- Main mode
- MMC
- packet
- Quick mode
- Transport Mode
- Tunnel Mode

Apply Your Knowledge

In this chapter, you have examined the basic implementation and troubleshooting of IPSec in Windows Server 2003. In the following exercises, you will practice some of the concepts and methods discussed in this chapter.

Exercises

8.1 Creating an IPSec Management Console

In this exercise, you will create a customized MMC console that can be used to implement, monitor, and troubleshoot IPSec.

Estimated Time: 10 minutes

1. Open a blank MMC by clicking Start, Run. Then type **`mmc`** to open a blank MMC.
2. In your new console, click the File menu and select Add/Remove Snap-in. The Add/Remove Snap-in dialog box opens.
3. Click the Add button to open the Add Standalone Snap-in dialog box.
4. Scroll down the list, select IP Security Monitor, and click the Add button.
5. Select IP Security Policy Management and click the Add button. You are prompted to choose the scope that the snap-in will manage.
6. For this example, choose Local Computer from the Select Computer or Domain page. Notice that you have the option to select the Active Directory domain that this computer is part of, another Active Directory domain, or another computer. Click Finish to complete the addition of the IP Security Policy Management snap-in to your console.
7. Click Close on the Add Standalone Snap-in dialog box.
8. Click OK on the Add/Remove Snap-in dialog box. Your completed IPSec management console is shown.
9. Save your newly created console by clicking File, Save. Enter a suitable name, such as **`IPSec Management Console`**, and click Save. By default, the console is saved in the Administrative Tools folder of the currently logged-in user.

8.2 Examining Kerberos Ticket Information

In this exercise, you will download, install, and use the `kerbtray.exe` utility to examine the Kerberos tickets in effect on your server.

Estimated Time: 20 minutes

1. Go the Microsoft Downloads Web site at www.microsoft.com/downloads and search for "Windows Server 2003 Resource Kit Tools."
2. Download the Windows Server 2003 Resource Kit Tools to your server.
3. Install the Windows Server 2003 Resource Kit Tools to your server.
4. Click Start, Programs, Windows Resource Kit Tools, Command Shell to open a command shell in the installation directory.

5. Start the `kerbtray.exe` utility by entering the command **`kerbtray.exe`** and pressing Enter.
6. The application starts and appears in your server's tray area, near the clock.
7. Double-click on the tray icon to open the Kerberos Tickets dialog box.
8. In the scrolling section, examine the various tickets your session currently has.
9. Use the bottom section to examine the properties of each ticket.

Exam Questions

1. You are the systems administrator for Joe's Crab Shack, a regional restaurant chain. You have recently begun to implement IPSec to secure communications on the internal network segments. You have just completed the configuration and implementation of the Richmond office network segment. Users in Richmond are now complaining to you that they can connect to their network resources from some computers, but not from others. What do you suspect is the most likely cause of this problem?

   ❍ **A.** The computers do not have basic network connectivity.

   ❍ **B.** More than one IPSec policy is in place.

   ❍ **C.** The domain controller is not responding.

   ❍ **D.** The Kerberos key distribution center is not responding.

2. You are the systems administrator for Widgets and Hammerstein, LLC. Andrea, one of your users, has called you and says that she cannot connect to one of the network servers that requires secured communication. What can you do to quickly verify the IPSec policy in use on that computer?

   ❍ **A.** Use the IP Security Monitor snap-in to see what IPSec policy is in use on the computer.

   ❍ **B.** Use the Network Monitor to see what IPSec policy is in use on the computer.

   ❍ **C.** Use the IP Security Policies snap-in to see what IPSec policy is in use on the computer.

   ❍ **D.** Use the `ipconfig/all` command to see what IPSec policy is in use on the computer.

3. You are the systems administrator for Sunny Day, Inc. You are creating a new IPSec policy for your internal network's financial subnet. When creating your new policy, which items can you specify as part of the IP filter? (Choose all that apply.)

   ❍ **A.** Source IP address

   ❍ **B.** Destination IP address

   ❍ **C.** Network protocol

   ❍ **D.** Operating system

4. You are the systems administrator for Herb's Happenings, a public relations firm. You want to create a new IPSec policy for traffic on your private network that provides the strongest secret key possible. In Windows Server 2003, what is the maximum Diffie-Hellman value that can be used?

❍ **A.** 512 bit

❍ **B.** 768 bit

❍ **C.** 1,024 bit

❍ **D.** 2,048 bit

5. You are a technical architect for Little Faith Enterprises, a venture capital company. You have recently been assigned a new security intern who will be assisting you over the summer months to implement a company-wide IPSec solution on your networks. In talking with your intern, Allison, you discover that she is a little weak on IPSec and its relevant components, so you decide to teach her about how Authentication Header (AH) and the Encapsulating Security Protocol (ESP) work. When discussing ESP, which of the following header fields is responsible for ensuring that a replay attack will not be successful?

❍ **A.** Security Paramters Index (SPI)

❍ **B.** Sequence Number

❍ **C.** Padding

❍ **C.** Padding Length

❍ **E.** Next Header

6. You are a technical architect for Little Faith Enterprises, a venture capital company. You are still training your newly assigned security intern, Allison, about how Authentication Header (AH) and the Encapsulating Security Protocol (ESP) work. When discussing AH, which of the following header fields is responsible for ensuring the integrity of the message?

❍ **A.** Next Header

❍ **B.** Length

❍ **C.** Security Paramters Index (SPI)

❍ **D.** Sequence Number

❍ **E.** Authentication Data

7. From the list of header components given, what is the correct order of header components for an IP packet with the ESP header inserted in tunnel mode? (All options will be used and will need to be arranged in the correct order to correctly answer this question.)

   ❍ **A.** New IP header

   ❍ **B.** IPSec ESP authentication

   ❍ **C.** TCP header

   ❍ **D.** IPSec ESP trailer

   ❍ **E.** Packet data

   ❍ **F.** IPSec ESP header

   ❍ **G.** Original IP header

8. From the list of header components given, which one is signed but *not* encrypted in an IP packet with the ESP header inserted in transfer mode?

   ❍ **A.** IPSec ESP trailer

   ❍ **B.** Packet data

   ❍ **C.** IPSec ESP header

   ❍ **D.** TCP header

9. You are the systems administrator for Herb's Happenings, a public relations firm. While examining the IPSec statistics in the Main Mode node of the IP Security Monitor snap-in, you notice that you have a very low number of IKE Main Mode SAs and a very high number of Soft Associations. What is typically the problem that causes this to happen?

   ❍ **A.** SAs were not formed with computers due to credentials or permissions mismatches.

   ❍ **B.** SAs were formed with computers that do not support IPSec or were not able to negotiate successful IPSec connections.

   ❍ **C.** SAs were not formed with computers due to Service Pack level mismatches.

   ❍ **D.** SAs were formed with computers that do not have a valid domain account in Active Directory.

10. You are the systems administrator for Widgets and Hammerstein, LLC. You have been directed by the network manager to secure all communications between servers and workstations in the financial department. All of the server and workstations are on a single, isolated subnet. What would be the easiest way to ensure that non IPSec-enabled (and configured) computers could not establish any communications with your servers?

❍ **A.** Create a custom IPSec policy.

❍ **B.** Assign the Client (Respond Only) policy.

❍ **C.** Assign the Server (Request Security) policy.

❍ **D.** Assign the Secure Server (Require Security) policy.

11. From the list of header components given, what is the correct order of headers for an IP packet with the ESP header inserted in transfer mode? (All options will be used and will need to be arranged in the correct order to correctly answer this question.)

❍ **A.** IPSec ESP header

❍ **B.** IPSec ESP trailer

❍ **C.** IP header

❍ **D.** Packet data

❍ **E.** IPSec ESP authentication

❍ **F.** TCP header

12. What tool can you use to graphically monitor the Kerberos tickets that a user has in his or her temporary cache?

❍ **A.** `kerbtray.exe`

❍ **B.** `klist.exe`

❍ **C.** IP Security Monitor

❍ **D.** pathping

13. From the list of header components given, what is the correct order of headers for an IP packet with the AH header inserted in transfer mode? (All options will be used and will need to be arranged in the correct order to correctly answer this question.)

❍ **A.** Packet data

❍ **B.** TCP header

❍ **C.** IP header

❍ **D.** IPSec AH header

Answers to Exam Questions

1. **B**. More often than not, when you have some computers able to create IPSec connections and others that cannot, you have more than one IPSec policy in place. If you are intentionally using multiple policies, you need to ensure that you have at least one common authentication and security method between them; otherwise, communications will fail. Basic network connectivity, while always a potential problem, does not appear to be the problem here; thus, Answer A is incorrect. The status of the domain controller is not an issue here; thus, Answer C is incorrect. The status of the KDC is also not an issue here; thus, Answer D is incorrect.

2. **A**. You need to use the IP Security Monitor snap-in to examine what IPSec policy, if any, is currently assigned to the computer. Network Monitor and the IP Security Policies snap-in will not show you what IPSec policy is assigned, and neither will the `ipconfig/all` command; thus, Answers B, C, and D are incorrect.

3. **A**, **B**, and **C**. You can specify the source IP address, destination IP address, source port, destination port, and network protocol in your IP filters. The operating system is not part of the filters; thus, Answer D is incorrect. For more information, see the section "Configuring and Implementing IPSec."

4. **D**. Windows Server 2003 provides the increased Diffie-Hellman option of 2,048 bits; thus, Answers A, B, and C are incorrect. The Diffie-Hellman group is used to determine the length of the base material that is actually used to generate the IPSec secret key. This increased length increases the secret key strength and thus makes it more difficult for an attacker to break.

5. **B**. The Sequence Number field provides the anti-replay functionality of ESP; thus, Answers A, C, D, and E are incorrect. The sequence number is an incrementally increasing number (starting from 0) that is never allowed to cycle and indicates the packet number. The machine receiving the packet checks this field to verify that the packet has not been received already. If a packet with this number has already been received, the packet is rejected. For more information, see the section "Understanding the Architecture and Components of IPSec."

6. **E**. The Authentication Data field contains the Integrity Check Value (ICV) used to verify the integrity of the message, which is a calculated hash value; thus, Answers A, B, C, and D are incorrect. The receiver calculates the hash value and checks it against the ICV to verify packet integrity. For more information, see the section "Understanding the Architecture and Components of IPSec."

7. **A-1**, **F-2**, **G-3**, **C-4**, **E-5**, **D-6**, **B-7**. When an IP packet is sent with the ESP header inserted in tunnel mode, the packet headers are in the following order: New IP header, IPSec ESP header, Original IP header, TCP header, Packet data, IPSec ESP trailer, IPSec ESP authentication. For more information, see the section "Understanding the Architecture and Components of IPSec."

8. **C**. The IPSec ESP header is signed, but not encrypted, when an IP packet is sent with the ESP header inserted in transfer mode; thus Answers A, B, and D are incorrect. The remaining header items listed are all signed and encrypted. For more information, see the section "Understanding the Architecture and Components of IPSec."

9. **B**. When you see a high number of Soft Associations, this is typically an indication of SAs formed with computers that do not support IPSec or were not able to negotiate successful IPSec connections; thus Answers A, C, and D are incorrect. This problem can be an indication of mismatched security and authentication settings. For more information, see the section "Monitoring IPSec."

10. **D**. In this case, the easiest way to accomplish the required solution is to assign the Secure Server (Require Security) policy; thus Answers A, B, and C are incorrect. This policy is implemented on computers that require highly secure communications, such as servers transmitting sensitive data. The filters in this policy require all outbound communication to be secured, allowing only the initial inbound communication request to be unsecured. For more information, see the section "Configuring and Implementing IPSec."

11. **C-1**, **A-2**, **F-3**, **D-4**, **B-5**, **E-6**. When an IP packet is sent with the ESP header inserted in transfer mode, the packet headers are in the following order: IP header, IPSec ESP header, TCP header, Packet data, IPSec ESP trailer, IPSec ESP authentication. For more information, see the section "Understanding the Architecture and Components of IPSec."

12. **A**. `kerbtray.exe`, part of the *Windows Server 2003 Resource Kit* tools, is used to display the cached Kerberos tickets a user has. `kerbtray.exe` is used from within the Windows GUI. `klist.exe` performs the same function but from the command line. For more information, see the section "Monitoring and Troubleshooting Kerberos."

13. **C-1**, **D-2**, **B-3**, **A-4**. When an IP packet is sent with the AH header inserted in transfer mode, the packet headers are in the following order: IP header, IPSec AH header, TCP header, Packet data. For more information, see the section "Understanding the Architecture and Components of IPSec."

Suggested Readings and Resources

1. Davies, Joseph, and Lee, Thomas. *Microsoft Windows Server 2003 TCP/IP Protocols and Services Technical Reference*. Microsoft Press, 2003.

2. "Technical Overview of Windows Server 2003 Security Services," www.microsoft.com/windowsserver2003/techinfo/overview/security.mspx.

3. Davies, Joseph, and Thomas Lee. 2003. *Microsoft Windows Server 2003 TCP/IP Protocols and Services Technical Reference.* Redmond, WA: Microsoft Press.

4. Microsoft Corporation. 2003. *Microsoft Windows Server 2003 Resource Kit.* Redmond, WA: Microsoft Press.

5. Microsoft Corporation. 2003. *Microsoft Windows Server 2003 Deployment Kit.* Redmond, WA: Microsoft Press.

6. "Internet Protocol Security Overview," www.microsoft.com/technet/prodtechnol/windowsserver2003/proddocs/standard/sag_IPSECintroduct.asp.

CHAPTER 9

Maintaining and Troubleshooting a Network Infrastructure

In a utopian world, you could simply install an operating system and forget about it after that. Unfortunately, in the real world, you can't actually do that—Windows Server 2003, even as advanced and easy to use as it is, still requires you to have a basic level of monitoring and troubleshooting skills when things on the network aren't working quite right.

This chapter covers objectives from the "Maintaining a Network Infrastructure" section of Exam 70-291.

Objectives

Monitor network traffic. Tools might include Network Monitor and System Monitor.

- Many times, you might discover that you have a network traffic problem without knowing the cause. In cases such as these, you can use the Network Monitor and the System Monitor to monitor and analyze the system in an effort to determine where the cause of the problem lies. You can use the Network Monitor to monitor raw network packets traversing the network and look for items such as broadcast floods. The System Monitor's counter objects can be used to monitor various aspects of network performance.

Troubleshoot connectivity to the Internet.

- You will undoubtedly have problems reaching the Internet from time to time—connectivity problems are a fact of life in the ever-changing network-centric world in which we live. Several tools are at your disposal to determine where the connectivity problem lies.

Troubleshoot server services.

- **Diagnose and resolve issues related to service dependency.**
- **Use service recovery options to diagnose and resolve service-related issues.**
- Many times, the failure of one service can cause a domino effect, and dependent services can also fail or become stuck. The Services console provides the information and management tools you need to ensure that your server's services are operating correctly. In addition, you can use the Event Viewer to get additional information on a service that has failed to start properly.

Outline

Study Strategies

- Get familiar with the usages and limitations of the Network Monitor and the System Monitor. After doing so, you will realize that you can use these tools and other third-party applications to effectively monitor network traffic on a network.
- Get your hands dirty. The Step by Step exercises throughout this book provide plenty of directions and exercises, but you should go beyond those examples and create some of your own. If you can, experiment with each of the topics we discuss in this chapter to see how they work and why you would use each one.

Introduction

The Internet and private networks are complex entities that are constantly changing. Although change and configuration management, capacity planning and monitoring, and network and system performance monitoring are not new topics, they have never been more important to the health and proper operation of networks than they are today.

You will commonly find yourself troubleshooting network traffic problems and troubleshooting network connectivity to the Internet. In addition, you will likely spend some time ensuring that servers' services are running smoothly and responding as required.

All these monitoring and troubleshooting tasks might seem boring or even unnecessary in the stable and automated world of Windows Server 2003, but they have their place, just as much as or even more than they did before. This chapter examines a wide array of monitoring and troubleshooting topics that you will be expected to understand for Exam 70-291 and later use while managing a Windows Server 2003 network.

Monitoring Network Traffic

Objective:

Monitor network traffic. Tools might include Network Monitor and System Monitor.

As a network administrator, you will find that network traffic can directly influence your productivity and design of a network. You need to implement a solid plan to monitor existing traffic and then deduce how to manage that traffic. Your constant battle will be that when you add a new service, you will also lose a percentage of your available bandwidth. Fortunately, through planning, tweaking, and design, you can keep those lost percentages small.

Using the Network Monitor

Network traffic is any activity directed to or from a host on a network. Any packet that leaves a network card is contributing to network traffic. Network traffic increases with more hosts and more services. In addition, when a network is not segmented properly, network traffic increases as well.

Why is the issue of network traffic so important? A crowded network, like rush-hour traffic, clogs the speed of the network, causes the network to become a bottleneck, and can ultimately cause a network to fail. As a rule, the more you add network services, shares, and resources, the more network traffic you generate.

You can use lots of tools and third-party add-ons to monitor your network's activity. However, one tool is more powerful than any piece of software: your brain! If you plan your networks before you implement them, you'll be happier in the long run. The following are a few tips for designing a network while keeping traffic in mind:

- Get rid of unneeded protocols.
- Get rid of unneeded services.
- Organize your shares to create a swift and easy-to-navigate structure.
- Don't be afraid to segment a network. The more users there are in an environment, the more chatter—and contention—the network experiences. You can segment a network in various ways, such as by using routers and/or switches.
- Use Network Monitor to create a baseline of network activity. Use this baseline to determine how the network is evolving.

You can use Network Monitor to capture packets on a network. From these packets, you can troubleshoot network problems, discern how busy your network is, and predict how the network will grow.

Network Monitor is made up of two primary components:

- **Network Monitor**—Network Monitor is the tool you use to capture packets sent to and from a server. The version of Network Monitor that is included with Windows Server 2003 records only packets sent to and from the server it is running on and the LAN.
- **Network Monitor driver**—The Network Monitor driver is installed automatically when you install Network Monitor on a server. If you have Systems Management Server (SMS) installed in your network, you can install the Network Monitor driver on additional computers to allow monitoring of more of your network. However, if you do install the Network Monitor driver on additional computers, you should make a point to install it only once per subnet.

EXAM ALERT

Beware the Limitations of the Network Monitor When taking this exam, be sure to remember the limitations of the Network Monitor. Also, pay careful attention to where you opt to deploy the Network Monitor driver on other computers.

Installing Network Monitor

Network Monitor is not installed by default, but it's easy enough to add. Step by Step 9.1 walks you through the steps to install Network Monitor.

STEP BY STEP

9.1 Installing the Network Monitor

1. Select Start, Settings, Control Panel, Add or Remove Programs.
2. Click the Add/Remove Windows Components button. The Windows Components Wizard dialog box opens, as shown in Figure 9.1.

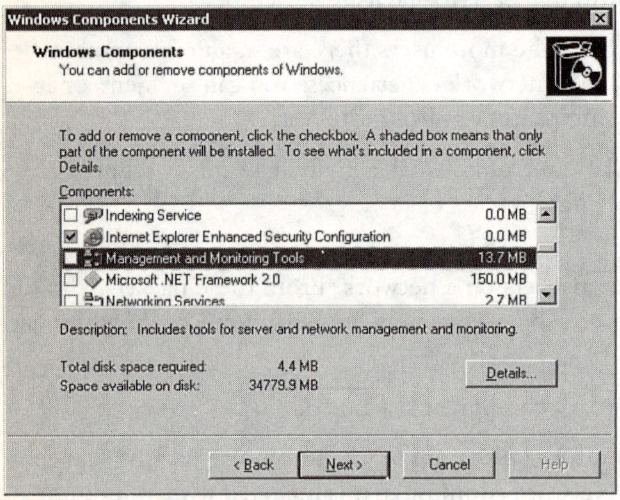

FIGURE 9.1 The Network Monitor components are listed under the Management and Monitoring Tools group.

3. Scroll down the list and select Management and Monitoring Tools by double-clicking it. The Management and Monitoring Tools dialog box, shown in Figure 9.2, opens.

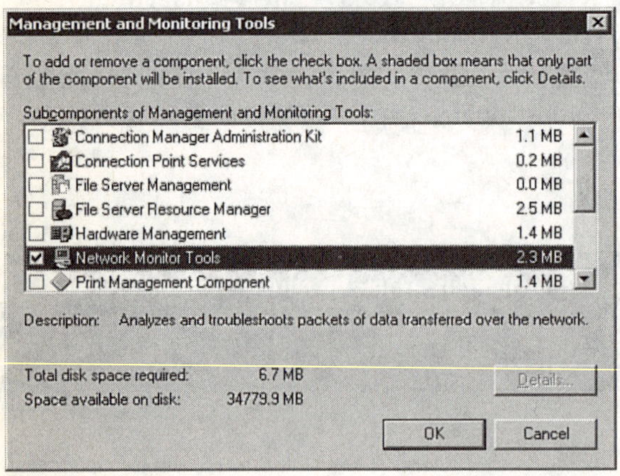

FIGURE 9.2 You can select the Network Monitor Tools option to install the Network Monitor.

4. Select the Network Monitor Tools option in the subcomponents list, click OK, and then click Next.
5. If asked to do so, provide your Windows Server 2003 CD or type a path for accessing the setup files.
6. Click Finish when prompted to complete the Windows Components Wizard.

Installing the Network Monitor Driver

If you need to monitor a different subnet than the one on which you have installed the Network Monitor or you need to support installation of SMS on a network, you need to add the Network Monitor driver. Step by Step 9.2 guides you through the process of adding only the driver.

STEP BY STEP

9.2 Adding the Network Monitor Driver

1. Open the Network Connections window by selecting Start, Settings, Network Connections.
2. Double-click the Local Area Connection icon to bring up the Local Area Connection Status dialog box.
3. Click the Properties button to open the Local Area Connection Properties dialog box.
4. On the General tab, click the Install button.
5. Choose Protocol from the list of available components and then click Add.
6. Select Network Monitor Driver and click OK. The necessary files are added.
7. If asked to do so, provide your Windows Server 2003 CD or type a path for accessing the setup files.

Using Network Monitor to Capture Data

Network Monitor, shown in Figure 9.3, captures frames, or packets, to and from the local computer and the network. Step by Step 9.3 walks you through the process of using Network Monitor and creating a simple capture. Later, we go into greater detail on creating a capture filter through Network Monitor.

The four panes in Network Monitor report information about the current network activity or captured file:

- **Graph pane**—The Graph pane reports percentages of activity in bar chart format.
- **Session Stats pane**—The Session Stats pane reports individual statistics of client-to-server activity during a capture or live activity.
- **Station Stats pane**—The Station Stats pane reports information on each workstation's activity on a network. Keep in mind that this is actually activity between the specific workstation and the server on which Network Monitor is installed.

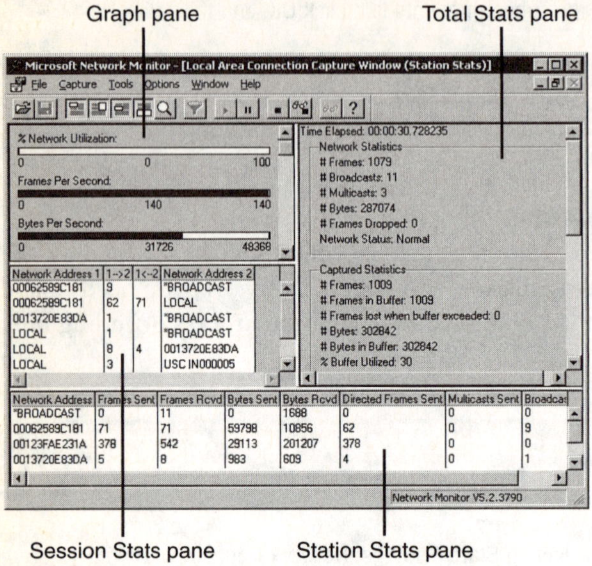

FIGURE 9.3 The Network Monitor has four panes that display information about network traffic.

- **Total Stats pane**—The Total Stats pane reports the totals of the stats for all other panes.

Now that you have seen how the captured data will be displayed to you, you can create your first network capture, as outlined in Step by Step 9.3.

STEP BY STEP

9.3 Creating a Network Capture

1. Select Start, Programs, Administrative Tools, Network Monitor. The Network Monitor window opens. If you are prompted to do so, select the network to be monitored.
2. Select Capture, Start to begin the capture session. Network Monitor records activity to and from this computer. You can generate some activity by sending a `ping` command or browsing the Internet.
3. Select Capture, Stop and View to examine the results of the network data capture. Figure 9.4 shows an example of captured network data.
4. Double-click any packet to examine it in greater detail, as shown in Figure 9.5. You can scroll through the list in the Summary pane and click any packet you want to examine in the Detail and Hex panes.

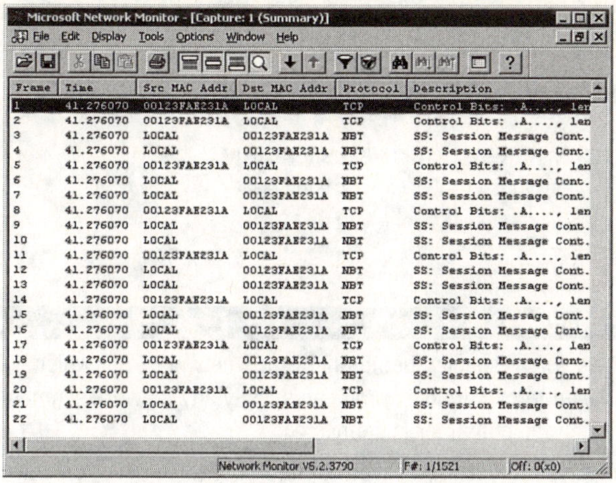

FIGURE 9.4 All network data that has been captured is listed sequentially.

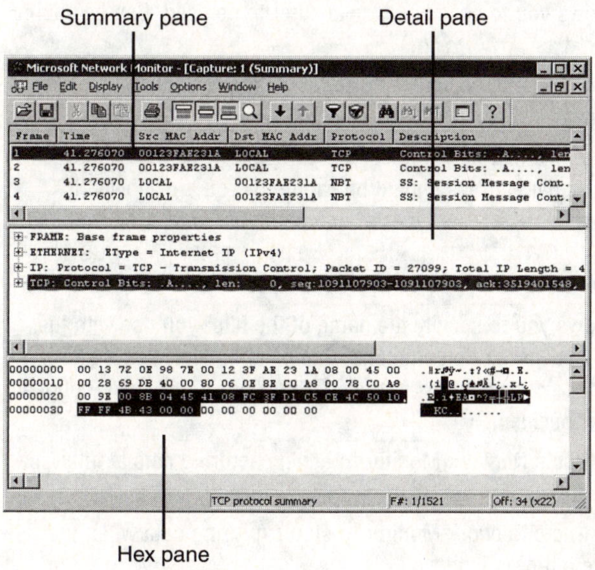

FIGURE 9.5 You can examine each packet captured during a network capture.

5. Close the Display window to return to the Network Statistics window.

Running Network Monitor from the Command Line

Like most other configuration and management tools in Windows Server 2003, you can run the Network Monitor from the command line. This is a more difficult and advanced method of performing captures, but it lets you script commands to be executed on multiple computers with little effort. The basic syntax of using the Network Monitor (`netmon`) from the command line is presented here and explained in more detail in Table 9.1:

```
start netmon [/net Number] [/capturefilter Path] [/displayfilter Path]
➥ [/buffersize Number]
➥ [/quickfilter {ATM ¦ ETHERNET ¦ IP ¦ IPX ¦ VINES ¦ TOKENRING ¦ FDDI},
➥ Address] [/quickfiltername FilterName] [/autostart] [/autostop]
```

TABLE 9.1 `netmon` **Command-Line Switches**

Switch	Description
`/net` *`Number`*	Allows you to specify the number of the network from which you want to capture data. You can specify any network segment to which the computer is connected.
`/capturefilter` *`Path`*	Allows you to specify a saved capture filter to be used. Can be abbreviated as `/cf` *`Path`*.
`/displayfilter` *`Path`*	Allows you to specify a display filter to be used. Can be abbreviated as `/df` *`Path`*.
`/buffersize` *`Number`*	Allows you to specify the size (in megabytes) of the capture buffer.
`/quickfilter {ATM ¦ ETHERNET ¦ IP ¦ IPX ¦ VINES ¦ TOKENRING ¦ FDDI},` *`Address`*	Specifies that only frames of a particular type and from a particular address should be captured. You are allowed to specify up to three types at one time. Can be abbreviated as `/qf {ATM ¦ ETHERNET ¦ IP ¦ IPX ¦ VINES ¦ TOKENRING ¦ FDDI},` *`Address`*.
`/quickfiltername` *`FilterName`*	Allows you to specify the name of the filter you use with the `/quickfilter` command. Can be abbreviated as `/qfn` *`FilterName`* and is not used if no `/quickfilter` options are specified.
`/autostart`	Instructs Network Monitor to begin capturing data at interface startup.
`/autostop`	Instructs Network Monitor to stop capturing data when the capture buffer is full.

Interpreting Captured Data

How you interpret captured data depends on the type of server with which you're working. What is the server's role in the domain? Is it a Domain Controller? An application server? A file server? Each of these roles has different traffic patterns. You need a filter to get an accurate picture of the activity for a server.

Filters allow you to strip away packets that may not be relevant to the server, capture, or packets types for which you're looking. Within Network Monitor, you choose Capture, Filter and the Capture Filter dialog box appears, as shown in Figure 9.6. The Capture Filter dialog box allows you to do the following:

- **Specify capture filter protocols**—You can designate which protocols you'd like displayed in the capture. You complete the SAP/ETYPE= field by designating the protocol(s) you'd like displayed.
- **Specify address pairs**—You can choose up to three pairs of addresses that have sent and received packets from each other.
- **Specify frame data patterns to capture**—You can build your own variables to display captured data. You can display frames that contain a designated pattern.

Step by Step 9.4 walks you through the steps for configuring filtering for a capture before you start the capture. The advantage of using this method is that it cuts down on the amount of captured data. The disadvantage is that it captures only the type of traffic for which you are filtering.

STEP BY STEP

9.4 Configuring Capture Filters Before a Capture

1. Select Capture, Filter to open the Capture Filter dialog box, which is shown in Figure 9.6.

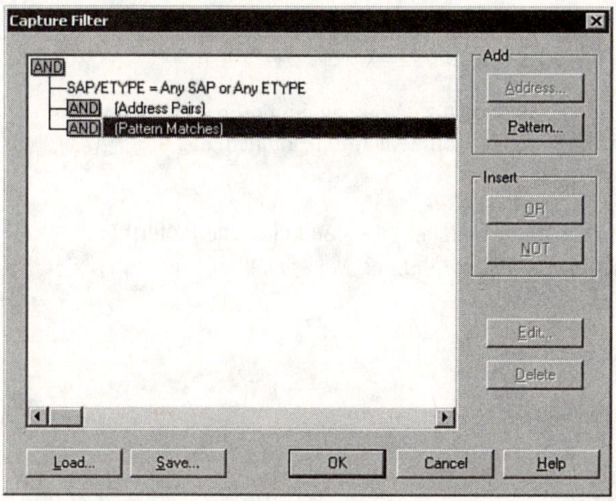

FIGURE 9.6 You can filter out unwanted packets by creating capture filters.

2. Click the SAP/ETYPE= line and then click the Edit button to open the Configure Filter SAPs and ETYPEs dialog box, which is shown in Figure 9.7. Typical options might include IP or NetWare. By default, all items are enabled. You might want to click Disable All and then enable the specific items for which you are looking. When you are done, click OK.

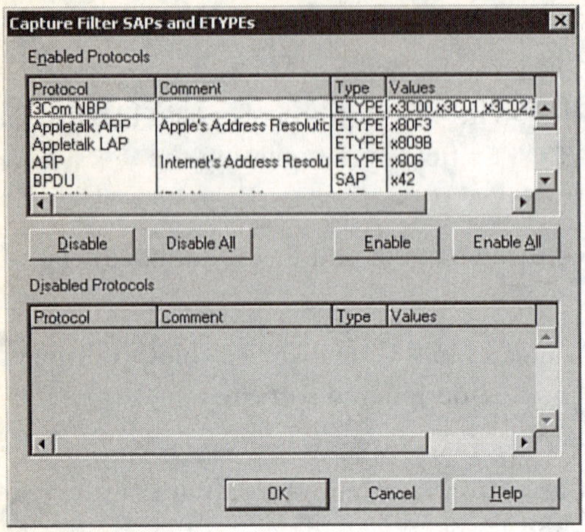

FIGURE 9.7 You start out by configuring the SAPs and ETYPEs for which you want to see capture data.

3. If you want to specify any address pairs, do so by selecting the (Address Pairs) item and clicking the Address button to open the Address Expression dialog box, which is shown in Figure 9.8.

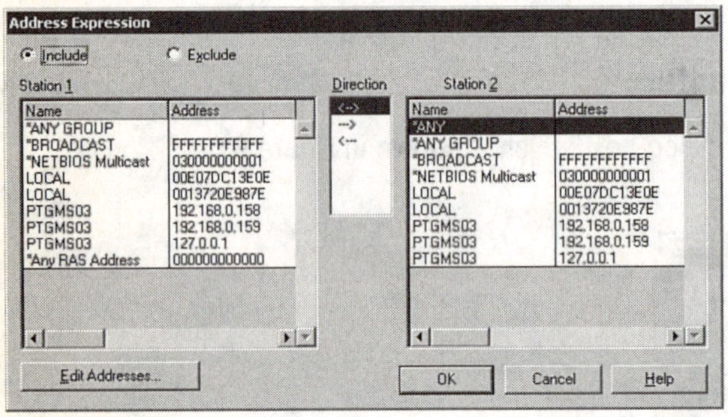

FIGURE 9.8 You can configure specific address pairs from which to examine data.

4. If you want to filter on data patterns, select the (Pattern Matches) item and click the Pattern button to open the Pattern Match dialog box, which is shown in Figure 9.9.

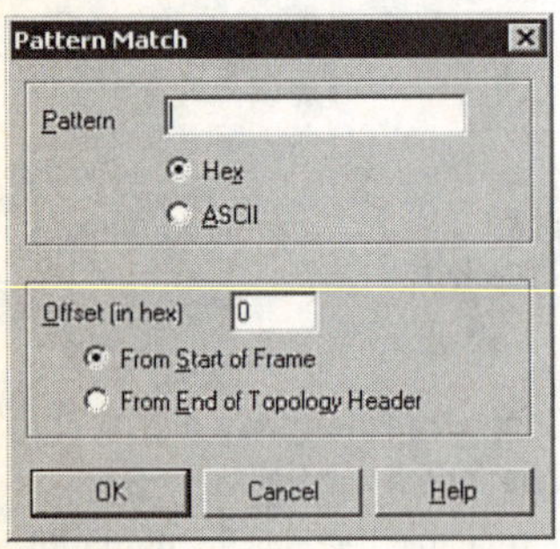

FIGURE 9.9 You can configure filter patterns to filter data by those specific patterns.

5. When you have configured the filters to your liking, click OK to close the Capture Filter dialog box. You can now perform a capture and get only the packets for which you are looking.

Sometimes you might have already performed a capture and want to filter out specific data from it. You can do this by clicking the funnel icon or by selecting Display, Filter. In either case, the Display Filter dialog box opens, as shown in Figure 9.10.

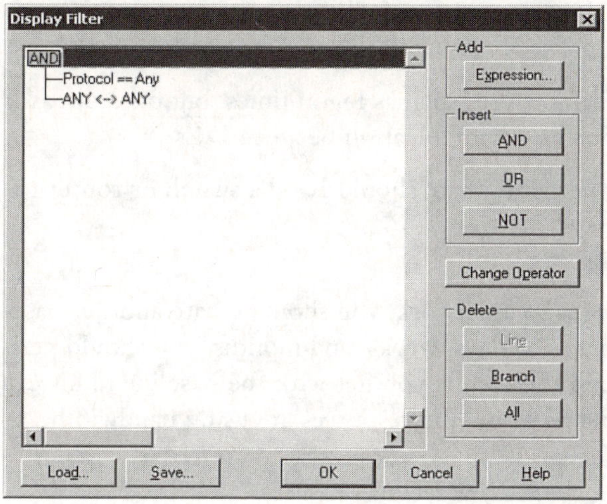

FIGURE 9.10 You can configure a filter for data that has already been captured.

By double-clicking the Protocol == Any item, you open the Expression dialog box, as shown in Figure 9.11. You can use this dialog box to configure a filter, and the most common filter is for a specific protocol type, such as ICMP.

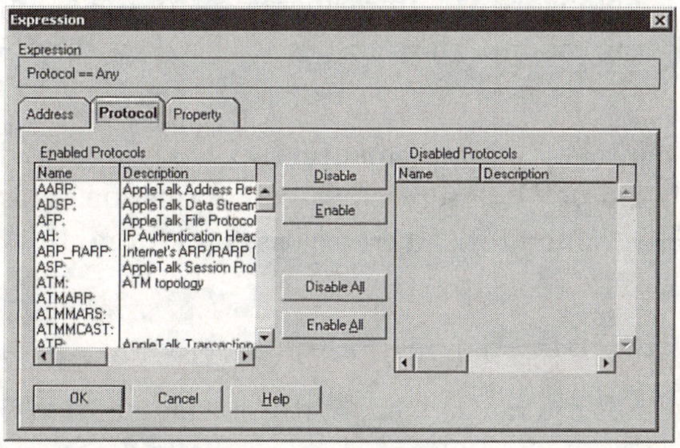

FIGURE 9.11 The Expression dialog box allows you to select how a filter should be constructed.

When you've determined the source of any problems with a network, you can begin to implement changes as required. Before you implement changes to a network, you should create a baseline. A *baseline* is a snapshot of how the network is operating under normal conditions.

After you create the baseline, you can make the desired changes and run the test again. After you run the test, you should ask yourself the following questions (among others):

- Did the changes help or hinder performance?
- If the changes hindered performance, have I configured all the options for this change properly?
- Has one area of network performance improved, such as logon times, but other areas of network performance worsened, such as communication between DCs?
- Is the network capacity more than 75 percent? If so, should I add a switch or router to break up the network?

After you've added and configured the changes to a network, you should create another baseline as a snapshot of the system. Over the next few days, weeks, and months, you should periodically run the same test again and compare the results you get with the baseline. This can help you predict how the network is growing and how the resources are using bandwidth.

Using the System Monitor

Sometimes you might encounter network problems that the Network Monitor doesn't help troubleshoot. Recall that the version of Network Monitor included in Windows Server 2003 can be used only to capture network traffic going to or from the server on which it is being run. Although there are many capable third-party network sniffers available for you to use, Exam 70-291 is only concerned with the included Network Monitor. Therefore, for the exam, you need to know how to use the System Monitor to monitor the statistics associated with network interfaces.

The System Monitor is discussed in Chapter 2, "Implementing, Managing, and Troubleshooting DHCP," as it applies to monitoring DHCP server-related information. This chapter examines how to use the System Monitor to monitor and create baselines for network interface statistics.

The following counters are listed under the Network Interface performance object:

- **Bytes Received/Sec**—This counter measures the rate at which bytes, including framing characters, are received over each network adapter. This counter is a subset of the Bytes Total/Sec counter.

- **Bytes Sent/Sec**—This counter measures the rate at which bytes, including framing characters, are sent over each network adapter. This counter is a subset of the Bytes Total/Sec counter.
- **Bytes Total/Sec**—This counter measures the rate at which bytes, including framing characters, are sent and received over each network adapter.
- **Current Bandwidth**—This counter measures an estimate of the current bandwidth of the network interface, in bits per second.
- **Output Queue Length**—This counter measures the length of the output packet queue (in packets). If this counter is greater than two, there are delays, and you should find and eliminate the bottleneck, if possible.
- **Packets Outbound Discarded**—This counter measures the number of outbound packets that were chosen to be discarded even though no errors had been detected to prevent transmission. One possible reason for discarding packets could be to free up buffer space.
- **Packets Outbound Errors**—This counter measures the number of outbound packets that could not be transmitted because of errors.
- **Packets Received Discarded**—This counter measures the number of inbound packets that were chosen to be discarded, even though no errors had been detected to prevent their delivery to a higher-layer protocol. One possible reason for discarding packets could be to free up buffer space.
- **Packets Received Errors**—This counter measures the number of inbound packets that contained errors that prevented them from being deliverable to a higher-layer protocol.
- **Packets Received Non-Unicast/Sec**—This counter measures the rate at which non-unicast packets are delivered to a higher-layer protocol.
- **Packets Received Unicast/Sec**—This counter measures the rate at which unicast packets are delivered to a higher-layer protocol.
- **Packets Received Unknown**—This counter measures the number of packets received through the interface that were discarded because of an unknown or unsupported protocol.
- **Packets Received/Sec**—This counter measures the rate at which packets are received on the network interface.
- **Packets Sent Unicast/Sec**—This counter measures the rate at which packets are requested to be transmitted to subnet-unicast addresses by higher-layer protocols.
- **Packets Sent/Sec**—This counter measures the rate at which packets are sent on the network interface.

- **Packets/Sec**—This counter measures the rate at which packets are sent and received on the network interface.

EXAM ALERT

Don't Get Tricked! When taking this exam, carefully read each question—especially those that deal with performance monitoring—to ensure that you select the correct answer. Because many of the monitoring options sound and look similar to each other, you might find several similar answers being presented, but only one of them will be correct.

You can access the System Monitor from the Administrative Tools folder by selecting Start, Programs, Administrative Tools, Performance. When it is initially opened, the Performance console appears as shown in Figure 9.12.

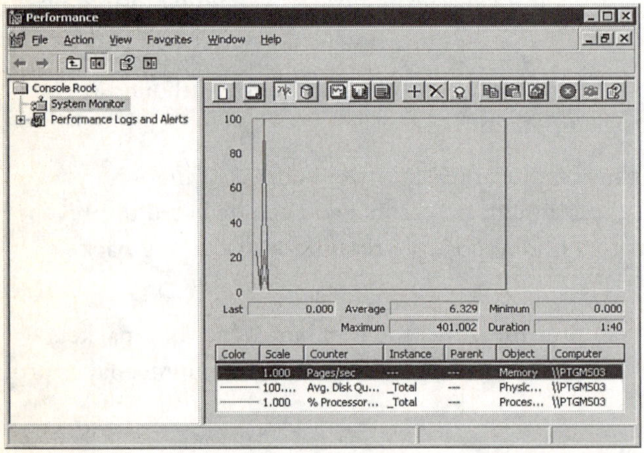

FIGURE 9.12 The Performance console in its default state monitors three basic items.

Monitoring Performance by Using the System Monitor

Configuring the Performance console to monitor and collect data about the network interface(s) in a server is a simple process, as described in Step by Step 9.5.

STEP BY STEP

9.5 Monitoring Network Adapter Statistics

1. Select Start, Program, Administrative Tools, Performance to open the Performance console.
2. Click System Monitor, as shown in Figure 9.12.
3. To add counter items to the System Monitor, click the + icon. The Add Counters dialog box, shown in Figure 9.13, opens, allowing you to begin adding counters.

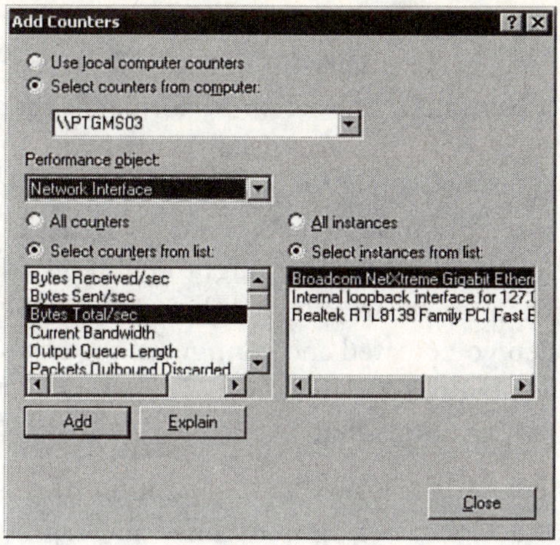

FIGURE 9.13 You can add counters to begin monitoring the network adapter statistics.

4. Select Network Interface from the Performance Object drop-down list box. The counters that relate to network interfaces and that are available for selection appear. If you need to know what a counter does, select the counter and click the Explain button.
5. Be sure that you are adding counters for the correct network interface in your server and not for the loopback interface. You can do this by selecting the Select Instances from List option and then selecting the correct network interface (as shown in Figure 9.13).
6. When you have decided what counter you want to monitor, click Add. You can add multiple counters either by selecting each counter and clicking Add or by holding down the Ctrl key while you select all the counters you want to monitor and then clicking Add.
7. Click Close when you are finished. Your counters are graphed like those shown in Figure 9.14.

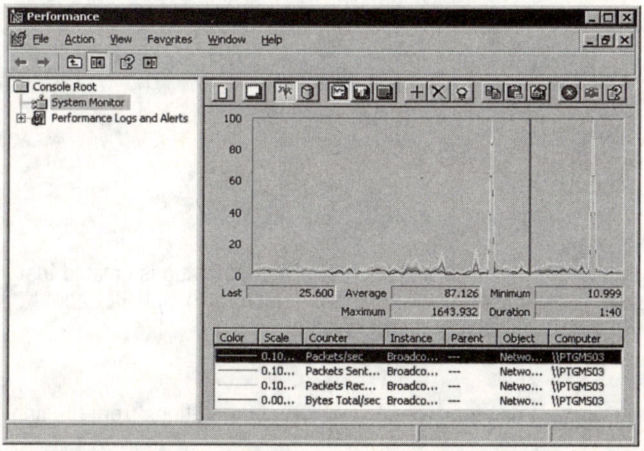

FIGURE 9.14 You can monitor the selected network interface statistics in real time.

Creating Baseline Counter Logs

Of course, monitoring the present operation and statistics of network interfaces will present you with only half of the picture. You need to create a baseline of the server performance that can be used to compare against the current performance statistics. You need this baseline to locate problematic areas. This can be very useful when you're performing troubleshooting, and it also aids during periods when configurations are being modified. When creating baseline logs for later comparison, be sure to include all of the counters you might be interested in. When you go to examine the baseline log sometime in the future, you'll only be able to see the counters you configured and obtained data for when you created and configured the baseline in the first place. Typically you will want to include not only network-related counters, but also counters for disk utilization, memory usage, and CPU utilization.

To create a baseline, you would create a counter log from the Counter Logs option of the Performance Logs and Alerts node. The creation of a Counter Log is outlined in Step by Step 9.6.

STEP BY STEP

9.6 Creating and Using a Baseline Counter Log

1. Select Start, Program, Administrative Tools, Performance to open the Performance console.
2. Expand the Performance Logs and Alerts node and click the Counter Logs entry, as shown in Figure 9.15.

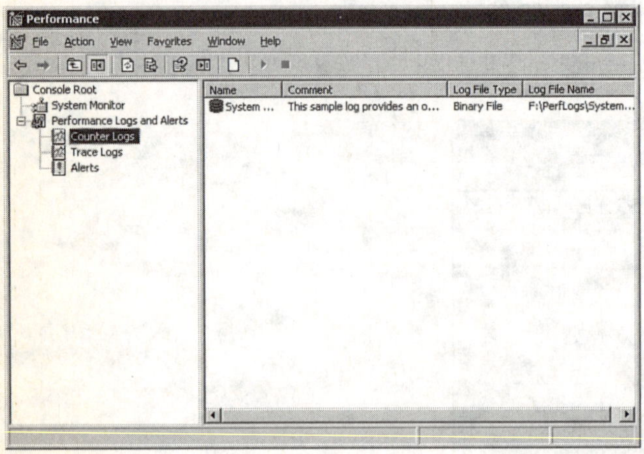

FIGURE 9.15 A counter log is created to keep baseline (historical) statistics about performance.

3. To add a new counter log, right-click the Counter Logs entry and select New Log Settings from the context menu.
4. Enter the name of the new counter log, as shown in Figure 9.16, and click OK. The Network adapter performance dialog box appears (see Figure 9.17).

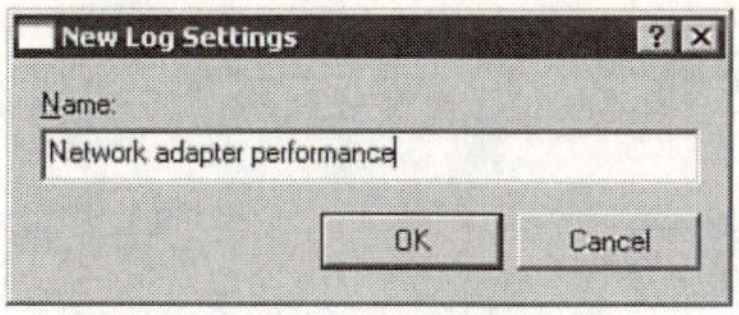

FIGURE 9.16 You should enter a descriptive name for the new counter log.

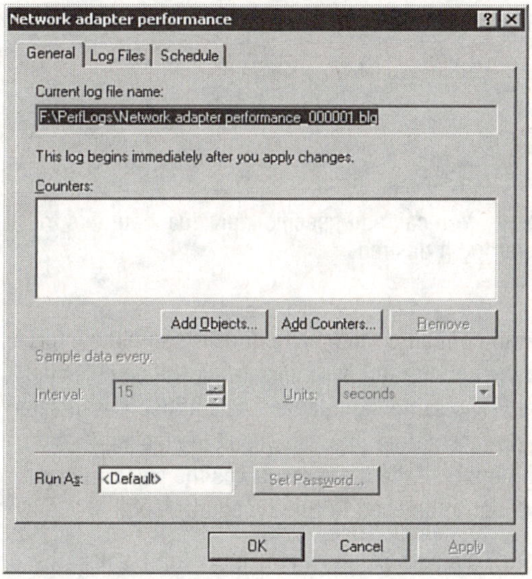

FIGURE 9.17 You must configure objects or counters on the new counter log before proceeding.

5. Configure new entire objects to be monitored by clicking the Add Objects button to open the Add Objects dialog box (see Figure 9.18). Alternatively, you can add individual counters by clicking the Add Counters button to open the Add Counters dialog box (see Figure 9.19). Then, add the objects or counters you desire to the counter log.

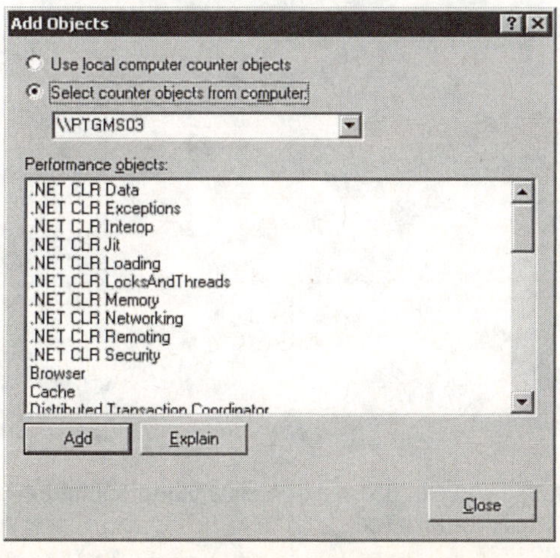

FIGURE 9.18 You can add entire objects to the counter log if desired.

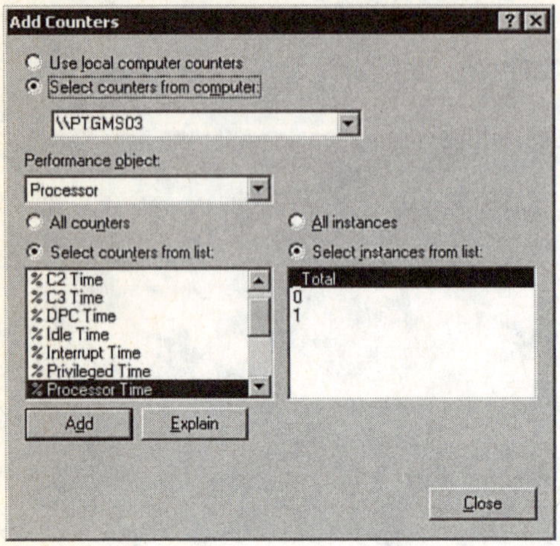

FIGURE 9.19 You can add specific individual counters to the counter log if desired.

6. After you have added some objects or counters, you can configure the options for the sampling interval. The default is every 15 seconds—meaning that while the counter log is running, data will be collected every 15 seconds from the computers being monitored. The sampling interval has a tradeoff associated with it: Smaller intervals mean larger, more accurate log files; larger intervals result in smaller, less accurate log files. In addition, the smaller the sampling interval, the more resources the performance monitoring consumes. You can also configure the account to be used to run the counter log.
7. On the Log Files tab of the Network adapter performance dialog box, shown in Figure 9.20, select the type of log file to be created as well as the numbering system to be used. The default settings are Binary file and nnnnn. The available options are explained after this Step by Step in Tables 9.2 and 9.3. In addition, you can enter a comment that will help identify the counter log.

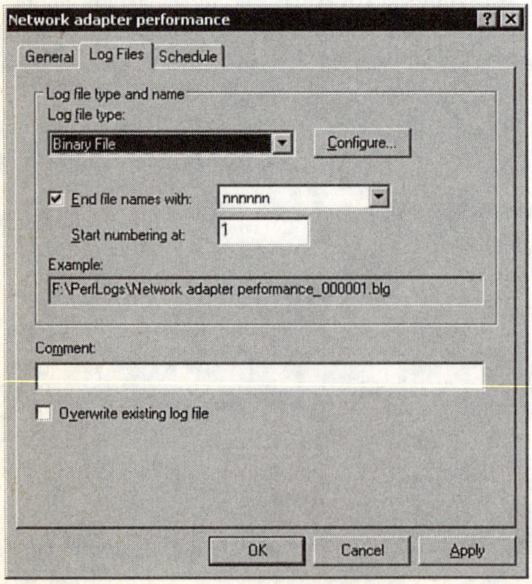

FIGURE 9.20 You can use the Log Files tab to configure how the log is to be saved.

8. Click the Configure button to open the Configure Log Files dialog box, as shown in Figure 9.21. From here you can change the path of the log file and its maximum allowed size. Click OK after you make your changes.

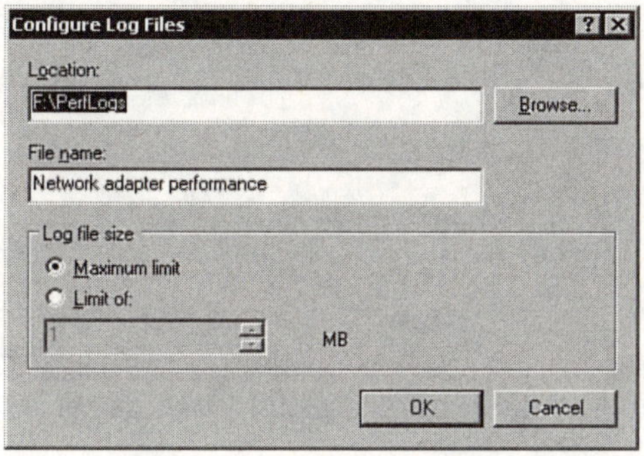

FIGURE 9.21 You can use the Configure Log Files dialog box to configure the maximum log file size as well as its path.

9. On the Schedule tab of the Network adapter performance dialog box, shown in Figure 9.22, you can configure how and when the counter log is to run. Typically you will run it manually, although you might opt to have it run automatically at a configured time.

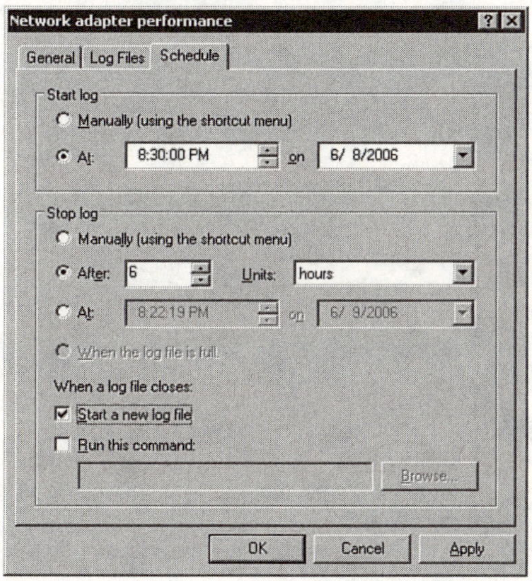

FIGURE 9.22 The counter log can be configured to start and stop automatically if desired.

10. After you make all your configurations, click OK to save the counter log settings. Back at the Counter Logs node, seen previously in Figure 9.15, select the new counter log object and start it by clicking the start (right arrow) button in the menu. If you configured the counter log to start automatically, as seen in Figure 9.22, it will start at the configured time and run as configured, as seen in Figure 9.23.

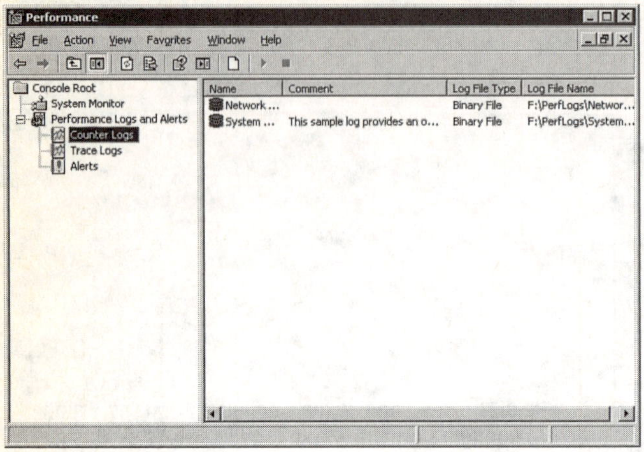

FIGURE 9.23 The counter log automatically starts if you configured it with a start time.

11. After the counter log has run for some time (or for its scheduled time), click the square stop icon to stop it.
12. Click the System Monitor node to switch back to the System Monitor. Click the database icon to open a log file, as shown in Figure 9.24. The System Monitor Properties dialog box opens, showing the Source tab (see Figure 9.25).

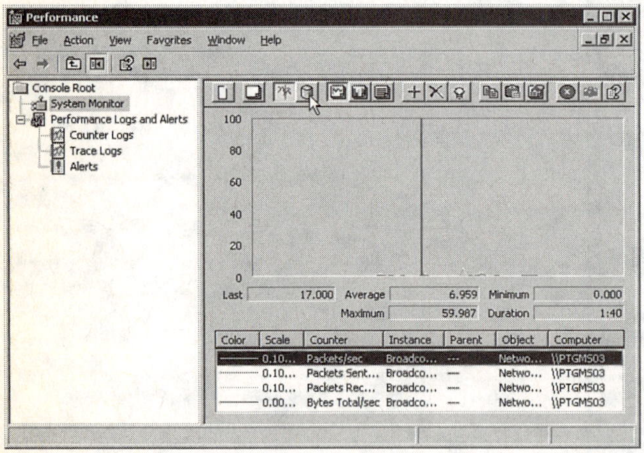

FIGURE 9.24 You need to load the counter log file into the System Monitor to examine it.

13. Select the Log Files radio button and click the Add button to locate and add the counter log file.
14. Switch to the Data tab, as shown in Figure 9.26, and ensure that all counters for which you are interested in seeing data are added. You will see data displayed only for counters that are selected here.

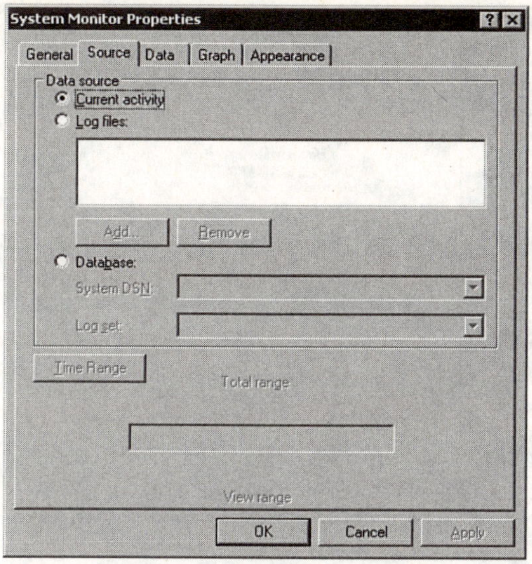

FIGURE 9.25 You can add one or more counter logs to the System Monitor.

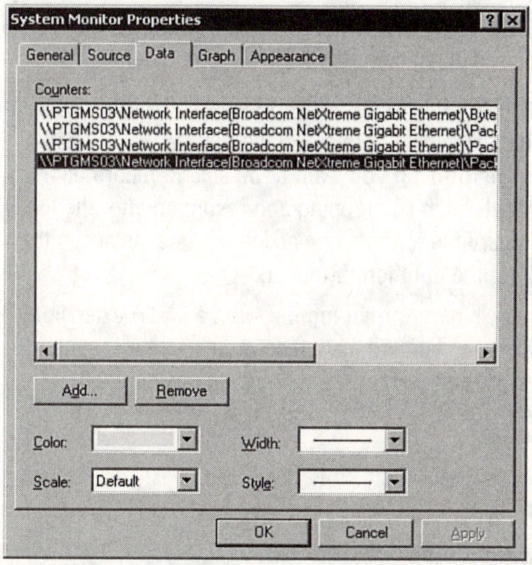

FIGURE 9.26 You need to ensure that all counters have been added for viewing.

15. The counter log data is displayed in the System Monitor, as shown in Figure 9.27. If you need to display only a certain portion of the data, you can do so by configuring the Time Range option on the Source tab of the System Monitor Properties dialog box (refer to Figure 9.25). The counter log options are listed in Table 9.2, and numbering systems are listed in Table 9.3.

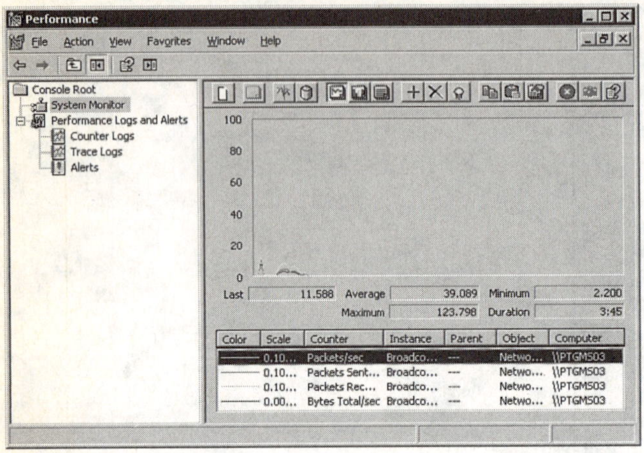

FIGURE 9.27 After you make the correct configurations, you can examine the historical counter log data.

TABLE 9.2 Counter Log File Format Options

Option	Description
Text File (Comma Delimited)	This option defines a comma-delimited log file (with a `.csv` extension).
Text File (Tab Delimited)	This option defines a tab-delimited log file (with a `.tsv` extension).
Binary File	This option defines a sequential, binary-format log file (with a `.blg` extension). You should use this file format if you want to be able to record data instances that are intermittent—that is, stopping and resuming after the log has begun running. Only binary file formats can accommodate instances that are not persistent throughout the duration of the log.
Binary Circular File	This option defines a circular, binary-format log file (with a `.blg` extension). You should use this file format to continuously record data to the same log file. This option overwrites previous records with new data when the file reaches its maximum size.

TABLE 9.3 Counter Log Numbering Systems

System	Example
nnnnnn	`Network Adapter Performance_000007.blg`
mmddhh	`Network Adapter Performance_042011.blg`
mmddhhmm	`Network Adapter Performance_04201126.blg`
yyyyddd	`Network Adapter Performance_2003111.blg`
yyyymm	`Network Adapter Performance_200304.blg`
yyyymmdd	`Network Adapter Performance_20030420.blg`
yyyymmddhh	`Network Adapter Performance_2003042011.blg`

System Monitor Tips and Tricks

Microsoft provides some helpful tips and tricks that you should keep in mind when working with the Performance console to solve performance-related problems. Through careful analysis of data, you might be able to identify problems with the network that are not otherwise seen. (These include excessive demands on resources that result in bottlenecks.) These problems can slow network performance to the degree that users begin to notice that something is wrong.

EXAM ALERT

Saving Time by Saving Your Configuration No one wants to reinvent the wheel. This holds true even when you are configuring System Monitor with a set of counters. You can save a good amount of time and effort by setting up the System Monitor with the counters and options you desire on one server and then saving the configuration file and distributing that file to each of your other servers. This saves you from re-creating the configuration each time you want to monitor the same items.

The following are some of the most common causes of bottlenecks that you might encounter while troubleshooting your network:

- The current level of provided resources is inadequate, thus requiring additional or upgraded resources to be added to the network.
- The available resources are not utilized evenly, thus requiring some form of load balancing to be implemented.
- An available resource is malfunctioning or stopped and needs to be repaired or restarted.
- An available resource is incorrectly configured, thus requiring a configuration correction.

After you have identified a problem, you should take care to avoid creating new problems while correcting the old one. You should make one change at a time to avoid masking the impact of changes. After each change, you should perform additional monitoring to determine the result and the effect of the change and reevaluate the status and condition of the previously identified problem(s). In addition, you can compare the performance of applications that are run over the network to their performance when run locally to determine how the network is affecting performance.

The following are some basic network configuration tips that you can implement while troubleshooting and correcting network-related problems:

- As often as possible, ensure that resources are located on the same physical subnet as the users using the resource.
- Uninstall or unbind network protocols that are not in use.
- Configure the network protocol binding order to place the most commonly used protocols higher on the list.
- Use multiple network adapters in high-use servers to increase effective network throughput.
- If you're going to monitor disk, CPU, and/or memory utilization as well, you'll want to monitor those items from a remote server or workstation. Monitoring of disk, CPU, and memory utilization can actually add load on these items if monitored locally, possibly making the output of the monitoring invalid or inaccurate.

EXAM ALERT

Don't Forget the Task Manager Even though it's a simple tool, don't underestimate the usefulness of the Task Manager. You can quickly launch the Task Manager to get a real-time look at network utilization (and process performance) without having to open the System Monitor and configure counters.

Troubleshooting Internet Connectivity

Objective:

Troubleshoot connectivity to the Internet.

Just when you thought you were done troubleshooting network connectivity problems, along comes the Internet—the Wild West of network connectivity. Although there are no tools designed specifically for troubleshooting Internet connectivity problems in Windows Server 2003, the full toolbox of network troubleshooting tools with which you are already familiar can be used to help alleviate any problems you might have.

When you need to troubleshoot Internet connectivity problems, you can use `ping`, `tracert`, `nslookup`, `pathping`, and the Network Diagnostics tool. `ping` and the Network Diagnostics tool are discussed in Chapter 1, "Configuring and Troubleshooting TCP/IP Addressing." `nslookup` is discussed in Chapter 3, "Implementing and Managing DNS."

The `pathping` command acts as the equivalent of the `tracert` command by allowing you to identify which routers are in the path that the packets take. It also acts as the equivalent of the `ping` command by sending `ping` requests to all the routers over a specified time period and then computing statistics based on the packets returned from each router. `pathping` displays the amount of packet loss at each router or link, allowing you to determine which routers and links (subnets) might be causes of connectivity troubles.

This is the basic syntax of the `pathping` command:

```
pathping [-g host-list] [-h maximum_hops] [-i address] [-n]
➥ [-p period] [-q num_queries] [-w timeout] [-4] [-6] target_
```

Table 9.4 explains the switches of the `pathping` command.

TABLE 9.4 `pathping` **Switches**

Switch	Description
`-g` *`host-list`*	Specifies that Echo Request messages are to use the Loose Source Route option in the IP header with the set of intermediate destinations specified in *`host-list`*. Successive intermediate destinations can be separated by one or multiple routers. *`host-list`* is a series of IP addresses (in dotted-decimal notation), separated by spaces.
`-h` *`maximum hops`*	Specifies the maximum number of hops in the path to search for the target. The default is 30 hops.
`-i` *`address`*	Specifies the source address.
-n	Specifies that addresses are not to be resolved to host names.
`-p` *`period`*	Specifies the number of milliseconds to wait between consecutive `pings`. The default is 250 milliseconds.
`-q` *`num queries`*	Specifies the number of Echo Request messages sent to each router in the path. The default is 100.
`-w` *`timeout`*	Specifies the number of milliseconds to wait for each reply. The default is 3,000 milliseconds.
-4	Specifies that `pathping` use IPv4 only.
-6	Specifies that `pathping` use IPv6 only.
`target`	Specifies the destination, either by IP address or hostname.

The following is an example of the output that you might expect to receive when using the `pathping` command:

```
C:\>pathping quepublishing.com
Tracing route to quepublishing.com [63.240.93.132]
over a maximum of 30 hops:
  0  ptgms03.corp.quepublishing.com [192.168.0.158]
  1  192.168.1.254
  2  68.152.202.125
  3  68.152.202.105
  4  205.152.246.25
  5  axr00msy-7-0-0-3.bellsouth.net [65.83.237.76]
```

```
  6  pxr00msy-0-0-0.bellsouth.net [65.83.236.32]
  7  so-2-0-0.gar2.Dallas1.Level3.net [67.72.4.1]
  8  ae-23-52.car3.Dallas1.Level3.net [4.68.122.47]
  9  att-level3-oc48.Dallas1.Level3.net [4.68.127.106]
 10  gbr1-a30s8.dlstx.ip.att.net [12.123.16.30]
 11  tbr1-cl6.sl9mo.ip.att.net [12.122.10.89]
 12  tbr1-cl4.wswdc.ip.att.net [12.122.10.29]
 13  tbr2-cl27.wswdc.ip.att.net [12.122.9.150]
 14  tbr2-cl15.n54ny.ip.att.net [12.122.10.53]
 15  ar1-p30.n54ny.ip.att.net [12.123.0.53]
 16  mdf1-gsr12-2-pos-7-0.nyc3.attens.net [12.122.255.162]
 17  mdf2-bi8k-2-gig1-1.nyc3.attens.net [63.240.64.166]
 18     *        *        *
Computing statistics for 450 seconds...
            Source to Here   This Node/Link
Hop  RTT    Lost/Sent = Pct  Lost/Sent = Pct  Address
  0                                           ptgms03.corp.quepublishing.com
[192.168.0.158]
                                0/ 100 =  0%   |
  1    1ms     0/ 100 =  0%     0/ 100 =  0%  192.168.1.254
                                0/ 100 =  0%   |
  2   42ms     1/ 100 =  1%     1/ 100 =  1%  68.152.202.125
                                0/ 100 =  0%   |
  3   49ms     0/ 100 =  0%     0/ 100 =  0%  68.152.202.105
                                0/ 100 =  0%   |
  4   48ms     1/ 100 =  1%     1/ 100 =  1%  205.152.246.25
                                0/ 100 =  0%   |
  5   70ms     0/ 100 =  0%     0/ 100 =  0%  axr00msy-7-0-0-3.bellsouth.net
[65.83.237.76]
                                1/ 100 =  1%   |
  6   65ms     2/ 100 =  2%     1/ 100 =  1%  pxr00msy-0-0-0.bellsouth.net
[65.83.236.32]
                                0/ 100 =  0%   |
  7   86ms     2/ 100 =  2%     1/ 100 =  1%  so-2-0-0.gar2.Dallas1.Level3.net
[67.72.4.1]
                                0/ 100 =  0%   |
  8   81ms     3/ 100 =  3%     2/ 100 =  2%  ae-23-52.car3.Dallas1.Level3.net
[4.68.122.47]
                                0/ 100 =  0%   |
  9   ---    100/ 100 =100%    99/ 100 = 99%  att-level3-oc48.Dallas1.Level3.net
[4.68.127.106]
                                0/ 100 =  0%   |
 10   ---    100/ 100 =100%    99/ 100 = 99%  gbr1-a30s8.dlstx.ip.att.net
[12.123.16.30]
                                0/ 100 =  0%   |
 11   ---    100/ 100 =100%    99/ 100 = 99%  tbr1-cl6.sl9mo.ip.att.net [12.122.10.89]
                                0/ 100 =  0%   |
 12   ---    100/ 100 =100%    99/ 100 = 99%  tbr1-cl4.wswdc.ip.att.net [12.122.10.29]
                                0/ 100 =  0%   |
```

```
 13  ---     100/ 100 =100%    99/ 100 = 99%  tbr2-cl27.wswdc.ip.att.net [12.122.9.150]
                                0/ 100 =  0%   |
 14  ---     100/ 100 =100%    99/ 100 = 99%  tbr2-cl15.n54ny.ip.att.net [12.122.10.53]
                                0/ 100 =  0%   |
 15  ---     100/ 100 =100%    99/ 100 = 99%  ar1-p30.n54ny.ip.att.net [12.123.0.53]
                                0/ 100 =  0%   |
 16  ---     100/ 100 =100%    99/ 100 = 99%  mdf1-gsr12-2-pos-7-0.nyc3.attens.net
[12.122.255.162]
                                0/ 100 =  0%   |
 17  131ms     1/ 100 =  1%     0/ 100 =  0%  mdf2-bi8k-2-gig1-1.nyc3.attens.net
[63.240.64.166]
                               99/ 100 = 99%   |
 18  ---     100/ 100 =100%     0/ 100 =  0%  ptgms03.corp.quepublishing.com [0.0.0.0]
Trace complete.
```

The output of `pathping` shows you not only what routes experience packet loss, but also which routers drop packets. This is valuable information when you're trying to track down an Internet-related connectivity problem.

EXAM ALERT

Be Aware of Misleading Results Sometimes, what appears to be a router failure might not be a router failure at all, but simply a firewall that is configured to block ICMP packets. You can test this configuration by trying to `ping` www.microsoft.com. Microsoft has been blocking ICMP packets for years now as a means of preventing denial-of-service (DoS) attacks on its networks.

Challenge

You have been hired by Sunshine Pastries, LLC to perform a traffic analysis on the company network. The owner of the company has informed you that he is especially interested in the traffic that is going into and out of three different file servers on the network. Several users have complained that the file servers seem to be sluggish and unresponsive at times, even though they appear to be running properly. The owner suspects that some of the older legacy Windows clients on the same subnet as these three file servers may be overwhelming the subnet with broadcast traffic. Your job is to determine what type of traffic the file servers see.

Your task is to perform the required network traffic captures for Sunshine Pastries and determine what, if any, changes should be made.

Try to complete this exercise on your own, listing your conclusions on a sheet of paper. After you have completed the exercise, compare your results to those given here.

(continues)

(continued)

Answers

In this scenario, you'll want to use the Network Monitor to capture and analyze the traffic flowing into and out of the three file servers in question. Specifically, you'll need to do the following:

- Determine what kinds of traffic are crossing the network adapters of the three file servers.
- Filter out broadcast traffic from unicast traffic and isolate it to its source.
- Use the Network Monitor supplied in Windows Server 2003 to capture traffic sent to or from the computer on which it is running.

By installing, configuring, and running the Network Monitor locally on each of the three servers, you can start the analysis of what type of traffic might be slowing down the servers.

If you plan on capturing traffic for some time, say two or three hours, you will most likely want to configure the capture filter before you actually start capturing data. This will allow you to quickly analyze only the pertinent types of traffic for which you are looking. The downside to filtering traffic while capturing it is that you will see only the traffic that meets the filter criteria. On the other hand, if you decide to filter traffic after the capture, you will be able to see all packets that traversed the server's network adapters. The downside to this method is that your capture files will be very large.

No matter which way you plan on capturing the traffic, you will be well on your way to determining the type of broadcast traffic the servers see, as well as the sources of the traffic. You will be able to help Sunshine Pastries increase the speed and efficiency of its network by providing it with the information it needs to prevent the excessive broadcasting on that subnet.

Troubleshooting Services

Objective:

Troubleshoot server services.

- Diagnose and resolve issues related to service dependency.
- Use service recovery options to diagnose and resolve service-related issues.

This section discusses dealing with service-related server issues. *Services* are applications that run in the background to provide critical functions on both workstations and servers. Most of the time, services run quietly and cause no problems. However, if a conflict is found between two services, Windows Server 2003 often stops one or both of them. In addition, services hang from time to time, causing various problems with the network and network resources. For example, if users start having a problem with a printer that functioned normally previously, the problem may be that the Print Spooler service has become stuck—a common problem many network administrators have experienced.

Server services are managed from the Services console, as shown in Figure 9.28. You can find the Services console in the Administrative Tools folder after you select Start, Programs, Administrative Tools, Services.

EXAM ALERT

Locating the Services Console—You can find the Services console in the Computer Management console, which is also located in the Administrative Tools folder. The Computer Management console is a preconfigured console that contains several of the most commonly used administrative tools, including the Event Viewer.

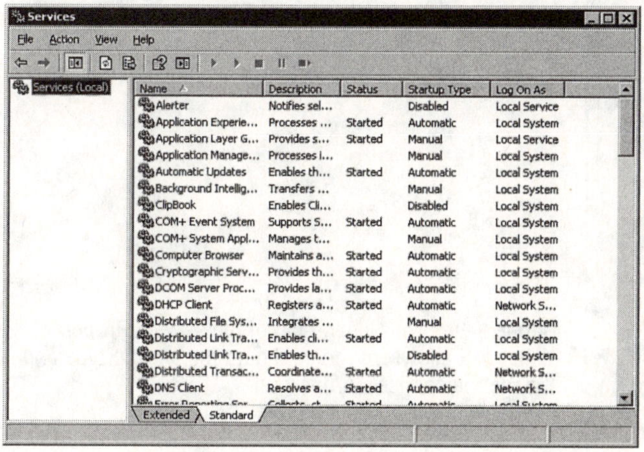

FIGURE 9.28 The Services console allows you to manage and configure server services.

The right pane of the Services console displays basic information about the configured services in the following columns:

- **Name**—Displays the name of the service.
- **Description**—Displays a short description of the service and its intended purpose.
- **Status**—Displays the current status of the service, such as Started, Paused, or Stopped.
- **Startup Type**—Displays the startup type for the service, such as Automatic or Manual.
- **Log On As**—Displays the account with which the service logs on to the network when it starts.

You can configure most of a service's properties by right-clicking its name and selecting Properties from the context menu, as discussed in the following paragraphs. You can also start, stop, pause, resume, and restart a service (as applicable, depending on its current status) from the context menu. In the case of a stuck service, such as a printer that stops functioning, using the restart option may clear up the problem and is a good first corrective action to try.

As mentioned, you can configure the properties of a service by right-clicking the service's name in the Service console and selecting Properties from the context menu. The Properties dialog box opens, with the General tab selected, as seen in Figure 9.29.

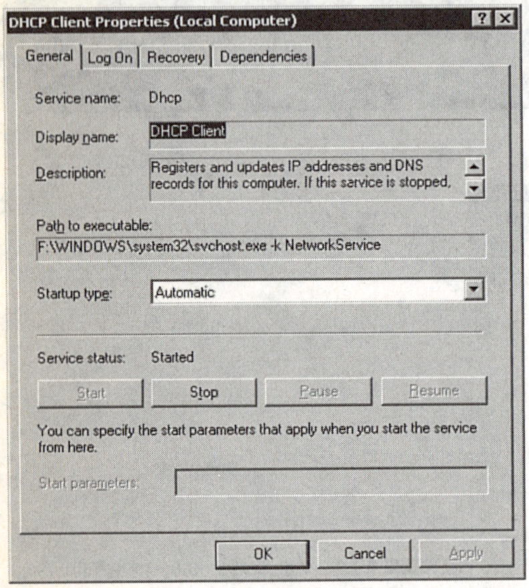

FIGURE 9.29 The General tab of the service Properties dialog box allows you to configure the startup type and change the service's properties.

The Log On tab, which is shown in Figure 9.30, allows you to configure the account that the service uses to log on to the network. If the incorrect account or password is supplied here, the service is either not able to start or is not able to function properly. In most cases, you should leave the default configuration as is.

The Recovery tab, which is shown in Figure 9.31, contains options that allow you to configure how the service is to respond after a failure occurs.

You can configure recovery options for the first, second, and all subsequent failure events the service experiences. These are the available options:

- **Take No Action**—No recovery actions will be taken if the service fails.
- **Restart the Service**—The service will stop and then start again.
- **Run a Program**—A program, script, or batch file can be run.
- **Restart the Computer**—The computer will be shut down and restarted.

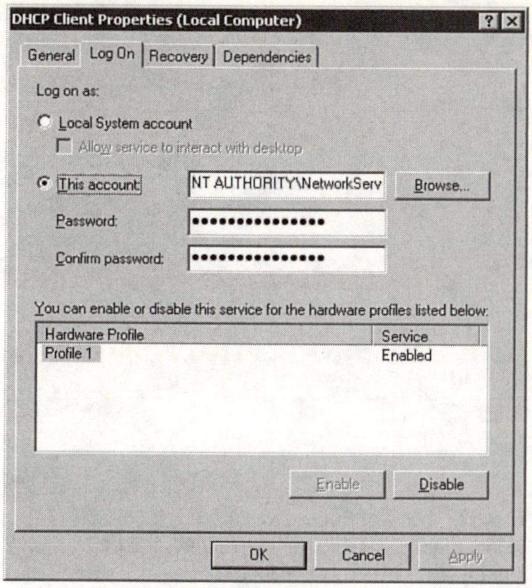

FIGURE 9.30 The Log On tab of the service Properties dialog box allows you to configure the logon account and password the service uses.

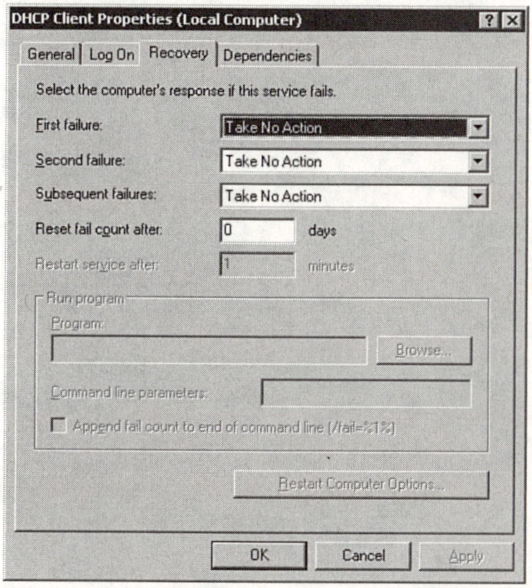

FIGURE 9.31 The Recovery tab of the service Properties dialog box allows you to configure what actions the service is to take upon failure.

The Dependencies tab, which is shown in Figure 9.32, allows you to view the dependency nature of the service. You can view components on which the service is dependent as well as the components that are dependent on the service. This information can help you troubleshoot why services are not functioning properly.

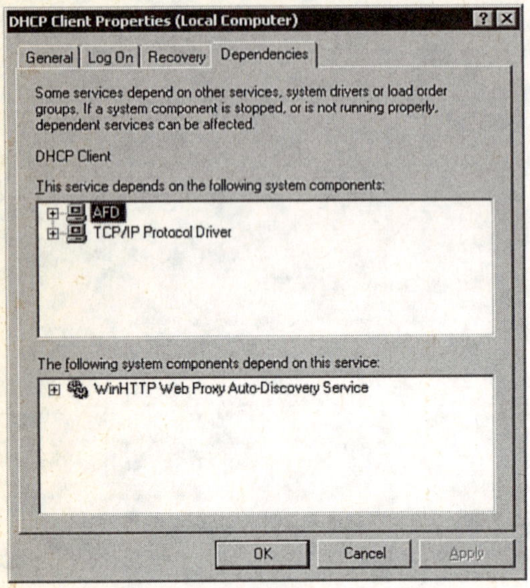

FIGURE 9.32 The Dependencies tab of the service Properties dialog box allows you to view the dependency relationship with other services.

Chapter Summary

This chapter covers a wide array of topics that all have one thing in common: network connectivity monitoring and troubleshooting. Unfortunately, it is a fact of life that nothing is ever perfect—networks included. The ability to use the various monitoring and troubleshooting tools that are at your disposal is key to your passing the exam. It is also key to your continued success as a network administrator for Windows-based networks.

Network troubleshooting issues come in many flavors, as discussed in this chapter. Everything from capturing network traffic with the Network Monitor to monitoring and troubleshooting performance falls under this broad category. Even some unconventional items, such as server services, play an important role in keeping the network running smoothly. Ultimately, the job of keeping your network running smoothly will fall on your shoulders. Knowing where to go and how to isolate problems will make your task an easier one.

Key Terms

- Baseline
- Binary circular file
- Binary file
- Capture filter
- Counter Log
- .CSV
- Frames
- Network Monitor
- Packet
- `pathping`
- Service
- System Monitor
- .TSV

Apply Your Knowledge

In this chapter, you have examined some basic means to troubleshoot problems in Windows Server 2003. In the following exercises, you will practice some of the concepts and methods discussed in this chapter.

Exercises

9.1 Creating a Baseline Counter Log

In this exercise, you will use the Performance console to create a baseline counter log. You will then be able to use the baseline as a comparison point for future performance monitoring.

Estimated Time: 30 minutes

1. Open the Performance console.
2. Expand the Performance Logs and Alerts node and click the Counter Logs entry.
3. Create a new counter log and name it `BASELINELOG1`.
4. Add entire objects or specific counters as desired. For this example, add the Packets Sent/Sec, Packets Received/Sec, and Packets Received Errors counters.
5. Leave the default data collection rate and account settings as is.
6. Configure the type of log file to be used as binary. Choose the numbering system of your choice.
7. Leave the default schedule of manual activation as is.
8. Click OK to save the counter log settings.
9. Allow the counter log to run for approximately 20 minutes and then stop the counter log.
10. Switch to the System Monitor node and click the database icon to open the counter log for viewing.
11. Click the Add button to locate and add the counter log file.
12. On the Data tab, ensure that you have configured all the same counters to be displayed as you used in the counter log itself. Click OK. The counter log data is displayed in the System Monitor.

9.2 Monitoring Performance

In this exercise, you will monitor the current performance characteristics of a computer's network adapter.

Estimated Time: 15 minutes

1. Open the Performance console.
2. Click System Monitor.
3. Click the + icon to open the Add Counters dialog box. Add the counters you want to monitor on your computer. These might include Packets Sent/Sec, Packets Received/Sec, and Packets Received Errors.
4. Click Close when you are finished. Watch the configured counters for 10 minutes while performing various activities that require network transfer to and from your computer.

9.3 Capturing Network Traffic

In this exercise, you will use the Network Monitor to capture traffic going to and from a Windows Server 2003 computer.

Estimated Time: 15 minutes

1. Open the Network Monitor. If prompted to do so, select the network to be monitored.
2. Click Capture, Start to begin the capture session. Network Monitor records activity to and from this computer. You can generate some activity by sending a `ping` command or browsing the Internet.
3. Select Capture, Stop and View to examine the results of the network data capture.
4. Double-click any packet to examine it in greater detail. You can scroll through the list in the Summary pane and click any packet you want to examine in the Detail and Hex panes.
5. Close the Display window to return to the Network Statistics window.

Exam Questions

1. You are a network consultant and have been hired by Fruity Flavor Beverage Distribution Group, Inc. You have been brought in to determine what protocols are running on the network that do not need to be running. What should be the first tool that you use to determine what network protocols are and are not required on the Fruity Flavor Beverage Distribution Group network?

   ❍ **A.** System Monitor

   ❍ **B.** `kerbtray.exe`

   ❍ **C.** Counter logs

   ❍ **D.** Network Monitor

2. You are the systems administrator for Bob's Boom Shack, a stereo retailer. You have recently completed a network capture using the Network Monitor. You did not set any capture filters before beginning the capture, and now you have more than 100,000 packets of capture data. You need to be able to quickly discard all packets except those related to AppleTalk. What can you do?

❍ **A.** Create a capture filter and start a new capture.

❍ **B.** Click the Protocol column heading to sort the packets by protocol.

❍ **C.** Create a display filter to filter out all protocols except those related to AppleTalk.

❍ **D.** Purchase the full version of Network Monitor that comes with SMS.

3. You are an assistant network technician for Joe's Jackhammer, Ltd. For some time now, you have been collecting reports about a general slowdown in network performance. You suspect that some of your legacy Windows 95 and Windows 98 workstation computers may be flooding the network with broadcast traffic. What tools could you use to determine how much broadcast traffic is being seen at specific Windows Server 2003 computers on the network? (Choose two.)

❍ **A.** Application log

❍ **B.** Network Monitor

❍ **C.** System Monitor

❍ **D.** `pathping`

❍ **E.** `nslookup`

4. You are an assistant network technician for Joe's Jackhammer, Ltd. You have decided that you will use the Network Monitor to gather information about why one of the network's Windows Server 2003 computers seems to be responding slowly despite showing no memory or CPU problems. You suspect that the cause of the problem is a flood of broadcast traffic from some of the Windows 95 computers located on the same subnet as the Windows Server 2003 computer. From where do you need to perform the installation of the Network Monitor?

❍ **A.** The Manage Your Server window

❍ **B.** The Windows Components Wizard

❍ **C.** The SUPPORT\TOOLS folder on the Windows Server 2003 CD

❍ **D.** The Windows Server 2003 Resource Kit

5. You are the systems administrator for Not Quite Evil Enough Enterprises, Inc. You have just completed a 30-minute Network Monitor capture on one of the network's Windows Server 2003 computers. During this time, you have accessed several Internet Web sites, performed file transfers, and `ping`ed this server from another workstation. You are trying to monitor DNS and browser traffic to and from this server, but when you look at the capture log, you see nothing for these two protocols. What is the most likely reason for this problem?

   ❍ **A.** You did not specify that these protocols were to be captured.

   ❍ **B.** You created a capture filter that excluded these protocols.

   ❍ **C.** You created a display filter that excluded these protocols.

   ❍ **D.** The capture buffer overflowed and dumped the data for which you were looking.

6. You are the third-shift systems administrator for Bob's Bull Riding College. You have just completed the installation and configuration of a new Windows Server 2003 file server. What should you do on this new computer over the next day or so to provide troubleshooting guidance in the future should network traffic problems occur?

   ❍ **A.** Remove all unnecessary protocols from the server's network adapters.

   ❍ **B.** Create a baseline counter log that documents what the server's performance was like at the time it was placed on the network.

   ❍ **C.** Check the event logs to ensure that no abnormal events occurred when the computer was joined to the network.

   ❍ **D.** Configure and implement IPSec to secure network traffic to and from the file server.

7. You are trying to monitor the performance statistics of your Windows Server 2003 computer's network interface. You have only one network interface installed on the computer. After you have selected the desired counters from the Network Interface object and returned to the System Monitor, you see no performance statistics displayed for the selected counters, even though you have been accessing Internet Web sites and transferring files across the network. What is the most likely cause of this problem?

   ❍ **A.** The network interface is disabled.

   ❍ **B.** The network interface does not support the System Monitor.

   ❍ **C.** You have selected the internal loopback network interface.

   ❍ **D.** You did not click Add to add the counters to be monitored.

8. You have recently completed the configuration of a baseline counter log that you will use to collect data about the performance of a new server you have just placed on the network. You configured a maximum log file size of 1MB. You let the counter log run for approximately six hours before stopping it. When you look at the data you have collected, you see only a fraction of this total time displayed—the last 45 minutes or so that you had the counter log catching data. What is the most likely reason for this problem?

- ❍ **A.** There has not been enough activity to generate more data than this.
- ❍ **B.** You configured the file type as binary.
- ❍ **C.** You configured the file type as binary circular.
- ❍ **D.** The computer was experiencing operating system instability problems that prevented the collection of more data.

9. You are configuring a counter log that is to run automatically each day and collect information about the performance of the network interface installed in your file server. Which of the following log numbering systems would most likely make the resulting counter logs easy to track back to the date and time they were created?

- ❍ **A.** *nnnnnn*
- ❍ **B.** *yyyymm*
- ❍ **C.** *mmddhhmm*
- ❍ **D.** yyyymmddhh

10. You are the systems administrator for Joe's Crab Shack, a regional restaurant chain. Your in-house development team is currently developing a new Point of Sale (POS) application that operates in a client-server arrangement. Because the application is still in development, the developers want to be informed every time one of the application's services stops. What can you do to ensure the developers are automatically informed of service failures?

- ❍ **A.** Configure the services so that they automatically restart upon a failure.
- ❍ **B.** Configure the services to run a program upon failure.
- ❍ **C.** Configure the services to restart the server automatically upon a failure.
- ❍ **D.** Configure the services to use a different logon account.

11. You are the systems administrator for Widgets and Hammerstein, LLC. You have a 10-node Windows Server 2003 Web cluster that provides a Web-based application to your internal network. The Web-based application is a custom-developed application that sometimes causes the SNMP service on the servers to stop. In the past, this service has been very difficult to restart after a failure caused by this application. You need the SNMP Service running to facilitate status monitoring on your server. How can you configure the service to ensure it will be restarted after a failure occurs?

   ❍ **A.** Configure the service so that it will automatically restart upon a failure.

   ❍ **B.** Configure the service to run a program upon failure.

   ❍ **C.** Configure the service to restart the server automatically upon a failure.

   ❍ **D.** Configure the service to use a different logon account.

12. You are a network consultant hired by Claire's Clown Colleges, Inc. Claire, the owner, has asked you to help her systems administrators determine what, if any, servers on their network are transmitting usernames and passwords in clear text during FTP sessions. Which tool should you use to collect the information you need to provide Claire with her answer?

   ❍ **A.** Application log

   ❍ **B.** Network Monitor

   ❍ **C.** System Monitor

   ❍ **D.** Counter logs

Answers to Exam Questions

1. **D**. The first tool you would normally use to analyze the network for nonrequired, and usually troublesome, networking protocols is the Network Monitor. Recall that the version supplied in Windows Server 2003 can be used only to capture traffic sent to or from the computer on which it is running. The System Monitor, and any Counter Logs it might create, would not be useful in troubleshooting unneeded network services; thus Answers A and C are incorrect. The `kerbtray.exe` tool is useful for monitoring and troubleshooting Kerberos ticket issues; thus Answer B is incorrect. For more information, see the section "Using the Network Monitor."

2. **C**. In this case, the best option is to create a display filter that shows only AppleTalk-related protocols. You will not actually be losing any data—just filtering it out. You've already run the capture; thus there is no real reason to do it again. Therefore, Answer A is incorrect. Sorting will not eliminate any data; thus Answer B is incorrect. There is no need to use the Network Monitor included in SMS, as you have already performed the capture; thus Answer D is incorrect. For more information, see the section "Interpreting Captured Data."

3. **B**, **C**. You can use both the Network Monitor and the System Monitor to determine how much broadcast traffic a particular server is being subjected to. The Network Monitor also allows you to determine the source and contents of the broadcast traffic, which can be helpful when you're performing additional troubleshooting. The Application Log in the Event Viewer is not going to have any useful information about what you need to see; thus Answer A is incorrect. The `pathping` and `nslookup` tools won't help you determine how much traffic a server is receiving; thus Answers D and E are incorrect. For more information, see the sections "Using the Network Monitor" and "Using the System Monitor."

4. **B**. The scaled-down version of the Network Monitor that is included in Windows Server 2003 can be installed from the Windows Components Wizard under the Management and Monitoring option group; thus Answers A, C, and D are all incorrect. For more information, see the section "Installing Network Monitor."

5. **B**. The most likely reason that you are not seeing any DNS or browser traffic in the capture logs is that you inadvertently filtered (excluded) the logs from being captured through a capture filter. Capture filters capture only protocol types that are enabled; thus Answer A is incorrect. Conversely, a display filter can be used after a capture has been completed to display only specific protocols; thus Answer C is incorrect. The buffer may dump some traffic if it becomes full, but certainly not all of the traffic you're looking for in most cases; thus Answer D is incorrect. For more information, see the section "Interpreting Captured Data."

6. **B**. The best thing for you to do at this time would be to configure a counter log that collects information about the performance of the server over the next day or so to use as a baseline for future troubleshooting efforts. This baseline log should contain counters for any pertinent objects that you will likely want to monitor and troubleshoot later, including network, memory, and other objects. In addition, you should consider creating a document that lists all applications and services that are running on the server. This can be helpful later, when you are trying to determine what might be causing changes in performance over time. Removing any unneeded protocols is never a bad idea, but won't accomplish the goal stated here; thus Answer A is incorrect. Checking the event logs is also a good idea, but doesn't help for future troubleshooting; thus Answer C is incorrect. Configuring IPSec is not mentioned in the question and has no value in future troubleshooting efforts; thus Answer D is incorrect. For more information, see the section "Creating Baseline Counter Logs."

7. **C**. The most likely reason for this problem is that you have mistakenly selected the internal loopback interface instead of the actual network interface that the computer is using. By default, the loopback interface is selected if the name of the network interface starts with a letter after *l*. Although certainly possible, having the network interface disabled is not the most likely reason for this problem; thus Answer A is incorrect. Any network interface that is installed and operating properly in Windows can be monitored by the System Monitor; thus Answer B is incorrect. The problem statement indicates that you did in fact add counters and are seeing no activity on the counters; thus Answer D is incorrect. For more information, see the section "Monitoring Performance by Using the System Monitor."

8. **C**. Configuring the counter log file format as binary circular causes the log file to overwrite older information when it has reached its maximum allowed size; thus Answers A, B, and D are incorrect. For more information, see the section "Creating Baseline Counter Logs."

9. **D**. The *yyyymmddhh* log numbering format would provide the easiest method of determining the data and time each counter log was created. Using the *nnnnnn* format will produce logs that are sequentially numbered, but do not readily indicate the date and time they were created; thus Answer A is incorrect. Using the *yyyymm* format will only indicate the year and month the log was created; thus Answer B is incorrect. Using the *mmddhhmm* format is not a bad choice, but it does not indicate the year the log was created; thus Answer C is incorrect. For more information, see the section "Creating Baseline Counter Logs."

10. **B**. Because you need to provide the developers with notification each time a service fails, but you'd probably rather not manually inform them once you detect a service failure, your best course of action is to configure the services to run a program upon failure. As an example, many command-line SMTP mailers exist that can be called from a DOS batch (.bat) file that can send a notification to your Exchange server, and thus to your developers; thus Answers A, C, and D are incorrect.

11. **C**. Because the service is prone to failures caused by your Web-based application and the service is often difficult to restart after a failure, you should configure the service to restart the server upon a failure of the service; thus Answers A and B are incorrect. Because the servers are part of a 10-node Web cluster, they should be able to be safely restarted in the event of a failure of the service. Using a different logon account won't help if the service is running and then stopping due to another application; thus Answer D is incorrect. For more information, see the section "Configuring Service Properties."

12. **B**. You will need to use the Network Monitor, installed on each server, to collect network traffic. Once you have performed your captures (using no capture filters), you can configure display filters to include only TCP/IP and FTP traffic. The user names and passwords for the FTP sessions will be very easy to find after the filter is in place. The Application Log in the Event Viewer will not contain the information you need; thus Answer A is incorrect. The System Monitor and any counter logs it creates will not help you determine what you need to know; thus Answers C and D are incorrect. For more information, see the section "Using the Network Monitor."

Suggested Readings and Resources

1. Davies, Joseph, and Thomas Lee. 2003. *Microsoft Windows Server 2003 TCP/IP Protocols and Services Technical Reference.* Redmond, WA: Microsoft Press.

2. Microsoft Corporation. 2003. *Microsoft Windows Server 2003 Resource Kit.* Redmond, WA: Microsoft Press.

3. "Network Monitor," http://technet2.microsoft.com/WindowsServer/en/Library/ad2b59d1-0fb8-45e3-9055-a5aeba8817a91033.mspx.

PART II

Final Review

Fast Facts

Implementing, Managing, and Maintaining a Microsoft Windows Server 2003 Network Infrastructure

Now that you have finished reading this book and working through the exercises, you're ready for the exam. This section of the book is intended to be used as you're sitting in the testing center parking lot doing your "final cram" before you head in the door.

Organized by chapter, this section of the book is not only a summary, but also a concentrated review of the most important points. If you know and are comfortable with the content and concepts presented here, the odds are good that you are truly prepared for Exam 70-291, "Implementing, Managing, and Maintaining a Microsoft Windows Server 2003 Network Infrastructure."

Configuring and Troubleshooting TCP/IP Addressing

An IP address is a series of numbers that represents a computer (for example, 131.108.116.55). Each of the numbers in an IP address is an octet, which is made up of 8 bits; the whole IP address is 32 bits. IP addresses are typically displayed in a decimal format called dotted-decimal notation. Each host that requires connectivity on a TCP/IP network requires its own unique IP address.

If you were to look at 131.108.116.55 in binary, as the computer sees it, you would see 10000011 01101100 01110100 00110111. The easiest way to convert dotted-decimal notation to binary is to learn the mechanics of the binary system. By knowing that the smallest value that an IP address octet can take is 0 and the largest value that an IP address octet can take is 255, you can make a chart such as the one shown in Table 1.

TABLE 1 Decimal-to-Binary Conversion Basics

	128 (27)	64 (26)	32 (25)	16 (24)	8 (23)	4 (22)	2 (21)	1 (20)
255	1	1	1	1	1	1	1	1
0	0	0	0	0	0	0	0	0

Table 1 represents the 8 binary digits that make up a single IP address octet. If you have a value of decimal 255, its binary equivalent is 11111111, and if you have a value of decimal 0, its binary equivalent is 00000000.

IP addresses are organized by class. There are three basic classes: Class A, Class B, and Class C. Table 2 defines the range and number of hosts included with each class of addresses.

TABLE 2 IP Address Classes

Class	Address Range	Number of Network IDs	Number of Host IDs
A	1–126	126	16,777,214
B	128–191	16,384	65,534
C	192–223	2,097,152	254

A subnet mask effectively breaks an IP address into two parts: the network identifier and the host identifier.

When the subnet bits match, the host and destination host are on the same subnet, and no routing is needed. When the subnet bits don't match, the destination host is on a remote network, and the packets are sent to the router.

The Internet community has standardized default subnet masks for each of the three IP address classes. The subnet masks for these address classes are defined in Table 3.

TABLE 3 Default IP Class Subnet Masks

Address Class	Bits for Subnet Mask	Subnet Mask
A	11111111 00000000 00000000 00000000	255.0.0.0
B	11111111 11111111 00000000 00000000	255.255.0.0
C	11111111 11111111 11111111 00000000	255.255.255.0

If a computer has an IP address of 142.146.102.45 and a subnet mask of 255.255.0.0, the first two octets (142.146) identify the network, and the last two octets (102.45) identify a specific host on that network.

Using Variable Length Subnet Masks, also known as subnet addressing, allows you to borrow bits from the host ID portion of an IP address and apply them to the network ID.

Suppose that you have been assigned a Class B address of 172.18.0.0. Further suppose that you now need to create four separate networks from your one IP address range. To do so, you borrow 3 bits from the host ID field. These 3 bits let you configure six separate subnets.

A default gateway is the IP address of the router that the packets from a host should use to leave the subnet. The typical process of how a packet leaves a host and gets to a destination is as follows:

1. Computer A looks up the IP address of Computer E by using a query to a DNS server.
2. Computer A determines whether the IP address of Computer E is local or remote by comparing its own IP address to that of Computer E.
3. If the address is remote, Computer A sends the packets to the default gateway's MAC address. The MAC address of the default gateway is determined via an ARP broadcast.
4. The default gateway forwards the packets on to the next router, according to its routing table.
5. If Computer E's IP address is on the same subnet as Computer A, the IP address of Computer E is resolved to the MAC address through an ARP broadcast.
6. Computer A and Computer E then communicate with one another, and there is no need for routing.

Several changes and improvements have been made to TCP/IP in Windows Server 2003:

- `netsh` can be used to reset TCP/IP.
- `netstat` can display PIDs.
- Internet Group Management Protocol version 3 (IGMPv3) is supported.
- Interface speed route metric determination is possible.
- IPv6 is supported.

After you've performed the initial configuration of TCP/IP, you still might need to configure some additional settings on the protocol. If you click the Advanced button in the TCP/IP Properties dialog box, the Advanced TCP/IP Settings dialog box appears, and you can change settings on the following tabs:

- **IP Settings**—This tab displays the currently configured IP address and default gateway.
- **DNS**—This tab allows you to configure additional multiple DNS servers that the network connection should use and the order in which they should be contacted.

- **WINS**—The WINS tab allows you to configure the WINS servers that are to be used to resolve NetBIOS hostnames to IP addresses on the network.
- **Options**—The Options tab contains only one item in Windows Server 2003: TCP/IP Filtering. With this option, you can control the type of TCP/IP information that is sent to a computer.

Table 4 provides a list of common TCP port numbers. Table 5 presents some common UDP port numbers. Table 6 covers common Internet protocol numbers.

TABLE 4 Common TCP Port Numbers

TCP Port Number	Description
20	FTP data channel
21	FTP control channel
22	SSH Remote Login Protocol
23	Telnet
25	SMTP
53	DNS
69	TFTP
79	Finger
80	HTTP
109	POP2
110	POP3
137	NBNS
138	NetBIOS Datagram Service
139	NetBIOS Session Service
161	SNMP
443	HTTPS

TABLE 5 Common UDP Port Numbers

TCP Port Number	Description
20	FTP data channel
21	FTP control channel
22	SSH remote login protocol
23	Telnet
25	SMTP

TABLE 5 Continued

TCP Port Number	Description
53	DNS
69	TFTP
79	Finger
80	HTTP
109	POP2
110	POP 3
137	NBNS
138	NetBIOS datagram service
139	NetBIOS session service
161	SNMP
520	RIP

TABLE 6 Common Internet Protocol Numbers

Protocol Number	Protocol
1	ICMP
2	IGMP
3	GGP
4	IP in IP (encapsulation)
5	ST
6	TCP
7	CBT
8	EGP

Automatic Private IP Addressing (APIPA) allows a DHCP-configured computer to automatically assume an IP address from the range 169.254.0.1 through 169.254.255.254, with a subnet mask of 255.255.0.0, when a DHCP server cannot be contacted. Although APIPA does provide a client with an IP address if a DHCP server cannot be contacted, the only guarantee that is made is that the IP address the client uses will not belong to any other computer on its IP subnet.

APIPA does not provide any information to the computer beyond the IP address and subnet mask. This means that a computer possessing an APIPA IP address will not be able to communicate with other computers that are working with correctly assigned IP addresses and subnet masks. In addition, APIPA receives no default gateway and thus is unable to communicate outside its IP subnet.

There are several tools for troubleshooting TCP/IP problems, including the following:

- **`ping`**—The `ping` command is used to test basic network connectivity between two computers. This testing is done over local and remote networks.
- **`ipconfig`**—The `ipconfig` command can be used to quickly determine what settings have been configured for the network adapters in computers.
- **Network Diagnostics**—The Network Diagnostics tool is available in Windows XP and Windows Server 2003, and you can use it to perform many of the same tests that were reviewed in Chapter 1, "Configuring and Troubleshooting TCP/IP Addressing," plus many more, all from within the Windows Graphical User Interface (GUI).
- **`netsh`**—The `netsh` command is an advanced configuration and troubleshooting command that helps you to manage almost any networking-related component on your Windows Server 2003 computer; note, however, that it does require you to have knowledge of the result you're trying to achieve. The `netsh` command can be used interactively or via scripting to manage networking-related configurations such as those for the Windows Firewall, DHCP, WINS, TCP/IP configuration and IP Security (IPSec) settings, as well as many other tasks.

Implementing, Managing, and Troubleshooting DHCP

DHCP was the Internet community's answer to the problem of dynamically distributing IP addresses. Here's how a client computer gets an address:

1. The client computer broadcasts a `DHCPDISCOVER` message that is intended for the DHCP server(s) on the network. If a router sits between the DHCP server and the client, it needs to be configured with the IP address of the DHCP server. It also needs to be configured to forward BOOTP.
2. Each DHCP server that receives the `DHCPDISCOVER` message responds with a DHCP offer message, which includes an IP address that is appropriate for the subnet where the client computer is attached. The DHCP server determines the appropriate address by looking at the source subnet for the broadcast `DHCPDISCOVER` message.
3. The client computer considers the offer messages and selects one (usually the first offer it receives). It sends a request (`DHCPREQUEST`) to use the address to the DHCP server that originated the offer. If there are multiple DHCP servers, they need to be carefully configured. It is very easy to inadvertently configure servers so that they conflict; therefore, it is important if you have multiple DHCP servers on a network that they do

not have the capability to offer duplicate IP addresses. Because DHCP servers do not communicate with one another, they have no way of telling whether an address has already been issued by another DHCP server.

4. The DHCP server acknowledges the request and grants the client computer a lease to use the address.

5. The client computer uses the IP address to bind to the network. If the IP address is associated with any configuration parameters, the parameters are incorporated into the client computer's TCP/IP configuration.

6. When 50 percent of the configured lease time has elapsed, the client sends another `DHCPREQUEST` message to the DHCP server that granted its lease, asking to renew and extend its current lease.

7. If the DHCP server is reachable, it responds with a `DHCPACK` message to the client, renewing and extending the DHCP lease as requested.

8. If the DHCP server is not reachable, the client continues trying to reach it until 87.5 percent of the lease time has elapsed. At that point, the client attempts to renew its lease with any DHCP server that responds. If this is unsuccessful, the client starts the process of acquiring a new DHCP lease.

DHCP is not a new service in Windows Server 2003, but it has undergone some changes from both Windows 2000 and Windows NT 4.0. The following list summarizes some of the major changes between DHCP in Windows NT 4.0 (and Windows 2000 Server as well) and Windows Server 2003:

- **DHCP integration in DNS**—DHCP servers in a Windows Server 2003 environment can trigger dynamic updates in the DNS database for all clients to which it leases IP addresses. Windows 2000 and newer clients can automatically update their DNS records if they are authorized to do so. Legacy clients can have their records updated by the DHCP server if it is authorized to do so.

- **Rogue DHCP server detection**—Unauthorized, or *rogue*, DHCP servers can cause a wide variety of problems, including a Denial of Service (DoS) to clients. To prevent such problems, Windows Server 2003 requires an administrator to authorize DHCP servers before they can start to service client requests. In this way, only those DHCP servers that have been authorized can provide DHCP leases to clients. You must be an enterprise administrator to authorize a DHCP server.

- **Superscope and multicast scope support**—Superscopes allow you to group several standard DHCP scopes into a single administrative group without causing any service disruption to network clients. Multicast scopes allow you to lease Class D IP addresses to clients for participation in multicast transmissions. These include streaming video and audio transmissions.

- **Local security groups for DHCP management**—Two new local administrative security groups are created when the DHCP service is installed: DHCP Users and DHCP Administrators.
- **Improved monitoring and reporting**—Windows Server 2003 provides a full set of performance monitoring counters that can be used to monitor DHCP server performance.
- **Custom DHCP option classes**—User- and vendor-specified option classes can be used to distribute specific options to the clients that need them.

A scope is a range of IP addresses that are available for dynamic assignment to hosts on a given subnet. The scope for a particular subnet is determined by the network address of the broadcast DHCP request. In addition to address information, a scope can include a set of configuration parameters to be assigned to client computers when the address is assigned. This list of configuration parameters can include DNS servers, WINS servers, default gateways, the subnet mask, a NetBIOS scope ID, IP routing information, and WINS proxy information.

A supernetted network is a network that has multiple network addresses or subnets running on the same segment. This configuration is common in a network environment with more than 254 hosts on a subnet and in an environment in which certain hosts need to be isolated from the rest of the logical network for security or routing reasons. Superscopes support a local multinet or a multinet that is located across a router and configured to use the BOOTP forwarder service.

Windows Server 2003 makes use of the concept of a multicast scope. The DHCP service has been extended to allow the assignment of multicast addresses in addition to unicast (single-computer) addresses. MADCAP (Multicast Address Dynamic Client Allocation Protocol) is an IETF standard (RFC 2730) that defines multicast address allocation.

You can configure DHCP options at four different levels for each DHCP server:

- **Server**—These are DHCP options that are applied to all scopes on the DHCP server.
- **Scope**—These are DHCP options that are applied only to the specific scope on the DHCP server.
- **Class**—These are DHCP options that are applied only to clients identified as members of specified user or vendor classes.
- **Reservation**—These are DHCP options that are applied only to a specific computer.

Some of the more common DHCP scope options are presented in Table 7.

TABLE 7 DHCP Scope Options

Code	Option Name	Option Description
2	Time Offset	Specifies the offset of the client's subnet in seconds from UTC.
3	Router	Specifies a list of IP addresses for routers on the client's subnet.
4	Time Server	Specifies a list of RFC 868 time servers available to the client.
5	Name Servers	Specifies a list of name servers available to the client.
6	DNS Servers	Specifies a list of DNS servers available to the client.
9	LPR Servers	Specifies a list of RFC 1179 line printer servers available to the client.
15	DNS Domain Name	Specifies the domain name that the client should use when resolving hostnames via DNS.
27	All Subnets Are Local	Specifies whether the client can assume that all subnets of the IP network to which the client is connected use the same MTU as the subnet of the network to which the client is directly connected.
28	Broadcast Address	Specifies the broadcast address in use on the client's subnet.
44	WINS/NBNS Servers	Specifies a list of RFC 1001/1002 NBNS servers, listed in order of preference.
46	WINS/NBT Node Type	Allows NetBT clients, which can be configured as described in RFC 1001/1002.
47	NetBIOS Scope ID	Specifies the NetBT scope parameter for the client, as specified in RFC 1001/1002.

Microsoft-specific DHCP options are shown in Table 8.

TABLE 8 Microsoft-Specific DHCP Options

Code	Option Name	Description
1	Microsoft Disable NetBIOS	This option can be used to selectively enable or disable NetBT for DHCP-enabled computers running Windows.
2	Microsoft Release DHCP Lease on Shutdown	This option can be used to control whether DHCP-enabled computers running Windows send a release for their current DHCP lease to the DHCP server when shutdown occurs.
3	Microsoft Default Router Metric Base	This value is a specified router metric base to be used for all default gateway routes.

When you provide DHCP using Windows Server 2003, you can take advantage of the tight integration between DHCP and DNS and thereby ensure that all clients are automatically registered in DNS. You can configure the following settings for DNS integration:

- Dynamically Update DNS A and PTR Records Only If Requested by the DHCP Clients
- Always Dynamically Update DNS A and PTR Records
- Discard A and PTR Records When Lease Is Deleted
- Dynamically Update DNS A and PTR Records for DHCP Clients That Do Not Request Automatic Updates

There are three basic configurations in which you can set up a DHCP relay agent:

- The first involves entering the IP address or addresses of the DHCP server(s) into the router itself, instructing it to pass DHCP messages to a specified IP address for action.
- The second method involves using the Windows Server 2003 Routing and Remote Access (RRAS) component as a router (in place of a hardware-based router) and configuring the DHCP relay agent within it.
- The third solution is to use a Windows Server 2003 computer located on a subnet without a DHCP server to act as a DHCP relay agent. This option requires the use of the RRAS components, but it does not involve the creation or configuration of a router, as would be the case with the second solution. What's important to understand is that the server providing the DHCP relay agent service does not have to be dedicated to that purpose; it could be a file server, a print server, or any other type of Windows Server 2003 (or Windows 2000 Server) server on that subnet.

You can monitor the following DHCP statistics from the DHCP console:

- Start Time
- Up Time
- Discovers
- Offers
- Requests
- Acks
- Nacks
- Declines

- Releases
- Total Scopes
- Total Addresses
- In Use
- Available

DHCP server backup and restore is one of the new features found in the DHCP service in Windows Server 2003. Two types of backups from the DHCP console are supported:

- **Synchronous**—A synchronous backup occurs automatically on the configured interval. The default interval is 60 minutes and can be changed from the registry location `HKEY_LOCAL_MACHINE\SYSTEM\CurrentControlSet\Services\DHCPServer\Parameters\BackupInterval`.
- **Asynchronous**—An asynchronous backup is a manual backup that is performed by using the Backup command from within the DHCP console.

Backups of the DHCP data from the DHCP console include the following items:

- All scopes
- All reservations
- All leases
- All options, including server options, scope options, reservation options, and class options
- All registry data in the following registry location: `HKEY_LOCAL_MACHINE\SYSTEM\CurrentControlSet\Services\DHCPServer\Parameters`

Implementing and Managing DNS

DNS is a hierarchical database that contains names and addresses for IP networks and hosts and that is used almost universally to provide name resolution. This fact was not lost on Microsoft as Windows Server 2003 (as Windows 2000 Server was before it) is completely dependent on DNS as its name resolution method for Windows Server 2003 rather than WINS, as in the days of Windows NT.

The Windows Server 2003 DNS service supports three types of zones:

- **Forward lookup zones**—Forward lookup zones provide the hostname-to-IP address resolution for which DNS is most frequently used.
- **Reverse lookup zones**—Reverse lookup zones resolve IP addresses to hostnames.
- **Stub zones**—In Windows Server 2003, Microsoft introduced support for stub zones for the first time. A stub zone contains only those resource records that are necessary to identify the authoritative DNS servers for that zone. Such resource records include Name Server (NS), Start of Authority (SOA), and possibly glue host (A) records. (Glue host records provide A record pointers to ensure that the master zone has the correct name server information for the stub zone.)

Stub zones are frequently used for the following:

- **To keep delegated zone information up to date**—Because a stub zone is used to provide pointers to a delegated zone, updating the stub zone causes the DNS server that is hosting both the parent zone and the stub zone to maintain a current list of authoritative DNS servers for the delegated zone.
- **To improve name resolution performance**—Because a stub zone enables a DNS server to perform recursive resolution by using the stub zone's list of name servers, the DNS server making the request does not need to query any Internet name servers or internal name servers to get the resolution.

With zone delegation, one DNS server can assign the administration of a domain to another DNS server.

A zone transfer involves the copying of the zone database from one DNS server to another. This is typically done to ensure name resolution availability and DNS server fault tolerance.

A DNS server can perform several roles, based on its configuration and the requirements of the site or network to which the server is connected. These server roles include the following:

- Primary master server
- Secondary master server
- Caching-only server
- DNS forwarder
- DNS slave server

A DNS name server resolves a name to an IP address by using the following process:

1. The client computer makes a request to the local DNS server. This generally occurs when an application tries to make a connection by using a hostname. For example, this request to the DNS server occurs when you enter **`www.quepublishing.com`** into a Web browser and the resolution is not found in the client's DNS cache.

2. The DNS server looks in a local memory cache for names it has recently resolved. If the requested name is found in the local cache, the name server returns the IP address that the client computer requires. Most DNS servers cache both local and remote domain names in memory, so even a DNS request for a host on the local network may be in cache.

3. The name server looks in the DNS server's host tables to see if there is a static entry (or, in the case of DDNS, a dynamic entry) for the hostname-to-IP address lookup. If an entry exists, the DNS server forwards the IP address to the client computer.

4. If the request has not been resolved, the name server refers the request to a root name server. (Root name servers support the root of the namespace hierarchy.) At present, 13 computers support the root domain.

5. The root name server refers the request to a name server for the Top Level Domain (TLD) in the hostname. (For example, if you have requested a host address for the quepublishing.com domain, the root name server forwards the request to the quepublishing.com DNS server.) The TLD name server refers the request to a name server for the second-level domain in the hostname, and so on, until a name server is encountered that can resolve the complete hostname.

6. The first name server that can resolve the hostname to an IP address reports the IP address to the client computer.

Several common DNS record types are described in Table 9.

TABLE 9 Common DNS Record Types

Record Type	RFC	Description
CNAME	RFC 1035	Canonical Name record. A CNAME entry indicates an alias domain name for a name already specified as another resource type in this zone. CNAME is the acronym for canonical name.
ATMA	RFC 2601	ATM Address record. An ATMA record maps a DNS name to an ATM address.
A	RFC 1035	Address record. An A record maps a DNS name to an IPv4 address.
AAAA	RFC 1886	AAAA record. An AAAA record is similar to the A record. It is used to map a DNS name to an IPv6 address.

(continues)

TABLE 9 Continued

Record Type	RFC	Description
ISDN	RFC 1183	ISDN record. An ISDN record maps a DNS name to an ISDN telephone number.
MX	RFC 1035	Mail Exchanger record. An MX record is used to provide message routing to a specific mail exchanger host for a specific DNS name.
MINFO	RFC 1035	Mailbox or Mailing List Information record. An MINFO record specifies a domain mailbox name to contact. It can also specify a mailbox for error messages.
PTR	RFC 1035	Pointer record. A PTR record maps an IP address to a DNS name. This is typically used for reverse lookups or IP-address-to-DNS-name lookups.
RP	RFC 1183	Responsible Person record. An RP record specifies the domain mailbox for a responsible person for which text (TXT) records exist.
TXT	RFC 1035	Text record. A TXT record is used to hold a string of characters that serve as descriptive text to be associated with a specific DNS name.
SRV	RFC 2052	Service record. An SRV record allows administrators to use several servers for a single DNS domain, to easily move a TCP/IP service from host to host, and to designate primary and backup service hosts.
WKS	RFC 1035	Well-known service record. A WKS record is used to describe well-known TCP/IP services supported by a particular protocol (that is, TCP or UDP) on a specific IP address.
SOA	RFC 1035	Start of Authority record. An SOA is the first resource record in every correctly configured zone. It contains information about the zone and tells the DNS server that it is authoritative for a zone.

Windows Server 2003's DNS contains several significant improvements over standard DNS (including Windows NT's implementation of DNS). The improvements include the following:

- Integrated zone tables
- Incremental zone transfers
- Secure DNS updates
- DNS/DHCP integration
- Support for stub zones
- Conditional forwarding
- Enhanced debug logging
- DNSSEC extensions

- Additional round-robin DNS capabilities
- Support for application directory partitions

You can use the following tools to troubleshoot the basic operation of DNS:

- `ping`
- `nslookup`
- The DNS server service monitoring tool
- A Web browser
- The Event Viewer
- The Performance console

Standard DNS zone information is stored in flat text files located in the `%systemroot%\system32\dns` directory on your DNS server. Active Directory–integrated DNS zones actually store the DNS zone information within an Active Directory application partition. This makes the DNS zone information available to all Domain Controllers within a domain or even a forest that have the DNS service running on them. By using Active Directory–integrated DNS zones, every DNS server then becomes a master server for that zone, increasing security, reliability, and redundancy of that zone information. A standard DNS zone can be converted into an integrated zone after its creation, or you can create new integrated zones from scratch.

As you've no doubt noticed by now, DNS is an important network service. Active Directory, as you've also likely noticed by now, is the heart and soul of a Windows Server 2003 network infrastructure. Thus, it only stands to reason that Active Directory absolutely cannot function without a reliable and functional DNS implementation in place.

Here are some key points that emphasize the importance of DNS to Active Directory:

- Without a properly working DNS infrastructure, Domain Controllers will not be able to replicate information about the domain among themselves.
- Without a properly working DNS infrastructure, Windows 2000 and Windows XP client computers will experience very long logon times or possibly the inability to log on at all.
- Without a properly working DNS infrastructure, Exchange Server 2003 and Exchange 2000 Server will not be able to work, and servers will likely fail to start critical services properly.

In short, without DNS, you won't have an Active Directory implementation.

Aging and scavenging of resource records will be important to you if you have clients that come and go from your network or have clients that have IP address changes. In all reality, that statement describes almost 100 percent of all networks that use DNS today, so aging and scavenging are useful for almost every DNS implementation to help keep records clean and up to date. By default, aging and scavenging are not enabled or configured on a newly installed Windows Server 2003 DNS server, so you'll need to perform those tasks yourself or run the risk of slowly poisoning your DNS information with outdated and conflicting resource records.

In terms of DNS, *aging* is the process of placing a timestamp on a dynamically created resource record and then tracking the age of that record. *Scavenging*, in DNS, is the process of deleting any resource records that have timestamps on them that are found to be outdated. As a result, scavenging can occur only when aging has been enabled and properly configured. In order for aging and scavenging to work correctly, they must be configured on the DNS server and also on any zones residing on that DNS server for which you want aging and scavenging to occur.

When configuring aging and scavenging for your DNS servers, you will need to understand how these options come into play:

- **No-Refresh Interval**—This option controls the time between the most recent refresh of a record's time stamp and when the time stamp can be refreshed again. In a very dynamic network where computers come on and leave frequently, you might want to lower this from the default, which is 7 days.
- **Refresh Interval**—This option sets the time between the earliest moment that a record time stamp can be refreshed and the earliest moment a record can be scavenged.

You can perform two simple tests of your DNS server's operation within the Properties tab of the server itself:

- **Simple (iterative) query**—A simple query, also called an iterative query, is one in which the name server provides the best response based on what that server knows from local zone files or from caching. If a name server doesn't have any information with which to answer the query, it simply sends a negative response.
- **Recursive query**—A recursive query forces a DNS server to respond to a request with either a failure response or a success response. With a recursive query, the DNS server must contact any other DNS servers it needs to contact in order to resolve the request. This is a much more resource-intensive query mechanism than the simple query.

Although Active Directory–integrated zones with secure dynamic updates are fairly secure, there are some more advanced configuration changes that can be made in the interest of further securing the server. While not a complete listing of items by any means, the following list presents some of the more common items that you can use to increase security:

- **Network interfaces**—If your DNS server has multiple network interfaces, the DNS service will by default listen for and respond to name resolution queries on all of them. You can add some security to your DNS server installation by configuring it so that it listens only on the IP address that DNS clients will be using to contact it.
- **Disabling recursion**—Recursion is enabled by default in Windows Server 2003 DNS, which allows the DNS server to perform recursive queries to other DNS servers on behalf of its DNS clients and other DNS servers that have forwarded queries to it for resolution. If a DNS server is not intended to perform recursive queries, you should disable them to prevent recursion from being used as an attack vector on the DNS server.
- **Securing the cache against pollution**—This advanced server option is enabled by default to aid in ensuring that a server's DNS cache is secured against pollution. Cache pollution can result when a DNS query response returns incorrect, nonauthoritative, or malicious data. By keeping this option enabled, the DNS server will not accept resource records in a query response that were not requested in the original query. You should not disable this protection.
- **Removing root hints**—If you have configured an internal DNS root in your DNS infrastructure, configure the root hints on all of your other internal DNS servers to point only to your internal DNS root server. By removing the ability for the other DNS servers to contact root servers on the Internet, you remove the possibility of accidentally disclosing your private internal information on the Internet.
- **Use a private DNS namespace**—If your network clients will never need to communicate with the Internet, you can use a private DNS namespace, such as quepublishing.corp, along with an internal root DNS server and applicable firewall configuration to prevent DNS-related traffic from ever leaving your organization. Note, simply using a private DNS namespace does not eliminate the ability to communicate with the Internet.
- **Use a split DNS namespace**—If your network clients will need to communicate with the Internet, consider using a split DNS namespace. In this model, the Internet namespace may be something like quepublishing.com while the internal namespace is something like corp.quepublishing.com. Each section of the DNS namespace should be hosted on separate DNS servers located on the applicable side of your corporate firewall. Requests made by clients internally should be forwarded to your external DNS servers if the internal DNS servers cannot provide the requested query answer.

Forwarding would be accomplished by configuring your internal DNS servers to forward requests only to your external DNS servers. Additionally, you should configure your external DNS servers to forward requests only to your ISP's trusted DNS servers.

- **Use firewall rules**—You can configure and implement a firewall rule on your packet filtering firewall that allows TCP and UDP traffic on port 53 only between your internal and external DNS servers.
- **Harden servers**—You can get detailed information and assistance on hardening Windows Server 2003 servers from the *Windows Server 2003 Security Guide*.

Implementing and Managing WINS

If you are familiar with Windows NT 4.0 networks, you are undoubtedly familiar with the intricacies of a WINS infrastructure. With Windows Server 2003, WINS is intended and needed only for backward compatibility. A Windows Server 2003 network running in native mode does not need to use WINS at all as DNS is used to provide resole host names into IP addresses.

Until your network is running only Windows Server 2003 (or higher) and no applications on the network require NetBIOS name resolution, you will still need WINS to provide backward compatibility for legacy Windows operating systems, particularly with any NT domains.

Four elements can be found in a WINS network:

- **WINS servers**—When WINS client computers enter the network, they contact a WINS server using a directed message. The client computer registers its name with the WINS server and uses the WINS server to resolve NetBIOS names to IP addresses.
- **WINS client computers**—WINS client computers use directed messages to communicate with WINS servers. All versions of Windows since Windows for Workgroups can be WINS client computers.
- **Non-WINS client computers**—Older Microsoft network client computers that can't use direct WINS communications can still benefit from WINS. Their broadcast messages are intercepted by WINS proxy computers that act as intermediaries between clients that must broadcast and WINS servers. MS-DOS and Windows 3.1 client computers function as non-WINS clients.
- **WINS proxies**—All versions of Windows client computers since Windows for Workgroups can function as WINS proxies. They intercept broadcasts on their local subnets and communicate with a WINS server on behalf of the broadcasting client computer.

You can set the following intervals on your WINS server. These intervals determine how WINS records and the WINS database are handled:

- **Renew Interval**—Determines the frequency of record renewal.
- **Extinction Interval**—Determines the length of time before a released record is considered extinct.
- **Extinction Timeout**—Determines the length of time after a record has been marked as extinct before it is removed from the database.
- **Verification Interval**—Determines the frequency at which database records are verified for accuracy.

In most environments that rely on WINS for name resolution, you will want to have more than one WINS server for redundancy and increased availability. To ensure that each server has a current copy of the database, it is important to configure replication between your WINS servers. The following types of replication are available to be configured for the WINS service:

- **Pull replication**—In pull replication, your server pulls the database from the replication partner. A pull replication is time based and occurs at the time you have configured. You can decide whether to establish a persistent connection for replication, and you can set the start time and interval for replication.
- **Push replication**—In push replication, your server pushes its database to the replication partner. A push replication is event driven, and the number of database updates determines when the event occurs. You can decide whether to use a persistent connection for push activities, and you can set the number of changes in the version ID before replication.
- **Replication partner type**—The partner type can be push, pull, or push/pull, depending on your requirements. (In push/pull replication, database replication can occur using either push or pull.)

Whenever possible, it is preferable to communicate through directed messages. This cuts down on the amount of network traffic and ensures that only the affected hosts receive the message. This also ensures that the messages will propagate across routers. Specially, for WINS, Microsoft needed to ensure that WINS communicated primarily with directed messages. This requirement was accomplished by allowing several types of NetBIOS naming methods. These naming methods are commonly called *node types*. A *node* is simply a device on a network. Every computer running Windows is configured to use one of four node types. The node type determines whether the computer will register and resolve names through broadcast messages, directed messages, or some combination of broadcast and directed messages. The four node types include the following:

- **b-node (broadcast node)**—Relies exclusively on broadcast messages and is the oldest NetBIOS name registration and resolution mode. A host needing to resolve a name request sends a message to every host within earshot, requesting the address associated with a host name. b-node has two shortcomings: broadcast traffic is undesirable and becomes a significant user of network bandwidths, and TCP/IP routers don't forward broadcast messages, which restricts b-node operation to a single network segment.
- **p-node (point-to-point node)**—Relies on WINS servers for NetBIOS name registration and resolution. Client computers register themselves with a WINS server when they come on the network. They then contact the WINS server with NetBIOS name resolution requests. WINS servers communicate using directed messages, which can cross routers, so p-node can operate on large networks. Unfortunately, if the WINS server is unavailable or if a node isn't configured to contact a WINS server, p-node name resolution fails.
- **m-node (modified node)**—A hybrid mode that first attempts to register and resolve NetBIOS names using the b-node mechanism. If that fails, an attempt is made to use p-node name resolution. m-node was the first hybrid mode put into operation, but it has the disadvantage of favoring b-node operation, which is associated with high levels of broadcast traffic.
- **h-node (hybrid node)**—A hybrid mode that favors the use of WINS for NetBIOS name registration and resolution. When a computer needs to resolve a NetBIOS name, it first attempts to use p-node resolution to resolve a name via WINS. Only if WINS resolution fails does the host resort to b-node to resolve the name via broadcasts. Because it typically results in the best network utilization, h-node is the default mode of operation for Microsoft TCP/IP client computers configured to use WINS for name resolution. Microsoft recommends leaving TCP/IP client computers in the default h-node configuration.

The following counters are available for monitoring WINS server performance:

- **Failed Queries/Sec**—Gives you the number of failed WINS queries per second. If this number is very high or suddenly spikes, you might have an issue with WINS resolution.
- **Failed Releases/Sec**—Gives you the number of failed WINS releases per second. If this number is very high or suddenly spikes, you might have an issue with WINS resolution.

- **Group Conflicts/Sec**—The rate at which group registrations by the WINS server resulted in conflicts with the database.
- **Group Registrations/Sec**—The rate at which group registrations are being received.
- **Group Renewals/Sec**—The rate at which group registrations are being renewed.
- **Queries/Sec**—The rate at which queries are being received.
- **Releases/Sec**—The rate at which releases are being received.
- **Successful Queries/Sec**—The number of successful queries per second. This is useful if you are watching for trends in your WINS usage.
- **Successful Releases/Sec**—The number of successful releases per second. This is useful if you are watching for trends in your WINS usage.
- **Total Number of Conflicts/Sec**—This is the sum of the unique and group conflicts per second.
- **Total Number of Registrations/Sec**—This is the sum of the unique and group registrations per second.
- **Total Number of Renewals/Sec**—This is the sum of the unique and group renewals per second.
- **Unique Conflicts/Sec**—The rate at which unique registrations and renewals cause conflicts with the database.
- **Unique Registrations/Sec**—The rate at which unique registrations are received by the server.
- **Unique Renewals/Sec**—The rate at which unique renewals are received by the server.

The `nbtstat` command gives you statistics for NetBIOS over TCP/IP. The utility is used to determine which NetBIOS names the machine has cached and to which IP addresses those names resolved. You need to be aware of the options for using the `nbtstat` command, as outlined in Table 10.

TABLE 10 The `nbtstat` Command Switches

Switch	Description
-a	Displays the name table of a remote machine given its name.
-A	Displays the name table of a remote machine given its IP address.
-c	Displays the cache of NetBIOS names held by the local machine. This is useful for determining which names the local client has requested recently and how they were resolved.
-n	Displays a list of local NetBIOS names.

(continues)

TABLE 10 Continued

Switch	Description
-r	Displays a list of names that have been resolved by broadcast and via WINS.
-R	Purges and reloads the remote cache name table.
-s	Displays a sessions table, showing the name of remote machines.
-S	Displays a sessions table, showing only IP addresses for remote machines.
-RR	Performs a release and refresh by sending name release packets to the WINS and then starting a refresh.

One of the easiest ways to ensure that name resolution is working is to hardcode it into the local files that Windows first looks to for information. By entering the information in the local files, you can ensure that the computer does not attempt to resolve the name and will use the address you've specified. Two files are used for name resolution. The first file, the `hosts` file, resolves IP names into IP addresses and can be thought of as an alternative to DNS. The second file, the `lmhosts` file, resolves NetBIOS names into IP addresses and can be thought of as an alternative to WINS.

On a Windows Server 2003 computer, the `hosts` file is located in the `%windir%\system32\drivers\etc` directory. This is the file you must modify to change the hard-coded host resolution. Entries in the `hosts` file are simple; they begin with the IP address and are followed by the host name. If you open the `hosts` file on your system, it will already contain the special localhost name, which you can use as a template for adding new names.

The format of the `lmhosts` file is different than the `hosts` file, but it is located in the same `%windir%\system32\drivers\etc` directory as the `hosts` file. Unlike the `hosts` file, no default `lmhosts` file is created when you install Windows Server 2003. However, Windows Server 2003 includes an `lmhosts.sam` file that is a sample file you can rename to `lmhosts` and use as a starting point.

The `lmhosts` file is similar to the `hosts` file, except that it has these additional options:

- **#PRE**—Placed after an entry, it causes the entry to be preloaded. The effect of this is that the entry is permanently loaded into memory. This is a good idea for hosts that will be accessed frequently.
- **#DOM:<*domain*>**—Associates an entry with the domain given. It helps the computer locate a domain controller for the network.
- **#INCLUDE <*filename*>**—Includes the named file as if it were located in the `lmhosts` file. This is infrequently used because it incurs additional overhead to process the file.

Implementing, Managing, and Maintaining Network Security

Windows Server 2003 comes with a full set of preconfigured security templates that you can use to customize the security settings of the server (or other computers in the domain) to your liking. These preconfigured templates can be thought of in one of two ways: either as a starting point from which to make your own customized security templates or as a solution in of themselves.

These preconfigured templates have the extension `.inf` and are located in the `%systemroot%\security\templates` folder on a Windows Server 2003 computer. You can use the Security Configuration and Analysis snap-in, the `secedit.exe` tool, or the Local Security Policy console to apply these templates to a local computer.

Table 11 details the preconfigured security templates that ship with Windows Server 2003.

TABLE 11 The Preconfigured Security Templates in Windows Server 2003

Template (Filename)	Description
Default (`Setup security.inf`)	This template is created during the installation of Windows on the computer. This template varies from one computer to the next, depending on whether the installation was performed as a clean installation or as an upgrade. `Setup security.inf` represents the default security settings that a computer started out with and thus can be used to reset portions of security as required. This template can be applied to both workstations and member servers, but not to domain controllers (DCs), and it should never be applied via Group Policy due to the large amount of data it contains. Doing so can result in performance degradation.
Default DC (`DC security.inf`)	This template is automatically created when a member server is promoted to a DC. It represents the file, registry, and system service default security settings for that DC and can be used later to reset those areas to their default configurations.

(continues)

TABLE 11 Continued

Template (Filename)	Description
Compatible (`compatws.inf`)	This template allows members of the Users group to run applications that do not conform to the Windows Logo Program for Windows 2000 and above. Applications that were written for Windows NT 4.0 do not use the same security model that applications written for Windows 2000 and above use. Applications that do conform to the Windows Logo Program can be, in the majority of cases, successfully run by members of the Users group without any further modifications required. For applications that do not conform, there are two basic choices: You can make the users members of the Power Users group or relax the default permissions of the Users group. The Compatible template solves this problem by changing the default file and registry permissions that are granted to the Users group to allow them to run most applications that are not part of the Windows Logo Program. As a side effect of applying this template, all users are removed from the Power Users group because the basic assumption is that the template is being applied in an effort to prevent the need for that group. This template should not be applied to DCs, so do not import it into the Default Domain Policy or the Default Domain Controller Policy.
Secure (`securews.inf`, `securedc.inf`)	The Secure templates are the first ones to actually begin the process of locking down the computer to which they are applied. There are two different Secure templates: `securews.inf`, which is for workstations and member servers, and `securedc.inf`, which is for DCs only. The Secure templates prevent the usage of the LAN Manager (LM) authentication protocol. Windows 9x clients need to have Active Directory Client Extensions installed to enable NT LAN Manager version 2 (NTLMv2) to allow them to communicate with Windows 2000 and above clients and servers using these templates. These templates also impose additional restrictions on anonymous users, such as preventing them from enumerating account and share information. The secure templates also enable Server Message Block (SMB) signing on the server side. By default, SMB signing is enabled on client computers. If you apply this template, SMB packet signing will always be negotiated between clients and servers.

TABLE 11 Continued

Template (Filename)	Description
Highly Secure (`hisecws.inf`, `hisecdc.inf`)	The Highly Secure templates impose further restrictions on computers to which they are applied. Whereas the Secure templates require at least NTLM authentication, the Highly Secure templates require NTLMv2 authentication. The Secure templates enable SMB packet signing, and the Highly Secure templates also require SMB packet signing. In addition to the various extra security restrictions that are imposed by the Highly Secure templates, these templates also make several changes to group membership and the login process. All members of the Power Users group are removed from this group. In addition, only members of the Domain Admins group and the local administrative account will be allowed to be members of the local Administrators group. When the Highly Secure templates are used, it is assumed that only Windows Logo Program–compliant applications are in use. Therefore, there is no provision in place for users to use noncompliant applications because the Compatible template is not needed and the Power Users group has no members. Members of the Users group are able to use applications that are Windows Logo Program compliant. In addition, members of the Administrators group can use any application they want.
System Root (`rootsec.inf`)	This template defines the root permissions for the root of the system volume. If these permissions are changed, they can be reapplied by using this template. In addition, you can modify this template to apply the same permissions to other volumes. Explicitly configured permissions are not overwritten on child objects when you use this template.
No Terminal Server Use SID (`notssid.inf`)	This template is used on servers that are not running Windows Terminal Services. It removes all unnecessary Terminal Services security identifiers (SIDs) from the file system and registry. This, however, does not increase the security of the server.

The Security Configuration Manager is not one console or tool per se; it is actually a collection of tools and utilities that you can use to implement security solutions across a network.

The following are the components of the Security Configuration Manager:

- The Security Configuration and Analysis snap-in
- The Security Templates snap-in
- Group Policy security extensions
- The `secedit.exe` command

The Security Configuration and Analysis snap-in is an important tool in an administrator's security template toolbox. By using the Security Configuration and Analysis snap-in, you can create, configure, test, and implement security template settings for a local computer. However, this reveals its one real weakness: It can be used to work only with the settings of a local computer. You can, however, find ways to get around this limitation by using the other tools that are at your disposal, including `secedit.exe` and the security extensions to Group Policy, both of which are discussed later in this chapter.

The Security Configuration and Analysis snap-in can be used in two basic modes, as its name suggests: configuration and analysis.

You can analyze and configure the following areas by using the Security Configuration and Analysis snap-in:

- Account Policies
- Local Policies
- Event Log
- Restricted Groups
- System Services
- Registry
- File System

You can use `secedit` to perform the same functions as the Security Configuration and Analysis snap-in. In addition, it has a couple additional functions not found in the snap-in. The `secedit` command has the following top-level options available for use:

- `/analyze`
- `/configure`
- `/export`
- `/import`

- `/validate`
- `/GenerateRollback`

To analyze the current security configuration of the local computer, you would issue the `secedit.exe` command with the following syntax:

```
secedit /analyze /db FileName /cfg FileName /overwrite /log FileName
 /quiet
```

Windows Server 2003 provides the following areas in which you can enable auditing:

- Audit account logon events
- Audit account management
- Audit directory service access
- Audit logon events
- Audit object access
- Audit policy change
- Audit privilege use
- Audit process tracking
- Audit system events

The following are some of Microsoft's recommended practices for successfully implementing and maintaining a security auditing solution:

- Create an audit plan before you implement auditing.
- Collect and archive logs across the entire organization.
- Audit system events for success and failure events.
- Audit policy change events for success events.
- Audit account management events for success events.
- Audit account logon events for success events on DCs.
- Configure specific object access auditing.

The Security Configuration Wizard (SCW) is a new and more advanced security hardening tool for Windows Server 2003 SP1 and Windows Server 2003 R2. If you have servers running these latest versions of Windows Server 2003, the SCW is worth taking a look at. By default, the SCW is not installed on your Windows Server 2003 computer. Before you can work with it, you'll need to install it.

Although Windows Server 2003 provides native support for the Windows Server Update Service (WSUS) and the older Server Update Service (SUS), it does not by default include WSUS. It's easy enough, however, to acquire the WSUS installation package and get to work configuring and implementing WSUS on a network. But what, really, is WSUS? WSUS is nothing more than a locally controlled and managed Windows Update server. Instead of allowing the Automatic Updates client on your client workstations and servers to download updates directly from the Microsoft Windows Update servers, you can install and configure one or more WSUS servers on your internal network and point your client workstations and servers toward those WSUS servers.

As you might imagine, the ability to have your client workstations use an internal server for Windows Update can be a tremendous benefit to you because it means decreased bandwidth usage. As important as bandwidth savings might be, there is actually a larger benefit to be realized by implementing a WSUS solution on your internal network: the ability to approve specific updates that are to be installed on your clients. When you use Windows Update, your client computers install any available update that matches their needs, but with WSUS, you can specify which of the available updates are authorized to be pushed to the clients after you are satisfied that the update will pose no problems for the systems. This is a tremendous benefit that often goes unrealized.

The requirements to install WSUS on a Windows Server 2003 computer are as follows:

- The system partition of the server must be formatted with the NTFS file system.
- The partition on which you install WSUS must be formatted with the NTFS file system.
- The system partition must have at least 1GB of free space available.
- The partition where you install WSUS must have a minimum of 6GB of free space available; however, for best results, it is recommended that the partition being used have at least 30GB of free space available.
- The partition where WSUS setup installs the Windows SQL Server 2000 Desktop Engine (WMSDE) must have at least 2GB of free space available.
- The server must have Internet Information Services (IIS) 6.0 installed.
- The server must have the Microsoft .NET Framework 1.1 SP1 for Windows Server 2003 software installed.
- The server must have the Background Intelligent Transfer Service (BITS) 2.0 update installed.

- The Windows SQL Server 2000 Desktop Engine (WMSDE), which will be installed by the WSUS setup.

Clients to be updated by WSUS must fall into one of the following groups:

- Microsoft Windows 2000 Professional with SP3 or SP4.
- Windows 2000 Server with SP3 or SP4 or Windows 2000 Advanced Server with SP3 or SP4.
- Microsoft Windows XP Professional, with or without SP1 or SP2.
- Microsoft Windows Server 2003, Standard Edition; Windows Server 2003, Enterprise Edition; Windows Serve 2003, Datacenter Edition; or Windows Server 2003, Web Edition.

Implementing, Managing and Troubleshooting Network Access

The authentication protocols used in conjunction with Windows Server 2003 RRAS include the following:

- **PAP**—PAP uses unencrypted (plaintext) passwords for authenticating users on a PPP link.
- **SPAP**—SPAP is used to allow Shiva client computers to connect to a Windows Server 2003 server and to allow Windows 2000 client computers to connect to Shiva servers.
- **CHAP**—CHAP provides a more secure PPP authentication mechanism than PAP by negotiating encrypted authentication with Message Digest 5 (MD5).
- **MS-CHAP**—MS-CHAP is an extension of CHAP that increases CHAP's capabilities by integrating the encryption and hashing algorithms used on Windows networks.
- **MS-CHAPv2**—MS-CHAPv2 corrects several problems with the original version of MS-CHAP, including removing the support for the notoriously weak LAN Manager authentication, adding the ability for two-way authentication (which allows the client to authenticate the PPP host to which it is connecting), and adding support for much stronger cryptographic keys for the authentication process.
- **EAP**—EAP was developed in response to an increasing need for stronger authentication mechanisms for remote user access services such as remote access servers and VPNs. The number of mobile users has increased and the technical sophistication of attackers has also increased, and today user ID/password authentication is not secure

enough for many organizations. EAP provides a standard mechanism for support of additional authentication methods within PPP. These methods include token cards, one-time passwords, and public key authentication using smart cards or certificates. Unlike the user ID/password capabilities of the other PPP authentication protocols, EAP, in conjunction with external authenticators such as a smart card or token card, is not vulnerable to brute-force or dictionary password attacks.

- **RADIUS**—RADIUS is an authentication and accounting system that is used by many Internet service providers and is available in Windows Server 2003.

IAS is included as part of Microsoft Windows Server 2003, Standard Edition, Enterprise Edition, and Datacenter Edition. IAS is not included with the Web Edition of Windows Server 2003. IAS is the Microsoft implementation of the RADIUS server and proxy. Acting as a RADIUS server, IAS is commonly used to provide centralized authentication, authorization, and accounting for remote access and VPN connections. IAS can be used to forward authentication and accounting messages to other RADIUS servers, such as a central RADIUS server.

Windows Server 2003 uses three types of remote access policies to control access:

- Group policies
- Local IAS policies
- Central IAS policies

In conjunction with the remote access policy, there is also a component known as the *remote access profile*. This profile contains several variables that allow you to further refine the parameters of the remote access policy.

One of the most interesting features of Windows Server 2003 is the ability to implement packet filters. A *packet* is a portion of a message that is transferred across a network. For example, when you download Windows Server 2003 SP1, the file is broken into many smaller packets to be transmitted to your computer, and then it is reassembled after all the packets have been delivered. A packet filter acts as a crude form of firewall, permitting or denying traffic based on rules set in the filter. Packet filters work by looking at the makeup of each packet, comparing that composition to the list of filters, and then making a decision about whether to forward or drop the packet based on those rules.

Windows Server 2003 supports three types of routing interfaces:

- LAN interfaces
- Demand-dial interfaces
- IP-in-IP tunnel interfaces

You typically see demand-dial routing used in two instances: for redundant network links and for small office connections.

The Windows Server 2003 demand-dial router supports several types of connections, including the following:

- **Modem or ISDN connection**—With this type of configuration, the configured phone number is dialed.
- **VPN connection**—With this type of configuration, the configured host or IP address is used to establish either a PPTP or IPSec connection.
- **Direct serial or direct parallel port connection**—With this type of configuration, a direct connection is made between the calling router and the answering router over the serial port or parallel port. (This is almost never used outside a lab/test environment.)

There are two common types of VPNs that you will encounter: remote access VPNs and site-to-site VPNs. Windows Server 2003 supports two VPN protocols: PPTP and L2TP:

- PPTP uses the proprietary MPPE protocol to encrypt the link between the VPN client and server, and it uses the Generic Routing Encapsulation (GRE) protocol for the encapsulation of the encrypted PPTP data in the PPP frame, which can be an IP datagram, an IPX datagram, or a NetBEUI frame. One of the key benefits of PPTP is that because Microsoft helped develop it, it has been bundled with all current versions of Microsoft's operating systems. This caused some problems because some security experts felt that PPTP was not secure enough to be used for Internet-based VPN connections, but Windows Server 2003 contains an updated version of PPTP that is secure.
- L2TP is a combination of the best features of PPTP and the Layer 2 Forwarding (L2F) protocol. The L2F protocol was an early competing protocol for PPTP that was developed by Cisco Systems. Like PPTP, L2TP was designed as an extension of PPP to allow PPP to be tunneled through an IP network. However, L2TP defines its own tunneling protocol, based on L2F. L2TP support was first included in a Microsoft server product with the release of Windows 2000 Server, and it continues to be supported in Windows Server 2003. Prior to Windows 2000, PPTP was the only supported VPN protocol in the Windows operating system family. L2TP uses one of the IPSec protocols, Encapsulating Security Payload (ESP), for encryption. For this reason, L2TP under Windows Server 2003 is also known as L2TP/IPSec. The use of IPSec as the encryption mechanism allows L2TP/IPSec to utilize third-party encryption hardware to offload the encryption functions of the VPN connections from the VPN server.

Implementing, Managing, and Troubleshooting Routing

Routing is the process of forwarding a packet based on the destination IP address. Routing occurs at a sending TCP/IP host, which is known as host routing, and at an IP router, which is known as router routing.

For the host to send a packet to its destination via the router, it must first determine the address of the router to which to send the packet. This can be accomplished using one of the following methods:

- The default gateway address is determined and then the local ARP cache is queried to identify the physical address to be used to reach the desired router.
- An ICMP redirect message is sent by an IP router to the sending host, informing it of a better route to a destination host. The better route becomes a host route in the routing table.
- A TCP/IP host can "listen" to the routing protocol traffic used by routers. This is known as RIP listening or passive RIP.

With router routing, several variables determine the router to which to forward the packet. These variables include each of the network paths to the destination host, including the number of hops and the cost of each hop. Windows Server 2003 provides router routing through RRAS.

Routing tables can be manually configured (static) or created through the use of a dynamic routing protocol. Two dynamic routing protocols that are provided with Windows Server 2003 are RIP and OSPF.

Routing can employ either distance-vector routing or link-state routing technologies. The main differences between the two routing protocols are as follows:

- The routing information that is exchanged
- How the information is exchanged
- How quickly the internetwork can recover from a downed link or a downed router

Distance-vector routing is the oldest and most common routing algorithm. Distance-vector routers build their routing information tables based on information received from other routers.

Link-state routing protocols exchange information only about the specific routes that have changed. Routers using link-state routing protocols learn about their network environment by "meeting" their neighboring routers.

RIP is a distance-vector protocol that uses hop count as its metric for measuring the number of routers that must be crossed to reach the desired network. Following are some details about RIP:

- RIP is limited to 15 router hops, with 16 hops being infinity. What does this mean? Picture a LAN with a PC that needs to communicate with a server on another LAN that is 15 routers away. The routers keep a list of which subnets are no more than 15 routers away, and if you try to expand the network past the sixteenth router, communication does not happen. Remember: You have a 15-hop minimum between networks, and the sixteenth hop is deemed infinity.
- RIP has problems with subnetted networks. In Chapter 2, "Implementing, Managing, and Troubleshooting DHCP," we briefly covered how subnetted networks should appear in your design. RIP was created and deployed before networks were subnetted to the degree that they are today, and because they have no direct support for RIP, your networks cannot support it. It really comes down to the information that each router sends to the others and what that packet contains. If the routing update does not contain a field in the packet to allow for subnetted networks, it does not carry over the information you may need it to carry over. In other words, the RIP protocol is configured to look at the prefix of the IP address in the routing update and know whether it's A, B, or C—and nothing more. If you subnet, your subnet will not be supported because RIP understands only that if a packet with an IP address of 10.0.0.1 comes in, it's automatically assigned a subnet of 255.0.0.0, even if you have it subnetted down to 255.255.255.0.
- RIP is bandwidth intensive, and although that isn't a problem on most networks, a network with small WAN links (such as 32KB Frame Relay link) could feel the effect of constant broadcasts every 30 seconds, especially if the routing table is large. If the routing table is too large, more than one update could be sent every 30 seconds, making RIP even more bandwidth intensive. For the 70-291 exam, remember that, by default, RIP broadcasts to its neighbors every 30 seconds. These broadcasts contain lists of networks and subnets it can reach.
- RIP is not very secure. RIP contains no security features or configurable parameters to make it secure. Other protocols used today have configurable parameters to make them more secure; however, RIP does not contain any solution to make it secure by default.

RIP2, or RIP version 2, was created for RIP users to overcome problems with security. This version adds an option for authentication to the RIP packet. It also adds support for subnetted networks and allows for variable length subnetted networks to be passed through routing updates.

OSPF is a link-state routing protocol that functions by sending LSAs to all other routers within the same hierarchical area. OSPF has the following features:

- Better convergence than RIP.
- Calculates routes that are always loop free.
- Sends updates only when the routing changes, rather than sending routing updates periodically. This makes better use of bandwidth.
- Allows for logical definition of networks where routers can be divided into areas.
- Designed to advertise the subnet mask with the network. OSPF supports VLSMs, disjointed subnets, and supernetting.
- Allows for routing authentication using different methods of password authentication.
- Routes outside the OSPF autonomous system are advertised within the autonomous system so that OSPF routers can calculate the least-cost route to external networks.

OSPF divides the network (what it considers a routing domain) into areas. An area is a subdivision of the entire network and is given a label. Area 0 (zero) is considered the backbone of an OSPF network. If your network is small enough, you can set up the entire network to use Area 0, which is very important. For example, if the network becomes more subdivided (say you have three areas, including Area 0), you would need to know that if all traffic must travel between areas, the packets are first routed to the backbone, or Area 0. When you plan a network this way, the design keeps subnets consolidated to areas, thus reducing the size of the link-state database that is updated on every router in an OSPF network. This keeps your OSPF network running optimally.

The following is some important information to remember about OSPF:

- OSPF sends out hello packets to each adjacent router connected to the network. OSPF uses hello packets to verify that the network is always ready to work as advertised. These hellos are sent out of every router interface every 10 seconds, but they are so small in size that they do not affect your available bandwidth.
- Link-state advertisements can help in a situation in which a router does not hear from its neighboring router for more than 40 seconds. In such a situation, the router sends out LSAs, marking the other router as down so that all the other routers can adjust their tables with the change.

- Hellos can be adjusted. A hello has a timer value that, when configured properly throughout the OSPF network, allows proper and accurate communications to take place. It is important to know that if a hello timer is misconfigured (not all timers are identical), problems can occur. Make sure that when you plan an OSPF network, you ensure that all the hello timers match. They must all be consistent across all routers on a network segment.
- Because LSAs age, it is important to get a refreshed routing table (or database) from a neighboring router just in case anything has changed. If nothing has changed on a particular router for 30 minutes, the router flushes its information and seeks an updated database from its adjacent routers. This means that the network reconverges every 30 minutes—a far cry from the forced reconvergence in a RIP network. That forced reconvergence is every 30 seconds!

Three forms of traffic traverse a network:

- **Unicast**—When a single node on the network sends data to its destination node under one single packet, it knows where the destination node is and gets the data to it. Remember "uni" as being a single transmission.
- **Broadcast**—Broadcasting (think of the word "broad") occurs when the destination is not known or cannot be found. In this situation, the node (which needs to find the destination node) sends out packets to all nodes on the network segment to see whether it can find its destination node. This process leads to increased traffic, collisions on hubbed networks, and so on. Broadcasts are at times a necessary evil, but most of the time, you should prevent them from happening often or control their number. Basically, broadcast traffic adds overhead to your network and its devices by creating packets that the majority of hosts shouldn't ever see in the first place.
- **Multicast**—Multicast is the happy medium, but it still can cause problems. A multicast transmission is based on a group. In simple terms, think of 20 nodes on a network, 5 of which need to communicate at all times and 15 of which do not need to ever know what the other 5 are doing. Say these nodes are OSPF routers. OSPF routers send out updates to each other via a multicast, so you might ask, "What about devices that do not need to know this information?" If you use a multicast address, such as 224.0.0.5 for OSPF-based networks, only those devices will listen for transmissions from other nodes using this service. This reduces the problems caused by broadcast traffic and enables you to cause one sender to get information to multiple (group) nodes without that message going to every node on the network. Consequently, multicasting is good, but as with any other technology, it can cause problems or require an advanced level of administration to make it work properly.

Implementing, Managing, and Troubleshooting IPSec to Secure Network Traffic

The following are the standard features of the Windows Server 2003 IPSec implementation:

- IPSec in Windows Server 2003 is policy based. Thus, it cannot be configured without an IPSec policy being in place. The IPSec policy allows an administrator to more easily apply settings to groups of objects, such as computers or users.
- IPSec on Windows Server 2003 can use Kerberos v5, a digital certificate, or a shared secret (string) for user authentication.
- IPSec mutually authenticates computers prior to any data being exchanged.
- IPSec establishes a security association (SA) between the two host computers involved in the data transfer. An SA is the collection of a policy and keys, which define the rules for security settings.
- IPSec encrypts data using Data Encryption Standard (DES) or Triple DES (3DES).
- IPSec uses the MD5 or SHA1 algorithm for data hashing.
- IPSec is invisible to users. IPSec operates at the network level of the Open System Interface (OSI) model; therefore, users and applications do not directly interact with the protocol. After an IPSec tunnel has been created, users can connect to applications and services as if they were on the local network and not on the other side of a public network.

The IPSec Authentication Header (AH) provides three services as part of the IPSec protocol. First (as its name might suggest), AH authenticates the entire packet. Second, it ensures data integrity. Third, it prevents any replaying of the packet by a third party who might be trying to penetrate the IPSec tunnel. One service AH doesn't provide is payload encryption. AH protects your data from modification, but an attacker who is snooping the network would still be able to read the data. To prevent the modification of the data, AH uses two hashing algorithms to "sign" the packet for integrity:

- The Message Digest 5 (MD5) algorithm applies the hashing function to the data in four passes.
- The Secure Hash Algorithm 1 (SHA-1) is closely modeled after MD5. SHA-1 uses 79 32-bit constants during the computation of the hash value, which results in a 160-bit key. Because SHA-1 has a longer key length, it is considered more secure than MD5.

Encapsulating Security Protocol (ESP) provides confidentiality in addition to authentication, integrity, and anti-replay. This portion of the IPSec protocol encrypts the data contents of the packet. The format of the ESP varies, depending on the type and mode of encryption being utilized. ESP can be used alone or in combination with AH.

Policies allow you to quickly and easily configure IPSec based on the settings required within your organization. Windows Server 2003 comes with the following three preconfigured IPSec policies that may or may not meet your needs:

- **Client (Respond Only)**—This policy requires IPSec-provided security only when another computer requests it. This policy allows the computer to attempt unsecured communications first and switch to IPSec-secured communications if requested. This policy contains the default response rule, which creates dynamic IPSec filters for inbound and outbound traffic. The filters are based on the requested protocol and the port traffic for the communication that is being secured. This policy, which can be used on workstations and servers alike, provides the minimum amount of IPSec security.

- **Server (Request Security)**—This policy requests security from the other computer and allows unsecured communication with computers that are not IPSec-aware. The computer accepts inbound unsecured traffic, but always attempts to secure further communications by requesting IPSec security from the sending computer. If the other computer is not IPSec-enabled, the entire communication is allowed to be unsecured. This policy, which can be used on workstations and servers alike, provides a medium level of IPSec security. If desired, you can opt to use this policy on a workstation computer as well.

- **Secure Server (Require Security)**—This policy is implemented on computers that require highly secure communications. These computers include servers transmitting sensitive data. The filters in this policy require all outbound communication to be secured, allowing only the initial inbound communication request to be unsecured. This policy has a rule to require security for all IP traffic, a rule to permit ICMP traffic, and the default response rule to respond to requests for security from other computers. This policy, typically used only on servers, provides the highest level of IPSec security on a network. This policy can also be used on workstation computers if you want. Computers that are not IPSec-enabled cannot establish any communications with computers using this policy. This policy can also be used on a workstation if desired.

Filter actions define the type of security and methods by which security is established. The default methods are Permit, Block, and Negotiate Security. The Permit option passes the traffic without the requirement for security. This action is appropriate if you never want to secure traffic to which a rule applies. The Block action silently blocks all traffic from computers specified in the IP filter list. The Negotiate Security action specifies that the computer is to use a list of security methods to negotiate the appropriate security for the communication.

The IP Security Monitor snap-in is divided into three major areas: the Active Policy node, the Main Mode node, and the Quick Mode node. Table 12 explains each of the information items shown in the Active Policy node of the IP Security Monitor snap-in. The Active Policy is the IPSec policy that is currently in effect on the computer.

TABLE 12 Active Policy Node Items

Item	Description
Policy Name	Specifies the name of the active IPSec policy.
Description	Describes the active IPSec policy.
Policy Last Modified	Provides the date and the time that the active IPSec policy was modified.
Policy Store	Provides the storage location for the active IPSec policy. For a local policy, it reads Local Store, and for a domain policy, it reads Domain Store.
Policy Path	Applies only to domain policies and provides the LDAP path to the active IPSec policy.
Organizational Unit	Applies only to domain policies and lists the organizational unit to which the group policy object (GPO) is applied.
Group Policy Object Name	Applies only to domain policies and lists the GPO to which the active IPSec policy is applied.

Table 13 explains each of the information items shown in the Statistics folder in the Main Mode node of the IP Security Monitor snap-in. The Main Mode SA, also known as the ISAKMP SA, is used to protect the IPSec security negotiations.

TABLE 13 Main Mode (Internet Key Exchange) Statistics

Statistic	Description
Active Acquire	Specifies a request by the IPSec policy to have IKE perform a task. This number includes all outstanding and queued requests and is typically 1. Under heavy loading, this number increases.
Active Receive	Displays the number of IKE messages that have been received and are queued for processing.
Acquire Failures	Displays the number of times that an acquire has failed.
Receive Failures	Displays the number of times that errors have occurred in receiving IKE messages.
Send Failures	Displays the number of times that errors have occurred in sending IKE messages.

TABLE 13 Continued

Statistic	Description
Acquire Heap Size	Displays the number of entries in the acquire heap, which stores active acquires. This number increases with heavy loading and decreases as the heap is cleared.
Receive Heap Size	Displays the number of entries in the IKE receive buffers for incoming IKE messages.
Authentication Failures	Displays the total number of identity authentication failures that have occurred during Main Mode negotiation. This is a very useful indicator to determine whether the authentication methods do not match between two computers attempting communications.
Negotiation Failures	Displays the total number of negotiation failures that occurred during Main Mode or Quick Mode negotiation. This is a useful statistic to determine whether security and/or authentication methods do not match between two computers attempting communications.
Invalid Cookies Received	Specifies a value contained in a received IKE message that is used by IKE to find the state of an active Main Mode. If a cookie in a received IKE message cannot be matched with an active Main Mode, it is invalid.
Total Acquire	Displays the total number of requests submitted by IKE to the IPSec driver to establish an SA for securing traffic.
Total Get SPI	Displays the total number of requests submitted by IKE to the IPSec driver to obtain a unique Security Parameters Index (SPI).
Key Additions	Displays the number of outbound Quick Mode SAs added by IKE to the IPSec driver.
Key Updates	Displays the number of inbound Quick Mode SAs added by IKE to the IPSec driver.
Get SPI Failures	Displays the number of requests submitted by IKE to the IPSec driver to obtain a unique SPI that have failed.
Key Addition Failures	Displays the number of outbound Quick Mode SA addition requests submitted by IKE to the IPSec driver that have failed.
Key Update Failures	Displays the number of inbound Quick Mode SA addition requests submitted by IKE to the IPSec driver that have failed.
ISADB List Size	Displays the number of Main Mode state entries, including negotiated Main Modes, Main Modes in progress, and Main Modes that have failed and have not yet been deleted.
Connection List Size	Displays the number of Quick Mode state entries. This number indicates the load placed on the computer.
IKE Main Mode	Displays the total number of successful SAs created during Main Mode negotiations.

(continues)

TABLE 13 Continued

Statistic	Description
IKE Quick Mode	Displays the total number of successful SAs created during Quick Mode negotiations. There are typically multiple Quick Mode SAs created for each Main Mode SA; thus, this value may not necessarily match that of the Main Mode.
Soft Associations	Displays the total number of negotiations that resulted in the use of unsecured traffic (also known as *soft SAs*). Typically this is an indication of SAs formed with computers that do not support IPSec or were not able to negotiate successful IPSec connections. This can be an indication of mismatched security and authentication settings.
Invalid Packets Received	Displays the number of received IKE messages that were invalid. Most commonly, invalid IKE messages are a result of retransmitted IKE messages or unmatched shared keys between the communicating computers.

Table 14 explains each of the information items shown in the Statistics folder in the Quick Mode node of the IP Security Monitor snap-in. The Quick Mode SAs, also known as the IPSec SAs, are those security associations that have been created to protect the data sent between computers communicating securely using IPSec.

TABLE 14 Quick Mode (IPSec) Statistics

Statistic	Description
Active Security Associations	Displays the number of active IPSec SAs.
Offloaded Security Associations	Displays the number of active IPSec SAs that have been offloaded to hardware.
Pending Key Operations	Displays the number of IPSec key operations that are in progress.
Key Additions	Displays the total number of successful IPSec SA negotiations.
Key Deletions	Displays the number of key deletions for IPSec SAs.
Re-Keys	Displays the number of rekey operations for IPSec SAs.
Active Tunnels	Displays the number of active IPSec tunnels.
Bad SPI Packets	Displays the total number of packets for which the SPI was incorrect. SPIs are used to match inbound packets with SAs. If the SPI is incorrect, the inbound SA may have expired. If rekeying intervals are set very short, this number is likely to increase rapidly. Under normal conditions, a bad SPI packet does not mean that IPSec is failing because SAs expire normally.
Packets Not Decrypted	Displays the total number of packets that were not decrypted successfully. This may indicate that a packet has arrived for which the SA has previously expired. When the SA expires, the session key used to decrypt packets is removed. By itself, this does not indicate that IPSec is failing.

TABLE 14 Continued

Statistic	Description
Packets Not Authenticated	Displays the total number of packets for which data could not be verified, meaning that the integrity hash verification failed. Most commonly this is a result of an expired SA.
Packets with Replay Detection	Displays the total number of packets that contained a valid Sequence Number field.
Confidential Bytes Sent	Displays the total number of bytes sent using the ESP protocol.
Confidential Bytes Received	Displays the total number of bytes received using the ESP protocol.
Authenticated Bytes Sent	Displays the total number of bytes sent using the AH protocol.
Authenticated Bytes Received	Displays the total number of bytes received using the AH protocol.
Transport Bytes Sent	Displays the total number of bytes sent using IPSec transport mode.
Transport Bytes Received	Displays the total number of bytes received using IPSec transport mode.
Bytes Sent in Tunnels	Displays the total number of bytes sent using IPSec tunnel mode.
Bytes Received in Tunnels	Displays the total number of bytes received using IPSec tunnel mode.
Offloaded Bytes Sent	Displays the total number of bytes sent using hardware offload.
Offloaded Bytes Received	Displays the total number of bytes received using hardware offload.

Configuring the IP Security Monitor hasn't changed much since Windows 2000, except that the IP Security Monitor is now an MMC snap-in. You can open the IP Security Monitor properties for any server listed in the IP Security Monitor node by right-clicking it and selecting Properties from the context menu. You have the option to change the refresh interval for the display of the IP Security Monitor statistics and to decide whether you want to enable DNS name resolution, which comes into play when you're examining the SAs that are formed.

If you have problems with IPSec, you should first verify that any routers or firewalls that traffic may be passing through are configured to support IPSec traffic. You need to allow the following traffic:

- Protocol ID 50 and 51 or ESP and AH traffic
- UDP port 500 for IPSec negotiation traffic

Some other basic problems and troubleshooting tips for them are outlined here:

- **You are not able to establish any communications with a computer**—In this case, you should first verify that basic network connectivity exists between the computers in question by using the `ping` command. You should also ensure that all required network services, such as DHCP and DNS, are operating properly for both computers.

- **You are not able to establish any communications with a computer**—This may be a result of a computer having been removed from the domain. Whatever the cause, IPSec communications will fail.
- **Communications are occurring, but not as expected**—You need to ensure that you have the correct (and compatible) IPSec policies assigned on both computers.
- **No hard associations are being formed**—If there are currently soft associations in place, a hard association will not be formed. You need to completely stop all communications between the computers for approximately 5–10 minutes to allow the soft associations to time out. The easiest way to do this is to disable the network connection. After you have allowed the soft association to time out, you should check to see that a hard association has been formed. If a hard association still has not been formed, you need to examine the IPSec policy to verify that unsecured communications are not allowed.
- **IPSec communications are failing after you configure a digital certificate for authentication**—You must make sure that the required digital certificate is installed on the computers that are attempting to communicate by using that IPSec policy. This can also be a result of specifying an incorrect Certificate Authority (CA).
- **Some computers can create IPSec connections and some cannot**—This is most likely caused by not having the same IPSec policy applied to all the computers. If you are intentionally using different policies, you need to ensure that they share at least one common authentication and security method.

You should also be aware that IPSec-related problems can be found in the security log. You can view IKE events (negotiation successes and negotiation failures) by enabling success and/or failure auditing for the Audit Logon Events audit policy for the domain or the local computer. The IKE event category is also used for the auditing of user logon events in other services as well, but you can disable this by editing the registry. For more information on configuring and implementing auditing, refer to Chapter 5, "Implementing, Managing, and Maintaining Network Security."

When success and/or failure auditing for the Audit Logon Events audit policy is enabled, IPSec records the success and/or failure of each Main Mode and Quick Mode negotiation. The establishment and termination of each negotiation is logged as a separate event for easier analysis and troubleshooting. Be aware, however, that when you enable audit logon events, the security log will likely quickly fill up with IKE events unless you opt to disable auditing of those events through registry editing.

Although there are no default tools provided in Windows Server 2003 that allow you to monitor and manipulate Kerberos tickets, two *Windows Server 2003 Resource Kit* tools are available:

- **`kerbtray.exe`**—You can use the `kerbtray.exe` utility to view cached Kerberos tickets for the current computer from within the Windows GUI.
- **`klist.exe`**—The `klist.exe` utility is a command-line tool that is similar to `kerbtray.exe`. `klist.exe` allows you to view and delete cached Kerberos tickets.

You can download the *Windows Server 2003 Resource Kit* tools from www.microsoft.com/downloads if you search for "Windows Server 2003 Resource Kit Tools."

Maintaining and Troubleshooting a Network Infrastructure

Network Monitor is made up of two primary components: Network Monitor and the Network Monitor driver.

Like most other configuration and management tools in Windows Server 2003, you can run the Network Monitor from the command line. This is a more difficult and advanced method of performing captures, but it offers the advantage of letting you script commands to be executed on multiple computers with little effort. The basic syntax of using the Network Monitor (`netmon`) from the command line is presented here and explained in more detail in Table 15.

```
start netmon [/net Number] [/capturefilter Path] [/displayfilter Path]
➥ [/buffersize Number]
➥ [/quickfilter {ATM | ETHERNET | IP | IPX | VINES | TOKENRING | FDDI},
➥ Address] [/quickfiltername FilterName] [/autostart] [/autostop]
```

TABLE 15 `netmon` Command-Line Switches

Switch	Description
`/net` *`Number`*	Allows you to specify the number of the network from which you want to capture data. You can specify any network segment to which the computer is connected.
`/capturefilter` *`Path`*	Allows you to specify a saved capture filter to be used. Can be abbreviated as `/cf` *`Path`*.
`/displayfilter` *`Path`*	Allows you to specify a display filter to be used. Can be abbreviated as `/df` *`Path`*.
`/buffersize` *`Number`*	Allows you to specify the size (in megabytes) of the capture buffer.

(continues)

TABLE 15 Continued

Switch	Description
`/quickfilter {ATM	ETHERNET	IP	IPX	VINES	TOKENRING	FDDI}, Address`	Specifies that only frames of a particular type and from a particular address should be captured. You are allowed to specify up to three types at one time. Can be abbreviated as `/qf {ATM	ETHERNET	IP	IPX	VINES	TOKENRING	FDDI}, Address`.
`/quickfiltername` *`FilterName`*	Allows you to specify the name of the filter you use with the `/quickfilter` command. Can be abbreviated as `/qfn` *`FilterName`* and is not used if no `/quickfilter` options are specified.
`/autostart`	Instructs Network Monitor to begin capturing data at interface startup.
`/autostop`	Instructs Network Monitor to stop capturing data when the capture buffer is full.

The System Monitor can be used to monitor and create a baseline of network interface statistics.

The following counters are listed under the Network Interface performance object:

- Bytes Received/sec
- Bytes Sent/sec
- Bytes Total/sec
- Current Bandwidth
- Output Queue Length
- Packets Outbound Discarded
- Packets Outbound Errors
- Packets Received Discarded
- Packets Received Errors
- Packets Received Non-Unicast/sec
- Packets Received Unicast/sec
- Packets Received Unknown
- Packets Received/sec
- Packets Sent Unicast/sec
- Packets Sent/sec
- Packets/sec

The following are some of the most common causes of bottlenecks that you might encounter while troubleshooting a network:

- The current level of provided resources is inadequate, thus requiring additional or upgraded resources to be added to the network.
- The available resources are not being utilized evenly, thus requiring that some form of load balancing be implemented.
- An available resource is malfunctioning or stopped and needs to be repaired or restarted.
- An available resource is incorrectly configured, thus requiring a configuration correction.

The following are some basic network configuration tips that you can check while troubleshooting and correcting network-related problems:

- As often as possible, ensure that resources are located on the same physical subnet as the users using the resource.
- Uninstall or unbind network protocols that are not in use.
- Configure the network protocol binding order to place the most commonly used protocols higher on the list.
- Use multiple network adapters in high-use servers to increase effective network throughput.

When creating a Counter Log, you can choose what log file format you want to use, as detailed in Table 16.

TABLE 16 Counter Log File Format Options

Option	Description
Text File (Comma Delimited)	This option defines a comma-delimited log file (with a `.csv` extension).
Text File (Tab Delimited)	This option defines a tab-delimited log file (with a `.tsv` extension).
Binary File	This option defines a sequential, binary-format log file (with a `.blg` extension). You should use this file format if you want to be able to record data instances that are intermittent—that is, data instances that stop and resume after the log has begun running. Only binary file formats can accommodate instances that are not persistent throughout the duration of the log.
Binary Circular File	This option defines a circular, binary-format log file (with a `.blg` extension). You should use this file format to continuously record data to the same log file, overwriting previous records with new data when the file reaches its maximum size.

When creating a Counter Log, you can also choose what numbering system will be used, as detailed in Table 17.

TABLE 17 Counter Log Numbering Systems

System	Example
nnnnnn	`Network Adapter Performance_000007.blg`
mmddhh	`Network Adapter Performance_042011.blg`
mmddhhmm	`Network Adapter Performance_04201126.blg`
yyyyddd	`Network Adapter Performance_2003111.blg`
yyyymm	`Network Adapter Performance_200304.blg`
yyyymmdd	`Network Adapter Performance_20030420.blg`
yyyymmddhh	`Network Adapter Performance_2003042011.blg`

For troubleshooting connectivity issues, the `pathping` command acts as the equivalent of the `tracert` command by allowing you to identify which routers are in the path that the packets are taking. It also acts as the equivalent of the `ping` command by sending `ping` requests to all the routers over a specified time period and then computing statistics based on the packets returned from each router. `pathping` displays the amount of packet loss at each router or link, allowing you to determine which routers and links (subnets) might be causes of connectivity troubles.

This is the basic syntax of the `pathping` command:

```
pathping [-g host-list] [-h maximum_hops] [-i address] [-n]
➥ [-p period] [-q num_queries] [-w timeout] [-4] [-6] target_name
```

Table 18 explains the switches of the `pathping` command.

TABLE 18 `pathping` Switches

Switch	Description
`-g` *`host-list`*	Specifies that Echo Request messages are to use the Loose Source Route option in the IP header with the set of intermediate destinations specified in *`HostList`*. Successive intermediate destinations can be separated by one or multiple routers. *`HostList`* is a series of IP addresses (in dotted-decimal notation), separated by spaces.
`-h` *`maximum hops`*	Specifies the maximum number of hops in the path to search for the target. The default is 30 hops.
`-i` *`address`*	Specifies the source address.
`-n`	Specifies that addresses are not to be resolved to hostnames.
`-p` *`period`*	Specifies the number of milliseconds to wait between consecutive `ping`s. The default is 250 milliseconds.

TABLE 18 Continued

Switch	Description
`-q` *`num queries`*	Specifies the number of Echo Request messages sent to each router in the path. The default is 100.
`-w` *`timeout`*	Specifies the number of milliseconds to wait for each reply. The default is 3,000 milliseconds.
`-4`	Specifies that `pathping` use IPv4 only.
`-6`	Specifies that `pathping` use IPv6 only.
`Target name`	Specifies the destination, either by IP address or hostname.

Server services can be configured with recovery options for the first, second, and all subsequent failure events the service experiences. These are the available options:

- **Take No Action**—No recovery actions will be taken if the service fails.
- **Restart the Service**—The service will stop and then start again.
- **Run a Program**—A program, script, or batch file can be run.
- **Restart the Computer**

Practice Exam

Implementing, Managing, and Maintaining a Microsoft Windows Server 2003 Network Infrastructure

This practice exam consists of 65 questions that are meant to help you assess what you have learned from this *Exam Prep*. It also includes questions that are representative of what you should expect on the actual exam. You will find that the questions here are mostly multiple choice. Some of the question forms that you might see on the actual exam, such as those that appear with simulations, are difficult or impossible to implement in book form because of the limitations of pencil-and-paper testing. Still, this practice exam should help you find out how well you understood the material presented in this *Exam Prep* and give you some experience with Microsoft-style questions.

When you take the exam, you should treat it as you would the real exam: Time yourself (about 90–120 minutes), answer each question carefully, and mark the questions you want to go back and double-check. The answers and their explanations appear at the end of the practice exam.

After you have taken this exam, you should follow up with Que Certification's exclusive MeasureUp test engine that accompanies this book. For more information, see Appendix A, "Accessing Your Free MeasureUp Practice Test—Including Networking Simulations!," and Appendix B, "MeasureUp's Product Features."

Exam Questions

1. You are part of the team of systems administrators for Sunshine Networks. Your task is to segment the Class C IP address into three subnets. You have been assigned the IP address 210.115.64.0. You must allow for the number of networks to increase. The maximum number of hosts per subnet will never surpass 14 hosts. What subnet mask would allow you to segment the network and allow for the required growth?

   ❍ **A.** 255.255.255.224

   ❍ **B.** 255.255.255.240

   ❍ **C.** 255.255.255.248

   ❍ **D.** 255.255.255.0

2. You are the network administrator for JMS Technologies. You have a network with 100 computers running Windows XP Professional and 3 computers running Windows Server 2003. One of the servers is a DC, one is providing DHCP services, and the third is providing DNS services. When a Windows XP Professional client computer obtains an IP address from the DHCP server, what registers the computer's hostname with the DNS server?

   ❍ **A.** The client computer

   ❍ **B.** The DHCP server

   ❍ **C.** The WINS server

   ❍ **D.** Active Directory

3. You are the systems administrator for a branch office of Little Faith Enterprises, a multinational pharmaceutical company. The office network consists of 3 Windows Server 2003 servers and 50 workstations running Windows XP Professional. In order to improve Internet DNS resolution, you have installed DNS on one of the Windows Server 2003 servers and configured it as a caching-only DNS server. Where does the new DNS server store its zone files?

   ❍ **A.** The zone files are stored in the server's `%systemroot%\system32\etc\DNS` directory.

   ❍ **B.** The zone files are stored in the server's RAM.

   ❍ **C.** The zone files are stored in Active Directory.

   ❍ **D.** Caching-only servers do not have any zone information.

4. You are the administrator of a large Windows Server 2003 Active Directory network. The network consists of 1,500 Windows Server 2003 servers spread over 150 OUs that have approximately 10 servers each. You have just finished creating a customized security template that specifies the Account Policies and Audit Policy settings that are required by your organization's corporate policy for specific departments. What is the best way for you to apply this template to only the Sales, Marketing, Production, and Engineering OUs?

   ❍ **A.** Import the security template at the domain level into a GPO.

   ❍ **B.** Import the security template into each required OU by using a GPO.

   ❍ **C.** Script the `secedit.exe` command to apply the security template to the required computers.

   ❍ **D.** Manually apply the security template to each of the computers.

5. You are the systems administrator for Sunshine Networks, a home-office network equipment manufacturer. The network consists of 75 locations interconnected with Windows Server 2003 servers running RRAS. Business has been very good, and you have recently added a number of segments to the network in several of the offices. You have noticed lately that you are receiving an increased number of "host unreachable" error messages. You believe that your routing tables are inaccurate. What should you enable in the Windows Server 2003 Routing and Remote Access console to prevent routing loops and count-to-infinity problems?

   ❍ **A.** Distance-vector routing

   ❍ **B.** Split horizon

   ❍ **C.** Poison reverse

   ❍ **D.** Topological database

6. You are a systems administrator for the RollUp YoYo company. The network consists of 6 Windows Server 2003 servers running all network services. You have 200 desktop computers running Windows XP Professional on the LAN, and you have just purchased 30 laptops that need to be able to dial in to the network at night. You configure and install RRAS on one of the Windows Server 2003 servers. This server is a member of the production Active Directory domain operating at the Windows Server 2003 domain functional level. The new laptop users are unable to connect remotely. Which of the following is the most likely problem?

   ❍ **A.** Windows Server 2003 RRAS does not support dial-in from a Windows XP system.

   ❍ **B.** The Windows Server 2003 running RRAS has conflicting remote access policies, and the first one that is applied to the remote users prevents them from accessing the data.

   ❍ **C.** You did not enable MS-CHAP as the default authentication protocol.

   ❍ **D.** You did not modify the default dial-in policy, which restricts access unless it is modified.

7. You are in the process of configuring a counter log to create a baseline log for a new Windows Server 2003 computer that you are placing on the production network. You have configured the counter log to start and stop automatically each day. You now need to configure it so that the resulting log files will be easily identified by the date and time that they were created. Which log numbering style should you use to accomplish this?

❍ **A.** *nnnnnn*

❍ **B.** *yyyymmddhh*

❍ **C.** *yyyymm*

❍ **D.** *mmddhhmm*

8. As the administrator for a small legal firm, you are in the process of converting some IP addresses from decimal to binary. What would be the binary value of 209.168.241.158?

❍ **A.** 11010001.10101000.11110001.10011110

❍ **B.** 11001001.10101000.11110001.10011110

❍ **C.** 11010001.10101000.11101001.10011110

❍ **D.** 11010001.10101010.11110001.10011110

9. You are the systems administrator for Long Beach Networks. Your network contains 240 computers running Windows 2000 Professional and 225 computers running Windows XP Professional and uses Class C IP addresses. All the computers are located on the same network segment. Lynne, your supervisor, has asked you to automate the process of assigning IP addresses. What do you need to do?

❍ **A.** You need to install DHCP and configure DNS integration.

❍ **B.** You need to install DHCP and configure a scope.

❍ **C.** You need to install DHCP and configure a superscope.

❍ **D.** You need to install DHCP and configure BOOTP.

10. You are the systems administrator for Mount Abora Consulting, a small computer training company. The IT Department has decided to install a Windows Server 2003 server as a primary DNS server to replace the one that is currently supplied by an ISP. The network currently consists of 300 Windows 2000 Professional computers. You need to ensure that your users will be able to resolve both hostnames and IP addresses. What type of zones do you need to configure? (Choose two.)

❍ **A.** A forward lookup zone

❍ **B.** A stub zone

❍ **C.** A reverse lookup zone

❍ **D.** A delegated zone

11. You are the systems administrator of the Gidget's Widgets, LLC, corporate network. You have instructed Andrea, your assistant administrator, to configure file access auditing for all files in the CorpDocs folder on the file server. In which section of the Group Policy Editor will Andrea find the auditing options?

❍ **A.** Account Policies

❍ **B.** Local Policies

❍ **C.** Restricted Groups

❍ **D.** File System

12. You are the WAN administrator for IVS Technologies. The company network consists of 10 branch offices, in a hub-and-spoke architecture. There are no redundant connections. You have decided to use RIP as the network routing protocol, but your manager has questions. He understands the benefits of RIP, although he wants to understand the drawbacks as well before he approves your funding. Which of the following is the major disadvantage of using RIP as the network routing protocol?

❍ **A.** High cost of software

❍ **B.** Low overhead on the network

❍ **C.** Count-to-infinity problem

❍ **D.** A maximum of only 12 hops

13. You are the lead technician for Good Deal Enterprises, a Microsoft-certified training center. You are in the process of training Mary, a new administrator, to take over your administrative duties on the corporate network. The network consists of 16 training rooms with 30 PCs each, running a mix of Windows 2000 Professional and Windows XP Professional, as well as 16 Windows Server 2003 servers, which provide all network services. You are working with Mary on a remote access problem, and she wants to check the network to see if the policies have been deleted. Where should you tell her to look for these policies?

❍ **A.** Remote access policies are stored in the user properties in Active Directory.

❍ **B.** Remote access policies are stored in the computer properties in Active Directory.

❍ **C.** Remote access policies are stored on the global catalog server in Active Directory.

❍ **D.** Remote access policies are stored individually on every RRAS server.

14. One of your Windows Server 2003 printer servers has been responding oddly lately. The Print Spooler service often seems to get stuck, requiring you to restart either the service or the server. Performing the server restart is a time-consuming task because the server is located across town in another building that your company owns. What's the most efficient way to have this troublesome server restart after the second failure of the Print Spooler service?

- ❍ **A.** Write a batch script that monitors this service and have it force a server restart after the service has failed twice.
- ❍ **B.** Write a batch script that monitors the service and emails you after the service has failed the first time so that you can travel to the server and prepare to restart it.
- ❍ **C.** Configure the service to restart the server after its second failure.
- ❍ **D.** Configure the service to restart itself after its second failure.

15. As the administrator for a big construction company, you are in the process of converting some IP addresses from binary to decimal. What would be the decimal value of 11001100.10101110.00011101.11101010?

- ❍ **A.** 204.176.29.234
- ❍ **B.** 198.174.29.234
- ❍ **C.** 204.174.29.234
- ❍ **D.** 204.174.29.240

16. You are the systems administrator for JMS Technologies, and you are trying to determine what settings (in addition to an IP address with your DHCP server) can be assigned to client computers running Windows XP Professional. What settings can be assigned? (Choose two.)

- ❍ **A.** The IP address of the DNS server
- ❍ **B.** The IP address of the DHCP server
- ❍ **C.** The IP address of the file server
- ❍ **D.** The IP address of the default gateway
- ❍ **E.** The IP address of the Active Directory domain controller

17. You are the senior instructor for the Brighter Bulbs corporate training center, and you are teaching an introduction to Microsoft networking class to 30 students. This week you are working on DNS concepts. As part of the DNS module, you are trying to explain each part of an FQDN. What is the host portion of `sarah.training.urwrite.net`?

- ❍ **A.** `sarah`
- ❍ **B.** `training`
- ❍ **C.** `urwrite`
- ❍ **D.** `net`

18. You are the systems administrator for Good Faith Enterprises, LLC. You want to increase the security of the company's client workstations, which are all Windows 2000 Professional computers, without causing any adverse effect on network communications between computers. You have already completed this configuration action on all your DCs and member servers. Which security template should you use to accomplish your goal?

- ❍ **A.** `securews.inf`
- ❍ **B.** `securedc.inf`
- ❍ **C.** `compatws.inf`
- ❍ **D.** `hisecws.inf`

19. You are the systems administrator for Sunshine Networks. You have a network of 17 sites, running Windows Server 2003 servers and RRAS to provide routing, and you're using OSPF as the dynamic routing protocol. You recently installed a Layer 3 switch in the core of your headquarters network, and the help desk has been receiving calls about "host unreachable" error messages. After you make sure the hosts are up, you decide to look at a network capture to determine what the problem could be. You start Network Monitor to capture network traffic, but when you go to view the capture, you realize there is more information available than you need or want to see. What can you do to make it easier to find the information you're looking for?

- ❍ **A.** Create a capture filter.
- ❍ **B.** Create a display filter.
- ❍ **C.** Enable OSPF on the network adapter.
- ❍ **D.** Start Network Monitor from the command line using the `netmon` command.

20. You are the systems administrator for LFE Technologies, a leading LCD panel manufacturer. You are in the process of configuring your first Windows Server 2003 RRAS server, for use in conjunction with a VPN connection. You need to install and configure the protocols that use PPP to provide the original envelope for the data. Which protocols should you install and configure? (Choose two.)

- ❍ **A.** PPTP
- ❍ **B.** L2TP
- ❍ **C.** EAP
- ❍ **D.** SPAP

21. You recently have been having unexplained problems with the Print Spooler service on two of your Windows Server 2003 printer servers. You can find nothing wrong with the Print Spooler service itself, and you have restarted it numerous times, with no effect. What else might you consider examining to determine the cause of the problems for the Print Spooler service? (Choose two.)

❍ **A.** The currently installed drivers for the printers attached to the printer server

❍ **B.** The services that are dependent on the Print Spooler service

❍ **C.** The services on which the Print Spooler service is dependent

❍ **D.** The account with which the Print Spooler service is logging on to the network

❍ **E.** The cables being used to connect the printers to the printer server

22. You are part of the team of systems administrators for Sunshine Networks. Your task is to segment the Class B IP address 145.65.0.0 into 20 different subnets. You must allow for the number of networks to increase. The maximum number of hosts per subnet will never surpass 950 hosts. What subnet mask would enable you to segment the network and allow for the required growth?

❍ **A.** 255.255.255.252

❍ **B.** 255.255.0.0

❍ **C.** 255.255.240.0

❍ **D.** 255.255.252.0

23. A Windows XP Professional client computer will receive a DHCPACK broadcast message from the DHCP server after which of the following events?

❍ **A.** When the client computer first requests an IP address

❍ **B.** Successfully receiving or renewing a TCP/IP address from the DHCP server

❍ **C.** When a DHCP server offers it a lease

❍ **D.** When the client computer sends a request to use a lease it was offered

24. You are the systems administrator for MAC Technologies, a venture capital firm. Your network consists of 70 Windows XP Professional workstations and 2 Windows Server 2003 servers. One server is acting as the local DNS server, providing name resolution services to users. This morning the users are complaining that they cannot connect to www.quepublishing.com. They are able to access it by directly going to the IP address, so this appears to be a DNS-related problem. You go to your DNS server to determine what the problem could be. What is the order the DNS server should use to resolve a forward lookup request?

❍ **A.** Root server, cache server

❍ **B.** Cache server, zone server

❍ **C.** Zone server, cache server

❍ **D.** Cache server, root server

25. You are an assistant systems administrator for the Nimbus Flying Broom corporation. You are responsible for 75 Windows XP Professional workstations and 5 Windows Server 2003 member server computers. You have been directed to perform a security analysis on each computer, comparing its settings to those contained in the `hisecws.inf` template. How can you accomplish the assigned task with the least amount of administrative effort and the smallest number of trips to remote computers?

❍ **A.** The only way to perform this analysis is to physically visit each computer and use the Security Configuration and Analysis snap-in.

❍ **B.** You can create a script that runs Security Configuration and Analysis on each computer and collect the results in a central location for later viewing.

❍ **C.** You can create a script that runs the `secedit /analyze` command on each computer and collect the results in a central location for later viewing.

❍ **D.** You can analyze remote computers from the Security Configuration and Analysis snap-in by targeting it at the desired computer.

26. You are the WAN administrator for CMS Technologies. Your network consists of 20 Windows NT 4.0 servers and 30 Windows Server 2003 servers. Some of the NT 4.0 servers are configured as routers. You have just started to configure some of the Windows Server 2003 servers as routers, but you are having some problems. The new routers cannot communicate with the old routers. You confirm that all the routers are configured to use RIP. What could be the problem?

❍ **A.** You have to change the RIPv2 outgoing packet protocol to use broadcast instead of multicast.

❍ **B.** You need to install and configure OSPF.

❍ **C.** RIP does not propagate more than 15 hops.

❍ **D.** You have to change the RIPv2 incoming packet protocol to use only RIPv1.

27. You are the security administrator for Smith, Underwood, and Evens, Unlimited, a mid-sized legal firm. The company has about 50 attorneys on staff, and the majority of them work remotely, connecting to the headquarters office through broadband Internet connections and a VPN. The firm has just been hired to defend a high-profile technology company, and you are very concerned about case-related information being compromised and leaked to the press. You are already connecting by using a 3DES VPN connection through a Windows Server 2003 server running RRAS, but you are concerned about password integrity because of some problems you have had in the past with attorneys using weak passwords. You have decided to outfit each attorney with a smart card reader and a smart card to use for authenticating to the network. You have the card reader drivers working, but you need to configure the remote access server to recognize the smart cards. Which protocol is needed to add smart card support for the solution?

❍ **A.** PPTP

❍ **B.** L2TP

❍ **C.** IPSec

❍ **D.** EAP

❍ **E.** MS-CHAPv2

28. You are troubleshooting user complaints of slow Internet access to a partner Web site. You have been told by the partner that they are experiencing high latency on several links leading to their network. What tool can you use to determine exactly which routers and links are dropping packets and what the ping time is for each link?

❍ **A.** `ping`

❍ **B.** `nslookup`

❍ **C.** `pathping`

❍ **D.** Network Diagnostics

❍ **E.** `tracert`

29. Chris is the network administrator for Sprectronomical Productions, Inc. This morning she received a call from a user who said that he could not access any network resources. Upon investigation, Chris has determined that the workstation has an IP address of 169.254.170.145. What is the most likely reason for the user's inability to connect to any network resources?

❍ **A.** The network cable has been damaged and is no longer passing a signal.

❍ **B.** The computer was not able to contact a DHCP server and has assigned itself an APIPA IP address.

❍ **C.** The computer is not a member of the domain and is being refused an IP address.

❍ **D.** The TCP/IP stack on the computer is corrupt and needs to be reset.

30. You are the systems administrator for Balzac Petroleum. You currently have a supernetted network and would like to simplify the management of DHCP. What component should you configure in DHCP?

❍ **A.** Scope

❍ **B.** Superscope

❍ **C.** Multicast scope

❍ **D.** BOOTP scope

31. You are the systems administrator for Balzac Petroleum, a leading oil refiner. Your network consists of a mix of Windows 2000 Professional and Windows XP Professional clients, with seven Windows Server 2003 servers. Two of the Windows Server 2003 servers act as the DNS servers for the company. You need to create a second DNS entry for the intranet Web server, so that users can access it using an easy-to-remember name. What type of record do you need to add if you want to create an alias in DNS for the server?

❍ **A.** An A record

❍ **B.** An MX record

❍ **C.** A CNAME record

❍ **D.** A PTR record

32. Austin is the systems administrator for the Eternal Light Group, LLC. He is attempting to perform an analysis of a computer by using the Security Configuration and Analysis snap-in. Austin knows he needs to complete the following steps:

1. Select the security template to be used in the analysis.

2. Right-click Security Configuration and Analysis and select Analyze Computer Now.

3. Select the log file to be used in the analysis.

4. Right-click Security Configuration and Analysis and select Open Database.

5. Right-click Security Configuration and Analysis and select Configure Computer Now.

6. Select the database to be used in the analysis.

What is the order in which Austin should perform these steps?

❍ **A.** 2, 1, 3, 4, 6, 5

❍ **B.** 4, 1, 6, 2, 5, 3

❍ **C.** 4, 6, 1, 3, 2, 5

❍ **D.** 2, 6, 1, 3, 4, 5

33. You are the WAN administrator for JMS Technologies, and you are trying to decide what routing technology you should be using for the company. You finally decide to go with distance-vector routing. You are aware that one of the major problems with distance-vector routing is count to infinity. What are some avoidance mechanisms that could be implemented to prevent any problems? (Choose three.)

❍ **A.** Split horizon

❍ **B.** Split horizon with poison reverse

❍ **C.** Triggered update

❍ **D.** Link-state routing

❍ **E.** Dynamic DNS

❍ **F.** Strong user passwords

34. You are the systems administrator for FuelMeUp Petroleum, a medium-sized oil refiner. Your network consists of a central site with 60 local users, 120 remote sales representatives who travel 90 percent of the time, and 16 Windows Server 2003 servers providing core network services, including remote access using RRAS. Your sales representatives need the ability to dial in to access resources on the network while traveling. The problem you are having is that the sales organization is split into eight geographic regions covering eight time zones, and the sales representatives from each region are only allowed to make remote connections during specific hours. Each region has a Windows security group that contains all of the sales representatives in that region. What do you need to do to ensure that the sales representatives can connect the remote access server, but only during the allowed times for their regions?

- ❍ **A.** Create different remote access policies for the different users.
- ❍ **B.** Configure multiple RRAS servers with different local policies and get the different groups to dial in to their respective servers.
- ❍ **C.** Create local security policies with the Group Policy Editor.
- ❍ **D.** Give all remote users the same policy.

35. You have recently configured and implemented a networkwide IPSec solution for your company's internal corporate network. You are using multiple IPSec polices, each of which is tailored to the specific needs of the different groups within the network. While monitoring the IPSec statistics, you notice a high level of negotiation failures. What are the most likely causes of this problem? (Choose two.)

- ❍ **A.** IPSec is not enabled on the computers.
- ❍ **B.** There is no matching security method configured between the computers.
- ❍ **C.** The Domain Controllers are not responding.
- ❍ **D.** There is no matching authentication method configured between the computers.

36. You are the second-shift systems administrator for Rick's Rockets, Inc. You are attempting to troubleshoot and correct a network connectivity problem that was reported by users on the first shift between a server and several workstations. What communication troubleshooting tool should you start with to determine where the problem lies?

- ❍ **A.** `ipconfig`
- ❍ **B.** `nslookup`
- ❍ **C.** `ping`
- ❍ **D.** `telnet`

37. You are the network administrator for Balzac Petroleum. You just installed and configured a DHCP server. After the installation, the wizard asked you to activate the scope, and you did. Staff from your company are complaining, however, that they are not obtaining IP addresses. What could be the problem?

❍ **A.** You did not activate the server.

❍ **B.** You were not authorized to activate the scope; only administrators can activate the scope.

❍ **C.** You did not authorize the server.

❍ **D.** Your scope is misconfigured.

38. You are the senior instructor at U-Learn Fast, Inc., a corporate training center. As you are reviewing DNS parameters, someone asks how long a node in an FQDN can be. What is the answer?

❍ **A.** 43 characters

❍ **B.** 63 characters

❍ **C.** 255 characters

❍ **D.** 512 characters

39. You have just completed an analysis of a computer by using the Security Configuration and Analysis snap-in. When you examine the results, you notice several items that have red X icons next to them. What does this type of icon indicate?

❍ **A.** The item is not defined in the analysis database and was not examined on the computer.

❍ **B.** The item is defined in the analysis database and on the computer, and it matches the currently configured setting.

❍ **C.** The item is defined in the analysis database but not on the computer.

❍ **D.** The item is defined in the analysis database and on the computer, but it does not match the currently configured setting.

40. You are the LAN administrator for Gonzo Candy, a lollipop manufacturer. You have three office locations, each with its own Windows Server 2003 servers. Each office has a local LAN that is very stable, and the company has no plans to add locations for the next three years. There are plans to network the three locations by using the existing Windows Server 2003 servers and ISDN lines. You have been asked to design a solution that will have the lowest impact on the servers, with no requirements for redundancy or failover. What routing method should you select?

❍ **A.** Static routes

❍ **B.** RIP

❍ **C.** OSPF

❍ **D.** Autostatic updates

41. You are the systems administrator for a small nursing home, and you have 200 computers running Windows XP Professional. Of those, 30 are laptops that need to be able to dial in to the network at night. You configure and install RRAS on one of your Windows Server 2003 servers. Your Windows Server 2003 network is running at the Windows Server 2003 domain functional level. Because this is the first time you have configured RRAS, you first modify the default policy. Then, as part of your testing, you configure 12 additional remote access policies. After this, the users complain that they cannot successfully access any information on the network. What is the most likely source of the problem?

❍ **A.** You need to enable IPSec to ensure that the connections are encrypted.

❍ **B.** You have some conflicting policies, and the first one that the users apply refuses them access to the information on the network.

❍ **C.** You did not enable MS-CHAP.

❍ **D.** You did not modify the default dial-in policy.

42. While monitoring the IPSec statistics for your network, you notice a large number of soft associations. What is the most likely reason for this occurrence?

❍ **A.** The packets have data that could not be verified, meaning that the integrity hash verification failed.

❍ **B.** SAs are being formed with computers that do not support IPSec or were not able to negotiate successful IPSec connections.

❍ **C.** The IPSec policies are using unmatched shared keys between the communicating computers.

❍ **D.** The operating systems do not match between the two computers attempting communications.

43. You are in the process of configuring three new Windows Server 2003 servers that will be placed on an Active Directory network as file servers. The network is large and contains six different IP subnets with clients and servers spread out over all six subnets. The three new servers you are configuring will be communicating with clients and servers from all six subnets. Which of the following items will you need to configure on the Internet Protocol (TCP/IP) Properties dialog box to ensure that these three new member servers can communicate with all the computers on the network? (Choose all correct answers.)

❍ **A.** IP address

❍ **B.** Subnet mask

❍ **C.** Default gateway

❍ **D.** DNS server IP address

❍ **E.** DNS suffix

❍ **F.** WINS server IP address

44. You are the administrator of a very large multinational organization. You are getting some error messages from the DHCP server. What counter in the Performance Console would display the number of DHCPOFFER messages sent per second by the DHCP server to a client computer?

❍ **A.** Offers/Sec

❍ **B.** Discovers/Sec

❍ **C.** Acks/Sec

❍ **D.** DHCPAcks/Sec

45. You have been hired as a network consultant to install DNS in the new corporate headquarters of Zanzibar Sports, a large sporting goods manufacturing company. The network currently consists of 3,000 computers running Windows XP Professional and 4,000 computers running Windows 2000 Professional. The servers providing DNS for the network are presently located in the largest branch location, but you want to move them into the new corporate data center. You also want to ensure that all remote offices and manufacturing sites can perform DNS resolution queries without adding additional traffic on your WAN links. What should you do to ensure that the remote offices and manufacturing sites do not add additional traffic to your WAN links?

❍ **A.** Configure the DNS servers at the corporate data center as Active Directory integrated.

❍ **B.** Configure standard secondary zone DNS servers at all remote offices and manufacturing sites.

❍ **C.** Configure the DNS servers at the corporate data center with standard secondary zones.

❍ **D.** Create a stub zone at the corporate data center.

46. Christopher is preparing to use the `secedit.exe` command to analyze the security on one of his member servers. If Christopher is using the Secure Workstation security template as his comparison point and needs to ensure that the analysis database is clear before importing the security template, which of the following choices represents the correct command that Christopher should enter to perform the analysis?

❍ **A.**

```
secedit /analyze /overwrite /db c:\sectst\sectst1.sdb
➥ /cfg C:\WINDOWS\security\templates\securedc.inf /log
➥ c:\sectst\sectst1.log
```

❍ **B.**

```
secedit /configure /db c:\sectst\sectst1.sdb /cfg
➥ C:\WINDOWS\security\templates\securedc.inf /log
➥ c:\sectst\sectst1.log
```

❍ **C.**

```
secedit /analyze /db c:\sectst\sectst1.sdb /cfg
➥ C:\WINDOWS\security\templates\securews.inf /log
➥ c:\sectst\sectst1.log
```

❍ **D.**

```
secedit /analyze /overwrite /db c:\sectst\sectst1.sdb
➥ /cfg C:\WINDOWS\security\templates\securews.inf /log
➥ c:\sectst\sectst1.log
```

47. You are the LAN administrator for Zanzibar Dream Enterprises, a small technology reseller. You have two office locations, each with its own Windows Server 2003 server. The two locations have been networked with a T-1 connection that runs between the Windows Server 2003 servers, which are running RRAS. You just added a new network in the main location, and you need to add a static route on the far end to provide connectivity to the location; you are not using any dynamic routing protocols. The network address, which you are using as a Class C address, is 10.10.10.0. The correct gateway address is 10.10.10.254. What command do you need to use to add a static route?

❍ **A.**

```
ipconfig /addroute 10.10.10.0 mask 255.255.255.0
➥ 10.10.10.254 metric 2
```

❍ **B.**

```
route add 10.10.10.0 mask 255.255.255.0
➥ 10.10.10.254 metric 2
```

❍ **C.**

```
route /addroute 10.10.10.0 mask 255.255.255.0
➥ 10.10.10.254 metric 2
```

❍ **D.**

```
netstat add 10.10.10.0 mask 255.255.255.0
➥ 10.10.10.254 metric 2
```

❍ **E.**

```
netstat add 10.10.10.0 mask 255.255.255.252
➥ 10.10.10.254 metric 2
```

48. You are the lead engineer for Mount Abora Consulting, a small technical consulting shop. You have just hired an intern to assist with some of the routine duties around the shop, and you are explaining to the intern some of the differences between using PPTP and L2TP to create VPNs for customers. Which of the following are accurate statements regarding PPTP and L2TP? (Choose three.)

❍ **A.** L2TP requires an IP-based transit internetwork.

❍ **B.** L2TP supports header compression.

❍ **C.** PPTP supports header compression.

❍ **D.** L2TP supports tunnel authentication.

❍ **E.** L2TP requires IPSec for encryption.

❍ **F.** L2TP can be used only on Windows networks.

49. You are the WAN administrator for IVS Technologies. You are trying to decide what routing technology you should be using for the company, and you finally decide to go with distance-vector routing. What is one of the major disadvantages of distance-vector routing?

❍ **A.** It has problems with slow convergence.

❍ **B.** It involves high overhead on the network.

❍ **C.** It suffers from the count-to-infinity problem.

❍ **D.** A network that uses it can connect to a maximum of only 15 hops.

50. You are the LAN administrator for the Oui Find-em detective agency. You would like to be able to verify some entries on one of your Windows Server 2003 DNS servers. How could you verify the entries in the DNS zone?

- ❍ **A.** You could use the Properties dialog box of the DNS server in the MMC.
- ❍ **B.** You could type **`nslookup`** at a command prompt.
- ❍ **C.** You could type **`ipconfig`** at a command prompt.
- ❍ **D.** You could use Event Viewer.

51. You are the systems administrator for the ShoeBox Shoe company. The corporation is running a routed network with a centrally located Windows Server 2003 DHCP server. The server is able to issue addresses to users on the local segment but cannot issue addresses to any sites across a router. What is the most probable cause of this problem?

- ❍ **A.** The DHCP forwarder service is not enabled on the DHCP server.
- ❍ **B.** The BOOTP forwarder service is not enabled on the DHCP server.
- ❍ **C.** The DHCP forwarder service is not enabled on the routers.
- ❍ **D.** The BOOTP forwarder service is not enabled on the routers.

52. You are the network administrator for JMS Technologies, a small consulting company. After installing and configuring DNS on a Windows Server 2003 server, you set up an Active Directory–integrated zone. Where does the server store the zone information?

- ❍ **A.** In the `%systemroot%\DNS` directory
- ❍ **B.** In the `%systemroot%\system32\DNS` directory
- ❍ **C.** In Active Directory
- ❍ **D.** In the server's cache

53. Andrea is an administrator for Carmine's Circus Clowns, Inc. She was recently hired because the last administrator, oddly enough, ran off to join the circus. Carmine's network includes two Domain Controllers and three member servers that provide file, print, and backup/restoration services. Carmine, the president of the company, has instructed Andrea to implement a more secure configuration on all five Windows Server 2003 servers. Andrea has decided to use the secure templates, but is not sure what the current configuration is on each server because the last administrator did not keep any records. What is the best way for Andrea to get these servers configured with the secure templates?

- ❍ **A.** Andrea should apply the Default security template from one of her member servers to all five servers and then apply the `securews.inf` and `securedc.inf` templates to them.

❍ **B.** Andrea should apply the Default security template found on each computer to that specific computer. After doing this, she should apply the `securews.inf` template to the DCs and the `securedc.inf` template to the member servers.

❍ **C.** Andrea should reinstall Windows Server 2003 on all five servers and re-create the domain. After doing this, she should apply the `securews.inf` and `securedc.inf` templates to the servers.

❍ **D.** Andrea should apply the Default security template found on each computer to that specific computer. After doing this, she should apply the `securedc.inf` template to the DCs and the `securews.inf` template to the member servers.

54. You are the WAN administrator for Bifurcated Plumbing, a large plumbing manufacturer. You have 12 office locations, each with its own Windows Server 2003 servers. Today the corporate headquarters has a WAN connection to the warehouse, but none of the other sites have WAN connections outside dial-in access. There are plans to network the remaining locations by using the existing Windows Server 2003 servers and ISDN lines. You have been asked to design a solution that will be easy to set up and maintain and that will still allow for a failover connection between the headquarters and the warehouse. What routing method should you select?

❍ **A.** Static routes

❍ **B.** RIP

❍ **C.** OSPF

❍ **D.** Autostatic updates

55. You are the lead system administrator for the Zanzibar Dream Ice Cream company. The company has 200 end users running Windows XP Professional that need to be able to access the company's network remotely. Several months ago you installed a Windows Server 2003 server running RRAS to allow users to dial in to the server for remote access. This server is in the corporate Active Directory tree, and after you configured it, the profiles worked perfectly. Last weekend you added another Windows Server 2003 server with RRAS loaded to provide a failover access device in the event of a server crash. Both servers are in the same native-mode Active Directory domain, and test users are unable to log in to the new RAS server. What is the most likely problem?

❍ **A.** You can have only a single Windows Server 2003 server running RRAS in an Active Directory domain.

❍ **B.** The Windows Server 2003 RRAS service needs to be authorized in Active Directory.

❍ **C.** You need to add the new Windows Server 2003 server to the Global Remote Access Servers group in Active Directory.

❍ **D.** The remote access profiles are not shared and need to be re-created on the new Windows Server 2003 server before anyone can access the server.

56. You are the systems administrator for Gidget's Widgets, LLC. You are trying to explain DNS and reverse lookup zones to your co-workers. What should you tell your co-workers that reverse lookup zone allows users to resolve?

❍ **A.** An IP address to a hostname

❍ **B.** A hostname to an IP address

❍ **C.** An IP address to a MAC address

❍ **D.** A hostname to an FQDN

57. You are the WAN administrator for General Telecommunications, a large manufacturer of network equipment. When you started with the company, you had 10 office locations, each with its own Windows Server 2003 servers. These locations were networked using fractional T-1s and Windows Server 2003 servers running RRAS, and they used RIP for routing information. General Telecommunications now has 120 sales offices throughout the United States and Europe, and you have been tasked with networking these locations by using hardware routers. You have been asked to design a solution that will support both the Windows Server 2003 servers and the hardware routers. The solution must also support failover connections between the original 10 locations. What routing method should you select?

❍ **A.** EIGRP

❍ **B.** RIP

❍ **C.** OSPF

❍ **D.** Autostatic updates

❍ **E.** BGP

58. You are a consultant for Champagne Glasses Corporation, and you have been asked to simplify the process of configuring TCP/IP on all the client computers. The network consists of 40 computers running Windows 2000 Professional and 60 computers running Windows XP Professional. Installing and configuring what service of Windows Server 2003 will help you accomplish your task?

❍ **A.** DHCP

❍ **B.** DNS

❍ **C.** WINS

❍ **D.** BOOTP

59. You are the systems administrator for Dulcimer Heating and Plumbing. The company network consists of 3 Windows Server 2003 servers and 100 Windows XP Professional workstations. The Sales Department spends a lot of time doing Web research at a variety of supplier, customer, and competitor Web sites. You have been asked to provide a solution to speed up name resolution for these users. You configure a cache-only server. Which of the following will have the largest impact on the response time for DNS requests?

❍ **A.** The speed and type of the hard drive

❍ **B.** The speed of the network adapter card

❍ **C.** The processor speed

❍ **D.** The amount of RAM installed

❍ **E.** The speed of the network connection

60. Kirsten is the systems administrator for Ike's Spikes, Inc., a leading manufacturer of railroad spikes. She has recently finished configuring and implementing an auditing plan for the company network. Kirsten needs to be able to track unsuccessful user logon attempts to the company network because she suspects that someone is trying to perform a dictionary attack against several user accounts. After two weeks, she has not found any unsuccessful user logon attempts recorded in the security log, even though she tried password-guessing several users' accounts just this morning. What does Kirsten need to correct in her auditing implementation?

❍ **A.** Kirsten needs to ensure that she has configured failure audits for the Audit Logon Events option.

❍ **B.** Kirsten needs to ensure that she has configured success audits for the Audit Account Logon Events option.

❍ **C.** Kirsten needs to ensure that she has configured success audits for the Audit Policy Change option.

❍ **D.** Kirsten needs to ensure that she has configured failure audits for the Audit Account Management option.

61. You are the lead administrator for Red Rabbit Motors, a chain of car dealerships. Red Rabbit has 14 locations and is using OSPF as part of its WAN implementation. You are training a new WAN engineer to support the WAN. She asks you for the correct name of the area with an ID of 0.0.0.0. What do you call this area?

❍ **A.** The AS

❍ **B.** The LSDB

❍ **C.** The OSPF backbone

❍ **D.** The default route

62. You are the lead system administrator for the Mellow Music Guitar Company, a custom guitar manufacturing company. The company has 75 users running Windows XP Professional that need to be able to access the company's network remotely. You would like to be able to provide redundant remote access servers by using Windows Server 2003 running RRAS to allow users to dial in to the network, but you want to maintain only one set of remote access profiles. How can you accomplish this?

❍ **A.** Install both servers in Active Directory, and on the Profiles tab of each server's Properties dialog box, select the Store Profiles in Active Directory option. Configure each server to point at the same domain in the Profile Location field.

❍ **B.** Install both servers in Active Directory, and on the Profiles tab of each server's Properties dialog box, select the Store Profiles in Active Directory option. Make sure both servers are in the same domain.

❍ **C.** Install ISA Server and use it as the central repository for the profiles.

❍ **D.** Install IAS and use it as the central repository for the profiles.

63. As a junior systems administrator for Alph Construction, you have been assigned the task of identifying and correcting a problem with one of the Windows Server 2003 DNS servers. Computers running Windows 2000 Professional have not registered dynamically with the DNS server. You would like to force these computers to register with DNS as quickly as possible. What should you do?

❍ **A.** Reboot the system so that the computer is issued a new DHCP address.

❍ **B.** On each computer, at the command prompt, type **`ipconfig/renew`**.

❍ **C.** On each computer, at the command prompt, type **`ipconfig/registerdns`**.

❍ **D.** On each computer, at the command prompt, type **`ipconfig/renewdns`**.

64. You are the systems administrator for ZFE, Inc., a medium-sized box manufacturer. You are using Windows Server 2003 as the network operating system in all four of ZFE's locations. You are using a server in corporate headquarters and another in the Boston sales office to establish an ISDN-based demand-dial routing connection. In order to control costs, this has been implemented as an on-demand connection. During operation, however, you notice that the connection is coming up fairly regularly, even during the evening, when you know that there is no communication occurring between the offices. What could be the problem?

❍ **A.** This is normal; it is an indication that the demand-dial routing solution is functioning normally.

❍ **B.** Legitimate data is being transferred during the connection.

❍ **C.** A default route has been configured on the calling router, and anytime a packet is received, it is forwarded to the destination demand-dial router.

❍ **D.** A default route has been configured on the answering router, and anytime a packet is received, it is forwarded to the destination demand-dial router.

65. You are the systems administrator for JMS Technologies. You have just installed the DHCP service through the Windows Component Wizard. You now need to configure DHCP to support a scope that will be used for streaming multimedia delivery. In the MMC, you right-click the server icon under DHCP. What option should you select to configure the scope?

- ❍ **A.** New Scope
- ❍ **B.** New Superscope
- ❍ **C.** New IP Scope
- ❍ **D.** New Multicast Scope

Answers to Practice Exam

Answers and Explanations

1. **B**. Because you will never exceed 14 hosts per subnet, the correct subnet mask is 255.255.255.240. Using the subnet mask of 255.255.255.224 would allow for 14 hosts, but is wasteful since it actually creates subnets containing room for 30 hosts, thus limiting future growth; thus Answer A is incorrect. Using the subnet mask of 255.255.255.248 would result in only 6 usable IP addresses per subnet, thus Answer C is incorrect. Using the subnet mask of 255.255.255.0 would result in no subnetting at all, thus Answer D is incorrect. For more information, see Chapter 1, "Configuring and Troubleshooting TCP/IP Addressing."
2. **A**. Windows XP client computers interact directly with the DNS server to update their A resource records. The DHCP server will update the PTR records for Windows XP client computers and both the A records and the PTR records for non-Windows XP/2000 client computers; therefore Answers B, C, and D are all incorrect. For more information, see Chapter 2, "Implementing, Managing, and Troubleshooting DHCP."
3. **D**. When you configure a DNS server as cache only, the server does not have any zone information. As a result, no information is stored on the hard drive, nor in Active Directory; thus Answers A and C are incorrect. While there is a cache of resolution information in the server's RAM, there are not any zone files; thus Answer B is incorrect. For more information, see Chapter 3, "Implementing and Managing DNS."
4. **B**. The best way to apply the settings to only the computers that require them is to import the template into a GPO associated with all the OUs that require the settings. (You can have one GPO linked to multiple OUs if desired to increase administrative efficiency.) Importing the security template into the domain-level GPO would apply the settings to all computers in the domain, most likely with unwanted side effects; thus Answer A is incorrect. Scripting the `secedit` command or manually applying the template to each computer are both ways to accomplish the task, but neither of them is as efficient as importing the template into a GPO; thus Answers C and D are incorrect. For more information, see Chapter 5, "Implementing, Managing, and Maintaining Network Security."

5. **B**. Split horizon is a mechanism that prevents routing information from being sent back in the direction from which it was received. Distance-vector routing is a type of routing protocol, such as RIP; thus Answer A is incorrect. Poison reverse allows routes to be broadcast back to the interface from which they were received, and buy indicates that the network is unreachable; thus Answer C is incorrect. A topological database is used by OSPF routers to keep LSAs of other OSPF routers; thus Answer D is incorrect. For more information, see Chapter 7, "Implementing, Managing and Troubleshooting Routing."

6. **D**. If you did not modify the default dial-in policy, no users will be able to connect. The default policy's permissions are set to deny access for everyone. Windows XP is a supported client for RRAS connections; thus Answer A is incorrect. Although having multiple, conflicting, remote access policies will create a similar problem, it's more likely that the default policy was not modified to allow access in this scenario; thus Answer B is incorrect. It is not required to configure MS-CHAP as the authentication protocol; thus Answer C incorrect. For more information, see Chapter 6, "Implementing, Managing and Troubleshooting Network Access."

7. **B**. The *yyyymmddhh* log numbering format would provide the easiest method of determining the date and time each counter log was created. The log numbering formats given in Answers A, C, and D are all missing some information that you will need to accurately determine the date (year, month, and date) and time that the log was created. For more information, see Chapter 9, "Maintaining and Troubleshooting a Network Infrastructure."

8. **A**. When you're converting from decimal to binary, 209.168.241.158 is equal to 11010001.10101000.11110001.10011110; thus Answers B, C, and D are incorrect. For more information, see Chapter 1.

9. **C**. Answer B could be a good answer, but because 465 computers are on the same segment, you need to get two Class C addresses and configure a superscope. While you should take the time to ensure DHCP and DNS are properly integrated, you will still need a superscope; thus Answer A is not correct. BOOTP is not required for Windows workstations; thus Answer D is not required. For more information, see Chapter 2.

10. **A**, **C**. In order to ensure that users can resolve hostnames to IP addresses, you need to create a forward lookup zone. In order to ensure that users can resolve IP addresses to hostnames, you need to create a reverse lookup zone. Creating a stub zone or delegated zone are more advanced configuration options that will not help you get DNS name resolution working for a new installation; thus Answers B and D are incorrect. For more information, see Chapter 3.

11. **B**. The Local Policies node of the Group Policy Editor contains three subnodes: Audit Policy, User Rights Assignment, and Security Options. The Audit Policy subnode is where Andrea will find the auditing items she needs to configure; thus Answers A, C, and D are all incorrect. For more information, see Chapter 5.

12. **C**. One of the major problems with distance-vector routing is the count-to-infinity problem. The cost of the Windows software is typically comparable or lower than a hardware routing device, but this is not typically an item of great concern when choosing a solution; thus Answer A is incorrect. Distance-vector routing protocols actually have a high overhead on the network, which is another major problem they suffer from; thus Answer B is incorrect. Distance-vector routing protocols

such as RIP have a maximum hop count of 16, not 12; thus Answer D is incorrect. For more information, see Chapter 7.

13. **D**. Remote access policies are stored individually on each RRAS server; thus Answers A, B, and C are all incorrect. For more information, see Chapter 6.

14. **C**. The most administratively efficient solution is to configure the service (from the Recovery tab) to restart the server after the second failure of the service. Repeated problems with a service usually indicate deeper problems, such as other services that are failing. Only by restarting the server can you reset all services back to a known functional state. Long-term problems of this sort will likely require further troubleshooting and repair. Writing a batch script to perform an action is certainly possible, but since you only need to restart the server, you can do this more efficiently using the service's properties; thus Answers A and B are incorrect. Restarting just the service might well fix the problem as well in most cases, but typically when a server is having this type of problem, it's best to just restart the entire server if you can; thus Answer D is incorrect. For more information, see Chapter 9.

15. **C**. When you're converting from binary to decimal, 11001100.10101110.00011101.11101010 is equal to 204.174.29.234; thus Answers A, B, and D are incorrect. For more information, see Chapter 1.

16. **A**, **D**. The DHCP server's primary function is to assign a unique IP address to the requesting client computers. DHCP servers can also be used to assign the IP address of the DNS server, the default gateway, the WINS server, and various other options. The IP address of the DHCP server is certainly unknown to the client when it does its broadcast to search for a DHCP server; thus Answer B is incorrect. You cannot pass file server IP address information to clients via DHCP; thus Answer C is incorrect. Active Directory–aware clients (such as Windows XP and Windows 2000) will query DNS for the service record of the Domain Controller that should service them; thus Answer E is incorrect. For more information, see Chapter 2.

17. **A**. In the FQDN `sarah.training.urwrite.net`, `sarah` identifies the host part. `training` identifies a child domain, `urwrite` is the domain name, and `net` is the top-level domain; thus Answers B, C, and D are all incorrect. For more information, see Chapter 3.

18. **A**. By applying the Secure template, `securews.inf`, you can increase the security of the client workstations without adversely affecting network communications. The `securedc.inf` template is to be used for Domain Controllers, not workstations; thus Answer B is incorrect. The `compatws.inf` template will actually reduce the security of workstations it is applied to; thus Answer C is incorrect. The `hisecws.inf` template will increase the workstation security, but will likely cause adverse effects as well; thus Answer D is incorrect. For more information, see Chapter 5.

19. **B**. Since you've already performed the capture, the best thing to do would be to create a display filter that filters out the captured data. In doing so, you can view only the specific information you're looking for. Answer A is incorrect because capture filters are created before a capture is started. Answer C is incorrect because you cannot enable a routing protocol on a network adapter. Although you can start Network Monitor from the command line, Answer D is incorrect because what you need to do is create the display filter for the data you already have. For more information, see Chapter 9.

20. **A**, **B**. Both PPTP and L2TP, use PPP to provide the original envelope for the data. EAP and SPAP are remote access authentication protocols; thus Answers C and D are incorrect. For more information, see Chapter 6.

21. **C**, **D**. Services that the Print Spooler service is dependent on and that are not functioning properly can cause the Print Spooler service to function improperly—as noted in the question. In addition, a misconfigured or incorrect account that is being used by the service can lead to problems and the inability to perform its intended function. Bad printer drivers can cause problems for the server itself and cause printing to not function correctly for the printer using the drivers, but it will not likely cause problems with the Print Spooler itself; thus Answer A is incorrect. Services dependent on the Print Spooler will not function correctly when the Print Spooler is not functioning, but they will not cause the Print Spooler to malfunction; thus Answer B is incorrect. Cabling problems will not cause issues with the Print Spooler; thus Answer E is incorrect. For more information, see Chapter 9.

22. **D**. By using the first 6 bits of the third octet, you allow up to 1,024 hosts per network. You also allow for the network to be segmented into up to 62 subnets; thus Answers A, B, and C are incorrect. For more information, see Chapter 1.

23. **B**. The client computer will receive a `DHCPNCK` message after successfully receiving or renewing a TCP/IP address from the DHCP server. When the client computer first requests an IP address, it issues a `DHCPDISCOVER` message to find a DHCP server; thus Answer A is incorrect. It then receives a `DHCPOFFER` message from each DHCP server; thus Answer C is incorrect. It sends a request (`DHCPREQUEST`) to use the address to the DHCP server that originated the offer; thus Answer D is incorrect. For more information, see Chapter 2.

24. **D**. The logical processing order that the DNS server uses to resolve a FQDN to an IP address request is that it first checks the DNS server's local cache. If the DNS server cannot resolve the request from the cache, it then forwards the request to the appropriate root server; thus Answers A, B, and C are incorrect. For more information, see Chapter 3.

25. **C**. The easiest way to accomplish this task is to create a script that runs the `secedit /analyze` command on the computers and collects the results in a central network location. Visiting each computer is not going to be efficient; thus Answer A is incorrect. You can script the `secedit` command, but not Security Configuration and Analysis itself; thus Answer B is incorrect. Remote computers cannot be targeted by Security Configuration and Analysis; thus Answer D is incorrect. For more information, see Chapter 5.

26. **A**. You have to configure RIP to use broadcast, not multicast. OSPF is not required to solve this problem; thus Answer B is incorrect. RIP has a maximum hop count of 16, but this has no bearing on the problem at hand; thus Answer C incorrect. You do not need to change the incoming packet protocol; thus Answer D is incorrect. For more information, see Chapter 7.

27. **D**. EAP supports smart card authentication. None of the other listed authentication protocols are designed to work with smart cards; thus Answers A, B, C, and E are all incorrect. For more information, see Chapter 6.

28. **C**. The `pathping` tool acts as the equivalent of the `tracert` command by allowing you to identify which routers are in the path that the packets are taking. It also acts as the equivalent of the `ping` command by sending `ping` requests to all the routers over a specified time period and then computing statistics based on the packets returned from each router. `pathping` displays the amount of packet loss at each router or link and allows you to determine which routers and links (subnets) might be the cause of connectivity troubles. Using the `ping`, `nslookup`, or `tracert` commands won't show you where packet loss is occurring; thus Answers A, B, and E are all incorrect. The Network Diagnostics utility does not show packet loss either; thus Answer D is incorrect. For more information, see Chapter 9.

29. **B**. In the majority of cases in which a computer configured for DHCP suddenly cannot communicate with the rest of the network, the cause is due to the computer having assigned itself an APIPA IP address. APIPA IP addresses are assigned from the IP address range 169.254.0.1–169.254.255.254, with a subnet mask of 255.255.0.0. This, in most cases, completely prevents an APIPA-configured computer from carrying out any other normal communications on the network. Having a damaged network cable (or any other damaged network device) is certainly a possible cause of this problem, but it is not the most common one; thus Answer A is incorrect. A computer does not need to be part of the Active Directory domain to get a DHCP lease; thus Answer C is incorrect. The chances of the TCP/IP stack being corrupt are very small and not a likely cause; thus Answer D is incorrect. For more information, see Chapter 1.

30. **B**. You need to configure a superscope. You already have multiple scopes since you have multiple subnets; thus Answer A is not going to help. Since multicast was not mentioned as a need, you don't need to configure a scope for it; thus Answer C is incorrect. BOOTP is not required for Windows computers, thus Answer D is incorrect. For more information, see Chapter 2.

31. **C**. The correct record to add to the DNS server when you want to add an alias is the CNAME record. The A record is used to map a host name to an IP address; thus Answer A is incorrect. The MX record is used to specify SMTP servers; thus Answer B is incorrect. The PTR record is used to map an IP address to a host name; thus Answer D is incorrect. For more information, see Chapter 3.

32. **C**. The correct steps to be used to perform an analysis of a computer with the Security Configuration and Analysis snap-in are as follows: Select Open Database, select the database, select the security template, select Analyze Computer, select the log file, select Configure Computer; thus Answers A, B, and D are all incorrect. For more information, see Chapter 5.

33. **A**, **B**, **C**. There are many ways to prevent count-to-infinity problems, including using split horizon, split horizon with poison reverse, and triggered update. Link-state routing is another routing technology; thus Answer D is incorrect. Dynamic DNS won't help you with count-to-infinity problems; thus Answer E is incorrect. While strong passwords are always recommended, they won't help with this problem either; thus Answer E is incorrect. For more information, see Chapter 7.

34. **A**. You need to create a different remote access policy for each region using the security group for that region to allow access during the allowable times for that region. You will need to create a total of eight policies since each region has different times that they are allowed to access the network via RRAS. While it's always good practice to have redundancy in your server design, it is not required to have different RRAS servers for each group; thus Answer B is incorrect. You can't control RRAS remote access via local security policies; thus Answer C is incorrect. Giving all remote users the policy does not meet the requirements you face; thus Answer D is incorrect. For more information, see Chapter 6.

35. **B**, **D**. The Negotiation Failures statistic displays the total number of negotiation failures that occurred during Main Mode or Quick Mode negotiation. This is a useful statistic to use to determine whether security and/or authentication methods do not match between two computers attempting communications. IPSec, as a service, is running by default on Windows 2000 and XP computers; thus there is no need to "enable" it. You do need to configure it by applying one or more IPSec policies as indicated in this scenario, however; thus Answer A is incorrect. If your Domain Controllers were not responding, you'd have a lot bigger problems than those just dealing with IPSec policies; thus Answer C is incorrect. For more information, see Chapter 8, "Implementing, Managing and Troubleshooting IPSec to Secure Network Traffic."

36. **A**. Using the `ipconfig` command to verify that the workstations have the correct TCP/IP configuration would be the most efficient place to start your troubleshooting. Once you've verified the TCP/IP configuration, and the problem still remains, you'd likely next move onto using the `ping` command to test basic network connectivity between the server and workstations; thus Answer C is incorrect. The `nslookup` command would likely not be used until after using the `ipconfig` and `ping` commands, as it is for more specific name resolution issues; thus Answer B is incorrect. The `telnet` command, used for creating remote sessions on servers, won't likely help you troubleshoot this issue; thus Answer D is incorrect. For more information, see Chapter 1.

37. **C**. Before a Windows Server 2003 DHCP server can issue any IP addresses, it needs to be authorized. Only members of the Enterprise Administrators group have the right to authorize DHCP servers in Active Directory. DHCP servers are not activated; thus Answer A is incorrect. The scope was already activated during the creation and configuration process, thus Answer B is incorrect. The scope options are very straightforward and very difficult to misconfigure. Although it is possible, the most likely explanation is that you did not authorize the server; thus Answer D is incorrect. For more information, see Chapter 2.

38. **B**. The maximum number of characters that you can have in a node is 63; thus Answers A, C, and D are incorrect. An FQDN can have a maximum of 255 characters. For more information, see Chapter 3.

39. **D**. A red X icon next to an item in the Security Configuration and Analysis snap-in results indicates that the item is present in both the database and the computer, but does not match the currently configured setting. A question mark indicates that the item is not defined in the analysis database and was not examined on the computer; thus Answer A is incorrect. A green check mark indicates that the item is defined in the analysis database and on the computer and matches the currently configured setting; thus Answer B is incorrect. An exclamation point indicates that the item is defined in the analysis database but not on the computer; thus Answer C is incorrect. For more information, see Chapter 5.

40. **A**. Because you are working with a small, static network and you are tasked with using the solution that has the lowest impact on resources, using static routes is the correct solution. RIP and OSPF are both available routing protocols that are overkill for this scenario; thus Answers B and C are incorrect. An *autostatic update* is a request from a router for all known routes or services from the router on the other side of the connection; thus Answer B is incorrect. For more information, see Chapter 7.

41. **B**. Since you have 12 custom policies, plus the default policy, you most likely have some conflicting policies, and the first one that is applied is refusing the users access. IPSec does not need to be enabled; thus Answer A is incorrect. Configuring MS-CHAP for authentication is not the most likely problem; thus Answer C is incorrect. If you have not created any custom policies, then the default policy would likely be your problem. But, with all of the policies you've created, one of them is likely to blame; thus Answer D is incorrect. For more information, see Chapter 6.

42. **B**. Soft associations are an indication that SAs have been formed with computers that do not support IPSec or were not able to negotiate successful IPSec connections. Soft associations can be an indication of mismatched security and authentication settings; thus Answers A, C, and D are all incorrect. For more information, see Chapter 8.

43. **A**, **B**, **C**, **D**. At a minimum, each computer using TCP/IP must have a valid IP address and subnet mask. Because these servers will be communicating with computers on other subnets, a valid default gateway will also be required to route packets off the local subnet. The servers should also have one or more valid DNS server IP addresses configured on them to facilitate domain service lookups and user authentication. WINS server information or custom DNS suffixes are sometimes helpful information to have configured, but are not part of the required minimum configured; thus Answers E and F are incorrect. For more information, see Chapter 1.

44. **A**. The performance counter that counts the number of `DHCPOFFER` messages sent per second by the DHCP server to a client computer is Offers/Sec. The Discovers/Sec counter monitors the number of `DHCPDISCOVER` messages received per second by the server; thus Answer B is incorrect. The Acks/Sec counter monitors the number of `DHCPACK` messages sent per second by the DHCP server to client computers; thus Answer C is incorrect. DHCPAcks/Sec is not a real counter; thus Answer D is incorrect. For more information, see Chapter 2.

45. **B**. By configuring standard secondary zones for all remote locations, you can provide a local name resolution solution and reduce the additional traffic placed on the WAN links due to the DNS service. Each secondary zone server will perform zone transfers with the corporate data center DNS servers, which is still likely much less traffic than handling the individual name resolution queries. Although a good idea, simply configuring your zones as Active Directory integrated won't help out with the WAN link traffic concern; thus Answer A is incorrect. Putting secondary zones on the corporate data center DNS servers won't help out with the WAN link traffic concern; thus Answer C is incorrect. Stub zones aren't going to reduce the WAN link traffic either; thus Answer D is incorrect. For more information, see Chapter 3.

46. **D**. Only Answer D meets all the specified requirements that Christopher has for performing this analysis: He must use the Secure template for a member server (`securews.inf`), and he must ensure that the database is cleared before the security template is imported. Answer C appears to meet these requirements, but it does not provide for clearing the database before importing the security template. The command presented in Answer A is incorrect because it uses the `securedc.inf` template. The command presented in Answer B is incorrect because it is actually going to configure, and not analyze, security settings. For more information, see Chapter 5.

47. **B**. The only correct syntax for this command is `route add 10.10.10.0 mask 255.255.255.0 10.10.10.254 metric 2`; thus Answers A, C, and D are incorrect. For more information, see Chapter 7.

48. **B**, **D**, **E**. PPTP requires an IP-based transit network. L2TP requires only that the tunnel media provide packet-oriented point-to-point connectivity; thus Answer A is incorrect. L2TP supports header compression, whereas PPTP does not; thus Answer C is incorrect. L2TP supports tunnel authentication, whereas PPTP does not. PPTP uses encryption; L2TP requires IPSec for encryption. L2TP can be used on a variety of hardware- and software-based devices, not just Windows based, thus Answer F incorrect. For more information, see Chapter 6.

49. **C**. Answers A and B could also be good answers, but the best answer is Answer C, as one of the major problems with distance-vector routing is the count-to-infinity problem. The hop count is limited to 16; thus Answer D is incorrect. For more information, see Chapter 7.

50. **B**. Using the `nslookup` command would allow you to query the DNS server to verify entries. You won't find any zone entries on the server's Properties dialog or in the Event Log; thus Answers A and D are incorrect. While the `ipconfig` command is useful for many TCP/IP-related tasks, this is not one of them; thus Answer C is incorrect. For more information, see Chapter 3.

51. **D**. Before the IP addresses can cross over the router, you need to enable the BOOTP forwarder; thus Answer C is incorrect. There is not any such thing as a DHCP forwarder or BOOTP forwarder on a DHCP server; thus Answers A and B are incorrect. For more information, see Chapter 2.

52. **C**. When you configure an Active Directory–integrated zone, the information is stored in the Active Directory database file itself; thus Answers A, B, and D are incorrect. For more information, see Chapter 3.

53. **D**. In a situation in which you do not know what the current security configuration is, you should apply the Default security template to the computer. Each computer has its own Default security template. This default security template is created at the time of Windows Server 2003 installation for member servers and at the time of promotion for Domain Controllers. You should not apply the Default security template from one computer to any other computer; thus Answer A is incorrect. After you reset the security configuration back to a known state by using the Default template, the secure templates can be successfully applied to create the desired level of security. Recall that security templates are incremental and only build on the security configuration already configured—they do not reset the computers' security configuration back to the default settings before any changes were made. Andrea should not apply a workstation template to a server, much less a Domain Controller; thus Answer B is incorrect. Reinstalling Windows Server 2003 on the servers would certainly put them in a known state, but is way beyond what is needed here; thus Answer C is incorrect. For more information, see Chapter 5.

54. **B**. The best routing protocol for this situation would be RIP. Although there are some drawbacks to using RIP, it is easy to set up and maintain, and it allows for redundancy between sites. Using static routes for this environment would be too time consuming and error prone; thus Answer A is incorrect. Using OSPF is not required in this network due to its relative small size and simplicity; thus Answer C is incorrect. An *autostatic update* is a request from a router for all known routes or services from the router on the other side of the connection; thus Answer D is incorrect. For more information, see Chapter 7.

55. **D**. Profiles are stored locally and need to be re-created on the new server before users can authenticate. You can have as many RRAS servers as your environment needs; thus Answer A is incorrect. There is no authorization that you must perform for RRAS like for DHCP; thus Answer B is incorrect. A RRAS server in an Active Directory domain will add itself to the required security groups automatically; thus Answer C is incorrect. For more information, see Chapter 6.

56. **A**. A reverse lookup zone allows you to resolve an IP address to a hostname. Forward lookup zones are used for hostname-to-IP address resolution; thus Answer B is incorrect. You will need to use the `arp` command to compare IP addresses to MAC addresses; thus Answer C is incorrect. You can determine, more often than not, the FQDN of a host by simply `pinging` the hostname. In a fully functional DNS environment, the returned information will contain the FQDN of the host; thus Answer D is incorrect. For more information, see Chapter 3.

57. **C**. Although EIGRP and BGP are excellent protocols for a large WAN of this type, they are not supported by Windows Server 2003. The best routing protocol for the situation described would be OSPF; thus Answers A, B, and E are incorrect. An *autostatic update* is a request from a router for all known routes or services from the router on the other side of the connection; thus Answer D is incorrect. For more information, see Chapter 7.

58. **A**. The Windows Server 2003 DHCP service is used to automatically assign IP addresses to client computers. DNS is used to resolve hostnames and IP address; thus Answer B is incorrect. WINS is used to resolve NetBIOS hostnames and IP addresses; thus Answer C is incorrect. BOOTP is not needed for Windows computers; thus Answer D is incorrect. For more information, see Chapter 2.

59. **D**. RAM is the most critical resource on a cache-only server because all the cache entries are stored in RAM; thus Answers A, B, C, and E are all incorrect. For more information, see Chapter 3.

60. **A**. In order to track failed logon attempts, Kirsten needs to configure failure auditing to occur for the Audit Logon Events option. Configuring auditing for success events on the Audit Logon Events option won't help collect information about failed logon attempts; thus Answer B is incorrect. Since she needs to collect information about failed logon events, it won't help to configure auditing for other areas; thus Answers C and D are incorrect. For more information, see Chapter 5.

61. **C**. The area with the ID 0.0.0.0 is the OSPF backbone. An autonomous system (AS) is a collection of networks and routers that are under common administration and that share a common routing protocol; thus Answer A is incorrect. The Link State Database (LSDB) is used by OSPF routers as they accumulate link-state information; thus Answer B is incorrect. A default route has a destination address of 0.0.0.0 and a subnet mask of 0.0.0.0. The default route is used to route any packets that are destined for an address not explicitly listed in the routing table; thus Answer D is incorrect. For more information, see Chapter 7.

62. D. IAS is needed to provide RADIUS authentication for the remote access servers. IAS can be used as the central repository for the profiles; thus Answers A, B, and C are incorrect. For more information, see Chapter 6.

63. C. To get a client computer to register dynamically with a DNS server, you type **`ipconfig/registerdns`** at the command prompt. Rebooting the computer will likely also solve the problem, but will take more time than simply using the `ipconfig/registerdns` command; thus Answer A is incorrect. The `ipconfig/renew` command is used to renew a DHCP lease; thus Answer B is incorrect. The `ipconfig/renewdns` command is not a valid command; thus Answer D is incorrect. For more information, see Chapter 3.

64. C. Although the default route can be used to simplify configuration of static routing over on-demand connections, you must consider its implications. The default IP route effectively summarizes all IP destinations and becomes the route used to forward IP packets when another more specific route is not found. This can cause traffic to be routed across the on-demand connection. It is not normal for a demand-dial connection to just connect without data to transmit; thus Answer A is incorrect. It is already known that no communication is occurring between the offices; thus Answer B is incorrect. A default route on the answering router would not cause this behavior; thus Answer D is incorrect. For more information, see Chapter 6.

65. D. To configure a new multicast scope, you must select the option New Multicast Scope. The New Scope option configures a normal DHCP scope; thus Answer A is incorrect. The New Superscope option will configure a superscope that contains multiple normal scopes; thus Answer B is incorrect. You can't create a new IP Scope; thus Answer C is incorrect. For more information, see Chapter 2.

PART III

Appendixes

APPENDIX A

Accessing Your Free MeasureUp Practice Test—Including Networking Simulations!

This Exam Cram book features exclusive access to MeasureUp's practice questions, including networking simulations! These simulations are yet another excellent study tool to help you assess your readiness for the 70-291 exam. MeasureUp is a Microsoft Certified Practice Test Provider, so these simulations validate your hands-on skills by modeling real-life networking scenarios via the use of simulated networking devices. MeasureUp's simulations also assess your ability to troubleshoot and solve realistic networking problems. If you are planning to take the certification exam for 70-290 or 70-291, you should expect to see performance-based simulations on the exam. MeasureUp's Microsoft simulations will ensure you are prepared.

To access your free practice questions and simulations, do the following:

1. Retrieve your unique registration key, which is on the inside of the back cover of this book.
2. Go to www.measureup.com.
3. Create a free MeasureUp account or log in to your existing account.
4. On the Learning Locker Toolbar, click Register Products.
5. Read and consent to the License Agreement by clicking the checkbox below the License Agreement.
6. Type your registration key number in the Key box. Do not remove any dashes or substitute any numbers.
7. Click Register.
8. Click the Learning Locker button to display your Personal Test Locker.
9. Click the Practice Test link, and follow the instructions to start your test or the Learning Locker tab to return to your Learning Locker.

For more details about MeasureUp's product features, see Appendix B, "MeasureUp's Product Features."

APPENDIX B

MeasureUp's Product Features

Since 1997, MeasureUp has helped more than 1 million IT professionals achieve certifications from the industry's leading vendors. Created by content developers certified in their areas and with real-world experience, MeasureUp practice tests feature comprehensive questions (some with performance-based simulations), detailed explanations, and complete score reporting. As a Microsoft Certified Practice Test Provider, MeasureUp's practice tests are the closest you can get to the certification exams!

Multiple Testing Modes

MeasureUp practice tests are available in Study, Certification, Custom, Missed Question, and Non-Duplicate question modes.

Study Mode

Tests administered in Study Mode allow you to request the correct answer(s) and explanation for each question during the test. These tests are not timed. You can modify the testing environment *during* the test by clicking the Options button.

Certification Mode

Tests administered in Certification Mode closely simulate the actual testing environment you will encounter when taking a certification exam. These tests do not allow you to request the answer(s) or explanation for each question until after the exam.

Custom Mode

Custom Mode allows you to specify your preferred testing environment. Use this mode to specify the objectives you want to include in your test, the timer length, and other test properties. You can also modify the testing environment *during* the test by clicking the Options button.

Missed Question Mode

Missed Question Mode allows you to take a test containing only the questions you missed previously.

Non-Duplicate Mode

Non-Duplicate Mode allows you to take a test containing only questions not displayed previously.

Question Types

The practice question types simulate the real exam experience, and include

- Create a tree
- Select and place
- Drop and connect
- Build list
- Reorder list
- Build and reorder list
- Single hotspot
- Multiple hotspots
- Live screen
- Command line
- Hot area
- Fill in the blank

Random Questions and Order of Answers

This feature helps you learn the material without memorizing questions and answers. Each time you take a practice test, the questions and answers appear in a different randomized order.

Detailed Explanations of Correct and Incorrect Answers

You'll receive automatic feedback on all correct and incorrect answers. The detailed answer explanations are a superb learning tool in their own right.

Attention to Exam Objectives

MeasureUp practice tests are designed to appropriately balance the questions over each technical area covered by a specific exam.

Technical Support

If you encounter problems with the MeasureUp test engine, you can contact MeasureUp at 678-356-5050 or email support@measureup.com. Technical support hours are from 8 a.m. to 5 p.m. EST Monday through Friday. Additionally, you'll find Frequently Asked Questions (FAQs) at www.measureup.com.

C

APPENDIX C

Review Questions and Answers

Chapter 1

Review Questions

1. What are two requirements for a valid IP address in a Windows Server 2003 environment?
2. How does TCP/IP know whether packets are local to a network or need to be forwarded to another network?
3. Why should a company choose to use DHCP over manually assigning IP addresses?
4. Why is it important to have a DNS server's IP address for a client computer in a Windows Server 2003 network?
5. What is the disadvantage of using VLSM to break up IP address ranges?

Answers to Review Questions

1. Two *minimum* requirements for a valid IP address in a Windows Server 2003 environment are a valid IP address and a subnet mask. With that having been said, you will typically always also configure a default gateway as well. For more information, see the section "Configuring TCP/IP."
2. The subnet mask defines the network ID portion of the IP address. If the destination of the packet has a different network ID, the packet is forwarded to the gateway. For more information, see the section "Subnets and Subnet Masks."
3. DHCP allows the dynamic assignment of IP addresses and provides greater flexibility in address management than manually assigning IP addresses. For example, a client computer using DHCP does not have a statically assigned IP address and can be moved to another network segment without the TCP/IP configuration needing to be manually modified. For more information, see the section "Configuring TCP/IP."

4. A DNS server provides the capability of resolving hostnames to IP addresses. Without a DNS server, you would need to know the actual IP address of the target computer. Also, with Windows Server 2003 Active Directory and DHCP, DNS can be dynamically updated. For more information, see the section "Configuring TCP/IP."

5. Although VLSM can be used to break up larger blocks of IP addresses into smaller, more customizable (and manageable) blocks, it causes you to lose usable IP addresses in the process. For example, when applying the VLSM 192.168.211.0/26, you would create four subnets, each with 62 usable addresses, for a total of 248 usable addresses. In this case, you would lose seven addresses. For more information, see the section "Variable Length Subnet Masks (VLSM)."

Chapter 2

Review Questions

1. You are the systems administrator for Exponent Mathematicians, and you have been asked to implement DHCP on a multinetted network segment. What should you do to ensure that you do this successfully?

2. You are the administrator of the DHCP server for the Get Bux pawnshop chain. You are getting complaints from users that they keep getting address conflict messages when they turn on their computers. What DHCP counter might help you identify the problem?

3. You are the administrator for Fly Away Travel. When administering Fly Away's DHCP server, you notice that the number of DHCP requests is very high for the number of users on the network. Where is the first place you should look for a server-related problem?

4. You're the administrator of the DHCP server for Little Faith Enterprises. You notice that the DHCP server is running sluggishly during peak hours. When you check the Performance utility, you notice that the DHCP Conflict Check Queue Length counter is very high. What could be causing the DHCP server to be running slowly?

5. You're the administrator of the DHCP server for Little Faith Enterprises. You have just installed the DHCP service and created your first scope by using the New Scope Wizard. You are trying to provide DHCP addresses to a group of users that are two router hops away. What do you still need to do?

Answers to Review Questions

1. To successfully implement DHCP in a multinetted environment, you should consider using a superscope to ease the management of the scopes for each of the multinetted networks. For more information, see the section "Understanding DHCP Superscopes."

2. You should check the Declines/Sec counter in the Performance console for the DHCP object. The number of `DHCPDECLINE` messages received per second by the DHCP server from client computers can be used to see whether the DHCP client computer has declined the IP address issued by the server. You see this number rise when client computers start having address conflict problems, and it could indicate a network problem, computers with static addresses also being part of a scope, or a rogue DHCP server being on the network. For more information, see the section "Troubleshooting DHCP Server Authorization Problems."

3. You should check the length of the DHCP lease. If the lease has been set to a very short duration, client computers would need to request addresses frequently. For more information, see the section "Creating a DHCP Scope."

4. There are either a lot of DHCP requests occurring during peak hours or the Conflict Detection Attempts parameter is set too high. If that parameter is enabled, the Windows Server 2003 DHCP service issues an address, and it checks whether any IP address conflicts exist. This can put a lot of additional overhead on the server and drive up the DHCP conflict check queue length. For more information, see the section "Troubleshooting DHCP Server Authorization Problems."

5. First, you need to authorize the DHCP server in Active Directory. The DHCP server cannot provide addresses until that occurs. You also need to configure the BOOTP forwarder on any routers between the DHCP server and the client workstations so that the routers know where to forward DHCP messages. For more information, see the section "Authorizing a DHCP Server in Active Directory."

Chapter 3

Review Questions

1. You are the systems administrator for Exponent Mathematicians, and you have been asked to implement DNS for a purely Windows environment, taking full advantage of the benefits of Windows Server 2003. How should you do this and why?

2. You are the systems administrator of the Get Stuffed Taxidermists chain DNS server. You are getting complaints from several field locations that it takes a long time to resolve addresses. All the sites complaining are across slow (128Kbps) WAN links. What should you do?

3. What must you create and configure to ensure that the `nslookup` command will work properly on your network?

4. You're the systems administrator of the Windows Server 2003 DNS server for Little Faith Enterprises. An end user is trying to download the 128-bit version of the Windows Server 2003 Service Pack 3. Microsoft's Web site keeps denying him access, saying that his domain cannot be resolved. What can you do to fix this?

5. You're the systems administrator for the Think About IT Consulting Services company. You are running a Windows NT 4.0 domain architecture and have just implemented your first Windows Server 2003 client computers. You have configured the client computers to perform dynamic updates to DNS, but they are not appearing in the table. Why are they not appearing, and what should you do to fix the problem?

Answers to Review Questions

1. Placement of the DNS servers is dependent on the network infrastructure of the company, but you need a Windows Server 2003 DNS service. Windows NT 4.0 DNS does not support the DDNS, and although other DNS servers support DDNS, the requirement for a purely Windows environment leaves them out. Although there may be benefits to some of the other platforms, a single-platform solution is not uncommon in environments where the administrators are most familiar with Windows NT. For more information, see the section "Configuring Zones."
2. You should place a secondary master DNS server at each of the complaining sites. This will give the sites local DNS resolution and a local cache of commonly visited Internet addresses. For more information, see the section "Installing and Configuring the DNS Server Service."
3. You must create and properly configure one or more reverse lookup zones in order for the `nslookup` command to function properly. By default, no reverse lookup zones will be automatically created for you; you will need to ensure they are created on your own. For more information, see the section "Reverse Lookups."
4. You need to make sure the end user had an entry in your reverse lookup table. Microsoft's site is trying to verify his location based on your domain and needs to be able to do a reverse lookup. If you do not have a reverse lookup zone, you need to create one. For more information, see the section "Reverse Lookups."
5. Windows NT 4.0's DNS server does not support DDNS updates. You need to upgrade to Windows Server 2003 DNS or migrate to a third-party implementation of DNS that supports dynamic updates. For more information, see the section "Configuring Zones."

Chapter 4

Review Questions

1. You are the network administrator for a small company with several sites, each with host computers. You are in the process of migrating to Windows Server 2003, but you want to be sure that all your legacy Windows NT 4 computers can browse the network. What should you do?
2. You have successfully deployed WINS in your environment, and it is working. Your users can browse the network. How does the WINS database get populated to make this possible?

3. After the WINS is fully implemented and the database is populated, how are entries deleted from the database?
4. What is the major difference between push replication and pull replication?
5. You're the administrator of Little Faith Enterprise's Windows Server 2003 servers, and you are considering setting up WINS. You feel you need a better understanding of how NetBIOS works and how the various node types work. What are the four NetBIOS node types, and how do they work?

Answers to Review Questions

1. You need to deploy WINS in your environment. Depending on your environment, you might be able to deploy redundant WINS servers in your central site, or you might need to deploy WINS servers to each location. In either event, you must configure replication between the servers. For more information, see the section "Installing and Configuring WINS."
2. The WINS database is populated by the WINS client computer. When the WINS client computer comes on the network, it registers its name and address with the WINS server automatically. After the client computer is registered, it receives a time to live for its registration. For more information, see the section "Configuring WINS."
3. There are two automated mechanisms for removing entries. When a client computer shuts down gracefully, it sends a release request to the WINS server. The entries are also removed when the time to live for that client computer's registration expires. For more information, see the section "Configuring WINS Replication."
4. The main difference between push and pull replication (besides the direction the database is replicated) is the trigger for the event. In the case of a push replication, the trigger is event based. When a specified number of changes are made to the database, the replication is triggered. A pull replication is triggered by the time configured for the replication. This is user configured. For more information, see the section "Configuring WINS Replication."
5. There are four node types, and the main differentiator between the types is the methods they use for name resolution (broadcast versus direct connection). They are as follows:
   - **b-node (broadcast node)**—Relies exclusively on broadcast messages and is the oldest NetBIOS name resolution mode. A host needing to resolve a name request sends a message to every host within earshot, requesting the address associated with a host name. b-node has two shortcomings: Broadcast traffic is undesirable and becomes a significant user of network bandwidths, and TCP/IP routers don't forward broadcast messages, which restricts b-node operation to a single network segment.
   - **p-node (point-to-point node)**—Relies on WINS servers for NetBIOS name resolution. Client computers register themselves with a WINS server when they come on the network. They then contact the WINS server with NetBIOS name resolution requests. WINS servers communicate using directed messages, which can cross routers, so p-node can operate on large networks. Unfortunately, if the WINS server is unavailable or if a node isn't configured to contact a WINS server, p-node name resolution fails.

- **m-node (modified node)**—It's a hybrid mode that first attempts to resolve NetBIOS names using the b-node mechanism. If that fails, an attempt is made to use p-node name resolution. m-node was the first hybrid mode put into operation, but it has the disadvantage of favoring b-node operation, which is associated with high levels of broadcast traffic.
- **h-node (hybrid node)**—It's also a hybrid mode that favors the use of WINS for NetBIOS name resolution. When a computer needs to resolve a NetBIOS name, it first attempts to use p-node resolution to resolve a name via WINS. Only if WINS resolution fails does the host resort to b-node to resolve the name via broadcasts. Because it typically results in the best network utilization, h-node is the default mode of operation for Windows clients configured to use WINS for name resolution. Microsoft recommends leaving TCP/IP client computers in the default h-node configuration.

For more information, see the section "Configuring NetBIOS Name Resolution."

Chapter 5

Review Questions

1. You are trying to explain to your CIO why using security templates to configure security is a better idea than directly configuring a GPO. What are some reasons that you might present to him to support your position?
2. You are the systems administrator of a large campus-wide community college network. Your network is comprised of computers running every version of Windows from Windows 95 to Windows Server 2003. Is WSUS a good solution for your network, to ensure that all computers are up-to-date with the latest security patches?
3. You have instructed your assistant administrator to configure auditing on the network. The next morning you come in and attempt to examine the security log on a DC, only to find out that it has shut down over night. What is the most likely reason for this situation?
4. You have configured WSUS for your network, but now several client computers are not getting updates. You determine that these computers are running a Japanese localized version of Windows XP Professional. What should you do to allow them to get updates from your WSUS server?
5. Your CIO has instructed you to implement a WSUS solution for your corporate network. He is concerned, however, about making unsecured connections to the WSUS server. What can be done to provide connection security?

Answers to Review Questions

1. By using security templates, you can perform configuration and testing on a computer that will not result in changes being applied across the network until they are ready. In addition, by using a security template, you are in effect using a script: You can ensure that all changes will be identical to all computers to which they are applied, even if they are in different OUs or domains. For more information, see the section "The Security Configuration and Analysis Snap-in."
2. If you have large numbers of pre-Windows 2000 computers (that is, legacy clients), WSUS is probably not the best solution for your updating needs. In this situation, you would most likely want to examine a solution such as SMS or a third-party solution that provides the same type of functionality. For more information, see the section "Implementing Windows Server Update Services (WSUS)."
3. Your assistant most likely caused this problem through the combination of two acts. First, he most likely enabled too much auditing, which created a flood of audit entries into the security log. Second, he most likely configured Group Policy to shut down the computer when the security log was full. This security option is designed to limit and contain the amount of damage an attacker can do. Shutting down a system when the security log fills up removes the system, and thus the target of opportunity, from the network when its security log has been filled to maximum capacity. In this case, the overzealous decision to audit too many things has created the same type of event flood condition. For more information, see the section "Configuring Auditing."
4. This is a relatively easy problem to solve: You simply enable support for the languages that you will be supporting from the WSUS Synchronization Options page. In this case, you should select the Japanese language option. For more information, see the section "Implementing Windows Server Update Services (WSUS)."
5. You can enable SSL support on the WSUS Web site and thus require that all connections be SSL secured. For more information, see the section "Implementing Windows Server Update Services (WSUS)."

Chapter 6

Review Questions

1. You are the network administrator for Exponent Mathematicians, and you have been asked to review the authentication protocols being used by your RRAS server. What are the available protocols, and how do they work?
2. You are the administrator of the Get Stuffed Taxidermists chain RRAS server. You have users who are utilizing the Windows Server 2003 VPN, using both IPSec and PPTP. What are those protocols, and which of them is the industry standard?

3. You have just installed RRAS for providing VPN services to 100 of your end users. You are able to get the first five users connected, but then the server denies access. What is the problem, and how do you fix it?
4. You're the LAN administrator for the Think About IT Consulting Services company. You have just installed your first RRAS server, and your users are connecting without a problem. You want to see how much traffic is being added to the network because of the additional users. How can you check?
5. If you use autostatic updates, what must you do the first time you connect to a remote router?

Answers to Review Questions

1. The authentication protocols available include the following:
    - **EAP-TLS**—EAP is an extension to PPP. EAP provides a standard mechanism for support of additional authentication methods within PPP, such as smart cards, one-time passwords, and certificates. EAP is critical for secure Windows Server 2003 VPNs because it offers stronger authentication methods (such as the use of smart cards) than relying on the user ID and password schemes used traditionally.
    - **CHAP**—CHAP negotiates encrypted authentication by using MD5, an industry-standard hashing scheme. CHAP uses challenge response with one-way MD5 hashing on the response. This allows a user to authenticate to the server without actually sending his or her password over the network. Because CHAP is an industry-standard authentication method, it allows Windows Server 2003 to securely connect to almost all third-party PPP servers.
    - **MS-CHAP**—Microsoft created MS-CHAP, an extension of CHAP, to authenticate remote Windows workstations, increasing CHAP's functionality by integrating the encryption and hashing algorithms used on Windows networks. Like CHAP, MS-CHAP uses a challenge-response mechanism with one-way encryption on the response. Although MS-CHAP is consistent with standard CHAP as much as possible, the MS-CHAP response packet is in a format specifically designed for computers running Windows operating systems. MS-CHAPv2 is also available. This new protocol provides mutual authentication, stronger initial data encryption keys, and different encryption keys for sending and receiving.
    - **SPAP**—Shiva Password Authentication Protocol (SPAP) is used specifically to allow Shiva client computers to connect to Windows Server 2003 servers and to allow Windows 2000 client computers to connect to Shiva servers.
    - **PAP**—PAP uses unencrypted (plaintext) passwords for authenticating users and is considered the least secure authentication protocol available. PAP is usually used as the authentication method of last resort—when a more secure form of authentication is not available. You might need to use this protocol when you are connecting to a non-Windows-based server.

    For more information, see the section "Configuring Remote Access Authentication Protocols."

2. Understanding the differences between IPSec and PPTP is important. These points should help you distinguish between the two:

    - **IPSec**—IPSec is a suite of cryptography-based protection services and security protocols used to provide a secure VPN connection. IPSec provides machine-level authentication, as well as data encryption, for L2TP-based VPN connections. Unlike some other IPSec-based VPNs, Microsoft's implementation uses the L2TP protocol for encrypting the usernames, passwords, and data, whereas IPSec is used to negotiate the secure connection between a computer and its remote tunnel server. All authentication under a Microsoft IPSec VPN occurs through L2TP connections, which use all standard PPP-based authentication protocols to authenticate the user after the secure IPSec communication is established.
    - **PPTP**—PPTP is Microsoft's legacy protocol for supporting VPNs. Developed jointly by Microsoft Corporation, U.S. Robotics, and several remote access vendor companies, known collectively as the PPTP Forum, PPTP encountered some security problems in its original form. PPTP has been revised by Microsoft, but it has never been widely accepted by the security community. Although still supported on a variety of vendors' VPN servers, PPTP is rapidly being overtaken by the more widely adopted IPSec protocol.

    For more information, see the section "Supported VPN Protocols."

3. By default, RRAS is configured with five connections for the VPN. You need to open the RRAS application, go into the port properties, and add additional ports as needed. For more information, see the section "Managing Devices and Ports."

4. To find out the raw numbers on bandwidth through the server, you need to use the Performance console. You go to the RAS Total object and add the Total Bytes Received and Total Bytes Transmitted counters. Then you add the counts of the two counters to get the total additional traffic. For more information, see the section "Troubleshooting Tools."

5. Autostatic updates do not occur automatically on initiation of a demand-dial connection. Rather, the autostatic update must be manually initiated or a schedule must be put in place to update routes. After the routes have been sent, the two routers do not exchange updates of routing information unless a manual request to update is made or a scheduled request occurs, depending on how autostatic updates are configured within the environment. Therefore, the first time a connection is made, an autostatic update must be manually initiated to configure the router with proper routes to the destination network. For more information, see the section "Autostatic Updates."

Chapter 7

Review Questions

1. What is a topological database?

2. What is one reason link-state protocols are more efficient than distance-vector algorithms?

3. Which parameter of the `route` command clears all existing routing table entries?

4. What ID is reserved for the OSPF backbone?

5. What is one of the major problems with distance-vector routing?

Answers to Review Questions

1. A topological database is essentially an overall picture of networks in relationship to routers. A topological database contains the collection of LSAs received from all routers in the same area. In a very large AS with a large number of networks, each OSPF router must keep the LSA of every other router in its topological database. Each router in a large OSPF AS has a large topological database. The SPF calculation of a large topological database can require a substantial amount of processing and can result in very large routing tables. To prevent this, ASs are divided into areas. For more information, see the section "Working with OSPF."

2. A link-state routing protocol is generally more efficient than a distance-vector protocol. The fact that LSAs contain only information about the neighbors of a particular router leads to smaller routing tables. For large networks, the LSAs contain only neighbor information, and therefore the impact on the network is much less than it would be on a network using a distance-vector routing protocol. With a distance-vector routing protocol, all the routes in a routing table are propagated, resulting in more usage of bandwidth than link-state protocols. In addition, because link-state information is not exchanged after the network has converged, it does not have the impact on the network that distance-vector routing does. By default, distance-vector routing broadcasts its information on a periodic basis, whether the information is required or not. For more information, see the section "Routing Protocols."

3. The `-f` parameter is used to clear the routing tables of all entries. For more information, see the section "Using the `route` Command to Configure Static Routes."

4. An OSPF backbone has a reserved area ID of 0.0.0.0. An OSPF backbone is responsible for distributing routing information between areas. There is at least one backbone per OSPF internetwork. It consists of all area border routers, networks that are not in any one area, and their attached routers. The backbone has to be at the center of all areas within the AS. That is, all areas have to be physically connected to the backbone. This is because OSPF expects all areas to inject routing information into the backbone, and in turn the backbone will disseminate that information into other areas. For more information, see the section "Working with OSPF."

5. The count-to-infinity problem is one of the major disadvantages of distance-vector routing. This condition is caused when a router (or a link to a router) becomes unavailable. The convergence time is slow and, therefore, incorrect routing information is propagated through the system. For more information, see the section "Routing Protocols."

Chapter 8

Review Questions

1. What IPSec policies does Windows Server 2003 provide by default?
2. Why is IPSec so important in a routed environment?
3. What is Kerberos used for in Windows Server 2003?
4. You are planning a new IPSec policy for use on your internal network between your Financial subnet and your Accounting subnet. What authentication methods will you have to select from when creating this new policy?
5. What functions does AH provide in IPSec?

Answers to Review Questions

1. Windows Server 2003 comes with the following three preconfigured IPSec policies that may or may not meet your needs:
    - **Client (Respond Only)**—This policy requires IPSec-provided security only when another computer requests it. This policy allows the computer to attempt unsecured communications first and switch to IPSec-secured communications if requested. This policy contains the default response rule, which creates dynamic IPSec filters for inbound and outbound traffic based on the requested protocol and port traffic for the communication that is being secured. This policy, which can be used on workstations and servers alike, provides the minimum amount of IPSec security.
    - **Server (Request Security)**—This policy requests security from the other computer and allows unsecured communication with non IPSec-aware computers. The computer accepts inbound unsecured traffic but always attempts to secure further communications by requesting IPSec security from the sending computer. If the other computer is not IPSec-enabled, the entire communication is allowed to be unsecured. This policy, which can be used on workstations and servers alike, provides a medium level of IPSec security.
    - **Secure Server (Require Security)**—This policy is implemented on computers that require highly secure communications, such as servers transmitting sensitive data. The filters in this policy require all outbound communication to be secured, allowing only the initial inbound communication request to be unsecured. This policy has a rule to require security for all IP traffic, a rule to permit ICMP traffic, and the default response rule to respond to requests for security from other computers. This policy, typically used only on servers, provides the highest level of IPSec security on a network. This policy can also be used on workstation computers if you want. Non-IPSec-enabled computers cannot establish any communications with computers using this policy.

You can opt to either use one of the preconfigured policies that comes with Windows Server 2003 or create your own policy. You can also modify the preconfigured policies to suit your needs if you want. For more information, see the section "Configuring and Implementing IPSec."

2. IPSec provides data integrity between two host IDs. The data and identity are safe and kept from being changed or read by other users through intermediary software. For more information, see the section "Monitoring and Troubleshooting Network Protocol Security."

3. The Kerberos version 5 protocol is used for user authentication in Windows 2000 and newer networks. For more information, see the section "Monitoring and Troubleshooting Kerberos."

4. IPSec on Windows Server 2003 can use Kerberos v5, a digital certificate, or a shared secret (string) for user authentication. For more information, see the section "What's New with Windows Server 2003 IPSec."

5. The IPSec AH provides three services as part of the IPSec protocol. First (as its name might suggest), AH authenticates the entire packet. Second, it ensures data integrity. Third, it prevents any replaying of the packet by a third party who might be trying to penetrate the IPSec tunnel. One service AH doesn't provide is payload encryption. AH protects your data from modification, but an attacker who is snooping the network would still be able to read the data. For more information, see the section "Authentication Header (AH)."

Chapter 9

Review Questions

1. What is a baseline and why is it important to create one?

2. When troubleshooting network or server problems using the Network Monitor, and assuming you're not sure what exactly you're looking for, when should you configure your filters?

3. What is the difference between using the Performance console's System Monitor and the Performance console's Counter Logs?

4. Why can broadcast traffic become a problem on large or busy networks?

5. What limitation is imposed on the version of Network Monitor that is included with Windows Server 2003?

Answers to Review Questions

1. You need to create a baseline of the server performance that can be used to compare against the current performance statistics. You should create this baseline before making any changes and again after you've verified any changes made were successful. You need this baseline to locate problematic areas. This can be very useful when you're performing troubleshooting, and it also aids during periods when configurations are being modified. For more information, see the section "Creating Baseline Counter Logs."

2. In cases when you are using the Network Monitor and you are not absolutely certain of the type of traffic or protocol for which you are looking, you will want to capture all traffic to or from the server and then filter it during the display phase. The downside to filtering traffic while capturing is that you will see only the traffic that meets the filter criteria. On the other hand, if you decide to filter traffic after the capture, you will be able to see all packets that traversed the server's network adapters, giving you the ability to examine the traffic in greater detail. For more information, see the section "Using the Network Monitor."

3. When you use the System Monitor portion of the Performance console, you are monitoring and viewing performance statistics in real time for your server. When you use the Counter Logs portion of the Performance console, you are creating log files containing performance statistics for your server that can be played back at any time in the future. For more information, see the section "Creating Baseline Counter Logs."

4. Because broadcast traffic is sent to all computers on a subnet, it causes excessive amounts of network traffic. Although some communications rely on broadcasts, such as ARP resolution and DHCP leasing, the majority of traffic does not need to use broadcasts. For more information, see the section "Using the Network Monitor."

5. The Network Monitor version included in Windows Server 2003 can capture only traffic being sent to or from the specific computer on which it is installed. For more information, see the section "Installing Network Monitor."

Glossary

Numbers and Symbols

`%SystemRoot%` A universal reference to the directory in which the Windows system files are installed. Typically, `%SystemRoot%` is `C:\Winnt` or `C:\Windows`. By default, clean installations of Windows Server 2003 use the Windows directory. If multiple copies of Windows are installed in a multiboot system, each copy has its own `%SystemRoot%` directory.

3DES (Triple Data Encryption Standard) A more secure variant of the DES standard that encrypts data by using three different 56-bit keys in succession. 3DES thus extends the DES key to 168 bits, providing approximately 6.2×10^{57} different keys.

A

Active Directory The directory services included with Windows Server 2003. Based on the DNS hierarchy, Active Directory provides a domain-based directory service for organizing all the objects and services in a Windows Server 2003 network.

Active Directory Users and Computers An MMC management console provided in Windows 2000 and Windows Server 2003 Active Directory domains that can be used to administer Active Directory objects.

address pool The available IP addresses within a scope for dynamic assignment by the DHCP server to DHCP clients.

address reservation *See* reservation.

adjacency A term in routing that refers to the record that a router keeps about the state of its connectivity with a neighbor and the attributes of the neighboring router.

administrative share A hidden share, created by the Windows installation process. Administrative shares may not be permanently removed and are identified by a trailing $ in the name (for example, C$, D$). Any share name appended with a $ is a hidden share. Only shares created at installation are considered administrative shares.

aging The DNS-related process of placing a timestamp on a dynamically created resource record and then tracking the age of that record.

AH (Authentication Header) A protocol in the IPSec suite that is used to authenticate IP traffic. The AH is inserted into the original IP packet immediately after the IP header.

area In an OSPF routing environment, a logical grouping of routers within the OSPF hierarchy.

area border router A router with multiple interfaces that participates in multiple areas.

ARP (Address Resolution Protocol) A protocol that is used to provide address translation from an IP address of a host to the host's physical address on the network. A host that wants to obtain a physical address broadcasts an ARP request onto the TCP/IP network. The host on the network that has the IP address in the request then replies with its physical hardware address.

ARP (Address Resolution Protocol) table The table of IP-to-MAC address translations that is used by a router to identify the physical addresses of devices on a local subnet.

AS (autonomous system) A collection of networks that are under common administration and share a common routing strategy. Each AS can be further divided into areas, with areas being linked by an OSPF backbone, which is also an area.

auditing The process of logging information about network activities such as user logins, system shutdowns, and file access.

authentication The process of verifying a user's identity on a network.

authoritative zone server A DNS name server that supports the name database for a domain.

Automatic Updates The client-side portion of the WSUS solution. Automatic Updates can be configured to work with the Microsoft Windows Update Web servers or with internal WSUS servers.

autostatic update A request from a router for all known routes or services from the router on the other side of the connection. After the request is received, the router adds the requested routes to its routing table. An autostatic update is a one-time, one-way exchange of routing information.

B

B-node (Broadcast Node) A NetBIOS name resolution method that relies exclusively on broadcast. A host needing to resolve a name request sends a message to every host within earshot, requesting the address associated with a hostname.

baseline A set of collected data that is representative of the normal or beginning performance statistics. You can compare the current performance statistics against a baseline to troubleshoot problems.

BGP (Border Gateway Protocol) An IP routing protocol that enables groups of routers (organized in ASs) to share routing information to create efficient routes. BGP is commonly used by ISPs as an Internet routing protocol. BGP is defined in RFC 1771.

binary circular log A logging file format used by counter logs that record data continuously to the same log file, overwriting previous records with new data when the file reaches its maximum size. Binary circular logs have the .blg extension.

binary log A logging file format used by counter logs that allows you to record data instances that are intermittent. Only binary file formats can accommodate instances that are not persistent throughout the duration of the log. Binary logs have the .blg extension.

BOOTP (Bootstrap Protocol) An Internet protocol that enables a diskless workstation to discover its own IP address from a BOOTP server. BOOTP is still used to allow DHCP requests and responses to traverse a routed network.

bridge A device that works on the physical layer (that is, Layer 2) of the OSI model to connect two network segments. A bridge listens to traffic on both segments and builds a list of MAC addresses that reside on each. It forwards packets from one segment to the other if the destination system is known.

C

CA (Certificate Authority) A service that issues digital certificates to users and computers. In addition, CAs maintain a current list of revoked certificates that are no longer considered valid.

caching A high-speed access mechanism in which routes, addresses, logon/authentication data, or DNS resolutions are stored in memory to speed further requests for the information.

caching-only server A DNS server that does not have authority for any zone because it does not store any zone information. It doesn't provide authoritative answers for other DNS servers, but it responds with the information in its cache.

callback A feature of RRAS that allows RRAS to call a user back by initiating a new connection to the user's predefined phone number after the user's initial modem connection has ended. Callback is used mostly for security reasons, and it can also be used to minimize the user's long-distance charges.

capture filter A filter that can be configured for the Network Monitor and that filters out packets not specifically configured for capture.

cell *See* packet.

certificate A credential that is used to authenticate the origin, identity, and purpose of the public half of a public/private key pair. A certificate ensures that the data sent and received is kept secure.

CHAP (Challenge Handshake Authentication Protocol) An encrypted authentication scheme in which an unencrypted password is not sent over the network. CHAP is defined in RFC 1994 and is supported by RRAS to allow legacy and non-Windows clients to dial in and authenticate to a Windows Server 2003 remote access server.

child domain A Windows Active Directory domain that exists directly beneath a parent domain in a tree hierarchy.

CIDR (classless interdomain routing) A more efficient IP address management system than the original class-based system of Class A, B, and C networks. CIDR is typically used by routers and gateways located on the Internet backbone for routing packets across the Internet. CIDR allows any number of contiguous bits in the IP address to be used at the network ID, resulting in more IP addresses becoming available.

Class A network The largest of the classes of IP networks. There are 126 Class A networks, each capable of addressing up to 16,777,214 hosts. Class A networks have a first octet between 1 and 126, with a default subnet mask of 255.0.0.0.

Class B network The second-largest class of IP networks. There are 16,384 Class B networks, each capable of addressing up to 65,534 hosts. Class B networks have a first octet between 128 and 191, with a default subnet mask of 255.255.0.0.

Class C network The smallest class of IP networks. There are 2,097,152 Class C networks, each capable of addressing up to 254 hosts. Class C networks have a first octet between 192 and 223, with a default subnet mask of 255.255.255.0.

cluster A technology that allows for multiple servers to provide fail-over of services.

CNAME (Canonical Name) record A record in a DNS zone file that acts as an alias for another entry in the DNS zone, allowing a single server to be mapped to multiple names. For example, a CNAME record could be used to map server a51svr3842.area51partners.com to the alias www.area51partners.com.

Compatible template A security template that provides a means of allowing members of the Users group to run applications that do not conform to the Windows Logo Program by modifying the default file and registry permissions that are granted to the Users group.

conditional forwarding A new feature in Windows Server 2003 DNS that allows administrators to direct DNS requests to other DNS servers based on domain. Also known as intelligent forwarding.

convergence A state in which all the routers in a network are aware of all available routes. Convergence is usually referred to in conjunction with the RIP, OSPF, or BGP TCP/IP routing protocols.

counter log A log that can be created by using the Performance console for later viewing and comparison against current performance statistics.

CSV (comma-separated values) A file format that is used by text files that contain fields of data separated by commas and carriage returns.

D

DDNS (Dynamic DNS) A process in which a workstation's name and address are entered into the DNS table when an IP address is obtained through DHCP. DDNS is a new addition to Microsoft's DNS implementation.

Default DC Security template A security template that is automatically created when a member server is promoted to DC. It represents the file, registry, and system service default security settings for that DC and can be used later to reset those areas to their default configurations.

default gateway The configured router on a TCP/IP-enabled system that allows all packets destined for a remote network to be forwarded out of the local network. If a packet is bound for a remote network but no route is specified, the packet is sent to the default gateway address. Also known as the default router.

default route A route that is configured and used to reduce the size of routing tables because they can be used to summarize all routes external to the area into a single route. The default route has a destination address of 0.0.0.0 and a subnet mask of 0.0.0.0. The default route is used to route any packets that are destined for an address not explicitly listed in the routing table.

default router *See* default gateway.

Default Security template A security template that is created during the installation of Windows on a computer. This template varies from one computer to the next, depending on whether the installation was performed as a clean installation or an upgrade. This template represents the default security settings that a computer started out with and thus can be used to reset portions of security as required.

demand dial routing A routing and remote access connection that typically is connected as needed and then disconnected when the need is gone.

DES (Data Encryption Standard) A symmetric encryption scheme that requires the sender and the receiver to know the secret key. DES uses a 56-bit key that provides approximately 7.2×10^{16} different key combinations.

designated router A router in an OSPF environment that acts as the hub for the distribution of link-state information, maintaining the synchronization of the topological database and controlling adjacencies between routers within the network.

DHCP (Dynamic Host Configuration Protocol) A standards-based method of automatically assigning and configuring IP addresses for DHCP clients.

DHCP client Any computer that has DHCP settings enabled and is requesting addresses from a DHCP server.

DHCP server A server that provides the automatic assignment and management of IP addresses to network clients.

DHCPACK An acknowledgment from a DHCP server to a DHCP client that indicates that the request for a lease (or renewal) was successful.

DHCPDISCOVER A message sent from a DHCP client to the network broadcast address. This is the beginning of the lease process, which causes any appropriately configured DHCP server to offer a lease.

DHCPNACK A negative acknowledgment from a DHCP server to a DHCP client, which indicates that the request for a lease (or renewal) was not successful.

DHCPOFFER A message from the DHCP server to the client that has sent a discover message, which indicates an available address.

DHCPREQUEST A message sent from a DHCP client to the server to request an offer or renew an IP address lease.

distance-vector routing A type of routing that calculates the best path in an RIP environment.

DNS (Domain Name System) A service that dynamically provides name and address resolution services in a TCP/IP environment.

DNS client Any host that utilizes a DNS server for name resolution services.

DNS server A server that runs DNS to provide name and address resolution services in a TCP/IP environment.

domain A container in the DNS name hierarchy or the network organizational unit for Windows Server 2003 networks.

dynamic routing A process that provides an automatic mechanism for routers to learn available routes. This is done by using a routing protocol such as RIP, OSPF, or BGP.

E

EGP (Exterior Gateway Protocol) The original exterior protocol used to exchange routing information between networks that do not share a common administration.

encryption A mechanism for securing data in which data is translated into a secret code, which can be read only with the correct key to translate the secret code back to the original data.

ESP (Encapsulating Security Payload) A protocol that is used in the IPSec suite to handle data encryption. ESP is usually used with AH to provide the maximum level of security and integrity for data transmitted in IPSec transmissions. ESP uses DES encryption by default, but it can be configured to use 3DES.

Ethernet A network standard that uses CSMA/CD on a bus topology. Ethernet currently runs at 10Mbps, 100Mbps, and 1Gbps.

exclusion A process in which IP addresses and address ranges are removed (excluded) from a DHCP scope.

Extensible Authentication Protocol (EAP) An extension to the Point-to-Point Protocol (PPP) as specified in RFC 2284 that provides a means for the primary authentication method to be negotiated during the initiation of the PPP session.

F

failure event An audited event that has been completed unsuccessfully, such as a user failing to successfully log in to a network.

forest An Active Directory structure that contains all domain trees. The forest shares the same domain configuration but does not share the same DNS namespace. Forests form the security boundary for Active Directory.

forward lookup In DNS, a name-to-IP address resolution.

forwarder A DNS server that has been configured to send name resolution requests to another DNS server.

FQDN (fully qualified domain name) The complete DNS name of a host, including the hostname and all domains that connect the host to the root domain. The FQDN is typically expressed without a trailing period, with the root domain assumed.

frame *See* packet.

frame type The data format for frames that are placed on a network when IPX/SPX is being used.

G

GC (global catalog) A partial replica of every object in an Active Directory database that is used to speed searching.

GPO (group policy object) A collection of security and configuration settings that are applied to a container in an Active Directory domain.

Group Policy Editor A subset of the Active Directory Users and Computers console that allows the editing of group policy objects.

H

H-node (Hybrid Node) A hybrid NetBIOS name resolution mode that favors the use of WINS for NetBIOS name resolution.

hierarchy A database structure that is based on the principle of categories and subcategories, typically represented in the form of an inverted tree. Each hierarchy has exactly one master category, typically called the root, and all other categories are subcategories of the root category. Categories can contain subcategories as well as data.

Highly Secure template A security template that imposes further restrictions on computers it is applied to. Whereas the Secure templates require at least NTLM authentication, the Highly Secure templates require NTLMv2 authentication.

hive A collection of six or more sets of files that hold registry data. Each hive consists of two files: a data file and a log file.

hop count A common metric used with routing that measures the networks that a message traverses on a route.

host A device that is attached to a TCP/IP network.

host ID The portion of an IP address that uniquely identifies a host on its local TCP/IP network.

host record The most common record in a DNS zone file (also known as an A, or alias, record). It allows a host's DNS name to be resolved to an IP address.

HOSTS A static database file that is used to resolve names on TCP/IP networks.

I–J

IAS (Internet Authentication Service) The Microsoft implementation of the RADIUS standard. RADIUS is used to provide network authentication for users attempting to connect to a network. RADIUS has traditionally been used for dial-up connections, but it has recently begun to see usage in a variety of connection scenarios including wireless network clients.

ICMP (Internet Control Message Protocol) A protocol in the TCP/IP suite of protocols that is used for testing connectivity. ICMP supports packets that contain error, control, and informational messages and is used by applications such as ping and tracert.

IGMP (Internet Group Management Protocol) One of the core protocols in the TCP/IP suite, a routing protocol that is used as part of multicasting.

IGP (Interior Gateway Protocol) A protocol that is used to pass routing information for routing networks that are under a common network administration.

IKE (Internet Key Exchange) An encryption scheme that allows disparate VPN servers to share encryption key information and make the IPSec protocol practical in today's environment.

Integrated Services Digital Network (ISDN) A type of channelized connection (also known as a multiport device). A Primary Rate Interface (PRI) ISDN connection can support two data channels, known as B-channels (short for bearer channels). Each of these B-channels can act as the port for a point-to-point connection. There is an additional 16KB D-channel (short for delta channel) that is used for session control and error handling.

intelligent forwarding *See* conditional forwarding.

IP (Internet Protocol) The portion of the TCP/IP suite that is used to provide packet routing.

IP address The 32-bit binary address that is used to identify a TCP/IP host's network and host ID. IPv6 IP addresses are 128 bits in length.

ipconfig (Internet Protocol Configuration) A command-line utility that can be used to view the configuration details for the host's TCP/IP properties on all installed network adapters. ipconfig can also be used to release or renew an address leased from a DHCP server as well as to display and flush the local DNS cache.

IPSec (IP Security) A Layer 3 TCP/IP that provides end-to-end security for data in transit.

ISAKMP/Oakley (Internet Security Association and Key Management Protocol/Oakley) A protocol that is used to share a public key between sender and receiver of a secure connection. ISAKMP/Oakley allows the receiving system to retrieve a public key and then authenticate the sender by using digital certificates.

iterative query A DNS query sent from a DNS server to one or more DNS servers in search of the DNS server that is authoritative for the name being sought.

K

kerbtray.exe A GUI-based Kerberos monitoring utility that can be used to display the currently cached tickets.

klist.exe The command-line equivalent of the `kerbtray.exe` utility. `klist.exe` can also be used to purge currently cached Kerberos tickets.

L

L2TP (Layer 2 Tunneling Protocol) A VPN protocol that is created by combining the PPTP and L2F tunneling protocols. L2TP is used as the transport protocol in the Windows Server 2003 VPN service in conjunction with IPSec.

LDAP (Lightweight Directory Access Protocol) A lightweight version of the X.500 directory standard that is used as the primary access protocol for Active Directory.

leaf The end object in a hierarchical tree structure.

lease The length of time a client computer can use a dynamically assigned IP address.

link-state routing Dynamic routing that tests the condition of a connection (link) between routers. OSPF is a link-state protocol.

LMHOSTS A static database file that is used to resolve names on NetBIOS networks.

M

M-node (Modified Node) A hybrid NetBIOS name resolution mode that first attempts to resolve NetBIOS names using the B-node mechanism. If that fails, an attempt is made to use P-node name resolution. M-node was the first hybrid mode put into operation, but it has the disadvantage of favoring B-node operation, which is associated with high levels of broadcast traffic.

MAC (Media Access Control) The physical address of a NIC. The MAC exists at the data link layer in the OSI model.

Main Mode The first phase of the IKE two-phase operation to establish a secure communication channel. During this phase, the two computers establish a secure, authenticated channel called the Phase I (Main Mode) SA.

medium A vehicle that carries data between a server and a client. Network media include copper cable, optical fiber, microwaves, and light pulses.

metric A number that assigns a preference to a route within routing protocols. The route with the lowest metric is the preferred route.

MIB (Management Information Base) A database of information that organizes a set of manageable objects for an installed service or device. MIBs are used in conjunction with SNMP.

MMC (Microsoft Management Console) A Microsoft Windows framework used for hosting administrative tools.

modem (modulator/demodulator) A hardware device that is used to convert digital signals to analog and vice versa. A modem allows digital communications to occur over regular (analog) phone lines.

MS-CHAP (Microsoft Challenge Authentication Protocol) A Microsoft-specific variation of the CHAP. MS-CHAP is more secure than CHAP and comes in two variations: MS-CHAPv1 and MS-CHAPv2. MS-CHAPv1 supports one-way authentication and is used by Windows NT 4.0. MS-CHAPv2 is used with Windows 2000 or later and supports mutual authentication.

multicast scope A range of IP multicast addresses in the range 224.0.0.0 to 239.254.255.255. Multicast addresses in this range can be prevented from propagating in either direction (send or receive) through the use of scope-based multicast boundaries.

multicasting A method of sending a series of packets to a group of computers instead of to a single computer or all computers on a network. IGMP support is required to use multicasting.

Multilink A capability that is included in Windows Server 2003 that allows the aggregating of multiple modem connections.

MX (Mail Exchange) record A record in the DNS zone file that indicates which host in the network will receive mail.

N

NetBIOS name The computer name for NetBIOS networking. This name can be 16 characters long: The first 15 characters provide the hostname, and the 16th character represents the service registering the name.

NetBIOS name cache A list of system NetBIOS names that a host has resolved or that have been preloaded from the LMHOSTS file.

NetBIOS node type The node type that determines the order of name resolution for NetBIOS names. There are four types: B-node, P-node, M-node, and H-node.

NetBIOS over TCP/IP (NBT or NetBT) The name given to the process of running NetBIOS network services over TCP/IP.

`netsh` An advanced command-line utility that allows you to display and configure network configuration items on a Windows Server 2003 computer.

Network Basic Input/Output System (NetBIOS) An Application layer networking protocol that works at the Application, Presentation, and Session layers of the OSI model. Legacy Microsoft networking used NetBIOS as the default Application layer protocol.

network ID The portion of an IP address that identifies the network to which a host is attached.

Network Monitor A software-based protocol analyzer that is included with Windows 2000 and Windows Server 2003. The Network Monitor tool can be used to troubleshoot network problems by capturing and analyzing traffic going into and out of a particular computer.

node A device that communicates on a network and is identified by a unique address. In hierarchies, a node is a container that can house other containers and data.

O

octet A group of 8 bits in network addresses, such as an IP address. A 32-bit IP address consists of four octets.

OSPF (Open Shortest Path First) A routing protocol that allows routers to share their routing information, making them dynamic routers.

P

P-node (Point-to-Point Node) A NetBIOS name resolution method that relies on WINS servers for NetBIOS name resolution. Client computers register themselves with a WINS server when they come on the network.

packet The basic unit of information that is transmitted over a network. Packets are also known as frames, datagrams, and cells.

paging The process of swapping data between RAM and disk-based virtual memory.

paging file A temporary file that is used to support virtual memory. Paging files are created on one or more hard drives in a computer and can be used to store data that is not currently needed in RAM.

PAP (Password Authentication Protocol) A clear-text authentication scheme that provides no security for information passed over the connection. PAP is defined in RFC 1334.

parent domain A domain that has one or more child domains under it that share the same DNS namespace.

partition A physical subdivision of a disk drive that can be formatted with a file system.

`pathping` A command-line tool that provides the equivalent of the `tracert` command by allowing you to identify which routers are in the path the packets are taking. `pathping` also acts as the equivalent of the ping command by sending ping requests to all the routers over a specified time period and then computing statistics based on the packets returned from each router. `pathping` displays the number of packets lost at each router or link, allowing you to determine which routers and links (subnets) might be causes of connectivity troubles.

ping (Packet Internet Groper) utility A utility that is used to troubleshoot TCP/IP problems. ping sends a packet with data, asking the remote system to echo the packet to the sender.

port, TCP *See* TCP port.

PPP (Point to Point Protocol) A standard transport method for point-to-point links, which are commonly called dial-up connections.

PPTP (Point-to-Point Tunneling Protocol) A protocol that is used by Microsoft and others to create VPNs.

primary DNS server The name server that contains the master copy of a zone file. Also called a primary master.

primary master *See* primary DNS server.

primary zone A DNS zone that contains the master copies of resource records for a domain.

principle of least privilege An administrative principle which states that users are given only the minimum privileges required to perform the specific set of tasks they have been assigned.

private IP address An IP address range reserved for private (non-Internet-connected) networks. There are private address ranges in the Class A, Class B, and Class C address blocks.

PTR (Pointer) record In DNS, a host entry that is used in a reverse zone file to allow IP address-to-FQDN resolution.

public IP address An IP address for use on the Internet or a private network that must be assigned via an organization or ISP so that no duplicates exist.

pull replication The act of replicating a copy of the WINS database from a WINS replication partner by pulling data from the partner's database to the local database.

push replication The act of replicating a copy of the WINS database to a WINS replication partner by pushing data from the partner's database to the local database.

push/pull replication The act of replicating a copy of the WINS database to a WINS replication partner by allowing the replication partners to push and/or pull.

Q

QoS (Quality of Service) A set of standards used to ensure that bandwidth is prioritized on a user or application basis for data transmissions across a network.

Quick Mode The second phase of the IKE two-phase operation to establish a secure communication channel. During this phase, the two computers establish the rules for communication called the Phase II (Quick Mode) SA. During the second phase, a new shared key is created for use. After the Phase II SA is in place, IPSec secured communications can occur.

R

RADIUS (Remote Access Dial-in User Service) An industry-standard security protocol that is used to authenticate client connections.

record type One of the various types of entries that can be created in a DNS table.

recursive query A DNS query that is used to request an authoritative answer or an answer indicating that there is no resolution for a DNS lookup.

registered IP address Any block of addresses registered with IANA.

registry key A container for data in the registry data hierarchy.

remote access policy A policy that is configured on a Routing and Remote Access (RRAS) server that defines conditions that must be met to grant remote access to the network via the server.

remote access profile A configuration made on a Routing and Remote Access (RRAS) server that contains a number of variables that allow you to further refine the parameters of the remote access policy.

repeater A physical device that takes a signal from one interface and retransmits it to another. This allows a network segment to be extended beyond the normal distances dictated by the limits of the topology.

replication partner A server in a WINS architecture that sends or receives a copy of the WINS database from another WINS server.

reservation A permanent address lease assignment from the DHCP server to a specified client.

resource record A data record in a DNS zone. Many types of resource records are available. For example, an address resource record is the data record that describes the address-to-name relationship for a host.

reverse lookup In DNS, an IP address-to-name resolution.

RFC (request for comments) A document that is used to make notes about the Internet and Internet technologies. RFCs are typically used as the official way to introduce a new Internet standard.

RIP (Routing Information Protocol) A protocol that dynamic routers use to share their routing tables. Similar to the OSPF and BGP protocols, RIP is an older, less-efficient routing protocol.

root In a hierarchy, the container that holds all other containers.

route (routing table) utility A utility that allows you to view and modify the routing table on a Windows computer.

router A system or device that forwards or drops packets between networks, based on the entries in its routing table.

routing protocol A type of protocol that is used by dynamic routers to share their routing tables with other routers.

routing table A table that describes routing decisions that a host can make. Minimum entries in the routing table include routes to each local network and a default route.

RRAS (Routing and Remote Access Service) A service that allows for remote connection to a server.

S

scavenging The DNS process of deleting any resource records that have timestamps on them and are found to be outdated.

scope The full, consecutive range of possible IP addresses for a network.

`secedit.exe` The command-line equivalent of the Security Configuration and Analysis snap-in.

secondary DNS server A server that provides name resolution for a zone but cannot be used to modify the zone. It contains a read-only copy of the zone file. Also known as a secondary master.

secondary master *See* secondary DNS server.

Secure template A security template that increases the level of security configured on a computer above the default configuration, but is not expected to cause problems with the computer's ability to communicate on the network. Secure templates prevent the usage of the LAN Manager (LM) authentication protocol. Windows 9x clients need to have Active Directory Client Extensions installed to enable NTLMv2 to allow them to communicate with Windows 2000 and above clients and servers using these templates. These templates also impose additional restrictions on anonymous users, such as preventing them from enumerating account and share information.

Security Configuration and Analysis snap-in An MMC snap-in that is used to configure, analyze, and implement security templates on a local computer. It can be used to create templates that are imported into GPOs for application to larger groups of computers.

Security Configuration Wizard A new, advanced, security configuration and implementation wizard first available in Windows Server 2003 Service Pack 1.

security log A log that is found in the Event Viewer and that contains auditing entries.

security template A text file that contains settings that configure the security settings of the computer or computers that it is applied to. Several preconfigured security templates come with Windows Server 2003, and you can edit and create your own custom ones as required.

Security Templates snap-in An MMC snap-in that can be used to safely create and modify security templates without danger of accidentally applying them to the local computer or the network.

service An application that runs in the background of the operating system to provide specific functionality to the network.

snap-in A tool that you can add to the MMC.

SNMP (Simple Network Management Protocol) A Layer 7 protocol that is used to facilitate network management of computers and network devices such as routers, switches, and firewalls.

SOA (Start of Authority) record In a DNS zone file, a record that is used to provide the zone parameters to all the DNS servers for the zone. The SOA record also provides the name of the primary server and the person in charge of the domain.

socket The unique combination of an IP address and a TCP port number that identifies a particular process running on a particular TCP/IP computer.

SPAP (Shiva Password Authentication Protocol) An encrypted password authentication protocol that was introduced for Shiva remote access servers.

split horizon A mechanism that is used with RIP to prevent routing loops. Split horizon blocks information about routes from being advertised by a router out any interface from which that information originated.

split horizon with poison reverse A mechanism that allows routes to be broadcast back to the interface from which they were received, but they are announced with a hop count of 16, which indicates that the network is unreachable.

static route An item in a routing table that is entered manually and that doesn't change based on information received from a routing protocol.

subnet A subdivision of a TCP/IP internetwork that communicates with other subnets through routers.

subnet mask In TCP/IP, a mask that is used to determine what subnet an IP address belongs to. A subnet mask enables a host or a router to determine which portion of an IP address is the network ID and which is the host ID. The host can then use this information to determine whether to send a packet to a host on the local network or to a router.

success event An audited event that has been completed successfully, such as a successful user login to a network.

suffix A domain extension that indicates the root domain. For example, .com is a domain suffix.

supernetted network A network that has multiple network addresses or subnets running on the same segment.

superscope A grouping of scopes that are used to support multinetted IP subnets on the same physical network.

System Monitor The portion of the Performance console that can be used to monitor the performance statistics of a computer in real-time.

T

TCP port A software address that lets the TCP/IPs deliver messages to the correct process on a computer. Each process running on a TCP/IP computer must be associated with a unique combination of an IP address and a port number. The combination of an IP address and a port number is called a socket.

TCP/IP (Transmission Control Protocol/Internet Protocol) The suite of communications protocols used to connect hosts on the Internet.

TCP/IP (Transmission Control Protocol/Internet Protocol) filter A filter that is used to prevent certain addresses or protocols from traversing a router.

TLD (top-level domain) A domain that exists directly underneath the root domain.

token ring A networking technology that is comparable to Ethernet, in which a token is used to determine who can send traffic onto the network. The data circulates through the ring until the system that it is intended for receives it and marks the token with an acknowledgment. The token then circles back to the sending system, which releases the token to the other stations on the ring.

tracert (trace route) utility A command-line utility that traces the route that packets travel between the local host and the destination host and displays it to the screen.

Transport Mode The use of IPSec not in a tunnel (with two configured endpoints). Commonly used on a private network between two hosts.

tree A logical group of Windows Server 2003 domains that share a common DNS namespace.

triggered updates Allows a router to announce changes in metric values almost immediately, rather than wait for the next periodic announcement. The trigger is a change to a metric in an entry in the routing table.

TSV (tab-separated values) A file format that is used by text files that contain fields of data separated by tabs and carriage returns.

Tunnel Mode The use of IPSec in a mode where two endpoints have been configured to create a tunnel, such as when a VPN tunnel is created.

U

UDP (User Datagram Protocol) A connectionless protocol that is part of the TCP/IP suite and is frequently used in broadcasts.

UNC (Universal Naming Convention) A naming convention that is used to define a resource on a Windows Server 2003 server network. A share named DOCS on the server SERVER1 could be accessed by using the UNC path \\SERVER1\DOCS.

unicast address A TCP/IP address that is used for host-to-host communications. Unicast addresses are the most commonly used types of TCP/IP addresses.

V–W

virtual link Created and used in cases where an OSPF area cannot have direct physical access to the backbone. In this instance, it is necessary to configure a connection from the new area to the backbone through a connection called a virtual link. The virtual link gives the disconnected area a logical path to the backbone. The virtual link has to be established between two area border routers that have a common area, with one area border router connected to the backbone.

VLSM (variable-length subnet mask) A subnet mask that is used either to split a large network into smaller pieces (subnetting) or combine smaller networks into a larger one (supernetting).

VPN (virtual private network) A mechanism for providing secure, private communications, utilizing a public network (such as the Internet) as the transport method. VPNs use a combination of encryption and authentication technologies to ensure data integrity and security.

Windows Internet Naming Service (WINS) A service that runs on a Windows Server 2003 server to provide NetBIOS name resolution. When you use WINS, name resolution is performed using directed transmissions, resulting in a reduction in broadcast traffic and the capability to find systems on different subnets. WINS replaces the LMHOSTS file in a fashion similar to the way DNS replaced the HOSTS file.

WSUS (Windows Server Update Services) An add-on service for Windows 2000 and Windows Server 2003 networks that provides the functionality of a Windows Update Web server on the internal network. WSUS allows you to select which available updates are authorized for distribution to network clients, thus ensuring that only the updates you have tested and approved are installed.

X–Y–Z

zone A domain for which a DNS server is authoritative.

zone transfer The process of copying DNS resource records from a primary zone to a secondary zone.

Index

A

B

C

D

E

F

I-J

K

L

M

O

P

Q

R

S

U

V

W-Z